SWING, SWING, SWING

The Life & Times of BENNY GOODMAN

Ross Firestone's previous biographies include
Actress: Postcards from the Road
(with Elizabeth Ashley)
and *Going My Own Way* (with Gary Crosby).
He is the editor of *A Book of Men,*
recently republished as *The Man in Me.*

Benny Goodman, 1936. Ken Whitten Collection

SWING, SWING, SWING

The Life & Times of
BENNY GOODMAN

ROSS FIRESTONE

W·W·NORTON & COMPANY·NEW YORK·LONDON

The text of this book is composed in Baskerville
with the display set in Broadway Engraved.
Composition and manufacturing by the Haddon Craftsmen, Inc.
Book design by Jacques Chazaud.

Library of Congress Cataloging-in-Publication Data

Firestone, Ross.
Swing, swing, swing: the life & times of Benny Goodman /
by Ross Firestone.
p. cm.
1. Goodman, Benny, 1909–1986. 2. Clarinetists—United States—
Biography. 3. Jazz musicians—United States—Biography.
I. Title.
ML422.G65F6   1992
781.65′092—dc20
[B]   92–9485

ISBN 0-393-31168-6

W.W. Norton & Company, Inc., 500 Fifth Avenue, New York, N.Y. 10110
W.W. Norton & Company Ltd., 10 Coptic Street, London WC1A 1PU

2 3 4 5 6 7 8 9 0

To my wife, Gail,
and
the memory of my mother,
Ray M. Firestone

Contents

Acknowledgments

Special thanks to my wife, Gail Firestone, for her unstinting encouragement and patience, James T. Maher for his wisdom, friendship and generosity, and Dan Conaway for being the kind of editor they don't make anymore.

My gratitude to the many others who have also helped make this book possible: Bob Altshuler, Jeff Atterton, George Avakian, Danny Bank, Ira Berkow, Bob Cato, John Clement, Mrs. Henry Colbert, Helen Oakley Dance, Robert Dugan, Larry Eanet, Charlotte Fisher, Herb Friedwald, Will Friedwald, Mort Goode, Norman Gorin, Buddy Greco, Marty Green, Chris Griffin, Victor Hirsh, Jane Hovde, Keith Ingham, the Institute of Jazz Studies, Jerry Jerome, Steve Jordan, Stanley King, Blanche Kolsby, Dr. Arthur Localio, Marvin Longton, Jimmy Maxwell, Jimmy McPartland, Marian McPartland, Toots Mondello, Dan Morgenstern, Jeff Nissim, Carol Phillips, Mel Powell, Howard Press, David Rose, Jeff Rund, Leon Russianoff, Harold E. Samuel, Bill Savory, Loren Schoenberg, Marian Seldes, Nat Sobel, Jess Stacy, Abner Stein, Eric Swensen, Paul Tobin, Freddie Townsend, Jeremy Townsend, Helen Ward, Dr. William J. Welch, Jerry Wexler, Ken Whitten, and the Yale University Music Library.

I don't see why anybody wants to know about me.
There's nothing to me. It's just the band.
—BENNY GOODMAN, 1937

There really is no such thing as Art. There are
only artists.
—E. M. GOMBRICH, *The Story of Art*

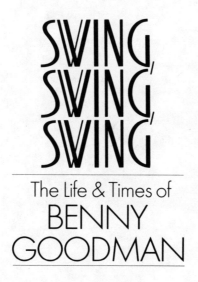

SWING,
SWING,
SWING

The Life & Times of
BENNY
GOODMAN

Benjamin David Goodman, age ten, about the time of his first clarinet lessons. Ken Whitten Collection

1

The Kid in Short Pants

ou know, I don't talk much about my childhood," he said. "Many times I've been asked to talk in depth about it. But I've resisted. I don't know why. I guess there are things that I simply want to block out. Probably because I never found it all that enjoyable. Growing up poor. Living in certain parts of Chicago. I'm not a great one for remembering."

It was 1975, and Benny Goodman was being interviewed by Ira Berkow for a book about the Maxwell Street ghetto, the Chicago slum where the clarinetist was born and raised. They were sitting in the living room of Benny's penthouse apartment on East Sixty-sixth Street, far above the crowded sidewalks and congested traffic of midtown Manhattan, a lifetime away from the dismal tenements where Benny had spent his first sixteen years. Everything about his immediate surroundings—the tastefully underplayed decor, the grand piano in the corner, the Picasso and the Monet on the walls—bore solid witness to just how far he had traveled from the privations and uncertainties of his youth. Yet Berkow's line of questioning was making him uncomfortable, and he was finding it difficult, even painful to go back there again.

Benny was never an easy interview, and as the writer pressed him for anecdotes and details, he began whistling to himself, retreating into the sanctuary of the music while he shuffled distractedly through the pile of papers on his desk. "Go ahead, I'm listening," he said, but now his attention wandered to the bowl of peanuts nearby, and he started working his way through them as though some faint memory of those early days when he still knew what it was like to go hungry had suddenly resurfaced. Quite abruptly, without explanation, he rose to his feet and disappeared into the bathroom down the hall, signaling, perhaps, that the audience had come to an end. A few minutes later he returned, all smiles and charm now, ready to bring the interview to a proper close.

"Playing music, well, maybe it was a great escape for me from the poverty," he conceded. "I don't know. I wanted to do something with myself. And the music was a great form for me. I was absolutely fascinated by it. So I set out at an early age to do what I could—and devote my efforts to it, and enjoy it."

Benny had carried few mementos of his childhood with him, but one thing that did survive was his first clarinet lesson book. "It was on parchment paper," he said. "And I've had it redone in antique style."

David Goodman and Dora Rezinsky were part of the first great wave of Eastern European Jews that landed upon the American shore in the closing decades of the nineteenth century. He was from Warsaw, and she was from Kovno (Kaunas) in Lithuania, both then under the rule of the Russian Empire, and like the five million other Jews living under Russian domination, their families had long endured the crippling oppression and enforced poverty that were their common lot.

They met and married in the port city of Baltimore in 1894 and had their first three children, Lena, Louis and Morris. David was a tailor, and in 1902 he moved the family to Chicago, where the burgeoning garment industry held out the promise of steady employment. Chicago was the second-largest manufacturing center in the nation and probably its fastest-growing metropolis. In 1860 the population numbered under a hundred thousand. By the turn of the century it was approaching two million. Four-fifths of its inhabitants were immigrants or the children of immigrants—Irish, Germans, Scandinavians, Slavs, Poles, Italians and now Russian Jews. Back in 1843 the entire Jewish population of Chicago consisted of two families. Between 1881 and 1900 some fifty thousand Jewish refugees, largely from Eastern Europe, poured into the city. Most of them, like the Goodmans, took up residence in the Maxwell Street ghetto, an overcrowded slum near the railroad yards and surrounding factories, about a mile southwest of downtown Chicago.

Writing about the immigrant slums of the city in 1910, the great social reformer Jane Addams offered this sobering description of the sort of neighborhood David and Dora found waiting for them: "The streets are inexpressibly dirty, the number of schools inadequate, sanitary legislation unenforced, the street lighting bad, the paving miserable and altogether lacking in the alleys and smaller streets, and the stables foul beyond description. Hundreds of houses are unconnected with the street sewer. The older and richer inhabitants seem anxious to move away as rapidly as they can afford it."

The Goodmans moved into what is now 1227 South Sagamon, and David found a job plying his trade. Chicago contained some two hundred clothing factories, but most of the Jewish and Italian tailors worked in the more than seventeen hundred contractors' shops—the notorious sweatshops—where they had taken over from the Irish, Germans and native-born Americans who had moved a peg up and no longer were forced to submit to the miserable pay and horrendous working conditions. The hours were long. Employment was irregular, subject to the whims of fashion and the unfathomable laws of supply and demand. The work was often dangerous and ultimately ruinous to one's health. But it was, in a manner of speaking, a living.

David did the best he could. Dora tended to the children. Over the next six years five more babies were born: Ida, Ethel, Harry, Freddy and Mary. The family moved about from tenement to tenement, finding a larger, somewhat more comfortable place to live when it could afford it, then falling back on less desirable quarters when things took a turn for the worse. (A contemporary report on the Chicago slums observed that "tenants evicted for nonpayment of rent form a floating population of some magnitude.") In 1905 the Goodmans were living at 1242 West Fourteenth Street. By 1909 they were at 1342 Washburne. It was at this address on May 30 that the ninth of their twelve children, Benjamin David Goodman, was born.

"My memory of those early days is hazier than that of most kids because we moved around quite a bit," Benny recalled. "But I can remember when we lived in a basement without heat during the winter, and a couple of times when there wasn't anything to eat. I don't mean *much* to eat. I mean *anything.* This isn't an experience you forget in a hurry. I haven't ever forgotten it."

Money was always a problem. Even in the best of times David Goodman rarely made more than twenty dollars a week, and he was often out of work. Breakfast for everyone usually consisted of rolls and black coffee. With so many mouths to feed, milk was a luxury beyond the family's reach. New shoes and socks for the children were major expenditures that had to be scrimped and saved for, and then, Benny remembered, "Pop would go out shopping with us after supper." Mom was so busy with the kids she might not leave the house for weeks at a time, so Pop also did the marketing for the next day's meals on his way home. One of Benny's earliest recollections was the image of his father staggering into their flat with a big basketful of apples and bananas, uncommon delicacies purchased at a local pushcart that left an indelible impression on the mind of the young child.

Nor did Benny ever forget, though he kept the memory secret, the demeaning, spirit-sapping kind of labor that his father was reduced to when no tailoring jobs were to be found. "Benny and I were having lunch about a month before he died in 1986," his good friend Jim Maher recalls. "Benny had become much more contemplative the last year or so of his life, and as we sat there together in this rather elegant restaurant, he began reminiscing about his father. Benny had been in excellent spirits, but now he suddenly leaned his head back as though he had a kink in his neck, closed his eyes and canted his head over to one side. He was clearly finding it difficult to discuss whatever had just crossed his mind, but he started to tell me about it, then he stopped, then he started again.

" 'You know, Pop sometimes worked in the stockyards,' he said. I said, 'No, I never heard that before.' He said, 'Yes, I know. He worked in the stockyards. He shoveled the guts that were made into lard. And it was terrible. He'd come home in the evening still wearing those high boots, and when he walked in the house, he'd be so tired.' Benny began to hunch his shoulders again; then he went on. 'The stink was awful. It was sickening. It smelled so bad.' Then all of a sudden he fell silent. His eyes were closed, and he leaned over to one side. I sat there and waited, and gradually he began to relax. Then he looked at me, he looked straight at me for a while and, without saying another word, he just shook his head.

"It was obviously a horrible, horrible memory for a boy to carry with him through life: his father, a skilled craftsman, a Jewish man who kept a kosher home, forced to slog around all day in the entrails of swine. And now here Benny was on the eve of his death finally able to talk about it."

By the time Benny was nine years old the Goodmans were living at 1125 Francisco Avenue, a three-story tenement with dark stairways and cramped, sunless rooms on the edge of the Italian district. His sister Mary had died of a brain tumor three years before, but two younger brothers, Irving and Gene, had also come along, bringing the number of children in the house up to ten. Yes, they were a close-knit family, Benny answered an interviewer many years later. "We *had* to be close-knit. We all lived in the same apartment."

Though Benny remembered Francisco Avenue as "a pretty hopeless neighborhood," the Goodmans were just a bit better off now than they had been before. Benny's oldest brothers, Louis and Morris, were out working and contributed to the family's support. His sister Ida at the age of fifteen had taken a job as a stenographer and was also able to help out. Ethel, one year older, was becoming a bookkeeper. Benny's mother had gone to work when she was eight years old and never learned to read and write. The way she saw it, the children were ready to go out into the world and start earning a living by their thirteenth or fourteenth birthdays.

There was nothing at all unusual about this way of thinking; it simply reflected the harsh realities of immigrant life in the Chicago slums of that day. As the pioneering study *Hull-House Maps and Papers* reported, "In this neighborhood, generally, a wife and children are sources of income as well as avenues of expense. . . . The theory that 'every man supports his own family' is as idle in a district like this as the fiction that 'every man can get work if he wants it.' " Children were legally bound to remain in school only until the age of fourteen, but the law was not rigorously enforced, and many dropped out even earlier. Child labor was common, and the brutal exploitation of children by Chicago's rapidly expanding industries was one of the great shames of the city. The Hull House report concluded:

It is a lamentable fact, well known to those who have investigated child labor that children are found in greatest numbers where the conditions of labor are most dangerous to life and health. Among the occupations in which children are most employed in Chicago, and which most endanger the health, are: The tobacco trade, nicotine poisoning finding as many victims among factory children as among the boys who are voluntary devotees of the weed . . . ; frame gilding, in which a child's fingers are stiffened and throat disease is contracted; button-holing, machine-stitching and handwork in tailor or sweatshops, the machine-work producing spinal curvature, and for girls pelvic disorders also, while the unsanitary condition of the shops makes even hand-sewing dangerous; bakeries, where children slowly roast before the ovens; binderies, paper-box and paint factories, where arsenical paper, rotting paste and the poison of the paints are injurious; boiler-plate works, cutlery works and metal-stamping works, where the dust produces lung disease; the handling of hot metal, accidents; the hammering of the plate, deafness. In addition to diseases incidental to trades, there are the conditions of bad sanitation and long hours, almost universal in the factories where children are employed.

But David Goodman had a different sort of future in mind for his children.

Some new neighbors had moved in next door. One night the sound of music was heard coming from their flat. Benny's father went over to investigate and discovered that the boys in the family attended high school and picked up some money on the side playing their instruments at various local functions. David Goodman had always loved music. He took the kids to the free band concerts in Douglas Park on Sunday afternoons—it was the first music Benny ever heard—and he'd long thought it would be good for them to learn how to play something someday. But now it was suddenly brought home to him that even youngsters could make money at music, and that struck him with the force of a revelation. "Pop was constantly scheming things that would make life go a little easier for all of us," Benny maintained, and now another one of his schemes began to take form. The boys next door didn't earn much. But whatever it was, it had to be better than the dismal prospects that the factories and sweatshops had to offer.

The following Sunday Pop went out for a walk and happened to stroll a bit farther than usual. Once again his attention was caught by the strains of music, coming at him now from somewhere in the distance. His steps led him to the Kehelah Jacob Synagogue, about a mile or so from home. Going inside, he found a group of small boys, the synagogue band, struggling their way through a tune under the direction of a Mr. Boguslawski, an elderly gentleman who was a professional musician. Pop asked some questions. No, there was no charge for the instruments. The *shul* lent them to the youngsters, who met for rehearsals several times a week. Before each rehearsal Mr. Boguslawski instructed them in the rudiments. The price for a lesson was twenty-five cents. Sure, bring the kids down. We'll find something or other for them to learn on.

Benny was ten years old and going to the Sheppard Grammar School across the alley from home with his brothers Freddy and Harry. Freddy was eleven and Harry was twelve, and the three of them always did everything together. The day of the next rehearsal Pop took the boys over to the synagogue. Harry was the biggest and given either a tuba or trombone. Freddy, the next in size, was given either an alto horn or a trumpet. Because Benny was the youngest and smallest, he was, in this decisive moment of his young life, handed a clarinet. "I wonder what it would have been like," Freddy later speculated, "if he had been given a trumpet or violin."

Mr. Boguslawski could teach every instrument, and to pick up a few extra dollars, he offered the boys private lessons on the side. Benny and his brothers talked it over at home, and Pop decided they should have them. Once a week after school Benny, Harry and Freddy walked the two miles to Mr. Boguslawski's house for their lessons. Two of them waited outside while the third received instruction in the basement. By the time they walked back home the day was over. About a year later the synagogue ran out of money and had to do away with the band. The lessons with Mr. Boguslawski also ended. But David Goodman was determined that their musical education would continue.

The boys' band at Hull House, the settlement house founded by Jane Addams over on Halsted Street, had recently started up again. The band was originally formed about 1908 under the leadership of James Sylvester, a talented music educator who, it was said, had the ability to take perfectly green boys who were unable to read a note and in a few weeks have them produce something in the way of music. By 1914 it consisted of seventy members. But then during World War I Sylvester and thirteen of his young musicians joined the band of the local National Guard regiment and were shipped to France. The financial support that had kept the boys' band going also dried up as its benefactors shifted their attention to aiding the war effort.

In 1920, the same year Benny stopped taking lessons at the synagogue, the band was revived as part of a Hull House campaign to cope with "the boy problem"—the wave of lawlessness and crime that swept across the Chicago slums following the end of the war. "Never in my experience has there been such a time in this neighborhood when there has been so much lawlessness," a Hull House fund raiser wrote in a pamphlet soliciting money to repair the old uniforms and replace the instruments that had been stolen or lost. "In a short period of a few months there have been seven bomb explosions, six murders and a large number of robberies and holdups; the majority of at least the latter have been committed by boys and young men. Even the young boys from eight to twelve years of age seem to be infected with this spirit of lawlessness."

The Maxwell Street neighborhood where Benny lived had long been a breeding ground for violence and crime and was commonly known as Bloody Maxwell. There were Jewish gangs in the ghetto, the Irish Valley Gang to the south and to the north, a few blocks away, the Italian 42 Gang, led by an enterprising youngster who was to go on to achieve his own sort of eminence, Sam ("Mo") Giancana. One of the games Benny played all the time was cops and robbers, but "a funny thing about this," he said, "was that the cops always got the worst of it. . . . What I might have become if I didn't play an instrument—I never stopped to think about that. Judging from the neighborhood where I lived, if it hadn't been for the clarinet, I might just as easily have been a gangster."

The Hull House band confronted "the boy problem" in two ways. It provided "wholesome recreation" to lure the young gangsters-in-the-making away from the lawlessness of the streets. More pragmatically it also prepared them for an "interesting and diverting occupation" by imparting the skills needed to earn a decent living playing music in the many dance halls around Chicago. Though Benny and his brothers were mostly attracted by the new instruments and the snappy red uniforms and military caps (supplied, after much beseeching, by the head of Sears, Roebuck), it was this promise to turn the boys into working professionals that had the greatest appeal to their father. The settlement house was several miles away, but Benny remembered how "during the winter Pop used to put us all on a sled and drag us over for our lessons." Benny also recalled that "he was very proud of our being able to play even a little bit, and whenever somebody came to the house they would have to hear us."

Membership in the band not only provided the Goodman boys with a golden opportunity to go on with their lessons at virtually no cost but also entitled them to spend two weeks in the country every summer at the Bowen Country Club, the Hull House summer camp near Waukegan, Illinois. A sprawling woodland retreat of over seventy acres, with a swimming pool, playgrounds, vegetable gardens and deep ravines filled with wild flowers, it gave Benny and his brothers a welcome break from the steamy pavements and dusty alleys of the Maxwell Street ghetto, something they looked forward to all year long. "It was only about fifty miles from Chicago," Benny remembered, "but we prepared for it from one year to the next as if we were going to the North Pole." The annual vacation in the country also underscored rather dramatically the sorts of luxuries that music could make possible.

Benny's fellow students included such future jazz names as the bassist Milt Hinton and the pianist Art Hodes, but jazz was not a regular part of the Hull House music program. The boys learned to play by practicing marches like "Semper Fidelis" and "Under the Double Eagle" and slightly more ambitious numbers like "Poet and Peasant Overture," then performed them at holiday parades, church picnics and the like. But Benny and his brothers began to hear the music elsewhere, and it affected them deeply.

"The way we first heard jazz was when we'd be passing a ballroom, coming home from seeing a movie maybe," Freddy remembered. "We'd hear music. It would be real exciting, and we'd sneak in. I'll never forget the thrill I got listening to a trumpet player who used a wah-wah mute. One time Benny just jumped up onstage, grabbed the guy's clarinet and started to play. He was a natural, that's all. He could do whatever he pleased, whatever he felt like playing, even then. He would just get aroused within."

Jazz also began to seep in through phonograph records. Benny's oldest brother, Louis, now known as Charlie because he worked in a place where someone else was named Louis, had gotten hold of an old windup Victrola and started bringing home recordings. Along with the Carusos and other classical artists, there were a few more or less jazz numbers by the Original Dixieland Jazz Band and the popular clarinet-playing vaudevillian Ted Lewis. "We figured [Ted Lewis] was a pretty hot clarinet player," Benny said, and "Charlie used to play this thing by the hour." In no time at all Benny was able to duplicate Lewis's solos note for note.

Benny's Ted Lewis imitations led to his first professional engagement. Mr. Boguslawski's son Ziggy was the director of the Central Park Theater, the Balaban and Katz vaudeville house on Roosevelt Road and Central Park Avenue. When Charlie discovered that Ziggy was now putting on amateur Jazz Nights every Thursday, he hustled Benny over to the theater to do his impersonation. Benny was gotten up in a Buster Brown collar and bow tie and was wearing knee pants. He was too young to play on the stage, so he performed in the orchestra pit standing on the conductor's podium.

Benny did well enough so that when one of the theater's acts canceled out at the last minute a few weeks later, Ziggy sent his father out looking for him to fill in for the day. Benny was playing shinny in the street when Mr. Boguslawski found him, but he grabbed his clarinet and, still in knee pants, rushed over to the theater. Benny was still playing a C clarinet rather than the more common B flat instrument, which is pitched a whole tone lower, and the orchestra had to transpose everything to his key. But Benny wasn't nervous, Freddy claimed. "Benny was never really nervous." He played "I Never Knew," "St. Louis Blues" and Ted Lewis's current hit, "When My Baby Smiles at Me." It brought down the house. Benny was twelve years old. He had been playing clarinet for all of a year and a half.

"The applause was nice," Benny reminisced, "but the five bucks they paid me was even better, because it was the first money I ever earned playing clarinet. . . . Nobody ever had to remind us kids that someday we'd have to go out on our own and earn a living. The idea was with us almost from the time we were old enough to talk."

While he continued on at Hull House, Benny also began taking private lessons from Franz Schoepp, one of the best-known classical clarinet teachers in the city. Schoepp had taught at the prestigious Chicago Musical College from 1906 to 1920 and may have played in the Chicago Symphony. The college's catalog maintained that the faculty for orchestral instruments were all members of that orchestra, and though Schoepp is not listed in any of the symphony's programs for this period, he probably performed with it from time to time as a substitute.

Benny was, as his brother Freddy said, a natural. He had an inborn talent for the clarinet that allowed him to progress with the sureness and speed of the authentic prodigy. But it was Franz Schoepp who gave him the foundation in legitimate clarinet technique that enabled him to actualize all his still-dormant potential, transforming him from a precocious youngster into a mature musician of unusual virtuosity. The two years he spent with Schoepp were, Benny claimed, "the only real teaching I ever had," and Schoepp "probably did more for me musically than anybody I ever knew."

Benny remembered his teacher fondly as "a wonderful old gent," "a small man quite white-haired . . . [who] used to look over his glasses at me." Schoepp was German by birth, and following in the exacting tradition of that musical heritage, he was a stern disciplinarian. "He was very strict about details," Benny said, "and never allowed a mistake to pass without being corrected," characteristics that Benny himself came to embody in the years ahead. Benny went to Schoepp's home on the North Side near Wrigley Field about once a week and paid him something like fifty cents a lesson—not very much but enough to put a strain on his father's meager income. Under Schoepp's tutelage he worked his way through the standard instructional texts for clarinet by Baerman, Klosé and Cavallini. "He used all German editions of his books," Benny recalled. "One day I said to him, 'Mr. Schoepp, why do you have everything in German? Why don't you have anything in English? We're here now.' And he said, '*Dummkopf*! Pretty soon *everything* will be in German.'"

Schoepp's faith in the coming supremacy of German *Kultur* was completely untainted by any prejudicial feelings about class or religion or race. Not only did he give lessons to this poor Jewish boy from the ghetto, but he also gave them to any black students who wanted them, something virtually unheard of in the Chicago of that day, which was still recovering from the shock of the so-called race riots that had taken place only a few years earlier. "I guess that sort of impressed me," Benny would say, "because there was plenty of prejudice about such things." A number of factors were involved in Benny's precedent-shattering decision to hire black musicians in the 1930s, but his old teacher's indifference to anything other than exclusively musical considerations should certainly be included among them.

Schoepp liked to have the student who was coming in for a lesson play a few duets with the student who was finishing up, and it was through such casual interchanges that Benny became acquainted with Buster Bailey and Jimmie Noone. Some seven and fourteen years older than Benny, Bailey and Noone were working professionals who had already established solid reputations in Chicago performing with the bands of, respectively, Erskine Tate and King Oliver. They were probably the first black jazz musicians Benny ever met. They were certainly the first jazz musicians he knew who were as dedicated to mastering the technical aspects of their instruments as to honing their improvisational skills, which is what had brought them to Schoepp's home for further instruction.

Buster Bailey had studied extensively with concert-trained musicians while growing up in Memphis and did not learn to play jazz until he acquired a solid grounding in technique. One suspects that if the color barrier had not limited his opportunities, he would have pursued a career on the concert stage rather than in dance halls and nightclubs, where he achieved considerable acclaim for his work with Fletcher Henderson and John Kirby.

Jimmie Noone had taken lessons back in New Orleans from Lorenzo Tio, the celebrated teacher of several generations of Creole clarinetists. As Albert McCarthy observes, he "undoubtedly possessed the most impressive technique of any of the great New Orleans clarinetists. His tone had a delicacy that was unique, his phrasing was subtle, and his control in all registers was exemplary. The finest of his solos are so logically developed, with technique and content in perfect balance, that they have great formal unity." The story is told that when Maurice Ravel heard Noone perform in a Chicago night-club, he was so struck by his virtuosity that he transcribed several of his solos. When he showed the transcriptions to a classical clarinetist back in France, for all his great skill, the clarinetist was unable to duplicate them.

Through their frequent meetings at Schoepp's home Benny came to know Bailey and Noone fairly well. And by their examples these older clari-netists showed him just how important it is for a musician who plays jazz to have complete mastery of his instrument, something not all jazz musicians of that day were overly concerned with. When Benny was asked to name his favorite clarinetists in 1941, he included both of them on his list and singled them out for their technical facility. Bailey, he said, is "unquestionably the fastest man on his instrument, and his tone is very good. He is probably the greatest technician of his race." Noone "was one of the early technicians. He had remarkable control of his instrument in a day when the clarinet was not as well handled by jazzmen as it is today."

Jimmie Noone probably had the greatest single influence upon Benny's development as a jazz musician, as both a stylistic model and a musical inspiration. Albert McCarthy's point about Jimmie's ability to hold technique and content in perfect balance would be an equally apt description of Benny's own mature solo work. "I loved Jimmie Noone's clarinet playing," Benny maintained. "He was an excellent clarinet player, period." Coming from Benny, there was no higher praise.

"Some of the guys I played with in those days didn't go around learning more about their instruments from an intellectual point of view," Benny recalled. "All they wanted to do was play hot jazz, and the instrument was just a means. I'd imagine that a lot of them criticized me—said my technique was too good. Something like that. But I've always wanted to know what *made* music. How you do it and why it sounds good. I always practiced, worked like hell."

It was during his studies with Schoepp that this constant, almost obses-sive practicing began, and it continued unabated throughout the rest of his life. David Goodman encouraged the boys in their music, and the more Benny practiced, the happier it made him, but sometimes his mother had enough of the racket and sent him outside to join the other youngsters in their games. "But I'd always tell her," Benny said, "that if I stayed any longer than a certain time she should call me, so I could go back to the clarinet."

Combined with his natural talent, Benny's fierce devotion to his instru-ment moved him along rapidly. About a year after he began studying with Schoepp, the teacher presented him in a student recital at a public school on the North Side. Benny's father and his sister Ida came to hear him play, and after the performance Schoepp embraced the three of them, then took Mr.

Goodman aside and told him he had great hopes for the boy's future. "I know this must have made Pop very happy," Benny said.

Benny's fast-developing skills stood him in good stead over at Hull House, where he quickly progressed beyond the beginner and intermediary levels to the advanced classes. Jimmy Sylvester also led the band at the 124th Regiment Field Artillery, and he used his best Hull House students to fill out its ranks. This gave Benny valuable experience playing with older professionals. It also enabled him to bring home some money. Benny recalled with considerable satisfaction that "when we played a parade we'd get five dollars for the day's work." This was more than his father was making.

When the Hull House Boys' Band played church picnics on Sunday afternoons, Benny and his brothers stuffed themselves with hot dogs and potato salad, then went off to the woods with some of the other youngsters to jam on tunes like "Darktown Strutters' Ball" and "Wabash Blues." After rehearsing with the artillery band, Benny hung around the armory and played jazz with the older musicians. For a while the Goodman boys also had their own little band, made up of other kids from the neighborhood. "We rehearsed on Friday nights, playing from stocks," Benny recalled, "but we didn't stick to them much after we got a chorus or two worked out. I always liked to play free, even from the very start, and when we got hold of a new chord or a good lick, that was a thrill like nothing else." The rehearsals were held at different members' homes every week, but when their parents had to have some peace and quiet for the evening, the Goodman flat was always available. "My father was always glad to have us, just as he was always glad to do anything for us kids that he could."

Benny's all-consuming passion for music kept him from being much of a student, but he managed to graduate from Sheppard Grammar School and moved on to Harrison High. It was there that he "began to know some kids who were a little better off in the world than I was. . . . That didn't mean anything to me from what you might call a social angle, but they had a little different idea about the world than I did, probably expected a little more from it, and that had its effect on me." One of the boys in the next class, the son of a fruit and vegetable peddler, was Arthur Goldberg, who was to become a member of John F. Kennedy's cabinet and a justice on the United States Supreme Court.

During his first year in high school Benny also came to know a group of somewhat older youngsters over at Austin High who were as taken with "playing free" as he was. The so-called Austin High Gang—which originally included Jimmy and Dick McPartland, Bud Freeman, Frank Teschemacher and Jim Lanigan, a twenty-year-old who was going with the McPartlands' sister—had stumbled upon jazz quite by accident when they were hanging out at the local soda shop after school and happened to put on a record by the Friars Society Orchestra, a band of white jazz musicians largely from New Orleans, soon to become better known as the New Orleans Rhythm Kings. "They brought a new kind of music to us," Freeman remembered. "It was something we had never heard or felt before. We didn't know what it was . . . didn't even realize that it was to any extent Negroid. All we knew was that it had a feeling to it and that we liked it and wanted to play like that." Jimmy McPartland claimed they were so overwhelmed by what they heard they decided then and there to become jazz musicians themselves and form their own band.

Jimmy, the most outgoing and assertive of the bunch, decided he would play cornet. His brother Dick picked the banjo and guitar, Teschemacher the clarinet, Lanigan the tuba, and Freeman, at the McPartlands' urging, took up the C-melody saxophone. All but Freeman had studied violin as children, so they already had some musical training, and by copying the Rhythm Kings' records a few bars at a time and practicing diligently, they soon began to develop a certain amount of proficiency. A short time later they were joined by Dave North, another Austin High student, on piano and the drummer Dave Tough from nearby Oak Park. Most of these youngsters were to form the nucleus of an expanding circle of young white jazz enthusiasts who are credited with developing Chicago-style jazz and would go on to become important figures in the history of the music.

There are several stories about how Benny and the Austin High Gang first met, but according to a 1987 conversation with Jimmy McPartland, it happened at the Columbus Park Refectory, a boathouse in the park with a space on the second floor that the city rented out for dances.

"I had worked with a piano player named Charlie Podolsky—everyone called him Murph because he looked so Jewish—and I'd heard that there was this kid who was terrific, a great little clarinet player. I finally got to hear him when he came to listen to us play at Columbus Park. I was putting on dances for the high school kids—*thés dansants* we called them to make them sound fancy. My girl friend collected the money at the door, and I'd give the guys three to five bucks apiece and keep the rest. The money didn't really matter that much to us. A lot of times we played for nothing. So one day I see this kid in short pants standing in front of the bandstand, listening to us and smiling away. It was Benny Goodman. I asked him if he wanted to sit in, and the little son of a gun knocked us all out. Benny could *play*! Gosh almighty, as young as he was he could get all over that horn."

Bud Freeman remembered Benny as "a very pleasant little guy who hadn't the faintest idea of the extraordinary talent he possessed. We all learned quite a bit from him because he was much more of a pro than any of us. . . . He played the clarinet so beautifully! It was not to be believed. He had the technique of a master and a beautiful sound to go with it!" But though Benny was always welcomed and frequently jammed with the gang, he never became a full-fledged member.

It wasn't so much the difference in backgrounds, though the differences were substantial. The Austin High kids were solidly middle-class. The McPartlands' father had a good job with the railroad, as did Frank Teschemacher's. Dave Tough's father was a physician. Bud's father was sufficiently well off to be able to tell his sons, "You boys don't have to worry. . . . Go and do what you want to do. Be happy." With the exception of Freeman, who was half Jewish, all of them were also Gentile. Jimmy maintained that none of this really mattered. "Benny wasn't hung up about being poor or Jewish. Who cared about any of that? It was all about music. If you could play jazz, you were in."

What did matter, though—and it ultimately shaped the divergent careers they went on to pursue—was the difference in priorities that followed from this difference in backgrounds. As Richard Hadlock points out, "Benny was primarily a *clarinetist*, and jazz was his favorite mode of expression." And the reason he became a clarinetist was to be able to make a living. For the Austin High kids, playing jazz was the most important thing, and the instruments they played were almost incidental. "I started out just loving this new music," Bud maintained, "and, frankly, I doubt very much that I would have become a musician at all if I had not been interested in jazz."

If it was mainly the artist's drive for perfection that led Benny to work so obsessively on improving his musicianship, he was also aware that the better he played, the better he could compete in the marketplace. Most of the Austin High crowd also worked hard on their instruments, but in their case it was because they were determined to become more accomplished improvisers. Spared the kind of privations Benny had known, they were not overly concerned about getting jobs and making money. ("A lot of times we played for nothing.") Although Benny enjoyed jamming with the gang, he never lost sight of the fact that music was, first of all, a way to earn a livelihood and help support his family.

Jimmy McPartland was the most entrepreneurial of the gang and the most professionally minded. Along with his after-school *thés dansants* in the park he worked a lot of fraternity parties at the University of Chicago and Northwestern, and he began using Benny regularly.

"To be able to improvise in those days was quite an accomplishment," he explained. "Most musicians just sat down with the music stands in front of them and read off the notes, so if you could improvise and play a little jazz, you were really something and the college boys would hire you. Teschemacher was our regular clarinetist, and he was good, but Benny was far ahead of him. He was already a polished musician, so whenever I had a job, I would try to get him rather than Tesch because he was that much better. Benny was just so good. His brother Harry was a nice quiet guy but a plodder. He did all right, but he wasn't in Benny's class. Neither was his other brother Freddy.

"Sometimes Benny and I worked three or four jobs a week and brought home as much as ten or fifteen dollars a night, which was quite a lot of money. My mother used to worry about that and would ask me, 'Are you sure they're paying you all this just for playing music?' She thought I was a little hoodlum and couldn't really believe it. I had an old Ford, and I would drive over to Benny's place to pick him up. His mother always had me sit down with them for dinner. There were so many mouths to feed I don't know how she managed to put food on the table. But there was a lovely family feeling in the house. You could feel the affection there. And I was always welcome. Benny's mother was wonderful to me. I was the nice little Christian boy who got Benny work. After the job we'd stop back at his house and have something to eat. Mrs. Goodman was a real Jewish mother, and she'd make me *gribbenes*—fried chicken fat—and eggs. Then the next morning we'd get up and go to school."

Benny was still only thirteen years old, but now he also began playing dates for Murph Podolsky, who led his own band and operated a successful booking office. This brought the youngster into the mainstream world of the Chicago music business, and Podolsky insisted he join the musicians' union. "I think I had to falsify my age," Benny recalled. "I think you had to be sixteen." Podolsky also sent Benny out to get some long pants. Jimmy McPartland claimed he took him down to Marshall Field's to buy his first pair. A tuxedo was another requirement, and since Benny was too small to buy one off the rack, his sister Ethel had the clothing company where she worked as a bookkeeper make one up for him, paying for it herself by putting in some overtime. "That was the first tuxedo in the Goodman family, a very big thrill," Benny remembered.

Ethel had previously helped Benny buy his first clarinet, "a swell Martin," and now, to make himself more marketable, he bought himself a saxophone. The family had some objections to the expenditure, but Benny was already thinking like a real professional and realized that being able to double would get him more work. Benny was completely self-taught on the instrument, and the saxophone never assumed the same importance for him as the clarinet. Yet when Bud Freeman heard him play it at a jam session a few years later, he was, he said, amazed. "He had the best sound I have ever heard, before or since." Benny had also taught himself to play a little trumpet. According to McPartland, "He had no tone, but he could run all over that thing, just like he did on the clarinet."

"I was holding my own pretty well" playing with more experienced older musicians, Benny maintained. "Nobody would have had any part of me if I didn't." The money was good, and it made Benny proud to be able to help out at home. But all those late nights took their toll on his schoolwork. Benny often fell asleep on the train coming back from the job and was too exhausted to get up the next morning.

Dave Tough suggested Benny join him over at Lewis Institute, a private school where you could schedule your classes so you didn't have to show up until almost noon. Benny's parents thought it was a good idea despite the tuition costs, and in the spring of 1923 Benny made the switch. Tough was from a well-to-do family, and the other students at Lewis shared similar backgrounds. The guitarist Eddie Condon, who had recently fallen in with the Austin High crowd, remembered Davy describing it to him as "a prep school for two kinds of people: those who can't go to the best schools and those who get thrown out of them." Benny could not have been very comfortable there, and in any case he was working almost constantly by now. The following fall, having reached the legal dropout age of fourteen, he put his formal education behind him after completing only one year of high school.

But education of a different sort was just beginning.

On the previous Fourth of July Benny had played a job with Podolsky at Colt's Electric Park opposite a black band that included the pianist Lil Hardin, Baby Dodds on drums and Baby's older brother Johnny on clarinet. They were such a hit with the crowd nobody was interested in what Podolsky was doing, so he packed up and went home. "Murphy was really angry, but I stayed to listen and I was fascinated by the music," Benny recalled. This was his first exposure to the great New Orleans clarinetist, and he stood there absorbing every chorus, every phrase, every inflection. "Johnny gave me one of my most important lessons on clarinet," he said. "His tone was clear and beautiful, his ideas exciting, his interpretation of the blues especially moving. . . . I have never forgotten [him]."

The following month Benny was asked to fill in at the last minute in the band the pianist Bill Grimm was leading on an excursion boat that ran from Chicago to Michigan City, and he played for the first time with the cornetist Bix Beiderbecke. Bix was only nineteen years old and still six months away from making his debut recordings with the Wolverines that were to bring him to the attention of jazz fans throughout the country, but he already had a strong reputation among the musicians in Chicago. "I had heard so much about Bix Beiderbecke in those days that he was practically a legend to me already," Benny said. "I was wearing short pants, and I went up to the bandstand. When he saw me sort of fooling around he wanted to kick me out because he thought I was just a little kid who was monkeying around with the instruments. Somebody had to persuade him that I was playing with the band.

"I think my first impression [of Bix] was the lasting one. I remember very clearly thinking, 'Where, what planet, did this guy come from? Is he from outer space?' I'd never heard anything like the way he played—not in Chicago, no place. The tone—he had this wonderful, ringing cornet tone. He could have played in a symphony orchestra with that tone. But also the intervals he played, the figures—whatever the hell he did."

Benny had reason to remember that the encounter took place on August 8, 1923, because when he returned home, he found that his youngest brother, Jerome, had just been born. He also remembered coming home so seasick that his sister Lena urged him not to accept Grimm's offer to finish out the season. "If the boat goes, I go with it," was his answer, and he continued playing with Bix and learning from him through the end of the summer. When Bix's records started to come out, Benny studied his solos until he could play them by heart on trumpet. "Everyone was influenced by Bix," Jimmy McPartland explained. "He was so musical, so fluid, and he had such a beautiful sound."

That fall, at the age of fourteen, Benny got his first steady job playing four nights a week in the band led by Jules Herbevaux at Guyon's Garden, a dance hall not far from the apartment on California Avenue where his family was now living. "It was strictly a stock band and not much good," Benny said, but he was making forty-eight dollars a week and was able to bring home money regularly. Another good thing about the money, even more important than it might have seemed at the time, is that it gave Benny the wherewithal to continue his education.

The dance halls and cafés over on the South Side provided employment to large numbers of black jazz musicians. The music was so plentiful and its quality so high that Bud Freeman was able to claim that "Chicago, not New Orleans, was the town that really cradled jazz." Along with his brother Harry and sometimes Jimmy McPartland, Dave Tough and the cornetist Muggsy Spanier, Benny began spending his nights off at places like the Entertainers' Café at Thirty-fifth and Indiana, where Jimmie Noone was playing in the band that backed Bessie Smith ("When she sang the blues, it took you right out"), and the Lorraine Gardens, where he got to hear Buster Bailey and the New Orleans trumpet man Freddie Keppard. The Lincoln Gardens, a large cabaret on Thirty-first Street, was a particular favorite, for this was the home of King Oliver's Creole Jazz Band, a miraculous ensemble that included Lil Hardin, the Dodds brothers and Louis Armstrong. While going about its main business of entertaining the regular customers, the Oliver band tutored a whole generation of young white jazz enthusiasts like Benny. "Aspiring white jazz musicians used to go there all the time, and the people there were wonderful," Bud remembered. "The big, black doorman weighed about 350 pounds, and every time he saw us he would say, 'I see you boys are here for your music lessons tonight.' He knew."

Along with Jimmie Noone, Johnny Dodds and Buster Bailey, Benny also listened to Leon Roppolo, the brilliant white clarinetist featured with the New Orleans Rhythm Kings, who were playing over at the Friar's Inn, a basement cabaret frequented by the likes of Al Capone and Dion O'Bannion. He also paid close attention to Volly de Faut, who replaced Roppolo in the band and frequently worked around town with Muggsy Spanier, and to Frank Tesch-emacher. Although Tesch's dissonant, rasping tone and biting attack seem the very antithesis of the smooth, legato style Benny went on to perfect, Benny always spoke highly of Tesch's abilities and included him among his favorite clarinetists. "Tesch hadn't an unusual amount of technique and his intonation wasn't always of the best, but he was a fine musician, perhaps the most inventive it has ever been my privilege to hear."

The musicians Benny couldn't hear in person he sought out on records. "I would sit in a record shop for three and four hours a day listening to music that was coming from wherever it came from. In those days you used to have to look as a sort of connoisseur, digging things up that a lot of other people weren't interested in that would have a good trumpet solo or a good sax solo or something else that intrigued you."

The joy and self-fulfillment that jazz had to offer were tugging Benny in one direction, but the need to make a steady living was pulling him in quite another, taking him to jobs that paid well but brought little in the way of personal gratification. Benny's ability to negotiate the most difficult score and play "correct clarinet," as he called it, carried its own sort of satisfactions and kept him working regularly. But the youngster's first experience of the peren-nial conflict between art and commerce generated a certain tension that had him moving about uncertainly from one band to another. "I was pretty restless," he said, "and never stayed on a job very long if a new one came along where I might get a little more money or sit in with better players."

Jules Herbevaux's "stock band" was able to hold him for only a few months. Then Benny left to join Arnold Johnson's orchestra at the Green Mill Gardens. "There was nobody of much account in the band," he remembered, but he hung on until the spring, dutifully playing commercial dance music and backing the floor show that included among the chorus girls the future *Ziegfeld Follies* stars Helen Morgan and Ruth Etting, then struggling with their own career problems. Although Benny was able to convince himself that "playing with bands like that was all right in several ways, particularly in money and as far as getting ahead was concerned," the need to perform the kind of music he respected and loved finally got the better of him. According to John Steiner, chronicler of the Chicago music scene of the 1920s, Benny was eventually fired "because he was too hot for the show atmosphere at the Green Mill." The same sort of problem recurred that summer, when Benny went out to Neenah, Wisconsin, to work a job at Waverly Beach. "The piano player who had the date was Billy Goodheart, but we didn't get along too well because he didn't like my style of playing. It was too crazy, he said—which meant that I played hot, and he didn't go for it."

That fall Benny took a big step up, both musically and professionally, when he joined the orchestra at the Midway Gardens, a large dance hall on the South Side across from Washington Park. The musical director at the Gardens was Elmer Schoebel, an accomplished musician who had played piano for the New Orleans Rhythm Kings and written their arrangements. Schoebel is considered one of the first important composer-arrangers in jazz; among his many compositions are such standards as "Farewell Blues," "Bugle Call Rag" and "Nobody's Sweetheart." The Midway Gardens orchestra included a number of other Rhythm Kings veterans as well as the fine saxophonist and clarinetist Danny Polo and the trumpet player Murphy Steinberg. When Benny joined the band, it was being fronted by Art Kassel, who is best remembered now for the rather dreary commercial dance band he led in the 1940s ("Art Kassel and his Kassels in the Air"), but according to the drummer Ben Pollack, another Rhythm Kings alumnus, during his early days in Chicago Kassel was known as "the hottest clarinet man in town." Over the previous year the orchestra had achieved some prominence through its numerous recordings. John Steiner tells us that its job at the Midway Gardens was "to provide dance music with a lilt. That might mean some dynamic restraint, but within that limitation, it was a fine jazz band."

Probably because of that inevitable "limitation," Benny's own opinion of the Midway Gardens orchestra was somewhat less enthusiastic. It played "pretty good music," he said, and he liked the job "all right." Still, he was working with other "hot" players for a change and being paid well for his efforts, so it wasn't that hard to curb his restlessness. But then about six months later he was approached by the saxophonist Gil Rodin.

Rodin was part of the new band that Ben Pollack had formed out in Venice, California, and he had come to see Benny at Pollack's request. They were looking for a new clarinet and saxophone player. Would Benny be interested? Benny was aware of Pollack's reputation as one of the first white drummers in Chicago able to play good jazz, and now Rodin told him how they were beginning to put together the first real large white jazz band. The money would be good. The prospect of California had its own appeal to a young man who had never been more than a hundred miles from home. "O-o-oh, I'd love to come!" Rodin remembered him answering. Rodin promised to get back to him soon. Benny returned to the Midway Gardens and waited out the months. Late in the summer of 1925 the offer finally came through, and Benny Goodman, all of sixteen years old, headed west to play the kind of music he wanted.

Ben Pollack and His Park Central Orchestra, 1929.
Along with Benny on clarinet and saxophones *(fifth from the right),*
the band included Jack Teagarden on trombone and
Jimmy McPartland on cornet *(top row, third and fourth from the left).*
From the Benny Goodman Archives in the Music Library at Yale University

2

The Two Bennys

Ben Pollack was a short, intense, fast-talking young man only six years older than his new clarinetist but already a respected veteran of the Chicago jazz scene. He was "a marvelous drummer," Bud Freeman maintained, one of the first white Chicagoans to understand jazz and absorb the lessons of King Oliver and Baby Dodds. Benny claimed he was also one of the first "to hit all four beats in a measure with the foot pedal on the bass drum in a fast tempo, something which made a big change in the way music was played."

At the age of nineteen Pollack was playing with the New Orleans Rhythm Kings over at Friar's Inn. By 1924 he was working with Harry Bastin's dance band at the Venice Ballroom outside Los Angeles. Pollack had begun leading his own bands while still in grammar school, playing weddings and wakes and Kiwanis Club outings, and when Bastin fell ill, he was asked to take over the orchestra. He immediately began revamping the band's personnel to make it more jazz-oriented. When Pollack's brother died, Gil Rodin traveled back east with him for the funeral, and they decided on the trip home to look around for some good local talent they could break in on the Coast, then eventually move the band to Chicago to be closer to their families. Pollack was sitting *shivah* with his parents, mourning his brother's passing, the night Rodin dropped by the Midway Gardens to check out the young clarinetist Pollack had recommended.

Pollack had first heard Benny as a kid when he was still doing his Ted Lewis imitations, but then he heard him again only a few years later and was struck by the young clarinetist's remarkable progress. Benny "was playing a mixture of Jimmie Noone, Leon Roppolo, Buster Bailey and other great clarinet players," Pollack recalled, but was already forging these disparate influences into his own distinctive style. Out of admiration for Roppolo, Benny had adopted the clarinetist's idiosyncratic way of sitting on the bandstand, stretched out on the chair so far he was practically on his back, and this also made an impression. Their first night back in town Pollack sent Rodin out looking for the youngster who "played clarinet lying down, like Roppolo." More than a decade later Rodin still remembered the impact Benny had on him when he walked into the Midway Gardens: "I heard the most astounding clarinet I had ever heard coming from a kid who wore short trousers—short trousers before and after work—long ones to play in. His technique at that time was as clean and exciting as it is today."

In August 1925 Pollack wired Benny that the job was now waiting for him and offered him something like one hundred dollars a week, more than he had ever made before. Benny's parents were against his moving so far away from home, but he was determined to go. To bring the folks around, he quit his job at the Midway Gardens, then told them he was fired and would be out of work if he didn't accept Pollack's invitation. All through the long train ride west Benny kept thinking about orange groves and palm trees and how he'd probably be playing in some glamorous hotel on the beach. Pollack met him at the station and whisked him out to the Venice Ballroom to start rehearsing with the orchestra. When Benny stepped from the car and got his first view of the Venice Pier, he was crestfallen. "Oh, boy. It was the sleaziest place," he recalled. "Rides, roller coasters and all that. I just looked around and I thought, 'What the hell did I come *here* for?' "

The Pollack band, though, was not a disappointment. Comprised of two trumpets, one trombone, a three-man saxophone section and four rhythm, it was not strictly a jazz band but a large dance band that incorporated jazz soloists and featured jazz-influenced arrangements. Rodin cited King Oliver's Creole Jazz Band as "the first colored band in Chicago that played arranged hot music and still kept swinging," and as Richard Hadlock points out, "Pollack's idea was a kind of sophisticated extension of the King Oliver band approach: over a steady, swinging rhythmic foundation, make the music *sound* impromptu, but base the improvisation on a real structure, with interesting scored passages worked out in advance." Arrangements were central to Pollack's concept, and he had to have musicians who were skillful readers as well as good improvisers, a combination of talents then in very short supply. Benny's ability to satisfy both requirements made him an especially important addition.

Fud Livingston was the band's principal arranger and set its basic style. But about the time Benny arrived Pollack had also hired Glenn Miller, a twenty-one-year-old trombone player who was languishing in the pit band at the Forum Theater and teaching himself arranging on the side. Pollack and Rodin were not overly impressed with Miller's trombone work when he sat in with them, Rodin recalled, but "We asked him to bring a few of his arrangements to rehearsal, and we liked them. He would copy riffs he heard on records—records by the Wolverines and Ray Miller's band—and then drop them into his own arrangements."

Benny was delighted with the kind of music he was now playing. "Fud and Glenn left room in their arrangements for jazz improvisation, which was right down my alley. It gave me an opportunity to let out, to be myself." The audience also liked what they were doing. Pollack claimed, "It wasn't long before we had the top-notch band on the Coast." According to one of the orchestra's fans, "Musicians used to congregate in crowds at both ends of the bandstand, [listening] with wonder."

The band remained at the Venice Ballroom until the beginning of the year. It was a great five months for Benny. The music was good. He got along well with Pollack and found Gil Rodin "one of the most decent fellows I've ever met." After sending money home, he still had enough left over to explore the California night life with Glenn Miller and the trumpet player Harry Greenberg. Despite the occasional hangover and upset stomach, "we had a lot of fun and plenty of laughs," Benny recalled, and he loved this newfound feeling of independence. "Just being with that gang and playing with them was a privilege in itself, and I learned plenty about music—as well as other things—in those first few months." When Benny arrived in California in August, Rodin had to lend him one of his own suits until he could buy some decent clothes. By the time the band returned to Chicago in January Benny had filled out so much he couldn't get the coat on his back.

The bass player decided to remain out west, so Benny persuaded Pollack to hire his older brother Harry. After a few other changes the band's personnel was in place, and Pollack was ready to take Chicago by storm. But the band's reputation had not followed it east, and there were no bookings to be found. Pollack tried to hold the orchestra together, but as the weeks went by, the men began drifting away. Benny joined Benny Krueger's stage band at the Uptown Theater, playing a little jazz but mostly the usual overtures and operatic arrangements. "It wasn't the kind of playing I cared much about," he said, but the California adventure was over, and it brought in a steady paycheck.

Benny rejoined the Pollack band briefly when it scored a two-week engagement at Castle Farms, a roadhouse near Cincinnati, then went back to Benny Krueger. When Pollack received another offer from the Southmoor Hotel, a major Chicago night spot that normally booked name orchestras like Roger Wolfe Kahn, Benny considered it too risky a proposition and decided not to return.

The Pollack band without Benny opened at the Southmoor's Venetian Room in May 1926. Pollack recalled, "They wanted to put on the dog opening night and wanted a big name, [so] I went to see [the orchestra leader] Paul Ash, who was the rage in Chicago at that time, and he told me he would be delighted to help out." The engagement was billed as "Paul Ash Presents Ben Pollack and His Orchestra," and Ash made a personal appearance at the opening. A few days later, Pollack said, he received a bill from Ash's wife for $250, a sizable chunk of the $1,050 a week the band was being paid. But it was money well spent. Opening night drew some nine hundred customers at $5 a head, and the band was a solid smash. Some weeks later Benny dropped by with Benny Krueger and ended up sitting in. Rodin implored him to come back, and since Benny saw that "things were looking pretty good in the room," he agreed, but then Rodin had to persuade Pollack to rehire him. "Ben rather felt that I should have come right on the job and done the opening with them," Benny explained, "and there wasn't the same closeness between us that there had been before."

This strain in their friendship did not get in the way of their musical compatibility. During the stay at the Southmoor Pollack began featuring Benny and himself in extended clarinet and drum duets, anticipating the sort of audience-rousing routines Benny worked out with Gene Krupa years later on numbers like "Sing, Sing, Sing." "Pollack and I used to sit right next to each other on the stand, and sometimes we'd get off on a tune like 'I Want to Be Happy' and play by ourselves, just clarinet and drums, for ten or fifteen choruses," Benny recalled. "We had our disagreements, but the fellows always liked to hear the two Bennys (as they called us) get off together." It was also an effective bit of showmanship that kept the customers entertained. Pollack would lean over the drums, yelling at Benny to "take another one, take another one," and whenever there was someone in the house he wanted to impress, he'd call out, "Give it the personality, kid," or "Let's hear you in the lower register—a million notes a minute." According to Benny, "Nobody else at the time was doing it. We did it a lot."

Pollack's concern with showmanship and presentation was something that was expected of every bandleader of that time, even those jazz musicians who were most esteemed by the purists. "In the early days, jazz wasn't

considered an art, it was song-and-dance music," the trumpet player Max
Kaminsky reminds us. "In 1926 at the Sunset Cafe in Chicago, Louis [Arm-
strong] and these other musicians, including Earl Hines, used to close the floor
show by doing the Charleston—and they really did it. . . . These jazzmen
thought of themselves as entertainers and they used comedy routines as a
regular part of their performances." But Pollack's new emphasis on such
matters also reflected his anxiety about sustaining the band's current popularity and a growing uneasiness about its future. As it settled into the Southmoor,
it began to attract the attention of established leaders like Roger Wolfe Kahn
and Red Nichols and the big band impresario Jean Goldkette, who were
always on the lookout for new talent. The night Goldkette dropped by the
hotel "I was scared to death he had come to 'look over' the band and would
take some of my men," Pollack remembered, "so I hurried over to his table
and pleaded with him to leave my band intact."

As the son of the millionaire financier Otto Kahn, Roger Wolfe Kahn
didn't have to worry very much about such mundane matters as expenses. His
band "had a million instruments: all sorts of woodwinds like oboes and flutes
and things," Benny recalled. "And it looked sharp! Well, Pollack took one look
at them and decided we had to have all that stuff, too. They cost a fortune."
Though the instruments were added primarily for their visual appeal, Benny
took his flute and oboe work seriously. To learn the oboe correctly, he began
studying with a teacher who had played with the Chicago Symphony. "I used
to bring the oboe in and play hot choruses on it," he said, "driving Ben Pollack
nuts."

The same seriousness about his playing also led Benny around this time
to shift over from the Albert (the so-called simple system) clarinet favored by
Jimmie Noone and the other New Orleans clarinetists to the more technically
advanced Boehm system. The different fingering arrangements on the Boehm
forced Benny to make a radical adaptation in his accustomed way of playing,
but the Boehm gave him the means to continue developing the virtuoso
approach to the instrument that became the hallmark of his style.

For all of Pollack's apprehensions, he continued to do well at the Southmoor and remained there until the spring of 1927. Benny was one of the
band's brightest stars. His name was prominently displayed in its advertise-
ments, and when it began recording for Victor toward the end of 1926, he
emerged as its strongest soloist.

Benny and Harry were bringing home pretty good money by now, so
their father was able to stop working, but rather than retire, he opened a
newspaper stand near his home at 4349 Jackson Street. He liked having
something to do, and after all those years cooped up in the sweatshops, he
enjoyed being out in the fresh air. "Benny told me several times," Jim Maher
recalls, "how he went over to the newsstand one day and said to his father,

'Listen, Pop, you don't have to do this anymore. I'd like to take care of things.'
He said his father reached out and put his hand on his arm and said, 'Benny,
you're a good boy. And that's very nice. But you take care of your life, and
I'll take care of mine.' Benny said it was a very sweet and loving moment, and
then it was over. He didn't even say, 'Okay.' He just looked at his father, and
they started talking about something else, and he never mentioned it again."

On the evening of December 9, 1926, David Goodman was on his way
home for supper when he was struck down by an automobile at the intersec-
tion of Madison and Kostner. His skull was fractured, and he died in the
hospital the next day without gaining consciousness. He was fifty-four years
old. Benny's father never learned that Ida had just given birth to his first
grandchild. Nor did he ever hear Benny play at the Southmoor. He had felt
his clothes were too shabby and wanted to wait until he got around to buying
himself a new suit. Benny described his father's death as "the saddest thing
that ever happened in our family," and the sadness remained with him for
many years to come. Benny was not an emotionally demonstrative person, but
in unguarded moments the recollection of the loss was enough to bring tears
to his eyes. What made it all the worse for him was that it happened just as
he was beginning to achieve the sort of success Pop had hoped he would find
someday when he took him to the Kehelah Jacob Synagogue for his first
clarinet lessons. Years later Benny dedicated his autobiography, *The Kingdom
of Swing*, "To the Memory of My Father David Goodman."

In the fall of 1926 a scout for Victor Records named Roy Shields
dropped by the Southmoor with Jean Goldkette and told Pollack he was
looking for some novelty material to record. Pollack was happy to oblige and
brought out a small novelty group within the band, consisting of Fud Livingston on "foot organ," Benny on clarinet, Lou Kessler on banjo and Pollack
himself on "kazoo in a glass." This was hardly the best the band had to offer,
but it was the sort of thing Shields was looking for, and he signed Pollack to
a contract. Pollack went into the studio on September 14 to record the novelty
item and two sides by the full band, one featuring a vocal trio of Pollack and
two sidemen and the other the first of Pollack's many dismal solo vocal efforts.
According to one account, the vocal trio was so dreadful the band collapsed
in laughter during the playback. Victor didn't think much of the entire session,
and all three sides were scrapped.

Pollack was given a second chance, and on December 9 he recorded two
arrangements by Glenn Miller. Miller, Gil Rodin said, "wrote more in the
pop vein for us," and was a great fan of Roger Wolfe Kahn's commercial
dance band, especially the way it employed strings. To emulate the Kahn
band's sound, he persuaded Pollack to add two violins for the session. A
straight reading of a current pop tune called "When I First Met Mary" with
a vocal chorus by one Joey Ray was deemed releasable; " 'Deed I Do," with
another of Pollack's vocals, was not. The following week Pollack returned to

the studio for several more run-throughs of " 'Deed I Do" and recorded two additional sides, "You're the One for Me," with a vocal by Ilomay Bailey, and "He's the Last Word," featuring the singing Williams Sisters. Victor had some reservations but decided to issue them.

None of these recordings really represents the more adventuresome jazz band aspect of the Pollack orchestra. According to Jimmy McPartland, who joined the band the following year, when it came to his record dates, "Pollack always wanted things a little on the commercial side, more and more as time went on." Jimmy maintained: "It was all right with us, as long as it was good music. Trouble is, I don't think any of our records really shows what the Pollack band could do, the way we could get goin'. You had to hear us on the job for that."

Pollack's decision to downplay the jazz on his records was entirely typical of the white leaders of that day. As Albert McCarthy points out, not one of them "really set out to gain public recognition on the strength of [his band's] jazz potential," but they pursued "an eclectic musical policy aimed at pleasing as wide a public as possible." Yet Pollack's desire for commercial success and the several near failures he had already encountered led him to bend over backward to ingratiate himself with the larger, less musically aware portion of his audience. ("May it please you—Ben Pollack" was the sycophantic tag line he took to using to close some of his recordings.) By his own account, the inclusion of Ilomay Bailey and the Williams Sisters on the December 17 record date was his idea, and Victor disliked them so intensely it actually threatened to cancel his contract.

Benny was not a jazz purist like the more adamant members of the Austin High Gang inner circle, and he shared Glenn Miller's high opinion of Roger Wolfe Kahn. (Kahn "knew who the good musicians were," he said, "and had one of the best bands of the time.") Nor did he appear to have been displeased with the band's early recordings. Interspersed between all the vocals and the conventional, often stilted orchestral passages, the band and its soloists do have their moments, and on " 'Deed I Do" and "He's the Last Word" Benny was given a chance to shine. Other than for a few primitive, barely audible home recordings, these are the first recorded examples of his playing that we have. Benny solos with great enthusiasm and remarkable assurance for one still so young, and we can hear the mature Goodman style already being formed out of boyhood influences like Jimmie Noone. But as Pollack's need for popular acceptance led him farther and farther away from the band's real strengths, Benny became increasingly disenchanted with his leadership and distrustful of his judgment.

Though the Austin High crowd had reservations about the Pollack band, they occasionally dropped by the Southmoor on their Sunday nights off from the

White City Ballroom. "All the musicians came in to hear us," Rodin remembered. Bix Beiderbecke and Frank Trumbauer drove in frequently from Detroit, where they were playing with Jean Goldkette. Benny liked to tell the story about the time he and some of the other Pollack sidemen joined Bix on a heady tour of the South Side clubs after work, then, when "a mellow mood had descended on all of us," decided to take the next night off so they could go back to Detroit with him to hear him play at the Greystone Ballroom. "The boss thought we were absolutely out of our heads. Imagine, taking a night off just to go see a trumpet player. But we did. That's how much we were interested in music. It was all we were interested in. We'd go anywhere to hear it. And there were quite a lot of places to hear it too."

That there were. Louis Armstrong was working with Earl Hines in Carroll Dickerson's orchestra over at the Sunset Cafe at Thirty-fifth and Calumet, and playing more brilliantly than ever. (Max Kaminsky found him so dazzling that "I felt as if I had stared into the sun's eye. All I could think of doing was to run away and hide till the blindness left me.") Across the street at the Plantation Café King Oliver led a band that included the wonderful New Orleans clarinetists Albert Nicholas and Barney Bigard. Jimmie Noone was playing right next door at the Nest, a little upstairs joint that opened at three in the morning and kept going until dawn. "Thirty-fifth and Calumet was jacked up every night, with Louis and Oliver and Jimmie all playing within a hundred feet of each other," Eddie Condon recalled. "Unless it happened in New Orleans I don't think so much good jazz was ever concentrated in so small an area. Around midnight you could hold an instrument in the middle of the street and the air would play it. That was music."

If the Lincoln Gardens and the Entertainers' Café had completed Benny's high school education a few years earlier, the Sunset and the Plantation and the Nest were his university. Like all the other white jazz musicians in town, he frequented them regularly. "Most of the clubs and hotels where the white musicians played closed between one and two o'clock, and they'd come down either to King Oliver at the Plantation or where we were. Benny Goodman used to come with his clarinet in a sack," Earl Hines remembered. "Whatever section they wanted to sit in, why, a musician would step out from his chair. We all got a kick out of listening to each other, and we all tried to learn. We sat around waiting to see if these guys were actually going to come up with something new or different."

Benny also did a lot of sitting in with the extended Austin High Gang, which had come to include the pianist Joe Sullivan and the eighteen-year-old drummer Gene Krupa as well as Eddie Condon and Mezz Mezzrow. They had their own following by now and their own hangout at the Three Deuces, a hole-in-the-wall speakeasy at 222 North State Street, where they held nightly jam sessions in the dank, unfinished cellar. "Sometimes when you'd go in there sober, it almost knocked you off your feet," Benny recalled. "I remember one session there that began about two in the morning and lasted well into the daylight hours."

Like Pollack's other sidemen, Benny had his musical differences with the gang. "The boys that hung out at the Three Deuces were terrifically talented guys," he said, "but most of them didn't read, and we thought their playing was rough—we didn't pay them much mind, although we liked to jam with them." For their part, "the boys" suffered from their own sort of elitism. "We were so damn cocky!" Krupa remembered. "If a guy went with a breadwinning band, he immediately became commercial. . . . If . . . Benny would bring in some other Pollack sidemen to our jams, when they'd go on the stand, we'd walk off, pretending to rest!"

Pollack remained at the Southmoor a full year, until April 1927, then moved over to the Rendezvous Café, a gangster hangout on the South Side that paid him $1,850 a week, $600 more than he'd been making. "The syndicate owned the place and had their own barber chair and their own barber," Rodin remembered, "and when a guy got a shave or a haircut, he'd be protected by their own guys with machine guns." Benny claimed the gangsters liked the band and treated everyone well, serving up free dinners and drinks whenever they stayed late to rehearse. He had worked in mob-run speakeasies since the age of fourteen, and his experience was "the bigger the gangster, the better the treatment and pay." Still, he recalled that Pollack had a couple of very bad weeks before he got up the nerve to tell the boss he wanted to move on to the Blackhawk to play for the college crowd.

The Blackhawk was a large restaurant on Wabash near Randolph that featured two-dollar lobster dinners and charged a one-dollar cover on weekends. The Pollack band opened in the middle of May and remained there until the start of the summer, when the college kids went off on vacation. The band decided to take a vacation, too, and headed back to California, financing the trip by playing two weeks in Omaha, then returning to the Venice Ballroom for a month. All the sidemen were paid the same ninety dollars a week, no more than they had made two years earlier and perhaps a bit less, but it was easy work, and Benny had plenty of time to go to the beach and learn to play golf.

Pollack reopened at the Blackhawk in September with a revised personnel that included Jimmy McPartland. On December 7 the band recorded three more sides for Victor: "Waitin' for Katie," a pop tune with a vocal trio, W. C. Handy's "Memphis Blues" and a "California Medley," which Victor chose not to release. Unencumbered by a string section and sparked by McPartland's enthusiastic presence, the band was finally able to express a bit more of its jazz-playing abilities, especially, surprisingly enough, on "Waitin' for Katie," the more commercial of the two issued sides.

After a brief introduction by the ensemble, Benny leaps in with his solo and instantly commands our attention with an ebullient, beautifully executed chorus full of good ideas, revealing just how far he has come in establishing his own identity since "He's the Last Word" and " 'Deed I Do." The Jimmie Noone influence is still apparent, and on "Memphis Blues" he adopts a thinner, more acerbic sound in the Teschemacher vein, indicating that he is still in the process of consolidating his influences, but he is clearly on his way.

Benny's work on this date did not go unnoticed. The saxophonist Arthur Rollini, who became one of the stars of the early Goodman orchestra, remembers listening repeatedly to Benny's "magnificent solo" on "Waitin' for Katie" while touring Great Britain a year or so later. In the spring of 1927 the music publisher Walter Melrose had issued a folio of *One Hundred Jazz Breaks by Benny Goodman,* and this was also bringing him to the attention of musicians beyond Chicago.

The band continued at the Blackhawk until the end of the year, then went off on a short but intense tour of one-nighters that took it as far afield as Nashville, Tennessee. Benny thoroughly disliked this sort of work, though he managed to put up with it once he had his own orchestra, and he claimed that his aversion to the one-nighter grind was a major reason he decided to leave Pollack for Isham Jones when he came back to town. More to the point, Jones had offered him a formidable salary of $175 a week, too much to turn down. Jones "wasn't the kind of band that I liked very much," Benny said, "but they let me play my style, and the pay was good."

If Benny's second defection alienated him even further from Pollack, he continued to be close with his former bandmates. When Walter Melrose offered to subsidize Benny's first recording session under his own name to promote a couple of Melrose-owned tunes, the seven-piece group Benny assembled consisted almost entirely of Pollack sidemen like Jimmy McPartland and Glenn Miller. The date, which was held on January 23, 1928, produced two rather different but equally interesting performances.

"A Jazz Holiday" is reminiscent of the coolly self-contained, elegantly "sophisticated" sort of jazz that Bix Beiderbecke and Frank Trumbauer had started recording in New York the previous year. If Glenn Miller's arrangement seems a little too self-consciously tricky at moments, on the whole it is a relaxed, swinging, utterly charming debut that offers fine solos by Benny, McPartland and Miller and even manages to satisfy the music publisher's needs by providing an ensemble chorus that spells out the basic melody clearly.

Befitting the nature of the material, Jelly Roll Morton's "Wolverine Blues" is a much hotter performance. The Beiderbecke influence still dominates, but there are also some similarities to the more intense, hard-punching approach favored by the Three Deuces crowd, especially in the Chicago-style "explosion" of the final ride-out chorus, where the ensemble begins softly, then increases the tension as it raises the volume, lowers it again, then proceeds to a final all-out finish that culminates with someone's audible gasp of delight. Doubtlessly inspired by Jimmy's marvelous chorus, Benny solos brilliantly in a voice that is unmistakably his own. As George T. Simon observes, all the different musicians who had left their mark on his playing are here "fused for the first time in a polished, unerringly self-confident clarinet style."

A New York booking agent named Bernie Foyer had been talking with Pollack about taking the band to New York and had lined up an engagement at the Little Club, a popular night spot on West Forty-fourth Street. To make the strongest possible impact in their assault upon Manhattan, the men in the band wanted Benny to come with them. Whatever their personal differences, Pollack did, too, and held off on his decision until Benny's return could be arranged. As it happened, Benny had already been thinking about leaving Chicago. The way he saw it, "Times were pretty good and getting better, and New York was certainly the place to take advantage of the fact." Rejoining Pollack gave him the way to get there. Before leaving Chicago, Pollack also hired Bud Freeman, giving the band yet another strong soloist.

The Pollack band's emigration to New York in February 1928 was part of a more general exodus taking place around this time. Work in Chicago was starting to dry up, especially for jazz musicians, and over the last year or so New York had emerged as the dominating force in the music business. King Oliver had left Chicago for New York in 1927. By 1929 Louis Armstrong was playing at Connie's Inn in Harlem and doubling in the Broadway revue *Hot Chocolates*. Shortly after the Pollack band hit town, Mezz Mezzrow, Eddie Condon, Frank Teschemacher, Gene Krupa and a number of other young white Chicagoans also showed up to try their luck.

Benny checked into the apartment he was sharing with his brother Harry, Glenn Miller and the guitarist Dick Morgan at the Whitby, the musicians' hotel on West Forty-fifth Street, then went out to see the sights. New York was a little overwhelming at first, a cold, impersonal place full of tall buildings and busy, unfriendly people. "When I first arrived it seemed to me the most terrifying city in the world," he said. "I remember walking on Broadway, looking up at this huge, mountainous place—and being so lonely. But things started to clear up when I met a few people in the street whom I'd met before—all of a sudden there got to be a certain familiarity about the place, and the terror kind of evaporated."

On February 29, 1928, a large ad in *Variety* announced that "THE BIG ORCHESTRA WITH THE LITTLE LEADER" was "BREAKING INTO THE BIG CITY." The Pollack band opened at the Little Club on March 6, playing dance music for the club's well-heeled clientele and backing a floor show that included the singing Lane Sisters and the daughter of a millionaire ink magnate who wanted to be a dancer. "They used to charge a three-dollar cover, a lot in those days," Rodin remembered. "But the band was a smash." The Pollack orchestra quickly became a favorite of top-echelon New York musicians like Red Nichols, Miff Mole, Eddie Lang, Adrian Rollini and Tommy and Jimmy Dorsey, who came around regularly Sunday evenings to listen and sit in and, according to Bud Freeman, "get very drunk." All this attention angered the star of the show, Rodin claimed, "and she and the band used to have a lot of fights."

"The big orchestra with the little leader" had most definitely arrived. "We were suddenly on top of the music business after having it tough in Chicago for so many years," Bud recalled. He and McPartland shared a room at the posh Mayflower Hotel, but the money didn't matter. Everyone was earning more than enough to explore all the pleasures the city had to offer. "There were a lot of speakeasies in New York," Benny remembered. "And a lot of nightclubs." There was also Fletcher Henderson over at the Roseland Ballroom, Fats Waller and the other stride pianists up in Harlem and Duke Ellington, whom Benny "liked enormously," at the Cotton Club. Once the band settled in, it began to make more recordings. The high-spirited self-confidence everyone was feeling comes through clearly in Benny's solo on "Singapore Sorrows," which simply refuses to be brought down by the corny, overcomplicated arrangement and Pollack's dreadful vocal. Benny was also starting to get some session work from Victor backing commercial pop singers like Johnny Marvin and Irene Beasley. On the two Johnny Marvin sides he soars above the inferior musical surroundings with defiantly jubilant solos on clarinet and alto saxophone, the first recorded example of his solo work on that instrument.

Variety did not get around to reviewing the band until May 2, but the review was a solid rave, praising the orchestra for producing "the most danceable dansapation extant in the midtown nite life." Yet just one week later the paper reported that Pollack had had a tiff with the owner of the club, who "objected to Pollack's allegedly overlong intermissions between dance sessions," and ended up walking out.

Two months after its triumphant opening in New York, the band was out of work once again with no meaningful prospects in sight. Jimmy and Bud moved out of the Mayflower and into the apartment at the Whitby Benny was sharing with Harry, Glenn and Dick Morgan. Cocktail parties were still plentiful, so there was always something to drink, but food was less easy to come by. Jimmy hadn't eaten for three days when he ran into Bix Beiderbecke at a party over on Park Avenue. "Bix was working with Paul Whiteman, and he laid a hundred and fifty dollars on me. I told him, 'I'll pay it back to you.'

'That's okay, kid,' he said. 'If you have it, fine. If you don't, don't worry about it.' " Benny and Glenn took to swiping empty milk bottles from the hallway and cashing them in to buy breakfast.

Everyone took turns staying close to the telephone so as not to miss any calls for work. Pollack managed to pick up a theater date in Brooklyn, a few radio shows for NBC and a couple of one-nighters out of town, but the men had lost confidence in him and were thinking about breaking away and having Benny or Glenn take over fronting the band. Meanwhile, they grabbed whatever jobs they could find. "The boys had been idle almost six weeks," Pollack said, "when Paul Ash opened at the Paramount with a bad band and wanted some of my men. Four of the boys joined him," including Glenn Miller.

At the beginning of June Benny scored a much-needed record date for Walter Melrose and hired most of the Pollack band as his sidemen, including Pollack himself on drums. Some of the men were a little rusty because of the layoff, and this is reflected in their playing. But Benny seems to have used the session primarily as a kind of calling card to advertise his versatility as a multitalented instrumentalist who could perform a wide variety of distinctive styles. Along with the clarinet, he plays a bit of cornet on the Ellington-inspired "Jungle Blues," baritone saxophone on the more straight-ahead Chicago-style "Room 1411" (named after his apartment at the Whitby) and both baritone and a beautifully crafted Bix-like solo on alto saxophone on the sentimental ballad "Blue," which is more in the Beiderbecke-Trumbauer manner. At the end of the session the musicians were kidding around with Tommy Dorsey, who had come in for another record date, and started playing some deliberately corny Dixieland. The recording supervisor rushed out of the control booth and told them, "That's it! That's what we want, just what you're playing there!" The result was a fourth side, a rowdy send-up of "St. Louis Blues" released under the title "Shirt Tail Stomp." "We played it corny and had a big hit," Jimmy recalled, still shaking his head in disbelief some sixty years later. "Everybody liked that crap." Later that week Benny happened to back the crooner Gene Austin in his deadly earnest rendition of the same W. C. Handy tune.

A few days after the Gene Austin date Benny and Harry picked up a week's work playing with Sam Lanin's orchestra at a convention at the Congress Hotel in Chicago. While he was home, Benny recorded two sides under his own name for Vocalion, "That's a Plenty" and "Clarinetitis," with Mel Stitzel on piano and Bob Conselman on drums. Though the clarinet-piano-drums format anticipates the Goodman Trio of the mid-1930s with Teddy Wilson and Gene Krupa, the session is really more of a nostalgic journey back to Benny's past. He had worked with Stitzel in Art Kassel's orchestra at the Midway Gardens in 1924 and with Conselman while he was with Isham Jones. "That's a Plenty" was an old New Orleans Rhythm Kings number, and Stitzel had been the pianist on the original Rhythm Kings recording. Jelly Roll Morton had employed the same instrumentation a year earlier on a 1927 session with Johnny and Baby Dodds that was also recorded in Chicago. Benny's playing here is so redolent of Dodds, Jimmie Noone and Frank Teschemacher, and seems so much more raw and unpolished than his recent work with Pollack, that some Goodman fans have reasonably concluded these are very early recordings done well before the move to New York. Benny's discographer Russ Connor, however, is sure they were made during the visit with Lanin, and Benny himself remembered it that way.

Toward the end of June Pollack's luck finally changed, and following four one-nighters in Pennsylvania, he was booked into a long engagement at the Million Dollar Pier in Atlantic City. Benny and most of the other sidemen returned, but Glenn Miller decided to remain with Paul Ash, so another trombone player was needed. The choice was obvious.

Jack Teagarden had turned up in New York the previous November, and the Pollack musicians discovered him soon after they opened at the Little Club. "The drummer Ray Bauduc came in and told us about him," McPartland recalled. " 'Come on, Jimmy, you gotta come with me tonight and hear this guy Jack Teagarden at a jam session.' 'Who's Jack Teagarden?' 'A trombone player.' 'Okay, terrific.' So we were all drinking and smoking a little pot, and we went to hear him. Teagarden had his trombone in a cloth sack. Somebody got out a guitar and Ray Bauduc picked up his sticks and Teagarden started to play. Holy mackerel, we were all knocked out of our minds, including Glenn Miller! He blew us all around. We never heard anything like it. Such style and good taste and the way he knew his harmonies. It was such a wonderful feeling inside to hear someone do something so well."

Teagarden's warm, richly melodic, blues-drenched playing was completely unlike the technically accomplished but emotionally remote approach to the instrument favored by Miff Mole, the premier white jazz trombonist up to now who was emulated by most other white trombone players, including Glenn Miller. Teagarden's impact upon the Pollack musicians and the rest of the jazz community in New York, black as well as white, can hardly be exaggerated. Gil Rodin thought he was the best trombonist he'd ever heard and claimed that the main reason Miller didn't return to the band was that he was humbled by Teagarden's hands-down superiority and knew everyone else really wanted him.

Benny and Teagarden took to each other's playing immediately. "Benny has always thrilled me," Teagarden said. "When we worked together in the old Ben Pollack orchestra . . . he used to leave me so weak I couldn't hardly get out of the chair." For Benny, Teagarden "was an absolutely fantastic trombone player, and I loved to listen to him take solos." According to

Pollack, "Benny Goodman was getting in everybody's hair about this time, because he was getting good and took all the choruses. But when Jack joined the band, Benny would turn around and pass the choruses on to Teagarden."

"I got about as many kicks out of hearing Jack play as any musician I've ever worked with," Benny maintained. But the peculiar remoteness that eventually became such a puzzling part of Benny's personality kept it from seeming that way at the beginning. "Benny used to worry me," Teagarden recalled. "He'd keep looking at me all the time, and it got on my nerves. One day I asked him, 'Say, you keep staring at me all the time. Do I annoy you—or is anything wrong?' Benny laughed and said, 'My gosh, no. But the things you play just keep surprising me!' " "Benny *was* hard to read," McPartland agreed. "He'd get a look on his face, and you really didn't know what he thought about anything. But he meant no ill will." "I never was much of a hand for talking about things I like, especially in those days," was Benny's comment on the incident. Bud Freeman claimed that Teagarden's advent changed the style of the band and left a permanent mark upon Benny's playing. "Benny Goodman, up to the time of hearing Jack, had not played much melody. He became a strong melodic player. I'm certain that this influence contributed strongly to Benny's greatness."

The Atlantic City job proved to be a real turning point. The engagement lasted through Labor Day and paid so well Pollack was able to raise the salaries of everyone who had been with him early on. Teagarden discovered some good jazz musicians from New Orleans working at a nearby club, and Benny remembered, "We used to spend a lot of time there after work drinking and jamming." The one thing that marred the summer was a falling-out between Pollack and Bud Freeman, who then left to join the ship's band on the *Île de France*. McPartland took Bud's part in the dispute and also walked out but returned a few weeks later. After finishing up at the Million Dollar Pier the band moved on to Pittsburgh for a couple of weeks. Then, following a brief layoff, on September 28 it opened at the Florentine Grill of the Park Central Hotel in midtown Manhattan.

The Park Central insisted that Pollack add a string section, which displeased Benny and the other jazz players, but by way of compensation there were some new charts by the great black arranger Don Redman. *Variety* reviewed the band favorably, though it took issue with the hotel for putting on the ritz with fawning waiters and oversolicitous maître d's. The Park Central's pretensions were dramatically deflated one Saturday evening in early November, when the gambler Arnold Rothstein staggered downstairs from his room on the third floor and died of gunshot wounds in the lobby, right under the balcony where the Pollack band was performing. The notoriety, though, did nothing to hurt business.

The band was, as Jimmy McPartland said, "a sensation," a huge hit with the college crowd and fellow musicians. It remained at the Park Central for almost a year and became so closely identified with the hotel through its nightly live radio broadcasts that its Victor recordings began to carry the name Ben Pollack and His Park Central Orchestra. Through an arrangement with the music publisher Irving Mills, a slightly scaled-down version of the band also started recording for a great variety of other labels under such euphonious pseudonyms as The Whoopee Makers, The Hotsy Totsy Gang, The Dixie Daisies and Mills Musical Clowns. "Whoopee Stomp" and "Bugle Call Rag," recorded for Mills soon after the Park Central opening, provide splendid examples of just how well it could swing when unencumbered by strings, bad tunes and mediocre singers. But this newfound success only exacerbated the band's internal tensions.

Bernie Foyer, a man who shared Pollack's cockiness and taste for long cigars, had taken over as his manager and had big plans for his future. Convinced that Pollack could be the next Rudy Vallee, he talked him into giving up the drums so he could stand out in front of the band and concentrate on his singing. At Teagarden's urging, the fine New Orleans drummer Ray Bauduc took over his place in the rhythm section. Foyer also had some ideas about pepping up the band's presentation. When they played "Tiger Rag," Bauduc had to put on a tiger head, and for "St. James Infirmary" he dressed up as an undertaker. During "She's One Sweet Showgirl" some of the men came out in hula skirts and camped around the stage in a mock striptease.

"It was so stupid," McPartland recalled, wincing in distaste. "We all wanted to quit, and eventually we did. But that was New York for you. It was much more about business than Chicago. Chicago was freewheeling. New York was commercial. It was about making money."

While continuing at the Park Central, the band took on another well-paying engagement toward the end of 1928, playing in the pit of the new Broadway musical *Hello, Daddy!* The show starred and was produced by Lew Fields, of the old Weber and Fields vaudeville team, and was very much a Fields family affair. The book was written by his son Herbert and the lyrics by his daughter Dorothy, who along with her partner, Jimmy McHugh, had supplied the songs for the hit revue *Blackbirds of 1928* earlier that season. The songwriters were great fans of the Pollack band and had recommended it for the job.

Hello, Daddy! went into rehearsal in late November and opened at Lew Fields's Mansfield Theater the day after Christmas. "It was the private opinion in the band that it wasn't so hot," Benny maintained. He and Gil Rodin were so certain the show would flop that rather than throw out eighty-five dollars on the formal evening clothes they were required to wear, they rented what turned out to be waiters' uniforms. Most of the critics shared the band's opinion, dismissing it as "a routine entertainment, mostly unfunny and lagging." The band had been enlarged to nineteen pieces for the engagement, and though one reviewer praised the "large, expert and amorous orchestra," another found it much too noisy. But everyone raved about the showstopping duet by Betty Starbuck and Billy Taylor on "In a Great Big Way," and this one routine was enough of a draw to keep the customers coming. *Hello, Daddy!* played almost two hundred performances and continued running until the middle of June.

The band was earning, Benny said, "more money than we knew what to do with," but it was a tough grind. They started at six-thirty in the evening at the Park Central, where they performed a nightly radio broadcast and played until eight, worked *Hello, Daddy!* from eight-thirty to eleven, then returned to the hotel until one-thirty in the morning. During the day they played matinees twice a week, and their other afternoons were often spent in the recording studio. Between the opening of the show on December 26 and its closing less than six months later Benny took part in two dozen record dates that produced some sixty-seven sides. Five of these sessions were with the Pollack band for Victor, including a small group date that was issued under the name of Ben's Bad Boys, a clear enough indication of how Pollack was feeling about his more troublesome sidemen. More than twice as many were done with "the Pollack band without Pollack," as it was called, offering up competing versions of the score from *Hello, Daddy!*, further run-throughs of "Shirt Tail Stomp" and endless Tin Pan Alley ephemera, but also some uncompromising jazz performances like "Dirty Dog" and "It's Tight like That." "We'd play the date the way [the recording executive] wanted it, in other words very commercial, if he'd let us make one side the way we wanted to make it," Ray Bauduc explained. "And that's how "Tight like That" and so forth—good jazz records—came out." Benny was also beginning to pick up a good bit of free-lance work on his own, recording with established New York musicians like Red Nichols and the saxophonist Jack Pettis as well as pop singers like Sammy Fain, the Crooning Composer.

On many of these sessions Benny plays alongside Jack Teagarden, who proves to be, as Bud Freeman maintained, a constant source of inspiration. Benny follows Teagarden's commanding yet utterly relaxed half chorus on Pettis's "Sweetest Melody" with a beautifully rendered, unusually bluesy and melodic solo that perfectly captures the soulfully reflective mood that Jack has just established. Benny also comes in right behind him on the Pollack band's "My Kinda Love," recorded the following month, and "It's Tight like That," done ten days later, and here again he meets the implicit challenge Teagarden has laid down for him with his own marvelous choruses. Benny's solos on these two sides are played in the rougher, grittier style of his early Chicago days, but on "Sweetest Melody," as on the date with Sammy Fain, we hear the more polished, full-toned approach characteristic of his later playing. The differences appear to be more a matter of conscious choice than natural evolution. Listening to the recordings Benny made over these few months, one is struck by his remarkable versatility and ability to adapt himself to whatever the music calls for. How easily he moves from the "old" style to the "new" and back again, from playing it perfectly straight on a commercial effort like the Whoopee Makers' "Honey" to the lower-register romp reminiscent of Jimmie Noone on the Ten Freshmen's "Bag O'Blues" to the strident Tesch-emacher-like urgency of Red Nichols's "Indiana." Not yet twenty years old, Benny had already acquired the seasoned professional's understanding of the need to match the style to the occasion and had all the skill necessary to implement whatever choice he deemed best.

Shortly before *Hello, Daddy!* finished its run, Pollack was asked to play a dance at Princeton but was unable to fit it into his schedule. Over Pollack's objections, Benny took the night off and put together his own band for the date, using men like Joe Sullivan, Dave Tough and Max Kaminsky. This was the first time Kaminsky worked with Benny, and he found him "a very unassuming, plain, quiet fellow, until he started to play." Benny ended up with about seven hundred dollars for the night's work. "This was plenty good," he recalled, "much better than blowing notes for somebody else," and it "probably put the idea in my head for the first time of having a band of my own some day."

Benny's insistence on taking the Princeton job placed a further strain on his relations with Pollack. Pollack's relationship with his other sidemen was also deteriorating. As Benny observed, "Pollack was a wonderful fellow when times were tough and we were scuffling, but as soon as the breaks started coming his way, he didn't need anybody. As a result, the spirit in the band was far from what it should have been." To cheer themselves up, shortly before the show closed, the band concocted a practical joke and smeared Limburger cheese on the megaphone Pollack sang through on his big number in the entr'acte. He was not amused.

The Park Central engagement ended in July, and after a few theater dates everyone took off on a much-needed two-week vacation. While he was home in Chicago, Benny recorded two sides for Brunswick under his own name, "After Awhile" and Kid Ory's "Muskrat Ramble," which somehow came out as "Scramble" on the record label. A small group jazz date that included Wingy Manone, Bud Freeman and Joe Sullivan, it is very much in the Chicago-style manner. Benny rasps out his solo on "After Awhile" as if Teschemacher were looking over his shoulder. When the band reconvened in August, it played a short tour of vaudeville theaters in the New York area. It was at the Fox Bushwick in Brooklyn that the inevitable happened, and all the bad feelings that had been building up between Benny and Pollack finally came to a head.

"Benny and I used to play handball on the roof between shows," Jimmy McPartland explained. "Benny was a hell of a handball player, the best in the band. We had to wear black-and-white shoes onstage, and one afternoon we were in such a rush to get back our shoes were still dirty. I used to come out and sing something with a trio behind Pollack, and when we got off the stand that day, he was very angry. 'You're fired, McPartland!' he said to me. 'Look at your shoes!' Benny looked over at him and said, 'Did you just fire Jimmy?' He said, 'Yes, I did!' 'Well, look at *my* shoes," Benny told him. 'I quit!' "

After a four-year apprenticeship that saw Benny evolve from a talented sixteen-year-old to a fully formed young veteran with a growing reputation, the two Bennys came to an abrupt parting of the ways over a relatively trivial display of bad temper. For Gil Rodin, Benny's departure from the Pollack band was a terrible loss. "He was a great inspiration to all of us, and needless to say, we sadly needed him both for his playing and [for] himself. I had been his close companion for a long time and dreaded the thought of not hearing his clarinet each night." For Pollack and Benny, though, the split-up was almost a relief. "I said it was all right with me," Pollack maintained, "as he was getting a little hard to handle." Benny acknowledged that "Pollack had done a lot for me, and I appreciated every bit of it, but I felt the time had come to go out on my own."

Benny's departure was followed by other disruptions. The band lost its Victor contract in November. While playing the Silver Slipper nightclub in New York the following month, Pollack sensed "there was an awful lot of undercurrent stuff going on" and claimed to have discovered that Benny and Dick Morgan were conspiring to take the orchestra away from him. When Pollack hired his girl friend Doris Robbins, a former *Ziegfeld Follies* show girl, to sing with the band, the morale sank even lower. "She and Pollack used to sing moist-eyed duets that made [us] cringe," the trumpet player Yank Lawson recalled. Convinced that Robbins had the makings of a star, Pollack focused all his attention on promoting her career, turning down jobs that didn't put her in the spotlight and alienating club owners with complaints about her billing. The men were increasingly resentful, and sometimes tempers flared. When Pollack criticized Ray Bauduc's playing one evening, Bauduc jumped off the bandstand and took a swing at him. During a record date for a small label in the spring of 1930 Pollack had some unkind words about Jack Teagarden's singing. By the end of the summer Teagarden was gone.

The band limped along until 1934, working sporadically between layoffs, held together by Pollack's promises of upcoming radio shows, record dates and nightclub jobs that usually failed to materialize. At the end of a Thanksgiving engagement at the Cotton Club in Los Angeles, Pollack announced he would be staying in California to continue his efforts to get Doris Robbins, now his wife, into the movies. There had been, as Gil Rodin said, "much unhappiness and dissatisfaction with [Pollack's] musical policies" even before they went west, but this was the final straw. The men turned in their arrangements and walked out en masse. Pollack claimed that Benny had enticed them into leaving by offering them jobs on his new "Let's Dance" radio series on NBC. Harry Goodman did join his brother's band, and Gil Rodin played one or two broadcasts, but most of Pollack's musicians had plans of their own that had nothing to do with Benny. After a quick vacation they re-formed in New York as a cooperative orchestra under Rodin's leadership. The following June they made Bob Crosby their front man and, as the Bob Crosby band, went on to become one of the Swing Era's more notable commercial and musical successes.

Pollack's scheme to turn his wife into a movie star failed to work out, and by 1936 he was leading another orchestra that included the wonderful New Orleans clarinetist Irving Fazola and an exciting new trumpet discovery named Harry James. It was an excellent band, and Pollack had high hopes for its future. "I can truthfully say that I have the nucleus of what I hope will be the greatest swing band, all around, I have ever had," he proclaimed, citing the wealth of "new world swingsters" like Fazola and James that his ear for talent had enabled him to bring together. "I have always been very proud of being able to take nobodies and make them good men," he said, a boast that contained a fair amount of truth. But by the time his remarks were published in March 1937 Harry James had already left to join the Benny Goodman orchestra, now riding high on the crest of the swing craze, and the new Pollack band was already beginning to fall apart.

In 1939 Pollack announced that he was suing Benny Goodman and the Bob Crosby band for half a million dollars, charging them with plagiarism, infringement and breach of contractual rights. His main grievance against Benny was that "without permission, sanction, knowledge or agreement" he had appropriated the Pollack band's arrangement of the old New Orleans Rhythm Kings' standard "Bugle Call Rag."

The origins of the arrangement Benny came to play can, in a sense, be traced back to Pollack. The Pollack musicians had worked out a loose head arrangement of the number at least as early as 1928, when they recorded it for Irving Mills on a Whoopee Makers date. Yet this recording bears hardly any resemblance to the later Goodman version. It was Pollack's arranger Deane Kincaide who developed the head into its familiar, fully orchestrated form when he committed it to manuscript sometime after he left the band in 1932. The chart came into Benny's possession in the summer of 1934, while he was looking for personnel and arrangements for the new orchestra he was organizing to open Billy Rose's Music Hall. Kincaide was now working in a band led by Jerry Johnson, another Pollack veteran, and it caught Benny's attention when he happened to drop by a rehearsal.

"I guess he liked what I had done with it," Kincaide recalled. "He wanted it right away, so maybe it was foolish, but anyway I made a trade with him. He got the parts for two pop tunes we needed for our book. But what happened was this: When we ran the arrangements down we found out that they were useless—really terrible. Benny got the better part of the deal, and he recorded it fairly quickly."

Pollack argued that the arrangement was the greatest single factor in Benny's phenomenal rise to success, but the suit really had more to do with his bitterness at being excluded from the mass acceptance now being accorded other white swing bands that had built upon his foundation than with some legally culpable transgression. There's no question that "Bugle Call Rag" was a big hit for Benny, and the reviewer for *Melody News* did detect "a distinct Pollack flavor" in the 1936 Victor recording when it was first issued. Yet Benny's huge popularity can hardly be attributed to any one piece of material. In any case, the same arrangements were often played by different orchestras; it was common practice. The lawsuit withered away in the courts and never came to trial.

By 1942 Pollack had given up leading his own big band to direct the orchestra backing Chico Marx on a theater tour. During the course of the tour he discovered a seventeen-year-old drummer and singer named Mel Tormé and was instrumental in furthering his career. In 1943 he opened a booking agency and formed Jewel Records. Pollack recorded Kay Starr for the first time and the musically advanced Boyd Raeburn orchestra a few years later, but the company eventually folded, and by the end of the decade he was back to playing drums with a small Dixieland band at the Beverly Caverns in Los Angeles. His last real shot at national exposure was a small part in *The Benny Goodman Story*, the 1956 film that celebrated his former sideman's rise to fame and fortune. "I wore William Powell's old toupee," he said with a certain caustic humor.

Pollack's final years were marked by further disappointments and failures. His marriage to Doris Robbins ended in divorce. By the mid-1960s he was running a beer bar called Easy Street West in Palm Springs. The bandleader Charlie Barnet was a neighbor and sometimes dropped by to visit. "We'd reminisce about the old days and the great musicians who had come out of his band," Barnet recalled. "He always seemed to have some scheme in mind to make a killing. None of them was viable, but that didn't stop him. He rode up to Anaheim one day when I was playing there and sat in for a set. Although his style of drumming was *passé*, he still kept real good time and swung after a fashion."

By 1971 Pollack's health had given out on him, and his customary optimism was gone. On June 7 he hanged himself in his bathroom shower.

The United Press reported that the "former bandleader, who was known as the 'father of swing' during the 1930s and 40s, . . . had left two notes complaining of despondency because of financial and marital problems." "The old beer bar has been vacant ever since he passed on, just as though it were haunted," Barnet said, "and I get a twinge of sorrow every time I drive by it."

3

The Free-lance Years

"It was hard leaving Gil, Jack, my brother Harry and the others," Benny said about his decision to quit the Pollack band and go out on his own, "but I was feeling pretty confident at the time." Considering the cataclysmic events about to take place, Benny's confidence in his future hardly seemed warranted. He left Pollack late in the summer of 1929, a few months after his twentieth birthday. Within a matter of weeks, on October 29, the Wall Street crash sent stock prices plummeting, signaling the onset of the Great Depression. Show business, like every other American industry, was devastated by the trauma. WALL STREET LAYS AN EGG, the October 30 *Variety* proclaimed in a soon-to-be-famous headline, and the accompanying story was filled with frontline reports of its immediate impact on the world of entertainment: millionaire showmen now suddenly bankrupt; movie stocks falling to small fractions of their previous values; hit Broadway shows playing to empty houses; expensive mistresses forced overnight to move out of their fancy apartments. There could not have been a less propitious time to give up a steady salary and try to establish oneself as a free-lance musician, a notoriously precarious way to earn a living even in the best of times.

All in a day's work: Benny *(fourth from the right)* **as he appeared in a 1933 Warner Brothers short with radio conductor Dave Rubinoff.**

From the Benny Goodman Archives in the Music Library at Yale University

Yet if money was no longer flowing as freely as it had before the stock market fell apart, the demand for entertainment did not dry up altogether. Records were still being produced, though not nearly as many as before. New Broadway musicals were still being mounted, though the 1929–1930 season saw their number dwindle to the lowest in over a decade. The elite eastern colleges still held dances and house parties on the weekends. Network radio was just coming into its own, even if most radio stations were operating at a loss. All these enterprises required musicians, and a small cadre of top white New York players were called upon regularly to supply the needed product. Helped by the strong reputation he had established during his years with Pollack and the foothold he had gained as a part-time free-lancer during the band's stay in New York, Benny displayed the same instinct for survival that had kept him working steadily since he took out his union card at the age of thirteen. During the first few years of the depression he not only endured but prospered.

Soon after leaving Pollack, Benny joined Glenn Miller for a brief stay in Eddie Paul's pit band at the Paramount Theater. Having to perform the same tired mélange of pop tunes and "symphonic" arrangements day after day was no more appealing now than it had been when he worked with Benny Krueger at the Uptown Theater back in Chicago, and the heavy schedule of shows limited his recording opportunities. But "there was nothing better in sight just then," he explained, and by way of compensation, always an important factor for Benny, "the pay was $175 a week." By early October he had his fill and joined the band the cornetist Red Nichols was putting together to open the new Hollywood Restaurant on Broadway. The Nichols orchestra was a definite improvement, but Benny's move was motivated as much by business as by musical considerations. Nichols was one of the busiest leaders in New York and always had plenty of outside work for his sidemen. And Benny's days would be free, allowing him time to get on with his free-lance activities.

Four years older than Benny, Red Nichols was, as Max Kaminsky said, "a highly proficient and well-schooled cornetist with a great command of his horn." He had come to New York in 1923 and quickly established himself as one of the most accomplished and versatile session men in town. Nichols pursued a lucrative career playing in dance bands and theater and radio orchestras, but it was as the organizer of recording dates that he demonstrated his strongest skill and achieved his greatest popular success. Starting in 1925, he began turning out a seemingly endless flow of records under such names as The Red Heads, The Arkansas Travelers, The Louisiana Rhythm Kings, Red and Miff's Stompers and finally, toward the end of 1926, Red Nichols and His Five Pennies, a generic designation for a wide variety of different pickup groups ranging in size from five to as many as nineteen musicians. Nichols had a keen ear for jazz talent and has rightly been credited with giving exposure to many important players. On his earlier sessions he used top white New York jazzmen like Jimmy Dorsey, Fud Livingston, Eddie Lang and his longtime associate Miff Mole. In 1928 he began drawing upon recent arrivals like Joe Sullivan, Gene Krupa, Glenn Miller, Jack Teagarden and Benny Goodman, who made his first records with Nichols in February 1929, while he was still with Ben Pollack.

Nichols was a perfectionist and a strict disciplinarian not much given to displays of spontaneity, and in keeping with his temperament and taste he insisted upon a carefully organized, tightly controlled approach to the music. According to Jimmy McPartland, who admired his musicianship, he was not an authentic improviser but always had to plan out his solos in advance before going into the recording studio. To hard-core Chicagoans like Mezz Mezzrow and Bud Freeman, for whom spontaneous creativity was everything, this was an unpardonable shortcoming. "In the opinion of our group Red Nichols was a synthetic player," Bud said. "He was a clever musician and made a lot of records, but he . . . copied every line he had ever learned in jazz from Bix." Nichols was extremely sensitive to the charge that he plagiarized from Beider- becke, a common enough opinion among many musicians and critics. Though he conceded "Bix made a tremendous impression on me and I'd be the last one to deny that his playing influenced mine," he claimed to have evolved his own style quite independently. "Only a person who is musically ignorant finds any marked similarity between my work and that of Bix," he insisted.

Benny acknowledged in *The Kingdom of Swing* that "musicians differed on Red's ability as a hot [cornet] player," and though he discreetly sidestepped giving his own opinion, it does not seem to have differed substantially from that of Freeman and the other Chicagoans. Writing about the night Nichols bawled him out for kidding around on the clarinet during a performance of *Girl Crazy,* Benny claimed he popped off with the comeback "You know how I sound when I'm kiddin'? Well, that's how you sound all the time." But their professional relationship was mutually beneficial, and it continued, on and off, for a year and a half, taking in two major Broadway musicals, radio transcrip- tions, nightclub jobs and many recordings. As Benny said, "Because he was a good promoter and usually had plenty of work lined up, musicians were glad to tie up with him."

One of the things that attracted Benny to Nichols was his involvement with the Broadway theater, a good source of well-paying steady employment. A month after Benny joined him Nichols was asked by George Gershwin to put together the orchestra for the new production of *Strike Up the Band,* George S. Kaufman's satirical send-up of American militarism and big business that had closed on the road back in 1927. Along with Benny, Nichols hired Glenn Miller, Gene Krupa and the saxophonist Babe Russin, who made it, in Benny's opinion, "just about the best lineup of hotmen that had yet played a Broadway show."

Following tryouts in Boston and Philadelphia, *Strike Up the Band* opened in New York on January 14, 1930. The reviews were mostly positive, and it settled down at the Times Square Theater for a solid five-and-a-half-month run. Gene Krupa was now so flush that every payday he took his Chicago pals uptown to hear Luis Russell's great band at the Saratoga Club. Benny, though, through an uncharacteristic miscalculation, wasn't around long enough to benefit from the show's success.

Benny estimated that "because I pulled one of the dumbest things in my life," he didn't play more than a dozen performances. During the Philadelphia tryout Gil Rodin confided that the Pollack musicians were planning to go out on their own and wanted him to come with them. A booking at the Park Central Hotel was practically set. There was even some talk about having Benny front the band as the nominal leader. Benny was sharing an apartment on West Fifty-eighth Street with Jimmy Dorsey and arranged to have Jimmy take over his chair for two weeks while he explored the possibilities with his old band mates. But there was some difference of opinion about whether Benny would be the right front man, especially on the part of Glenn Miller, who was also in on the scheme. And at the very last minute the Park Central was unable to secure the all-important radio line everyone was counting on to give them the necessary exposure. Pollack maintained that a friendly executive at NBC withheld the line from the hotel as a personal favor to help quash the mutiny. Benny tried to return to the show, but Nichols was perfectly happy with Dorsey and saw no reason to make another change. When the dust from all this wheeling and dealing finally settled, Benny found himself out of work.

As resourceful as ever, by the end of January he was headed back to Broadway as part of the orchestra assembled by Donald Voorhees for *The Nine Fifteen Revue*. On paper at least, it looked as if the show couldn't possibly miss. It was produced by Ruth Selwyn, wife of the producer of *Strike Up the Band*, and though this was her first theatrical venture, she was able to draw upon the talents of a vast array of eminent show business friends, including Anita Loos, Noël Coward, Ring Lardner, George Gershwin, Cole Porter, Vincent Youmans, and Rodgers and Hart. Yet the opening night reviews were disastrous. The *Sun* liked the "expertly noisy orchestra" that filled the theater with "the Spirit of Jazz," and a few of the critics praised Harold Arlen's terrific new song "Get Happy," but the overall opinion was that Mrs. Selwyn's friends had done her no service by dredging out long-abandoned material from the bottom of their trunks. The show closed six days later on February 17.

What came out of it for Benny, though, was an ongoing and highly profitable relationship with Donald Voorhees that moved him into the top echelons of radio work. The twenty-six-year-old Voorhees had begun exploring the new medium of radio as early as 1925, and by 1928 he was concentrating on it almost exclusively as a free-lance musical director, only occasionally taking time out for theater work like *The Nine Fifteen Revue*. The orchestra he had put together for the show "was a pretty remarkable outfit," Benny recalled, and during the spring and summer of 1930 Voorhees used it frequently on his various radio programs. Benny sometimes did as many as two and three a day for him. He found the work challenging and in its own way, as a test of his musical skills, rather satisfying. "We played a lot of stock orchestrations, and you had to be able to transpose and be quick on the draw about doing everything with him. He demanded it of you. I must say it was a wonderful experience for me." The music itself was not especially satisfying. Other than for an occasional solo, there was hardly any chance to play jazz. But as Benny said, in what has by now become a very familiar refrain, "The work paid well, and it was fairly steady."

Once he established himself with Voorhees, Benny had no trouble finding employment with other high-placed radio conductors like Frank Black, Dave Rubinoff, Al Goodman, André Kostelanetz and Paul Whiteman. Network radio was a good place for a free-lancer to take cover in as the depression gathered force. It provided much-needed free entertainment of a higher quality than most people could otherwise afford, and the audience was growing. By 1930 more than fifty million listeners tuned in nightly. Along with early situation comedy hits like "Amos 'n' Andy" and "The Rise of the Goldbergs," syncopated dance music was one of the most popular attractions. Paul Whiteman and Guy Lombardo had their own weekly radio series. Musical variety programs like "The Rudy Vallee Show" and "Show Boat," which Voorhees conducted and Benny played, drew enormous audiences. Music was also employed on comedy shows like Ed Wynn's "Fire Chief" and Eddie Cantor's "Chase & Sanborn Hour."

Benny appeared on all sorts of programs, including the "City Service Concerts," which had him performing symphonic music as well as current Tin Pan Alley ditties. With a busy schedule that kept him moving around from one studio to the next, often in the company of Tommy Dorsey, he had every reason to believe that "a musician's future was going to be tied up" with the medium, as he put it, and he would be able to "find a pretty secure living in that field." To hone his skills, he began taking lessons in musical theory from Joseph Schillinger. To make himself more salable to potential employers, he became much more concerned with developing a "legitimate" style of playing that would be suitable for just about any kind of musical occasion. It is probably the demands of his radio work that explain why starting around this time, Benny largely abandoned the rougher, more acerbic Chicago style playing he had sometimes favored on his recent recordings and committed himself to the smoother, more readily identifiable "Benny Goodman style."

If the depression was ultimately beneficial for radio, it was disastrous for records. Two days after the stock market collapsed, the Thomas A. Edison Company announced it had discontinued the sale of records and phonographs and would now limit itself to radios and dictating machines. RCA, whose stock plummeted from 114 to 20 over the next few weeks, virtually ended its production of phonographs, dropped many of its recording artists, pared its record advertising to the bone and instituted stringent new procedures in the recording studio, such as limiting each tune to a single take. Columbia and Brunswick also canceled many contracts, and Brunswick's parent company was so discouraged by the prospects for its record division that in 1930 it sold the label to Warner Brothers Pictures, which quickly passed it along to the American Record Company at a bargain basement price. The abiding pessimism about the future of recordings was confirmed by the bottom line. Record sales for 1930 fell by 39 percent. In 1931 they slipped even further, and by 1932 they had dropped to ten million by one estimate, six million by another, in either case a small fraction of the one hundred million discs that had been sold in 1927.

Yet despite steadily declining sales, Benny's recording career actually took off and flourished during this period. Along with a small handful of other top New York session men who knew how to perform any kind of popular music efficiently and well, there was a constant demand for his services, and his appointment book was filled with as many as seven record dates in a single week. In 1930 alone he participated in more than three dozen sessions that yielded over one hundred issued sides.

Benny's ability to find steady employment in the recording studios is attributable in no small part to the connection he had established with Ben Selvin, the recording director at Columbia. Still in his early thirties, Selvin already had two decades of experience in the music business as a violinist, an orchestra leader, a songwriter, a music contractor, a radio conductor and a recording artist. His 1918 rendition of "Dardanella" is said to be the first record to sell more than a million copies. As recording director for Columbia Selvin organized sessions for popular singers like Ruth Etting, Ethel Waters and Kate Smith and produced dates by studio groups that were sometimes released under his own name, sometimes under such pseudonyms as The Columbia Photo Players and The Midnight Minstrels. Benny began working for him in December 1929, and the majority of Benny's recordings over the next few years were done under Selvin's supervision.

Benny's cohorts on the Selvin sessions regularly included Tommy Dorsey, the trumpet virtuoso Manny Klein, bass saxophonist Adrian Rollini, Rube Bloom on piano and Eddie Lang on guitar. All these men played good jazz, but relatively little jazz was played. Selvin was the epitome of the businessman-musician; a 1934 interview was aptly titled "How to Make Money as a Musician." His choice of personnel suggests he had some feeling for jazz, but he also knew what the market would bear. A novelty number like Rube Bloom and His Bayou Boys' "The Man from the South (with a Big Cigar in His Mouth)" might offer up some unexpectedly heated choruses, and every so often Benny was allowed to get off a hot solo, but the main order of business was to provide commercially acceptable renderings of current pop tunes and unobtrusive background accompaniment to the big name singers.

Several of the 1930 record sessions Benny did for other companies had even greater jazz potential, but once again the depression-driven need for commercial acceptability kept it from being fully realized. The band on the two sides he recorded with Hoagy Carmichael on May 21 included Bix Beiderbecke, Bud Freeman, Eddie Lang, Joe Venuti, Gene Krupa, Tommy and Jimmy Dorsey and Duke Ellington's former trumpet star Bubber Miley. "This was probably the greatest aggregation of names ever assembled at one time," Carmichael rightly claimed, "and all they got was twenty dollars each." The first tune of the date was Hoagy's "Rockin' Chair," and what with solos by Miley, Tommy Dorsey, Venuti and, briefly but effectively, Bix Beiderbecke, the jazz content was fairly high. For the second side, though, Victor insisted upon a corny novelty item called "Barnacle Bill the Sailor." The tune was written in strict march tempo, which reminded Benny of the old days back in the Hull House Boys' Band, but Hoagy's arrangement switched into "one-step," as he called it, during Bix's and Benny's solos to give them a chance to cut loose. Both of them solo well, yet the side is most notable for its slaphappy good humor, especially at the very end when, instead of the expected tag line "Barnacle Bill the sailor," Venuti intones in a loud basso voice that somehow escaped Victor's notice, "He's Barnacle Bill the shithead." Carmichael's assessment of the session seems accurate. "These were not great jazz records except for a few spots here and there. We had the men to do it and I could have made the orchestrations accordingly, but Victor was rather intent upon commercialism."

Ironically, considering the low opinion many jazz purists had of him, it was Red Nichols who offered Benny the greatest opportunity to play jazz on records during this first belt-tightening year of the depression. Though Benny was out of *Strike Up the Band*, he recorded two pickup dates for Nichols toward the end of the show's run and began recording with him frequently after it closed. In his own way Nichols was as much of a businessman-musician as Ben Selvin, and some of these sessions were clearly calculated to appeal to the broadest possible public. They included violin- and vocal-laden arrangements of current pop tunes ("Yours and Mine"), saccharine instrumental dance music ("By the Shalimar"), a novelty item ("Bug a Boo") and a big choral production number ("On Revival Day"). Yet even on these largely commercial efforts Nichols used the best white jazz musicians in New York and gave them plenty of room to stretch out. Benny can be heard to excellent advantage on all these sides, soloing in the legato "legitimate" style he now was favoring.

Nichols was certainly aware that the interest in jazz was waning, but perhaps because he still had an audience for this kind of music, perhaps simply because that was what he wanted to do and still had the clout to get away with it, a number of the other recordings he made with Benny during this period were straightforward jazz records without any mitigating commercial elements. "China Boy," "The Sheik of Araby" and "Shim-Me-Sha-Wabble," recorded early in July with an all-star pickup group that included Jack Teagarden and his brother Charlie on trumpet, Glenn Miller, Joe Sullivan and Gene Krupa, are unrelievedly hot and deserve the high reputation that has led to their frequent reissue. "The Sheik" even takes a humorous swipe at the lowest-common-denominator sort of product that jazz musicians were now obliged to manufacture. Teagarden interrupts the deliberately corny crooning that starts the side off ("Wait, wait, wait, man! What in the world are you singin' about?"), then moves on to his own bluesy reworking of the lyric. On the following chorus Miller's rigidly straight dance band reading of the melody is juxtaposed behind—and quite overwhelmed by—Jack's gloriously unconstrained improvisation. Nichols had recorded "Shim-Me-Sha-Wabble" two years earlier with a small group that also included Sullivan and Krupa as well as Frank Teschemacher, the supreme Chicago-style clarinetist. It was probably the hottest record he ever made, and his decision to do the tune again can be seen as a personal stand against the forces that currently kept such records from being produced. Benny's solo here has a by now uncharacteristic Teschemacher-like roughness that makes its own sort of statement.

In the fall of 1930 Nichols offered Benny a job playing in the pit band he was putting together for the new Gershwin musical *Girl Crazy*. Benny was doing a lot of free-lance radio and record work, but he realized "a show was still a good thing to be in on" and made room in his busy schedule. The orchestra was even better than the one Nichols had assembled for *Strike Up the Band*—"a pit-full of experts in syncopation," the *New York Times* called it—and included Charlie Teagarden, Gene Krupa and Glenn Miller, who also arranged some jazz inserts and ride-outs that were incorporated into Russell Bennett's orchestrations. Toward the end of his life Benny recalled with some pride that Gershwin was so taken with his playing that he wrote a special clarinet part

into the overture specifically for him, and after he left the show, the passage
had to be removed because nobody else could execute it properly.

Following a tryout run in Philadelphia, *Girl Crazy* opened at the Alvin
Theater on October 14, with Gershwin himself conducting. "The theater was
so warm I must have lost three pounds perspiring," the composer recalled.
"[But] the opening was so well received that five pounds would not have been
too much. With the exception of some dead head friends of mine, who sat in
the front row, everybody seemed to enjoy the show tremendously, especially
the critics. I think the notices, especially of the music, were the best I have ever
received." The praise was entirely warranted. Gershwin's score included some
of the finest American popular songs ever written: "I Got Rhythm," "Em-
braceable You," "But Not for Me," "Bidin' My Time." And the strong cast,
headed by Ginger Rogers, the comedian Willie Howard and a twenty-one-
year-old newcomer named Ethel Merman, did them full justice. Merman
belted out "I Got Rhythm" with such electrifying abandon she was trans-
formed into a star overnight. Some of the critics took issue with the rather
ordinary book, which had none of the adventuresomeness of *Strike Up the Band*.
But between Gershwin's music, his brother Ira's lyrics and the expert singing
and dancing, there were more than enough high points to make the show a
solid hit "destined to find a profitable place among the luxuries of Times
Square, if not the necessities," as the *Times* reviewer put it.

Girl Crazy settled into the Alvin for a thirty-four-week run. This time
Benny had the sense to stay put and was able to add a substantial weekly
paycheck to his other outside income. But as the months went by, his personal
relationship with Nichols began to unravel in much the same way it had with
Ben Pollack. Benny was, by his own account, "getting a little bit cocky," and
toward the end of the run Nichols accused him of making fun of the oboe
player, snickering during her solo passages and lampooning what he took to
be her exaggerated vibrato and corny phrasing. They argued about it, and it
soon reached the point where Nichols went to the union to try to break
Benny's standard run-of-the-play contract. Benny further antagonized Nichols by refusing to play a dance with him after the show at the University of
Pennsylvania because he had booked his own job at Princeton for substantially more money. In the spring of 1931 the growing strain between them
gave way to a final break.

Nichols was home in bed, recuperating from an attack of pleurisy, when
the notice was posted backstage that *Girl Crazy* would be closing in June. To
keep the band working, he set up a tour of New England colleges and
ballrooms. But before he was well enough to return to the theater, Glenn
Miller telephoned him and rather casually announced that once *Girl Crazy*
closed, he no longer had a band. Practically everyone was going with Benny
Goodman to play a new show called *Free for All*. As the ongoing hassles with

Nichols and, before him Ben Pollack, suggest, Benny was finding it increasingly difficult to serve as someone else's sideman. He'd had a small taste of leading his own pickup bands on college weekends, and now he was beginning to think about something more permanent. It seemed to him that putting together a pit band for a Broadway musical would be the best way to get started, and while Nichols was away, he arranged an audition with *Free for All*'s producers, taking along most of Nichols's best musicians. The audition went well, and the band was hired. After rehearsals and an out-of-town tryout in New Haven, they were to open in New York in September.

Nichols, of course, was furious and severed his ties with Benny. The recording session of April 24 was the last date they did together; on his subsequent recordings he went back to Jimmy Dorsey. Nichols is said not to have spoken to Benny again until 1946, when his former sideman dropped by to hear him play at the Morocco Club in Hollywood. The meeting was brief. The wound still rankled. "It's nice to shake the hand of the guy who stole my band," Nichols told him.

Free for All looked as if it had a great deal of potential. Richard Whiting composed the score. The lead was played by Jack Haley, who had been a big hit in the enormously successful *Follow Thru* a few seasons earlier. Oscar Hammerstein staged the production and coauthored the book. More a comedy with music than a musical comedy, the show made an admirable attempt to bypass the clichés of the genre by dispensing with the usual line of chorus girls and taking on such up-to-date topics as parlor bolshevism, psychoanalysis and free love. Yet none of this seemed to work. The critics found the production "sophomoric and seldom funny" with little "that will make either conservatives or radicals laugh," a "slow-paced and labored affair" that left them with the opinion that "musical comedy, for all the unimaginative artificiality of its formula, is sometimes not so bad, after all." A few chorus girls might have helped. *Free for All* opened at the Manhattan Theater on September 8, and the closing notices went up as soon as the reviews hit the newsstands. "We renamed the show *Freeze and Melt,*" Benny recalled. Two weeks later, after only fifteen performances, "Ben Goodman and His Recording Orchestra," as it was billed, came to an end.

Stung by the band's sudden demise, Benny gave up any further thoughts about leading his own orchestra and went back to the studios. Despite the deepening depression, such work was still plentiful and very well paying for the small group of musicians in Benny's favorable position. It had enabled him to bring his mother and younger brothers in from Chicago the previous summer and set them up in a large apartment he shared with them in Jackson Heights out in Queens. Now that his father was gone, "Benny automatically became head of the family when it came to making decisions," his brother Irving recalled, "and he needed us near at hand." Between March 1930 and

March 1931 the number of unemployed had doubled from four to eight million, yet Benny claimed that "there were few weeks when I didn't earn between three-fifty and four hundred dollars," a remarkable sum for a twenty-two-year-old clarinet player hardly anyone outside the music business had ever heard of. College graduates his age lucky enough to find jobs couldn't reasonably expect to earn one-tenth that amount.

A good part of Benny's income now, as much as eighty dollars a day, came from recording movie sound track music at the Paramount studio out in Astoria. Though overshadowed by Hollywood, New York was still an important filmmaking center, accounting for almost one-fourth of all the movies produced in the United States. Located just across the East River from Manhattan, Paramount's Astoria division was able to draw upon the wealth of writers, directors and performers who primarily worked on the Broadway stage. Many of the Astoria productions, like the Marx Brothers' *The Cocoanuts* and *Animal Crackers,* were direct adaptations of recent Broadway hits. Astoria was also the main production center for Paramount shorts, which frequently starred New York-based radio entertainers like Jack Benny, Rudy Vallee, and George Burns and Gracie Allen. Benny remembered doing "a lot of tunes for the movies" around this time but was vague on the specifics, probably because he just rushed through whatever had to be played so he could get out to the Long Island beaches for some swimming and sun. Benny also worked for the animated cartoon studios, which were still centered in Manhattan, and played on some of the music tracks that were being dubbed onto the old silent comedies.

Benny continued to record prolifically after *Free for All* closed, immediately picking up the momentum he established earlier in the year by doing two sessions for Ben Selvin the day after the show finished its run. Nineteen thirty-one was the busiest year in the recording studio Benny would ever have. He played over fifty dates for Selvin, some issued on Columbia, many more on the cut-rate Harmony, Velvetone and Clarion labels the company had started to boost its declining sales. He also recorded some two dozen sides for American Record's comparable Melotone line, which sold for a quarter instead of the usual seventy-five cents. Most of the Melotone sides were released under the name of Benny Goodman and His Orchestra, which was something of a misnomer. His "orchestra" was strictly a recording group made up of Red Nichols sidemen and fellow session players like Tommy Dorsey, Eddie Lang and the young trumpet player Bunny Berigan, who was just beginning to move into the inner circle of New York free-lancers. And despite the presence of such sterling jazz musicians and the occasional brief solo by Benny, they are very commercial recordings, routine stock arrangements of routine pop tunes that express virtually nothing of his musical personality. As far as Benny himself was concerned, "the first [date] in which I put across something like a style of my own" was the Charleston Chasers session he organized for Columbia in February that produced "Basin Street Blues" and "Beale Street Blues," two acknowledged masterpieces.

Benny was still playing in *Girl Crazy* when he put the session together, and he hired many of the same Nichols musicians he used for his Melotone dates, including Charlie Teagarden, Glenn Miller and Gene Krupa. The big difference was that he also brought in Jack Teagarden and was allowed to pick the tunes and play them the way he wanted. For "Beale Street Blues" he employed the same arrangement Glenn Miller had written five months earlier for a recording by a Ben Pollack group led by Gil Rodin that also included Teagarden. For "Basin Street" Miller worked out a new arrangement and, with Teagarden's assistance, added lyrics and a verse ("Won'tcha come along with me/To the Mississippi . . .") that soon became standard parts of the song, though Miller was never really credited for his contributions. Unlike the elaborate orchestrations he usually produced for Pollack, both of Miller's arrangements were pared down to the bone—"There was very little written, just little notes here and there, a background," the trumpet player Ruby Weinstein recalled—and mainly serve to set off the soloists. And it is the quality of the solo work, especially Jack Teagarden's forceful singing and playing, that makes these sides such classics. Teagarden was in inspired form that day and dominates the proceedings. Benny solos on "Basin Street" but on "Beale Street" rather uncharacteristically limits himself a brief obbligato behind Jack's vocal. Close to half a century later Benny still remembered the session with enthusiasm. "A really good record," he called it, "and it was a great date."

Over the course of 1931 Benny also did a lot of recording with the vaudevillian Ted Lewis. Lewis liked jazz and, to his credit, regularly employed the fine cornetist Muggsy Spanier and the former New Orleans Rhythm Kings trombonist George Brunis. But Lewis was no jazz musician himself, and his own clarinet playing was considered something of a joke. Bud Freeman recalled that when Jimmy Dorsey and Fud Livingston came down to the Little Club to sit in with the Pollack band, they would try to outdo each other's efforts to perform the corniest Ted Lewis parody. Benny shared their opinion and was not above entertaining the crowd with his own wicked impression. But business was business. "The days when I thought Lewis was something on clarinet were long past," he explained, "but the dates paid good money and I was glad to pick them up."

The dates produced some very peculiar music, an improbable mélange of old-fashioned show business hokum and driving hot jazz. One moment Lewis is sprechspieling his way through a sentimental heart tugger or a piece of happy-days-are-here-again uplift. ("All aboard for the Sunshine Special. This train is headin' for Better Times.") The next moment Benny or Muggsy steps out front and turns up the heat. Yet these recordings are, in their own strange way, quite appealing, and a few of them are considerably more than that.

The sessions of March 5 and 6 benefit enormously from the catalyzing presence of Fats Waller. According to Waller's son Maurice, Lewis had to be talked into using him on the dates because he was concerned that he might be upstaged. Fats is kept under wraps on "Egyptian Ella," the first tune up, while Benny offers a dead-on imitation of Lewis that verges perilously close to parody. But on the next number, Waller's own "I'm Crazy 'bout My Baby," Fats takes charge from the opening notes of his piano introduction, singing and playing with a joyful ebullience that sparks Benny's solos and the all-out jam band finish. It is a wonderful record. "Dallas Blues" and "Royal Garden Blues," recorded the following day, are no less hot. Here again Lewis has the good sense to stay out of the way, limiting his contribution to croaking over Waller's solo on "Dallas Blues," "Play it boy! Play it!" and registering a territorial claim with his trademark tag line "Is everybody happy? Yes, sir!" Lewis also encourages Benny on during the equally torrid "Dip Your Brush in the Sunshine" recorded a few weeks later: "Paint it, Benny! Paint it! Paint it blue, Benny! Sky blue, Benny!" Whether because of or despite Lewis's exhortations, Benny digs in with a ferociously swinging solo that is matched by Muggsy's growling chorus. Lewis must have admired what he heard. He wisely kept his own clarinet playing to a minimum when Benny was in the studio, but on their next date together later that week he edged up to the microphone and shouted over Benny's solo on "Ho Hum," "Play it, Ted! Play it!"

Most jazz fans would agree that the high point among all the many recordings Benny made in 1931 was the session cut for Vocalion on October 22 with an eight-piece pickup group led by Eddie Lang and Joe Venuti. Venuti and Lang were among Benny's favorite musicians. He considered Venuti "the first fiddle player to make sense in a jazz band" and maintained that Lang's innovative approach to the guitar "was pretty much responsible for its taking the place of the old banjo." Benny had recorded with them frequently over the past year, as he had with Jack and Charlie Teagarden, who were also on hand for the date. But unlike most of the other sessions they did together, this time they were unconstrained by the usual commercial imperatives. Venuti and Lang picked four good jam session standards, sketched out a few unobtrusive head arrangements and divided up the solo spots with Benny and the Teagardens. "Nobody was out to compete with anyone else," Benny recalled. "We were there to make good music and have a good time." Both aims were accomplished. One is struck by the relaxed affability that pervades the entire session and contributes so much to making it such a success. Following a jaunty "Beale Street Blues," they move on to "After You've Gone," which begins as a lazy ballad and ends with a surging up-tempo solo by Venuti that leads into the sprightly ensemble ride-out. The pace continues unabated on the fiery run-through of the New Orleans Rhythm Kings' "Farewell Blues," then settles back down for the mellow but no less high-spirited and swinging "Someday Sweetheart," the final tune of the date. For the jazz critic and historian George T. Simon, these four sides "are probably the first records by a white band to swing as consistently hard as those by the best black bands of the period." They are also the last jazz records Benny would make for the next two years.

The depression continued to deepen over the course of 1932 and by the middle of the year had reached its nadir. More than 12 million people were now out of work. In New York City alone almost one-third of the city's 3.2 million working population was looking for employment. Industry was operating at about half the volume of 1929, and the record business was doing even worse. Sales for 1932 were down 40 percent from the year before. Far fewer records were being produced, and there was almost no interest at all in jazz. In 1931 Benny had recorded close to 250 sides. In 1932 he had a grand total of three record dates, two for Ted Lewis and one for Ben Selvin.

Network radio, though, was largely unaffected by the rest of the country's economic woes—NO DEPRESH FOR RADIO, a *Variety* headline announced—and Benny continued to pick up jobs in the studio orchestras, frequently playing with Dave Rubinoff on the "Chase & Sanborn Show" and even appearing as a featured soloist on one of Paul Whiteman's NBC programs. There was still some movie sound track work around. And during the spring of 1932 he was hired to put together a dance band to be fronted by the popular crooner Russ Columbo.

Benny was drifting way from jazz, but the Columbo offer seemed to ignite some of his old enthusiasm, and he filled the band with good jazz musicians like Gene Krupa, Babe Russin and Joe Sullivan. Benny did not appear with the band on all its engagements, but when it was booked for the summer into the Woodmansten Inn, a roadhouse just outside Manhattan, he took over as musical director, allowing Columbo to mix with the customers when he wasn't singing. *Variety*'s review of the May 5 opening praised the high quality of the band's music, calling it "dance inspiring," but unhappily for Benny, Columbo's manager, Con Conrad, did not share this enthusiasm. "It was a good little band," Benny said. "But Conrad wound up getting mad at me because whenever we played for dancing people seemed to really like it. I mean, we'd play *Between the Devil and the Deep Blue Sea* or some song like that, and all of a sudden the joint was rocking. He'd say, 'Hey, wait a minute—you guys aren't supposed to be the attraction here,' and he meant it." The experience did nothing to encourage Benny to try his hand again at leading his own orchestra, and at the end of the summer he returned to the decidedly unrocking anonymity of the radio studios.

By the early months of 1933 radio had become just about Benny's only source of steady work. But now that, too, was starting to fall off. Many of the big network shows had turned to established name orchestras like Guy Lombardo and Fred Waring, and there was much less need for high-priced free-lancers. Nor did it help matters that Benny was acquiring a reputation for being a rather arrogant, thorny personality.

When Benny entered the free-lance marketplace back in 1929, he still thought of himself primarily as a jazz musician, and he shared his fellow jazz musicians' disdain for those who played only straight commercial music. "None of us had much use for what was known then, and probably always will be, as 'commercial' musicians," he recalled. "The saddest thing always was a recognized hot man who went in for that sort of work because he made good dough and got steady work around the studios." Yet over the next few years that is precisely what Benny himself became. By 1933 the boredom and frustration endemic to "that sort of work" had finally caught up with him and were beginning to cause him serious problems. He was having a particularly hard time getting along with those radio conductors who liked to throw in a bit of jazz now and then as long as it was performed exactly the way they wanted. Benny simply had no patience for being told how to play the kind of music that, in a sense, continued to be the bedrock of his identity even though he hardly played it any longer. At the beginning of the year Benny was still earning about two hundred dollars a week, a very good income for 1933. But word was getting around that he had become hard to handle, and the telephone was no longer ringing so steadily. By that fall he was down to just one radio show a week.

"I guess I was doing something that didn't really satisfy me, and that's where a lot of the trouble came in," Benny admitted. It was time for a change, time to move on to something that did satisfy him and maybe pointed the way to some kind of more tolerable future. The opportunity presented itself in the most unlikely manner.

4

Ain'tcha Glad?

n the fall of 1933 the Onyx Club was still a cramped and noisy speakeasy hidden away in the back of the parlor floor of the old brownstone at 35 West Fifty-second. Presided over by a genial bartender named Joe Helbock, it catered almost exclusively to the white musicians who worked at the NBC and CBS radio studios nearby. During business hours they played whatever had to be played to grind out a living, but once that was disposed of, they repaired to the Onyx to pick up their mail and telephone messages, talk shop and bend an elbow or two. And whenever the spirit moved them, they broke open their instrument cases, took out the tools of their trade and played the kind of music that no one with money in his pockets seemed interested in listening to anymore.

At first glance the young man with the brushed-back crew cut and unmistakable air of privilege and wealth must have looked as if he'd lost his way as he headed toward this inelegant hangout. Surely he'd have been more at home sipping a quiet glass of sherry in one of the baronial mansions at the Fifth Avenue end of the block. And, in fact, the imposing edifice on the southwest corner of Fifty-second and Fifth had been built by his maternal grandfather, William Henry Vanderbilt of the steamship and railroad for-

**Benny and John Hammond in 1975,
some forty years after they began their association.**

From the Benny Goodman Archives in the Music Library at Yale University

tunes, and he'd passed many a pleasant Sunday afternoon there as a boy, chauffeured to and from from his home on East Ninetieth Street in his parents' Brewster or Pierce-Arrow. Yet the self-assured way he bounded down the basement steps that late September evening, moved briskly along the darkened hall, climbed the flight of stairs in the back and rapped on the silver-painted door made it clear he was hardly a stranger to the Onyx Club and its boisterous goings-on.

Nor was any other place in New York where live jazz could still be heard foreign to him. Even before he dropped out of Yale in his sophomore year, he'd taken to wandering around Harlem at night, searching out the music in night spots like Small's, the Bamboo, the Hole in the Wall, the Saratoga Club and the Savoy Ballroom. Unlike the forays of others of his class who occasionally sojourned uptown in their limousines, these excursions had nothing to do with "slumming." A well-developed social conscience made such cheap sensation seeking repugnant to him. He did not drink. He was not interested in the free and easy sex that was part of the Harlem night life. The lure was all in the music, and he sought it out with the same fierce determination with which his great-grandfather Commodore Vanderbilt had piled up his many millions.

An eye appeared in the peephole. The password was given: "I'm from eight-oh-two," the number of the New York musicians' union. The silver door swung open. And John Hammond stepped through.

Hammond was here tonight on a matter of some personal urgency. He'd just arrived back in New York from England and came straight to the Onyx as soon as he cleared customs. It was imperative that he see Benny Goodman immediately. Chances were he'd be dropping by sometime over the course of the evening.

While visiting with his sister, Alice, in London, Hammond had been introduced to Sir Louis Sterling, head of the Columbia Graphophone Company, and been asked to record a year's supply of jazz records for the English Columbia and Parlophone labels. Though jazz records were a dead issue in the States, they were still selling fairly well in Britain. Since American Columbia was all but out of business, Sir Louis needed someone to supply him with new product for the British market. Despite his youth (he was only twenty-three), Hammond was a logical choice.

He had been writing about jazz for the past two years in the English *Gramophone* and *Melody Maker* magazines, reporting on American musicians and records with an authoritative, sometimes violently opinionated zeal that conveyed both his knowledge and his enthusiasm. Though far from experienced as a record producer, he had, at the age of twenty-one, recorded pianist Garland Wilson at his own expense, then gone on to supervise some excellent sessions by Fletcher Henderson and Benny Carter for English distribution. When Spike Hughes, recording director of English Decca, visited New York the previous spring, Hammond had quickly assembled a superb all-star band of black players to record Hughes's compositions. Besides, Hammond fervently wanted to carve out a place for himself in the record business and wasn't overly concerned about the paltry remuneration he'd been offered for his services. By the end of his negotiations with Sir Louis, he contracted to produce some sixty sides over the next few months by men like Fletcher and Horace Henderson, Coleman Hawkins, Benny Carter, Joe Venuti and Benny Goodman.

There was only one problem. In committing himself, he had also committed the musicians without ever consulting them. This probably wouldn't matter to Carter and the Hendersons and most of the others. Hammond had worked with them before, written glowingly about them in his columns, established some kind of personal relationship. He wouldn't have to explain that record dates were few and far between these days and any opportunity was to be welcomed. Goodman, though, could present a serious obstacle.

Hammond barely knew him. They had met only briefly the year before, when Benny was leading the band backing Russ Columbo at the Woodmansten Inn up in Westchester, and they hadn't really connected. At the time Hammond wasn't particularly impressed by Benny's playing. He thought he was all right, on a par with Jimmy Dorsey, perhaps, but not up to the level of a lot of black clarinetists. Nor had he any sympathy for hot musicians who took on commercial work that betrayed their talents. If Benny didn't sense this lack of enthusiasm at their meeting, it would have been painfully clear to him when he read Hammond's review in the *Melody Maker* a few weeks later:

> We devotees of improvisation in "jazz" were all excited when we heard that Benny Goodman had organised a band in which were to be featured Babe Russin on tenor; Joe Sullivan, piano; Gene Krupa, drums; Harry Goodman, bass; Max Ceppos, violin, and others, good but less important. Last night I journeyed in the rain out to Woodmansten Inn, where the band is playing under the direction of that irrepressible crooner, Russ Columbo. Mr. Goodman, I fear, has forgotten all about the fact there are actually individual human beings in the band. The result is painful, and the band is merely another smooth and soporific dance combination. Poor Krupa does his best to keep up his spirits, but he is allowed by Goodman only the use of brushes. Even the elegant piano playing of Sullivan the leader tries to conventionalise. All this goes under the name of "commercialism," but I venture to say that the Inn will not stay open a day longer because of the dull and dry performances of the band.

Most musicians ignored such reviews, never even bothered to read them. But Benny was different. Spike Hughes, who reviewed records for the *Melody Maker* under the name of Mike, was struck by his unusual sensitivity to criticism when they ran into each other during Hughes's American visit. "I had a long and interesting conversation with Benny Goodman on the subject of an unfavorable criticism of one of Benny's records by my *alter ego*," he recalled. "Benny Goodman was the only musician I ever met in the Onyx who took 'Mike' seriously; but then Benny was a very serious young man. . . . He was so clearly upset by whatever it was I had written about his playing in the *Melody Maker* that I could have kicked myself for having written it—particularly because I later changed my whole opinion of Benny Goodman and his contribution to music."

The hours were passing, and Benny still hadn't appeared. Then, about ten-thirty, he finally strolled through the door. Masking his anxiety behind the ingratiating smile that hardly ever left his face, Hammond stepped up and reintroduced himself, then got down to business. "Hi, Benny. I'm John Hammond, and I want you to know that I've got a Columbia recording contract for you."

If Benny did indeed remember that scornful review of the Russ Columbo band, the memory was overshadowed by the utter implausibility of Hammond's offer. In his nervousness, Hammond hadn't made it clear that he was talking about English Columbia, not its American counterpart. And only last week Benny had gone to see Ben Selvin about some record work and been turned down flat. The company was practically bankrupt, Selvin told him. A record contract was out of the question.

Hammond quickly cleared up the misunderstanding, but Benny remained skeptical. The money was nothing much. Hammond argued that the session might eventually be released in the United States, so there could be some royalties later on. But what he had in mind was a straightforward jazz date without any of the usual commercial concessions. No charts. A mixed band of black and white players, no less, featuring men like Coleman Hawkins and Benny Carter.

Benny had responsibilities. He was trying to earn a living. He still dropped by the Onyx with some regularity, but he'd pretty much given up on jazz by now. It had been many months since he played the kind of music Hammond insisted upon recording.

"I guess I was in kind of a bad groove mentally at the time," he explained some years later, "with not much desire other than to make money, keep the place going for my mother and the kids, and have as much fun as possible. . . . I sort of broke away from the fellows I had been with since I came to New York, seeing them for the most part only when we worked on a job together."

As Hammond went on arguing, explaining, promising and cajoling, Benny's deeply entrenched cynicism got the best of him.

"Well, I don't know, John," Hammond remembered him saying. "I'll tell you what. I'm rehearsing a band now for a radio show. I'd like you to hear it and tell me what you think, because I think it's just what you're going to like."

Hammond could barely contain his excitement. Then, as throughout his life, the lure of hearing some great unknown talent was too strong to resist, and he temporarily put aside his earlier plans for the date. But when he showed up at the Gotham Studios the next day, he found that the band Benny had waiting for him was "worse than the Russ Columbo Orchestra, the dreariest group of musicians I had ever listened to." This wasn't what he had in mind at all. If Benny insisted upon using this tired bunch, the record deal was off.

Benny was surprised that this pleasant young man could be so adamant. After much arguing back and forth he agreed to go along with Hammond's original idea. But there were certain conditions. Jamming was out. There would have to be written arrangements, and he wanted Arthur Schutt to do them. At least two of the four sides would have to be current pop tunes to balance the blues and the original Hammond insisted upon. As for the personnel, they would need to find some white sidemen to replace Benny Carter and Coleman Hawkins. "If it gets around that I recorded with colored guys," Hammond claimed Benny told him, "I won't get another job in this town."

Given Benny's well-deserved reputation for breaking down racial barriers in music a few years later, this refusal to work alongside black musicians may seem shocking. But such was the shameful state of affairs in the New York music business in 1933, especially in the radio studios. Benny Carter recalls those days with great clarity:

> Radio staff and studio orchestras were closed to us and these were steadier jobs paying hundreds of dollars weekly at a time when the union scale at places like the Savoy was thirty-three dollars. . . . Of course many white musicians, making more than we did, came to listen to us and play with us. We welcomed them and enjoyed the jamming. But we couldn't go downtown and join them. We learned from each other and we didn't much blame the white musicians—we did envy them though. What was holding us back was not just the individual differences but a whole system of discrimination and segregation involving musicians, audiences, bookings, productions and so on.

Mixed record dates, as they were called, weren't exactly unheard of in the early 1930s, but they were still extremely rare. Jelly Roll Morton had done two sessions with the New Orleans Rhythm Kings back in 1923. Six years later Jack Teagarden, Joe Sullivan and Eddie Lang recorded the splendid "Knockin' a Jug" with Louis Armstrong. Fats Waller had used Jack Teagarden and Eddie Condon on a few sessions. Teagarden also used Waller, and Condon had brought Coleman Hawkins and a number of other black players into the recording studios. Benny himself had taken part in the Hoagy Carmichael session that included Bubber Miley and the Ted Lewis dates that featured Fats Waller. There were a few other precedents but not very many. For all practical purposes, the uptown and downtown jazz worlds remained firmly segregated.

John Hammond felt as strongly about racism as he did about jazz. Over the past two years he had reported frequently in the *Nation* on the Scottsboro Boys, nine black youths falsely accused of raping a white woman in Tennessee, and had contributed to their defense fund. But even he had to concede that Benny was probably right. Things *were* that bad. Helped along by Hammond's prodding, mixed record dates would soon become fairly common. Right now this one, at least, would have to wait.

While Hammond continued arguing with Benny about the details of the session, he began recording some of the other musicians he promised to deliver. In less than two weeks he produced more than a dozen sides by Fletcher Henderson, Joe Sullivan, Coleman Hawkins and Joe Venuti. The Venuti date was planned with an unusual front line of violin, clarinet, tenor and bass saxophones, and Hammond hired Benny for the clarinet spot. Perhaps it was just a coincidence, but in bringing Benny back together with the violinist with whom he'd made his last real jazz records, it seems likely that Hammond was deliberately trying to rekindle his interest in jazz and put him in a better frame of mind about his own upcoming session. If that was Hammond's strategy, it partially succeeded. The four sides are no match for the earlier Lang-Venuti All Stars date, but Benny plays wonderfully, with a real sense of involvement and urgency, especially on the old jam session standards "Jazz Me Blues" and "Dippermouth Blues" (called here "In De Ruff").

Hammond and Benny finally settled on a personnel that included their mutual favorites Jack Teagarden and Gene Krupa. Both men were out of town working in Mal Hallett's dance band up in New England. Hammond told Benny he would pay their train fares down to New York, then traveled up to Boston to talk them into doing the date. Teagarden agreed readily. He "loved to make records," Hammond remembered, "and any excuse to get away from the Hallett band for a day suited him just fine."

Krupa, though, turned out to be somewhat less enthusiastic. "I'll never work for that son of a bitch again," he told Hammond flatly. "When he hired me for the Columbo band he would only let me play with brushes." There was, by some accounts, rather more to it than that. Benny recalled that he "drove a pretty hard bargain with some of the boys" in the Columbo orchestra, "which they resented." According to one widely circulated story, his hard bargaining extended to putting the raise Columbo gave the band into his own pocket. When Krupa discovered what happened, he was outraged. But Hammond kept insisting that Benny was different now, and Gene finally relented.

Benny was adamant about using Manny Klein on first trumpet and Art Karle on tenor saxophone. Karle's primary virtue was that he was a good reader who would be able to cut Arthur Schutt's complicated arrangements. Klein was a brilliant studio musician who could play anything, but according to Hammond, Benny wanted him mainly because he was the leading contractor in New York and might throw some work in Benny's direction.

Then Benny went around to the music publishers to pick out the tunes. He eventually came back with "Ain'tcha Glad?," an amiable but minor Fats Waller-Andy Razaf collaboration, and a splendid new song Harold Arlen and Ted Koehler had written for the current Cotton Club revue, "I Gotta Right to Sing the Blues." As practical as ever, Benny talked Arlen's music publisher Irving Mills into paying for the arrangement. For the original, Dick McDonough, the guitar player on the date, contributed a lightweight novelty called "Dr. Heckle and Mr. Jibe" that was no better than the title suggests. The fourth side, to Hammond's relief, was to be a blues featuring Jack Teagarden called "Texas Tea Party," "Tea" being both a play on Teagarden's name and current slang for marijuana. ("Now Mama, Mama, Mama, Mam-oh, where did you hide my tea? . . . Now come on, Mama, Mama, Mam-oh, and quit that holding out on me.")

"My hopes for a jazz date were out the window by this time," Hammond recalled, "and I was horrified by the thought of what the English fans and critics would say."

His misgivings seemed justified when the musicians assembled at the old Columbia studio around the corner from his Sullivan Street apartment on the morning of October 18 and began running through Schutt's arrangements of "Ain'tcha Glad?" and "I Gotta Right to Sing the Blues." The charts were, by Benny's account, "nothing wonderful." In Hammond's view, they were a lot worse than that, "filled with commercial introductions and pat transitions."

But then something quite unexpected happened. Inspired, perhaps, by the presence of Jack Teagarden and the other fine jazz players grouped around the microphone (Joe Sullivan, Gene Krupa, Charlie Teagarden and the bassist Artie Bernstein), Benny suddenly abandoned the commercial considerations that had dominated his thinking about the date up to now and began to tear the arrangements apart, setting riff backgrounds here, assigning solo spots there, giving himself over to the spirit of the music that Hammond had been trying so hard to instill in him. By the time he was done with the

Harold Arlen tune, it had become essentially a solo vehicle for Teagarden's magnificent singing and playing, with an improvised jam session feel that made it seem it was all happening right on the spot. Maybe because time was running short, maybe because Benny couldn't quite bring himself to forget altogether about the pop music market, "Ain'tcha Glad?," the second tune of the date, retained much more of the formality of Schutt's rather stilted arrangement. But here, too, Teagarden was spotlighted heavily, and Benny played a wonderfully high-spirited obbligato behind his vocal.

With all the last-minute changes, the three-hour session was over before they got around to the final two sides, and Krupa and Teagarden had to rush back to Boston. Hammond sent a cable to London explaining he would have to go over budget and schedule another date and managed to persuade the company to pick up the tab for their return. Perhaps to justify these additional expenses, perhaps to stir up some interest among the British fans, perhaps just to express his genuine enthusiasm and relief, Hammond also wired the *Melody Maker* a glowing report about the session. "Benny Goodman and his band made a couple of sides the other day including 'I Gotta Right to Sing the Blues' and 'Ain'tcha Glad?,' " he wrote, blithely ignoring any possible conflict of interest. "The rhythm section was probably the finest that exists anywhere. . . . [It is] just about the best white band to record in many years. The records are really the goods."

The band reconvened at the Columbia studio nine days later on October 27. The personnel was the same, except that Joe Sullivan had gone off to California and was replaced by Frank Froeba. Once again Benny subordinated himself to Teagarden. Once again, one side, "Dr. Heckle and Mr. Jibe," was more carefully arranged with an eye toward the commercial market, and the other, "Texas Tea Party," seemed largely improvised.

"The results were not what I had hoped for, but not bad, either," was Hammond's final judgment about these recordings. As the years went by, though, Benny came to regard them with a special fondness. Half a century later—only a month or so before his death—Benny was visited by Bob Altshuler, an executive at CBS Records and a longtime jazz fan. "The premise of the visit," Altshuler says, "was to get some ideas from him about which of his recordings he would like to see out on compact discs. I thought we would be listening to the Eddie Sauter period and the sextet with Charlie Christian, but he wanted to play me some recordings that date back to 1933 that featured a great deal of Jack Teagarden. He had apparently been listening to them again in recent days and was convinced they were some of the best recordings he had ever done. He professed tremendous admiration for all the musicians on the dates and kept playing the records over and over. There was such an expression of joy on his face. Of all the things he did during this period, they were obviously closest to his heart."

These records were made on the most threadbare of shoestrings. The sidemen earned twenty dollars for each three-hour session, and Benny didn't receive much more. Yet through an unexpected stroke of luck, they turned out to be a real turning point for both Benny and Hammond.

American Columbia was all but out of business, but it still needed product. Since the Goodman dates were already bought and paid for by English Columbia, it could issue them in the United States by just paying its British affiliate a few cents in royalties. Ben Selvin thought "Ain'tcha Glad?," the most commercial of the four sides, had possibilities and decided to schedule it for release backed by Clyde McCoy's horrendously corny "Sugar Blues." Marshaling his considerable powers of persuasion, Hammond enlisted the support of Columbia's sales and promotion managers and eventually convinced Selvin to pair it with "I Gotta Right to Sing the Blues." When the record was released in November, it became a minor hit, selling five thousand copies and drawing a good bit of attention. *Metronome* magazine named it one of the best records of the month.

As a result of this success (plus the fact Benny was willing to work for scale), Selvin signed him to a Columbia contract, so he was back in the record business again. Of more far-ranging importance, the surprising sales showed Benny, as he put it, "that there was still a lot of interest in hot music, especially among college boys." The seeds were planted. It wouldn't take long for them to sprout.

The success of "Ain'tcha Glad?" was just as important to Hammond. Though not the millionaire everyone thought him to be, he did have a more than comfortable private income. He was able to vacation in Europe. He was able to buy a new Hudson convertible every year and drive wherever the music called him. He was able to invest in interesting projects and give money to worthy progressive causes. What he did not have was a career, a real outlet for his tremendous energy and idealism, something that would enable him to make his mark in the world and find a place where he belonged. And he desperately wanted one. His mother, an heir to the Vanderbilt and W. and J. Sloane fortunes, was an earnestly religious woman who arose by six-thirty every morning to begin the day's good works. His father was a hardworking banker and lawyer and chairman of several railroads who took the subway to the office.

Up to this point in his life Hammond's efforts to follow their footsteps in his own fashion had not led to much success. He invested in a downtown theater that presented black musicians and variety acts, but it closed within two weeks when the discovery of a sudden shrinkage in the corporation's finances was followed by a mysterious backstage fire. He worked for a while as a disc jockey on a socialist radio station owned by the *Jewish Daily Forward* and financed on-the-air jam sessions out of his own pocket. But that came to an end when the station moved to new quarters and the landlord insisted the black musicians use the freight elevator. He tried his hand as a Broadway producer, backing a socially conscious play about reform school inmates. But the curtain rang down for the last time after a dozen performances.

Writing about music for the *Brooklyn Eagle* and *Melody Maker* was fun and not unsuited to his talents. He had some musical training and was an amateur violist. Nor was he ever short of opinions. But the very nature of the observer's role put him on the periphery of things, and he was already too much of an outsider. What he needed to do was get closer to the center. And "Ain'tcha Glad?" allowed that to happen. Ben Selvin asked him to produce some record dates for American Columbia. Irving Mills hired him to edit *Melody News,* the house organ for Mills Music, and to supervise record sessions by musicians Mills managed, playing songs he published, to be leased to the various record companies he supplied with product. Hammond was finally on his way.

Benny had a major part to play in Hammond's new career. Hammond supervised Benny's sessions for Selvin. When the company soon ran out of funds and canceled Benny's contract, Hammond talked him into joining the Mills stable, and they went on working together. They were friends by now as well as business associates, a relationship that would continue for many years to come. There would be recurrent personal and musical differences and tempestuous flare-ups that drove them apart in bitter acrimony, yet their lives remained so closely intertwined it is impossible to trace the course of one without crossing paths with the other.

It was, on the face of it, a peculiar, most unlikely sort of friendship. On one side, the gentleman amateur, the highborn Presbyterian from Hotchkiss and Yale whose passion for jazz and social justice had led him to reject the comfortable options readily available to his class. On the other, the poor Jewish boy from Chicago who had raised himself up from the ghetto by dint of talent and ambition and unrelenting hard work. Yet each gave the other something he needed.

Hammond offered Benny enthusiasm, support and a renewed clarity about his talent at a time when he was in serious danger of losing his way. He was, in effect, Benny's musical conscience. Benny offered Hammond the chance to help shape and mold and participate more fully in a music he loved and understood but could not himself play, as well as the opportunity to merge his own career with that of an important musician who he correctly foresaw had a brilliant future ahead of him. Certainly, Benny's underclass origins also had their appeal. Hammond is almost wistful in his autobiography when he considers the possibility that some Jewish blood may actually run through his own veins. Close friendship with Benny would link him to the proletariat ever so much more directly than all the petitions he signed and checks that he wrote and articles he published in the *Nation*. Nor can one ignore the likelihood that Benny, never unmindful of social approval and acceptance, was also drawn to Hammond because of the upper-class background that was an undeniable part of his presence, however much he seemed to play it down.

As 1933 moved toward a close, Benny was still working in the radio studios for Al Goodman and Johnny Green and doing whatever commercial record dates came his way. But now he and Hammond began spending their evenings together, listening to the Fletcher Henderson and Benny Carter bands and going uptown to places like the Harlem Opera House, Pod's and Jerry's Log Cabin and Small's Paradise—wherever good jazz was being played. As a result of Hammond's influence, Benny also started recording with black musicians.

On November 27 he played behind Bessie Smith as part of a handpicked mixed band Hammond had assembled that included Frankie Newton, Chu Berry, Buck Washington and Jack Teagarden, the only other white musician on the date. The details of this session are perplexing. Benny insisted he was present on all four sides, but he can be heard, very faintly, only on the out chorus of one, "Take Me for a Buggy Ride." Hammond claimed he found Bessie in horribly reduced circumstances, working "in a miserable little gin-mill in North Philly as a hostess, singing pornographic songs for tips." Yet Bessie's biographer Chris Albertson maintains, "None of the people close to her at the time ever recall Bessie working in a speakeasy, much less as a hostess," and though no longer the high-priced headliner she had been in the 1920s, she still toured and played theaters with some regularity.

Still, these were the first records anyone had asked this very great artist to make in over two years, and they also were to be her last. No one, not even the English jazz fans, was interested in blues singers any more, and Hammond had to talk American Columbia into recording her for its low-priced Okeh label for a flat fifty dollars a side. (According to Albertson, he paid for the session himself.) Bessie was so discouraged about her prospects she refused to do any blues songs and had her friends Coot Grant and Socks Wilson write some vaudeville-type tunes for the date. The records are classics now, with or without Benny's audible presence, but when they were first released, they didn't sell at all. Four years later, in 1937, Smith was killed in an automobile accident in Mississippi.

Three days after the Bessie Smith session Benny cut another record, her first, with a frightened seventeen-year-old Billie Holiday. Hammond had stumbled upon her quite by accident earlier in the year when he'd gone uptown expecting to hear the singer Monette Moore. Transfixed by Billie's sound, by her phrasing, by her musician's ear, he was convinced by the end of the evening that "she was the best jazz singer I had ever heard."

Hammond dragged everyone he knew up to Harlem to listen to her, enthused about her in the pages of the *Melody Maker*, tried hard to get her a record date. None of the record companies was interested, but the opportunity finally presented itself when Benny went back into the studio to begin a series of record sessions under his new Columbia contract. On November 27 he put together a band to accompany Ethel Waters on a couple of numbers and, probably at Hammond's urging, brought Billie down to sing on the final side, a run-of-the-mill pop tune from *Lew Leslie's Blackbirds of 1934* called "Your Mother's Son-in-Law."

Billie sounds young and inexperienced and very, very nervous, hardly anything at all like the glorious singer who emerged on the first of her landmark collaborations with pianist Teddy Wilson less than two years later. "Benny came up to get me and took me to the studio downtown. When we got there and I saw this big old microphone, it scared me half to death," she explained. "I'd never sung in one and I was afraid of it." But Billie was a fast learner, and by the time she returned to the studio to cut "Riffin' the Scotch" with Benny a few weeks later she was already much more at ease and beginning to reveal some of the unforced authority and subtle swing that marked her mature style.

The band Benny put together for the two Billie Holiday sessions included most of the same men he had used on the "Ain'tcha Glad" dates. The one difference was that instead of Manny Klein, he brought in Shirley Clay, a black trumpet player from Don Redman's orchestra. This was a minor enough change, but a clear indication that he was no longer quite so reluctant to have black musicians record with him. He was still making his living in radio, but the studios and their prejudices were getting to be less important. The next session under his own name included Coleman Hawkins. The one after that brought him together for the first time with the pianist Teddy Wilson. Largely thanks to John Hammond, Benny was beginning to see some other possibilities in his future.

Singing waiters serenade the dinner crowd at the Billy Rose Music Hall, August 1934. AP/Wide World Photos

5

Music Hall Rag

he repeal of Prohibition at the end of 1933 radically altered the character of Manhattan's night life for the privileged few who could still afford one. The speakeasies closed their doors and immediately reopened as nightclubs, some of which—El Morocco, The Stork Club, "21"—affected an air of genteel exclusivity that belied their less than reputable origins. The Rockefellers opened the Rainbow Room, that art deco fantasy in the clouds, on top of the RCA Building in Rockefeller Center. Hotels like the Waldorf-Astoria, which had been teetering on the edge of bankruptcy, found new solvency as the center of social life for the carriage trade, offering cocktail hours, floor shows and dance bands that attracted well-heeled local residents as well as out-of-towners.

None of this, though, had much relevance to ordinary New Yorkers who, despite the belt tightening of the Great Depression, might still find a place in their budgets for an occasional night out. It was all much too pricey. And now that alcohol was legal there was no real need to leave home. There were liquor stores on every corner, and the radio provided plenty of free dance music and entertainment.

For most Manhattan night spots, business was seriously down. B'WAY

NITERIES PRAYING FOR GOOD OL' PROHI DAYS; AIN'T NO DRINKIN', *Variety* proclaimed in a front-page headline, then went on to analyze the situation. "The niteries now realize that booze is no longer an attraction. They must give [the customers] something else—or else. . . . No couverts, no $1-a-drink tariffs, but more genuine basic appeal must be the standard of things if nite spots are to draw. . . . On the whole, the show or the dance music, along with some basic atmospheric appeal, must pull 'em—not just the booze."

There was an opportunity here for the taking—which is all Billy Rose ever required.

The diminutive showman first made his mark as a shorthand speedwriting champion, then as a songwriter, then as a nightclub operator and a high-priced, if unproduced, screenwriter and theatrical impresario and husband of *Ziegfeld Follies* star Fanny Brice. He was a master of ballyhoo; selling it, he claimed, brought him "such fame as has not been achieved in the show business since Phineas Barnum brought the original Jumbo to this country and put a sign over the exit of his museum saying: 'This way to the Egress.' " A shameless self-promoter; "Without his name in the paper, Billy felt nude," his friend Ben Hecht observed. A restless, hard-driving force of nature always on the lookout for the next big thing that would challenge his boundless energy and talent.

In December 1933 Rose had taken over the bankrupt Gallo Theater on West Fifty-fourth Street and turned it into a large theater restaurant called the Casino de Paree. For a moderate two-dollar minimum one could have dinner, watch a vaudeville show, gawk at the scantily clad show girls and dance to the music of the Don Redman and Ben Pollack orchestras. This was something quite new in New York, "tony but with an undercurrent of 'honky tonk,' " as Rose himself described it, and it was an immediate success, grossing between thirty and thirty-five thousand dollars a week. As imitators announced their plans for similar establishments in Chicago, Cleveland and Baltimore, it looked as if he had started something of a national trend, but Billy had already turned his mind to other matters. His new idea took the Casino de Paree concept and developed it one step farther. He would open another theater restaurant that would be bigger and more extravagant and even more of a bargain and pitch it to the family trade the other nightclubs ignored.

Bankrolled by mobsters in the beer business, Billy rented the old Hammerstein Theater at Fifty-third and Broadway, ripped out the seats and had the space redesigned to copy the elaborate nightclub set in the current Al Jolson movie *Wonder Bar*. He also planned to appropriate the name of the film, but when a cabaret in Union City, New Jersey, grabbed it first, he came up with "Billy Rose's Music Hall." He ordered a huge electric sign that would spell out his name over Broadway in letters eighteen feet high, then went to work fleshing out his vision.

The Music Hall was to seat a thousand people and be open from 11:00

in the morning until 4:00 A.M. the next day. It offered a fifty-cent luncheon that included a dance band and a show. During the afternoon there were newsreels and drinks. Dinner cost $1; supper $1.25. The evening show was a multimedia extravaganza unlike anything Broadway had ever seen. Headlined by comedian Ben Blue and his stooges, it featured the midgets Olive and George, a trained seal, dancers, chorus girls, a waterfall and Oscar the flea. There was also a Small Time Cavalcade of Vaudeville that brought back every conceivable kind of old-time vaudeville act that could still wobble across a stage. The overture was a filmed paean to national recovery and the American spirit. The finale blended footage from D. W. Griffith's 1919 epic *The Fall of Babylon* with a nude tableau.

While all this was coming together, Benny's brother Harry was playing bass in Ben Pollack's orchestra down the street at the Casino de Paree. Harry was living with Benny and the family out in Jackson Heights, and when he heard about Billy's new venture, he urged Benny to put together a band and audition for the Music Hall job. So did Oscar Levant, who had worked with him on "The Hoffman Ginger Ale Hour," and the agent Arthur Michaud, who had frequently hired him to lead the pickup dance bands he booked into the eastern colleges. "Benny was always a not too easy chap to get along with but was an exceptional band leader, punctual, reliable and knowledgeable," Michaud recalled, and having seen Benny's largely untapped organizational abilities first hand, he thought the Music Hall opening would give him a good opportunity to take the next step forward and assemble an orchestra on a more permanent basis.

Even with all this encouragement Benny wasn't so sure. Preparing for an audition he wasn't even certain he could get was highly speculative at best—and Billy Rose was no jazz fan. He would have to start completely from scratch: find good musicians who were willing to go along with him, scrounge up arrangements, schedule rehearsals, try to whip the band into some kind of shape. It all might come to nothing, and Benny wasn't really in any position to take that risk. He was back down to one radio show a week playing fourth saxophone for Al Goodman, which paid him about forty dollars.

Yet the prospect of forming his own band did have a certain appeal, and Benny had, in fact, been toying with the idea for some months. The record dates he had done with John Hammond did more than reawaken his interest in jazz. They also gave him a small taste of what it was like to be a leader and express his own musical ideas through a relatively large ensemble of like-minded players. "Nothing much came of my thinking," he recalled. "I wasn't quite convinced that the public was ready for the kind of band I dreamed of leading."

What Benny dreamed of leading was a big dance band that played jazz, something like the original Ben Pollack orchestra. And the reason he considered it a dream was that there were hardly any white bands playing that kind of music anymore. There was certainly no shortage of black jazz orchestras. Duke Ellington, Fletcher Henderson, Don Redman, Chick Webb, Jimmie Lunceford and Bennie Moten were just the top of the list. But now that Pollack had become so commercial, about the only white dance bands doing anything at all like what Benny had in mind were the Casa Loma Orchestra and the new band Tommy and Jimmy Dorsey had recently started rehearsing.

The Casa Loma Orchestra had moved to New York from Detroit in 1929. Though nominally led by Glen Gray, it was actually a cooperative corporation, with all the members owning an equal share of stock. As such, the band had an unusually stable personnel, which enabled it to execute Gene Gifford's demanding arrangements with great accuracy and skill. According to manager Cork O'Keefe, the tone for the Casa Loma's music was set by trombonist Billy Rausch, who had "an obsession for meticulous perfection and who insisted that the band play with machinelike precision." *Machinelike* is the operative word here. Gifford's charts were filled with the riffs and call-and-response patterns that were the main orchestral devices employed by the swing bands to come, but the emphasis on precision was achieved at the expense of looseness and relaxation, those other essentials of big band swing, and it led Gifford to write arrangements that were often overly flashy and too packed with ornate detail. "I don't know if it's a good band," Fats Waller told the singer Helen Ward. "But it sure is a busy band." Ward herself puts it more bluntly. In her judgment, "It just didn't swing."

Not that the Casa Loma didn't have its fans. A John Hammond might dismiss the band's recorded output as "junk," but the combination of showy flag-wavers like "White Jazz" and moody ballads like "Smoke Rings" had made it a great favorite among the college crowd, who sought out its records, avidly followed its weekly radio show on CBS and packed the ballrooms for its personal appearances. In the middle of 1934 a full-page ad in *Variety* reprised the band's many triumphs over the first half of the year and heralded its current record breaking stand at the Glen Island Casino in New Rochelle.

The Casa Loma's success did not escape Benny's notice as he continued thinking about whether or not to try out for the Music Hall job. Nor was it overlooked by Benny's fellow free-lancers Tommy and Jimmy Dorsey. They were weary of studio work, too, and prodded by Glenn Miller, who was to become their chief arranger, they canceled their radio gigs and started rehearsing their new band early in 1934.

Like the Casa Loma, the Dorsey Brothers Orchestra featured precision-tooled ensemble work and elaborate arrangements. Managed by the same powerful Rockwell-O'Keefe agency that steered the Casa Loma, it was carefully groomed for similar success. After an extended period of rehearsals and a few weeks of one-nighters, it was booked into the Sands Point Casino on Long Island, where it was able to broadcast its music nationally through the casino's NBC radio hookup. The agency then signed the band to the recently formed Decca record company, which was already thriving on the best-selling records of Bing Crosby, another Rockwell-O'Keefe client, and over Tommy's objection, made Bing's kid brother, Bob, the band's male singer.

Benny had nothing resembling this kind of high-powered financial and managerial backing. He was essentially on his own. But with the radio work all but gone, he eventually came to the decision that he had nothing much to lose. Oscar Levant arranged an introduction to Billy Rose. An audition was set for March. And with John Hammond's assistance, Benny began looking for musicians.

"I had definite ideas about how I wanted my band to sound," Benny remembered. "First, I was interested only in jazz. I wanted to create a tight, small-band quality, and I wanted every one of my boys to be a soloist. The band had to have a driving beat, a rhythmic brass section, and a sax section that would be smooth but with lots of punch."

The first person Benny thought of was Jack Teagarden, but he had recently signed a lucrative long-term contract with Paul Whiteman. Some of the other men he had in mind were also making decent money in the studios and sweet commercial dance bands and weren't willing to give up the security of steady employment. Others, though, were either out of work or attracted to the idea of getting off the commercial treadmill for once and performing the kind of music they had a chance to play only after hours. Benny had a strong reputation among his fellow musicians in New York, and that also helped. So did Hammond's enthusiasm and powers of persuasion.

One man at a time, they began to assemble an orchestra. Tenor saxophonist Arthur Rollini had just returned to town from a dismal tour with George Olsen, and a single phone call from Benny was enough to capture his attention. Hammond discovered Hank Wayland playing bass in a chop suey joint on Lexington Avenue. Pianist Claude Thornhill and the guitar player George Van Eps had worked with Benny in the studios. The studios also yielded up trumpet players Russ Case and Sammy Shapiro, who became better known as Sammy Spear when he went on to conduct for Jackie Gleason. Third trumpet was Jerry Neary, who had briefly replaced Charlie Spivak in the Dorsey Brothers band.

Scouting the hotels and ballrooms, Benny found Red Ballard playing trombone with Isham Jones at the Commodore, and Jack Lacey, "the nearest thing to Jack Teagarden I had heard," with Joe Reichman at the Arcadia. The Gene Kardos orchestra at Roseland brought him drummer Sammy Weiss and alto saxophonist Hymie Schertzer. For lead alto, he was able to get a commitment from Ben Kanter, who had played with Leo Reisman.

Benny had no money for arrangements and had to get them wherever he could. The record dates done over the past few months provided a small handful of charts by Deane Kincaide, George Bassman and Arthur Schutt, and he reached back to a 1931 session with Teagarden for Glenn Miller's orchestration of "Basin Street Blues." The rest had to be borrowed haphazardly anywhere he could find them. Edgar Sampson, who was writing for the Chick Webb band, let him use "Stompin' at the Savoy." Charlie Barnet gave him a few charts. So did Deane Kincaide and Benny Carter.

Benny now started rehearsing. The rehearsals were mostly held during the afternoons so the musicians who were working at night could get to their regular jobs. Benny also took whatever free-lance work he could find, but as he struggled to mold the band into shape, it began to absorb just about all his energy and attention.

This was essentially the first time he had ever stepped out in front of his own orchestra. His college prom bands were casually assembled pickup groups, and the musicians read off the stock arrangements as best they could or just jammed. The *Free for All* pit band had played the assigned orchestrations and been conducted not by Benny but by one John McManus. The Russ Columbo band had operated under similar limitations. And now that Benny was, as he put it, "working with a bunch of musicians to get some unity out of a dozen different ways of playing," he began to discover what it actually meant to be a leader.

It was one thing to work as a sideman and be responsible for properly executing your own part within a larger ensemble. It was quite another to be responsible for the intonation, phrasing, tempo and orchestral blend of twelve other musicians. But Benny took to this new role with a zeal that disclosed a natural talent he probably didn't even realize he possessed. His sidemen weren't being paid for rehearsing, so he was hardly in a position to be too demanding, yet that never seemed to occur to him. "I didn't just ask for good musicianship; I insisted on it," he said. "Nothing less than perfection would do; I lived that music, and expected everybody else to live it, too," an expectation all Benny's future sidemen would have to learn to live with as long as a Benny Goodman orchestra continued to mount the bandstand.

The audition for Billy Rose took place in the early spring. Since the Music Hall was still under construction, it was held around the corner at the Casino de Paree during the afternoon. "If there's anything more depressing than an empty night club during the night," Benny recalled, "it's an empty night club during the daytime." Rose was not overly impressed. He was auditioning bands every day and asked Benny to come back a few weeks later.

To make the most of this second audition, Benny got in touch with the singer Helen Ward. They had met briefly the previous year when they auditioned with Al Goodman for a new radio show under consideration by

Lucky Strike cigarettes. The other musicians Al Goodman assembled included Tommy and Jimmy Dorsey, Artie Shaw, Bunny Berigan and Artie Bernstein—the absolute cream of the New York radio free-lancers—but the audition was a disaster. The potential sponsor was George Washington Hill, the autocratic head of the American Tobacco Company, and he fell sound asleep as soon as they started playing.

Benny and Helen became better acquainted a few months later, when they were reintroduced by the arranger George Bassman. They hit it off immediately, and Benny asked her out to dinner. There was some mix-up about the time, and when Helen arrived home, she found that Benny had been patiently sitting there for hours, chatting with her mother. He brought Helen flowers. He couldn't wait to show her the new Ford he'd just picked up in Connecticut. "He was like a young kid," Helen remembers. "He was so proud of it."

"Moody and inarticulate" was the way Oscar Levant described Benny during this period. Most of the other musicians who knew him then tended to share that opinion. But as Benny and Helen continued seeing each other, he was able to let down his guard a little and expose the warmer, more open and vulnerable side of his nature. Benny brought her out to Jackson Heights and played Louis Armstrong records for her to teach her about jazz. During dinner one night at Mamma Leone's he started reminiscing about his father, and as he told her about David Goodman's hard life and early death, tears filled his eyes, and he quietly began to sob. "It was the first and last time I ever saw Benny give vent to his feelings so emotionally," Helen says. "He adored his father. His heart was still broken from the memories of that poverty and the terrible accident that ended his father's life when he was still such a young man."

Helen was singing with Enrique Madriguera's band at the Waldorf-Astoria when Benny asked her to audition for the Music Hall job. "I said, 'Sure, but I'm not going in there.' I was only seventeen years old and had never worked in a real nightclub. I had a picture of show girls and fat guys with cigars, and it just didn't appeal to me." Maybe Helen's presence helped tip the balance in Benny's favor. Or maybe Billy Rose thought Benny had followed his earlier suggestions about improving the brass section. (He hadn't.) But at the end of the audition Benny was hired.

The band was paid union scale, about $850 a week. When Benny figured out his expenses, he realized he was actually losing money. But he was doing what he wanted and felt certain the kind of music he was playing "was something real and genuine, which the public would go for if they had a chance to hear it." He still had some savings in the bank. He would borrow whatever he had to.

"Benny Goodman's orchestra is busily rehearsing at the new Billy Rose

Music Hall," Hammond reported in the July *Melody Maker*. "Although the names of the guys are all but unknown, with few exceptions, the bunch will probably have more swing than any whites in New York. In other words, it's a helluva good band."

The rehearsals, in fact, did not go all that smoothly. Along with providing dance music, Benny was required to back the elaborate floor show, and right from the start he ran into problems with that part of the job. "We were terrible," he recalled. "I don't know why, but we couldn't seem to work our way through the score." Arthur Rollini offers a rather terse explanation: "Benny could not conduct." According to Jim Maher, "Benny later made a remark that still sends the hair up the neck of expert pit men: 'I thought the dancers and acts were supposed to follow *us*.' " Rose eventually had the alternating dance band led by Harold Arlen's brother Jerry take over the show, and he hired an experienced pit band leader named Lou Foreman to conduct it.

Following several postponements, the Music Hall finally opened its doors on June 21, 1934. Heralded in *Variety* as introducing "a new phase in the evolution of post-repeal show business," it showed every sign of living up to Billy Rose's grandiose expectations, and he was already hard at work setting up similar establishments in half a dozen other cities. What with the one hundred singing waiters and the fire-eaters and strong women and Oscar the flea, Benny's band was barely noticed in the opening night reviews. But the musicians and more musically alert listeners soon became aware that something rather special was happening. BENNY GOODMAN AND ORCH. BIG SUCCESS ON BROADWAY, read the headline of *Down Beat*'s September issue, which went on to enthuse, "The management of Billy Rose's Music Hall certainly chose wisely and well when they selected Benny Goodman for their spot at 52nd and Broadway."

Most of the Music Hall clientele did not share this enthusiasm. The music was too loud for them. They couldn't figure out how to dance to it. It would still be awhile before the lindy hop traveled downtown from Harlem's Savoy Ballroom and jitterbugging became a national pastime, and the customers just milled around the bandstand or sat at the tables, stomping their feet. Rose was about to give Benny notice when it was explained to him that this was the kind of music some people just liked to listen to.

The band also had its own internal problems. "We worked seven nights a week from seven P.M. until three A.M., at the lowest salary that I had ever worked," Rollini remembers, and Benny frequently called rehearsals for the afternoon. A number of musicians left, as did some of the men who replaced them. The comings and goings took their toll, yet Benny remained hopeful.

The band was broadcasting over WMCA several nights a week and was beginning to attract attention. Sometimes it went on early before it had a chance to warm up and played painfully out of tune. But as the months went by, the quality of its performance gradually improved.

"The band was getting better and better," Benny recalled. "I was still working in radio during the daytime hours, and one evening I had a broadcast with Leo Reisman's orchestra that made me late for work at the Music Hall. The boys started off without me, and they were playing when I walked in. I remember thinking, 'Gee, this gang sounds pretty good.' Two days later we got our notice."

While Rose was vacationing in Europe, the dress manufacturer fronting for the mobsters who owned the Music Hall had decided to restage the show himself and fired the Goodman band along with the dancer and future movie star Eleanor Powell. "When I got back from Europe, I insisted on an immediate pow-wow with the backers," Billy explained. "I met them at three A.M. in the office over the cafe. 'You guys have broken my contract,' I said. 'It specifically states you are not to interfere with the operation.' The natty little Italian who headed the mob spoke up. 'I wouldn't depend on that contract if I were you. While you were in Europe I shot out most of the clauses.' "

Billy soon had his fill of "the broken-fingernail set," as he called it, and by the end of 1934 the Billy Rose Music Hall was show business history. Resilient as always, he moved on to his next big venture, a musical circus extravaganza called *Jumbo*. For Benny, though, the loss of the Music Hall job was devastating: "This was probably the toughest blow I ever received, because the Music Hall had represented some sort of pinnacle to me. I had actually gotten together a band, rehearsed it, got a job, and held it for three months, and then had it kicked out from under me for no reason at all. About this last point, I was really convinced. I realized the band had weaknesses and shortcomings, but I felt we had tried to put across something new and had won a certain amount of acceptance from the public."

The public *was* starting to accept the band, not only in New York but across the country. On August 16 Benny had recorded four sides with the Music Hall orchestra for Columbia, and though he wasn't especially pleased with the results, the records were selling briskly. *Variety*'s September Music Survey included "Take My Word" and "It Happens to the Best of Friends" among the label's half dozen top sellers. When "Bugle Call Rag" and "Nitwit Serenade" were released in October, they did even better. "Bugle Call Rag" was Columbia's number one title in Chicago and Los Angeles and ranked third in New York City.

When one listens to these records now, the reason for their appeal is apparent. Will Hudson's "Nitwit Serenade" and Deane Kincaide's arrangement of "Bugle Call Rag," for example, offer some of the same attractive features as the popular Casa Loma Orchestra's recordings: short, stabbing riffs interspersed with solos, played at an extremely fast tempo calculated to show off the band's slick ensemble work and generate immediate excitement. Compared with air checks of the Casa Loma's 1934 "Camel Caravan" broadcasts, the Goodman band doesn't perform with anywhere near the same precision, but it digs in so much deeper and swings ever so much harder, especially when Benny is playing. The same can be said for "Music Hall Rag," a thinly disguised version of "The World Is Waiting for the Sunrise," recorded in November 1934, a month after the Music Hall job ended but with largely the same personnel. Benny solos with such bite and fire it's hard to believe Arthur Rollini's claim that compared with what he did with the tune on the job every night, his performance here is relatively lackluster.

Benny was handed his notice in the middle of September 1934 and had just four weeks to figure out what to do next. Some of his advisers suggested he go back to playing in the studios. Others thought he should try to hold the band together but make it more commercial, more like all the other white dance bands in New York. There was also a third option that might have reset his course on an entirely new direction.

"I remember this as clearly as though it were right now," Charlie Barnet recalled. "Benny Goodman was trying to have a band at Billy Rose's joint on 53rd Street, and he was having a rough time. He and Benny Carter were rather disgusted with the reception of jazz . . . of big band jazz particularly . . . and we sat one time at a table there at the Park Central Hotel seriously plotting to go to Europe and set up shop."

It was something that merited serious consideration. There was a growing interest in jazz on the other side of the Atlantic. Louis Armstrong and Duke Ellington had recently made triumphant tours of the Continent, drawing the kind of attention and appreciation they seldom received at home. Earlier that year, only weeks after recording with Benny as a sideman, a discouraged Coleman Hawkins had quit Fletcher Henderson's struggling orchestra and moved to Europe, where he was playing to universal acclaim. Perhaps the time was ripe for such a radical change.

The conversation with Charlie Barnet was more than idle talk born out of disappointment and frustration. The following May Benny Carter did, in fact, emigrate to Europe, and he remained there until the Nazis marched into Austria three years later. And when Carter and Goodman sat together with Barnet that day, they were already involved in a project that would have them take a temporary leave of absence from their regular jobs to travel overseas to Great Britain.

The plan was first announced on the front page of the *Melody Maker* on

July 7, less than three weeks after the Music Hall opening. BLACK, WHITE
AMERICAN STARS FORM GREATEST OUTFIT EVER, the headline read, and the
accompanying story more than justified this attention-grabbing hyperbole.
The idea was to bring over to England a truly all-star band of black and white
musicians, consisting of Doc Cheatham, Charlie Teagarden and Bill Coleman
on trumpet; Jack Teagarden, J. C. Higginbotham and Will Bradley on trombone; Benny Carter, Edgar Sampson and Chu Berry on saxophones; and a
rhythm section of Teddy Wilson on piano, Lawrence Lucie on guitar, Hank
Wayland on bass and Gene Krupa on drums. Added attractions would include Bessie Smith, Red Norvo and the dance team of Red and Struggie. The
clarinetist and leader would be Benny Goodman.

The idea, jointly credited to Goodman, Carter and John Hammond, was
fantastically ambitious, worthy of Billy Rose at his manic best. Nothing
remotely like this had ever been tried before. Black and white musicians might
casually sit in with each other now and then, but an interracial orchestra, even
one formed on a temporary basis, was absolutely unheard of. And quite apart
from race, the logistical problems were all but overwhelming. Most of the
listed musicians were featured sidemen in various bands working in different
parts of the country. Leaves of absence would have to be negotiated, suitable
replacements found, schedules adjusted and readjusted before they could even
be brought together to start rehearsing. Labor permits would also have to be
obtained to allow the band to work in England, and the right sort of bookings
arranged. This was a high-priced package of talent, and only the largest halls
would be able to handle the expenses. Still, if the project did materialize, it
would be, as the *Melody Maker* ballyhooed, "the greatest and most convincing
exposition of modern dance music and band entertainment ever presented in
this country, or, indeed, in any part of the world."

The *Melody Maker* announcement was attributed to an unnamed "Special
Correspondent" in the United States, but like the follow-up reports, it was
almost certainly written by John Hammond. In all likelihood the idea for the
tour was primarily Hammond's, too. Interracial orchestras were one of his pet
personal causes. Goodman and Carter already had their hands full trying to
hold their own bands together.

There was an immediate demand for tickets. In the weeks that followed,
Hammond kept the appetite of the British jazz fans whetted with all the fervor
of an advance man for the Second Coming.

July 21: "BENNY GOODMAN BLACK AND WHITE BAND OFFERED CONTRACT.
Mecca Agency Steps in and Cables Terms for Six Weeks. Band Is in Rehearsal Stage." The English tour would begin the middle of October. The
band might then move on to tour the Continent.

August 4: "GOODMAN FANTASY BAND NEARER ENGLAND. Black and White
Principals Accept Cabled Terms. Rehearsing Now in New York." All that

remained was to obtain the necessary permits from the Ministry of Labor, but "they should be granted without question as this combination is the most significant which the world has ever known, and its educational value for British musicians is beyond dispute."

August 25: "The spirit of the guys is swell. Jack Teagarden could hardly be more excited, and Benny Goodman has a new idea every moment. The rest are equally happy, and I suspect that October 15 is going to be something in the history of swing music."

But then, as October 15 drew nearer, the barrage of publicity suddenly ended. There was a passing remark in Hammond's September 29 column that the fate of the band "is to be decided this week," the first and only indication that there might be some problems, but after that only silence. Hammond, in fact, suddenly disappeared from the *Melody Maker*'s pages. A brief news item in the October *Down Beat* offered a partial explanation: Labor permits could not be obtained, and the tour had been canceled.

The following spring *Down Beat* printed a front-page interview with Hammond detailing at length his version of what happened. The idea for the band, he now claimed, originated with the head of the English Selmer Company, who had promised to supply the start-up money and get the English bandleader and promoter Jack Hylton to sponsor the tour. On the basis of this encouragement, Hammond secured the commitment of Benny Goodman and the other musicians. When Hylton came to New York in September, he agreed to arrange the bookings, Hammond said, and he was to cable all the necessary information as soon as he returned home. But no cable ever arrived. Nor did Hylton ever answer the repeated requests for an explanation. "Hylton broke a definitive promise to me," Hammond concluded, "and I, for one, will never forgive him for it."

The response of the *Melody Maker* was immediate and impassioned. "The story is so fantastically inaccurate as to demand refutation," wrote the editor. Back in July "Hammond gave us to understand that the band was formed and rehearsing, and when Hylton, later, went to America, he expected to hear the band in the flesh. . . . To Jack's surprise, however, Hammond was still only talking about the proposition; the band had not materialised at all and had never met, nor could it meet, since most of the members were scattered over America in various outfits." Of course, Hylton didn't book any dates or bother to answer Hammond's cables since "the band existed only in the ambitions of a free-lance American. . . . John Hammond is a young man of means who has devoted much of his life to the cause of the oppressed Negro in the U.S.A., and his intense enthusiasm for the cause undoubtedly results in him conceiving schemes sky-high and almost as unattainable."

This would seem to be the final word on the subject. Hammond did not even mention this ill-fated project in his 1977 autobiography, *John Hammond on Record.*

One can sympathize with Hammond's embarrassment. He was, after all, still a relatively inexperienced young man, and his enthusiasm, his zeal, his need to make things happen and become part of something important led him soon enough to any number of very real and substantial accomplishments. But for Benny, the collapse of the English tour involved a good bit more than a temporary loss of face. It was the second major disappointment within a month, his second serious career setback. "A tragedy," he called it. The Music Hall job was about to end. He was running out of time. There were no real prospects in sight. Nor had he been able to find a clear sense of direction.

Benny's last night at the Music Hall was October 17, 1934. Arthur Rollini asked him to take part in a record date his brother Adrian had contracted with Decca the following week, and Benny accepted. He was paid union scale, about twenty-five dollars, and, according to Rollini, was quite unhappy about it. There were a few other things that may have caused him to grumble. It was all too evident that Adrian hadn't touched his bass saxophone in months and was struggling with a badly warped reed. Though Jack Teagarden managed to breathe some life into the music, especially on "Somebody Loves Me" and "Riverboat Shuffle," the overall playing was stiff and uninspired and thoroughly unswinging, and the old-fashioned arrangements were more like the sort of thing Red Nichols had done five years earlier than what Benny had been moving toward at the Music Hall. He was back to being a free-lance sideman, and the session must have been a depressing reminder of what lay in store for him if he continued in this line of work.

Benny tried to keep the band going. He managed to book a few dance dates around New York, but there just weren't enough of them. Ben Kanter returned home to Boston. Claude Thornhill and Jack Lacey joined Freddy Martin's orchestra at the St. Regis Hotel and picked up some radio shows with André Kostelanetz. Benny went to see Tommy Rockwell about representing the band, but Rockwell already had the Casa Loma and the Dorsey Brothers and wasn't interested. Benny felt he was fighting a losing battle and didn't know what more he could do.

But then in the beginning of November he received a phone call from a man named Josef Bonime, and his luck began to change.

The Kehelah Jacob Synagogue band, where it all began. From the Benny Goodman Archives in the Music Library at Yale University

A family snapshot of Benny with his mother and some of his brothers. From the Benny Goodman Archives in the Music Library at Yale University

Benny shortly after the Ben Pollack orchestra arrived in New York in 1928. From the Benny Goodman Archives in the Music Library at Yale University

Benny leading a 1934 record date that included the great tenor saxophonist Coleman Hawkins. From the Benny Goodman Archives in the Music Library at Yale University

Benny and fellow "Let's Dance" leaders Kel Murray and Xavier Cugat, November 1934. Frank Driggs Collection

6

Let's Dance: 1

n 1920, when Benny was eleven years old and still struggling with the rudiments of the clarinet, there was only one radio station broadcasting in the entire United States. By 1927, the year before he went off to New York with Ben Pollack, there were close to a thousand. Almost overnight radio had grown from an interesting experiment with an uncertain future into a huge and powerful industry:

Great things have happened to the radio in a remarkably short time [Charles Merz observed in 1928]. It is only eight years since the first grand opera star trilled a few notes condescendingly into a microphone; now there is no opera star who has not fought . . . for a wave-length. It is only eight years since the first church service was broadcast from Calvary Church in Pittsburgh; now the air is filled with sermons every Sunday morning. It is only eight years since Congresswoman-elect Alice M. Robertson of Oklahoma was persuaded to say a few words at the first hotel banquet broadcast by KDKA; now no President—no up-to-date Vice President—would think of shaking hands with a farmer from the corn belt without making certain of his hook-ups.

The radio industry continued its rapid expansion into the 1930s. If anything, the depression only accelerated its growth and strengthened its hold on the American public. A survey conducted by something called the National Recreation Association ranked it just below the reading of newspapers and magazines as the most frequent leisure time activity. According to a poll of some eighty-eight thousand homes commissioned by the Columbia Broadcasting System, by 1934 more than fourteen million radio sets were turned on daily across the United States. Over 90 percent of American homes owned one, and they were played on the average four and a half hours a day.

During the summer of 1934 the competing NBC radio network conducted its own less formal survey of listener tastes and preferences by handing out questionnaires to its studio audiences. Upon tabulating the eighteen thousand replies, it discovered that dance music was far and away the most popular type of program on the air, winning more votes than all the runners-up (comedy, drama, symphonic music, news and variety shows) combined. These results shouldn't have been too surprising. Dance music of one sort or another had long been a major staple of radio programming. During the 1920s it filled a good two-thirds of the broadcasting hours on large stations and small; currently it occupied over 30 percent of NBC's own broadcasting schedule.

Metronome magazine reported this survey with a certain amused skepticism. The McCann-Erickson advertising agency, though, regarded it a good bit more seriously. After selling the National Biscuit Company on the idea, it began developing what turned out to be the most ambitious radio program of dance music that had ever been aired.

The show was to be called "Let's Dance." Originating in NBC's recently completed Studio 8H, a huge auditorium that could seat a thousand people, it would broadcast three hours of live dance music coast to coast every Saturday night over the network's more than fifty local stations. To appeal to the widest possible audience, three different orchestras would be used, alternating with one another in short sets. There would be a sweet band for commercial dance music, a Latin band for rhumbas and, for the youngsters who had turned the Casa Loma into such a great success, a hot dance band playing what was just starting to be known as swing.

The person in charge of putting all this together was Josef Bonime, a highly regarded radio conductor and contractor who was also the music consultant for McCann-Erickson. Benny had free-lanced for Bonime on the Dill's Best "One Night Stands" program, and when he heard Bonime was lining up bands to audition, he invited him down to the Music Hall. Bonime accepted and arranged to drop by on Benny's closing night.

Benny's musicians had already started to leave him. The trumpet player Sammy Shapiro had to be talked into doubling from the band at the Casino de Paree down the street and spent the entire evening running back and forth between the two gigs. Benny also had to work his way around the problem of having so few special arrangements. There were only about twelve or fourteen of them in his entire library. The rest consisted of ordinary stock charts of current pop tunes, which could be heard all over town. To get through this crucial preliminary audition, Benny decided to play all his special arrangements in a single set, which would last about thirty or forty minutes, then get off the bandstand fast before Bonime realized he had exhausted his repertoire. He hoped Bonime would be impressed enough by then not to have to hear any more.

Bonime showed up as planned along with his wife and Dorothy Barstow, head of the McCann-Erickson radio department. Benny was a little panicky when he spotted them in the audience, but the set went extremely well. "We never sounded better than we did that night," he remembered. "The band played with real authority, and when I shot a glance at Joe and his colleagues, I could see they were eating it up."

During the break Benny stopped by Bonime's table. "Sounds pretty good," Bonime told him. "You'll hear from me." Then, to Benny's relief, he paid the check and left. On the way down Broadway, Bonime turned to Dorothy Barstow and asked whether they should invite Benny to a formal audition. She shrugged her shoulders and casually answered, "Why not?" She explained some years later: "I was always saying 'Why not?' in those days." It was a great stroke of good fortune for Benny that she did. Anything less positive, Bonime recalled, and the invitation wouldn't have been extended.

As it was, Benny had to wait several long, nerve-racking weeks before the promised phone call finally materialized. Bonime was busy listening to all the other orchestras around New York, trying to come to some decisions about whom else to audition. He abhorred what he called the "gushified" music played by Paul Whiteman and his imitators, so that kind of band was out. Eventually he decided to assemble his own orchestra for the sweet dance band spot, drawing on the wealth of free-lance talent already working at NBC, men like Manny Klein, Benny Baker, Arnold Brilhart, Henry Wade, Dick McDonough and Arthur Schutt. It would be led by the violinist Murray Kellner, who for the purpose of the show changed his name to Kel Murray.

Bonime's first thought for the Latin band was Enrique Madriguera, but Madriguera was very much a part of the same café society crowd he entertained and considered the job beneath him. Bonime's next choice was Xavier Cugat, who was starting his second season as the house band at the Waldorf-Astoria. Cugat is probably best remembered now for his wives, his chihuahua and the watered-down version of Latin music he played in the 1950s, but according to all accounts his 1934 band was outstanding. He won the "Let's Dance" competition with votes to spare.

Benny had just about given up hope when the telephone rang and Bonime asked him to come down to the network. The audition was held on Thursday morning, November 7, without benefit of an audience. The music was piped into the boardroom, where a dozen or so agency people, Nabisco representatives and NBC secretaries listened and tried dancing on the thick carpet. At the end of the performance a ballot was cast (yet another survey), and when the results were counted, Benny had won—by a single vote.

After being fired from the Music Hall and the collapse of the British tour, he was off to a fresh start.

Reminiscing about this major turning point in Benny's career some two decades later, John Hammond wrote, "How Benny got the job must remain a mystery, because of the libel laws." Hammond was a good bit less mysterious in private conversation, confiding that Benny had agreed to kick back to Bonime part of his weekly paycheck. This rumor has persisted, even finding its way into Marshall Stearns's standard history *The Story of Jazz,* but it's highly unlikely that's what happened.

Kickbacks were as common in the music business of 1934 as they were during the highly publicized payola scandals of the 1950s, so this sort of under-the-table finageling wouldn't have been anything especially unusual. But Bonime produced at least three other shows for McCann-Erickson, and the few dollars he might have been able to squeeze out of Benny's tight budget would have been meaningless to him. Moreover, he was personally fond of Benny and seemed bent on doing him a good turn. Had Benny failed the audition, he was prepared to offer him the third saxophone chair in Kel Murray's orchestra.

Most significantly, Josef Bonime needed Benny Goodman as much as Benny needed Bonime. The show sold to the National Biscuit Company called for a swing band, but where were such bands to be found? The racism pervading the radio networks at the time meant that none of the magnificent black orchestras playing around New York—Duke Ellington, Fletcher Henderson, Benny Carter, Jimmie Lunceford, Chick Webb and so on—could even be considered for the spot. That left only the smallest handful of white possibilities. Bonime tried to interest the Dorsey Brothers, but they were busy working at the Rockland Palace. The Casa Loma was also tied up. Benny was almost the only choice he had left. Bonime did manage to find another band (no one remembers which) to compete against him at the audition, but according to Jim Maher, it failed to show up, and he was forced to play a phonograph record—a straight dance tune by Enrique Madriguera—to go through the motions of a real contest. When Benny eked out his narrow victory, Bonime must have been just as relieved as Benny himself.

"Let's Dance" was set to premiere the night of December 1. Benny had a little over three weeks to pull the band together and begin to assemble a library of original arrangements. Now that he had a thirteen-week contract with the network, with a possibility of renewal if everything clicked, Benny was able to make a firm commitment to some of the musicians from the Music Hall band before they drifted away. His personnel for the opening broadcast included seven or eight holdovers, including the trumpet player Pee Wee Erwin, the trombonists Jack Lacey and Red Ballard and the saxophonists Arthur Rollini and Hymie Schertzer. For the important lead alto chair, he managed to secure the services of the highly regarded Toots Mondello, then working at the McAlpin Hotel with the Joe Haymes orchestra. For lead and solo trumpet, he accomplished another major coup by hiring Bunny Berigan, easily the best white jazz trumpet player in New York.

Another important addition was the singer Helen Ward. "One of the toughest problems for any band that wants to play with swing," Benny would say, "is finding a vocalist who can sing with the band. It's particularly hard since it is almost entirely a matter of feeling . . . [and] the field is pretty limited." Helen Ward had that feeling, quite possibly more than any other singer who ever worked for him, and her warm jazz-inflected vocals were a major contribution to Benny's eventual success. The male singer spot was filled for the moment, rather less satisfactorily, by Buddy Clark, who was to go on to achieve his own popularity as a solo performer.

This personnel was far from fixed. There were frequent substitutions as well as a certain amount of coming and going. Gil Rodin, Benny's bandmate from the Ben Pollack orchestra, was around briefly. Ben Kanter and Benny's brother Freddy occasionally sat in on saxophone and trumpet. But even with these fluctuations the band was beginning to take on a permanent form. What it had not yet developed was its own distinctive identity.

Benny's contract for the show included a budget for eight new charts a week, an incredible windfall for a band in Benny's position. "This was what we needed more than anything else," he recalled, "and in the long run, it turned out to be the most valuable thing about the program." In the short run, though, a great deal of writing had to be accomplished very quickly, so Benny was farming out the orchestrations to a variety of arrangers, including Joe Lippman, Fud Livingston, Gordon Jenkins (whose "Good-bye," became Benny's signoff theme), Spud Murphy (who produced a large number of scores, as many as four a week), Deane Kincaide, Benny Carter and Edgar Sampson.

These were all excellent writers but all quite different. If there was a center to Benny's taste, it ran toward the Dixieland sort of orchestrations provided by Kincaide and Murphy. The only problem with this style of writing was that it resembled too closely what the Dorsey Brothers were already doing. If Benny was to match their success, much less equal what the Casa Loma had achieved with Gene Gifford, he needed to be just as easily identifiable. What he had to do, Mildred Bailey argued with him after the first few broadcasts, was find someone to give the band its own immediately recognizable style. And the most likely candidate would almost certainly be one of the good black arrangers currently working around town.

Benny Carter must have seemed like the logical first choice. He and Benny already had a good working relationship, and Benny was especially pleased by the chart of "Take My Word" he had written for the Music Hall orchestra. But Carter was struggling to hold his own band together and may already have begun making plans to move to Europe. Don Redman was also leading his own band. Edgar Sampson had done a bit of writing for Benny and was to do more in the months to come, but as both an arranger and a player he was an indispensable member of Chick Webb's orchestra. Duke Ellington was Duke Ellington. Who could even consider asking him to become part of someone else's arranging staff?

The road led, inevitably, to a single destination.

John Hammond remained one of Fletcher Henderson's biggest fans despite the difficulties Henderson's laxity as a leader had caused him in the past. In the spring of 1932 Hammond had become involved in a project to present black musicians and variety acts in a theater downtown and booked Henderson to star on the opening bill. "When they so desired, their playing excelled that of any other band in the world," he reported in the *Melody Maker*. "But, alas, stage discipline is not a part of this band's make-up, with the result that the boys would struggle in late more often than not." By the end of the first week they had piled up something like sixty infractions of the show schedule and, to Hammond's regret, were replaced by Luis Russell.

The following December Hammond recorded the Henderson band for release in England. It was his first professional record date, and he was filled with excitement about working with what he considered "the greatest band of the era." Hammond remembered:

> The session was scheduled for ten A.M., and everyone had been warned that promptness was essential. At 11:30 there were exactly five men in the studio, and my realization came that this was a band with little or no morale. It was not until 12:40 P.M. that John Kirby finally arrived with his bass and the date actually started. Miraculously, three of Henderson's greatest sides were cut

in the space of 45 minutes: "Honeysuckle Rose," "New King Porter Stomp," and "Underneath the Harlem Moon."

Hammond did not discuss how Henderson reacted to his orchestra's almost hopeless lack of discipline and serious purpose, but it's likely to have been with the same strangely passive, rather bemused indifference he seemed to have had about his career as a bandleader from the very beginning.

Eleven years older than Benny, James Fletcher Henderson was born in Cuthbert, Georgia, on December 18, 1898. (He later changed his name to Fletcher Hamilton Henderson, Jr., because he thought "James" was associated too much with domestic service.) Both his parents were educators. At their insistence he began studying piano as a child, and though he is said to have resented taking lessons, he showed real promise. When he graduated from Atlanta University in 1920, the school yearbook prophesied a brilliant career in music: "His playing and compositions are sure to make him the most widely sought musical genius in America. He will be a regular contributor to *Etude* and other musical magazines. Before he has attained the heights of his success his works will be classed with Rachmaninoff and other noted musicians."

Henderson's involvement with jazz didn't really begin until he moved to New York to do graduate work in chemistry at Columbia University and took a part-time job as a song demonstrator with Pace and Handy, the pioneering black music publishing company. When Henry Pace left the firm in 1921 to found Black Swan records, Henderson went with him as musical director. His plans to become a chemist were behind him by now, and he began to make records backing blues singers, playing solo piano and leading the Black Swan house band. After work he sometimes also played with the Harlem Symphony.

One of the singers Fletcher worked with was a very young Ethel Waters. When Waters's first few recordings became hits, Pace sent her on tour with Henderson and the Black Swan Syncopaters. "Fletcher Henderson wasn't sure it would be dignified enough for him, a college student studying chemistry, to be the piano player for a girl who sang blues in a cellar," she recalled. "Before he would go out Fletcher had his whole family come up from Georgia to look me over and see if it would be all right." According to Waters, it was during this trip that Henderson made a begrudging commitment to the kind of music he'd be associated with the rest of his life:

Fletcher wouldn't give me what I call the "damn-it-to-hell bass," that chump-chump stuff that real jazz needs. All during the tour I kept nagging at him. I said he *couldn't* play as I wanted him to. When we reached Chicago

I got some piano rolls that Jimmy Johnson had made and pounded out each passage to Henderson. To prove to me he could do it, Fletch began to practice. He got so perfect, listening to James P. Johnson play on the player piano, that he could press down the keys as the roll played, never missing a note. Naturally, he began to be identified with that kind of music, which isn't his kind at all.

In the spring of 1923 Henderson began leading his own orchestra. The band was formed in a typically offhanded manner when after a record date Fletcher and the other musicians dropped by the Roseland Ballroom to say hello to some friends and were told the Club Alabam on West Forty-fourth Street was looking for a black band to play for the floor show. They auditioned with the same numbers they had just recorded and were immediately hired. "We decided to make Fletcher the leader," the saxophonist and arranger Don Redman explained, "because he was a college graduate and presented a nice appearance."

The Club Alabam engagement lasted a year, and during this period the Henderson orchestra began to evolve into what is considered the first big band to play jazz. The job mainly called for straight commercial dance and show music, and Fletcher used a lot of prefabricated stock arrangements. But there was also a certain amount of room for experimentation. Drawing upon influences as diverse as Paul Whiteman and King Oliver's Creole Jazz Band, whose records were just beginning to be heard around New York, Henderson's arranger, Don Redman, started working out a style that blended the formalism of written orchestrations with the freedom, intensity and emotional expressiveness of improvised jazz, incorporating some of the qualities of improvised solo playing in the fully scored passages of his charts.

"He used the saxophones as a section, much as other arrangers of the time were doing," Samuel B. Charters and Leonard Kunstadt explain, "but instead of simply harmonizing the melody for the section, he began writing solo passages, often very complex, for the section playing as a group. The melodic line was divided between the brass instruments and the saxophones, one section often beginning a phrase and the other finishing it." In time these devices, elaborated and refined, provided the basic approach followed by virtually all the big bands of the Swing Era.

The Henderson orchestra moved on to Roseland in September 1924 and took a tremendous leap forward when Fletcher managed to lure Louis Armstrong away from King Oliver in Chicago that October. "Nobody had ever heard so much horn-blowing before," Duke Ellington remembered. "He almost caused a riot."

Armstrong's virtuosity set a new standard for the Henderson soloists, and his drive and swing imparted a spirit to the ensemble that raised it to an entirely new level of excellence. "Louis, his style and his feeling changed our whole idea about the band musically," Don Redman later said. They also had a decisive effect on Redman's own writing. Louis had brought along some of the tunes he'd played with Oliver, and Redman immediately made an arrangement of "Dippermouth Blues" to showcase the young trumpet star. Retitled "Sugarfoot Stomp" when it was recorded the following May, the arrangement represents, as Richard Hadlock observes, "the culmination of Henderson's early period and the completion of the task of catching up to the New Orleans-dominated bands in Chicago. Riffs, 'organ' chords, a good grasp of the blues idiom, loose-jointed but precise ensemble playing, and first-rate solo power all come together in this performance to place the Fletcher Henderson band—and its chief arranger, Don Redman—ahead of all its competitors."

Fletcher gradually increased the number of players in the orchestra until he had five brass, three reeds and four rhythm, which approximated the standard instrumentation of the swing bands to come. The enlarged personnel gave Redman more to work with, and his arrangements became even more interesting. The orchestra continued to develop and improve, and its popularity was growing. At one point it was so in demand Fletcher formed a second band to work under his name. But then, in 1927, everything began to fall apart.

In March of that year Don Redman accepted an offer to become musical director of the McKinney's Cotton Pickers orchestra in Detroit, and Fletcher was suddenly left without an arranger. Borrowing scores wherever he could cost the band some of its hard-earned individuality, and he began to rely more on head arrangements. Benny Carter came in the following year as Redman's replacement, but Henderson also had to start doing some of the writing himself.

And then, when the band went on tour in the summer of 1928, Fletcher was seriously injured in an automobile accident. His head was deeply gashed, and his left collarbone was broken. Some years later he became paralyzed on his left side, but the immediate psychological effects were almost as devastating.

"Believe me Fletcher was never the same after he had that automobile accident down in Kentucky," his wife, Leora, maintained. "That was the only accident he ever had, and after that—why, he just changed. Everything would seem comical to him and he never achieved to go higher than he was. He never had much business qualities anyhow, but after that accident, he had even less. And worst of all, he would get careless. He had a wonderful ear and if a bell would strike somewhere in the street, Fletcher would tell you what note it was. But one day I went to a rehearsal and the boys were blowin' and I said, 'Fletcher, can't you tell, one of them horns is out of tune.' But he didn't seem to care much. It was the men in the band that kept up the morale then."

John Hammond believed that "the color bar crippled his ambition and made him cynical of the intentions of all white people," but perhaps, as Leora Henderson claimed, it was that accident that accounts for Henderson's peculiarly self-defeating passivity that allowed him to let the control of his orchestra slip through his hands. According to his younger brother, Horace, who joined the band as pianist and arranger in 1931, "Everybody knew he was an easygoing guy, and the greatest harm he ever did to anybody was to himself by being too easy with his musicians."

Henderson's fortunes continued to decline during the early 1930s, and he was forced to take to the road on a series of increasingly unprofitable tours and one-nighters. There were occasional good jobs, but the band was not well managed, and the men frequently found themselves between engagements. The Duke Ellington and Cab Calloway orchestras were thriving now under the expert guidance of Irving Mills and beginning to take the spotlight away from him. Fletcher's recordings had never sold especially well, but from the end of 1928 to the end of 1930 he hardly made any records at all. And when he started recording again in 1931, he was saddled with a lot of dubious tunes and inferior pop singers in an unsuccessful attempt to make him more commercial.

By the winter of 1934 the Fletcher Henderson orchestra had reached the end of the line and was forced to disband. The hellishly ironic thing was that at the time of the breakup it sounded absolutely wonderful. It was filled with great soloists like Red Allen, Buster Bailey, Ben Webster and Hilton Jefferson. And Fletcher had finally come into his own as an arranger. Moving beyond the relatively simple organization of head arrangements he first favored, he had gone on to perfect the innovations introduced by Don Redman and became the band's principal writer. A new recording contract with Decca in the fall of 1934 allowed him to demonstrate some of his recently acquired maturity and self-assurance. Charts like "Down South Camp Meeting" and "Wrappin' It Up" forge together into a single glorious entity improvisationlike ensemble choruses, call-and-response dialogue between saxophone and brass sections and high-spirited interplay between soloist and larger ensemble—all the elements that characterized big band writing for years to come. Yet for the first time in over a decade Fletcher Henderson was without an orchestra.

John Hammond visited Fletcher toward the end of the year and asked if he'd be interested in writing for Benny on an ongoing basis. The "Let's Dance" budget allowed him to offer a fee of $37.50 an arrangement. This was far from the $100 a score Paul Whiteman had paid Don Redman back in 1927, but Benny wasn't in Paul Whiteman's position, and Fletcher found it acceptable.

Because of the tremendous contribution the Henderson charts were to make to Benny's eventual success, later commentators have sometimes criticized Goodman harshly for exploiting the down-on-his-luck arranger. Benny bristled when questioned about it in a 1974 interview. "Fletcher never did think so," he argued, adding, "I was underpaid too." And according to Leora Henderson, "Nobody could have done more [for Fletcher] than John and Benny." Still, the fact remains that through no fault of his own, Benny was the beneficiary of a dozen years of experimentation, development and gradual perfection of a style of big band arranging that was to give him the identity he needed.

Fletcher began by sending Benny some of the charts already in the Henderson book. Benny recalled that the first two he received were "King Porter Stomp" and Horace's "Big John [aka "Big John's] Special." "As far as I know," he said, "it was the first time they had been played by a white orchestra, and it was one of the biggest kicks I've ever had in music to go through these scores and dig the music out of them, even in rehearsal."

The process of "digging out the music" appears to have begun at these initial readings. Benny had a distinctive way of rehearsing his musicians. Instead of letting the band as a whole run the tune down from top to bottom, he often had the individual sections—saxophones, trumpets, trombones—play their parts separately. "That was Benny's way," Helen Ward explains, "because any flaw, any weakness, is going to stand so revealed. You don't have a cushion. By the time he got through, I knew the tune without looking at the music. I just needed the music for the words."

It is often remarked that the basic difference between Benny and Fletcher is that Benny insisted his musicians play with much greater precision. In a sense, that was perfectly true. He wanted—and succeeded in getting—more accurate intonation, more carefully articulated phrasing, cleaner section work and a better blending of the overall ensemble. But he was also after something else. "We were rehearsing one time," Helen Ward recalls, "and I remember Benny saying to the guys, 'You don't need the arrangement. Don't *read* the notes; *play* 'em.' In other words, be more expressive." The idea was to evolve a style of performance that was tight but also loose, controlled yet also free, precise and predictable yet also open to individual inspiration. And to find music like Fletcher's that allowed itself to be played that way.

"He was just a marvelous arranger," Benny reminisced some three decades later. "After I heard one or two of his arrangements, I just couldn't get enough of them. Each one was a little classic."

The format of "Let's Dance" required Benny to play a lot of pop tunes and standards, and he persuaded Fletcher to try his hand at this sort of material. "He had to be convinced of it himself," Benny remembered, "but once he started he did marvelous work. These were the things, with their wonderful easy style and great background figures, that really set the style of the band." During the early weeks of the show Fletcher began turning out orchestrations of songs like "Three Little Words," "Am I Blue?" "Sweet and Lovely" and "I've Got My Love to Keep Me Warm." A number of his scores in this vein—"Sleepy Time Down South," "Blue Skies" and, above all, "Sometimes I'm Happy"—provided the basis for some of Benny's most highly regarded recordings.

Spud Murphy was still the band's most prolific writer, but Benny kept after Fletcher to get as many charts out of him as he could. He was doing about three arrangements a week, and many of them had to be produced at the very last minute. Horace Henderson vividly recounted the tremendous pressure this placed upon his brother: "I used to be in New York at our house on 139th Street, and I'd come in from my job around 3:30 in the morning. I've been off for two hours, and there's poor Fletcher at the piano. Benny had just called up and said, 'I need an arrangement for nine o'clock. We're recording so-and-so.' This is for twelve, fifteen pieces we're talking about. Poor Fletcher. And he's sitting up all night, man, and sleeping at the piano. I'd wake him up sometimes and help him undress. He's so tired, but he says, 'I've got to finish this for Benny.' Benny would think nothing of calling you up at four in the morning, telling you, 'I've got to have this by ten.' Oh, he was an arranger's nightmare.

"Fletcher was so swamped. Sometimes he said to me, 'I just can't do it. Can you make something up for Benny?' I was tickled to death to think that Fletcher asked me to write something for Benny Goodman. It was an honor. 'Sometimes I'm Happy'—there's a beautiful thing he and I made together. The reed chorus was a legend, the way it flowed. Fletcher wrote this early in the morning, and then he called me downstairs. I was asleep. He asked if I'd come down and finish the arrangement. I wrote the brass chorus—that's me. This happened many times."

Benny's urgent 4:00 A.M. telephone calls reveal a growing single-mindedness of purpose about the band and his budding career as a leader, as well as his hunger for Fletcher's arrangements. Certainly Fletcher needed the money, but his responsiveness to Benny's sometimes unreasonable demands also suggests, strangely enough, a personal involvement with the Goodman band he may never have had with his own orchestra. "I can only say this," Helen Ward offers by way of an explanation. "The very same arrangements that Fletcher's band played, put them in Benny's hands and my God, it was another world. The notes were there, they were all there in Fletcher's scores and up here in Fletcher's mind, but he couldn't whip it all together the way Benny did. He was a much gentler soul. He didn't have that sense of discipline in him. He was too soft. The guys took advantage of him. So he had never heard his music played so well before—the way it was supposed to be played, the way he conceived it. It was a perfect marriage of talents. It really was." Toots Mondello, Benny's great lead alto player, remembers that when, during the record session that produced "Sometimes I'm Happy," he announced he was leaving the band, Fletcher chased him around the studio to try to get him to stay.

There was never any question in Benny's mind that Fletcher's arrangements played a major part in his artistic and commercial success. As the years went by, he returned to these same Henderson scores over and over again, sometimes to the exasperation of younger sidemen, who thought it was time to move on to more contemporary writing. Nor was Benny ever unstinting in his praise. "Fletcher's ideas were far ahead of anybody else's," he wrote in his 1939 autobiography. "Without Fletcher I probably would have had a pretty good band, but it would have been something quite different from what it eventually turned out to be." And almost half a century later, a few months before he died, he dedicated his last television special to Fletcher's memory. "The fascination with his arrangements was endless," he said. "I really thought he was a genius."

The Goodman band in performance on the ''Let's Dance'' show, December 1934. *Bottom row:* Benny, Barry McKinley, Helen Ward. *Second row:* Dick Clark, Hymie Schertzer, Toots Mondello, Arthur Rollini. *Third row:* Frank Froeba, Harry Goodman, George VanEps, Jack Lacey, Red Ballard. *Top row:* Jerry Neary, Sammy Shapiro, Pee Wee Erwin, **Gene Krupa.** Ken Whitten Collection

7

Let's Dance: 2

lthough Fletcher Henderson's arrangements "convinced me more than ever which way the band should head," Benny recalled, "we still didn't have the right band to play that kind of music." Hammond put it more directly: "The only trouble with Benny's band at the beginning of the 'Let's Dance' broadcasts was that it did not swing." The main problem, Hammond thought, was the rhythm section, particularly the drummer. Benny agreed with him: "It has never been possible to have a band with swing unless you had a really good rhythm section. This was one of our main ideas right from the start. . . . [But] our drummer was merely adequate."

Stan King had taken over the drum chair from Sammy Weiss during the last days of the Music Hall engagement. King was one of the most sought-after drummers in New York, in constant demand for his skillful radio and record work, but though he was a good steady timekeeper, he did not drive the band through those Henderson charts with anywhere near the swing Walter Johnson had brought to Fletcher's orchestra. "We called him a strictly society type of musician," Helen Ward remembers. "Everything he played was boom-cha, boom-cha. There was no fire there." The drummer who could give the band the fire it needed was working in Chicago. After talking it over with Benny, Hammond went off to hire him.

Gene Krupa was now playing with the orchestra fronted by Buddy Rogers, the movie star turned bandleader. The Rogers band had a number of excellent jazz musicians, including the saxophonist Dick Clark, who was to join Benny shortly, but the band itself was much less than the sum of its better parts. "Atrocious" is how Hammond described it in his review for the *Melody News*. Krupa was initially resistant to Hammond's offer. He still harbored some bad feelings toward Benny from the Russ Columbo engagement, nor had he forgotten that only a few months earlier Hammond had tried talking him into joining that all-star tour of England that had failed to materialize. If the Rogers job wasn't exactly inspiring, at least it paid well, and he had recently married and was in considerable debt.

"At that point Gene had to play for the floor show," Hammond remembered, "during which Buddy Rogers went through his usual act, playing a variety of instruments, each worse than the last. At the next break Gene returned to my table and said, 'All right, John. I'll come.' "

Benny was jubilant when Hammond reported his mission had been successful. "He kept telling me, 'Gene Krupa's coming in from Chicago! Just wait till you hear this guy!' " Helen Ward recalls. "And I made this silly remark to him, 'So what? So what's the big deal with a drummer?' Because I was only used to oom-cha, oom-cha. Wow! Did I change my mind once I actually heard him! Gene was a revelation. Everything he did was right. He had such a feeling for phrasing it was almost like he was playing the melody. When Benny took a solo, Gene almost played the notes with him. He inspired Benny. He inspired everybody."

Gene Krupa's drumming was not without its limitations. He could be loud. He could be overbearing. He had a tendency to rush. But he was the perfect drummer for the Benny Goodman band, one of those rare musical matches made in heaven like Sonny Greer and Duke Ellington or Jo Jones and Count Basie. "Gene's arrival marked a musical turning point in the Goodman organization," Hammond maintained. "Fletcher Henderson's arrangements began to take on excitement, and the other studio musicians acquired a small bit of the relaxation and verve of the old Henderson band."

Krupa's contributions to the Goodman orchestra extended far beyond his considerable technical abilities. A small, compact man (like a number of other powerful drummers: Dave Tough, Buddy Rich, Art Blakey, Roy Haynes), he was movie star handsome with longish dark hair and a Tyrone Power profile. Enormously likable, his personality projected itself effortlessly across the bandstand and into the audience. In the tradition of Chick Webb and Sid Catlett, he was also very much of a showman, with a flashy visual style that gave physical form and substance to the musical abstractions he produced on his drum kit. John S. Wilson described it nicely in the obituary published in the *New York Times* following Gene's death in 1973:

> He hunched over his drums, chewing gum in vigorous tempo with the beat, a dangling lock of black hair waving back and forth in front of his eyes, which filled with an almost fiendish zest as he flailed away at his snare drum, tom-toms and cymbals. Suddenly he would rear back, holding both arms in the air as he pounded his bass drum with a foot pedal. And then, perspiration dripping from him like a tropical rainfall, his arms and drumsticks became a blur of motion as he built his solo to a crashing climax.

Krupa brought to the Goodman band the glamour and personal magnetism that Benny himself lacked. He gave the musically unsophisticated in the audience something to grab hold of that they could comprehend, turning the drums into a central attraction for people who never heard of Baby Dodds or Chick Webb. In a very short time he became the star of the band, and once that happened, the door was open for other sidemen to become stars as well. His impact on future generations of drummers was enormous. He was, Buddy Rich said some two decades later, "the inspiration for every big-band drummer in the business today." Krupa reflected toward the end of his career: "I'm happy that I succeeded in doing two things. I made the drummer a high-priced guy, and I was able to project enough so that I was able to draw more people to jazz."

Krupa joined Benny shortly before Christmas 1934 in time to play the fourth broadcast. Probably because Benny had promised to feature him, his drums were conspicuously placed downstage in front of the orchestra. He was so overpowering no one could hear the rest of the band, and by the following week he was back with the other members of the rhythm section, where he remained, serving nobly, for the next three years.

The "Let's Dance" show was preceded by an ear-shattering barrage of advance publicity. McCann-Erickson pulled out all the stops, hyping the show as the world's greatest dance program, the program all America said it wanted to hear, the lengthiest sponsored broadcast since radio began, the most important step forward for dance music that had ever been taken. The National Biscuit Company sent out counter displays to all its retail outlets promoting the idea of an at-home Saturday night dance party and encouraging shoppers to lay in a fresh supply of crackers and cookies. "Let's Dance" posters appeared on the company's delivery trucks. Stockholders received postcards imploring them to "join in by having a dance party in your home to help this program achieve quick popularity." Celebrities were rounded up to attend the

December 1 premiere—actress Mae Murray, fan dancer Sally Rand, stars of the Metropolitan Opera and the *Ziegfeld Follies*. There were klieg lights, loudspeakers, clicking cameras, traffic jams. The show was sent out over shortwave to ships in the Atlantic and Pacific oceans and the Panama Canal, and they radioed back to the studio audience that they were hearing the music just fine and enjoying every minute of it.

The music and show business press was largely unamused by all this artfully staged delirium. McCann-Erickson's "handling of the 'Let's Dance' affair brought little credit to the agency," *Variety* intoned, dismissing it as "a species of showmanship that smacked of 1928." Reviewing the opening broadcast, which it rated only "Fair," *Metronome* magazine pointed out that "there is nothing new about dance music on the air. Anyone can tune in on Sat night especially and get all they want." This was perfectly true. Radio station WNEW in New York broadcast six hours of live dance music every Saturday evening from various hotels and ballrooms, and the other local stations and networks did much the same, without the intrusion of Nabisco's extensive and overly cute commercial interruptions. "Is there any reason why the National Biscuit Company program should be preferred to that of the non-commercial sustainings?" *Billboard* asked. "Add a chorus of 'No, No, a Thousand Times No.' "

But despite the bad reviews and dire prognostications that it was bound to fail, the audience for "Let's Dance" built steadily from week to week. Nabisco experienced the desired upsurge in the sale of its crackers and cookies. When the initial thirteen-week commitment ended, it quickly renewed its option for a second thirteen-week run. And as the show settled in, musicians and other musically alert listeners across the country began to plan their Saturday nights so they could be close to a radio and hear what this new Benny Goodman orchestra was sending out over the airways.

The fans in New York crowded into Studio 8H to hear the band in person. "A truly great outfit," *Metronome* raved. "Fine arrangements, and musicians who are together all the time. . . . Wonderful." *Down Beat* was even more enthusiastic: "Benny's performance is magnificent. The band is the smoothest and fastest thing heard yet, and the soloists are not to be improved upon. . . . Benny himself never played any better than he is playing today. . . . This is the band of the year. It's not to be beaten." The *Down Beat* encomium appeared without a by-line but was almost certainly written by John Hammond. He was a regular contributor by now and, as he confessed, "wrote about the band tactlessly and in great detail," adding, "Because of my connection with the sheet, I may have wielded more influence with Benny than I deserved."

Though most of McCann-Erickson's hyperbole shouldn't be taken too seriously, one of its claims was no more than a simple statement of fact. "Let's

Dance" *was* the most ambitious and elaborate program of dance music ever put on the air. Nothing on this scale had ever been tried before. The logistics were all but overwhelming.

Since it was broadcast live from coast to coast, the show had to be scrupulously organized to accommodate the demands of four different time zones. It went on the air at 10:30 P.M. in the East and signed off three hours later at 1:30 in the morning. At 10:30 eastern time it was picked up by the states in the central zone, where it was only 9:30, and continued on the air until it was 12:30 central time (1:30 A.M. in the East). At 11:30 New York time the stations in the mountain states joined in. At 12:30 A.M. the Pacific Coast stations were added. To air three hours of dance music across the country, the broadcast went on for a full five hours in the New York studio, and split-second timing had to be worked out to cut in the appropriate commercials, station breaks and other announcements at just the right moment. This became even more complicated in the spring, when daylight savings went into effect in some—but not all—parts of the country and some—but not all—of the cities in the areas where it was generally followed.

To make all this halfway manageable, the show was structured as a series of thirty-minute self-contained segments. For the most part each of the three bands appeared in each segment, first Kel Murray, then Xavier Cugat, then Benny. Since Xavier Cugat was also working at the Waldorf, at several points in the evening he had to miss his turn in the rotation to get over to the hotel. "You can imagine how hectic my Saturdays were," he recalled. "It meant playing a dance session at the hotel, then dashing for the broadcast, then back to the Waldorf, then back again to go on the air and another quick return to the hotel. My ingenious brother, Albert, solved the difficulty by corralling, each Saturday night, a fleet of taxicabs, waiting in gear, to whisk us back and forth. Thanks to Albert, I was never late for a broadcast nor for a set of dances." Jim Maher asked Albert Cugat many years later: " 'My God, how did you ever do it?" He was a rather thin, gentlemanly soul, and he just looked at me then raised his eyes to Heaven. As he brought his eyes back down he said, 'Do you know the Latin American temperament?' "

The musicians in Kel Murray's saxophone section had their own scheduling problems to contend with. They were simultaneously working another NBC broadcast that went on about two minutes after they finished their opening set. As soon as they hit the last note, they had to dash offstage (with saxophones in hand) to where a freight elevator was waiting to whisk them downstairs to the other studio, then run to the bandstand, take their seats and immediately start playing.

The difficulties were endless, according to Jim Maher, who has researched the show extensively. This was the first year Studio 8H was open. The following year Arturo Toscanini was to take up residence with the NBC

Symphony, but right now there were still numerous problems with engineering and acoustics, especially when Benny's band started blasting. The musicians had to wear tuxedoes and look their best in front of the large studio audience, but many of Benny's men had recording sessions and rehearsals for other programs earlier in the day, and by the time they showed up they needed someplace to take another shave. Since they were there from nine-thirty in the evening until three- or four-thirty the following morning, they also had to eat, and when the hall was designed, no one considered there might be a need to feed a huge cast of approximately seventy musicians, singers and announcers. By the second week Joe Bonime and Dorothy Barstow had rigged up some trestle tables backstage and brought in a caterer. "A few of the boys would sneak downstairs for a fast one," Maher says, "but Benny kept his eyes on them. This was his big chance, and he didn't want anyone coming back drunk."

The dancing part of the "Let's Dance" show was handled by three pairs of professional ballroom dancers, one for each of the orchestras. The thousand fans who jammed into Studio 8H each Saturday night had to be remain in their seats, no matter how much the music stirred them. Sometimes Helen Ward might do a bit of fox-trotting between vocals. "Benny was very tolerant about that. I had made it clear to him that I didn't just want to sit on the bandstand doing nothing when I wasn't singing. It made me feel like a dummy." Her partner was the singer Ray Hendricks, who had replaced Buddy Clark by the eleventh broadcast. Helen remembers that Hendricks was "a great little dancer," but on the rare occasions Benny could be coaxed onto a dance floor he moved around awkwardly in tight little circles, like a kid suffering through his first day of dancing class. Curiously, John Hammond claimed that "one of the reasons Benny Goodman set such perfect dance tempos was that he could dance so well himself." This would seem to be either a minor lapse of memory or a very private joke.

Since the Goodman orchestra was primarily a dance band, it was important to get out of the studio and gain some experience playing before crowds of actual dancers. A few times without any advance publicity Benny took the band up to the Savoy Ballroom, where it worked opposite Chick Webb. He also began booking some one-nighters out of town. The band's reputation was growing, but it still wasn't popular enough to command much money, and some of the gigs were for as little as two hundred dollars. Toots Mondello, Pee Wee Erwin and George Van Eps were frequently busy with other commitments and had to send in substitutes, diluting the band's homogeneity, but Benny was not yet in a position to demand that his men give up their outside interests. For Pee Wee Erwin, "Playing with Benny was just another part of the week's work." Benny expected his musicians to share his commitment to making the band a success, and he found that sort of casual attitude infuriating.

The Goodman orchestra played low-profile one-nighters in places like Scranton, Pennsylvania, White Plains and Binghamton, New York, and Nutting-on-the-Charles near Boston. The Binghamton job in upstate New York, which took place on Christmas Day, was especially rough. As Arthur Rollini tells the story, they made the trip in an ancient four-cylinder Coney Island sight-seeing bus that Benny was able to hire very cheaply.

> Everything was fine until we got about thirty-five miles north of New York City, and then the bus had trouble climbing the hills. They became steeper and steeper, and the driver was in low gear. Finally we all had to get out with our instruments and walk up the hills. We reached the top before the bus. This went on repeatedly, and it was terribly difficult for the drummer. . . . We finally arrived at the dance hall at 11 P.M., quite disheveled and perspiring profusely, even though it was winter. A girls' band was playing, but we finished the date. Fortunately it was downhill going back to New York City.

Despite such vicissitudes, which were a fairly standard part of life on the road, these in-person engagements proved enormously valuable. They gave the band a chance to interact with live dancers and, as Benny put it, "really find its groove." They gave the musicians an opportunity to rehearse in public and reach the high level of performance Benny expected of them by the time they went on the air Saturday night. They also allowed the band to plow its way through the huge number of new arrangements and tunes being thrown at it every week and discover which ones worked best. Along with the charts Benny commissioned out of his "Let's Dance" budget, he was also being supplied with arrangements by some of the big music publishers in the hope he would give their tunes national exposure by broadcasting them on the show. "New songs were coming in like coffee out of a grinder," Helen Ward recalls. "Benny had a fantastic feel for good tunes, so he would dutifully go through everything and pick out the ones he thought had possibilities. Then he would try them out on the road. The ones that seemed to work would be played on 'Let's Dance.' The best ones, the ones he really believed in, would eventually be recorded."

These one-nighters also supplied Benny with some much-needed experience in dealing with the public. He was basically a reserved, intensely private man, with neither the temperament nor the taste for the easygoing show biz bonhomie audiences expected of a bandleader. At this point in his career he even found it hard to make announcements. Conducting the orchestra with the exaggerated theatricality many leaders affected was absolutely out of the question. Helen Ward remembers the great difficulty he had coming to terms with the most common sort of audience rudeness. "On one of these dates Benny was looking through the library to pick out tunes, and this kid came up to the bandstand and pulled on his coattails. Benny turned around, grabbed his clarinet and was ready to clobber him. I told him later on, 'Benny, this is your public. You've got to learn to be a little tolerant.' " Some musicians are naturally endowed with what it takes to be a public personality, but Benny was not one of them. At the beginning at least, it required a tremendous act of will to place himself in front of an audience and adapt to the role of "entertainer."

Among the many fans who showed up regularly at the "Let's Dance," broadcasts was a young MCA agent named Willard Alexander. One year older than Benny, Alexander had graduated in 1930 from the University of Pennsylvania, where he studied music and fine arts, led a dance band and booked outside orchestras for various college functions. His own band played strictly commercial music, but he knew and loved jazz and was an avid follower of Benny's work as a sideman. After graduation Willard became a full-time bandleader, like his father before him. Working such places as the Shelburne Hotel in Atlantic City and the Walton Roof in Philadelphia, he displayed a great deal of personal style and flair. The trumpet player Chris Griffin recalls that "although he didn't have much money at the time, he would hire a limousine to drive him up to the hotel, get out with his high hat on and his wonderful tuxedo with tails, then stride into the ballroom. He was a mediocre violinist, I understand, but he sure knew how to show it."

By 1935, Willard had become an agent with the Music Corporation of America (MCA), which had built its business on very commercial dance orchestras like Guy Lombardo, Bernie Cummins and Wayne King. Billy Goodheart, who was now vice-president of the agency, had turned Benny down when he went to see him about representation in February after the "Let's Dance" show was renewed. But Willard Alexander was a much younger man and saw things differently. The jazz fan in him loved Benny's music. The astute businessman shared Benny's conviction that the Casa Loma's popularity in the colleges had created a new market for jazz-oriented big bands that was yet to be satisfied.

Benny was suspicious at first when Willard approached him about becoming his agent. "Most of the people I had come in contact with in the music business [were] pretty hard-boiled, with not much interest in anybody except to figure out how much they can make on them." Nor was Goodheart at all receptive when Alexander tried to sell him on the idea. But Willard was, as Helen Ward described him, a "go-getter of the first order." He eventually brought both of them around and signed Benny to a long-term contract with the agency, even though it meant putting his own job very much on the line.

"I remember very well first meeting with John Hammond," Alexander told Jim Maher in 1961. "It was at lunch with Benny Goodman at the old Park and Tilford, which used to be located where Tiffany's jewelry store is now. We got along great, all three of us." Hammond's response to Alexander was equally positive: "From my observation of the business, I could not conceive of a band agent as anything but musically ignorant, out to exploit all musicians, and without the slightest concern for, or ability to guide, their careers. Willard Alexander was . . . the exception to this stereotype, and he became as important to Benny Goodman's early career as anyone."

"Anyone" may be taken to mean Fletcher Henderson, Gene Krupa and Hammond himself. And this would be a fair statement. Hammond reawakened Benny's musical conscience and brought him back to jazz, then served as his unofficial talent scout and adviser. Fletcher created the arrangements that set the band's style and gave Benny his musical identity. Krupa sparked the band to life with his playing and provided a dramatic visual counterpart to the music's excitement. But big bands were more than music. They were also a business, and Willard Alexander guided Benny through the twists and turns and unexpected pitfalls of that business with uncommon enthusiasm and skill.

"Benny had always been a high-priced individual musician who only thought about himself," he explained. "But when he started leading a band I tried to make him conscious that he had to make the transition from an independent musician to a responsible overall businessman, a switch that was essential if he was going to become successful. This is one of the great transitions that many of the top musicians could not make for some reason or other, but Benny switched over very responsibly and adapted himself very well. I would say he was the easiest person I ever handled. Ninety percent of all the musical ideas came from him, but he abided almost completely by what I said managerially."

The "Let's Dance" band's first recordings were done for Irving Mills in January and February 1935 and released on Columbia. As with his earlier record dates for Mills, Benny was encouraged to play tunes Mills had published and was paid a flat fee. But then in the early spring he entered into a much more favorable arrangement with Victor. Victor was owned by RCA, the giant corporation that also owned the NBC network that broadcast "Let's Dance," and it was headed by Ted Wallerstein, a big Goodman fan. Overcoming the resistance of the other Victor executives, Wallerstein insisted that

Benny's contract include a clause paying him an ongoing royalty. This is said to be one of the first royalty deals ever given a jazz artist and came about because Wallerstein believed creative musicians should share in the marketing of their talent. It was also an unusually farsighted piece of business thinking. Benny remained with the label for the next four years, recording well over two hundred sides, including all the landmark hits that made him a household name. Had he not been given a share of the very substantial profits, he might well have been lured away by one of Victor's competitors.

Over the past few years Victor had recorded a number of other jazz-oriented big bands but hadn't really made any long-term commitment. In 1933 Duke Ellington, Fletcher Henderson, Jimmie Lunceford and Cab Calloway were all on the label, but by the spring of 1934 they were gone. About the only jazz artists still left were Willie Bryant and Fats Waller, both of whom were required to perform a lot of run-of-the-mill popular songs. During Duke Ellington's brief stay with the company in 1933 and 1934, he also did his share of forgettable commercial material along with such enduring masterpieces as "Daybreak Express," "Solitude" and "Stompy Jones." All of which serves as a reminder that the perceived market for unfettered jazz records was still extremely small. It also helps explain the decidedly commercial cast of Benny's first record date for the label on April 4.

Three of the four sides recorded that day—"Hooray for Love," "I'm Living in a Great Big Way" and "Hunkadola"—were breezy pop tunes featured in current movies. The fourth was a remake of the Johnny Mercer novelty "The Dixieland Band," which Benny had recorded for Columbia less than three months earlier. (Eli Oberstein, Victor's recording director, thought the label could turn the tune into a hit, and it did.) Only one of these sides, "Hunkadola," was an instrumental with a substantial amount of solo work, and it was arranged, probably by Deane Kincaide, in a mannered Dixieland style that reminded the *Down Beat* reviewer of "the Casa Loma band ripping through one of its mechanical hot arrangements."

None of these sides is without interest. The band digs in admirably, performing the remake of the Mercer tune with much more assurance and swing than on the original version. It had come a long way in a very few months. And Benny plays extremely well whenever he solos. But on the whole, there isn't that much here to explain why jazz fans and the music magazines were hailing the Goodman orchestra as the band of the year.

The vocals on "The Dixieland Band" and "Hooray for Love" were sung by Helen Ward. She continued to be heavily featured on future record sessions as well as on Benny's radio shows and live appearances and became one of the band's strongest assets. But she remains convinced that if Benny had followed his own personal tastes rather than the dictates of the market-place, she would not have been there at all.

"Singers were a necessary evil to Benny," she says. "I faced that a long time ago. The real McCoy that he was after came in the instrumentals. But it was an absolute necessity that we play the pop tunes of the day. Half the people would sit down at 'Bugle Call Rag,' let's face it. So there had to be what we called commercial music in between. And that's where the girl singer came in. But he never cared for girl singers. Never. Or for boy singers either. He didn't like singers, period. Commercial music, you know. Benny was strictly the jazz hound. But he felt he had to have them."

Benny came a lot closer to "the real McCoy" on his second record date two weeks later, probably because Jack Teagarden was sitting in. Jack leads the trombone section masterfully through the opening chorus of "Japanese Sandman" and takes a long solo on "You're a Heavenly Thing." Three of the four tunes were arranged by Fletcher or Horace Henderson, and the fourth, the superior Sam Coslow ballad "Restless," contains beautifully written ensemble passages for the saxophone section by Spud Murphy very much in the Henderson vein. "Japanese Sandman" and "Always," the two instrumentals on the date, were released back to back, suggesting that Victor was becoming a little more confident in the less commercial side of the Goodman band's music. *Metronome* magazine selected it as the number one record of the month, praising "Always" as "the last word" and "Sandman" as "another 4-star revival of a 4-star old favorite by a real 4-star band."

Benny's new records were starting to sell, and "Let's Dance" continued to draw enthusiastic audiences throughout the country. But on May 25, 1935, five days before Benny's twenty-sixth birthday, the show suddenly went off the air. A strike had closed down the Nabisco factories, and now that it had no product to market, the company decided against renewing for another thirteen weeks. Once again the band was out of work.

To keep the orchestra from falling apart, Benny needed another booking quickly. And since a number of key men held down other jobs in New York, it had to be something in town. About the only possibility available just then was the Grill of the Roosevelt Hotel at Forty-fifth and Madison.

MCA had controlled the bookings at the Roosevelt for the past five and a half years, ever since it brought Guy Lombardo in from Chicago in October 1929. Before then the agency had operated successfully in its home base of Chicago and throughout the Midwest, but it had not yet managed to gain a foothold in New York. It tried various times to establish itself as a presence in the New York music business by sending out midwestern dance bands like Wayne King and Abe Lyman, but all these efforts had failed. Working closely with Lombardo, Jules Stein, the head of MCA, planned out his 1929 assault on Manhattan with great deliberation and care, eventually choosing the

Roosevelt over the St. Regis and New Yorker hotels because it was more suited to the young college crowd that had been Lombardo's biggest fans back in Chicago and Cleveland. The strategy proved enormously successful for both Lombardo and MCA. By 1935 Lombardo had become an almost permanent fixture at the Roosevelt, attracting a staid, middle-aged clientele of out-of-towners who danced to the "Sweetest Music This Side of Heaven" between courses of their expensive suppers.

Lombardo's manager at the time was a young agent named Sonny Werblin, who went on to become a major sports figure as owner of the New York Jets and president of the New Jersey Meadowlands and Madison Square Garden. In 1935 he and Willard Alexander were roommates as well as fellow agents at MCA, sharing what John Hammond called "a swinging apartment" at the Alrae Hotel. Werblin also booked the other bands at the Roosevelt when Lombardo went on the road, and Willard implored him to put Benny into the hotel to replace the Lombardo-like Bernie Cummins orchestra, which was going on tour. Everyone was aware that this was hardly the ideal room for Benny's kind of music, but there was really no other choice. "We wanted to get work for the band," Alexander explained. "Hell, we would have booked the Holland Tunnel."

Had Benny matched Lombardo's earlier triumph, the Roosevelt would have gone down in the history books as the birthplace of the Swing Era, and writers could have had a fine time holding forth about how the power of righteous jazz drove the false music of Guy Lombardo and his ilk out of the temple. Unfortunately nothing like this happened. No carefully thought-out strategy was brought to bear this time around, no calculated maneuvering to boost a client's career. It was simply a matter of getting the band a gig. Some gigs work out; some do not. This one didn't.

The Roosevelt Grill was a fairly small room designed on a number of different levels to encourage a sense of intimacy. The bandstand was built to scale and could barely contain the full Goodman aggregation. Benny did make some effort to adjust to the room and its customers by featuring Helen Ward on ballads like "It's Easy to Remember." But as she says, "The place was impossible for what we were trying to do. How softly can you play 'King Porter Stomp'? The people were absolutely, totally unnerved. They were used to this sweet music, and now they couldn't hear each other over dinner." Arthur Rollini recalled: "The management had never heard anything like this before. The waiters were rattling dishes, knives and forks, and holding their fingers in their ears." According to Hymie Schertzer's head-shaking memory of that opening night, "It was a horror, a horror!" At the beginning of the second set the manager rushed into the Grill, bawled out Willard Alexander, Benny and the MCA executives, then ended his tirade by giving the band its two weeks' notice.

Big Band,
Small Band

tremendous amount of progress
had been made during the twenty-six weeks the "Let's Dance" show remained
on the air. Starting pretty much from scratch, Benny had brought a remarkable new orchestra into being, begun to build up an enthusiastic coterie of
fans, signed with the powerful MCA booking agency and acquired a new
record contract with Victor. But when the unexpected cancellation of "Let's
Dance" was immediately followed by the loss of the job at the Roosevelt Grill,
he suffered a serious double blow that broke his momentum and left his future
uncertain.

The one really positive note was that "Hunkadola" and "The Dixieland
Band," Benny's first Victor release, were selling briskly, especially in the New
England college towns and, for some reason or other, out in California. As a
result, the West Coast office of MCA approached him about booking the band
into a new dance hall near Los Angeles called the Palomar Ballroom. Benny
did not find the prospect especially appealing. He wanted to remain in New
York. The Palomar job would last only about a month and was three thousand miles away. But this was about the only significant engagement being
offered him right now, and he had to do something to hold the band together.

Benny with Teddy Wilson and Gene Krupa,
the groundbreaking Benny Goodman Trio, 1937.

Ken Whitten Collection

To make the California trip more attractive, Willard Alexander got busy trying to set up some bookings along the way. He also managed to arrange a few one-nighters in the New York area. Benny returned to Binghamton (without the Coney Island sight-seeing bus this time around), and six hundred people, double the number of his Christmas Day appearance, showed up to hear him. Another one-night stand out in the boondocks was even more successful. "The crowd of country whites was so excited by the band," *Down Beat* reported, "that they behaved like a bunch of 'sailing' Harlemites at the Savoy."

These were encouraging signs, but the band would not be leaving New York until the middle of July, and still had a lot of idle time on its hands. To take up some of the slack and help meet his payroll, Benny began to do a good bit of recording. On June 6, 1935, he brought his musicians into the NBC studio to cut some electrical transcriptions, sixteen-inch 33⅓ rpm plastic discs leased to radio stations for airplay, to be issued under the generic name of the Rhythm Makers Orchestra. The band started running through its book at nine-thirty in the morning, doing one quick take after another, substituting instrumental solos for the singers whenever they came to a vocal chorus. By the time the exhausted sidemen put their instruments away at five-thirty that afternoon they had piled up fifty-one sides. Pee Wee Erwin remembered it as one of the strangest recording sessions of all times: "I may be wrong, but to my knowledge it may still stand as the longest record date in terms of number of tunes recorded at one sitting." Arthur Rollini recalled that "we received a grand total of fifty-one dollars—one dollar per tune."

A couple of weeks later Benny undertook his third recording session for Victor. Along with a pop tune featuring Helen Ward and a fairly straight reading of Hoagy Carmichael's "Ballad in Blue," the band also performed two out-and-out jazz charts, Fletcher Henderson's arrangement of "Blue Skies" and his brother Horace's "Dear Old Southland." "Blue Skies" turned out especially well, in no small part because of Bunny Berigan's return to the trumpet section. After playing the first six "Let's Dance" broadcasts, Bunny had dropped out of the band. He was in constant demand for his session work—everyone in New York wanted to use him—but it seems likely that his heavy drinking had hastened his departure.

"One of the things Benny would not put up with was any drinking on the job," Helen Ward tells us. "Yet one night at the 'Let's Dance' show Bunny got so drunk he literally fell off the bandstand, and Manny Klein had to sit in and sight-read his part. Why Bunny did things like that I don't know. You could tell how much he enjoyed playing. But that's the way he was. One time he showed me a beautiful new horn case he just had made to order. He opened the thing up, and here's a place for the mouthpiece and a place for the horn and a separate compartment for his gin bottle lined in red velvet."

Bunny's appearance on the "Blue Skies" date was reported as "an added attraction," but he returned the following week when Benny recorded "Sometimes I'm Happy" and "King Porter Stomp." The projected road tour was shaping up by now, and since Pee Wee Erwin had decided to remain in New York, Benny needed a permanent replacement. Despite his misgivings, he offered Bunny the job, and though it took some doing, Bunny finally accepted. "Benny had to overlook Bunny's drinking problem because of his greatness," Helen explains. "He was the one exception."

"King Porter Stomp" and "Sometimes I'm Happy" are marvelous records, the first fully realized expressions of what Benny was trying to achieve. Fletcher's orchestrations, with their gorgeous writing for the saxophone section, are played at just the right tempo with a relaxed self-assurance that reveals all their excitement and charm. Krupa is indisputably *there* throughout both performances, as solid as a rock as he drives the band forward and fills in behind the soloists in a kind of ongoing dialogue that both supports and inspires the other end of the conversation. Bunny is simply breathtaking, playing at the bottom of the horn and then at the top, now muted, now open, with the full, rich sound, deeply felt emotion and boundless flow of ideas that characterize his best solo work. Benny himself almost bubbles over with delight on "King Porter," placing his flawless technique at the service of a throaty, raspy sound that hints back to the clarinet players of his Chicago youth.

"Without a doubt this record represents the band at its best and beats anything it has made on wax previously," *Down Beat* proclaimed. "Colossal," the *Melody Maker* called it. "It's a waste of time trying to describe this band; you will simply have to listen to it yourselves."

It took a few months before the record was released and the reviews were published. In the meantime, while the band's future still remained very much in doubt, Benny made several other landmark recordings of a very different nature.

One night in early June, after he had finished up for the evening at the Roosevelt Grill, Benny had driven out to Forest Hills to attend a party being given by Red Norvo and his wife, Mildred Bailey. Mildred enjoyed cooking for her friends and frequently invited a crowd of fellow musicians over to the house for her southern fried chicken and a little after-hours jamming. The other guests that night included the omnipresent John Hammond, Mildred's cousin Carl Bellinger, a test pilot who was also an amateur drummer, and the young black pianist Teddy Wilson, who was currently working in Willie Bryant's orchestra. "Knowing how good Benny and Teddy were, and how naturally their styles and ideas met," Mildred recalled, "I suggested they join forces with the drummer-cousin for a spot of trio playing."

The results were electrifying. Teddy and Benny had played together before. At Hammond's urging, Benny had used him on a few record dates the previous year, and on the May 1934 session featuring Teagarden, Teddy took an especially lovely solo on "Moonglow." But now that it was just the two of them, supported by Bellinger's unobtrusive wire brushes keeping time on an empty suitcase, it was as if Benny heard what he could really do for the first time. "Teddy and I began to play as though we were thinking with the same brain," is the way he explained it many years later. "It was a real kick."

Everyone in the room was bowled over by the almost telepathic rapport these two great musicians shared with each other as they jammed away into the dawn, especially that professional enthusiast John Hammond. The next day he fired off an eyewitness report to the *Melody Maker,* calling it "about the most exciting evening musically that I can ever remember."

Hammond had been talking up Teddy Wilson to anyone who would listen ever since he first happened to hear him with Clarence Moore's band on a radio broadcast from Chicago's Grand Terrace in 1932. Moore was substituting for Earl Hines that night, and Hammond was immediately struck by how this anonymous piano player was "absolutely unique, with a cleaner and more elegant sound than Hines', never flashy, but swinging and with an excellent left hand." Reaching for the telephone, he put in a long-distance call to the radio station to find out his name.

In the fall of 1933 Benny Carter was looking for someone to replace the pianist in his band, and Hammond suggested Teddy Wilson. Carter remembered hearing Teddy work in a piano duo with Art Tatum in Toledo, Ohio, and when he agreed he'd be the perfect choice, Hammond took out his wallet and handed him $150 to bring Teddy to New York.

The day Teddy hit town Hammond rushed him into the recording studio to make his first records, four sides for English Parlophone as part of a mixed band billed as the Chocolate Dandies. Six days later he recorded him again with Carter's orchestra and the following May, a week after the Goodman "Moonglow" session, arranged to have him cut four piano solos for Columbia. Hammond felt certain these first recorded examples of Teddy's unaccompanied solo work were "highly commercial" as well as "magnificent," but Columbia found them "monotonous" and refused to release them. Frustrated but undaunted, Hammond continued to promote further record dates for the young pianist, including two wonderful all-star sessions led by Red Norvo that Hammond financed out of his own pocket.

"To me, Teddy was the ultimate chamber music player, and chamber music was my great love," Hammond recalled. "I was terribly impressed by him, both as a pianist and a person. He was the first young black musician I had come across who was the child of intellectuals. His mother was the chief librarian at Tuskegee Institute in Alabama, and his father was the head of the English department there. . . . I knew that, with his education, he was going to be *the* guy to break down racial barriers. He had the musical skills, the technique, the reading ability—and the manner."

Hammond also recognized that Teddy would be the perfect musical partner for Benny Goodman. "I saw in Teddy Wilson the only piano player I could conceive of with the same technical facility Benny had—and who thought and was cool in the same way." After that evening at the Norvos, Benny no longer needed any convincing. "I don't know how many tunes we played that night, but when we finished everybody said it was a shame we didn't have records of what we played. We felt the same way about it, and as soon as possible we arranged to go down to Victor . . . and make some stuff."

Teddy had recently signed an exclusive contract with the competing Brunswick record company. After much arm twisting, Hammond had managed to sell Brunswick on the idea of having Wilson head up an ongoing series of small band sessions featuring Billie Holiday, another of his great musical loves. Hammond explained:

> In 1934, Homer Capehart came out with the first juke box. By 1935, there were a couple of hundred thousand juke boxes in existence. It was as fast as that! . . . Suddenly all those black bars had juke boxes. I got around enough to realize that their machines didn't have the right material to go in them, so I was able to convince Harry Grey [a top Brunswick executive] that it would be smart to make the pop tunes of the day acceptable to the black audience. They would be performed without arrangements, by the greatest soloists and a superb vocalist. "We can do four sides for two-hundred-and-fifty to three hundred dollars," I added as an inducement. 'We'll need only six or seven musicians. The publishers are not going to crack down on us, because you'll already have covered the numbers with Eddy Duchin, Kay Kyser and the rest. They won't squawk if we take a little liberty with the tunes."

The Brunswick contract came at an ideal time for Teddy. Willie Bryant had recently walked out on a commitment to tour New England, and it looked as if his subsequent legal problems might force him to disband. The arrangement with Brunswick guaranteed Teddy three sessions a month over the next year as a leader, soloist or sideman, giving him the exposure he needed to go out on his own.

Hammond frequently stated that because of Brunswick's contractual hold over Teddy, it would allow him to record with Goodman only if Benny reciprocated by playing on Teddy's upcoming debut session. This has become the accepted version of what happened, but the way Hammond explained it in his autobiography strongly suggests that Brunswick had very little to do with it and that Hammond himself personally engineered the trade-off to advance Teddy's career: "I had no difficulty persuading American Brunswick to allow Teddy to record with Benny for Victor, because the association with Goodman, who was now beginning to sell, could only enhance Teddy's own reputation and sales on Columbia's Brunswick label. But I also wanted the favor returned. I wanted Goodman in the Wilson group for the Billie Holiday recordings, and I also managed that."

This probably explains Benny's strong reluctance to take part in Teddy's first Brunswick session on July 2. Certainly the paltry twenty dollars he'd receive for the afternoon's work wasn't much of an enticement, but he also must have resented being needlessly forced into the role of sideman again through the machinations and divided loyalties of his trusted adviser. In any case, there was a fierce, if short-lived, flare-up between the two friends, which, incredibly enough, Hammond made fully public in his *Melody Maker* column: "The recording was set to start at 5:30 sharp. Two men had not shown up at that time. At 5:35 the phone rang, and Benny Goodman was on the wire, busily explaining that he would not be able to come, despite his earlier promises. Just at that moment I put on a greater burst of temperament than the New York Telephone Company has ever before had to suffer. Result: in ten minutes Benny was sitting and playing in the studio better than ever."

One has to wonder how Benny reacted to this extremely tactless disclosure, with its clear implication that when John Hammond whistled, Benny Goodman came running. People who were close to Benny agree that he was always put on edge by the ongoing rumor that Hammond was the real power behind the throne and that when it came to deciding what moves to make or which musicians to hire, he was little more than Hammond's puppet. If Hammond didn't always foster this impression, neither did he always do that much to dispel it.

Fortunately for the rest of us, the personal tensions of the afternoon dissipated quickly the moment Benny unpacked his clarinet and began to play. The three sides he and Teddy did together that day—"I Wished on the Moon," "Miss Brown to You," and "What a Little Moonlight Can Do"—are among the most enduring jazz records ever made.

This was the first time Billie Holiday had been in the studio since she recorded "Riffin' the Scotch" with Benny back in December 1933. Her talent had ripened and matured remarkably in the intervening year and a half, and now she bursts forth at the height of her powers, singing with a gutsy swing, fullness of feeling and wonderful bittersweet sound that more than justify Hammond's claim that she was the best singer he ever heard. The band, handpicked by Hammond and Wilson, could hardly be improved upon. Along with Benny, the front line included Roy Eldridge's exuberant trumpet and Ben Webster's broad-shouldered tenor saxophone. The hard-swinging rhythm section was made up of John Kirby on bass, John Trueheart on guitar and Cozy Cole on drums.

"I Wished on the Moon" and "Miss Brown to You" are given much the same treatment. Teddy and Benny split the first chorus, alternating statements of the theme with improvised variations, working together closely in a way that takes full advantage of their extraordinary compatibility. Billie then sings a full chorus backed by Teddy or some combination of the horns. On "Miss Brown," Teddy follows her up with a solo chorus of his own. ("Yes, yes," she calls out to him, encouraging him on. "Knock it down.") Both sides end with Roy Eldridge at his hottest riding herd over the other players at the outer limits of his instrument. It is a simple but totally effective format, cramming a tremendous amount of very exciting music into the three-minute limitations of a 78 rpm ten-inch record.

Perhaps the most exciting of the three sides is "What a Little Moonlight Can Do." Fellow pianist Dick Katz has observed that Teddy Wilson "was the first authentically cool and controlled—but deeply involved—solo and ensemble pianist. He proved, as did Lester Young, that understatement can swing. But when called upon, Wilson could also generate terrific heat." And that's what happens here.

"Moonlight" is taken at a much faster tempo than the other two sides, and right from his opening introduction Teddy is an absolute terror, playing with an intensity and abandon that become increasingly, almost unbearably heated as he drives Benny, Billie and Ben through their solos, solos himself, then plunges headlong into the wild all-out finish that brings the performance to its spectacular close. Though Teddy dominates the record from beginning to end, Benny also plays marvelously, starting his solo in the lower register with a softly voiced, more or less straightforward statement of the melody but quickly ascending to the upper range of his horn as he creates what Hammond (and many others) considered one of his best improvisations.

The Brunswick executives were less than thrilled with the final product. They were displeased that Benny left early before the fourth tune, "A Sunbonnet Sue," got around to being made. They were unhappy they weren't allowed to advertise his name on the label. And amazingly, they didn't care very much for Billie's singing. But the sales were good enough to keep the series going, and over the next six years Teddy and Billie turned out dozens of masterpieces together with all-star pickup groups drawn from big bands like Duke Ellington and Count Basie. On several occasions Benny joined them, sometimes using the pseudonym John Jackson. By 1936 Billie had become sufficiently popular to start recording under her own name for Vocalion, Brunswick's lower-priced subsidiary, singing two choruses now instead of just one. Teddy also appeared behind her on many of these dates, serving as her musical director as well as her pianist.

On July 13, 1935, eleven days after the first Wilson-Holiday date, Benny brought Teddy and Gene Krupa into the Victor studio to record the first historic sides by the Benny Goodman Trio. Avoiding the Tin Pan Alley ephemera Teddy was required to perform on his own recordings, Benny selected some good solid standards, just the sort of tunes he and Teddy had played together that night at Mildred Bailey's party. Jazz musicians had been jamming on "Someday Sweetheart" and "After You've Gone" for years. Benny had recorded both of them on the Eddie Lang-Joe Venuti All Stars date back in 1931, and the memory of the remarkable music that session produced may well have led to his decision to do them again. Jerome Kern's "Who?" and Johnny Green's "Body and Soul" were also vintage numbers, dating back to 1925 and 1930. The familiarity of all this material meant that Benny did not have to concern himself with selling melodies to the public and could go wherever his inspiration took him. The results rank with the Wilson-Holiday date and should remind us that although the big bands gave the Swing Era its commercial popularity, it was casually assembled small group sessions like these that produced much of its most inspired music.

With Krupa's drums as the only other instrument, Benny and Teddy work together even more closely than before, alternating solos, splitting choruses, interweaving phrases, exchanging breaks, clearly having a wonderful time with each other as they negotiate the routines they worked out in the studio to give shape to their ongoing dialogue. "Who?" is an especially high-spirited performance, full of ebullient good humor and fun as Teddy romps through his opening solo in an almost Fats Waller-like manner, Gene takes a Chicago-style stop time chorus of his own and Benny playfully bats the melody around first in the upper register and then in the lower.

Perhaps the most striking quality of these collaborations is their unruffled elegance and virtuosity, which soon brought the term *chamber jazz* into vogue. As Dick Katz points out, "Prodded by Gene Krupa's 'hot' brushes, Goodman and Wilson took collective improvising to a new level of clarity and precision, and attracted listeners who had previously thought of jazz (quite wrongly, to be sure) as a crude and even primitive musical idiom."

Benny was particularly pleased with "Body and Soul" and "After You've Gone." "I still think of [these two sides] as ranking with the best I ever did," he stated some twenty years later. And his high opinion was shared by the music critics when they were originally released back to back in the summer of 1935. *Down Beat* called it "a record that should be in the library of every hot fan." *Metronome* singled it out as the record of the month. "Body and Soul," it promised, "will give you fellows goose flesh and no maybe—slow, potent, with plenty of stuff." "Who?" and "Someday Sweetheart" drew similar raves when they were issued that fall. "I like this second disc even better than the first one," the *Down Beat* reviewer enthused. "But why waste any more words on this? You'll probably buy the record anyway."

The trio recordings did, in fact, sell surprisingly well, and Victor pressed Benny for more. But for the time being that would have to wait. Teddy was still in New York, doing his own record dates and playing intermission piano at the Famous Door on Fifty-second, but the Goodman band was now out on the road in the middle of its first national tour.

9

On the Road for MCA

By the end of June Willard had lined up a string of engagements that would take the Goodman orchestra out to the Palomar Ballroom in Los Angeles. The prospects for the band weren't especially bright, not after the Roosevelt Hotel disaster, and a number of key sidemen chose to remain in New York. Newcomers included Allan Reuss on guitar and Bill De Pew on alto saxophone. Arthur Rollini remembers that Benny auditioned the very nervous young saxophonist while everyone stood around watching. When he heard De Pew play clarinet, an instrument he would have to double on in some of the arrangements, Benny exclaimed, "He sounds like me!" and hired him on the spot.

The pianist Frank Froeba also decided to stay close to home because of a family illness, and Benny was faced with the considerable difficulty of finding a suitable replacement. Once again John Hammond was ready with a recommendation. If musical considerations were all that mattered, the obvious choice would have been Teddy Wilson. But as Hammond himself acknowledged, "Despite Benny's recognition of Teddy as the best pianist in jazz, custom and prejudice decreed that there was no place for him in the band." But there was this *marvelous* white piano player out in Chicago. . . .

The Goodman band at a happier moment during the disastrous engagement at Elitch's Garden in Denver, 1935. *Bottom row:* Jess Stacy, Dick Clark, Hymie Schertzer, Gene Krupa, Jack Lacey, Bunny Berigan, Bill DePew, Arthur Rollini, Ralph Muzzillo, Red Ballard, Allan Reuss. *Top row:* Harry Goodman, Joe Harris, Helen Ward, Benny, Nate Kazebier. From the Benny Goodman Archives in the Music Library at Yale University

While visiting Chicago the previous year, Hammond had found Jess Stacy working with Muggsy Spanier and the drummer George Wettling in what he described at the time as "a real low dive called The Subway, where the hours are from eleven to seven in the morning." A few months later he praised him as "far and away the best pianist in Chicago." Then in January 1935, while the Goodman band was beginning to settle down on the "Let's Dance" show, Stacy appeared on four superb small group sides led by the trumpet player Paul Mares. Hammond's ears pricked up at the sound of the elegant but hard-driving playing of the unnamed pianist, and he placed another long-distance telephone call to Chicago, this time to Helen Oakley, the young jazz fan who had supervised the date. Clearly this was the piano player Benny Goodman needed.

"I thought somebody was playing a prank on me when I heard Benny's voice asking me to come with him," Jess recalls. "It seemed too good to be true. I hadn't known Benny personally, but I used to go to the Southmoor Hotel when he was working with Benny Pollack and listen to him there. Even then he was a hell of a good clarinet player; his reputation among the Chicago musicians was tops. And of course, I'd heard his band on the 'Let's Dance' show. I said, 'Well, if you really are Benny Goodman, then send me a wire.' So he sent me a wire, and I went off to New York. I really wanted to get out of Chicago. I was only playing for gangsters.

"Before I left town, a friend told me, 'I hope you'll get along with Benny. He's supposed to be kind of an odd guy.' I had heard that, too, so I went there prepared. When I met Benny in New York, I sort of had to audition for him. He asked me to sit down at the piano and play some old popular tune he must have done when he was working those Princeton college dates. I said, 'I don't know how it goes.' He said, 'Well, play it anyhow.' I didn't have the sheet music, so I had to fake it. I guess he must have liked me. I got the job."

Benny may not have handed out any compliments, but Stacy was an enormous improvement over Frank Froeba, and Benny eventually conceded, "Needless to say, that's another change that I've never regretted." Helen Ward explains: "Froeba did some wonderful things behind the vocal when we recorded 'Between the Devil and the Deep Blue Sea,' but he was too busy for Benny's taste, and Jess was just perfect. He had such feeling and delicacy, and he was a heavenly accompanist. And he was such a sweet, easygoing guy. I don't think I ever saw him lose his temper or get out of sorts."

In the middle of July, a few days after the trio session with Teddy Wilson, the band hit the road and headed west. The itinerary consisted almost entirely of one-nighters. Some of the jobs were for as little as $250 a night. There was no money for a bus, so the musicians used their own cars and were reimbursed at the rate of two or three cents a mile. Until they reached the Palomar, the only real break from the grind would be a three-week stopover in Denver.

"Oh, those one-nighters." Helen Ward laughs. "We were always hungry and tired, and the cars would break down in the middle of nowhere. I constantly had to worry about where I was going to get my dress pressed when we finally reached wherever we were going because they usually rolled up the sidewalks by seven o'clock. And the distances we had to travel! I remember driving through one state after another to get to the next location. We'd all start singing in the car—what else was there to do?—and one time we made up this song to the tune of 'On the Road to Mandalay.' I still haven't forgotten the words.

> *On the road for MCA.*
> *Many places do we play.*
> *We're in Dallas, Texas, on a Wednesday.*
> *Thursday, York, PA.*
> *On the road for MCA.*
> *Don't lose the places that we play.*

"In those days we used to say, 'Don't lose it,' about anything that was bad. It made no sense, but that was the expression. And there were some terrible places.

> *When the dawn is waking*
> *We'll be breaking*
> *Our necks for MCA.*

"But it was also wonderful. We were so young, and everyone was so enthusiastic. It was a way of starting out, and we were doing what we wanted to do. The feeling at the beginning is hard to put into words, but it was inspirational. Every night was something different, something new. Benny would play something we never heard before, or when one of the guys took a particularly good solo, he'd say, 'Take another,' and everybody would flip and giggle and laugh. It was never the same old notes night after night. And the band kept getting better and better."

The way Jess remembers it, "There wasn't a whole lot of optimism about what might happen when the tour hit the road. It was really a panic band from the beginning, though we were all enthusiastic about the music. We knew it was a great band, and everybody played their best all the time. It was such good music we hoped something good might come out of it, but we sure didn't have much confidence that it would."

These misgivings seemed confirmed as the caravan proceeded westward.

Some of the stopovers in Pennsylvania and Ohio drew a reasonable turnout of youngsters. The two nights in Milwaukee seemed to go fairly well. The dance hall was packed with musicians who had driven in from as far away as Chicago, and the band drew a two-column rave in *Down Beat* from Helen Oakley, who praised it as "immeasurably superior to any other outfit playing today." But Helen Oakley and the musicians who crowded around the bandstand were hardly typical of the general public who came to the local ballroom for an evening's entertainment. And it was their support that was needed if the band was to succeed or even keep going. And for some reason or other, most of the time people just weren't showing up. "I began to wonder what happened to all those radio listeners who'd written us fan letters," Benny reflected.

Everyone had been looking forward to Denver, where they'd finally be able to get off the road and settle down for a few weeks. They were booked into Elitch's Garden, a dance hall outside town, and would be staying at a nearby country lodge, where they could go fishing and horseback riding and spend their days out in the sunshine instead of pressing on to the next gig. But half an hour into the first set on opening night the manager came racing out of his office in a frenzy. The noise from the bandstand was driving the customers away, and they were demanding their money back. "I hired a dance band!" he ranted. "What's the matter—can't you boys play any waltzes?" The most popular bands in Denver, it seems, were Bernie Cummins, the same orchestra Benny had replaced at the Roosevelt Hotel with equally dire results, and Griff Williams, whose musicians wore funny hats and did comedy routines. That's what Benny'd better start doing, too, the manager advised.

Benny remembered the evening as "about the most humiliating experience of my life." The next morning the ballroom's manager called Willard Alexander in New York and asked to be let out of his contract. Willard listened patiently to his complaints about the lousy, undanceable music and how the hard-nosed leader fluffed off all his suggestions, then said he would speak to Benny. Maybe they could work something out. He did not mention they would *have to* to keep the band alive. If this job fell apart, there would be a three-week layover until the next booking, and the rest of the tour would probably be canceled. Benny was beginning to think that might not be such a bad idea. Maybe there was no real audience for this kind of music after all. After arguing with Benny for close to an hour, Willard finally calmed him down and got him to agree to smooth things over a little.

Trying to be pragmatic, Benny sent out for a hundred stock arrangements and cut them down to accommodate the ballroom's staff of three-dances-for-a-dime hostesses. According to the saxophonist Dick Clark, he also "worked up a few novelty numbers, with Joe Harris dancing in front of the band in funny hats." Clark recalled: "It didn't go over at all. He got no cooperation from us." Helen Ward was a pretty good pianist, so that night Benny had her play a couple of waltz sets accompanied by Bunny, Harry and Gene. They even threw in some tangos. But none of this did much good. There were fifteen or twenty couples on the dance floor during the week and maybe a hundred on the weekends. Everyone else was across the lake listening to Kay Kyser. "He used to play hokum numbers," Hymie Schertzer remembered. "All the guys in the band wore these crazy hats and did Ish Kabibble things. They were drawing the crowds."

"It was a fiasco, a terrible fiasco," Helen says. "And it really got to Benny. He was so heartbroken he stayed alone in his hotel room in downtown Denver all day." According to Jess Stacy, "He was about ready to throw it in. I was driving him back to the hotel one night, and he told me he was going to give up the band and go back to working on radio. I talked to him like a Dutch uncle and said, 'Well, why don't you take the band across the mountains over to Colorado and see what happens there? And if it's still a bust, give up then.' "

The other musicians were just as demoralized. Despite Benny's strictures about boozing on the job, some of them, especially Bunny Berigan, were drinking heavily. "Berigan used to complain about Goodman all the time," Jess remembers. "Berigan was playing lead trumpet and hot solos, and finally, every night about eleven, after those difficult Fletcher Henderson arrangements and all the solos, he'd say, 'This is impossible,' and take the last drink—the law-of-diminishing-returns drink—and wipe himself out."

When word got around that Benny was bombing in Denver, the MCA executives in California wanted to cancel him out of the Palomar. Willard managed to talk them out of it, and the band continued limping along. Some of the one-nighters went reasonably well; others were disastrous. In Grand Junction, Colorado, there was wire netting up in front of the bandstand to protect them from the whiskey bottles thrown by the audience of drunken Indians. In Salt Lake City Bunny got so wasted he couldn't play, and Benny fired him, only to hire him back again the next day.

At the age of twenty-six, Benny had, in his own way, negotiated the classic three-step ascent out of the ghetto accomplished by some of the other immigrant sons of his generation. From holding down a job with someone else (sideman in Ben Pollack's band), he had gone to work for himself (his years as a New York free-lancer), then moved on to open his own business (the Benny Goodman orchestra). With each hard-earned step up the ladder, there was greater freedom and financial reward and a broader outlet for his talents, but there was also more uncertainty and risk as well as the pressure of ever-increasing responsibility. The fact that Benny was drawn to a kind of music that held out very little promise of financial gain complicated things for him considerably. But starting around the time John Hammond came into his life, it suggested a direction that might just possibly give him both the economic security he wanted and the artistic fulfillment he also needed.

The overall failure of the cross-country tour, climaxed by the humiliating fiasco at Elitch's Garden, put the practical businessman-musician in Benny at odds with the creative artist. The success of the "Let's Dance" show and the popularity of some of his recordings had made it look for a while as if they might be able to work in harmony for their mutual benefit. But the weeks of stock arrangements and waltzes and three dances for a dime seemed to prove otherwise. Benny now had only three options open to him, none of them very appealing. He could continue playing his kind of music in the face of indifference and hostility until the jobs ran out and the band died a natural death. He could break up the band and return to the radio studios, moving a large step down the ladder he had worked so hard to climb. Or he could figure the angles, play down the jazz numbers and try to keep the customers satisfied.

Watching the way Kay Kyser "put it across" in Denver, Benny recalled that "maybe for a minute I wished I could do it too—but as far as the music was concerned, I couldn't go for it." And as he surely must have realized from watching Ben Pollack put himself through all those ill-conceived contortions in his efforts to win mass acceptance, watering down his music to make it more accessible was no guarantee of commercial success and might easily open the door to other uncertainties and perils. And Ben Pollack wasn't the only example of the dangers that come with that sort of thinking. Reviewing the faltering Dorsey Brothers band in the current issue of *Down Beat,* John Hammond wrote, "It has always been a mystery to me that the brothers Dorsey didn't take advantage of their golden opportunities to start a band which would have both musicianship and simple guts. At least part of the blame for the actual result may possibly lie at the door of their manager Tommy Rockwell, who is a demon for knowing 'what the public wants.' "

Benny's efforts to reach some kind of clarity about his future were totally disrupted when the band pulled up to MacFadden's Ballroom in Oakland. "Mobs of people were milling around in front of the place waiting to get in," Helen Ward remembers. "There were mounted police on the sidewalk. Then we saw this huge poster of Guy Lombardo out in front, and Benny said to me, 'My God, we're here on the wrong night!' "

Benny was ready to fire off a telegram to Willard Alexander bawling him out for the mixup when someone with a big smile on his face stepped up and began pumping his hand. It was the manager of the ballroom, overjoyed at the turnout. Yes, Guy Lombardo would be playing there soon, but tonight the crowd was here for Benny Goodman. Benny recalled:

It was impossible for me to believe that so many people had come to hear us. I was still sure they had us confused with some other band. We set up our instruments sort of warily, half expecting the other band to walk in the door.

When the manager finally opened the door to the public, the crowd surged inside and jammed up tight against the bandstand. I thought, "If it's a mistake, it's a mistake. I might as well make it a real mistake." I called for "King Porter Stomp," one of Fletcher's real killers. That number started off with Bunny Berigan playing a trumpet solo, the saxophones and rhythm behind him. Before he'd played four bars, there was such a yelling and stomping and carrying on in that hall I thought a riot had broken out. When I went into my solo, the noise was even louder. Finally the truth got through to me: *We* were causing the riot. What was even more amazing, the fans seemed to get wilder and wilder as the night wore on. I was positive it was a fluke, and that we'd just had the good luck to be booked into a jazz-mad town.

It looked as if Benny might be right when they moved down the coast to Pismo Beach, the last leg in the long journey to the Palomar. "We played in a fish barn," Helen recalls. "I mean that literally. The place stank of fish." The reaction was "worse than Elitch's," according to Dick Clark. "[When] we pulled into L.A. the next day to rehearse that afternoon, Benny was scared to death again because of the lousy reception."

The Palomar was a huge ballroom out on Vermont and Second formerly known as the Rainbow Gardens. Recently redecorated, it had an enormous dance floor and a separate section with tables for dining and drinks. A fairly good crowd had turned up, including a lot of local musicians and some old friends like Joe Sullivan and the composer Victor Young. But Benny hadn't played anywhere quite like this before and didn't know what to expect. He wasn't expecting much.

"By the time we finished our three weeks at Elitch's Garden, I was pretty discouraged," he reminisced in a 1975 interview celebrating the fortieth anniversary of the Palomar opening. "The West had a reputation for being corny. They had all those sort of Mickey Mouse bands out on the Coast. So I said, 'Well, this has got to get worse the farther west we go. I don't see any kind of future in this at all.' . . . I thought we'd finish the engagement in California, then take the train back to New York and that would be it. I'd just be a clarinetist again."

Benny began the evening cautiously, playing some of his sweeter, more commercial arrangements for the first few sets. There was no sense ending the tour with another Elitch's Garden or Pismo Beach. The kids standing in front of the bandstand seemed to recognize the musicians and know their solos, but the audience as a whole was far from enthusiastic. They weren't throwing whiskey bottles, but the band was still dying, slowly this time, by inches. As they prepared for the next set, one of the sidemen—it might have been Bunny Berigan or maybe Gene Krupa—told Benny what the hell, as long as they were going down, they might as well go down swinging. Benny nodded his head and broke out the Fletcher Henderson arrangements.

"From the moment I kicked them off [the boys] dug in with some of the best playing I'd heard since we left New York," Benny recalled. "To our complete amazement, half of the crowd stopped dancing and came surging around the stand. . . . That was the moment that decided things for me. After traveling three thousand miles, we finally found people who were up on what we were trying to do, prepared to take our music the way we wanted to play it. That first big roar from the crowd was one of the sweetest sounds I ever heard in my life, and from that time on the night kept getting bigger and bigger, as we played about every good number in our book."

The next morning Taft Schreiber, MCA's West Coast booker, called the New York office to report on Benny's triumph. Billy Goodheart summoned Willard Alexander into his office to hear the news over the telephone loudspeaker. According to the writer Mort Goode, Schreiber's voice wasn't coming through clearly, and it sounded as if he were saying the band had bombed. "Willard sunk lower and lower as Goodheart seemed to gloat, yelling back at Taft how he and his partner, Jules Stein, knew it would happen. Then Taft shouted, 'What do you mean—bombed? The band is the biggest thing that ever hit the West Coast!' "

The date of the Palomar opening—August 21, 1935—has gone down in the history of popular music as the night the Swing Era was born. This is something of an exaggeration. There were plenty of swing bands before Benny (though only few of them were white). Duke Ellington had issued his famous dictum that "it don't mean a thing if it ain't got that swing" a good three years earlier. Nor was the Goodman band's future yet all that secure. The rest of the country still lay ahead, and it would have to keep proving itself on the return trip east. Still, that evening at the Palomar was a lot more than one good night like Oakland that might be canceled out the next day by another Pismo Beach. A real breakthrough *had* taken place.

What caused this to happen? The standard explanation offered by most observers, including Benny himself, is that the time difference between New York and California brought the "Let's Dance" show to the West Coast three hours earlier, so it was able to attract a much larger audience of the youngsters who were the band's principal fans. But this isn't really the way it worked.

NBC scheduled the broadcast to take account of the various time zones, cutting in different parts of the country at more or less the same local hour. "Let's Dance" went on the air at 10:30 P.M. in New York, but the West Coast stations didn't pick it up until 9:30 their time, not 7:30. And while this was one hour earlier than it could be heard in the East, that hardly seems significant enough to explain away the Palomar triumph.

What seems more to the point is that California caught the last three of the five hours Benny actually performed in the studio. The band had warmed up by then and was able to hit its stride on numbers like "Down South Camp Meeting" and "Sugarfoot Stomp" that showed it off at its best. (This still doesn't account for why it laid an egg in nearby Pismo Beach.) Another contributing factor was that the Los Angeles disc jockey Al Jarvis liked Benny's records and had been playing them regularly on his "Make Believe Ballroom" show, creating an audience of fans who were eager to catch the band in person. Jarvis's enthusiasm probably also explains why Benny's records had been selling so well in Southern California in the first place, giving MCA the ammunition it had needed to set up the Palomar booking. Benny believed he also may have been helped by the fact that Louis Armstrong had played several long engagements in Culver City a few years earlier, opening the ears of white Angelenos to big band jazz.

Whatever the reasons (and none of these seems wholly convincing), the Palomar stand was an unqualified success. The crowds that jammed into the ballroom kept getting bigger and bigger, and Benny's contract was extended for another three weeks. Monday, when the local musicians were usually off, was set aside as "Musician's Night," but as Jess Stacy remembers it, they were there *every* night, whether they were supposed to be working or not. Along with the musicians and kids, the band also began to draw movie stars and the rest of the Hollywood set, who may or may not have understood what Benny was up to but knew it was the place to be. Remote broadcasts from the Palomar helped spread the word up and down the coast. Saturday afternoons the band played for football rallies at some of the nearby colleges, and that added to the lines building up in front of the box office.

GOODMAN WAKES UP WEST COAST WITH "SWING" STYLE, *Down Beat* proclaimed. And now that it had been raised from its slumbers, it not only danced but listened. According to *Metronome*, someone visiting the Palomar might well have asked "whether he was attending a dance in a ballroom or some new and weird type of orchestral recital in a music hall. The dancers literally swarmed the platform, and though they came to dance, they stood around to listen and applaud." Hymie Schertzer said: "It was unbelievable. They stood in front of the band by the hundreds. They knew the charts. They loved it."

But even after breaking the Palomar's attendance records, Benny couldn't quite believe what had happened and continued to be apprehensive about what might happen next. He'd been through this before in his Ben Pollack days and had seen how overnight success could leave you scrounging for breakfast money the next morning. "Every night we kept expecting that the kids and other fans would have run out of money and the crowds would fall off," he recalled. "[Los Angeles] was only one little part of the country, and elsewhere we weren't much better known than we had been before. . . . The future was pretty much of a blank."

**Benny, Helen Ward and the Goodman band
at the Congress Hotel in Chicago, March 1935.**

From the Benny Goodman Archives in the Music Library at Yale University

10

Swing Is Here

Benny stayed on the road for the next month, working his way back east on another stretch of one-nighters. As a result of the Palomar success, he drew a good turnout of dancers everywhere he appeared, and his records were doing nicely, especially on the West Coast. For the month of October the trio's recording of "Body and Soul" was Victor's number one seller in Los Angeles, "King Porter" was number two and in anticipation of the coming holiday season, Spud Murphy's rousing arrangement of "Jingle Bells" ranked third. Some of the earlier Columbia sides like "The Dixieland Band" and "Music Hall Rag" were also still moving briskly. All this was encouraging, but what the band needed now was an extended engagement in some major ballroom or hotel that would allow it to stay in one place for a while and capitalize on the momentum that had begun to build up at the Palomar.

After weighing several offers, Benny decided on the Joseph Urban Room at the Congress Hotel in Chicago—a booking Willard Alexander was dead set against. The room had been closed for months and had done terrible business for two years before then, ever since some of the guests visiting the Chicago world's fair in 1933 came down with amoebic dysentery from the hotel's faulty plumbing. The hotel's reputation was in ruins, and it was very close to declaring bankruptcy. But while Willard was home sick, Benny approved the contract on his own, and the band moved on to Chicago for its November 6 opening.

As it turned out, Harry Kaufman, the manager of the Congress, was no fan of Benny's music and had booked the band almost by accident. While trying to decide between Benny and a sweet dance band MCA also offered him, he solicited the opinion of some of the musicians working in the Congress Grill. They had heard Benny on the radio and wanted to see him in person, so they assured the manager that he was bound to be a terrific draw.

The opening went surprisingly well. Squirrel Ashcraft and Helen Oakley, moving forces in the Chicago Rhythm Club, both were socially connected and had rounded up a large turnout of the Chicago elite. The local newspapers gave the band good reviews, even if they didn't completely understand what it was up to. (Benny remembered one of the reviewers saying his rhythm was "comparable to Eddy Duchin's.") Business built steadily from night to night, and Kaufman began thinking about extending Benny's run another four weeks.

The Chicago-based *Down Beat* also got behind the band and helped spread the news of its success nationally. It received further exposure from its early-evening broadcasts from the Congress five nights a week. Most of these remotes were aired locally over station WGN, but some were picked up by the networks and could be heard across the country. George T. Simon, *Metronome*'s jazz ears in New York, was an avid listener and praised the band's progress in his monthly column, calling it "without a doubt the greatest swing band in the country."

Swing band was a relatively new term. It wasn't, in fact, until the Congress engagement that the Goodman orchestra started using it in its billing. Benny recalled that the idea probably came from Gene Krupa a few months before while they were still suffering through the Denver fiasco.

"We were sitting around talking one day, and I think Gene Krupa was sitting next to me. Someone asked me, how come you just call yourselves Benny Goodman's Band. There's Waring and his Pennsylvanians, Lombardo and his Royal Canadians. Your name just doesn't sound complete. And Gene said, well, why don't you call it a swing band. That's it, we agreed: Benny Goodman and his Swing Band."

For all the offhandedness with which he arrived at this decision, Benny was surely aware that *swing* was a word that was now coming very much into vogue.

For some time there had been a growing dissatisfaction with *jazz* as an adequate term for the kind of improvised music currently being played. It was too old-fashioned, too redolent of the bygone *Jazz Age* of the 1920s, suggesting, on the one hand, the more "primitive" New Orleans-Chicago improvisational approaches that were no longer really in style and, on the other, the overly sophisticated "symphonic" dilution of the music epitomized by Paul Whiteman, the putative "King of Jazz" who had also reached his peak of popularity some years before. The word's earlier connection with "sex," which it had never fully outgrown in the minds of the general public, also led to a feeling in some quarters that it was too crude and unrespectable a term for a music that merited more dignified associations. The orchestra leader Don Bestor had generated considerable publicity for himself in 1934 by campaigning to outlaw "jazz" from the English language and find an apt substitute to take its place in the next edition of *Webster's Dictionary*.

Swing was commonly used among musicians as a verb to refer to the flowing rhythmic pulse that was an essential element of good jazz playing. ("He really swings!") Sometime around 1934 it also began being employed as a noun standing in for what was still commonly called jazz. One can't really pin down exactly how this happened, though the *Melody Maker* appeared to be perfectly serious when it took credit for originating this use of the word in a 1935 editorial deploring its subsequent abuses.

On November 6, 1935, the same day Benny opened at the Congress, *Variety* introduced a new weekly column by Abel Green titled "Swing Stuff," a sure sign that the word had by now entered the show business mainstream and that the music it referred to was, after a long dry spell, beginning to register a significant commercial impact. The column presented a series of breezy news items about such matters as Louis Armstrong's opening at Connie's Inn, Teddy Wilson's new record session with Billie Holiday, and the appearances of Wingy Manone at the Hickory House and Red Norvo at the Famous Door. The Hickory House and the Famous Door were, along with the Onyx, the major jazz clubs on New York's Fifty-second Street, and it was Swing Street's recent popularity, more than anything, that called both the word and the music to *Variety*'s attention.

The Famous Door had swung open the previous February. The first band to work there was led by the trumpet player Louis Prima, who had recently arrived from New Orleans. Prima was, in those days, a very good jazz musician, but he was also an extremely entertaining performer, peppering his sets with a lot of amusing jive vocals and good-humored patter. (In his later years he became king of the Las Vegas lounge acts.) To the consternation of the musicians and jazz purists in the audience, Prima's effusive showmanship soon began drawing crowds of big spenders who were less interested in his improvising than in his comedy. But they turned the Famous Door into the hottest club in town.

Prima's success was followed by that of fellow New Orleans trumpet player Wingy Manone, a regular attraction at the Hickory House, when much against his will, he was made to record a dreary English ballad called "The Isle of Capri." Wingy maintained that Benny had the recording director of Vocalion force the tune on him as a practical joke, and after a night of heavy drinking, trying to figure out what to do with it, he came up with an irreverent jive version that to everyone's surprise became a big hit. "[It] really put me on top. People came to New York from all over the country to hear me play and sing 'Ol' Capri on the Isle.' . . . Man, that record sold over a drillion copies."

The biggest draw on Fifty-second Street, though, was two jazz musicians with a special penchant for uninhibited knockabout comedy. Trombonist Mike Riley and trumpet player Eddie Farley were working at the Onyx with the singer Red McKenzie's five-piece band when, two months before Benny opened at the Congress, they happened to record a novelty number for Decca called "The Music Goes 'Round and Around." Decca had been in business for only a year and was still struggling to stay alive, even though its roster included Bing Crosby. But the record was an overnight sensation, selling some hundred thousand copies and transforming the fledgling company into a major label.

Once "The Music Goes 'Round" took off it could be heard everywhere. Teddy Wilson recalled that on his way home from his job at the Famous Door that New Year's Eve, "all the drunks on 52nd Street were singing it." The tune was quickly recorded by any number of other artists, including Louis Armstrong, the Boswell Sisters and Wingy Manone. Versions also appeared in Yiddish, Italian, Spanish, Hungarian, German, Polish, Ukrainian, Greek and pig Latin. The song attracted such huge crowds to the Onyx, where Riley and Farley now led their own group, that there was hardly any room for the real jazz fans. And it helped make the kind of music just becoming known as swing the latest national fad.

There are several very substantial ironies here. Although the Swing Era is commonly thought of as the era of big bands, it was small groups headed by Prima, Manone and Riley-Farley that first brought attention to the word and gave the music its initial popularity. Further, while Prima, Manone and, to a lesser extent, Riley and Farley were accomplished jazz musicians, it was their flair for good-natured comedy and show business hokum that captured the public's attention. Most curious of all, although swing was clearly the coming thing by the end of 1935, no one, least of all the musicians who played it, seemed very clear about what it was. Abel Green observed in the January 1, 1936, *Variety:*

The swingos think that swing is marking an indelible notation on the evolution of jazz. With them it's a creed, a code and something of a state of coma. That's why the swing addicts seem so glazed and dazed in their nth degree appreciation of this here swing business. . . . So what is swing? Ask any of the swingologists and they all vamp off, "Well, swing is something like—" But none seems able to define just what it is. . . . Says Mike Riley, "It's a jam, but arranged." Explains Red McKenzie: "It's an evolution of Dixie (i.e., the Original Dixieland Jazz Band's style). It's the difference between the old and the new music. It's carefully conceived improvisation." Says Wingy Manone: "It's a livelier tempo; you know, swingy like."

A similar survey by *Metronome*'s Gordon Wright produced similarly vague results and led him to conclude that "SWING CANNOT BE DEFINED." But the quest for a definition continued. In the following months *Metronome* readers took up Wright's challenge and deluged the magazine with their own efforts without any notable success. The music educator Otto Cesana did not do much better when he made a stab at it, and neither did drum manufacturer William F. Ludwig or *Down Beat*'s Carl Cons in an extended essay full of abstract argumentation that went on for pages. At a press conference for Fats Waller, "What is swing?" was one of the first questions put to him. His answer—"It's two-thirds rhythm and one-third soul"—did not really satisfy the assembled reporters, and they pressed him for something more definite. "Fats wiped off a few beads of perspiration from his brow," we are told, "and opined that authorities had not yet arrived at complete accord."

There is an obvious enough reason for all this inconclusive fumbling about. When the modern jazz revolution took place in the mid-1940s, it was necessary to introduce an identifying tag like "bebop" to distinguish it from the jazz that came before it and call attention to its own distinctive character. This was also true of the "free jazz" revolution two decades later. But swing did not really involve any radical break in the jazz tradition. One may argue that the rhythm section became more supple and flowing and the soloists tended to be more technically proficient and that there was a different approach to ensemble playing. But though this may be so, it was a gradual, orderly, evolutionary change that never actually defied the existing norms the way bebop did with earlier jazz and free jazz did with bop. They used to call it ragtime, Louis Armstrong observed. "Later on in the years it was called jazz music, hot music, gutbucket, and now they've poured a little gravy over it and called it swing music." Dick Voynow, former leader of the Wolverines, the band with which Bix Beiderbecke made his first recordings in 1924, argued much the same point in less diplomatic terms: "All this hullaballoo about Swing Music is so much nonsense. There isn't anything new about the idea at all, and the present crop of swing musicians have not originated any new styles but are still duplicating the efforts of the old timers."

Essentially, *swing* was a word in search of a meaning. But it was a good word, a word with strong commercial potential that people seemed to like, so some sort of meaning had to be sought and found.

The fad popularity of the word explains why Benny took it up as well as why he was so wary about too close an association, especially after the more enthusiastic members of the press dubbed him the King of Swing sometime in 1936. Not that it would have been easy to have escaped such an identification. Whatever swing was, it was definitely here, and Benny was fast becoming its most popular practitioner.

The January 1936 issue of *Metronome* selected the Goodman orchestra as "the outstanding swing band as well as the sensation of the year." The same week the magazine hit the stands a full-page ad on the back cover of *Variety* proclaimed it the greatest swing band in the country and extolled Benny in the following rather overwrought superlatives: "Not since the year 1920, epochal in American musical history, when Paul Whiteman and Art Hickman created a new, startling jazz music . . . has a bandsman so thrilled the nation as this brilliant young maestro. . . . Young and old alike . . . radio, stage and dance fans . . . hail his individual hot-sweet 'swing' style."

The use of *swing* in quotation marks (printed "as if it was something in a foreign language," is the way Benny put it when he talked about the promotional campaign for his Congress engagement) seems to have been a conscious and deliberate decision, a way to distance Benny from the term as well as connect him into it. "At the time we didn't regard [the word] as anything very important, just a tag that would associate us with something definite in the public mind," he explained. "I wanted to play that down and keep the expression 'king of swing' out of our publicity, because I didn't know how long this was going to last, and I didn't want to be tied down to something people might say was old-fashioned just because they got tired of the name, in a year or so. But there was no way of avoiding it, so we had to go along with what the public wanted to call us."

Benny's caution was well advised. The swing craze was not to reach its frenzied heights for another year, but a minor sort of backlash was already under way. The December-January issue of *Down Beat*, that bastion of jazz fans and Goodman supporters, contained a crotchety attack on the music that singled out Benny as a major culprit. That September the bandleader Fred Waring had published an article titled "The Swing Mania Annoys Me," in which he prophesied it would soon become extinct. And in a letter to *Metronome* an irate reader vehemently disputed Benny's claims to the music's throne: "I certainly don't think Goodman is all that he's proclaimed to be. 'King of Swing'—fuie! . . . Although I am not colored, I believe the colored boys ought to get piles of credit and praise. Personally I think this Goodman band is just a passing fad, and that before six months have elapsed, it will have passed into oblivion."

Be that as it may, the customers continued packing the Congress Hotel night after night, wiping away any lingering uncertainty that the Palomar success was just a fluke. And through its radio broadcasts, extensive coverage in the press and many excellent new records, the band began to attract growing numbers of fans across the country. "It wasn't until the engagement at the Congress that it really became established," recalled Pee Wee Erwin, who rejoined the trumpet section in March. "All of a sudden a national reputation began to develop, and it was obvious from all of the activities that were going on it was getting to be a whale of a popular band, not only with the jazz fans but the general public too." Erwin was also struck by how dramatically the band had improved since he'd played with it on the "Let's Dance" show the year before. Back then it was essentially a loosely knit collection of studio players, but all those months on the road and Benny's unrelenting drive for perfection had made everything come together, and now it had jelled into a real orchestra with a stable personnel and a style and sound of its own.

Benny was booked into the Congress for one month and ended up staying half a year. Toward the end of 1935 the band started doing weekly broadcasts from the hotel over the NBC network. The following March it picked up its second sponsored radio series, NBC's "The Elgin Review," for the Elgin Watch Company. It also put in a lot of time at Victor's local recording studio. Over the course of the Congress stand it turned out almost two dozen new sides, including such classics as "Stompin' at the Savoy" and "Goody-Goody." (Helen Ward was initially resistant to singing this last tune, though it turned into one of her biggest hits. "I thought it was silly. I hated it so much the first time I heard it I almost cried.") With all this activity and exposure, Benny needed more and more new charts, and he began commissioning orchestrations from two Chicago-based arrangers.

Some years later David Rose became extremely well known for his radio and record work and such popular compositions as "Holiday for Strings" and "The Stripper." When he began stopping by the Congress every night, he was employed as a staff pianist at NBC and playing some jazz on the side with musicians like Muggsy Spanier, Irving Fazola and George Wettling.

"I had just started writing," he recalled. "Roy Shields, the musical director at NBC, encouraged me to try my hand at it, and that's how I learned. I did about ten or twelve arrangements for Benny, including 'It's Been So Long' and an original called 'Transcontinental,' which was quite a fancy title for that time. There's an interesting story connected with 'It's Been So Long' because it seems to have given Glenn Miller his famous trademark sound. When I first showed the arrangement to Benny, he said, 'Don't let me just stand there after Helen's vocal,' so for the saxophone passage that segued into his solo I made his clarinet the lead instrument and inverted the rest of the saxophones. I noticed the similarity in the voicing Glenn Miller used when he started to become popular but didn't think much about it. Then Benny's brother Irving told me he had seen Miller come into the Congress one night and really focus in on that arrangement, so evidently that's where he got the idea. The writing I did for Benny did a lot for my reputation mainly because the band played my arrangements so beautifully. The same scores never would have sounded as good performed by some other orchestra. By the time it got to Chicago Benny's band was really outstanding. All the musicians in town thought it was tops, the very best."

Benny's other new writer was the black tenor saxophonist and arranger Jimmy Mundy. Mundy was a mainstay of the Earl Hines band over at the Grand Terrace, a club with close mob affiliations frequented by gangsters like the Capones, John Dillinger and Pretty Boy Floyd. Like Fletcher Henderson, Mundy was a well-schooled musician with a solid background in the classics. At one time he had some thoughts about becoming a concert violinist, but as his career unfolded, he taught himself tenor saxophone and arranging and pursued a direction more open to the black musicians of his generation. While working with Earl Hines in New York, Mundy had submitted some charts to Benny for possible use on the "Let's Dance" show. Benny bought at least one of them, a superior up-tempo instrumental called "Madhouse" that had been written for Hines. Benny liked it enough to record it just before he left the Palomar, and now that he needed an ongoing supply of new orchestrations, he hired Mundy away from Hines as a full-time staff arranger.

Although Mundy maintained a long working relationship with Benny, they never hit it off on a personal level. "Benny and I didn't get along too well," the arranger maintained, "so I was always quitting, but then he would sweeten the pot. This went on quite a while, until 1939, when I had my own band for a time." It's possible Mundy resented the way Benny took coauthor credit for some of his original compositions, though however unsavory, this was standard music business practice. Hines had, in fact, appropriated credit for Mundy's "Cavernism" when he first hired him.

Mundy was an extremely fast and prolific writer. Benny estimated he produced some four hundred charts during the three years he remained with the band, more than forty of which were recorded. During 1936 Mundy was turning out five arrangements a week, writing his ideas directly onto the score sheets without resorting to a piano. His output included standards-to-be like "These Foolish Things," "In a Sentimental Mood" and "There's a Small Hotel" as well as the more transient pop tunes of the day. But his most important contributions were original instrumentals like "House Hop," "Jam Session" and "Swingtime in the Rockies"—hard-driving, fiercely intense jump tunes that aimed for and succeeded in achieving a white-hot excitement. Quite different from Fletcher Henderson's more relaxed writing, though they employed much the same orchestral language, Mundy's blistering arrangements brought the term *killer-diller* into the swing fan's vocabulary and established a taste for up-tempo flag-wavers that was catered to by just about every swing band worthy of the name.

Curiously, Mundy's arrangement of Louis Prima's "Sing, Sing, Sing" provided only the germ for what turned out to be Benny's most famous and enduring killer-diller. It was originally conceived as a vocal for Helen Ward, but the band kept changing it in performance, adding solos, incorporating strains from Chu Berry's "Christopher Columbus" and so on, until it bore only the slightest resemblance to the original score. The way Helen remembers it, the process began wholly by accident during the band's return visit to the Palomar that summer. "One night Gene just refused to stop drumming when he got to the end of the third chorus, where the tune was supposed to end, so Benny blithely picked up the clarinet and noodled along with him. Then someone else stood up and took it, and it went on from there." By the time Benny recorded the expanded head arrangement in 1937, it had grown to be over eight minutes long and covered both sides of a twelve-inch 78 rpm record.

Fletcher Henderson continued feeding arrangements into the band, though somewhat fewer than before. He had originally planned to join Benny in California and write for him full time, but the exposure he'd received through the "Let's Dance" show and Benny's recordings led to a renewed interest in his work, and in the spring of 1935 he decided to start up his own orchestra again. The reformulated Henderson band played a few months at Roseland to very mixed reviews; then with a revised personnel sparked by trumpet player Roy Eldridge and tenor man Chu Berry, a much-improved edition replaced Earl Hines at the Grand Terrace in Chicago in January 1936.

It was reported that Benny had made the Terrace booking possible, and he continued to use his influence to stir up local interest in the band. He frequently dropped by to visit, and when one of Fletcher's musicians quit without notice, Benny took his place in the saxophone section for that evening's broadcast. Sometimes after the closing set he would go off with Eldridge and Berry to jam for a few hours. In technique and ideas and emotional intensity both these brilliant musicians were Benny's peers, and they provided the sort of musical challenge he thrived upon. All that is apparent on the small group recording date the three of them did together under Gene Krupa's leadership that February, especially on the side titled, with dead-on accuracy, "Swing Is Here." The virtuoso solo work, razor-sharp riffing and unrelenting excitement generated by their performance throw more light on the nature of swing and swinging than all the discussions in the magazines and newspapers put together.

The 1936 Henderson band was one of the strongest he ever led, and its marvelous recording of "Christopher Columbus" gave him that rarity of rarities, a hit record. But in typically self-defeating fashion, Fletcher refused to capitalize on its success. "Fletcher was hot," the trumpet player Joe Thomas remembered. "Everyone was asking for him. Duke came by one night and told him. Fletcher should have gone out on the road then, [but] by the time he got ready . . . somebody else had something big, and Fletcher couldn't get started." The band dragged along for another three years, fettered by Fletcher's characteristic lack of resolve and inability to maintain discipline; then, in 1939, he finally gave it up and joined Benny's arranging staff.

In a way Fletcher's work for Benny hindered as much as it helped his own efforts as a leader. Benny had a powerful support system behind him—the MCA booking agency, Victor Records, the NBC radio network—and it was his versions of Fletcher's arrangements that were brought to the public's attention. And since Benny embodied all the qualities of the perfectionist and disciplinarian that Fletcher himself lacked, a comparison of how the two bands executed the same material tended to show Fletcher at a disadvantage. This demoralizing state of affairs was apparent to some of Fletcher's own sidemen like Garvin Bushell: "Once we were scheduled to follow Benny Goodman at the Savoy Ballroom. But Goodman's book was the same as Fletcher's; every time Fletcher made an arrangement for Goodman, he'd keep it for himself. So we couldn't go on after Goodman and make fools of ourselves. What good would it do, since Goodman had better musicians than we did, and could play the arrangements better?"

A month after the Congress opening the Goodman band further solidified its success by playing its first jazz "concert." There was very little precedent for presenting this sort of music in a setting where people came not to drink or dance but solely to listen, and the event attracted a great deal of national publicity that helped increase the public's awareness of Benny and his musicians. The concert took place at the Congress Hotel on Sunday afternoon, December 8, and was produced by the Chicago Rhythm Club, one of the growing number of hot clubs springing up around the country. Ironically, Benny was totally resistant to the idea when the Rhythm Club's Helen Oakley first approached him about it, and she recalls that it took all her determination to bring him around:

"Benny had been doing the 'Let's Dance' broadcasts from New York, and they were terrific. Chicago was a musical wilderness in those days, so when we listened to those broadcasts, they lightened our hearts and gave us hope. It was the only time I ever did this, but I dropped Benny a line saying, 'This is great. This must be kept up.' He always said it was his first fan letter.

"Well, when I heard that he was booked into the Congress, I thought something should be done to guarantee it would be a success, because if it were a success, that could be a stepping-stone to New York. The band's whole future could hinge on it. I talked it over with a group of friends from the Rhythm Club, and we agreed that somehow or other we would try to put on a concert. By the time Benny arrived in town, I had already discussed the possibility with the Chicago musicians' union. At first they were very sticky about it, but they finally agreed that if we made it a benefit, it would be all right. And that's when I ran into the Benny Goodman problem.

"I had assumed Benny would react like a normal person and say, 'Well, gosh, that's a great idea. It's wonderful publicity. We should definitely do it.' Instead, I was up there in his hotel room in the Congress listening to a lot of objections. He didn't like the whole idea of playing a concert. Why should he take on all the extra work? Since this was a benefit, how would the musicians be paid? And so on. I thought to myself, 'This man is mad, and I'm going to argue like heck with him,' which I did. I was really quite insulting, telling him things like 'I never knew such a dummkopf!' Both of us laughed, and he eventually agreed to go along with it if we took care of the arrangements. Harry Kaufman, the very nice man who ran the hotel, gave us his full cooperation. The Chicago Rhythm Club people had never done anything like this before, but they were extremely enthusiastic and started peddling tickets everywhere, even on street corners."

By the day of the concert only 200 tickets had been sold, but that afternoon a huge crowd lined up at the door, and some 800 people crammed into the Urban Room, a relatively small space that normally held no more than 550. The audience was a mix of society people, musicians and jazz fans, and the band was so inspired by their cheers and applause it played without letup for three and a half hours. The concert was an unqualified triumph. *Time* magazine wrote about it glowingly a few weeks later in a major piece on the resurgence of jazz that acclaimed Benny "the Man of the Hour."

Encouraged by this success, the Rhythm Club put on a second concert in March with Fletcher Henderson's band and packed the Urban Room again. "Although Fletcher's band is both rough around the edges and unpolished," *Down Beat* reported, giving voice to the racial stereotyping that sometimes still informed even the most well-intentioned discussions of the music, "the aggregation 'swings it!' as no similar white musicians could do. There is something still primitively 'alive' in the heart of every Negro . . . that no white man without that jungle ancestry can ever approach." Despite the lack of proper ancestry, Benny sat in with the band for a few numbers at the end of the afternoon, trading choruses around the microphone with Chu Berry and Roy Eldridge. Benny maintained that this was "the first time, probably, that white and colored musicians played together for a paying audience in America." Although earlier precedents can be found, this was hardly an everyday occurrence, and it helped set the stage for an occasion of historic significance that took place five weeks later.

The Rhythm Club had booked Benny for a second concert at the Congress on Easter Sunday, April 12. Benny's trio recordings with Teddy Wilson had received excellent reviews and were selling extremely well, so Helen Oakley approached him about bringing Teddy in from New York and presenting the trio as part of the afternoon's program.

"I felt it would be a real breakthrough if we could get Teddy there and have black and white performing together publicly," she explains. "I also felt it would produce some terrific music. Benny played his best with black musicians like Teddy because most white jazz musicians at that time hadn't caught up yet. In a sense, Benny was handicapped playing with his own band, as good as it was, because most of the guys simply weren't on his level. And whenever he worked with black musicians he liked, his own playing became really inspired. Benny probably had never played with a pianist as good as Teddy Wilson, so I went over to the Congress to talk to him about it.

"Benny was extremely dubious. He was not an adventurous person and certainly wasn't interested in sticking his neck out. He just wanted to go along doing what he knew how to do best and try to make a success out of that. Racial integration was not a personal cause with Benny. Charlie Barnet was much more concerned about it than he was. Not that Benny was against it. He just couldn't envision what might be and was only interested in cold, hard facts, and he was afraid that if he and Teddy played together in public, it might not be found acceptable. 'The hotel will never allow it,' he told me. I said, 'What if I can get Harry Kaufman to agree to it, and we bring Teddy out here?' Benny's answer was, 'All right, then we'll talk.' I didn't have a straight yes from him, but neither did I have a straight no, and that gave me enough to go on.

"I reached Teddy on the phone and asked if he'd be willing to come. He was playing intermission piano at the Famous Door, but nothing much was really happening for him, so he said, sure, he'd be glad to. Then I spoke to Harry Kaufman. I explained to him about the trio records and said, 'What Benny ought to do is have the trio come on in the intermission as a kind of entr'acte. It would be a phenomenal presentation of talent, and nobody could really object.' Kaufman was a sensible man, and he believed in me by now because the previous concerts had done so well. He answered, 'Yes, I don't see any problems with that. People who buy tickets will know what they're going to hear.' Then I sent Teddy the fare, which I paid for myself, and told Benny everything was set. 'Why don't you just do it?' I said to him. 'You have a wonderful chance to do something absolutely different, and it will be marvelous music.' Benny finally agreed, so we went ahead with our plans."

For all of Benny's apprehensions, the walls of the Congress did not shudder and shake at the sight of black and white musicians sharing the same bandstand, though they might well have vibrated a little from the fine music that was generated. The afternoon was not without its dissonant moments, but they took place offstage before the concert began.

The Rhythm Club had invited John Hammond to attend as its guest. Although Hammond served in no official capacity with either Benny or the club, he did have his own ideas about how things ought to be done, and some of the plans for the afternoon did not meet with his approval. The English bandleader Jack Hylton was in town, fronting an orchestra of American musicians at the Drake Hotel, and the club had asked him to stop by and say a few words about the splendid job Benny was doing making swing music acceptable to the general public. Hammond still smarted from the run-in he'd had with Hylton when the all-star tour of England fell through a year and a half earlier. After a heated argument with Oakley he cloistered himself back-stage with Benny for an hour and persuaded him to drop Hylton's opening remarks from the program.

Nor did Hammond care for the selection of material Benny had chosen to perform. There were too many "bombastic" numbers like "Bugle Call Rag," as he put it at the time, that appealed to "the faddists and would-be society folk" in the audience and not enough of "the more subtle and quiet Henderson creations." There were also too many Helen Ward vocals for his taste, and he pressed Benny to omit her usual choruses, which led to a further dispute with Oakley, one of Helen's biggest fans.

All this backstage unpleasantness "didn't help our mood along any," Benny recalled, "and the whole thing came pretty near not going on at all." The concert had been oversold, and he was also put off by the attendant confusion and noise and the fact that "quite a few [of the ticket holders] had come just because it was the fashionable thing to do and . . . were more interested in each other than the music." But none of that mattered once he took the stage with Teddy and Gene. "We were all picked up so much by the chance to play together (after the lapse of almost a year) that we got off by ourselves and just let go. The three of us worked together as if we had been born to play this way, and one idea just came after another. What surprised us, though, was the great response from the audience, because there was nothing sensational in the playing, just music."

The audience response was so positive and Benny so thrilled to be playing with a musician of Teddy's caliber in a small group format that allowed him much more creative freedom than he had with his orchestra that he decided to make the trio permanent and hired Teddy to remain on in Chicago. (According to Hammond, Harry Kaufman must also be credited for insisting that Benny keep the trio at the Congress for the rest of his engage-

ment.) This was the first time a black musician became a permanent member
of an established all-white orchestra, and as Leonard Feather reminds us, "it
was an historic precedent, the magnitude of which can hardly be appreciated
today in correct perspective."

One of the things that's hard to keep in perspective is that, strictly
speaking, Teddy was not part of the orchestra at all but a kind of extra
attraction. During the remainder of the Congress stand he played intermission
piano, then was joined by Benny and Gene for a special trio segment before
the band took the stage. This arrangement, originally conceived by Helen
Oakley for the Rhythm Club concert, was maintained over the next three
years Teddy remained with Benny. Looked at today, it may suggest a halfhearted cautiousness that veers uncomfortably close to a sort of musical
apartheid. Yet one need look no farther than the music business itself to see
what Benny and Teddy were up against. The Chicago musicians' union was
still rigidly segregated into two separate locals. Black musicians could work the
clubs on New York's Fifty-second Street, but black patrons were unwelcome.
Quite apart from its musical merits and its commercial appeal to bookers, who
got two "acts" for the price of one, the trio arrangement provided a way to
push back the boundaries of Jim Crow as far as the times allowed without
driving away potential customers hung up with their own racial problems.

"There had been a lot of interracial record sessions," Teddy said some
years later. "But this—playing in public with Benny—was a breakthrough. I
knew of the pressures that were pulling Benny the other way. Guys in the
music business were telling him he'd ruin his career if he hired me. They
weren't necessarily antiblack; they were businessmen."

One can imagine Teddy's disdain for this sort of thinking. "Teddy was
a well-educated, highly cultured man very much ahead of his time," explains
Helen Oakley, who became a close lifelong friend. "He knew he was on a par
with everybody else in every conceivable way. When he ran into racial
prejudice and unpleasant situations that could not be avoided, he would never
deign to show the slightest emotion however much he loathed them. He rose
above everything with the same deadpan expression and ramrod-straight
posture with which he sat at the piano.

"Most black musicians at that time had a great deal of warmth and
humor, so Benny was probably a bit mystified by Teddy's rather chilly
reserve, especially since they played so well together. Teddy tended to be like
that with everyone, and he was certainly that way with Benny. They never
really hit it off temperamentally. They could never have become buddies. I'm
sure Teddy must have sized Benny up and found him lacking in many ways.
Benny still had a lot of rough edges on him at this point in his life. He was
very unpolished and sometimes quite coarse. He didn't really give a hoot
about it—he didn't see where it mattered—and you have to admire him for

that. But Teddy's own background was so different. His mother probably would have found Benny shocking."

The Congress engagement was going so well Benny probably could have stayed on indefinitely. But his network radio show for the Elgin Watch Company was shifted to New York, and he was forced to leave the hotel in May. The band played a number of one-nighters on the return journey east, and the response was overwhelming. "I had never seen such crowds before," Pee Wee Erwin remembered. "Benny, I'm sure, was being booked by MCA on the usual percentage basis, and he began to make so much money that handling it became a problem. Since we were always on the move, it wasn't always possible to get to a bank, and I know of at least one instance where Eugene, Benny's younger brother, who drove the instrument truck wearing coveralls, had $70,000 concealed under them." When the Goodman orchestra left New York the previous July, it was, as Jess Stacy called it, "a panic band," uncertain whether it would be able to keep going from one night to the next. When it returned ten months later, it was the hottest thing in the music business.

The Goodman band pulls in the crowds
at Atlantic City's Steel Pier, September 1936.
Left to right: Chris Griffin, Ziggy Elman, Gene Krupa, Red Ballard,
Hymie Schertzer, Bill DePew, Helen Ward, Benny,
Murray McEachern, Zeke Zarchey, Vido Musso,
Arthur Rollini, Harry Goodman, Jess Stacy.

From the Benny Goodman Archives in the Music Library at Yale University

11

Making It

"If I were inclined to be sentimental," Benny reminisced, "I could say something about the way I felt having our first real success in Chicago, where I was born and all that. It would have been swell no matter where it happened, but the fact that it was in Chicago, that we had come into the place on a few weeks' trial and stayed on for [close to] seven months, well, that just made it all the better."

Strolling around the old neighborhood, stopping to talk with people he hadn't seen in years, Benny could take justifiable pride in how far he'd come since he left home as a nineteen-year-old sideman with Ben Pollack's band and headed off to New York. The unheated basement flat where the Goodman family shivered through the remorseless Chicago winters, the Francisco Avenue tenement with its dark stairways and tiny, sunless rooms, the long, dismal days when his father was out of a job and the kids had to go hungry— all that was behind him now. Through hard work and perseverance and unrelenting dedication to making the most of his natural abilities, the poor Jewish boy from the Maxwell Street ghetto had fulfilled the immigrant dream of a better life for the children, had indeed raised himself up even beyond where David Goodman might have dared hope when he dragged Benny and his brothers off to their first music lessons. Universally admired by his fellow musicians, adulated by fans across the country who snapped up his records and clustered around the radio to listen to his broadcasts, welcomed into the homes of the Chicago gentry who packed the Congress every night, Benny had prevailed over the impediments of the music business, and without compromising his talent or taste or desire to play the kind of music he loved, he had made himself a success.

Yet who could say for certain how real any of this was or how long it might last? The road to the Congress had been paved with so many false starts and heart-wrenching near misses. Why should the string of disappointments and unexpected reversals end here? Today Benny was on top of the world, but who knew what might happen tomorrow—or even tonight?

"It was during these months that Ben Pollack passed through Chicago and dropped in to hear the band," Benny recalled. "Folks around town had been boosting us to him, and he was curious to find out what the fuss was about. Well, when I saw Ben sitting there, listening to me out in front of my own band, I couldn't play a note. I think it was the only time in my life that I was ever really nervous to the point where I hadn't an idea in my head. To top it all, I split a reed, and that just about finished me. When Ben left I could tell from the way he acted that he didn't think much of what he had heard."

Benny had never forgotten how just as he was beginning to do well and could finally start giving his parents some of the things they never had, his father was struck down by a car and killed. When Benny returned to Chicago, he invited his sister Ida to the Congress opening, only to learn that her husband was in the hospital and her kids had come down with scarlet fever. A few days before Ida's husband had been walking down the street and was caught in a collision between two automobiles. Both arms and legs were broken, and it was doubtful if he would ever be able to return to his dental practice. This near repetition of his father's fatal accident was Benny's homecoming. Who could be sure of anything?

Everyone agrees that it was during his stay in Chicago that Benny began to change.

JESS STACY: Even at the beginning Benny was a taskmaster. And after we went into the Congress and he had some success, he got tougher.

HELEN WARD: He became even more dedicated and even more imbued with the idea of making it. Nothing else seemed to matter. He had to get there. It was like something weighing on him. He became much more serious. He didn't laugh at jokes as readily. He grew more inward and remote. Benny was a very outgoing guy when I first met him, but he was basically an introvert, and strangely enough, the more successful he got, the more introverted he became. He would say things he didn't mean, and sometimes he wouldn't say anything at all. It was very hard to communicate with him.

ARTHUR ROLLINI: Benny was more or less always aloof . . . and as he became more popular he became more critical with everybody. . . . Every time you played a solo he'd just look at the bell of your horn and expect to be knocked out of this world. The band sounded very relaxed, but everybody was [actually] very tense.

If Benny couldn't help the wrong bookings and disappointing turnouts and failed expectations that had undermined him in the past, there were certain places where he could exert some kind of control to keep his future from slipping away from him once again.

   After Chris Griffin quit his job at the CBS studio in New York to join the Goodman band at the Congress, he discovered that Benny was unwilling to pay him more than one hundred dollars a week, ten dollars less than he had been earning. And the hard bargain Benny drove with his new trumpet player was by no means untypical. As Jess Stacy puts it, "He was always on the verge of being cautious with a buck." When it came to family, Benny accepted the burden of responsibility that fell on his shoulders after his father died and made sure everyone was taken care of. The band was run almost like a family business. His older brother Harry played bass. Younger brother Eugene drove the instrument truck. Sister Ethel managed the band's payroll in New York. From time to time Irving and Freddy filled in on trumpet. "When Ida's husband had that terrible accident," Helen Ward remembers, "Benny saw to it that he got the best care money could buy, and he footed every bill. Nobody knows about that because Benny never talked about it." On occasion Benny could be just as secretively generous with his musicians. But most of the time the memory of those early years was too strong to overcome, and very little of the money that was now filling his bank accounts found its way into their pockets. "I've always been fairly frugal and sensible," Benny conceded. "A lot of people in our business make very simple and stupid mistakes. They go bankrupt."

   But it was by maintaining the strictest vigilance over the quality of his music that Benny had the best chance to gain some control over the uncertainties that had beset him in the past. For all his great fondness for Fletcher Henderson, he could not fail to see that Fletcher's easygoing nature and laxity with his sidemen had led him to betray his enormous talent and subvert a career that should have reached the heights. Tolerance for sloppy or indifferent playing, accepting less than one's best, putting up with any of the distractions that interfered with a total dedication to one's craft—not only were these sins against the vision of excellence inherent in the musician's calling, but considering the vagaries of the music business, especially in these shaky years of the Great Depression, they posed a serious threat to one's very survival. Always highly critical about his own playing, Benny became just as demanding with his sidemen.

"Benny was a real taskmaster," Chris Griffin says. "He would have us go over some new arrangement time and time again even though it didn't require that much rehearsing, and he would keep working on his own solo until he found just what he wanted. He was such a perfectionist. I had previously worked with Charlie Barnet for a while, and he was a wild man who loved to have fun with his musicians. The Goodman band, though, was a lot more formal."

Benny acknowledged that he "ran the band in a very orderly way," claiming, "I see no reason not to do that, no matter what business you're in. Seeing that we did get our training in radio, with people who were strict about our efforts, we demanded that from other people too. It wasn't anything unusual at all."

Maybe it wasn't. Tommy Dorsey was as much of a taskmaster, and so was Glenn Miller. (The story goes that Miller was such a martinet that when his plane went down in the English Channel during the Second World War, the men in his air force band actually celebrated.) And those leaders who took a more relaxed view of things usually had to pay the price. Everyone who worked for Bunny Berigan loved him, and his orchestra was infused with a camaraderie that helped keep it going when the paychecks ran out and the jobs fell through. "It was a tight little band, just like a family of bad little boys, with Bunny the worst of all," trombonist Ray Conniff recalled about his tenure with the Berigan orchestra in 1938. "We were all friends. In fact, Bunny wouldn't hire anybody he didn't like. And all of us would take turns rooming with him. Oh, it was a mad ball. You should've seen those hotel rooms! Ribs, booze and women all over the place." But the mad ball soon ended, and Bunny's subsequent efforts to head his own band were just as short-lived.

Big bands were a business, a difficult, high-pressure business, and the leaders who were determined to make it had no choice but to adapt themselves to what the business required of them, however much they had to change. According to Bud Freeman, Benny "was the finest man you would ever want to meet until he got into the big band thing and had all that pressure and nervousness on him. . . . For a man as talented as Benny Goodman to try to run a band takes its toll in some ways. You become hard and selfish and impervious to the feelings of others. But Benny knew what he wanted, and he was like a machine."

Jess Stacy puts it more succinctly: "Like they say, when you're a bandleader, you automatically become a prick. Automatically."

Benny was not easy to work for. "He was so hard to communicate with that half the time you couldn't figure out what he wanted," Chris Griffin remembers. "If you asked him about it, his standard answer would be, 'Just swing, that's all. Just swing.' Well, we knew *that*. We knew we're supposed to swing. But exactly what did he want us to do? 'Just swing'—that's all he would say."

When Benny was pleased by a musician's performance, he usually kept it to himself. "He was not a demonstrative person," Helen Ward explains. "The only way he would praise anyone was in a physical reaction. He'd giggle silently. If something was great, he would throw up his arms or even jump off the bandstand. But he could never express himself directly and say, 'I think that was wonderful.' Well, how many of us really can? And when you're very young, the way we were, and so much is happening so fast, you kind of take everything for granted and don't stop to appreciate what you have. You just go along from one day to the next expecting more."

When Benny was displeased, however, it was all too apparent. "Once, at the Congress Hotel, in Chicago," Jess remembers, "I was fooling around with a little blues before a set started, and he came over and stood next to me and listened awhile, and then said, *'That's* the blues?' I hadn't been with him very long, and I was crushed." Teddy Wilson agreed: "Benny didn't spare anybody's feelings. He switched solos and first parts in a minute, right in front of everybody. 'You give him that part. You let him play that. You lay out.'"

When the phrasing was off or the intonation a little shaky, Benny had a habit of peering over his glasses with a look of such icy disbelief that it could make strong men tremble. Someone, possibly trombonist Murray McEachern, who replaced Joe Harris at the Congress, was reminded of the "Paralysis Ray" in the *Little Orphan Annie* comic strip and started using the term for the formidable Goodman stare. The term caught on, and "the Ray" took its place alongside such other mystifying idiosyncrasies as Benny's endless quest for the perfect reed and his inability to remember his sidemen's names. The cruel contempt it seemed to convey may or may not have been always intended. According to Helen Oakley, "Benny was so enormously endowed I don't think he could ever get it in his head that no, other people weren't. It was more or less a matter of his thinking to himself, 'How could you? What's the matter with you?'" Still, "the Ray" upset his musicians terribly, undermining their confidence in their own abilities and nullifying the enthusiasm they brought with them when they first joined the band.

Benny's insistence upon the highest standards of musicianship produced the desired result. As Helen Ward says, "Benny wanted perfection, and he got it. That band breathed together. It was like one guy playing." Hymie Schertzer gave a telling example of the level of performance the Goodman musicians came to take for granted: "One night I somehow added an eighth note by mistake. It was the first time it ever happened to me. I couldn't tell you how or why. I do know it hit the band like a tank charge—the surprise of that extra moment threw everyone for a loop, including me. It was that unexpected from any member of the band."

Fletcher Henderson in 1934, shortly before he gave up his own orchestra and started writing for Benny. Frank Driggs Collection

Willard Alexander, Benny's champion at MCA. Institute of Jazz Studies

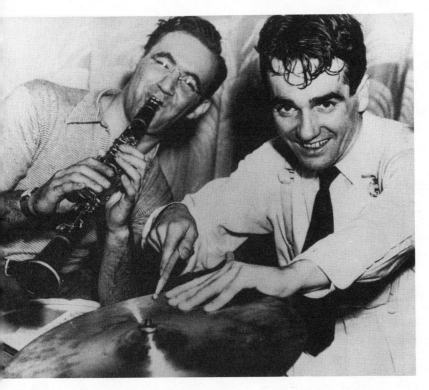

Benny and Gene Krupa, 1938. From the Benny Goodman Archives in the Music Library at Yale University

A glowing Benny shares a table with the pianist Joe Sullivan during the band's breakthrough engagement at the Palomar Ballroom in the fall of 1935. Ken Whitten Collection

NOTICE
Palomar All Sold
Out for Elks' Grand
Ball, July 14th

VERMONT at 3rd

The PALOMAR

PROGRAM
WEEK OF
JULY 6th

THE DINING . . . . . DANCING . . . . . and ENTERTAINMENT CENTER OF THE WEST

"Swing Music" Swings To The Top!

BENNY GOODMAN

LAST YEAR -- -- PALOMAR'S 'DIXIELAND - BAND' LEADER

THIS YEAR . . . . AMERICA'S FAVORITE 'SWING---MASTER'

Program announcing the return of "America's Favorite 'Swing–Master' " to the Palomar Ballroom in July 1936. Ken Whitten Collection

12

Return to the Palomar

argely as a result of Benny's grow-
ing popularity, swing music was attracting more and more fans and coming
to be seen as an increasingly viable part of the music business. A few days
before he returned to New York, the city was treated to what was vigorously
promoted as its "First Swing Concert." Produced by the Onyx's Joe Helbock,
the event filled every seat in the Imperial Theater and kept the audience
yelling for more until midnight as one band after another paraded across the
stage, played two or three numbers, then made way for the next.

One of the high points of the evening was an unusual small group Artie
Shaw put together that combined his clarinet with a string quartet and rhythm
section. Shaw's "dynamic clarinet work will probably keep Goodman awake
for several nights to come," *Down Beat* raved. "Absolutely masterful on technique and tone. . . . Rates with Goodman any day. . . . Applause tore down
house and necessitated many a bow." Shaw was still laboring in the radio
studios, making a good living as a free-lancer, but now he was suddenly
besieged with offers to form his own big band and go into competition with
Benny. He signed with the Rockwell-O'Keefe Agency, MCA's archrival, and
later that summer debuted his new orchestra at the Lexington Hotel. Shaw

included the string quartet in his lineup for a while, producing some subtly distinctive music unlike anything else being played, but early the next year he changed to a harder-swinging more orthodox format very much in the Goodman-Henderson mode.

Other big swing bands were also beginning to make their presence felt. Jimmy Dorsey could be heard on Bing Crosby's radio program every week and was turning out a lot of records for Decca. Tommy Dorsey was now working at Manhattan's Hotel Lincoln with a much improved orchestra that included Bud Freeman, Max Kaminsky and Dave Tough. Bob Crosby came into New York for the first time early in 1936, appearing at the Hotel New Yorker with an exciting Dixieland-style outfit filled with fine soloists like Yank Lawson, Eddie Miller and Matty Matlock. Charlie Barnet was booked into the prestigious Glen Island Casino for the summer and had a record contract with Bluebird, Victor's lower-priced subsidiary. Some other important big bands were to be heard from soon. Within the year Glenn Miller formed his own orchestra. Thanks to John Hammond's relentless enthusiasm and some encouragement from Benny, Willard Alexander was to sign the Count Basie band to MCA, raising it out of its present obscurity at the Reno Club in Kansas City.

Benny's crown remained secure. The Goodman orchestra won first place in *Down Beat*'s 1936 reader's poll, scoring almost three times the votes of its nearest competitor, and he was awarded the clarinet spot in the magazine's all-time swing band. His popularity only increased in the months to come. But the competition was starting to mass its forces, giving him something else to worry about.

Benny remained in New York until the end of June, finishing up the last Elgin radio broadcasts, playing one-nighters around the area, recording more Jimmy Mundy and Fletcher Henderson charts, occasionally sitting in with Tommy Dorsey at the Hotel Lincoln and Bunny Berigan's small group at the Club 18. Then he headed west once again back to Los Angeles. Willard had booked a return engagement at the Palomar at triple the price of the previous summer. The band was also scheduled to start doing another weekly radio program, the popular "Camel Caravan" show on CBS, sponsored by the R. J. Reynolds Tobacco Company. Benny couldn't help being pleased that he was replacing the Casa Loma Orchestra, which had played the show for the past three seasons. It was the Casa Loma's success that originally persuaded him to try becoming a leader. Now Benny's own star was in the ascendant.

While the band was on the road, Willard secured it a featured spot in the Paramount movie *The Big Broadcast of 1937*. "It was a tough period," Chris Griffin remembers. "Most of the time we were due on the set around six in the morning, and we'd go until maybe four in the afternoon under those white hot lights, just waiting until we had a break and could find ourselves some shade. When we finally finished up, we'd drive home and have a quick dinner and maybe close our eyes for a few minutes, then go off to the Palomar, where we'd play from eight o'clock at night until about two in the morning. This went on for about three weeks, and we were a total mess. Luckily we were young. If we had been older, I don't think we'd have been able to stand it." The pace became somewhat less hectic once the picture was finished, though along with their regular night's work at the Palomar they still had the "Camel Caravan" every Tuesday, weekly rehearsals for the new floor show and occasional recording sessions. Benny also began booking outside jobs on Sundays, their one day off.

The Big Broadcast of 1937 was the third in a series of *Big Broadcast* films spotlighting some of the popular radio personalities of the day, in this case Jack Benny, George Burns and Gracie Allen, Bob Burns and Martha Raye. The Goodman band can be seen backing a few of the vocalists and racing through Jimmy Mundy's killer-diller rearrangement of "Bugle Call Rag." Teddy Wilson did not appear. "They wanted me to do the recording for a musical sequence but have a white musician substitute for me when they shot the picture," he explained. "I refused to do that." The picture was a great success, topping all opening week attendance records when it played the New York Paramount toward the end of the year.

The Palomar engagement went extremely well, especially the part of every evening that showcased the trio. "When they performed, the people would be stacked in front of the bandstand," Pee Wee Erwin remembered. Behind the scenes, however, not everything was going so smoothly. Benny and his third trumpet player, Nate Kazebier, had been having their problems, and around the middle of August Kazebier suddenly left. About the same time saxophonist Dick Clark also disappeared. According to Arthur Rollini, Benny wanted a young-looking band and decided to get rid of Clark because he was prematurely bald. Clark was a good solid player, though Benny hardly ever gave him a chance to solo, but the saxophonist who replaced him more than made up for the loss.

Rollini had heard Vido Musso at the Rendezvous Ballroom in a band led by Gil Evans, the brilliant arranger who became best known for his collaborations with Miles Davis two decades later, and he suggested that Benny drive out to Balboa Beach and have a listen. "The combo was so-so—except for a piano man with some ideas, named Stan Kenton, and the tenor man, a thickset, tough-looking young Italian," Benny recalled. "I invited him to come around the next evening and sit in with us. He showed up while we were in the middle of our arrangement of 'Honeysuckle Rose,' and I beckoned him to take a chorus. He took twelve. The crowd was excited, but their reaction was nothing compared to mine; I jumped right off the stand."

Vido provided the sort of challenge and excitement Benny was always looking for. As John Hammond observed, "Despite Benny Goodman's talent as an improvisor and ensemble musician, he did need new inspiration every few months, the introduction of a new player with fresh ideas." The only problem with Musso was that he couldn't read music, a limitation that might seem to make him totally unsuited for a band that demanded the highest technical proficiency from its members. But Benny was determined to hire him anyway and had Rollini and Hymie Schertzer take him under their wing to help him get through the arrangements.

It was slow going, and when Benny asked Vido why he was making such little progress, he answered, "It ain't the notes that bother me, Benny. It's the rest-ess." There may have been something to it. According to Schertzer, the way Leora Henderson copied out the parts of Fletcher's orchestrations often made it difficult to distinguish between a quarter note and a quarter rest. (One can imagine Leora scribbling away frantically through the night, doing her best to get the charts finished in time for Benny's rehearsal the next morning.) Nevertheless, this became the first in a long line of Vido Musso stories that continue to delight Goodman veterans to the present day.

Vido had grown up in Sicily with very little formal education, and there was an off-center, almost surrealistic quality in the way he expressed himself in English. "We were sitting in someone's car taking five," Chris Griffin remembers. "The brakes started to slip, and the car was backing up slowly. Vido looked out the window and said, 'Gee, de oith's movin'!' Oh, he was something else." Benny recounted: "One day he came to work with a fearful boil on his neck. The next day it was gone. 'I had it glanced,' he said, 'and the Doc put some easy tape on it.' "

"Oh, how he mangled the language." Helen Ward laughs. "He couldn't spell or write at all, and I don't think he could read. Arthur Rollini used to write letters for him to his sweetheart back home. There weren't many characters in the band. Benny didn't put up with much nonsense. But Vido certainly qualified as one of them. He was a wonderful kid. And God, what a talent." Vido remained with the band until the end of 1937. His big, burly tenor can be heard to advantage on such recordings as "Jam Session," "Riffin' at the Ritz" and "I Want to Be Happy."

A few days after Vido Musso was hired, Benny came across another even more inspiring player. Four years younger than Benny, Lionel Hampton started out as a drummer, then, during a 1930 record date with Louis Armstrong, started fooling around with a vibraphone he happened to find in the studio. The vibraphone gave him an outlet for his tremendous skills at melodic and harmonic improvisation, and he gradually switched over, becoming the first jazz musician to make it his primary instrument.

By the summer of 1936 Hampton was leading his own nine-piece band at the Paradise Club, a seedy sailor bar at Sixth and Main that was beginning to attract an upscale Hollywood crowd lured by his playing and showmanship. Pee Wee Erwin and Hymie Schertzer stumbled across him in the course of their usual quest for good places to eat, were knocked out by what they heard and spread the word to the rest of the Goodman musicians. After Benny finished up at the Palomar one evening, he drove over to the club to see what everyone was talking about. Lionel remembered:

> Benny sits down at a table and starts listening to me. I was playing the vibraharp, and Benny was very amused at it because at that time the vibes weren't very popular or well known. The drummers just used it to play the pretty notes on—the "bing bong" they'd hang on the end of a tune. But I was playing jazz on it, and that night, with Benny there, I was inspired. He'd been in the house about half an hour, listening, when he came over and said, "Pops . . . I've been hearing a lot about you and I'd like to sit in with you." So he took out his clarinet and began blowing. We jammed about two or three hours. The place was supposed to close at three o'clock, but I think the whole house stayed till five that morning. The next night he brought Teddy Wilson, Gene Krupa and several other boys from the band. We jammed till five or six o'clock. Then Benny said, "Pops, how'd you like to make a record with me?" That thrilled me. Man, I was really gassed. I got home that morning after six, and about eleven Benny called and asked me to come out to the RCA Victor studio. I jumped out of bed right away and rushed down to Sixth and Main to pick up my vibes, [and] that was the birth of the Goodman Quartet.

Benny had a big band date scheduled that morning, and at the end of the session he had Lionel record one tune with the trio, the lovely Will Hudson-Eddie De Lange ballad "Moonglow." The performance is so relaxed and the four of them play together with such obvious empathy and enjoyment it sounds as if they've been doing it for years. As Benny said, "It was the story of the Trio all over again—one of those natural things that was just meant to be."

Five days later he brought Lionel back for more. This time they recorded "Dinah" and "Vibraphone Blues," with a vocal by Hamp and a grittier-than-usual clarinet solo by Benny. Benny also had him do a vocal chorus on the trio rendition of "Exactly like You." "It was a loose session," Hampton remembered. "Benny was feeling good that day. That's why he let me sing. One thing about Benny: he reflected all his dates. You had to fit in with his ideas and the way he was feeling. When you became a part of Benny Good-man's band, you became a part of Benny Goodman."

Hampton's exuberant improvising, always full of high spirits, heady emotion and finger-popping excitement, marvelously complemented Teddy Wilson's cooler, more controlled virtuosity. Between the two of them, they suggested the full range of expressive possibilities in Benny's own playing. Lionel joined Benny in New York that fall, and the new Goodman Quartet gave Benny yet another special attraction to add to his presentation. Hampton became an immediate favorite not only with musicians and jazz fans but also with the much larger, more commercially significant pop music audiences. His contribution to Benny's ongoing success was enormous. And as a result of the heavy exposure he received with Benny, the vibraphone came to be regarded as less of a novelty instrument and began to attract other musicians. In 1943 Red Norvo switched over from xylophone, the unamplified precursor of the vibes, with wood rather than metal keys. In 1945 Milt Jackson, the third important vibraphonist, bopped onto the scene with Dizzy Gillespie. Within a few years any number of other players emerged, and the vibraphone became a standard part of many jazz ensembles.

Hampton's arrival pushed back the established racial barriers that much farther. MCA had the expected apprehensions. When the Goodman band went south to play the Dallas Exposition in September 1937, there were predictions of impending violence, and Benny was advised to leave Teddy and Lionel behind. He refused to do that, but ostensibly because the opening show was running too long, he did omit the trio and quartet from his first set. Hammond reported what happened:

> When the crowd, many of whom had come hundreds of miles for the occasion, heard that they would not be able to hear Teddy and Lionel they were loud in their fury, and several of them even went so far as to demand a refund. After that, Benny knew that a Dallas audience was no different from any other in the country. Needless to say, when the Quartet was presented at the later show it was an enormous success, and there was not even the slightest hint of a protest during the entire eleven day stay from anyone in the audience.

According to Teddy, he and Lionel were welcomed by the Goodman musicians without hesitation. "There were Southerners in the band and Italians and Jews, but we were all like brothers. The whole outfit was as solid as a family. And we were all very much aware of what was going on. Every-body was a dedicated musician, and we believed in what we were doing, socially and musically. It was completely different from what Jackie Robinson had to put up with when he joined the Brooklyn Dodgers and had to fight the guys on his own team as well as the fans and the opposing players. As a matter of fact, the racial mixing turned out to be an asset. The jazz fans were hungry for this sort of thing. The interest in the United States was tremendous, and the audiences were so for it we never heard one negative voice.

"Of course, when we went on the road, Lionel and I couldn't stay in the white hotels, but it's hard to call that a problem because it was the norm of the day. And we didn't challenge that norm. If you made a battle of that in every town on every one night stand, you couldn't ever get to work. So Lionel and I would usually drive our cars over to the Negro district of town and check into a Negro hotel, and then we'd just go and do the job. In some areas, of course, our road manager could have sounded out the hotels and restaurants in advance to find out whether or not the entire group would be welcome, so we would know what we were walking into. But we just took every situation as we came to it. We were not going to fight City Hall. We went along with the tide the way it was because we had already opened the door a giant crack, and there was no need to make a big fuss. And I think it was correct to do it that way. The door gradually opened of its own accord."

Considering all the concern about whether or not the public was ready for a mixed band, the racial incidents were remarkably few and far between. But even the power of the quartet's music had its limitations, and every now and then something would happen. "One time we went down as far as Louisville and played just outside of town a little ways, and it got pretty rough there that night," Chris Griffin remembers. "Lionel and I kept watching each other to see if anybody was going to jump us. Another time was in, of all places, Canada. Teddy and I were at the bar having a drink, and some real red-neck walks up to him, spins him around and says, 'You niggers are everyplace. You're even coming up here.' With that he took a poke at Teddy, which Teddy ducked, and I jumped on him. I weighed about a hundred and forty pounds soaking wet, but then everybody jumped in. Benny came over and told the bosses, 'If there's any more of this sort of thing, I'll leave in the middle of the night with the whole band,' so it was quiet from then on. Those are the only two incidents I ever saw."

Benny may have had some initial reluctance about integrating the band. Teddy's exclusion from *The Big Broadcast* did not do him much credit. But once he committed himself fully by also hiring Lionel Hampton, he refused to back down or compromise himself in any way. If you hired Benny Goodman, you also hired his musicians, all of them. That was his policy, and his absolute clarity about it helped keep the unpleasant incidents to a minimum. And whenever they happened, he was always ready to tear up his contract and walk. "As far as I'm concerned, what he did in those days—and they were hard days, in 1937—made it possible for Negroes to have their chance in baseball and other fields," Hampton maintains. "He was a real pioneer, and he didn't grandstand about it. He used to tell me, 'If a guy's got it, let him give it. I'm selling music, not prejudice.' "

Benny's precedent-breaking challenge to the prejudice of the day did not automatically throw open the doors to other black musicians. His popularity gave him tremendous leverage, but the few less successful leaders who tried integrating their bands found the going a lot harder. Mezz Mezzrow made several attempts at leading a mixed orchestra during the 1930s but was never able to keep it working. Billie Holiday's tenure with the Artie Shaw orchestra in 1938 was a constant struggle with racism, and she left after eight months. Lena Horne joined Charlie Barnet in 1941 and was gone four months later. As Leonard Feather points out, integration crawled along for almost a decade, and every instance was viewed as a curiosity.

The two months Benny spent in California during the summer of 1936 were wonderfully eventful and productive. He returned to the Palomar and topped his previous success. Appeared in his first movie. Began broadcasting the "Camel Caravan" show. Added Vido Musso to the saxophone section. Discovered Lionel Hampton and made his first records with the quartet, as well as half a dozen sides with the big band. The work was good. The acclaim was loud. The money was plentiful. Yet there was no easing up in Benny's unrelenting single-mindedness of purpose. Whether or not the fearsome Goodman Ray was wholly intentional, the fact that it continued to inspire such dread in some of his musicians indicates clearly enough that his drive for perfection was stronger than ever. The band had to keep improving, getting ever closer to that ideal of transcendent excellence that Benny imposed upon his own playing. And it had to keep a tight hold on everything that had brought it to its present level of achievement and mass acceptance. Benny's determination about that was so fierce that it could, when threatened, ride roughshod over just about every other consideration.

Let Helen Ward tell her own story.

"One night after we finished up at the Palomar, a gang of us went down to the Paradise Club to hear Lionel Hampton. Benny started jamming with Lionel and then Teddy got in and then Lionel put his two-finger piano on top, and it was fabulous. I was with a date, a man I was seeing named Bill, and we stayed until the very end, then went over to the Brown Derby for pancakes and coffee. Bill and I were sitting there talking, and in walked Benny by himself and sat himself down at our table.

"Benny and I had dated off and on. We'd go out for a while, then we'd have a fight, then we'd get back together again—the usual sort of thing. I was so surprised Benny joined us because this was one of those off periods, and I was quite angry at him. In addition to our usual problems, Paramount had cast Martha Raye and Shirley Ross in *The Big Broadcast*, and Benny didn't once say, to my knowledge, 'Hey, do you want the band? Here's Helen.' I mean, I wasn't that ugly. I wasn't as gorgeous as some of the gals, but at least I was passable. That really hurt me.

"Well, when Benny sat down, Bill was telling me that he wanted me to stay in California after the band left, and without so much as a how-do-you-do, Benny turned to him and said, 'You know, I'm going to marry this girl.' It was completely out of left field. Yes, I was in love with him. I was in love with him, I think, from the first time I ever heard him play. And he knew it. But by now I had almost put Benny out of my head entirely as far as marriage or anything serious was concerned, and I couldn't imagine what brought this on.

"It was a very embarrassing moment. I must have said something like 'Hey, come on, we're having coffee.' And then Bill took me home. We kissed and said good-night; then a few minutes later Bill called me on the phone and said that on his way out he saw Benny downstairs sitting in his car, waiting for him to leave. Sure enough, about five minutes later the doorbell rings, and it's Benny. I let him in, and I'll never forget it. I sat down on the sofa. He did not sit down. I said, 'What's going on?' He's standing in front of me and looks down and says, 'I want to marry you.' Just like that. I said, 'Well, this is news to me. You've been going out with Jane, Joan, June, whomever, and I had no idea that's how you felt. When did you . . .' He said, 'Well, I want to marry you.' I said yes.

"After the Palomar we went back east, and on Labor Day weekend we played the Steel Pier in Atlantic City. I was standing on the end of the pier, looking out at the ocean, when Benny came over to me. He said, 'Helen, I'm not ready for marriage. I'm determined to make it, and I don't feel I should get married yet.'

"I really believe Benny liked me a lot. He was always very good to me, and we always had fun together when we weren't fighting. But I have to think the real reason he proposed was to keep me from leaving the band. After all, I did sing every other tune.

"I was furious. It would have been so easy to say, 'Aw, come on, Helen, I've got so much money invested in you, don't leave yet. Why don't you wait?' And maybe I would have listened. But his music meant more to him than anything, and how he hurt me didn't even enter into it.

"Benny could be terribly insensitive at times, but we always said, 'Well, that's Benny,' and let it go. At least I did. But this was too much. I called Willard Alexander in New York and told him, 'I'm going back to the Coast.' Willard drove down and somehow talked me out of it. But it just about broke my heart, and after that my feelings for Benny kind of petered out.

"We went into the Hotel Pennsylvania in the beginning of October, and I started seeing a man who had been my very first date when I was a kid. He really courted me. He was there every night. And he asked me to marry him. One evening before we went to work, I told Benny I was leaving. We were sitting at a little table for two there in the Madhattan Room. Benny was holding one of those oversize dinner menus, and he just flung it across the table in my face. That was his reaction."

13

Dancing
in the Aisles

he morning after Benny opened in
Atlantic City his new trumpet player Zeke Zarchey woke up with a bad lip
infection, and Benny said, "Let's get the kid from the house band to fill in."
The kid in question was a fast-talking, cigar-chomping twenty-two-year-old
named Harry Finkelman who went by the moniker of Ziggy Elman. Elman
was a natural musician gifted with perfect pitch, and there didn't seem to be
any instrument he couldn't handle. Chris Griffin recalls, "When Benny first
heard him he was playing trumpet in the top row of Alex Bartha's band, then
he jumped down to the second row and played trombone, then he jumped
down to the bottom row and played baritone saxophone. Benny just sat there
going, 'Jeez.' He could hardly believe all that power coming out of him."
Zarchey remembers: "Well, Ziggy played the next four days with both bands
and tore it up. Benny was ecstatic. Every time Ziggy stood up to solo he would
be standing there grinning." At the end of the week Benny hired him to
replace Sterling Bose, who had been helping Benny out temporarily and was
due to return to his regular job with Ray Noble's orchestra.

Ziggy Elman was a formidable presence both on and off the bandstand.
The *New Republic* writer Otis Ferguson was a big fan of his playing but found
him personally, at first, rather alarming:

Jitterbugs cut a rug at the Paramount Theater during the Goodman band's historic 1937 engagement. Ken Whitten Collection

I remember when I first used to see Ziggy Elman banging along on buses and trains and gambling for hours on end with that eight-inch cigar permanently in his teeth and talking the current obscene jargon of the day in that noisy gangster's voice of his, and when it was common knowledge he ran a liquor store in Atlantic City and had a brother in one of those fast-talk auction deadfalls along the boardwalk, he looked wrong enough to scare you. He didn't seem to have much connection with the finer arts, and when he played, he was a little fearsome, because he never had time to learn any non-pressure method, and when the brass was working, you could see the whole side of his head bulge out right down to his collar.

"He played all wrong, but he got marvelous results," Chris Griffin explains. "When he was warming up, he could barely tongue. Then he got out in the front, and when the time was with him, he could play as fast as anybody. He was same way with baseball. We had a softball team, and Ziggy played way out in center field, and he used to run at the ball the way a woman would run, holding his hands up over his head instead of loping over and then putting them up to make the catch. But he never missed. I remember playing Ping-Pong with him one afternoon up in Canada. He had never played before, and I play pretty good. He said, 'Well, how do you hold this thing?' and I showed him the easiest grip for a beginner. You know, he damn near beat me that very first game, talking a mile a minute the whole time. He talked like a son of a gun. I think Benny admired him more than anyone else in the band because of that raw ego."

Ziggy was an extremely loud and forceful player, and when the band moved on to the Ritz Carlton Roof in Boston, a small, sedate room that catered to the Back Bay elite, Benny became a bit apprehensive about his trumpet section's growing volume. "Zeke and I were fairly loud players"—Chris laughs—"but Ziggy was like a bus horn. So one day Benny gets him behind the bandstand and says, 'Ziggy, you're playing so loud and all.' And Ziggy says, 'Look, Benny, I didn't ask for you. You asked for me. Atlantic City is only a couple hundred miles down the way. I just left there very happy, and I'll be happy to go back there again. That's the way I play.' From then on I don't remember Benny ever saying a word to him about it."

The band opened at the Madhattan Room of New York's Hotel Pennsylvania on October 1, 1936. By the last week in November Zarchey had moved on to Artie Shaw's new orchestra, which was on its way to California to play the popular "Kraft Music Hall" radio show. "The band broke up after Dallas and never made it to the Coast," Zarchey recalls. "My first day back in New York I went to the Pennsylvania Hotel to see the guys. Chris and Ziggy and Hymie came over right away, and the first thing Chris says is, 'Wait till you hear this new guy who joined the band. He's really something.' When the band came on I heard Harry James for the first time, and I couldn't believe it. What a sound! Fire came out of that trumpet every time he picked up his horn. It was like a guy throwing a spear. And the approach that he had to the music. And the technique. And the flawless playing and the attack and the virtuosity. It was a tremendous thrill listening to him."

James's breathtaking brilliance put an end to any lingering thoughts Zarchey might have harbored about rejoining the band, and he would have to start looking around for another job. Though he had been with Benny only about three months and had chosen to leave him for a rival orchestra, what happened next provides a good example of the sort of quiet generosity Benny could sometimes rise to despite his abiding self-absorption.

"After the next set Benny came over and said, 'I want you to meet some friends of mine,' then took me back to a table where about six guys were sitting. He introduced me to everyone, and when someone asked me to sit down, Benny excused himself. One of the guys said, 'We're with the Bob Crosby orchestra and we're looking for a first trumpet player and Benny has recommended you very highly. Would you be interested in coming with us?' I said, 'Sure, why not?' So the next morning at nine o'clock I was down at Penn Station and part of the Bob Crosby band."

Zarchey's original replacement was Benny's twenty-two-year-old younger brother Irving, who lived out in Jackson Heights with the rest of the family. Although he occasionally filled in for someone in Benny's trumpet section, Irving always preferred keeping himself away from the long shadow cast by his well-intended but sometimes overbearing big brother, and he eventually engineered his release by selling Benny on Harry James. "I'd heard Harry playing on some Ben Pollack records and kept telling Benny about him. I finally convinced him, and Harry came in the band that January."

At the time of his arrival at the Pennsylvania Hotel, Harry James was a tall, gaunt twenty-one-year-old with a Texas drawl, the pencil-thin mustache of a riverboat gambler and a taste for flashy haberdashery inherited from his circus background. Harry's father, Everette, had played trumpet and led the band in the Mighty Haag Circus, a truck show that toured the South and Southwest. Though not a jazz musician himself, he was greatly admired by such early New Orleans trumpet men as Peter Bocage and Charlie Love for his technical virtuosity. Harry's mother, Mabel, was an aerialist who, so the story goes, continued doing her trapeze act until a month before she gave birth.

Harry began studying trumpet with his father when he was eight years old. By the time he was twelve he was good enough to be leading one of the bands in the Christy Brothers Circus. Like Benny, he was a musical prodigy totally dedicated to his instrument, practicing as many as six hours every day.

His seriousness about mastering the trumpet, solid grounding in technique and early experience blasting out circus marches provided him with the iron lip, spectacular range and distinctive biting sound that formed the basis of his bravura style.

Some four decades later Harry still remembered his first night with the Goodman orchestra:

> Well, Benny wasn't there for the first set. He and Gene and Teddy were somewhere with the Trio playing a benefit and Lionel was playing drums and sort of leading the band. I remember we were playing a stock orchestration of 'A Fine Romance,' and after the first ensemble everybody would play choruses. I took one and then Lionel called out, "Pops, play another!" And then he called out "Play another!" again, and the next thing you know I'm playing six choruses in a row at the dinner session! Finally Benny came in, and after the set I was standing in back, but I could hear Lionel saying excitedly to Benny, "Hey, hey, hey, Pops, this guy can *play!*"

Arthur Rollini was just as impressed. "Harry James was a genius. He could read all of the highly syncopated charts at sight, and he played fantastic jazz solos—different every time. . . . He was also a good conductor and a fine arranger."

Harry's conducting skills were put to excellent use on the "Camel Caravan" broadcasts. Benny always had trouble kicking off the tempo while reading the scripted announcement leading into the next number, and there would be an awkward moment of dead air while he readied himself to set the band's pace. The problem was eliminated when he began having Harry beat off the tunes in his stead. Nor did he let Harry's abilities as a soloist go to waste. Though Benny remained the dominant solo voice on the band's recordings, he featured Harry heavily, more than any of his other sidemen. As a result of this exposure, Harry won first place in the trumpet category of the 1937 *Down Beat* readers poll, coming in ahead of established stars like Bunny Berigan, Roy Eldridge and even Louis Armstrong. The previous year, as a relatively anonymous player in Ben Pollack's band, he had not received a single vote.

By January 1937, then, through the almost random process of comings and goings and casually hired replacements and all the other accidents of circumstance that commonly determined the course of a big band's personnel, the Goodman trumpet section finally completed its evolution and had formed itself into the classic triumvirate of Harry James, Ziggy Elman and Chris Griffin. This powerhouse trio, as it came to be called, played with a precision and drive and spirit-rousing joyfulness that added even more excitement to the band's performances, and it was the perfect vehicle for executing the

Jimmy Mundy killer-dillers that Benny was now favoring. For Hammond, who much preferred Fletcher Henderson's more subtle and relaxed approach to orchestration, "the loud, meaningless 'killer' arrangements which Benny instructs Jimmy Mundy to pound out in mass production each week are definitely detracting from the musicianship of the orchestra." But even he had to admit "there has never been a better trumpet section except in one of Fletcher Henderson's old bands."

This was not an uncommon opinion. Glenn Miller, for one, considered it "the Marvel of the Age." "The best compliment we ever got," Chris Griffin remembers, "is when Duke Ellington once said we were the greatest trumpet section that ever was, as far as his liking." Listen to how the section digs in on some of the live performances recorded during the two years it remained intact—"Down South Camp Meeting" and "Bugle Call Rag," for example, and "Minnie the Moocher's Wedding Day" and "Peckin' " and the Carnegie Hall concert version of "Sing, Sing, Sing"—and it should be perfectly clear what Glenn Miller and Duke Ellington meant.

There was a certain amount of playful competition among the three trumpet men. They had a standing bet of a dollar about who could learn his part in a new arrangement first, and the last one still to resort to the written score was always in for a kidding. But there was also a fierce camaraderie and shared pride in achievement that led them to close ranks whenever Benny tried to interfere with the section's operation. "We always tuned up a little sharper than the rest of the band to make it more brilliant," Chris recalls. "We could cut better that way. But Benny could never quite tune up to where we were, so one night he got the three of us behind the bandstand and said, 'Hey, fellas, it's so sharp I can't get it. Don't you think you ought to tune down, you know?' He looked at Harry—'Don't you?'—and Harry didn't say anything. Then he looked at Ziggy, and Ziggy looked at me, and neither of us said a word. Benny sort of went, 'Whew,' turned around and walked out. And we never changed at all."

In most trumpet sections one man played lead and the others held down the less demanding second and third trumpet chairs. In the Goodman band, though, the lead was alternated among all three players. "They switched the parts around because there were so many high notes for the trumpets they'd wear one guy out," Jess Stacy explains. "They *had* to switch the parts. If they hadn't, one guy would have died."

The Madhattan Room was the first major engagement the Goodman orchestra had played in New York in a year and a half. Willard had deliberately kept the band out of town to build up the anticipation that would ensure its success, and the fans were ready. Well-heeled college kids jammed the room every weekend and over their vacations. As the excitement began to spread, an older, musically more conservative crowd of big spenders also started showing up, helping the hotel set new attendance records. Benny remained at the Pennsylvania for seven heady months, until the end of April. He would return the following October and continue packing them in until he moved on again in January.

It was a hectic but exhilarating time for Benny. The band played the Pennsylvania every night but Sunday from seven to one-thirty. Three nights a week there were live broadcasts from the hotel, and the "Camel Caravan" show every Tuesday. Thursdays after work were set aside for rehearsals, which went on till four in the morning. *The Big Broadcast of 1937* also opened in October and brought him even more visibility. His records were selling better than ever, and every few weeks he was back in the studio turning out new ones. The four months between October and February produced some twenty-five new sides with the big band, over half arranged by Jimmy Mundy, and nine with the trio and quartet. His personal income for the year was estimated at one hundred thousand dollars.

Benny lived at the Pennsylvania during the band's engagement, in a three-room suite hidden off in a corner of the seventh floor that allowed him to maintain his privacy. Along with the usual hotel furniture there were some magazines and records and a phonograph but few other personal touches that might suggest even some degree of permanence. Benny's life out of the spotlight during these months had a low-key, businesslike regularity very much at odds with his burgeoning celebrity. He would get up about noon, have breakfast in the hotel dining room, then return upstairs to do some work. For the next few hours he'd go over the mail with his assistant Dwight Chapin, figure out the tunes he wanted to play that evening and listen to the recordings he'd had made of the band's recent broadcasts to monitor its progress. If he were free for the afternoon, he might take in a movie or matinee, then go back to the hotel and practice. On Sundays he always went out to Jackson Heights to visit his mother and the rest of the family. It was expected of him, and it grounded him in a familiar reality he found reassuring.

"Benny was extremely quiet to the point of being shy," says the veteran record producer George Avakian, then a seventeen-year-old prep school senior Benny had befriended when the knowledgeable young jazz fan came to interview him for the Horace Mann newspaper. "After the set he would just disappear and go up to his room in the hotel. Sometimes he'd invite me to come with him. He'd check the door, and every so often there'd be a girl sleeping in or on the bed, and I'd realize that was Benny's companion for the night. He'd say, 'Well, we can't disturb the lady, can we?' with that chuckle of his, and we'd go into another room. Benny didn't really mix with the public. He wouldn't go table-hopping. Even when there were friends of his in the audience, he'd just spend a moment or two with them and not even sit down. Benny was never at ease in social situations. He never enjoyed meeting strangers, which is too bad in a way, but I suppose it enabled him to maintain his concentration."

Maintaining his concentration was a constant struggle. As the newly annointed "King of Swing" Benny was the man of the hour, and everyone wanted a piece of him. Song pluggers hounded him to display their latest wares on his radio broadcasts and records. Newspaper and magazine writers, many of whom had very little understanding of jazz, besieged him with requests for interviews and, when they were granted, asked him the same routine questions and tried to evoke colorful opinions that would make good copy, which he had neither the temperament nor the inclination to give them. ("Unlike many swing musicians," one of them remarked somewhat ruefully, "he is not a 'personality' lad.") And of course, the fans were everywhere.

Cutting across the normal social and cultural boundaries, they included concert artists like Joseph Szigeti, who showed up regularly at the Madhattan Room, as well as sophisticated *New Yorker* literati like Robert Benchley, S. J. Perelman and E. B. White, who hung out in his hotel room listening to records and basked in his presence at late-night breakfasts at Reuben's restaurant. But the most passionate of all were the hordes of high school and college kids who just wanted to get close to him for a minute because they loved his music so. "It was very difficult for me to appear in public," Benny recalled. "Kids used to try to get into cabs with me, and even though I took off my glasses to keep from being recognized, they followed me everywhere. It was very tiring, but when I remembered that the kids had made us what we were, I tried to be as polite as possible—and most of the time, I must admit, I enjoyed it."

Benny handled the music publishers as best he could, forthrightly but without an abundance of tact. "I think I had a reputation of playing exactly what I wanted to play and nothing else. I couldn't care less who the song belonged to." Journalists often found him just as intractable. "He doesn't talk. He just won't," one complained. "I thought perhaps I wasn't scintillating sufficiently all over the table when I lunched with him the other day. Come to find out I didn't do so badly. He did bring forth the following: 'I don't see why anyone wants to know about me. There's nothing to me. It's just the band.' " Another writer reported:

> It takes a full hour to persuade him of your interest in his comments and observations, and even then there is a slow drawl (sounding definitely Negroid over the telephone and air waves) which betokens uncertainty and shyness. . . . Inability to articulate, and a combination of fear and modesty in delivering pronouncements, all run the greater danger of being interpreted as snobbish aloofness and unwillingness to participate in conversation. Benny has met this danger and taken it on the chin.

Benny's inability to muster up the sort of free and easy affability expected
of a newly successful public figure *was* generating a lot of negative feelings in
the music business as well as the press. Professing that "we don't want to see
one of the finest swing musicians that ever touched an instrument make the
tragic mistake of his life," the February 1937 issue of *Down Beat* took Benny
to task in a severely critical editorial published under the attention-grabbing
headline IS BENNY GOODMAN'S HEAD SWOLLEN?:

> We were frankly amazed at the universal expressions of dislike for Benny
> among musicians, bookers, publishers and other band leaders in New York.
> Even Benny's own musicians couldn't help betraying a certain discomfiture
> and lack of ease with him. Tales of petty snobbery by Benny are on the lips
> of Broadway. Whether they are just or not, we do not know, but where there
> is such a smoke or resentment, there must be some smoldering cause. . . .
> Whether Benny likes it or not, there is a certain cordiality demanded in an
> artist, a certain friendliness that he should genuinely feel towards his associ-
> ates whether he likes them or not. And a sporting spirit of give and take!!
> Your friends can make or break you, Benny, and in all fairness to yourself,
> you should accord them even more consideration than you did when you
> were on the way up!

Metronome quickly sprang to Benny's defense. Although it conceded that
"his music comes first in the thoughts of Benny Goodman, and very often he
is blind to circumstances that do not directly concern its quality," the competing monthly's survey of music publishers, rival bandleaders and other person-
ages in the New York music business supported its contention that the Chicago-based *Down Beat* simply didn't know "the true facts." Artie Shaw replied
with characteristic candor: "The statement is stupid. It's out of the question;
it's just not so. Benny has a lot more on his mind than he used to have, but
he still doesn't come close to having a big head. Anyway, anybody who makes
a crack like that is likely to make the same sort about any orchestra leader,
and I'm going to protect myself too!" Tommy Dorsey responded in much the
same vein: "Hey, that guy's so busy right now he doesn't know if he's coming
or going most of the time. I just saw him the other day, and he had nothing
even remotely resembling a swelled head!"

The most thoughtful and spirited defense of Benny's behavior came from
the pen of John Hammond and appeared in *Down Beat*'s own pages:

> Benny Goodman, like a few other human beings we know, has faults, but
> snobbishness and conceit are not among them. The editorial, which was
> undoubtedly written in good faith, burned me up, because it was asking
> Benny to become a hypocrite with a smile for those he detests. If Benny is
> bored or annoyed by somebody, whether it be the chief booker of the

Paramount Theater, his manager, myself or the editor of *Down Beat,* he makes no attempt to conceal the fact. As far as I've seen, Benny behaves the same way to people in all walks of life; he indulges in remarkably little kowtowing. He has his enemies: music publishers, who are annoyed by his playing standard numbers instead of their commercial tripe, rival bookers who knew him when, and Broadway musicians who resent his preference for Negroes. I believe that men are best judged by their enemies, and Benny has very few that I wouldn't be proud to acknowledge as my own. In the past there were undoubtedly times when he was needlessly avaricious, and that I deplore; but in comparison to the so-called nice guys along Broadway, Benny is a wing-sprouting angel. He is incredibly tactless, to be sure, but I wonder if that is a vice.

The popularity of the Goodman orchestra and of swing bands in general was given a tremendous boost by the emergence of a style of dancing that perfectly matched its exuberant, free-flowing rhythms. Like the music itself, the lindy hop originated in the black community, probably in Harlem, and appears to have taken form even before 1927, when Charles Lindbergh's celebrated solo hop across the Atlantic gave the dance its name.

Marshall and Jean Stearns observed in their seminal history of jazz dancing:

> In a sense, the Lindy is choreographed swing music. Unlike earlier Dixieland jazz, and the Toddle, which was danced to it—a bouncy, up-and-down style of dancing—swing music and the Lindy flowed more horizontally and smoothly. There was more rhythmic continuity. Again, swing music and the Lindy were more complicated, for while a Lindy team often danced together during the opening ensembles of a big band, they tended to go into a breakaway and improvise individual steps when the band arrangement led into a solo. The similarity is conscious and intentional, for jazz dancers follow the music closely.

The lindy (later also called the jitterbug, though this first seems to have been a term of derision for the jerky movements of white dancers who imperfectly imitated the black originators) was nurtured and brought to full maturity at the Savoy Ballroom, "the home of happy feet," to the music of hard-hitting black swing bands like Chick Webb. Under the canny, if tyrannical, supervision of the Savoy's bouncer, an ex-thug named Herbert White, the young dancers who came there to hone their skills and compete with one another for their own pleasure were eventually organized into semiprofessional troupes that were seen, then emulated by white audiences.

The first major step in this crossover was accomplished when White managed to have his lindy hoppers included in the *Daily News'* Harvest Moon

Ball dance competition held in Madison Square Garden in August 1935, the same month Benny broke through at the Palomar. Providing a dramatic contrast with the constrained formality of the waltzes, tangos and fox-trots performed by the other dancers, the uninhibited lindy hoppers created a sensation and were hired to strut their stuff in downtown clubs and even tour Europe. The following summer they achieved widespread national exposure when they appeared in the Marx Brothers movie *A Day at the Races*. By then the Savoy had become a favorite tourist stop for movie stars and other celebrities and was frequented by white youngsters who watched and learned and took their lessons home with them. "We didn't mind that people came from downtown to watch us," Norma Miller, one of the original lindy hoppers, maintained. "No white kids could ever cut us up on the ballroom floor, but we liked it that they tried. When they came close, we'd just ask the band to up the tempo."

It was during Benny's stay at the Pennsylvania Hotel that Helen Ward first became aware of the couples lindy-hopping on the dance floor: "Out on the Coast there were wall-to-wall people, and nobody could dance. They just stood there and yelled and hollered and screamed. Oh, here and there a few people would dance, but they just did the regular fox-trot. They didn't really start lindying until we came back to New York and went into the Madhattan Room. In the beginning they were all dressed up, but then when the lindy really caught on, the gals began wearing saddle shoes and the socks and the full skirts, which was the necessary gear to do all those gyrations. I was always very dance-conscious, so it was very exciting to me. I thought it was great because it was expressing the spirit the guys had in them up on the bandstand. It goes without saying that an appreciative audience that responds enthusiastically is the most inspirational thing that could ever happen to a band, and the better the reaction, the better the guys play. There's nothing more deadly than sitting in a studio and staring at the four walls. So the dancers made the music even more exciting. It used to kill me to have to stand up and sing while everybody else was out there dancing."

If the advent of the lindy stoked the fires of Benny's new popularity, what happened next caused a full-scale conflagration.

On March 3, 1937, the Goodman orchestra began a two-week engagement at the Paramount Theater on Times Square. Benny wasn't expecting anything much to come of it. It was Lent. He had worked only a few theater dates before, and they all had been, as he put it, "less than sensational." But there would be pretty good money and more exposure in the press, and the Paramount was having considerable success with its new big band stage show policy.

Big bands had started playing the Broadway movie houses at the beginning of the decade, but as Guy Lombardo, who preceded Benny at the Paramount, explained, "It turned out to be an expensive proposition for the theaters because of demands by union stagehands to be paid for moving the bandstand, the chairs, the instruments before and after the other acts." By 1934 the Paramount had dropped its stage shows and was playing only movies. Then the theater's manager, a young man named Bob Weitman, came up with a bright idea that was soon emulated by every other large movie theater in the country that also offered live entertainment. By installing a rising orchestra pit that ascended from the basement like an elevator and came to rest in the front of the stage, he not only cut down on the need for all those expensive stagehands but also sped up the tempo of the show and brought the bands closer to the audience.

Weitman reintroduced big bands to the Paramount over the Christmas holidays of 1935 by booking the Casa Loma for two weeks. The experiment proved wildly successful, grossing fifty-five thousand dollars the first week, as opposed to only eighty-five hundred the week before. In the months that followed, the theater also drew large crowds with Hal Kemp, Isham Jones, Eddy Duchin, Richard Himber, Fred Waring and Guy Lombardo. Apart from the Casa Loma, these all were sweet commercial orchestras that had almost nothing in common with the sort of music the Goodman band was known for. The Paramount was aware of Benny's growing popularity on radio and records but offered him the job mainly because it felt a hot band was needed to balance the somber picture it had scheduled, an unpromising Claudette Colbert drama about witch-hunts called *Maid of Salem.*

The band arrived at the Paramount at 7:00 A.M. to rehearse before the opening show. Several hundred youngsters had dragged themselves out of bed even earlier and were now lined up in front of the box office. Benny found this surprising but tried to make light of it. "We couldn't help feeling that every one of our most loyal supporters in the five boroughs was already on hand." But while the musicians waited in the basement, word came backstage that the huge theater was already sold out and the restless audience of youngsters was in unusually high spirits. Finally Claudette Colbert's tribulations came to an end. The men climbed aboard the bandstand and picked up their instruments. As the elevator brought them up to the stage, Benny kicked off the tempo on "Let's Dance," their familiar opening theme. When they came into view, they were greeted with an ear-shattering roar of clapping and whistling and stomping and yelling that sounded, Benny remembered, "like Times Square on New Year's Eve." "It was exciting," he recalled, "but also a little frightening—scary."

The band swung into "Bugle Call Rag," quieted things down a bit with "Star Dust," then after Edith Mann's brief tap dance routine, brought the energy level back up again with Jimmy Mundy's killer arrangement of "Ridin'

High." And riding high they were—Harry, Ziggy, Vido, Jess, Gene and the rest of the crew, madmen with a purpose wailing away at ten-thirty in the morning (who could believe it?) at the very top of their form. The audience cheered and screamed, crowded the stage, even began jitterbugging in the aisles. "Ladies and gentlemen . . . ladies and gentlemen," Benny beseeched them, trying to make himself heard over the din. But they would have none of it, so he just stood there with his finger raised like a teacher in front of an unruly classroom until they finally settled down enough for the show to continue. Frances Hunt, Helen Ward's replacement, sang a few songs; Fritz and Jean Hubert did their drunk dancing comedy turn; then it was time for the trio and quartet. Benny and Teddy and Gene started out sedately enough with "Body and Soul," but then Lionel joined them, and they turned up the heat, raising the temperature to a rolling boil as they served up chorus after steaming chorus of "I Got Rhythm." There seemed nowhere left to go, but now the orchestra reclaimed the spotlight and brought the crowd to full climax as it kicked out the jambs on "Sing, Sing, Sing," the killer-diller to end all killer-dillers. The swing-intoxicated throng was still pleading for more as the bandstand slid out of sight and the houselights were raised.

It was apparent to everyone—Benny and the band, the Paramount management, the assembled members of the press and the thousands of still-ecstatic youngsters—that something truly momentous had just taken place, that the Goodman orchestra's brief forty-three-minute sojourn on the Paramount stage was some kind of breakthrough that topped, and was different from, all its previous successes. What started out as just another stage show had turned into a kind of celebration of the spirit, a love feast of communal frenzy that was, as *Variety* observed, "tradition-shattering in its spontaneity, its unanimity, its sincerity, its volume, in the childlike violence of its manifestations."

What caused this to happen is, in retrospect, stunningly obvious. The school kids were among Benny's most zealous fans, and this was the first chance they had to hear him in person. The Hotel Pennsylvania was fine for the Ivy League college students who loved the band, too, but it was completely beyond the reach of the legions of ordinary youngsters who, up to now, could only listen to Benny on the radio or spring for an occasional record. As tough as things were for most of their families, it wasn't all that hard to get together the twenty-five cents it took to buy a ticket to the Paramount before one o'clock. And if it meant cutting school for the day, so be it; what better way to answer the call to freedom and abandon that was the underlying message of the music?

By the end of the day the Paramount had sold an astonishing twenty-one thousand admissions, even though many of the kids refused to go home and held on to their seats for two and even three shows. (No wonder the theater also sold a record-breaking nine hundred dollars' worth of candy.) The gross for the first week was fifty-eight thousand dollars, twice the amount brought in by Guy Lombardo's popular orchestra the week before. Ticket sales for the second week totaled forty-five thousand dollars, and Benny was held over for a third, delaying the return of Eddy Duchin. The band did a very good thirty-five thousand dollars, even though it was now Easter, and would have been extended again if it hadn't had other commitments.

As impressive as they are, these numbers tell only part of the story. Other bands had done as well at the Paramount and in a few cases slightly better. Eddy Duchin grossed $59,500 the week after Benny, only $100 less than the all-time high set by Ray Noble and the Cecil B. De Mille epic *The Plainsman*. But neither Duchin nor Noble nor any of the other bands generated the uncontrolled excitement of the Goodman orchestra, and it was this uninhibited emotionalism, more than anything, that captured the public imagination and the attention of the press and brought Benny up to a new plateau of popularity.

When Benny played his next theater date in May, there was a repeat of the same phenomenon. The *Boston Morning Globe* reported:

The Metropolitan Theater yesterday appeared to hold every boy and girl in Greater Boston who could beg a school "absent" excuse from a tolerant parent. Benny Goodman, King of Swing, is in town, which means that the youngsters of the city are in their seventh heaven of rapture. . . . What shrieks of joy as he played "Alexander's Ragtime Band" in his own swingy rhythms! What yells and whistles and stampings followed Gene Krupa's exhibitions!

And so it went throughout the rest of the country.

Looking back at the Paramount and its aftermath many years later, Benny characteristically shrugged off whatever excitement he may have felt at the time with faintly amused disdain:

When we got on the [Paramount] stage the first time the audience was in such hysteria and so enthusiastic we couldn't play, so we just sat there for four or five minutes and said, "When you get through applauding, well— we'll play." We looked at them, I guess, [as if] they were the show and we were the audience. . . . They always used to talk about the dancing in the aisles at the Paramount Theater, and we always would try to avoid it. I mean, if anyone came on stage or danced in the aisles, we thought it was rather ridiculous, and we'd try to stop it all the time—but the people succeeded in doing it anyway. . . . And then we'd go to another place like Philadelphia or Detroit, and the manager would say, "What about the kids dancing in the aisles?" I'd say, "Well, I don't know about the kids dancing in the aisles. What do we have to do with that?" He would be rather disappointed if the whole theater didn't get up and dance whereas we were always trying to curtail it and avoid it because it did interfere with the actual program that was going on.

The jazz purists, not to mention the guardians of public morality, were even more disapproving. But the kids dancing in the aisles remain to this day the single most powerful image of the Swing Era triumphant, sharing a place in the gallery of pop iconography with the bobby-soxers swooning over Frank Sinatra in the 1940s and the teenyboppers driven to hysterics by the Beatles two decades later. Curiously, though, as with Sinatra's swooning bobby-soxers, it was not as entirely extemporaneous as it first seemed.

Two months after the Paramount opening a one-line item buried in a *Down Beat* gossip column praised "the inspired move of Mr. McInnerney, purveyor of propaganda for the theater, who arranged for couples to dance in the aisles at the first show." This salient bit of information came and went without attracting much notice and has never been incorporated into the standard accounts of the Paramount triumph. But it appears to be perfectly accurate. The trumpet player Jimmy Maxwell, who joined Benny in 1939, tells us, "The guys in the band sort of laughed at me when I said something about the dancing in the aisles. Then I asked Benny's manager Leonard Vannerson, and he explained what happened. The first two or three people to get up and dance were ringers, and then the other kids started dancing spontaneously. And after it got in the newspapers, everybody started doing it."

Arthur Rollini still remembers the crowds of young girls waiting at the Paramount stage door who would "do anything" to have a date with the boys in the band and all the heated fan mail with telephone numbers and outright propositions and the endless requests for autographs and how Benny "stayed aloof."

For Hammond the best commentary on the Paramount success was that the theater's black patronage increased more than 500 percent. "Goodman's appeal to Harlemites is due not only to his music but to the fact that he is the first band leader to break down the color line in music," he explained. The following month he reported that the color line continued to fall even further. Because Lionel and Teddy were such a huge hit at the Paramount, Benny had been asked to appear with the quartet in his next Hollywood movie. "It is amusing to note that commercial success has a magnificent way of eliminating color segregation," Hammond concluded. "Maybe the comrades are right in saying that the root of all difficulty between the two races is a matter of economics."

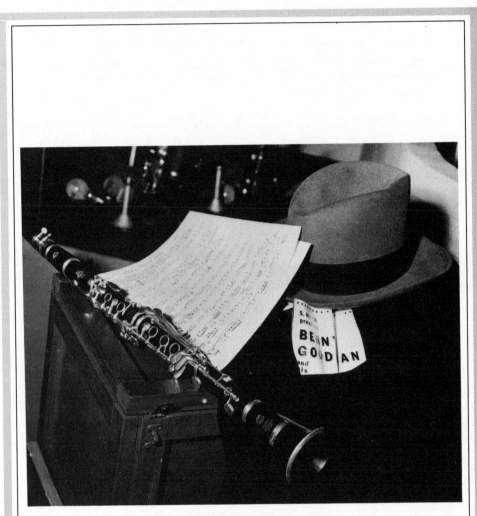

Carnegie Hall still life, January 1938.
From the Benny Goodman Archives in the Music Library at Yale University

14

Carnegie Jump

On the night of May 11, 1937, two weeks after he closed at the Pennsylvania, Benny took the band up to the Savoy Ballroom to engage in a battle of music with Chick Webb's mighty orchestra. The event was billed as the "Music Battle of the Century," and some ten thousand wildly enthusiastic swing fans crowded the sidewalk in front of the box office, trying to jam their way in. Only about four thousand succeeded, enough to set a new attendance record, and the rest spilled over onto Lenox Avenue, tying up traffic for hours.

"Music battles" were sometimes just a promoter's way of publicizing a joint appearance of two popular orchestras, but this was the real thing. Though Chick Webb was trapped in the hopelessly crippled body of a hunchbacked dwarf and in almost constant pain, he was a fiercely competitive bandleader as well as a very great drummer, and he neither asked for nor offered any quarter in encounters of this nature. And he had more than the usual reasons for wanting to emerge triumphant this particular evening. Webb's arranger Edgar Sampson had given Benny some of his biggest hits, including "Stompin' at the Savoy" and "If Dreams Come True," while his own orchestra struggled along playing the same charts without anything like the same adulation and commercial success. Nor could he have been too pleased that Benny had "borrowed" Ella Fitzgerald, his star vocalist, for a recording session six months earlier especially since it was Ella's growing popularity that was bringing him his first taste of national recognition. Nor, for that matter, could he have found it acceptable that Gene Krupa, who learned much from him, was widely regarded as the best drummer in the country. Chick Webb was, by all accounts, a kind and generous man, but he had his pride as well as the true champion's love of battle.

Benny started off in high gear with the Harry James killer-diller "Peckin'," and the crowd went wild. But the moment Webb opened up on his drums, it went even wilder. Benny regrouped during the intermission and began the second set with a rousing rendition of Jimmy Mundy's "Jam Session," one of his current big crowd pleasers. Chick, though, was waiting for him and cannily responded with his own version of the piece, which brought down the house. The grin that lit up Webb's face revealed he knew he had already won. For all practical purposes the contest was over.

Some listeners believed that the Savoy Ballroom defeat proved the Goodman band didn't really deserve all the acclaim that was now coming its way. And according to Hammond, it still seemed to be feeling the aftereffects when it played a night at Roseland the following week and "once again failed to give a proper account of itself." Yet it was right back on course by the time it engaged in another battle with Roy Eldridge in Chicago the next month. Roy's tenor man Dave Young remembers that "Roy was in great form that night, [and] we blew the ceiling off that place." But then the Goodman band "went right through the ceiling and the crowd went with them. Those white boys were playing those black arrangements with a togetherness you wouldn't believe."

The band had left New York the beginning of June. On June 29 it was to begin its third engagement at the Palomar Ballroom in Los Angeles, but before then it had to face a full month on the road. Aside from a few theater dates, the tour consisted almost entirely of one-nighters in widely scattered ballrooms across Pennsylvania, Ohio, Indiana and Iowa. There were endless problems with transportation, and the blazing midwestern heat forced the musicians to strip down to their shorts as the rickety chartered bus bounced them along to their next destination. Benny and Arthur Rollini both credit the orchestra's coolly efficient bandboy Pee Wee Monte with keeping the inevitable difficulties from getting too out of hand. Rollini also recalls the band's irritation when Benny kept them waiting on the bus for an hour and a half while he trysted with a young lady in his hotel room, then finally climbed aboard without the slightest apology.

However exhausting and filled with annoyance, the tour was an enormous success. Everywhere Benny went he was greeted with the same overwhelming enthusiasm. The temperature soared to 102 degrees the day he played the small farming town of Olwin, Iowa, but hundreds of musicians turned up from as far away as Minneapolis and Omaha, and the audience crowded twenty deep around the bandstand, urging him on to five, six, seven, eight encores. The response was equally ecstatic when he opened at the Palomar at the end of the month. The Casa Loma had set a house record the previous week, topping Benny's earlier draw of fifty-five hundred admissions, but the seven thousand Goodman fans who turned up that night established a new one. The huge ballroom was so packed there was no room to dance, but nobody really minded. They were just happy to be there, and they stood shoulder to shoulder, swaying to the band's rhythms like the waves ebbing and flowing on the Malibu shore.

A few weeks later Benny began shooting *Hollywood Hotel*, his second movie. Hammond was displeased that the film was financed by the right-wing newspaper publisher William Randolph Hearst and that his minion Louella Parsons had a strong hand in it. Yet even he had to admit the sound recording was "nothing less than perfection," and the band and quartet came through marvelously well in their featured spots.

Galvanized by Gene's and Lionel's almost manic exuberance, the quartet is so electrifying it practically leaps off the screen on "I've Got a Heartful of Music," a pop tune that incorporates the exciting stop-and-go routine it had worked out for "I Got Rhythm." The full band is equally exciting on "Sing, Sing, Sing," giving those of us born too late a heart-thumping approximation of what it must have been like to hear it in person. "They wanted us to record it first and then go through the motions of simulating playing to the music," Benny explained. "Well, we could never do that with 'Sing, Sing, Sing' because we would always improvise and we never knew exactly what we did. So we insisted that the only way we could possibly film it was to have four or five or half a dozen cameras going on at the same time, play it through once and that would be it. And that is exactly the way we did it."

So many other things were going on Benny hadn't set foot in a recording studio in five months, and now that he had settled down in California for the summer he began to make up for lost time. Working around the *Hollywood Hotel* shooting schedule, the band recorded a number of soon-to-be-classic instrumentals, including "Peckin'," "Sing, Sing, Sing" and Mary Lou Williams's boogie-woogie rave-up "Roll 'Em." Benny also did some sessions with the quartet as well as his final date as a sideman with Teddy Wilson. And on September 6, two days after he finished up at the Palomar and was preparing to go back on the road, he made the first two sides with his new singer, Martha Tilton.

Benny had tried out a number of vocalists after Helen Ward's departure, but it wasn't until he heard Martha Tilton with the Meyer Alexander Chorus on the "Camel Caravan" show that he finally found what he wanted. Tilton had worked with Jimmy Dorsey's orchestra earlier that year, so she already had some swing band experience. In addition to being a good, musicianly singer, she was an extremely attractive blonde and projected a warm, wholesome girl-next-door presence. She remained with the band for close to two years, taking part in some of Benny's more sizable pop hits like "Loch Lomond," "Bei Mir Bist du Schön" and "And the Angels Sing." These last two served up unmistakably Yiddish melodies, and on both recordings Ziggy Elman's old-country *fraylich* trumpet shared the spotlight with the *echt* WASP singer.

Benny returned to the Hotel Pennsylvania on October 11. As an added attraction, the dance entrepreneur Arthur Murray brought in a troupe of white jitterbugs to demonstrate the "shag break," "peckin' and posin'," "peel the apple" and all the other latest steps cribbed from the lindy hoppers uptown. On November 1 *Life* magazine, one of the most influential periodicals in the country, devoted its regular "Life Goes to a Party" feature to a four-page celebration of the Madhattan Room engagement. "A nightly scene of wild adulation," the magazine called it, "where intermittent dancing and dining is subordinated to the almost scholarly pleasure of listening to Benny 'feel his stuff.'" To make the most of this important national publicity, Benny christened a new Harry James jump tune "Life Goes to a Party," quickly recorded it and sent the lead sheet off to the *Life* letters to the editor column along with an effusive thank-you note.

Despite a few complaints from jazz purists that its striving for excitement was leading it into a dead end of sterile virtuosity, the Goodman band was riding higher than ever—broadcasting from the Pennsylvania at least once a night, kicking off the new season of the "Camel Caravan" show and turning out endless new records. Its personnel had remained essentially unchanged for close to a year, but during the fall of 1937 it suffered two important losses. Early in October the phenomenal trombone player Murray McEachern handed in his notice to go with the Casa Loma Orchestra. ("I got talked into leaving by Harry James. It turned out he wanted to get his friend Vernon Brown into the band. Harry was a great con merchant and sold me a bill of goods.") And then a month later Vido Musso suddenly disappeared. "I do not know to this day what happened," Arthur Rollini tells us. "Vido said no goodbyes but just vanished." Chris Griffin remembers: "His place was immediately taken by Babe Russin, an excellent but delicate player. We used to play behind Vido full and loud, and he'd always top it, and we did the same thing with poor Babe. His first night on the job he went over to a friend between sets with tears in his eyes and said, 'I don't know what to do. I can't play with this band. Those guys in the brass section are so loud I can't even hear myself.' But he eventually got used to it and stayed for quite a while."

It was a great winter for swing music in New York. Tommy Dorsey was playing across town at the Palm Room of the Commodore Hotel. After two years on the Coast his brother Jimmy returned east and replaced the Casa Loma at the New Yorker. Cab Calloway was at the Cotton Club. Mezz Mezzrow's short-lived all-star mixed orchestra played a brief engagement at the Harlem Uproar House. Chick Webb was still taking on all comers at the Savoy. Louis Prima and Art Tatum were holding forth at the Famous Door. In January Count Basie went into the Loew's State on Broadway.

Nevertheless, a number of sweet band leaders and unsympathetic journalists were beginning to prophesy that the swing craze was just about over. The professional moralists, though, weren't so sure and were starting to voice their alarm that swing's savage hold over the younger generation was transforming the youth of the country into uninhibited sexual maniacs. Their concern was given "scientific" credibility by one Arthur Cremin, director of the New York Schools of Music, in a series of experiments that showed when boys and girls were left alone, they conversed together as usual if classical music was played but started necking freely as soon as the music was changed to swing. Cremin's conclusion: There ought to be legislation outlawing the pernicious stuff before the morals of modern youth are corrupted beyond redemption.

It is these background murmurings of dissent that allow us to appreciate the sheer brilliance of the idea that, with one masterful stroke, reaffirmed the supremacy of the Goodman band in the face of growing competition, demonstrated the ongoing vitality of swing and conferred a cultural (and therefore moral) legitimacy upon the music that, at least for the moment, raised it loftily beyond the reach of those seeking to write it off or do away with it.

The idea was to present the Benny Goodman orchestra in concert at Carnegie Hall, and it was the brainchild of Wynn Nathanson, a publicist with the Tom Fizdale agency, which was handling the "Camel Caravan" account. Then, much more than now, Carnegie Hall was a bastion of musical propriety, "an import house of Old World traditions," as John McDonough puts it, "whose snobby smirks toward American culture had a way of making status-sensitive Yankees feel like Babbitts for comparing—or God forbid, preferring—Gershwin to Wagner or Tatum to Horowitz." If Nathanson's idea was basically a publicity stunt, it was also a serious bid for musical parity, a demand that Benny and the kind of quintessentially American music he represented be given the same attention and respect accorded the culturally sanctioned concert music of Europe.

Benny greeted Nathanson's suggestion with the same almost reflexive negativity he'd shown in the past when asked to break new ground. "You must be out of your mind!" he remembered telling the publicist. Not that he didn't have his reasons. The prospect of appearing in the same hall where Stokowski and Toscanini made their marks must have seemed a little intimidating. And as he explained some years later, "I didn't like the idea of playing concerts on the stage with a band. I kind of liked the feeling of the audience right close to you and more or less giving them their choice as to whether they wanted to listen or dance." Then, too, "Playing a job at a place like the Madhattan Room of the Pennsylvania Hotel, where we were then, or most any place, we'd usually start kind of quietly. Play dinner music, so to speak. Warm up a little. It wasn't until later that the band really got rocking. But in a concert you had to hit right from the top, bang!" And of course, if the bang turned into a fizzle, the failure not only would be a personal embarrassment but could also have damaging consequences for a career that was swinging along as hard as one of Jimmy Mundy's killer-dillers without Carnegie Hall.

Nathanson met Benny's objections, explaining that he could handle the concert in his own terms, doing what he always did, and Benny eventually came around. The publicist then moved on to the next phase of his plan, which was to persuade the impresario Sol Hurok to present the event under his auspices. Hurok had long been a major broker of high culture in New York, sponsoring distinguished attractions like the Ballet Russe de Monte Carlo, Anna Pavlova, Feodor Chaliapin, Isadora Duncan and the Moscow Art Players, and his imprimatur would add that much more cachet to the band's appearance. Irving Kolodin, the classical music reviewer for the *New York Sun,* who was also a Goodman fan, happened to be sitting in the office of Hurok's press chief Gerald Goode the December afternoon when Nathanson called. "What would you think of a concert by Benny Goodman's band in Carnegie?" Goode asked him, putting Nathanson on hold. "A terrific idea," Kolodin answered. Paul Whiteman had performed there in 1925. Louis Armstrong and Duke Ellington both had played successful concert engagements in Europe. And of course, Benny had already proved he could draw large crowds of serious listeners at his Sunday afternoon concerts at the Congress Hotel in Chicago. Goode passed the proposition on to Hurok. Hurok was dubious, but his misgivings were somewhat relieved when he went to hear Benny at the Madhattan Room. According to Kolodin, though Hurok was "quite taken aback by the uproar of the band, . . . so many well-dressed people spending money on an attraction was obviously a good omen."

Hurok booked Carnegie Hall for Sunday evening, January 16, the night after Benny finished his three-month stay at the Pennsylvania. Benny began planning the program. Kolodin, who had recently published a history of the Metropolitan Opera, was commissioned to write an elaborate set of program notes "addressed to those whose knowledge of swing is limited," explaining the music and giving a moment by moment analysis of each selection in the erudite style of classical concert guides. ("Don't Be That Way," for example, "features a graceful legato phrase, first heard from the saxophone section immediately after the introduction, punctuated by a rhythmic figure from the brass. The brass has the lead in the middle section of the thirty-two measure tune, thereafter reverting to the first pattern again." And so on.) The house was scaled, and the tickets were printed; prices ranged from a low of 85 cents for the upper balcony to $2.75 for the boxes, somewhat less than the $2 to $3 charged for the Philharmonic Symphony. The advertisements were placed. The handbills were distributed. "S. Hurok presents Benny Goodman and his Swing Orchestra in the first swing concert in the history of Carnegie Hall," they proclaimed, heralding the significance of the event in overheated prose of glistening purple hue:

> From Louisiana's swampland a trumpet blared and a clarinet screamed to trapdrum syncopation. Critics thought it vulgar, cacophonic, and scowlingly called it jazz. The infant idiom begged at the door of musical America. Refused admittance to the homes of pundits, it swirled clamorously into the life of the common man. Still yearning for acceptance by the tutored, it became "sweet" and "symphonic" in turn, a traitor to its origins. Losing finally its inferiority complex, it surged forward again, flying its own colors, but with a new name, "swing." Despite the mysticists, swing is jazz grown mature and strong. Its orchestrations and polyrhythmic structures have earned the admiration of such musicians as Stravinsky and Stokowski. . . . Benny Goodman . . . the leading innovator in America today of swing, and himself one of the world's greatest virtuosi of the clarinet . . . will render music which is the daily stimulus of fifty millions of Americans—music which centuries from now will be unquestioningly called American folk-music, compositions which are as indigenous to this life as a Bach passacaglia is to the eighteenth century.

No wonder Benny was nervous.

As January 16 approached, "I kind of got cold feet," he recalled, so he asked the fey British comedienne Beatrice Lillie, who had appeared with him on the "Camel Caravan" show, to warm up the audience with a few jokes. Hurok was appalled. "[I] believe it will bring about a certain amount of ridicule from the music critics—who are the very ones you should be seeking to impress," he wrote Willard Alexander in an icy letter that also took issue with the plans for dressing up the band in "theatrical costumes" and having it play against a background of black curtains and special lighting effects. ("This is contrary to musical tradition and will only serve to neutralize the very dignity which you are seeking to obtain.") Bea Lillie felt much the same way and, as Benny put it, "was smart enough to say no." The theatrical costumes and show biz presentation were also abandoned.

Benny insisted upon rehearsing the band in Carnegie Hall several days before the concert to familiarize himself with its particularly lively acoustics. The publicity for the concert was building, along with the personal tensions, and when Douglas Gilbert of the *World-Telegram* dropped by for an interview, Benny was wound so tight he practically snapped his head off. "Now that swing has achieved the dignity of Carnegie Hall," Gilbert started out, but Benny cut him short before he could even finish his question. "Listen," he shot back, "Szigeti and a lot of the top men have listened to me and recognize swing as modern and original stuff. They know it's got something. Why, if a lot of the concert stars had Lionel Hampton's rhythm, they'd be even greater. And the arrangements I play of Fletcher Henderson's are classics, and Jimmy Mundy's too." Benny was just as defensive when asked about swing's current state of health ("Maybe swing is dying, as some guy wrote. Maybe the public is getting tired of it. I can't prove it. I can prove the opposite") and about Gilbert's less than tactful query as to whether the band was good for another three years ("Three years? What the hell! That's a long time").

Any doubts Benny might have had about the band's future were considerably eased when *Hollywood Hotel* opened at the Strand Theater in Times Square on January 12, just four days before the concert. Goodman fans flooded the lobby and overflowed down Broadway, causing the police department to call out the reserves. According to the *New York Times:*

> Mr. Goodman could not so much as poke his clarinet into camera range yesterday without producing an ovation. His followers, whose name—as you have guessed—is legion, beat their hands as though they had toughened them in brine for days. They stamped their feet, and there didn't seem to be a rubber heel in the house. They whistled, they bleated, they cooed and they got rhythm and they almost drowned out the picture. . . . They were yowling for more when we left.

Benny had worked out a program that balanced some of the more familiar items in the band's repertoire ("Sometimes I'm Happy," "Blue Skies," "Swingtime in the Rockies," "Sing, Sing, Sing") with relatively new numbers only recently or not yet recorded (Edgar Sampson's reorchestration of "Don't Be That Way," Count Basie's "One O'Clock Jump," Harry James's "Life Goes to a Party, Claude Thornhill's "Loch Lomond"). To underscore the contribution made by the great American songwriters, he also commissioned Fletcher Henderson to write new arrangements of Rodgers and Hart's "Blue Room" and Jerome Kern's "Make Believe." (Only "Blue Room" was finished in time to be performed.) The trio and quartet were to close out the first half of the evening. In keeping with the special character of the occasion,

Benny decided to include two special presentations: a thumbnail history of hot music called "Twenty Years of Jazz," and an extended, let-the-chips-fall-where-they-may jam session that would feature some of the stars from the Count Basie and Duke Ellington bands along with his own soloists.

By the morning of January 16, all 2,760 seats in Carnegie Hall had long since been sold, and so had the 100 extra chairs set up on the side of the stage to provide for the overflow. When some of Benny's family decided at the last minute to come in from Chicago, he had to buy their tickets from a scalper. It was a bitter cold day, but around two o'clock in the afternoon a line began forming outside the box office for the standing room admissions that would go on sale when the doors finally opened. The *New York Times Magazine* had given the event a big write-up that morning ("Swing It! And Even in a Temple of Music"), and it had become the hottest ticket in town. Inside the hall the New York Philharmonic was playing one of its regular Sunday afternoon concerts. As the sun began to set, the Goodman musicians and guest artists started assembling backstage.

"Sure, I'm nervous," Harry James told the reporter from *Down Beat.* "You know—Carnegie Hall—after all. . . ." Babe Russin said he had fortified himself with a half gallon of blackberry wine. Teddy Wilson was as self-contained and impassive as ever. Benny claimed to be taking it all in stride, but as he leafed through some papers, his hands were visibly trembling. Duke Ellington's singer Ivie Anderson dropped backstage to say hello. "I guess this is the top," she told the musicians who were standing around comparing their respective degrees of nervousness. "Say, I was so nervous when I made my first movie, my knees knocked together!" To help ease the tension, she lifted her Persian lamb coat and gave everybody a demonstration. Back in the special dressing room normally reserved for the Philharmonic conductors, Jess Stacy was fooling around at the piano. Benny and some of the others joined him, and they started jamming together softly. Martha Tilton showed up in an expensive pink tulle party dress she had bought at Lord & Taylor especially for the occasion. Lionel Hampton was the last one to arrive. It was almost time to get started.

As the ticket holders converged upon Carnegie Hall, they were met by a picket line protesting Benny's support of the Loyalists in the Spanish Civil War. No doubt at Hammond's urging (Benny had no discernible politics), he had played several benefits while he was at the Pennsylvania. The past May he had also been one of the sponsors of a fund raiser put on at the Belasco Theater by the anti-Franco Theater Committee for Aid to Spanish Democracy. Although the pro-Franco pickets included a number of priests, no one is known to have turned around and gone home.

A scattering of Carnegie Hall regulars, including some older gentlemen in soup and fish and dowagers in evening gowns, had shown up for the concert. ("Remember, son," Paul Whiteman had wired Benny in his congratulatory telegram, "a clarinet sounds just as good to a lorgnette.") Helen Ward was there with her husband, Albert Marx, who had arranged to have the event recorded as a present for his wife, as was Bill Savory, whose brilliant restoration of the old acetates allowed them to be released commercially more than a decade later. There were also a number of classical musicians like Joseph Szigeti, the Metropolitan Opera's Rose Bampton and the Viennese harpsicordist Yella Pessl, who had been giving Teddy Wilson weekly lessons on the instrument. But the audience was predominantly youthful and dominated by Benny's usual fans—the same college students who came to hear him at the Pennsylvania and the adolescent schoolboys who cheered him on at the Paramount. So much for Irving Kolodin's elaborate program notes explaining swing to the uninitiated.

The concert began promptly at eight forty-five. Just before the musicians took the stage, Harry James was heard to mutter the now-immortal line "I feel like a whore in church." Olin Downes reported in the *New York Times* the next morning, "When Mr. Goodman entered he received a real Toscanini send-off from the excited throng. It took some minutes to establish quiet. There was a quivering excitement in the air, an almost electrical effect, and much laughter."

Benny set the tempo for "Don't Be That Way" and gave the downbeat. Still feeling a bit pressured, the band started out tense and unsettled, but then Gene Krupa took command with a forceful drum break that drew tremendous applause and put everyone in the right groove. "By the time we got to the end of the first piece," Chris Griffin remembers, "we were back home." After a flowing run-through of "Sometimes I'm Happy," Jess Stacy offered up the first great solo of the night with his four chorus lead-in to "One O'Clock Jump," foreshadowing what was to come at the astonishing climax of the concert and setting the pace for the fine solos that followed by Babe Russin, Vernon Brown, Benny and Harry. The band built steadily through chorus after chorus of the ensemble ride-out, eliciting more shouts and applause from the enraptured audience.

"The idea for the historical 'Twenty Years of Jazz' was, I'm afraid, mine," Kolodin explained in his notes to the recordings of the concert. "I apologize for it because it probably caused more trouble listening to old records and copying off arrangements than it was worth." A fair enough statement. The series of brief vignettes started off with a tribute to the Original Dixieland Jazz Band, five white New Orleans musicians who had achieved great commercial success when they appeared in New York back in 1917 but hardly merited such attention on either historical or musical grounds. The fine cornetist Bobby Hackett then made a guest appearance, playing Bix Beiderbecke's classic solo on "I'm Coming Virginia" at less than the top of his form.

("I was very frightened," Hackett recalled. "I got stuck with the assignment, which I didn't want to do and I'm sorry I did.") This was followed by Benny's deliberately corny send-up of Ted Lewis's "When My Baby Smiles at Me," which brought a spot of humor into the program but still seemed out of place.

Harry's homage to Louis Armstrong came next, an overly frantic killer-dillerized version of the final choruses of Louis's 1931 solo on "Shine." Then Duke Ellington's Cootie Williams, Johnny Hodges and Harry Carney joined the Goodman rhythm section for an absolutely gorgeous full-scale rendition of Duke's "Blue Reverie" that made the whole "Twenty Years of Jazz" gimmick worthwhile. According to a friend of Ellington's who was sitting next to him that night, Duke had been invited to present his own concert at Carnegie Hall the year before, but his manager, Irving Mills, rejected the offer because there wasn't enough money in it. Perhaps Mills did have half a point. Benny's expenses ran so high the concert went into the red even with every seat in the house sold out. But then again, the benefits in publicity and prestige far outweighed the financial loss. Understandably enough, Ellington was said to be looking "kind of disgruntled."

The band returned for a spirited reading of "Life Goes to a Party." Then it was time for the jam session. Benny, Harry, Vernon and Gene were joined by Johnny Hodges and Harry Carney and five guests from the Count Basie band: Lester Young, Buck Clayton and three-quarters of the Basie rhythm section, including Basie himself on piano. "It is understood that a hall of this size is far from the most appropriate setting for the best results in this type of playing," Kolodin had cautioned in his program notes. "Thus the audience is asked to accept the jam session in a spirit of experimentation, with the hope that the proper atmosphere will be established." Somehow, even with all this formidable talent sharing the stage, the proper atmosphere was not established, and the experiment proved less than successful.

If the jam session was one of the evening's disappointments, the trio and quartet performances that followed were one of its indisputable triumphs. Teddy was at his lyrical best on the trio's "Body and Soul," earning every decibel of the huge ovation that greeted him when he took his place at the piano. Lionel was astonishing on the three quartet numbers, electrifying the audience and Benny as well on "Avalon," then "The Man I Love" and finally "I Got Rhythm," which has to be one of the most exciting small group performances ever to have found its way onto a record. There was really nowhere left to go after that, and the first half of the concert came to its scheduled close.

"How long an intermission do you want?" Benny had been asked the day before. "I don't know," he answered. "How much does Toscanini have?" When the negotiated time had elapsed, the audience strapped themselves back in their seats, and the music took off once again. The band opened with

Fletcher's by-now classic arrangement of "Blue Skies." Then Martha Tilton came out for "Loch Lomond," the swing treatment of the traditional Scottish song originally introduced by Maxine Sullivan that summer. As the band swung its way into Fletcher's new chart of "Blue Room," it began to catch fire, and Jimmy Mundy's "Swingtime in the Rockies," which came next, sent the flames shooting even higher. "All of a sudden, blasting like hell, riding on high out of the ancient alcoves came Ziggy Elman with a trumpet passage that absolutely broke everything up," George T. Simon wrote in his review. "The crowd commenced to yell; the band began to blast at a pace it had never approached before Ziggy's outburst, and by the time the boys had wended their way out of the Rockies they had created a ruckus that must have been heard way out there." Benny turned down the heat just a little with "Bei Mir Bist du Schön," Sholom Secunda's Yiddish ditty that had somehow become a big hit for the Andrews Sisters. Benny had recorded it a few weeks earlier with Martha, Ziggy and the quartet, but this time Martha's vocal and Ziggy's *fraylich* trumpet were featured in a big band setting provided by Jimmy Mundy. The audience loved it. Even the old ladies in evening gloves and lorgnettes were seen clapping in time (more or less) to the music.

When the program notes were printed, the trio and quartet were slated to perform only in the first part of the concert, but now Benny brought them back out for an additional appearance. Picking up where they left off, Teddy, Benny and Gene sizzled their way through a ferociously up-tempo "China Boy," urging each other on through chorus after chorus ("Take one more, Benny" . . . "Take one more, Gene") that held the crowd on the edge of its seats for the next five minutes. Lionel joined them, and off they went again on an easy rocking "Stompin' at the Savoy." Then the four of them took everyone on a roller-coaster ride with the aptly titled "Dizzy Spells," a new addition to the quartet's repertoire.

Benny had decided to bring the concert to a finale with the surefire crowd pleaser "Sing, Sing, Sing." It was an astute, if almost unavoidable, choice, but even Benny couldn't have anticipated just how well it was going to work out.

Gene started things off on tomtom, and the band jumped in with the familiar opening theme. After a short soulful solo by Benny and more tomtom, the full ensemble returned with "Christopher Columbus," booted along by the trumpet section's incredible bite and drive, then moved on to variation upon variation evolved in the course of all those long nights on the road. By now the kids in the audience were jitterbugging in their seats, and even some of the gentry in the boxes and dress circle had gotten up on their feet and were shagging in the aisles. Gene's solo and a final ensemble ride-out that recapitulated Louis Prima's original theme seemed to bring the performance to an end, but it was only just beginning. Following a great burst of applause, Babe

Russin took off on tenor saxophone, and the band started building up another head of steam. Gene's drum break led into a long, dazzling solo by Harry James full of triple tonguing and bravura high notes. After another passage by the full ensemble, Benny entered quietly and, backed by Gene's toms and Jess's gentle chords and fills, began unfolding a wonderful blues-tinged solo that gradually worked its way up to a dramatic high C. As the applause swept over the bandstand, he motioned Jess to take one himself, thereby setting the stage for the moment that more than any other in that evening of memorable moments is most clearly remembered and cherished.

"Yeah, Jess," Benny called out in delight as Stacy began to dig in, causing the whole audience to break up. And in the two minutes that followed, Jess spun out the most miraculous solo of his career, an elegant, wistful, deeply moving meditation that was part blues, part some kind of almost classical music (he'd been listening to a lot of Debussy and MacDowell) and wholly unlike anything anyone ever heard him play before.

Jess had been regularly featured on "Sing, Sing, Sing" in the past, but then for some reason or other his solo was taken away from him, so Benny's signal came as a complete surprise. "If I'd have known it was coming, I would have probably screwed it up," he says with a smile. "It just happened. I think Benny liked what I was doing behind him that night. I wasn't getting in his way, but I was still goosing him a little bit. Then all of a sudden he pointed at me to play. It was very simple. Everybody had been knocking their brains out all night long, so I went the other way and it just fell into place."

Benny reminisced some two decades later:

> I remember Jess' solo vividly. It was brilliant. There was complete quiet when he was playing and he was completely engrossed in what he was doing, and I just looked at him and said, "Well, I'll be a son of a gun, of all the terrific players we have here tonight, this guy is really taking on the whole thing." He was stealing the show completely as far as I was concerned, and I think he really did. He sounded like a concert artist playing a big concerto that night, just improvising this little thing on "Sing, Sing, Sing."

As Jess completed his solo, Gene picked it back up, signaling with his cowbells for the band to come in with the final ride-out chorus that brought the performance and the scheduled program to a close. The cheers and applause went on for close to five minutes.

Lionel remembered Benny's telling him at the Paramount, "Once you stop a show, get off that stage and don't come back on. You might do a lot of encores, but hit one bad note and you spoil it all." But tonight the encores were unavoidable. Coming after "Sing, Sing, Sing" brought down the house, "If Dreams Come True" and "Big John Special" were almost bound to be anticlimactic, and they were. But no great harm was done. There had already been more than enough climaxes for one evening.

The reviews of the Carnegie Hall concert were decidedly mixed. Most of the New York newspaper critics simply didn't know what to make of it. Olin Downes of the *New York Times,* probably the most influential music critic in the country, claimed to be sympathetic to jazz (at least the Paul Whiteman "symphonic" variety) but found Benny and the band totally lacking in originality and interest despite their obvious technical virtuosity. "Nothing came of it at all," he complained, then went on to "venture the prediction that 'swing' of this kind will quickly be a thing of the past." The review prompted at least one outraged letter to the editor protesting Downes's incompetence ("Obviously you did not understand what was going on that night in Carnegie Hall; worse, you listened with an ear perverted by prejudice and bias"), which caused the *Times* to bring the matter to its editorial pages: "There seems to be no middle group who likes swing music a little. One either loves it to the point of distraction or takes to the hills to get away from it. It is of no use to argue about it."

More surprisingly, even those writers who did love swing "to the point of distraction" were far from unanimous in their praise. *Metronome*'s George T. Simon noted the concert's deficiencies and disappointments but was on the whole extremely enthusiastic. (BENNY AND CATS MAKE CARNEGIE DEBUT REAL HOWLING SUCCESS). The reviewer from *Down Beat,* though, saw the evening as a mixture of exciting highs and boring lows, and *Variety* regretted it hadn't turned out better. For Otis Ferguson, "Their average work was what was heard at Carnegie Hall. The superlative work, which just happens and over which they have no control, is done elsewhere and will be done again."

By the time the recordings Albert Marx had made of the concert were unearthed in 1950 and finally issued, the dissenting opinions were long since forgotten. Benny's older fans were dazzled by these rediscovered treasures. Younger listeners had never before heard this kind of music played with such freshness and intensity. *The Famous 1938 Carnegie Hall Jazz Concert* became one of the best-selling jazz albums of all time—and the night of January 16 came to be enshrined as the absolute pinnacle of Benny's career and one of the truly important landmarks in the whole history of jazz. Predictably enough, it was used as the dramatic climax of *The Benny Goodman Story,* the wretched film about Benny's life produced in 1954, since with a few typical Hollywood oversimplifications it could be made to demonstrate both his final glorious triumph over adversity and swing's acceptance into polite society.

Not that the evening wasn't a triumph. A lot of wonderful music did get played that night. It generated tremendous publicity and prestige. If anything, the critical controversy only strengthened the loyalty of Benny's fans. It even opened Carnegie's doors to other events of a similar nature: Before the year ended Ethel Waters also performed there; W. C. Handy's sixty-fifth birthday was celebrated by Jimmie Lunceford, Teddy Wilson, Lionel Hampton and a host of other swing musicians; Louis Armstrong, Artie Shaw and Raymond Scott appeared with Paul Whiteman; and Hammond put on the first "Spirituals to Swing" concert with a spectrum of jazz, blues and gospel artists that included Big Bill Broonzy, James P. Johnson, Sidney Bechet and Count Basie. But Benny himself seems to have struck the right chord when he stated in 1981, "Looking back on it, I sometimes think that the thing that really made the concert important was the album that came out. I don't know what would have happened if the concert hadn't been recorded. People would have remembered it, sure—but not like this."

Ten days after Carnegie Hall Benny returned to the Paramount, and the opening day frenzy was even more delirious than when he appeared there the previous March. The New York high schools were on mid-semester break, and by five o'clock in the morning some three thousand youngsters had jammed the sidewalks in front of the theater, causing the management to call out the mounted police. By seven-thirty the crowd was so enormous the theater had to open its doors and get the show started early. Swarming into their seats, the kids hooted and stomped through the newsreel and Mae West's *Every Day's a Holiday*, then, when the band finally came into view, began shagging and trucking down the aisles and up onto the stage. "The audience broke all records for mob hysteria," *Variety* reported. And all attendance records as well. By the end of the day the Paramount had sold an all-time high of twenty-six thousand tickets.

The frenzy continued through the rest of the week. The theater added on four shows, bringing the weekly total to an unprecedented thirty-nine, and supplemented the army of harried ushers with doctors and police. Benny tried his best to maintain his composure. "So they're crazy?" he told the *New York Post*. "So what? I am still sane. Look here. At the Pennsylvania Hotel they wear tuxes and orchids. Here they wear sweaters and middy blouses. What's the difference? A kid's a kid. All kids are crazy." But sometimes the crazy kids got so out of control he had to stop the band in the middle of a number and sit cross-legged on the stage with his clarinet between his knees until they simmered down. The Paramount's gross for the week was a sensational fifty-seven thousand dollars, more than double the amount Fred Waring brought in the week before and the third best business it had ever done under its present big band policy.

The three-week engagement at the Paramount was the crowning success in an incredible season of successes that brought Benny and his band up to a heady new peak of popularity. From October to January they had packed the Madhattan Room every night. In November there was the big picture spread in *Life* magazine. In January alone *Hollywood Hotel* was released, Benny played Carnegie Hall and once again had them dancing in the aisles at the Paramount. When pressed about his future by a skeptical reporter, he snapped back with justifiable irritation, "I don't worry about it at all, so why should you?"

As far as money was concerned, Benny was perfectly right: There *was* absolutely nothing to worry about. The Paramount was paying him close to $15,000 a week, perhaps not all that astonishing a figure when divided by thirty-nine shows and one considers the theater's share of the take, but it was a long way from the $1,750 he had taken home for a week at the Fox Theater in Detroit only a little over two years before. He was filling up the ballrooms and hotels everywhere he appeared. Debutante parties and college proms were bringing in $2,000 a night. But success for Benny wasn't entirely a matter of money and ongoing popular appeal. As important as they were to him— and he was too much of a pragmatist not to give them their due—they weren't more important than the music itself. And he knew perfectly well that his achievements as a musician ultimately had very little to do with the celebrity and wealth they had brought his way, however much he enjoyed them. "Hell, I'm a musician," he proclaimed backstage at the Paramount, cutting right to the crux of the matter when a journalist made the bad mistake of opening his interview with questions about money and being a celebrated social phenome- non. "And let me tell you something. I was just as good a musician ten years ago, when nobody knew me or made any noise or hullaballoo about me."

Ten years ago, though, Benny wasn't leading a band. And now that he was, he was also dependent upon the combined talents of all the other musicians who made up the orchestra. Despite Benny's growing remoteness and the occasional grumblings of his sidemen and the loss of Murray McEach- ern and Vido Musso, the personnel of the band had remained remarkably stable over the past year. And in a band like Benny's that combined an almost machinelike precision with a looseness and relaxation that only came from complete familiarity with the material it was called upon to perform, a stable personnel was essential. But a few weeks after the glorious season in New York ended and Benny returned to the road, there was a sudden, shockingly public clash of temperaments that disrupted the band's precious stability and set in motion a succession of further changes that would cast a dark shadow over its future.

15

Farewell Blues

he rumors had been building for well over a year: Benny and Gene Krupa just weren't getting along. According to the gossip around the business, Benny was becoming increasingly resentful of the way Gene's crowd-pleasing showmanship was taking the spotlight away from him. For his part, Gene was said to be getting awfully tired of being confined to the role of sideman and was starting to think seriously about moving on. The April 1937 *Variety* disclosed that even though he was the highest-paid "stick swinger" in "the biz," Gene was "reported anxious to organize his own swing crew and cash in on the name he has built for himself." The fact that his two-year contract with Benny was about to expire gave the rumor some credibility, and musicians and fans across the country began exchanging worried speculations about what might happen to the Goodman orchestra should he actually decide to leave.

Gene publicly denied there was any basis to this gossip and renewed his contract with Benny for significantly more money, so it looked as if the band would continue swinging along as usual for at least the next two years. This happy impression was confirmed by the enthusiasm Gene expressed about the way Benny and the band performed at Carnegie Hall in his monthly column

Despite some recent losses, Benny still holds the fans enthralled at a 1938 appearance in Burlington, Ontario. *Left to right:* Jess Stacy, Harry Goodman, Ben Heller, Benny, Chris Griffin, Dave Tough, Bud Freeman, Ziggy Elman, Harry James, Noni Bernardi, Dave Matthews, Vernon Brown, Red Ballard and Arthur Rollini. Ken Whitten Collection for *Metronome*, dashed off the day after the concert: "I'm telling you right now that Benny and the guys sent me more than they did anybody in the whole room. I've never heard them cut loose the way they did. I've never heard them play everything so perfectly." The truth of the matter, though, was that Benny and Gene *were* having serious problems, and despite the new contract and the success of Carnegie Hall, things were only getting worse.

For all their compatibility as musical partners, they hadn't ever really connected on a more personal level. "Benny was respectful," Chris Griffin says, "but there was never any great closeness there. The closest I ever saw Benny come to being a friend was one Christmas when he gave Krupa a check for three hundred dollars, which was quite a bit of money in those days and showed that he at least appreciated him." And the distance between them was only widened by Gene's growing popularity with the fans. "Gene Krupa was our spark plug, our showman," Jess Stacy explains. "The rest of us just sat there and played good music. And I believe Benny did have some problems with the way he emerged as the big star and crowd pleaser. I remember Benny saying one time out of the corner of his mouth, 'Gee, I think I take a good solo and nobody claps; then Krupa gets up there and tears it up.' The whole thing with the public was visual, and Gene Krupa was an excellent show-man—a good-looking guy with tousled hair and all that. Benny would play some terrific things, but nobody listened that much. I don't mean the people who love music, but how many people really love music?"

Chris Griffin agrees that Benny often found this troubling: "I saw many a time when kids would be wanting autographs, and they would rush right by Benny to get to Gene Krupa and Harry James, then come back, and I'd see this expression on his face: 'Why is this happening?' " To the saxophonist Jerry Jerome, who joined the band toward the end of 1938, the explanation was obvious: "Benny looked like a college professor up there with his big glasses, and he would never reach out to make contact with the people. He felt that playing the clarinet and having the band do what it did so well were enough. He certainly didn't object to the audience's enthusiasm, but I don't think he cared to share himself with them. He didn't think he had to. That was the point. He knew he was good, and he knew he didn't have to come on with a big show of personality. Some bandleaders needed to do that because that's all they had going for them. But Benny built a little cellophane barrier between himself and the audience, and they had to take him as he was and like it. The result was that he didn't even get the applause that a Harry James or a Ziggy Elman or Chris Griffin or maybe myself would get when we'd stand up, because we played to the audience more. I was out to make them like me. I loved to hear that roar. And I think Benny didn't give a damn. I'd rate Harry's solos seventy, mine fifty, Ziggy's seventy-five and Benny's a hundred, but it didn't come out that way on the applause meter, even though Benny was playing far better than anyone else."

Apart from any jealousy or resentment Benny might have felt for Gene's ability to stir up the crowds, the growing strain between them was, at heart, essentially musical—a matter of tempo and style and personal taste. "Benny was not too great at kicking off tempos," Helen Ward explains. "That was one of Gene's biggest beefs. Benny would set the tempo by just waving around his bent index finger, which was not much of a baton and certainly didn't give Gene much to go on. To make matters worse, sometimes Benny would kick off a tune too slowly or too fast, and Gene would try to settle into whatever the time was actually supposed to be. That got to Benny after a while. He really didn't like it."

According to Hammond, Benny was also having problems with the sort of music Gene's showmanship was almost forcing the band to play. Benny was too good a businessman not to encourage Krupa's exhibitionism on "Sing, Sing, Sing" and the other Jimmy Mundy killer-dillers, but his tastes were changing, and "the hysterical roars of the crowd which once had been sweet music to his ears first perplexed, then irked him." Hammond reported:

He [wants] his music to be appreciated for its essential worth, and not because of its fortissimo volume and crazy antics. But he [has] educated his public and a few of his musicians differently, and the going [has been] difficult for subtlety. For many months now Benny has felt that his band was not achieving real swing. . . . But the public was clamoring for noise, and the band felt obliged to give the public what it seemed to want. . . . The behavior of his audience has set the guy on edge for the last six months. I happened to catch the third show on the first day of his recent appearance at the New York Paramount. The crowd's exhibitionism at the earlier performances had so disgusted him that he could not even bring himself to face the well-behaved patrons at the quiet supper show. The audience sensed his hostility and simply didn't know what to make of it. . . . [Benny] genuinely wants the public to appreciate his music and he hates to see it "fooled" by tricky stunts—even though he has largely been to blame for the public's gullibility. There have been some harrowing experiences for Gene, trying to follow Benny's desires for him to relax and to play as a member of the rhythm section rather than as a soloist, but finding it all but impossible to disregard the crowd's pleas for more and more display of technique.

It all came to a head the last week of February during an engagement at the Earle Theater in Philadelphia. "The tension had been building," Chris remembers. "Benny thought that Gene was always racing and pulling ahead, not doing his time, and finally the boil burst right out onstage. Benny says to Gene, 'Come on, come on!' when they're doing the trio and quartet, and Gene answers, 'You're the King of Swing. Let's hear you swing. Go ahead, start swinging!' And that's how it went for the next three shows. The two of them were battling in public, really badly." According to Rollini, "This went on for a few days, and Gene couldn't stand it any longer. Finally, on stage, in full hearing range of all of us, Gene (who rarely swore) flared up and blurted, 'Eat some shit, Pops!' After the show he went to the dressing room and tore up his high-priced contract."

Gene's contract still had more than a year to run, but as in most unhappy marriages the split-up was mutual, and Benny relinquished whatever legal hold he had on his further services. Benny hired Dave Tough, who had been playing with Bunny Berigan and Tommy Dorsey, and had Lionel Hampton fill in on drums until Dave was able to join him at the Madhattan Room on March 19. Gene immediately signed with MCA and Brunswick records and began putting together a big band, which on the strength of his popularity was booked into the Steel Pier in Atlantic City during Easter week.

The Krupa band based its style on the audience-rousing flag-wavers that Benny himself was now trying to put behind him. Gene's head arranger and musical director was no less than Jimmy Mundy, who had stopped writing for Benny as soon as Gene left, and his featured soloists included Vido Musso, Benny's hard-driving former saxophone star who was a past master of excitation. The Atlantic City debut turned out to be a solid success, drawing some four thousand ecstatic swing fans, who cheered and shagged around the bandstand as Gene called out one killer-diller after another. Gene packed Buffalo's Glen Park Casino to capacity the following month, and a police guard had to be stationed in front of the bandstand to protect him from the overzealous audience. The reviews were good, but some qualifications were beginning to creep in. By the time he moved on to the Arcadia in Philadelphia, the honeymoon with the press was just about over. Most of his radio broadcasts from the restaurant "have not been worth listening to," *Metronome* claimed, and "the entire band was strangely lacking in lift." Gene's return to Philadelphia's Earle Theater grossed a less than earthshaking nineteen thousand dollars for the week, and now the critical response was almost entirely negative:

The emphasis is on screeching brass and ponderous chords and screwy runs. . . . It is not difficult to get a large outfit to pound and blare; for a while it may be thrilling to hear, but in a short time it becomes oppressive and monotonous. That Krupa should spend time in developing a style which both Goodman and Shaw abandoned, after having developed it further than Krupa can possibly do, seems rather pointless. At the rate at which the band is progressing, the style will probably be outmoded when Krupa has finally worked it into shape.

This prediction proved accurate. For all its early promise, the Krupa band of the late 1930s never did attain either the musical excellence or the popular appeal that had been expected. And its recordings tended to be even more disappointing, becoming increasingly commercial as the fad for killer-dillers finally ran its course. It wasn't until Anita O'Day and then Roy Eldridge joined the band in the early 1940s that it finally caught fire and found its way to the same distinctive, very satisfying high-voltage musicality that Gene was always capable of generating on the drums.

Dave Tough, Krupa's replacement in the Goodman band, was a very different sort of drummer altogether. A small, frail, often forlorn-looking man, he had none of Gene's star quality and personal magnetism and preferred elegant understatement to Gene's more blatant blasting. He was not a showman. He hated to solo. But in his own subtly unobtrusive, almost self-effacing way, he was one of the most musical and propulsively swinging drummers ever to set brushes to cymbal, a joy to every musician who had the good fortune to play with him. To Pee Wee Erwin, Davy's band mate in the Tommy Dorsey orchestra, he was "probably the greatest drummer I have ever worked with, although I can't possibly tell you why. I only know he was able to work some strange magic that could make you play over and beyond yourself. . . ."

Davy had gone to the Lewis Institute with Benny back in Chicago, and they joined the musicians' union on the same day. He was an unusually bright, sensitive, articulate youngster with a passionate interest in art and literature as well as jazz and at one point seriously considered becoming a writer. He was also from an early age a deeply troubled alcoholic, which led him to fall away from music in the early 1930s and reduced him to a street derelict begging for handouts. By 1935 he had pulled himself together well enough to return to the drums and move to New York, where he was promptly hired by Dorsey and Bunny Berigan, but this illness continued to bedevil him throughout his brief life and led to his premature death at the age of forty-one.

For all Davy's personal problems, his supple, understated drumming made him the ideal timekeeper for the simpler, more relaxed style of music Benny was intent on playing after Gene's departure. Leonard Feather still recalls the tremendous enthusiasm with which Benny looked forward to Davy's first recording session with the trio and quartet a week after he joined the band. "This is going to be the greatest thing we've ever done!" Benny had promised, and the session did go extremely well, producing five splendid sides in something like three hours. Benny started out by calling "Sweet Lorraine" for the trio, Jimmie Noone's classic clarinet feature that he and Davy must have heard Noone play dozens of times back at the Apex Club in Chicago. Then Lionel Hampton joined them for an impromptu two-part blues, "The Blues in My Flat" and "The Blues in Your Flat," notable for its easygoing good humor. At Benny's suggestion, the quartet moved on to the old Austin

High Gang favorite "Sugar," then ended with Lionel's "Dizzy Spells," which Gene had attacked with such manic energy at Carnegie Hall. In this run-through Davy plays with brushes rather than with sticks like Gene, and the result is a quieter, more laid-back and self-contained performance that perfectly realizes the musical qualities Benny was now after. Benny "seemed warm, human and as relaxed as I had ever seen him," Feather remembers. He was "so inspired by Tough's support that he burst into a profusion of uncharacteristic compliments, which Tough accepted with modest reluctance."

The Goodman musicians shared Benny's enthusiasm. "When Gene was with the band, I figured all the time that there was nobody on earth who could touch him—who could match his terrific drive and technique," Harry James remarked shortly after Tough came on board. "And then along comes Davy with a much simpler and yet just as terrific a drive. It's wonderful the way this Tough man remains unobtrusively in the background, at the bottom of everything, pushing you ahead gently but firmly from almost underneath your chair, staying with you at all times in everything you play. He gives you an entirely different kind of boot than Gene does—in fact, their styles of drumming are so different . . . that it's hard to believe that they're both drummers!" For some Goodman sidemen, like Chris Griffin, the change was all for the better: "Krupa was always for Krupa first of all, and the band was secondary. He was not conscious of playing with the band. But Tough was so nice and flexible. God, it just felt so good!"

Benny's new looser, leaner, less sensationalistic approach was heralded as an enormous improvement by the critics, who had grown as weary of the flag-wavers as had Benny himself, and they all singled out Dave Tough for his enormous contribution. For George Frazier, Davy was in many ways the hero of the evening when Benny re-created the Carnegie Hall concert at Boston's Symphony Hall. "Playing with an unbelievable rock and with impeccable taste, he won the gratitude of every true lover of jazz. His tempi were perfect, his composure [was] admirable. He is, of course, so fine that his tremendous worth is not likely to be appreciated by a public weaned on sensationalism."

Perhaps that was at the root of the problem. The musicians and true jazz lovers and *Down Beat* and *Metronome* reviewers may have appreciated what Davy was doing, but the larger public, "weaned on sensationalism," did not, and what it wanted—demanded, really—was more of the same frenzied showmanship that had originally attracted it to the Goodman orchestra. If Benny was to maintain his popularity, he needed the continuing support of those fans, however much they offended him, and as Jess Stacy sees it, he soon came to understand he'd lost something important when Gene Krupa left. "Benny had said he didn't want a showman, but then he realized that he needed a showman. The band still played great, but the guy up there wasn't breaking his neck on the drums, and the people weren't going for it. Krupa did rush sometimes—my left arm is still paralyzed from trying to keep up with him—and Benny had problems with that, especially toward the end. Then Dave Tough came in and just played good time, but you've got to do more than that if you want to get the public's attention. You've got to take your clothes off or something."

Benny's enthusiasm for his new drummer quickly began to fade. "We were playing a job in Cleveland," Jess recalls, "and we came in by bus and dogsled and everything else and had bags under our bags. Benny came in by plane and was fresh and rested, and before the curtain went up, he looked over at Dave Tough and says, 'Now I want you to send me this time.' And Dave says, 'Where do you want to be sent, Benny? I'm a directional sender.' A lot of things went on like that." "Oh, it got to be miserable," Chris Griffin agrees. "Benny started to get on Davy little by little, and it finally reached the point where he was just plain insulting. He'd say, 'Tough, leave the bass drum out.' So Davy takes his foot off the pedal. Then it was, 'Tough, use the flyswatters.' He didn't even say 'brushes.' And here's this big band making a lot of noise, and this guy is sitting back there playing flyswatters like Benny said. It tore his morale down terrifically. I'm surprised Davy didn't go back to drinking at that time, because he was dry. He'd been dry for a couple of years, and he never touched a drop the whole time he was with the band."

Jess remembers otherwise, but whether or not it was because Davy started drinking again, he was absent from several "Camel Caravan" broadcasts in July and may not have appeared at the Ravinia Park concert in Chicago that August. And Benny began freezing him out of both the live and recorded trio performances, having Lionel take over on drums and letting Davy play only when Hampton switched back to vibes for the quartet numbers. On October 26 Davy failed to show up for the band's opening at the Waldorf-Astoria, and Benny fired him.

Davy's tenure with the Goodman band lasted barely seven months. He was replaced by Buddy Schutz from the Gene Kardos orchestra. Schutz's stay was even briefer. When Buddy first joined the band, Benny praised him as just about the best white drummer he'd heard. And Buddy *was* good, Chris agrees. "He filled the bill. He was steady and never got in the way, and he wasn't flashy." Yet once again Benny soon became disenchanted, and Buddy was given his notice a few months later. "But Buddy was smart enough to get a one-year contract before he joined," Jerry Jerome recalls with a smile, "so even after Benny fired him, he kept showing up. One day Benny asked Leonard Vannerson, 'Why doesn't he go home?' and Vannerson told him, 'Because he has a contract,' so Benny started trying to humiliate him to get him to leave. He began calling him 'Adolf' because Buddy had a mustache that looked a little like Hitler's, and he thought that would make him angry, but Buddy just laughed and started putting Benny on. He'd do things like hang around backstage during rehearsals and say, 'Do you need anything, Benny? Can I go out and get you some coffee?' Oh, it was murder! Finally Benny couldn't stand it anymore, but the only way he could get rid of him was by paying him off. Buddy absolutely turned the Ray around on Benny. He's the only guy I know who ever did that. How Benny allowed himself to get sucked into a contract like that, I can't imagine."

Buddy Schutz was replaced by Nick Fatool, who, in Chris's opinion, was, "outside of Dave Tough, the best drummer we ever had as far as playing with and for the band." Yet the same thing happened again. "For some reason Benny just wasn't satisfied," Jerry remembers, "and he started giving Nick the Ray when we were recording in California. During the rehearsal he said to him, 'Lay out while we work on this,' which is a normal thing to do, and after we finished rehearsing without the drums, he had Nick come back in and play. But then he had him lay out again, and this time he turns around and says to the band, 'You know, I think it sounds better this way.' Now whether Benny meant this cruelly or whether this particular thing we were doing did sound better without the drums, I don't know, but Nick wanted to cut his head off with a cymbal. He was absolutely furious at being humiliated like that, and he subsequently left."

Benny's ongoing discontent with all his drummers after Krupa continues to mystify veterans of the 1938–1939 band to this day. Chris remembers, "He tried everybody in the world, including guys who weren't capable of playing with a big band. And in the middle of that whole mess of people he even tried a very young Buddy Rich. We were down at Atlantic Beach for a week, and this kid came in one night and sounded exactly like what Benny had just gotten rid of and didn't want. He listened to him for about two numbers and said, 'Okay, kid,' and that was the end of that. He didn't want anybody as flashy as Gene. He didn't want to go through that again. He was trying to find something else. But there was no such drummer as what he was looking for. I think maybe he just didn't like drummers."

In a sense, Benny's problem with drummers was emblematic of the larger problem he was now having with the band's overall personnel. Keeping track of all the comings and goings during this period is a little like trying to count the blur of Christmas shoppers swirling in and out of a department store's revolving doors.

Some sidemen left because they were fired. Others handed in their notices because they began to feel the brunt of Benny's displeasure and knew their time with the band was about over. Others grew weary of life on the road and were ready to settle into the better-paying, relatively unstressful jobs in the radio studios available to musicians who could place experience with the Goodman band at the top of their résumés. Or were lured away by competing leaders. Or were ready to try their hands at becoming leaders themselves. Some simply couldn't take Benny anymore and left because they'd had enough of the insensitive, often high-handed way they were being treated.

"You had to stand your ground with Benny," Chris Griffin maintains. "I don't know how some of the guys let him use them the way he did. He'd go over to one of the saxophone players and take a reed right off his stand without even looking at him, try it out, then break it in two and throw it on the floor. One time I even saw him reach over and take a guy's handkerchief, blow his nose on it and drop it back on the stand. The poor guy had a look on his face like, 'Oh, Jesus, why? Why is he doing this?' Because he let him. If he'd done that to me, I would have been out of there in five seconds and probably wouldn't have ever come back.

"Benny had heard a high-note trumpet player on the East Coast, I think his name was Olson, and when we were doing a theater in Chicago, he told Leonard Vannerson to get hold of him and bring him out. Well, the kid stood on the sidelines for about three or four days. Benny never even spoke to him. He finally says to Leonard, 'Who's that kid who keeps showing up here?' Vannerson says, 'That's the trumpet player I told you about three nights ago. You had me send for him.' Benny says, 'How's he play?' Leonard says, 'We don't know. You haven't let him play anything yet.' So Benny says, 'Hey, kid, sit in Chris's place,' It didn't mean that I was on the way out, but maybe it did. It was a rare period of time when I wasn't arguing with him. So he sat in and played a set and Benny said, 'Okay,' and then he got up. Leonard told me that two days later he asked Benny, 'What am I going to do about this Olson kid?' and Benny said, 'Oh, is he still here? Send him back.' In the meantime, the guy had left his job and made not one cent. That's the kind of thing Benny was capable of doing if you let him get away with it.

"I probably had more arguments with him than anybody. After Gene left the band, he was going to find someone he could pounce on for chewing gum, and I was chewing gum. I never had before, but I guess I just felt like it. He'd see me on the stand in the theater and say, 'Chris, take the gum out of your mouth!' and then I'd have a big fight with him on the elevator. 'What do you mean telling me to take the gum out of my mouth?' 'Well, it's my band!' Kid stuff. I quit about four or five times, and every time I got ready to leave he'd say, 'Aw, what do you want to go for, Pops?' And then he'd give me another ten- or fifteen-dollar raise, which doesn't sound like much now, but I wound up making almost as much as Harry James, who was a much more valuable asset than I was."

In March 1938, the same month Gene Krupa quit, George Koenig, Allan Reuss and Babe Russin also left. Arthur Rollini recalls that when he came to work one night at the Pennsylvania Hotel and happened to look over at the fourth saxophone chair, Russin had simply vanished and someone else was now sitting in his place. Reuss, who had played guitar in the band since it first hit the road back in 1935, was evidently fired after a bad row with Benny and went off to Paul Whiteman. It's not terribly clear why the alto saxophonist George Koenig left, but he was one of the few sidemen who refused to be intimidated by Benny, and according to Chris Griffin, they never really hit it off.

Koenig was replaced by Harry James's buddy Dave Matthews from the Jimmy Dorsey band. At Ziggy's recommendation, Ben Heller replaced Reuss. Bud Freeman gave up his position as Tommy Dorsey's star saxophone soloist and came in for Babe Russin. Tommy was reportedly furious, even though he'd been trying to make off with Benny's lead alto player Hymie Schertzer for some time and did in fact hire him a month later, after Benny turned over one too many of Hymie's parts to Dave Matthews.

This sort of personnel raiding was becoming increasingly common. White dance band musicians who played well, read fluently and knew how to swing were in very short supply, and as the big bands became more popular and began to proliferate, there was a growing demand for their services. The newer yet-to-be-established leaders, who were unable to match the salaries and prestige of the Goodmans and Dorseys, suffered the most. But the established leaders also had their problems with one another, and in the case of Benny and Tommy the mutual plundering of key sidemen aggravated a rivalry that was already putting a strain on their old friendship.

Tommy's band still played some jazz and, as always, contained a number of first-rate jazz musicians, but by the early part of 1938 it had become much more commercial than the Goodman orchestra, relying heavily upon smooth renditions of the pop tunes of the day and the vocals of Jack Leonard and Edythe Wright. This may have led jazz purists like John Hammond to lament that "his present group is just about the dullest big band on the market" and to reproach Tommy "for letting me and the rest of the public down with inferior musicianship and a basic lack of sincerity." But Tommy Dorsey was an astute businessman, and his rather tamed-down approach to big band swing gave the larger, less jazz-oriented public something that it wanted, bringing him up to a level of popularity and financial success that now challenged Benny's much-cherished supremacy.

Tommy was an aggressive, extremely competitive bandleader who had no qualms at all about trying to raid his own brother Jimmy's band, and he seemed to take particular pleasure in his growing rivalry with Benny. Chris Griffin remembers that when the Goodman band was at the Pennsylvania, "Tommy would come over from the New Yorker during his break along with Jack Leonard, Axel Stordahl and the rest of his entourage and sit as close to

Benny as he could get. Then he'd invite Ziggy or Harry or me to his table and say very loudly so Benny would be sure to hear him, "Why don't you join a good band? What do you want to stay with this heel for?" Benny, in his own way, was just as relentless. After taking Bud Freeman, he went after Tommy's guitar player Carmen Mastren, and he pressured Victor to withhold Tommy's recording of "It's Wonderful" to keep it from competing with his own recently issued version. A few weeks later Tommy was seen thumbing his nose at Benny at the Earle Theater in Philadelphia. Tommy claimed that his gesture was misunderstood and that everything between them was fine, but the rumor persisted that he was planning to launch a counterraid on Benny's band, starting with Jess Stacy.

Bandleader "feuds" were often just press agents' stunts calculated to generate newspaper coverage, but the feud between Tommy and Benny seems to have been genuine. Since they shared the same booking office, as well as the same record company, Willard Alexander had his hands full trying to get his two top money-makers to lay off each other. When Benny and Tommy both showed up at the Victor studios the morning of January 12, 1939, to take part in an all-star recording session of *Metronome* poll winners, it was said to be the first time in two years they had exchanged more than three-and-a-quarter curt how-do-you-do's.

Dave Matthews, Ben Heller and Bud Freeman all joined the Goodman orchestra the same month as Dave Tough, and the critics gave them a good share of the credit for the new looser, easier swinging style sparked by Davy's drums. Air checks of the band's live performances vividly reveal why the music press was so enthusiastic about its current direction. Curiously, though, with few exceptions, the studio recordings do not. The band's recorded output for Victor during this period is dominated by a lot of very ordinary pop tunes usually sung by Martha Tilton, well arranged but played in a straightforward, perfunctory manner that does nothing to make them any better than they are. Sides like "That Feeling Is Gone," "Why'd You Make Me Fall in Love?," "Don't Wake Up My Heart" and "What Goes On Here in My Heart?" fail to bring into play any of the band's real strengths and have virtually been forgotten by all but the most committed Goodman diehards.

Perhaps Tommy Dorsey's growing popularity caused Victor to steer Benny into such arid commercial territory. It's conceivable that his personal rivalry with Dorsey made him come to this decision himself in the hope that he could best Tommy at his own game. Commercial pop tunes may also have provided Benny with a needed respite from the killer-dillers he was tired of playing and given him a way to distance himself a little from the overdemonstrative swing fans he was beginning to find so irritating. It's possible, too, that the departure of his prolific arranger Jimmy Mundy left him short of new instrumental material, and he needed a stopgap until he could build up his

library again. The instrumental pieces he did put on record during this time
include "Big John Special," "Melancholy Baby," "Wrappin' It Up" and
"Farewell Blues," charts that had been in his book for as long as two and even
three years.

In July 1938 Benny sailed off to Europe for a much-needed three-week
vacation. While he was away, Artie Shaw took his band into the studio to
make his first recordings for Victor's lower-priced Bluebird label.

After Shaw's band had bombed out on the road early in 1937, he had
retreated to Boston and taken up residence at the Roseland-State Ballroom.
Dropping the string section that had given his music much of its individuality,
he began building a new orchestra along more conventional swing band lines.
Shaw claimed, with some bitterness, that he was planning to have "the loudest
goddam band in the world," but what evolved was far more subtle and
interesting than that. He auditioned musicians endlessly until he found the
right combination of big band veterans and young, untried talents that would
give him the kind of focused musicianship he wanted. He discarded his old
arrangements and began working closely with Jerry Gray on a new library of
material that shunned current pop tunes in favor of songs of the highest
quality by the best American composers like George Gershwin, Cole Porter,
Irving Berlin and Vincent Youmans. Letting the material itself dictate the style
of the arrangements, he had them orchestrated with a lean, uncluttered
simplicity that revealed all their musical substance with the crystal-clear trans-
parency he was seeking. Shaw also placed a heavy emphasis on jazz originals,
many of which he composed himself. Some evenings when the band really got
rolling, it would play "Moten Swing" for fifteen minutes or more, and "The
Blues" might go on for over half an hour.

By the end of 1937 the new Artie Shaw band was well on its way to
achieving its own distinctive identity. In the early spring its ranks were
strengthened substantially by the addition of Billie Holiday and the superb
trumpet player Max Kaminsky. The band was still based in Boston, but its
forays out on the road, Brunswick recordings and occasional air shots were
beginning to bring it some much-needed national attention. In June 1938 a
rave review in *Down Beat* hailed it as "the biggest hunk of jazz dynamite now
languishing in the shade of the old one-night stand." The following month
John Hammond awarded it his imprimatur. "I still think that Benny's revised
band has something that no other white band can touch," he said, "but the
combination of Artie and Billie makes me feel that Benny is going to have to
watch out for himself."

Artie's recordings for Brunswick had been well received by the reviewers,
but those who heard the band in person thought they didn't compare with its

live performances, and Artie himself was not pleased with them. The sides he recorded for Bluebird on July 24, however, finally succeeded in capturing what the orchestra was capable of doing and more than justified the critical buildup. It plays with a spirit and freshness befitting its youthfulness, and the half dozen sides it laid down that day offer a striking contrast with the Goodman band's current output, which seems to reflect the strain and fatigue of encroaching middle age. Shaw had wisely chosen to record some of the most appealing numbers in his library, including such future swing classics as "Indian Love Call," "Back Bay Shuffle" and "Any Old Time," the only recording Billie Holiday made with the band and one of her best. But it was the first tune of the session that really did it.

"I joined the band three weeks after 'Begin the Beguine' became available in the stores," the trumpet player Bernie Privin recalled. "Before I knew it, the band was the hottest thing in the country. The record was played everywhere. Because of it, Artie suddenly became a major celebrity." The crowds, the frenzy, the sudden financial success and mind-bending acclamation—it was the Benny Goodman story all over again.

Comparison between the two clarinet-playing leaders was inevitable. Musicians weighed their respective merits on the instrument, often concluding that Benny was the better jazz player but that Artie had the lovelier tone and greater skill in the higher register and was harmonically more interesting. Egged on by Rockwell-O'Keefe, Artie's booking agency, which billed him as the "King of the Clarinet," the fans divided into rival camps, arguing the superiority of one or the other with the same white-hot vehemence usually reserved for favorite baseball teams or heavyweight contenders. All this made terrific copy, and when Artie made his New York debut at the Lincoln Hotel on the same October 1938 evening that Benny opened at the Waldorf-Astoria, the music press played it up as a "contest for clarinet and swing supremacy."

Neither Artie nor Benny seems to have taken any of this hyped-up "rivalry" all that seriously. When a *Metronome* reporter misquoted Shaw as saying before he left Boston, "I'll be the King of Swing within a year!," Artie was appalled, and his letter of denial clearly stated his aversion to such pugnacious competitiveness: "There is room for twenty, even fifty swing bands, and I say more power to any contemporary leader who makes an outstanding success. If I were writing a novel I wouldn't particularly want to be known as the greatest novelist. I'd have satisfaction enough if my book were judged a success on its own and not on a basis of comparison . . . and that's how I feel about my music." Both bands were friendly and would get together for drinks, and Benny regarded Artie's playing very highly. A few years later he listed Shaw among his favorite clarinetists, praising him as "a fine musician with all-around ability." "He knows his instrument well, has extreme development in both registers and an amazing harmonic sense," Benny went on, citing some of the very skills in which Artie was sometimes said to excell him. "Benny took me to hear Artie Shaw at the Lincoln Hotel," Helen Ward remembers. "Benny admired Artie. He said he was damn good. He never made any bones about that. He thought Artie was a great clarinetist." Yet Benny also felt the pressure of the Shaw band's burgeoning popularity and made several efforts to compete with Artie's big hit. "Within a couple of weeks after 'Begin the Beguine' came out, Benny also had an arrangement of it," Chris Griffin says, "and he played it a lot." And the saxophonist Noni Bernardi recalls how Benny had him write an arrangement of the Spanish-tinged "Estrellita" because he was looking for something to match the tune's success. ("It didn't do it.")

Harry James had emerged as the band's star sideman after Krupa left, and it was only a matter of time until he also went out on his own. The move had been in the planning stages as far back as March 1938, only two months after Carnegie Hall, when Benny talked Harry into having MCA represent him whenever he started his own band. In return for this potentially valuable service, the agency agreed to pay Benny 5 percent of the commission fees it would collect on Harry's bookings. Harry remained with Benny until January 1939, and his decision to leave was accompanied by none of the bitter acrimony that marred Gene's departure. But then Benny had a strong financial interest in Harry's future. A few weeks after Harry turned in his notice, they signed an agreement that was very heavily weighed in Benny's favor. In exchange for a line of credit allowing Harry to borrow up to seven thousand dollars during the course of the year Benny was to receive one-third of Harry's net earnings over the next decade. The loan had to be repaid within twenty-four months. Benny would start taking in his full portion of Harry's net after ninety days.

    With the help of his close friend Dave Matthews, who also handed in his notice, Harry began putting together a band largely comprised of fellow Texans he had started bringing up to New York even before he left the Goodman trumpet section. He commissioned a library of swinging instrumentals from Andy Gibson, the black arranger who had been writing for Charlie Barnet. He secured a record contract with Brunswick, which had previously recorded several pickup sessions under his name produced by John Hammond. By February he was ready to step out into the spotlight and get on with his new career as a leader.

    The band's first important engagement was at the Benjamin Franklin Hotel in Philadelphia. *Down Beat* was thrilled by its hard-swinging, if still somewhat roughhewn, section work and Harry's own heavily featured trumpet playing. The hotel management, though, was not and demanded that Harry cut back on the jump tunes and do more of the softer, more danceable numbers favored by the room's clientele. This was not what he originally had in mind when he decided to style his band on the Goodman model, but like the sensible businessman he was already on his way to becoming, Harry agreed to keep the customers satisfied and limited his more unfettered playing to the late-night closing sets.

Within the next month or two, after working the Hotel Pennsylvania in New York and putting in some time on the road, Harry largely abandoned the wildly exuberant improvising that first brought him to the public's attention and began to call for more ballads like "I Surrender, Dear," "Just a Gigolo," "I'm in the Market for You" and "Black and Blue," which gave him the opportunity to play "prettier," less sensational trumpet. All four of these tunes were closely associated with Louis Armstrong, Harry's first influence, who recorded them between 1929 and 1931, a period when he, too, began to front a big band and turn toward a more commercially acceptable, if no less musically valid, repertoire. In following Louis's example, Harry appears to have been, like Louis himself, trying to find a way to maintain his authenticity as a jazzman and still survive in a marketplace where the sort of uncompromising blowing he'd been known for had only limited appeal. "One of my chief aims," he explained, is "to have a band that really swings and that's easy to dance to all the time," and these highly melodic, very danceable standards provided him with the means to do both.

There's no reason to believe that Harry was forcing himself into something he didn't prefer to do anyway. Benny wasn't the only musician in the Goodman orchestra who'd had his fill of the killer-dillers. " 'Sing, Sing, Sing'—God, I never got so sick and tired of anything in my whole life," Harry's section mate Chris Griffin remembers, and Harry had gotten to the point where he was psychologically incapable of playing it one more time. If the hard-core jazz fans were somewhat disappointed by the course he was now charting for the band, Harry himself was full of enthusiasm and optimism: "Of course, I can't expect to make as much in dollars and cents right off. A new band gives a guy plenty of expenses, and headaches too. I think in the long run, though, I'll be making out much better financially as well as spiritually. Playing what you want to play is good for a guy's soul, you know!"

The headaches and expenses continued to multiply as the months went by, and the expected success still eluded him. Writing about the band's appearance at Roseland in August 1939, George T. Simon called it "just about the most rhythmic white band dancebandom has yet known," but at the management's insistence the more rhythmic numbers had to be interspersed with rumbas, tangos and waltzes. When Harry finished up in New York, he was scheduled to play the Palomar Ballroom in Los Angeles, the scene of

Benny's own dramatic breakthrough, but the Palomar burned to the ground while the band was on the road, and it was booked into an upscale restaurant called the Victor Hugo. The owner deemed the music so loud that he ordered the brass section to muffle its sound with handkerchiefs, mutes and felt hats and had a canopy built around the bandstand. Back in June Harry had discovered a young singer named Frank Sinatra working out in Englewood, New Jersey, and had taken him on as his boy vocalist. Yet even with this considerable commercial asset, his records failed to sell. When his contract with Brunswick (now renamed Columbia) expired at the end of the year, it was not renewed. Eli Oberstein had left RCA to form his own Varsity label and agreed to sign Harry only on the condition that MCA would give him a chance at some of its more promising orchestras. Sinatra, by now, had been hired away by Tommy Dorsey.

Harry's fortunes began to take a turn for the better toward the end of 1940. He was still deeply in debt. The band was earning less than four hundred dollars a night, not nearly enough to cover its expenses. His Varsity recordings, like the label itself, had gone nowhere. But then Manie Sacks, an executive at MCA who had some faith in Harry's potential, became popular music director at Columbia and talked the company into giving him a second chance. Earlier that year Harry had threatened to add a string section to the band to make it more commercially palatable. Now, with the encouragement of Morty Palitz, his producer at Columbia, he proceeded to do so. And with the strings very much in evidence, he began turning out records like "Flight of the Bumblebee" and "Carnival of Venice," virtuoso showpieces for trumpet filled with a lot of triple-tonguing pyrotechnics but devoid of any jazz content. Harry's playing here harkens back to his childhood years in the circus, long before he'd even heard of Louis Armstrong. It had been foreshadowed, however briefly, in the opening chorus of "Ciribiribin," the first tune he recorded for Brunswick under his original 1939 contract. But in "Ciribiribin" the circus band razzle-dazzle seemed to have been intended halfway humorously and quickly gave way to a straight swing band reading of the tune in the same mode as the Fletcher Henderson arrangement Harry played while he was still with Benny. On "Carnival of Venice" and the like, he appears to be deadly serious. But the records sold.

A few months later, in May 1941, Harry recorded his first major hit, a throbbing, full-throated rendition of the old tearjerker "You Made Me Love You," recently given new life by a teenaged Judy Garland. Jazz purists were shaken by Harry's playing on the record. The overly broad, almost comically exaggerated vibrato, the thin, nagging tone, the overwrought emotionalism all too redolent of the Judy Garland version—what did any of this have to do with the brilliant jazz musician who had swung the Goodman band to such frenzy with his amazing choruses on "Sing, Sing, Sing" and "Roll 'Em"? But

Harry insisted he *liked* Garland's approach to the song and over the years continued to maintain he was only going where his taste and interest led him.

In September 1941 Benny's former bandboy Pee Wee Monte took over the management of Harry's band and began straightening out its tangled finances. By the following April Harry was able to buy back Benny's interest for something like twenty-five thousand dollars. Had Benny waited awhile longer, the return on his forty-five-hundred-dollar loan might have been even greater. Benefiting enormously from the addition of former Goodman singer Helen Forrest, whose fulsome vocals mirrored Harry's own current ballad work, the band soon began moving from one commercial triumph to another—movies, hit records, network radio shows, top-grossing theater, hotel and ballroom engagements. It could still manage to swing when it had a mind to, but that was no longer so important. In the summer of 1943 the young trumpet player from the Texas circus bands attained the very pinnacle of mainstream success by marrying the reigning movie star pinup queen of the day, Betty Grable.

Harry's decision to strike out on his own left the Goodman band without one of its galvanizing forces offstage as well as on. "It had been such a brotherly band, so full of camaraderie," Jerry Jerome remembers. "When I was with Red Norvo, there were certain guys who smoked pot and certain guys who drank, and that led to different cliques, but it wasn't that way at all with Benny. When we played the Waldorf-Astoria, everybody hung out together at the Waldorf men's bar and everybody ordered the same thing—Canadian Club, which was considered quite a classy drink. Then on Saturday nights Harry would get a porno film, and all the guys would go up to the musicians' room and watch those ridiculous black-and-white porno movies between the dinner and supper shows and get hysterical laughing. There were a lot of laughs, a lot of fun, and it was great. But after Harry left, the guys started to peel off, and it wasn't quite the same."

In March 1939, two months after Harry's departure, Teddy Wilson also left to start his own orchestra. Teddy's slightly scaled-down eleven-piece big band looked extremely promising. It included such splendid soloists as Ben Webster on tenor saxophone and Harold Baker on trumpet, both of whom went on to make their mark with Duke Ellington. It had a first-class rhythm section, consisting of guitarist Al Casey, bassist Al Hall and J. C. Heard on drums, and a good singer in Thelma Carpenter. Like Harry James and Gene Krupa, Teddy was being booked by the powerful Music Corporation of America and recording for Brunswick/Columbia, for which he'd done all those marvelous small group sessions over the past four years. Teddy's tenure with Benny had brought him a tremendous amount of public visibility, and he'd long since acquired his own enthusiastic following. There was every reason to believe that an orchestra under his leadership was bound to prosper. But for a variety of reasons it didn't, and a little more than a year and a half later Teddy was forced to disband.

One of the problems was that the market had recently become glutted with new bands hoping to cash in on the continuing swing craze. "Never before in the history of dancebandom have so many new orchestras sprung up as now," *Metronome* observed in a series of editorials cautioning ambitious sidemen to think twice before quitting their jobs to form their own outfits. "But where are all these bands going to work? There's not even a semblance of a proportionate increase in the number of spots into which they can be booked." Then, too, Teddy's orchestra was an extension of his own emotionally self-contained personality, and its elegant, highly organized approach to big band swing was not what was expected from black bands of that day. "The band simply didn't have much mass appeal," Teddy reflected some twenty years later. "We played good dance music, but we needed ten to twenty good *stomp* head arrangements to add to the excitement that was missing." Bassist Al Hall put it another way: "Everybody kept saying we sounded too white."

For a while the Wilson orchestra was, along with Andy Kirk, one of the resident bands at the Golden Gate Ballroom in Harlem. Yet there were months when it hardly worked at all, and Teddy was forced to dig into his own pockets to meet his weekly payroll. Rather than give up a large piece of the band to outside investors, he had financed it himself from the money he made with Benny. What with the cost of arrangements and uniforms and equipment and all the other expenses it took to keep a big band running, his savings were soon exhausted, and key sidemen like Ben Webster began to leave.

MCA quickly lost interest. So did Teddy's longtime benefactor John Hammond. Hammond "never liked my big band," Teddy recalled. "And with him not supporting it, it died a natural death." Hammond was now booking the talent for Café Society, Barney Josephson's new racially integrated nightclub in Greenwich Village, and he offered Teddy a job leading the small house band. Teddy's salary was only one hundred dollars a week, far less than the fifteen thousand a year he was reported to have earned with Benny. He had no say in the group's personnel. ("Hammond wouldn't take the men out of my big band. He didn't like them.") The job mainly consisted of backing singers like Lena Horne and providing incidental music for comics like Zero Mostel and Jimmy Savo. But at least it was steady work and gave Teddy a chance to climb out of debt.

The loss of stars like Teddy Wilson, Harry James and Gene Krupa, along with all the other changes in personnel, certainly affected the quality of the music

Benny was now putting before the public. Yet if the band was no longer operating at the same high level of excitement it had the year before, it was still playing well, and for the moment, at least, its popularity remained undiminished.

"I don't remember the band hurting," Jerry Jerome maintains. "Benny always seemed able to get good players who could do the gig. There were so many musicians like myself who were already tuned into the band and had no problems with the concept. All the new trumpet players could probably sing the first trumpet parts. Every first alto man who came in played pretty much the same way. So the band kind of went by itself. And despite all the changes, I think it was a very golden period in Benny's career because he was reaping the success of the band before mine, the really hot band that had broken it up at the Palomar. The hard work and the planning had already happened. By now all Willard Alexander had to do was pick up the telephone and say, 'Benny's available April thirteenth for a week,' and everyone would jump at the top price. Who knew about this guy replacing Dave Matthews or Jerry Jerome replacing Bud Freeman? *Down Beat* readers. But they weren't the main ones who supported the band. The people who lined up to hear Benny Goodman couldn't have cared less about who was playing first alto. When we went into the Paramount Theater, those kids were screaming their heads off when I stood up to take a solo, but they didn't know me. There was so much hysteria they couldn't even hear me, so there was no way of telling how well I did or didn't play. And then someone playing trumpet stood up and—whomp!—it was the same thing. The crowds were crazy. Crazy!"

16

What Swing Really Does to People

If Benny's popularity continued rolling along out of its own momentum, it also benefited enormously from the continuing growth of the overall swing craze in the final years of the decade.

The naysayers still kept insisting the fad had played itself out and would soon be replaced by a return to a gentler, more romantic style of music. But swing bands were doing even better business than they had a year or so before, piling up ever-larger grosses in ballrooms and theaters throughout the country. In May 1938 a "carnival of swing" at New York's Randalls Island drew a huge crowd of twenty-four thousand frenzied devotees, who gyrated ecstatically to the likes of Duke Ellington, Count Basie, Woody Herman and Chick Webb and almost caused a riot when the rumor began to spread that Benny Goodman was backstage waiting to go on. A few months later what was described as "an overwrought mob" of somewhere between a hundred and two hundred thousand jitterbugs jammed Soldier Field in Chicago for a free "swing jamboree."

For all the belt tightening of the depression, an estimated seven hundred thousand swing records were being purchased every month, and the musical instrument industry was flourishing. Trumpet sales had recently doubled, and

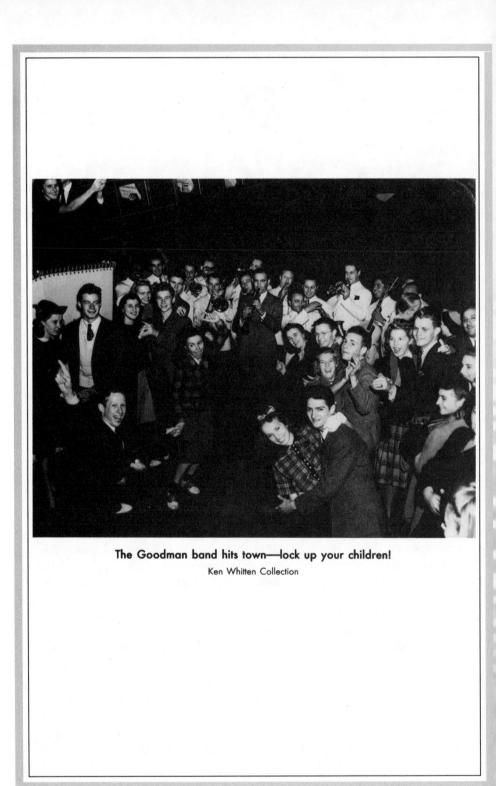

The Goodman band hits town—lock up your children!
Ken Whitten Collection

the sale of clarinets had tripled. New permutations of the basic lindy hop—the Big Apple, the Little Peach, the shag, trucking, bumping, clucking, the Suzy-Q, the dipsy doodle—were being introduced almost weekly. Along with the new dance steps came a new vocabulary of swing language, part authentic musicians' jargon and part press agents' fantastications, and mainstream publications like the *New York Times* and *Look* magazine took to printing lexicons of the latest lingo to help mystified parents decipher what their offspring were talking about with such impassioned intensity.

Metronome was right on the mark when it announced in the spring of 1938, "It seems there will be no post mortem on swing this year. And if the times are propitious, for some years to come. *O tempora! O mores!*"

Most jazz journalists found it distressing that the popular press focused its attention on the fans rather than on the music itself. But what could be more photogenic or make better copy than a bunch of Iowa high school kids trucking on down the staircase on their way to class or a teenage lovely writhing in private ecstasy at Benny's latest Paramount appearance? One suspects that hardly any of these writers were dancers themselves, and their disdain for those who did respond to the music with their bodies—"mental riff-raff," *Down Beat* called them—kept them from really appreciating the music's larger social impact. Not that there was any shortage of attempts to grapple with the significance of the swing phenomenon. Explaining what it all meant became a favorite pastime of social scientists and other pundits, and there was about as much unanimity of opinion as might have been expected.

"Swing is the voice of youth striving to be heard," claimed an enthusiastic correspondent to the *New York Times*, who was all for it. "Swing is the tempo of our time." But, no, according to one learned psychologist, the fad should be understood as "a *protest* against mechanization, a *release* from the drab monotony of the machine age." For the choirmaster of Chicago's St. James Episcopal Church, it "manifested a healthy exuberance" and was "completely sane." But in another psychologist's esteemed opinion, it was "merely an American manifestation of the restless hysteria which is sweeping the world in advance of the coming war," on a par with the shovel brigades in Nazi Germany and the youth marchers in Fascist Italy. Was the ongoing appeal of swing "a sign of our uncertain times," as the president of the Dancing Teachers Business Association would have it, and its devotees "the unfortunate victims of economic instability"? Or were they, rather, finding a joyful way of transcending the rigors of the Great Depression or, perhaps, as others claimed, expressing an emotional loosening up that reflected the way the economy was beginning to pull itself out of the doldrums? Nobody knew for sure, but almost everyone had an opinion.

Now that it was becoming clear that swing would continue to be around for some time to come, those who took a dim view of its influence upon American youth began to step up their campaign of vilification. As Paul Eduard Miller observed in *Down Beat*'s 1939 *Yearbook of Swing,* "No other music, to my knowledge, has suffered so much violent criticism nor has been the subject of so many spurious attacks by both professional and non-professional reformers of the world's morals."

One college president warned his graduating class that the "cacophony" of swing reflected the "current attitude prevailing in the political, economic and social fields, as music always mirrors the dominant feeling of an epoch." The newly installed head of the economics and social science department at Barnard College lectured an audience of undergraduates that "swing is musical Hitlerism." "There is a mass sense of 'letting one's self go,' " he maintained, which opens the way for a dictator who will promise to give the people a genuine mass thrill. Another commentator saw in the mass hysteria produced by the music a potential means of regimenting public opinion that could lead to a de facto dictatorship.

But it was the sexual rather than the political consequences of the music that many of its other detractors found most alarming. For the sweet bandleader Blue Barron, "Swing is nothing but orchestrated sex . . . a phallic symbol set to sound . . . music that cannot shake off its origins in the lowest sporting spots of the deep South." According to the *Chicago Sunday Tribune,* "Swing deals largely with eroticism—hence its restlessness and pain and gloom, its mad excitements and its profound despairs." One psychologist attributed swing's dangerously hypnotic effect to the fact that it is "cunningly designed to a tempo faster than seventy-two beats a minute—faster than the normal pulse," which causes a heightening of the emotions in young people that "can reasonably be expected to break down conventions and lead to moral weakness." A psychiatrist who viewed the swing craze as "an epidemic" produced by "mass contagion" advised parents to quarantine their still-healthy children from the infected jitterbugs who were the carriers of this deadly virus.

The conviction that something ought to be done to keep the contagion from spreading was sometimes accompanied by aggressive action. A bill outlawing swing was proposed in the New York legislature. In 1938 swing music was banned from the forthcoming St. Patrick's Day march up Manhattan's Fifth Avenue. That November a special meeting of clergy in Orangeville, Ontario, rejected a couple's request to be married to a swing version of the wedding march. In December the Star-Spangled Banner Flag House Association formed a movement to prevent dance orchestras from "swinging and jazzing" the national anthem. The next May "jitterbug tunes" were officially barred from Princeton University's annual songfest.

Following the great commercial success of swing versions of beloved traditional melodies like "Loch Lomond," "John Peel" and "Comin' Through the Rye," radio stations in Detroit, Cleveland and Beverly Hills took up arms and banned them from the air. In Newark, New Jersey, the Bach Society filed a protest to the Federal Communications Commission expressing the "distress" music lovers experienced when classical compositions were "destroyed by the savage slurrings of the saxophone and the jungled discords of the clarinet." So much for Benny's "Bach Goes to Town." "We would suggest," the president of the society continued, "that any station that violates the canon of decency by permitting the syncopation of classics, particularly Bach's music, be penalized by having its license suspended." The story made the front page of the *New York Times,* and the debate raged on for weeks, eliciting extended commentary from the music critic Olin Downes and other notables, as well as a slew of irate letters supporting the proposal. ("To think that these music distorters saw fit to place their slimy hands on the sacred music of the great masters! . . . Should we allow these musical ghouls to rob all music of its most beautiful moments?") The FCC dodged the issue, declining to rule officially on an orchestra's right to swing the classics, but urged radio stations to use "a high degree of discrimination" in their airing of such performances.

Swing fever had spread across the Atlantic by now, and the guardians of traditional culture were even more outraged than they were in the United States. A swing-hating passenger on a British cruise ship "went giddy" and threw the band's instruments overboard. (The ship's "alligators" donated eighty pounds to buy new ones when they landed at Gibraltar.) Sir John C. Squire, an author and editor, registered a complaint to the British Broadcasting Corporation that Benny Goodman's swing music was "an awful series of jungle noises which can hearten no man" and demanded that it stop playing his recordings.

The thinly veiled racism lurking behind such phrases as "jungle noises" and "savage slurrings of the saxophone" was expressed with far more brutal and consequential directness in Nazi Germany, which had a long-standing opposition to jazz. Not only was it American and Negro, but to the Reich's way of thinking it was also Jewish, a peculiar association that may have been borrowed from the anti-Semitic industrialist Henry Ford, who had been railing against jazz for years as a Jewish conspiracy to "Negrotize" American culture. In 1935 jazz was barred from German radio as part of the effort to do away with the "culture-destroying activities of the Bolshevistic Jews." Toward the end of 1938 the Nazi leaders in charge of the places of amusement in Württemberg declared that swing might be fit for Negroes and Jews "but not for us Germans," and in line with their "suggestion," the district of Pomerania agreed to ban it. Following the Nazis' lead, the Italian Fascists issued a regulation forbidding the broadcasting of any records composed or played by Jewish artists, and the Italian papers launched a sustained assault upon the "Negroid dances" that threatened "the flower of our race, the youth—the greatest hope of the country for tomorrow."

The ongoing controversy back in the United States led Benny's publicists to arrange for several pro-swing articles under his by-line in some of the more widely read popular magazines. The first appeared in *Look* in September 1938 and was a plea to "give swing a chance to prove it is not a flash in the pan, but the only really truly American music we have." The following May *Liberty* printed a second Goodman piece titled "What Swing Really Does to People," which, like the first, was addressed to the unitiated and defended the music against the charges currently being leveled against it by its opponents. Swing is not, Benny insisted, "expressed in sexy dancing" but is "a new brand of fun," the modern equivalent of "what old-time barn tunes were to jigging farmers, and strumming guitars and crooning were to black feet shuffling in the delta mud."

Curiously, though, the following February, when he appeared in *Collier's* magazine as the author of a lengthy article titled "Now Take the Jitterbug," Benny turned away from extolling the virtues of swing and, instead, devoted most of the space to a rather severe condemnation of its more vociferous fanatics, criticizing them for their insensitivity to the finer points of the music and plain bad manners. If Benny's position here is better-humored and far more understanding than that of swing's harshest critics, it moved him un-comfortably close to the enemy camp. Although the piece exhibits very little of Benny's own voice, it is almost certainly an accurate reflection of his current state of mind about the "hoodlum jitterbugs," as he now calls them, their childish jargon and the loud, unsubtle music they pressured him to perform over the past few years. "We learned to play against hell and high water. We played loud when we should have played soft and played louder when we normally would have played loud. . . . Musical subtlety, just coming to life, went out the window and the era of Sandblast Swing came in." The way Benny disassociates himself here from both his audience and his earlier killer-diller rave-ups provides further confirmation that he was feeling the need for a major change. The general tone of discontent running throughout the piece also strongly suggests that he was ready to start looking elsewhere for musical gratification.

17

Contrasts

enny's early studies with Franz
Schoepp had given him a certain amount of exposure to classical music, and
toward the end of 1935 he performed the Mozart Quintet at a musical
evening put on by John Hammond and his mother at the Hammond mansion
on Ninety-first Street. It was, Hammond maintained, "the first time [Benny]
had played a serious piece before an audience," and even though it was a
private social gathering and most of the performers were amateurs, he was
extremely nervous. Hammond, who played the viola part, claimed he had to
persuade Benny to try his hand at it—"I had visions of bridging the gulf
between classical music and jazz, which I thought could be important to
jazz"—though he acknowledged that Benny "always had an urge to do more
than improvise jazz." About a year later Benny made an uncharacteristically
casual attempt to record the composition with the Pro Arte Quartet. It turned
out to be, he recalled in chagrin, a "humiliating," "ridiculous" experience.

> I must have been more than slightly distracted at the time, as I normally
> take a very serious view of a serious venture. . . . I was on a one-nighter tour
> of the Middle West. The night before the recording date, my band and I

Benny recording Béla Bartók's *Contrasts* with Joseph Szigeti on violin and the composer on piano, May 1940. Sony Music

were playing in Wisconsin. When the engagement was over, we piled into a bus, drove through the night and arrived in Chicago at six A.M. Four hours later I breezed into the recording studio, met the Pro Arte members for the first time, sat down, took out my clarinet with the same reed in it which I had used the night before for the "One O'Clock Jump" and bashed right into the Mozart Quintet—and right out of the studio a few bars later!"

He had not done any preparation. The Pro Arte musicians spoke very little English. "After playing for maybe five minutes, I started saying to myself, 'What the hell am I doing here? This is nuts. I don't know this piece.' I just wasn't prepared. So I excused myself, saying, 'I'm sorry, gentlemen. Thank you, but this was my mistake.' "

On January 18, 1938, two days after the Carnegie Hall concert, Benny played the allegro movement of the Mozart with the Coolidge String Quartet on the "Camel Caravan" show. The performance was much more than just another good publicity stunt but reflected Benny's growing interest in the classics and his need to expand the boundaries of his talent. "I wanted something else to do to give myself a challenge," he explained some years later. "It's a sense of—well, growing up, I guess. If I hadn't done it, I probably always would have regretted it. . . . What are you going to do, go out and play 'Lady Be Good' again, forever and ever? How many times?"

The broadcast came off well enough to encourage Benny to try recording the Mozart again three months later with the Budapest String Quartet. Benny had done a lot of serious thinking after the Pro Arte fiasco and had by now "learned my lesson," as he put it. "I studied hard for weeks beforehand. I asked other musicians to listen and criticize me, and I couldn't even count the hours I spent looking for *the* perfect reed. After that, we had days of rehearsal going over every phrase again and yet again. I am happy to report that the results of this second recording date were very different from the first one."

Some years later Benny reflected: "Looking back, I suppose that it was at this moment that my [double] musical life started in earnest. Once I had become even slightly familiar with the other world of music, it was quite impossible for me to dismiss it."

The recording attracted a great deal of attention and, largely because of Benny's name, became a classical best seller. Reviewing the album in the *New Republic*, Otis Ferguson acknowledged that what he called "the freak quality" of the collaboration accounted for much of its popularity but found the performance itself entirely praiseworthy: "The Quintet is played the way the writing indicated, and for once perhaps the way it spun and lifted in the composer's head."

A few months after the recording session Benny began planning his public debut as a classical performer. During the summer of 1938 it was

announced that he would appear with the Budapest as an assisting artist at
two of its late-afternoon Town Hall concerts the following season, playing
Mozart and Brahms clarinet quintets on November 5 and some Prokofiev on
January 2. The Prokofiev was eventually dropped from the program, and then
so was the Brahms, but on the afternoon of November 5, after the Budapest
had performed string quartets by Brahms and Debussy, Benny stepped onto
the Town Hall stage and joined them for the Mozart. "In some classic breasts
this raised apprehension," Olin Downes reported in the *New York Times* the
next morning, "but the alligators and jitterbugs . . . [who] were not present
in overwhelming numbers . . . said that Benny would show them. And he did,
in the most legitimate manner." Although Downes thought that Benny was
"a little stiff" in the first movement and "disposed to be overcautious," he had
nothing but praise for "his sincerity, his proficiency and his earnest regard for
the music," singling out the "beautiful legato and fine feeling" he displayed
in the slow movement.

Two months later, on January 9, 1939, Benny took part in a Carnegie Hall
recital by the violinist Joseph Szigeti, playing the premiere performance of the
Rhapsody for Clarinet and Violin by the great modern Hungarian composer
Béla Bartók, a chamber piece for clarinet, violin and piano that he had
commissioned. The idea for the commission—"a brainstorm," he called it—
came from Szigeti, a musician of uncommonly wide-ranging enthusiasms that
encompassed both jazz and the still-controversial compositions of his fellow
countryman. Szigeti was a great fan of Benny's and had a long personal and
professional association with Bartók, who had dedicated his Rhapsody No. 1
to him back in 1928. Although the clarinetist and composer came from two
very different musical worlds, Szigeti evidently assumed that Bartók's deep
involvement in the folk music of Eastern Europe would inspire him to discover
some sort of common ground. Bartók did, in fact, tell him that the opening
movement of the work was suggested by the "blues" section of Ravel's violin
sonata, and to the critic Nicholas Slonimsky, the final result was "the Hungarian counterpart of the American blues."

After Benny had agreed to underwrite the project, Szigeti explained the
requirements to Bartók when they met at a music festival in London in the
summer of 1938. "It was as simple as that," the violinist recalled. "A few
months later, the two large sections entitled 'Verbunkos' ["Recruiting
Dance"] and 'Sebes' ["Fast Dance"] were finished." As pragmatic as ever,
Benny had expressed the hope that the work would be just long enough to fit
on both sides of a twelve-inch 78 rpm record. "This was not the case," Szigeti
tells us, "and Bartók was somewhat apologetic about the 'overweight.' . . .
Bartók wrote, when sending the score to Benny and me: 'Generally the

salesman delivers less than he is supposed to. There are exceptions, however, as for example if you order a suit for a two-year-old baby and an adult's suit is sent instead—when the generosity is not particularly welcome!' "

This was the first and only time Bartók included a wind instrument in one of his chamber pieces. According to his biographer Halsey Stevens:

> Had it not been for a commission, he would very likely never have concerned himself with one of them. . . . [S]ince the 1904 Quintet for piano and strings, he had combined the piano only with individual string instruments in the two Sonatas and the Rhapsodies, apparently having reached the conclusion that no real ensemble is possible between instruments of such pronounced differences in tone production. To add still another type of instrument—the clarinet—meant that there would be even less possibility of blending their sonorities; consequently he approached the problem from the opposite side: playing up the disparities.

Benny found the composition "quite a difficult piece to play, very modern . . . although I was enthralled and completely absorbed in it."

Benny was doing a full schedule of shows at the Paramount the week he gave the rhapsody its debut performance. Jerry Jerome remembers, "We'd pass Benny's dressing room and hear him rehearsing that impossibly difficult Bartók piece, and I'd say, 'How the hell can he do it?' It scared me. How do you run back and forth that way from one thing to another?" Reminiscing some two decades later, Benny wondered about that himself. "At the moment it strikes me as being absolutely nuts. But then I suppose I just took it in my stride and said, 'Well, so I do another show in between.' It was like an extra performance. When I think about some of the things we did then, it's almost hair-raising."

Benny was concerned that since Bartók was still considered a difficult, very avant-garde composer and the larger concert-going public had not yet come to terms with his modernity, no one would show up. "I had to get an audience over there some way by hook or crook. They knew we weren't going to be playing anything very commercial. So it was one of the few times I rather cajoled all the music publishers into buying tickets to the concert for some of the past favors I had done them."

There had been some talk that Bartók might come to the United States to perform the piano part, and some later accounts state that he did. But the trip failed to materialize, and the pianist was actually Endre Petri. Szigeti's E string snapped in the middle of the performance, but he quickly replaced it, and there were no further untoward incidents. Both the composition and the performance were well received. The *Times* reviewer found it an "earthy" and "rollicking," if demanding, piece of work, "as Hungarian as goulash," that "spared neither the fingers nor ears nor lips of the performers, nor cared little for what [it] asked from the harassed instruments." Benny was praised for being "artist enough to restrain himself from any insinuation of swing," as well as for "the purity of his style and the bright neatness of his technique." It was, the *Times* concluded, "an evening of high enthusiasm." We do not know how the shanghaied music publishers felt about it.

Bartók did visit the United States briefly the following spring, prior to emigrating here in the fall of 1941. What Szigeti calls his "unfailing sense of form" and "equilibrium" had led the composer to continue working on the rhapsody, and he had by now expanded the piece by adding a short middle section called "Piheno" ("Relaxation"), which separates the slow dance of the first movement from the fast dance of the second. Bartók had also decided the composition would benefit from a new, presumably more descriptive title. Szigeti remembered how "we sat for hours in my apartment on Park Avenue mulling over a suitable title to replace Rhapsody, he finally hitting upon "Contrasts.' " According to Halsey Stevens, the new title refers not to the contrasting tempos of the three movements but to the disparate sonorities of the three instruments.

Benny had left Victor for Columbia in the spring of 1939, and Szigeti suggested to Goddard Lieberson, the head of classical music at the label, that he undertake a recording of 'Contrasts' while Bartók was still in the United States. In May 1940, about a week before the composer returned home, he and Szigeti joined Benny in Los Angeles for the recording session. "Mr. Bartók was quite a wonderful little man. He was very quiet, very small. He couldn't have been more than five foot six," Benny recalled. "One day at rehearsal I said to him, 'You know, Mr. Bartók, I think I'm going to have to have three hands to play this particular part, it's so difficult.' And instead of raising a big fuss about it, he said, 'Well, Mr. Goodman, just approximate. Play as close as you can.' I thought that was quite something for one of the great composers of all time." When the recording was released that November on two twelve-inch 78 rpm records, it received a laudatory review from the *New York Times*' Howard Taubman, who praised Benny's prowess at negotiating the difficulties of this extremely demanding piece of work.

Contrasts was only the first of the classical compositions for clarinet that Benny commissioned. In the years to come there were numerous others, including Paul Hindemith's Concerto for Clarinet and Orchestra (1947), Aaron Copland's Concerto for Clarinet (1947) and Morton Gould's Derivations for Clarinet and Band (1956). Though Benny was primarily concerned with generating new repertoire for himself, the net result was to expand the very small body of clarinet literature, an accomplishment that has placed all classical clarinetists in his debt.

Between the debut of the Bartók in January 1939 and the time he recorded it sixteen months later, Benny's involvement with classical music continued to deepen. A week after the premiere he appeared at the Waldorf-Astoria with the Philharmonic Symphony Ensemble, about forty musicians drawn from the New York Philharmonic, playing the Mozart Clarinet Concerto at the first of a series of three Sunday evening dinner concerts. Later that month he brought Szigeti on to the "Camel Caravan" show to perform a short solo piece by Debussy. That August he played the Mozart Quintet with the Budapest at Mills College in Oakland, California. In November he performed the Mozart concerto with the Buffalo Philharmonic and the following May played it once more at the Hollywood Bowl at a concert conducted by Leopold Stokowski.

As far back as June 1938 it had been rumored that Benny was making plans to appear at Carnegie Hall as a soloist with the full Philharmonic Symphony. On December 12, 1940, the plan finally came to fruition, and Benny joined John Barbirolli and the orchestra for the Mozart concerto and Debussy's First Rhapsody for Clarinet, both of which he had recently performed upstate with the Rochester Civic Symphony. The *Times* reviewer found that although Benny approached the Mozart "rather warily" and moved through the Debussy with "greater assurance and freedom," he met the composition's most difficult passages with "the utmost ease and accuracy." If "the sounds of his clarinet often overbalanced the correctly discreet orchestral support," his phrasing was "impeccable," his legato "the smoothest."

Given Benny's limited background in classical music, he made the transition to the concert hall with remarkable ease. Yet as he realized himself, it would take years of further experience before he attained the confidence and sustained mastery he already had with jazz, which came as easily to him, he claimed, as "falling off a log."

Talking with Howard Taubman after the Philharmonic concert, Benny expressed his awe for Mozart's genius and compared playing the concerto to walking a tightrope. "Why, that fellow never uses more than the same seven notes or so, and look what he does with them. When I play a hot chorus, I might use every note I have on the clarinet. Just seven notes or so for Mozart. It ought to be a cinch after the stuff I've done, but it certainly is not. You know I'll have to play that Concerto a lot more. Because no matter how you sweat over it, there's one thing you can't forget—Mozart is still the boss."

Four days after the performance Benny recorded the Mozart and Debussy with Barbirolli and the Philharmonic. The Debussy was issued as planned. But whether because Barbirolli or Columbia or Benny himself was displeased with the result, the Mozart was judged unworthy and withheld from release.

Discussing his double musical life in 1951, Benny reflected:

> The greatest exponents of jazz are those with the most originality in ideas plus the technique to express them. In classical music, on the contrary, the musician must try and see into the composer's mind and play the way he believes the composer meant the piece to be played. To do this naturally requires many long hours of preparation and practice. I have learned to accept this fact during the past years, but apparently it has been more difficult for my family.
>
> I remember one occasion several years ago when my wife, who is a passionately enthusiastic gardener, had been listening to me through an open window repeating endlessly certain passages of a piece I was preparing for a concert. She finally came in and said, "Don't you ever get tired going over and over and over the same phrase?" I had been glancing out of the window from time to time while playing, so I replied, "It's funny you should ask me that. I have been watching you working in the broiling sun for hours on end, weeding, digging, planting, pruning, covered with dirt, and I've been thinking the same about you!"

The more open-minded concert artists like Szigeti, Leopold Stokowski and the Budapest Quartet welcomed the opportunity to collaborate with Benny. Those who looked down upon jazz and the musicians who played it did not. In July 1941 Benny was scheduled to perform the Mozart Clarinet Concerto at Philadelphia's Robin Hood Dell under the baton of the pianist and conductor José Iturbi. Two weeks before the concert Iturbi announced that he was unwilling to appear on the same stage with him. "He is a jazz band leader," Iturbi protested. "It would be beneath my dignity to conduct for him." The manager of the Dell offered to release him from the engagement. But Iturbi, who evidently did not feel it beneath his dignity to appear in a number of MGM musicals a few years later, whacking out a bit of boogie-woogie piano in *Thousands Cheer* to prove he was a regular guy, was adamantly opposed to this solution. "But I do not want to be released!" he shouted. "Why should I always be the one who has to give in? I want you to release Goodman. I am willing to help you out." The Dell's manager answered that he did not wish to be helped out. "Benny Goodman's contribution to American music is as important as any I know," he explained.

The Benny Goodman Quartet—Lionel Hampton, Teddy Wilson, Benny and Gene Krupa—tear it up in the 1937 movie *Hollywood Hotel.*

From the Benny Goodman Archives in the Music Library at Yale University

The Goodman orchestra blowing at the top of its form provided another good reason to check into the *Hotel. Bottom row:* **Vido Musso, Hymie Schertzer, Benny, Arthur Rollini, George Koenig.** *Middle:* **Harry Goodman, Allan Reuss, Red Ballard, Murray McEachern.** *Top:* **Jess Stacy, Gene Krupa, Harry James, Ziggy Elman, Chris Griffin and a ringer, sometime trumpet player Johnny ("Scat") Davis, who had an acting role in the movie.**

From the Benny Goodman Archives in the Music Library at Yale University.

A driving rainstorm wasn't enough to keep the fans from lining up in front of the
Paramount Theater for Benny's epochal 1937 engagement. Ken Whitten Collection

Harry Goodman, Gene Krupa and Harry James stompin' at the Savoy Ballroom in
the famous battle of swing with Chick Webb, May 1937. Ken Whitten Collection

Benny rehearsing the band at Carnegie Hall for its 1938 concert. Ken Whitten Collection

Benny visits Artie Shaw between sets during the Goodman orchestra's 1939 stand at the Waldorf-Astoria. Ken Whitten Collection

John Hammond, Benny, Charlie Christian and producer Morty Palitz at a 1940 recording session for Columbia. Ken Whitten Collection

18

The Changes Made

pril 1939 saw the publication of Benny's autobiography, *The Kingdom of Swing*, one month before his thirtieth birthday. A straightforward account of his Horatio Alger-like rise to prominence, its retrospective view of how Benny arrived at the present moment necessarily put his past accomplishments some distance behind him and left him looking at a future that contained its own share of uncertainties. Toward the end of the book Benny confronted the unavoidable question of whether or not the swing vogue was on its way out, and though he maintained it was not, he allowed that other bands could come along at any moment to take the play away from him. By way of confirming the music's ongoing vitality, he cited the recent arrival of a new generation of musicians like Harry James and Lester Young—a curious sort of passing the torch for a young man not yet out of his twenties who showed absolutely no signs of slowing down, much less withdrawing from the fray.

The Kingdom of Swing was only the second autobiography of an American jazz musician ever to be published—Louis Armstrong's *Swing That Music*, issued in 1936, was the first—and was written with the collaboration of Irving Kolodin, the highly regarded classical music critic for the *New York Sun*.

Kolodin had put together the elaborate program notes for the Carnegie Hall concert, and his participation here served a similar purpose, assuring that the project would have a certain quality and be taken seriously as something more than mere public relations flackery. Despite some minor caviling in the music press, the book received excellent notices. For *Tempo* magazine, "Though *The Kingdom of Swing* fails to give as good a picture of the Goodman character as it might, and Benny's accounts of some of the more important musicians with whom he associated are not as revealing as the reader could wish, his story is still a valuable document in a field where good histories are still lacking." Other reviews praised it as "a worthwhile addition to every swing fan's library" and a book that "the public, swing conscious or otherwise, will enjoy." Sales were strong enough to warrant a second printing the following January.

In the course of recounting the band's early struggles Benny gave due credit to Willard Alexander for the very important part he played in its eventual success. But by the time *The Kingdom of Swing* was published their relationship was over. Willard had left MCA early in the year to run the newly opened band department at the William Morris agency. According to Hammond, the Morris office had assumed that Benny Goodman and Count Basie would come with him. Basie did, but it was "a shock for Willard" when Benny decided to remain where he was.

The change turned out to be unsatisfactory for both of them. William Morris's interest in big bands was only halfhearted, and Willard eventually moved on to open his own agency. And without Willard to look after his interests, Benny's relationship with MCA deteriorated badly. By July it had reached such a sorry state that Benny and the booking office were no longer on speaking terms and he was refusing to sign any contracts or renewals. Benny stayed closemouthed on the subject but supposedly was still furious that the Bob Crosby band had been given his spot on the Tuesday "Camel Caravan" show, even though Camel subsequently sponsored him on a Saturday evening edition. The larger cause, it was said, was that now that Willard had gone, there was no one at MCA with the same sort of close personal involvement to whom Benny could go with his problems.

Benny's long association with Victor also came to an end that spring, when he switched over to the newly revitalized Columbia label. In December 1938 the Columbia Broadcasting System bought the faltering American Record Company for $750,000 and hired Ted Wallerstein away from Victor to become its president. The names of American Record's Brunswick and Vocalion labels were changed to Columbia and Okeh. To compete with Victor, which, like Brunswick, sold its popular recordings for seventy-five cents, Wallerstein lowered Columbia's price to half a dollar. Hammond tells us that "the

move caught Victor unprepared, and it put Columbia back into the competitive record market."

Early in the year Hammond had been hired by Wallerstein as associate
director of popular recordings. His responsibilities included the onerous task
of supervising sessions by commercial dance bands like Eddy Duchin, Kay
Kyser and Horace Heidt that he had previously scorned in his *Down Beat*
reviews. But he was also expected to search out more congenial talents and
bring into the Columbia fold some of the artists he had worked with in the
past, such as Count Basie and, especially, Benny Goodman. "John Hammond
was gung-ho about my going there," Benny recalled. "And it wasn't too smart
then; Columbia only had two distributors, I think. Instead of taking a salary,
with the fact that Columbia was really just getting started, I should have asked
for a piece of the company. But I wasn't too happy about the way things were
at Victor—I couldn't even find anybody to talk to."

In light of Benny's problems at MCA, this last factor was probably the
decisive one. Not only had Wallerstein, the executive who originally signed
him to Victor back in 1935, moved on to Columbia, but Eli Oberstein, who
had supervised his recordings for the label, was also gone. Victor's roster of
swing bands was overflowing with the likes of Tommy Dorsey, Charlie Barnet,
Artie Shaw and Glenn Miller's promising new orchestra, all of whom required
their fair share of attention. Benny was getting to be old news at the company.
It was time for a change.

Benny's final recording session for Victor was scheduled to take place on
May 2 and provided a less than glorious conclusion to a wonderfully productive alliance that had begun so auspiciously four years before. The band had
endured a 350-mile drive to Chicago after finishing up its night's work, then
spent the afternoon rehearsing that evening's "Camel Caravan" show. After
the broadcast it reconvened at the Victor studio and over the next two hours
recorded "Pick-a-Rib" and "You and Your Love." It was past midnight by
now, and there was still one more tune to go, but as it prepared for the final
number, one of the engineers came in with the embarrassing news that
something was wrong with the new recording equipment, and not one note
had been gotten down. Benny exploded, then went off to catch some sleep.
Two days later he returned to the studio, ran down the three tunes without
any further difficulties, and that was the end of that.

Writing in *The Kingdom of Swing*, Benny took a rather casual view of all the
recent turnovers in his band's personnel: "Of course, in the kind of music we
play, where so much depends on the way musicians get along together and
on the freshness of their own ideas, it's necessary to keep each man on his toes
all the time. That's why I think that an orchestra should be changed around
a little every so often, so that the men don't get stale from playing too much

together." But the same month the book appeared in the stores, what had been so temperately described as a minor and occasional "changing around" suddenly gave way to a massive exodus of sidemen that left the Goodman orchestra with hardly any familiar faces.

The first wave of departures took place in April and May. Buddy Schutz and Ben Heller were fired. Benny's older brother Harry, who had played bass with the band from the very beginning, also left and gave up performing to run his new Pick-a-Rib barbecue restaurant in New York and look after some of Benny's business interests. And then, to the shocked dismay of fans and sidemen alike, Benny told Martha Tilton that as long as the others were leaving, she might as well go too. "I was there when she burst into tears," Jerry Jerome remembers. "She was beside herself. I never saw the reason why, but Benny wanted to get rid of her."

Martha was replaced by Harry James's wife, Louise Tobin. Benny brought in Nick Fatool and George Rose as his new drummer and guitarist, replaced his brother Harry with Artie Bernstein and added Bruce Squires on third trombone. Then, while the band was out on tour, Arthur Rollini handed in his notice. He was tired of the road—"So were the other men," he recalled—and it seemed to him "the band was falling apart." When Benny returned to New York in June, he managed to entice the great lead alto player Toots Mondello into taking back his old chair, and Hymie Schertzer, who had recently returned from Tommy Dorsey, moved over to second alto.

Benny was extremely pleased with the way the orchestra was shaping up. "It'll be the greatest band I've ever had!" he promised. "The band was okay, I guess, but it just hadn't been kicking me as much as I wanted it to. So I made some changes." More were on the way. Hymie Schertzer and Benny's new guitar player George Rose were gone by July, and so was Jess Stacy.

When Fletcher Henderson broke up his band in early June, Benny had immediately hired him to head his arranging staff. Though Fletcher was no more than a competent pianist, Benny began having him take over for Jess in the trio and quartet, then on Fletcher's arrangement of "Stealin' Apples" and some of the other big band numbers. And according to Jerry Jerome, he started giving Jess a special version of the Goodman Ray.

"There was very little eye contact with Stacy because he was always very intent upon what he was doing and played looking down at the keys, so Benny began beating time on him by clicking his fingers. Stacy finally looked up and said, 'What the hell, is the old man giving me a tempo after all these years? My God, I must be getting the Ray!' He started increasing his alcohol content and soon left. We were all quite unhappy about that. Fletcher was a lovely gentleman, a wonderful guy and a fine arranger, but we weren't too impressed with his piano playing. I can't believe Benny thought he was better than Stacy."

Surely Benny didn't. But the band was going out to California for several months and, while it was there, would start recording again under its new Columbia contract, so there was a lot for Fletcher to do, and Benny wanted him close at hand. "The band was on the wane," Jess recalls. "The same interest wasn't there. Benny could see what was happening, and he was desperately trying to get back on top. Fletcher Henderson's arrangements had really made Benny's band, and he probably thought that if he could have Fletcher with him, he could bolster the band up again. Who knows what was going on in Benny's mind, but he had lost a lot of his key men. I wasn't jealous of Fletcher. Fletcher was a nice guy. I just left the band, that's all, and joined Bob Crosby. And that was a fun band. There was no pressure, no discipline— we just played. It was a very different feeling from being with Benny. And we played all the best jobs, too."

Lionel Hampton had filled in on drums from time to time, but Fletcher was the first black musician to become a regular member of the Goodman orchestra. This was still considered so controversial it warranted a banner headline on the front page of *Down Beat*. But as the magazine reported, although "mixed bands have never been successful with the American public," Benny paid no heed to that "accepted fact." On the first "Camel Caravan" show from San Francisco he introduced Fletcher to the radio audience and had him solo with the orchestra. Then without any further to-do, the new pianist simply took his place in the rhythm section. Much to the surprise of those who believed that this time Benny had gone too far, the sky did not fall, and the boundaries of racial segregation were pushed back that much farther.

Jess's departure left the Goodman band with only four members who had been there a year before: Chris Griffin, Ziggy Elman and trombonists Vernon Brown and Red Ballard. "Benny's motive is a mystery," a concerned *Metronome* writer commented. "When he started housecleaning on a small scale a short time ago, observers commended the move for psychological reasons, more than any other. But Benny's gone so far that now even his closest advisors are greatly alarmed." There was good cause for such alarm, since all this changing around had, inevitably, taken its toll on the band's level of performance. The saxophones were said to sound at times "amazingly sloppy," the intonation of the trombones "inconsistent," and the band's precision ensemble work was in tatters. The morale of the band was also suffering badly, and a whole new slate of complaints about Benny was starting to be heard around the business.

As discriminating as Benny was about his choice of material, he was still expected to play a lot of current pop tunes, and since the stock charts the music publishers provided as a matter of course were totally out of the question, he needed a capable arranger who knew how to make the most of this ephemera. Jerry Jerome and Chris Griffin both recommended Eddie Sauter.

The quiet, reserved twenty-four-year-old arranger had been writing for Red Norvo's bands and occasionally playing trumpet and mellophone with him for almost four years. Norvo was one of the most sophisticated, forward-thinking jazz musicians of his generation, and he encouraged Sauter to take a fresh, unhackneyed approach to arranging that bypassed the standard practices of the day. "Write linearly," he exhorted him, "not like Fletcher Henderson, where you write two lines and fill it in. The saxophone section should be just as easy and sound just as good with three as with four if you voice it so that the third part is just as interesting as the first." Eddie recalled: "Red and Mildred [Bailey] always encouraged me to experiment, to go one step further than I might have and to hell with whether it sold or not. I was only twenty, twenty-one and, naturally, limited in what I could do, and it meant a hell of a lot to me."

Sauter's arrangements for Red's slightly scaled-down big band were filled with unusual voicings, shifting rhythmic patterns, unexpected key changes and rich, sometimes dissonant harmonies that made it unique. Musicians and critics and the more alert jazz fans found the Norvo band's subtly complex, soft-spoken music enormously appealing, but its very virtues kept it from attracting a mass audience weaned on more blatant pleasures. By the spring of 1939 it was having trouble getting work.

Rather reluctantly Eddie accepted Benny's offer. He had recently married. Driven by a restless, questing intelligence that would never let him be completely happy in the commercial world of popular music, he had also begun studying classical composition at Juilliard and Columbia. "I think my main reason for going with Benny was to get enough money so I could pay those teachers," he explained. "I was having to put out about thirty, thirty-five dollars a week for lessons, and I couldn't do it with Red. Red was too sporadic, and Benny at least gave me the possibility of being somewhat steady."

Sauter joined the Goodman band toward the end of May, a few weeks before Fletcher arrived, and was assigned two or three pop tunes a week, some of which, he recalled, "were awful." He had brought with him the same uncompromising attitude toward orchestration he'd developed with Norvo—stretching the possibilities, pushing the limits, making a point of never falling back on the old familiar patterns—and now that he was writing for a larger ensemble that offered greater opportunities for exploration, his arrangements became even more adventuresome. This was not what was expected. "Benny had built his band around Fletcher's arrangements, and I was supposed to imitate that, I think. But I never really could."

"The guys wanted to kill me at first for recommending him." Jerry Jerome laughs. "His charts were so difficult and so involved, and they didn't sound like Benny's band. I didn't like them myself at the beginning and wondered what the hell he was doing. I had assumed Eddie would write in the Fletcher Henderson mode, like Jimmy Mundy and the band's other arrangers. Fletcher wrote in a very understandable, nice, easygoing style, and when you played one of his arrangements, the first time down was pretty much as good as it was going to get. It was fine. It just rolled. But when you started playing a Sauter arrangement for the first time—jeez! There'd be F sharps for tenor and you'd have to work out fingerings or B flats and you had to do some honking, and they were so restrictive. When Eddie sent in an arrangement, he'd even write on Benny's part, 'Play as is.' Benny would chuckle and say, 'Hey, look at this. The guy's telling me how to play.' But, you know, after about three weeks of rehearsing they would start to sound like something. And once we had them down, they got to be nice. They were fun."

If Fletcher's return brought Benny back to a comfortably familiar past, Eddie Sauter provided the fresh stimulation he also needed. Not that Sauter's arrival radically changed the direction of the Goodman orchestra, as has sometimes been assumed. Fletcher was still Benny's favorite arranger, and he did not feature Eddie's work all that extensively, certainly not at the beginning. Chris recalls that "we would play maybe one every couple of sets." The charts Sauter is best remembered for now, like "The Man I Love," "More than You Know" and the three dazzling originals "Benny Rides Again," "Superman" and "Clarinet à la King," were still a year or two away. Nor did Benny always allow Eddie's originality a completely free rein, which probably explains why the first recorded examples of his work for the band—"Rendezvous Time in Paree," "Comes Love," "Scatterbrain" and Rodgers and Hart's subpar "Love Never Went to College," all very ordinary pop tunes of the day—were orchestrated in a rather straightforward, conventional manner that reveals little of his distinctive style.

According to Jimmy Maxwell, who joined the trumpet section that August, "Benny used to edit his arrangements brutally—just brutally. He would take whole chunks out of them, leaving an open space for rhythm here, taking out this measure there, trying to make them swing. And he succeeded in doing that. Eddie's arrangements did swing in their own way, but it was a different kind of swing from Fletcher's. It was more like Duke Ellington—not a copy of Duke, but more that kind of feel. Eddie would be furious, and they would argue about it. At the time I was on Eddie's side. 'How dare you tamper with his arrangements!' But I realized later on that Benny was right, particularly after I listened to the Sauter-Finnegan band and heard how precious and involved he could get."

The band spent the month of July at the Golden Gate Exposition in San Francisco, then moved down the coast to Los Angeles. On August 10 it began a one-week engagement at the Victor Hugo restaurant in Beverly Hills. The afternoon of the opening Benny also made his first recordings for Columbia. In the three months since his final session for Victor the band had undergone very substantial changes. Three of the four saxophones had been replaced, and there was an entirely new rhythm section as well as a new vocalist. Hammond recalled that since Columbia did not have its own recording studio in Los Angeles, the session had to be held at the independent West Coast Recorders, where the "facilities were so poor I wondered when I saw them whether [Benny] would wish he had never left Victor." But to judge from the results, none of that seemed to matter.

The first tune up was the aptly titled "There'll Be Some Changes Made," and the whole band, particularly the saxophone section, sounds marvelous as it steps its way through Fletcher's arrangement of the old standard, playing with a spirit and involvement that reveal it has finally shaken off its torpor and come alive once again. Benny is in especially high spirits and sounds just as invigorated on the second number, Count Basie's irresistibly swinging "Jumpin' at the Woodside," which Basie had recorded for Decca the previous August. The last two sides of the afternoon, "Rendezvous Time in Paree" and "Comes Love," were pop tunes that offered the band less scope to strut its stuff, but it plays them well, with a greater sense of commitment than its comparable efforts for Victor a few months earlier.

The following day Benny returned to the studio to lay down four more sides. The first was Fletcher's reworking of "Stealin' Apples," the jaunty Fats Waller tune he had recorded with his own big band back in 1936 in a much less fully orchestrated arrangement. After a run-through of Chris Griffin's feature, "Boy Meets Horn," which reproduced almost note for note Duke Ellington's recording with Rex Stewart, the band moved on to Fletcher's ambitious, extremely imaginative adaptation of Ravel's *Bolero*. (Unfortunately, what with all the bad press "swinging the classics" had been getting, Ravel's estate would not allow it to be released, and it remained unissued for many years.) Five days later on August 16, just before the band returned east, it recorded four more sides, including Fletcher's rousing arrangements of "Night and Day" and Mendelssohn's "Spring Song," another exercise in swinging the classics, which managed to make its way to the public without interference. With these three sessions under his belt, Benny was very much back in the record business.

The most consequential thing to take place during Benny's two-week stay in Los Angeles, however, was not his debut recording sessions for Columbia, as important as they were, but the arrival of a young black guitar player straight off the plane from Oklahoma City, who showed up at the studio the afternoon of the first session with his guitar case in one hand and an amplifier in the other. Charlie Christian "was really a sight to see," Hammond recalled some thirty years later. "A [twenty-three]-year-old, scared kid with a big broad-rimmed Texas hat, very pointed yellow shoes, a green suit and a purple shirt with an outlandish tie. He might be in style now. He wasn't then."

Hammond had first heard about Charlie Christian four months before in the course of supervising a record date for Mildred Bailey. Mildred was being backed on this particular session by an all black pickup group that included two of the stars of the Andy Kirk band, pianist Mary Lou Williams and the guitar player Floyd Smith. Hammond admired Smith's acoustic work but found the sounds produced by the electrified metal Hawaiian guitar he sometimes also played "ghastly." Never one to keep his opinions to himself, he expressed his displeasure to the pianist. There is no reason to believe Mary Lou shared this opinion. She had, in fact, provided the arrangement for Smith's big electric guitar feature "Floyd's Guitar Blues," which they re-corded with the Kirk band sometime that same day. And Benny himself had been sufficiently intrigued by Smith's "ghastly" sounds to try to buy out his contract with Kirk. Mary Lou just shrugged and told Hammond, "If you really want to hear an electric guitar played like an acoustic guitar, you've got to go to the Ritz Cafe in Oklahoma City, where Charlie Christian works. He's the greatest electric guitar player I've ever heard." That was all Hammond had to hear. The game was afoot once again.

Hammond had to be in Los Angeles in August to supervise Benny's recordings for Columbia, so he arranged a side trip to Oklahoma City on the way out. He found Charlie's little six-piece band "pretty sad," but Charlie Christian himself was a revelation. Charlie played a regular acoustical instru-ment that he had hooked up to a primitive amplifier and small speaker, and this allowed him to phrase like a horn player, almost like a saxophone, without any of the slides and whines and tremolo Hammond had deemed so offensive in Floyd Smith's playing. And his solos were "as exciting improvisations as I had ever heard on any instrument, let alone the guitar. . . . I guess it was one of the most exciting days of my life."

Hammond felt certain that this amazing guitar player was just what Benny needed to spark his small groups, which hadn't been the same since Teddy Wilson's departure. Benny was skeptical when Hammond raved on about having just heard the greatest guitarist since Eddie Lang, but he finally agreed to send Christian the airfare when Hammond pointed out he could draw on the three-hundred-dollar weekly budget allotted for guest artists by the "Camel Caravan" show.

Although Charlie was earning only a miserable $7.50 a week, he had become something of a local legend, and his reputation was growing among the musicians in the many traveling bands that passed through Oklahoma

City. Other orchestra leaders, including, improbably enough, Henry Busse, had tried to get him to leave home without success, and he evidently had some reluctance about going off to California. "I think I was really the one who got him to join Benny Goodman," Mary Lou Williams maintained. "I used to jam with Charlie . . . when we passed through town with Andy Kirk's band, and one night in 1939 I asked him if he was going to take the Goodman job. I don't think he wanted to leave Oklahoma City, and I don't think his family wanted him to leave, either—maybe because they already knew [he was sick with tuberculosis]. All he said was, 'Mary, I'll join if you join, too.' There *was* some talk about my going with Goodman, but I told him go ahead anyway, and he did."

Charlie received a less than auspicious welcome when he showed up in Los Angeles on August 10 in the middle of Benny's first recording session. Benny was busy with the date. He had the Victor Hugo opening that evening. He was anxious to get some rest. One glance at this outlandish-looking character in the cowboy hat and purple shirt, and he went back to the business at hand. When the session ended and Benny was getting ready to leave, Hammond begged him at least to listen to the young man who had come all the way from Oklahoma to play for him. Without giving Charlie a chance to plug in his amplifier, Benny told him to chord behind him on "Tea for Two," and they played together for maybe two minutes. "At which point Benny left the studio thoroughly annoyed," Hammond said, "convinced that it was another of my 'pointless enthusiasms.' "

That evening, after the band had finished its opening set at the Victor Hugo, Hammond carried Charlie's amp and loudspeaker onto the stage while Benny was eating dinner. Then when the Goodman Quintet came on to play, he sneaked the waiting youngster in through the kitchen door. As Hammond told the story, "Goodman watched Charlie approach the bandstand, looked around the room until he spotted me and zapped me with the famous Goodman Ray. For candlepower I think this one has never been surpassed. . . . But before the opening-night audience there was nothing he could do but go along for at least one tune."

Benny called "Rose Room," a song he may have thought Charlie didn't know, but after Christian heard the opening statement of the theme, it was his, and when Benny signaled him to take a chorus, he ended up taking over twenty. The number went on for close to three-quarters of an hour. To make sure Charlie received an enthusiastic reception, Hammond had packed the bar with a claque of local musicians, but the precaution wasn't really necessary. "Everybody got up from the tables and clustered around the bandstand," he recalled, "and there could be no doubt that perhaps the most spectacularly original soloist ever to play with Goodman had been launched."

Though Hammond was much given to hyperbole, the favored rhetorical mode of the professional enthusiast, his claims for Charlie Christian's "spectacular originality" were no exaggeration. There had been a small number of important acoustical guitar soloists before him—Lonnie Johnson, Eddie Lang, Django Reinhardt and a handful of others. A few guitar players—Floyd Smith, Eddie Durham, Jim Daddy Walker, all from the Southwest, like Charlie—had begun experimenting with various forms of electrical amplification before he tried his hand at it. But as Leonard Feather observes, "With the advent of Christian, the guitar came of age in jazz," in one great leap forward transforming itself from a felt but seldom audible part of the rhythm section into a major solo voice capable of holding its own with the most commanding trumpet or saxophone. Christian's astonishing technique, harmonic sophistication, unwavering sense of swing and limitless flow of ideas, drenched in the blues but also looking ahead to the modern jazz revolution of the decade to come, set the pace for every guitar player who ever heard him, and with the exposure he gained from Benny, all of them did. "After I heard him, I could forget about everybody else," the guitarist Tiny Grimes maintained. "Christian was *it*." For Benny, he was "one of the most astounding musicians I think I've ever heard."

Benny hired Charlie on the spot, paying him something like $150 a week to play in his small group alongside Lionel, Fletcher, Artie Bernstein and Nick Fatool, which now became the first of the Goodman Sextets. Rather than record him immediately at the substandard studio Columbia was using in Los Angeles, Benny decided to hold off a few weeks until they returned to New York. Meanwhile, he played with Christian nightly and began featuring him on the "Camel Caravan" show. On the August 17 broadcast the sextet performed "Flying Home," the first of the many soon-to-be-classic riff tunes Charlie spun out with such ease, though he seldom received a fair share of the composer's credit. The guitarist Mary Osborne recalled hearing him play with a six-piece band led by Alphonso Trent in Bismarck, North Dakota, back in 1938 and maintained, "The sextet was doing everything that Benny Goodman did later and doing it even better. I remember some of the figures Charlie played in his solos—they were exactly the same things that Benny recorded later as 'Flying Home,' 'Gone with What Wind,' 'Seven Come Eleven' and all the others."

Charlie's arrival added another major soloist to the new Goodman Sextet, animating it in much the same way as all the recent changes in personnel had brought new life to the orchestra. Lionel Hampton recalled that "when Charlie Christian and I would play and get into a terrific groove, you could see tears come into [Benny's] eyes." Jimmy Maxwell agrees: "They were both very inspiring to him. If Benny had a solo after Lionel or Charlie, I'd often find him playing some of the things they had played just before. I know he didn't do it deliberately. He wasn't stealing from them. Everybody copies something they like. It was just that some of their phrasing would catch his fancy and sink into his computer bank, and it would come out in his next solo. That's how much he liked those guys. And they really did spur each other on. Sometimes when the sextet got going, we'd be off the stand for an hour or even longer because Benny wouldn't want to stop."

According to the novelist Ralph Ellison, who grew up with Charlie and his brothers in Oklahoma City, the great tenor saxophonist Lester Young probably provided the single most stimulating influence upon Christian's development as a soloist. "Lester first came to Oklahoma City in 1929, [and] left no reed player, and few young players of any instrument, unstirred by the wild, original flights of his imagination. It should be said that Lester Young didn't bring Charles Christian out of some dark nowhere. He was already out in the light. . . . Then he heard Lester and that, I think, was all he needed."

Jimmy Maxwell recalls how "Charlie would sit there in the back of the bus, singing Lester's solos over and over again. I believe he originally wanted to be a tenor sax player, but of course, he couldn't afford a saxophone. He couldn't even afford a good guitar. He had this old guitar of his uncle's and a little one-tube cigar box amplifier. The only thing he sang besides Lester's solos was 'Shimme Shewaba.' He loved that tune and would keep on it for hours, like some kind of Buddhist chant: 'She-*me* She-*wa*-ba. She'd throw it on the ceiling. She'd throw it on the wall. She'd throw it out the window, and catch it 'fore it falls.' " Charlie was a shy, quiet young man with a taste for marijuana that Benny had no choice but to overlook, and he spent a lot of his time in the back of the bus by himself, caught up in what Jerry Jerome calls "his own Charlie Christian world." "Shortly after he joined the band the Second World War broke out. One day one of the guys went back to talk to him and told Charlie about some of the latest things that were going on. 'Did you hear what the Nazis just did? They just dropped four hundred paratroopers behind the lines.' Charlie looks up and says, 'They did?' 'Yeah. What do you think about that?' All Charlie had to say was, 'Well, *solid!*' "

Most of the Goodman sidemen welcomed Charlie's arrival, but a certain number were privately critical of Benny for taking on yet another black musician, a view that was shared by enough other white players and leaders to warrant a feature article and editorial in *Down Beat* dealing with the question "Should Negro Musicians Play in White Bands?" Some of those who thought they shouldn't were against it for strictly pragmatic reasons: "It's not fair for Negroes to replace white musicians when there is so much unemployment." Others rationalized their objections by appealing to some vague sense of racial integrity: "When a Negro enters a white band, he loses his identity as a Negro musician." Yet others, protected by the anonymity they insisted upon, argued their case on more overtly racist grounds: "White people do not want to mix socially with Negroes. . . . There have been many instances of

Negro musicians making overtures to white women in the cafés they were playing. That alone is enough to incense a white man against the colored race." Or even more virulently: "The North has spoiled the Negro, and success has made him insolent and overbearing!"

Benny, of course, also had his defenders. They included Jimmy Dorsey, who said, "I think Benny should be congratulated for his courage. If anyone can make a mixed band acceptable, Benny Goodman can!" Artie Shaw insisted, "Every bandleader should be free to hire men on the basis of ability and ability alone." And Benny's former saxophone star Vido Musso offered a surprisingly shrewd observation about the commercial *benefits* Lionel, Fletcher and Charlie brought to the Goodman organization: "I not only admire Benny's musical taste in adding these men. I also think his using Negroes is a smart promotional and business move to buck all these good swing bands that are coming along to crowd him out of the limelight." Benny himself kept apart from the debate, simply saying he wanted to have the best band possible and had recently hired Christian and Henderson because "they are the best on their respective instruments."

The Goodman orchestra at Catalina Island shortly before Benny's
deteriorating health forced him to disband, June 1940.
Bottom row: Johnny Guarnieri, Les Robinson, Toots Mondello,
Red Ballard, Bus Bassey. *Top:* Artie Bernstein, Jerry Jerome,
Vernon Brown, Irving Goodman, Helen Forrest, Benny,
Nick Fatool, Jimmy Maxwell, Ted Veseley, Ziggy Elman.

Institute of Jazz Studies

19

The Hour of Parting

The band had improved dramatically over the past few months, but Benny still wasn't satisfied. Before leaving California that August, he replaced trombonist Bruce Squires and hired Jimmy Maxwell on trumpet.

"When Benny offered me the job, he had said, 'You can play first trumpet, can't you?' " Jimmy recalls, "and I said, 'Oh, sure,' when I should have said, 'I don't know, I never tried.' So I walked into the Harry James book, which was about three-fourths of the lead and at least half the solos, and to make matters worse, my first night on the job I didn't have my horn because the airline had lost it, so I had to play on strange equipment and didn't do very well. Chris said, 'You know, kid, you're in the big time now. You shouldn't be missing notes like that.' Then Ziggy jumped in. 'Tissue paper lip. You miss more notes in one hour than the rest of us do all night.' All those guys took a great deal of pride in their playing and were very conscious about being in a big name band. There were a lot of jokes about that—name band discounts and 'How about it, honey, would you like to go out with a name band musician?'

"Benny was extremely nice to me when I first came on board. He would even take me to the theater with him and invite me to have breakfast on the train. Ziggy said, 'The old man's giving you quite a honeymoon, isn't he?' I said, 'Yeah, it's really great the way he's taking me to all these places and everything.' Ziggy said, 'Who's paying?' That kind of stopped me in my tracks, and Ziggy said, 'Well, think about it.' I said, 'Well, most of the time he doesn't seem to remember his money.' Ziggy said, 'Yeah, you'd better watch him. He's not *going* to remember it either.' Benny was really funny that way."

About three weeks after Jimmy arrived, Chris Griffin quit the band once again, but this time he really meant it. "My wife, Helen, and I were expecting our second child, and we just wanted to have some kind of a life, so I decided to go back to CBS. I gave Leonard Vannerson formal notice while we were playing the New York World's Fair in Flushing. Leonard told Benny the next day when he was driving him out to the fair in Benny's new Cadillac, which was only about two days old. As they were going down Roosevelt Avenue, he says, 'How are you feeling, Benny?' Benny said, 'Okay, pops. Why?' 'Well, Chris gave me his notice last night. He wants to get through.' Just then a guy pulls out in front of them, and they mesh their fenders together. So Leonard gets out and looks at the damage, exchanges insurance information, straightens the fender so they can drive on and all the rest of it. All this takes some time, and Benny's still sitting there quietly slumped back in his seat. When they finally start moving again, Benny doesn't say anything about what happened to his brand-new car, but after they go about three blocks, he turns to Leonard, and the first words out of his mouth are, 'Aw, what the hell's Chris want to do that for?' "

Benny spent most of the fall of 1939 in New York, playing the world's fair for a week early in September, then settling into the Waldorf-Astoria for a long engagement on October 4. This gave him the opportunity to step up his recording work for Columbia, and between September and November the band stockpiled some twenty sides.

These included a few instrumentals like Fletcher's arrangements of "Down by the Old Mill Stream" and "Honeysuckle Rose" and his expansion of George Bassman's abbreviated chart of "Let's Dance," the band's familiar opening theme, but most of the material consisted of popular tunes of varying quality, given some jazz content by brief solos from Benny, Ziggy and Toots Mondello, who had become one of the band's main soloists as well as its lead alto. The preponderance of pop tunes may have been dictated by the recent popularity of the much more commercial Glenn Miller orchestra, which had finally come into its own that spring. Even Artie Shaw, who had started out adamant about playing only the very best American popular songs, was now recording his share of schlock.

Largely thanks to Charlie Christian, the musical high points of Benny's recording output that autumn were the two splendid sessions with his newly formed sextet. Charlie's presence added a third major soloist who was every bit the equal of Lionel and Benny himself, more than compensating for Fletcher's inability to match the earlier contributions made by Teddy Wilson and then Jess Stacy. Christian's knack for creating ingenious new riffs generated a repertoire of first-rate original material that Benny's big band currently lacked. And combined with Lionel's vibraphone and Benny's clarinet, his electric guitar helped create a fresh, wonderfully appealing ensemble sound quite unlike anything anyone had heard before.

The first Goodman Sextet session, which took place on October 2, placed Charlie very much in the center stage spotlight. Along with Lionel Hampton, Christian dominates "Flying Home," playing a long, loping bluesy solo that sounds as if it could go on forever. The impression that Charlie still has a whole trunkful of ideas to spare is confirmed by his chorus on the alternate take, which is just as good but completely different. Uncharacteristically, Benny relegates himself to a secondary role, confining his contributions to the ensembles that frame Charlie's and Lionel's choruses and two very brief solo statements on the opening and closing releases. The intricate unison riffing heard here, so elegantly executed that the three voices merge into one, serves as the prototype for the distinctive sextet sound also heard on "Soft Winds" and "Seven Come Eleven" recorded at the second session a month later and the other performances in this mode soon to come, like "Shivers," "AC-DC Current" and "Gone with What Wind."

The other two tunes Benny called on this date were, like "Memories of You" on the second session, standard ballads, familiar jam session fare that are appropriately played in a more open, less organized fashion. It could hardly be coincidental that "Rose Room" was the same tune that had brought Charlie and Benny together on the Victor Hugo bandstand two months earlier, and Charlie's wonderfully sunny improvisation, played with the languid phrasing and behind-the-beat relaxation favored by his idol Lester Young, can be seen as a happy look back at that momentous occasion.

The final tune of the day was "Star Dust," and once again Benny takes a back seat, splitting a single chorus with Lionel to allow Charlie room to re-create the solo that had so taken Benny's fancy he had him play it on the "Camel Caravan" show before a national audience. Alternating chords and single string work in a stunning recomposition of the familiar melody, Charlie's solo sounds so inevitably *right* that once it has been heard, it's hard to imagine the tune played any other way. There is no mystery to why Benny was so impressed, only why he chose to withhold the side from release until 1951. It is an absolutely gorgeous solo, and like a number of other great jazz solos, though it appears spontaneously conceived on the spot, it was, in fact, a carefully worked-out routine. When Charlie jammed the tune at an after-hours session in Minneapolis with Jerry Jerome and Oscar Pettiford a few weeks earlier, the results happened to be recorded by a local disc jockey, and he can be heard laying down the same set of ideas when he moves on to his second chorus. So much for the old canard that no true jazz musician ever plays the same thing twice.

On November 29, while he was still at the Waldorf-Astoria, Benny opened with the sextet at the Center Theater in *Swingin' the Dream*, a musical comedy extravaganza loosely based on Shakespeare's *A Midsummer Night's Dream*. Conceived by the German producer Erik Charell, the show was the theatrical equivalent of all those big band efforts at swinging the classics and was probably inspired by the two competing swing versions of Gilbert and Sullivan's *The Mikado* that had played for a while on Broadway earlier that year. The scene of Shakespeare's comedy was shifted from Athens to New Orleans, "The Athens of the Old South," as the program notes put it, the time updated to the 1890s, "At the Birth of Swing," and the elaborate plot of mistaken identities radically simplified to allow plenty of room for singing, dancing and comedy turns by the predominantly black cast.

The Center was a great white elephant of a theater directly across the street from Radio City Music Hall. Its five thousand seats had hardly ever been filled by the various productions tried there since it opened in 1932, and it was badly in need of a hit. Charell pulled out all the stops to give it one. Rarely had any Broadway show been so laden with talent.

Along with Benny, the star headliners were Louis Armstrong, who had an acting role as Bottom, now dressed in a fireman's outfit, and the popular singer Maxine Sullivan, who played Titania, Queen of the Pixies, making her entrance in a motorized guide's chair from the New York World's Fair. The huge supporting cast of 150 included Moms Mabley, Butterfly McQueen and Dorothy Dandridge, as well as a handful of white Broadway actors like Ruth Ford and Dorothy McGuire. The book was written by the noted author and jazz fan Gilbert Seldes in collaboration with Charell. Half a dozen new songs were contributed by Jimmy Van Heusen and Eddie De Lange, including the future standard "Darn That Dream." Agnes De Mille supervised the choreography. Herbert White's Lindy Hoppers were brought down from the Savoy Ballroom for a couple of specialty numbers. Walt Disney provided the artwork for the sets. As for music, there was the Goodman Sextet in a side box on the left of the stage, Bud Freeman's splendid Summa Cum Laude band on the right and a full orchestra conducted by Don Voorhees (Benny's brother Freddy was in the trumpet section) playing in the pit. Even the rehearsal pianist was no less an eminence than the great composer and stride pianist James P. Johnson.

There had been some concern that this tampering with a venerated classic would call down the same outrage from the purists as the swing bands' "profanations" of Bach. But if anything, the opening night reviewers found fault with the adapters for being overly respectful of the original Shakespeare text, and most of them were disappointed that what had seemed like such a promising idea hadn't worked out better. The Goodman Sextet, though, safely ensconced on the side of the stage away from the dialogue and machinations of the plot, received almost unanimous praise. "Nothing that is left in the hodge-podge of Shakespeariana that opened at the Center Theater last evening can hold a candle to the virtuosity of the Benny Goodman Sextet," Brooks Atkinson wrote in the *New York Times*. "Mr. Goodman's contribution is the only one that pulls loose from a poorly assembled show and unfailingly bursts into swing rapture. With Lionel Hampton skipping gayly over the vibraharp, Mr. Goodman and his musicians perform with extraordinary brilliance."

Gilbert Seldes's daughter, the actress Marian Seldes, still recalls the tremendous impact Benny's performance had on her as an eleven-year-old:

> I had never heard anyone play like Goodman and had never seen anyone like him on the stage. He seemed completely without ego, which does not mean without personality. I thought that even when he was playing he was smiling, but that of course must have been his eyes. And I remember he wore glasses, and that seemed strange to me. I had been to the theater a lot, but this man was not like any other. I realize now that what impressed me and stayed with me in memory was—the sounds he made. He played so purely. The music seemed to come from him, not just the instrument he played with such mastery.
>
> Years later—I think it was a year or so before he died—I met Benny Goodman at a party given for him by William Livingston's magazine *HiFi & Stereo Review*. Because of the tiny connection with *Dream* they brought me up to him and took our picture. I told him who I was, feeling rather shy. "Oh," he said, "I met you when you were a little girl when your father brought you backstage." He was soft-spoken and gentle and charming, and I was always glad I had the chance to tell him how much pleasure he had given me through the years and that he was the first and best and most brilliant clarinetist I had ever heard.

In the hope of attracting the largest possible audience, ticket prices had been scaled down to a very modest $2.20 top, with hundreds of orchestra seats going for as little as $1.65. But the bad reviews were just too damaging. *Swingin' the Dream* closed on December 9 after only thirteen performances. The reported loss was nearly $100,000, making it one of the costliest theatrical failures of recent years. Benny picked up the slack by returning to a full schedule of sets at the Waldorf, where Nat Brandwynne's orchestra had been substituting for him in the early part of the evening.

As 1939 drew to a close, Benny had almost completed the laborious task of reshaping the band's personnel—almost but not quite. "In spite of all the changes in his band in recent months, supposedly to make it more perfect than ever before, Benny Goodman is still not satisfied with the results," Leonard Feather reported in *Down Beat* that December. "Possibilities are that John Martel and Jimmy Maxwell will have been replaced by December 1." Martel had come in for Chris Griffin in September, and by February he was gone. From the look of things, it certainly seemed that Jimmy Maxwell was also on his way out.

"Benny fired me because of Duke Ellington." Jimmy laughs. "I was very much in awe of Benny, but at the same time I hung around his dressing room and talked to him a lot because I enjoyed hearing him tell stories. Well, it seemed to me that Eddie Sauter's arrangements were great but that Fletcher Henderson's had seen better days and we ought to get somebody else more in Eddie's vein. I couldn't really tell Benny that, but while we were talking one day I said to him, 'If you like colored arrangers so much, why don't you use some of Duke Ellington's charts?' Benny just looked at me, then said, 'Do you really *like* that band, pops?' I was amazed. I thought jazz musicians were always honest with each other, so I said, 'Sure, it's the greatest band that ever was.' He said, 'Yeah? Do you think so? I always kind of thought *my* band is.' I couldn't believe he was serious, so when he asked me, 'And who's your favorite clarinet player?' I told him Barney Bigard, who was playing with Ellington at that time. About an hour later Leonard Vannerson came over to me and said, 'The old man wants to see you.' I went back to Benny's dressing room, and he said, 'You know, pops, I don't think I want anybody in the band who doesn't think *we're* the best. I'm going to let you go.' I said I was sorry about that, but I thought we were being honest. So Benny put me on notice and started trying out new trumpet players. There were a whole bunch of them. He kept me on notice for about six months, but for one reason or another he never did get around to replacing me."

On December 11, though, two days after *Swingin' the Dream* drew its final gasp, Benny did replace Fletcher Henderson on piano. The strain of having to produce a constant flow of new arrangements while he was also holding down the piano chair in both the band and the sextet had proved too much for Fletcher's fragile health, and he had been after Benny to hire another pianist so he could concentrate on his writing. Although Benny bristled at the growing complaints that Fletcher was the one weak link in an otherwise admirable rhythm section, he couldn't really deny them, and after considering a number of possibilities, including Clarence Profit and Joe Bushkin, he decided upon a young piano player with a solid classical background though not much of a jazz reputation who was hidden away in George Hall's very commercial dance band.

"When I joined Benny Goodman, it was like a fulfillment of a beautiful dream for me. It was what I had lived and worked for," Johnny Guarnieri recalled. But this dream, too, was short-lived. "When I first joined Benny, he called me 'Fletcher' for three months before he could remember my name. And then he told me I was the worst piano player he'd had since Frankie Froeba. He didn't like my so-called 'imitating' other pianists."

"Johnny would sit there with Benny and start playing like Fats Waller, and Benny would say, 'Stop doing that!' " Jimmy Maxwell remembers. "Then he'd play like Teddy Wilson, and Benny would glare at him. Finally Johnny said, 'Well, who *do* you want me to play like?' and Benny said, 'Can't you play like Johnny Guarnieri?' Johnny had those styles *down*. He could also play like Alec Templeton, who had all those opera routines, and he would do them at intermission if Benny couldn't catch him in time. He was a funny guy. He knew all of Sherlock Holmes by heart and every baseball score back to the beginning of baseball. He was such a Sherlock Holmes fan he wore the deerstalker's cap and the inverness cape and smoked a meerschaum pipe. One time we walked into a restaurant in San Diego in the middle of summer, and everybody took a look at him in that getup and started laughing. Johnny stops and says, 'I ascertain I am the source of comic relief.' I'm afraid I have to take Benny's side about anything that happened to him in that band. He was a very eccentric character."

"I'll tell you, though," Guarnieri maintained, "both Lionel Hampton and Charlie Christian would tell me, 'Don't let Benny scare you. You're a *piano player,* Johnny—and you *swing.*' As a matter of fact, Lionel and Charlie were the only two guys in the band who would talk to me when I joined. All the other guys were 'big shots' and I wasn't." Johnny *did* swing, no matter what style he played in, and despite his differences with Benny, he continued with him off and on until 1941.

About the same time Johnny Guarnieri joined Benny at the Waldorf his new vocalist, Helen Forrest, also made her debut. Helen had been the featured singer with Artie Shaw's enormously popular orchestra, but three weeks earlier, on November 18, Artie walked off the bandstand of the Hotel Pennsylvania across town, got into his car and drove away from all the pressures that had made life so intolerable for him over the past year.

"I was going through a peculiar transition from musician to 'celebrity,' " Shaw explained some years later. "A celebrity was not something I was equipped to be. By mid-1939 the pressures were enormous and had been building for some time. . . . Progressively I moved away from my musicians. I couldn't seem to communicate with anyone. I found it impossible to articulate the problems at that time. I can't tell you how lonely I was. But I was determined to get out, to relieve the tension."

"At the stage I was in then, any little thing would have been sufficient," Shaw wrote in his autobiography, *The Trouble with Cinderella*, "and so, because of a slight unpleasantness with some idiot on the floor in front of the band, who was evidently trying to impress his partner by using me as a focal point for his witticisms, I suddenly decided I'd had it." Driving through a heavy snowstorm with no clear idea of where he was going, he headed south and ended up in Acapulco, where he spent the winter months swimming and fishing and loafing around in the sun while trying to put his career in some kind of perspective.

When Helen Forrest heard Benny was looking for a new vocalist, she telephoned him at the Waldorf. She recalled:

> He said I was his singer. I didn't even have to audition. All I had to do was accept a cut in pay from the $175 a week I'd been making with Artie to $85 a week with Benny. I took it. I wanted to work. I wanted to sing with Benny's band. . . . I don't know why Benny took me. A couple of years earlier he had walked out on me in Washington, saying I couldn't sing. Maybe I couldn't. Maybe I was singing better by the time he took me. But I don't know that he ever really listened to me. I think he took me because I was becoming a big singer and he had to have a singer and he didn't care about singers anyway, and he figured he could do worse.

By the middle of December the personnel of the band was finally in place. In an unusually candid interview with *Down Beat*, Benny was able to express both his satisfaction and his relief:

> A great many things have happened to my band during the past twelve months. Three out of four saxes were changed (Jerry Jerome alone remaining). A third trombone was added. Two out of three trumpets were changed, and the entire rhythm section was overhauled. . . .
>
> The changes were dictated by necessity. I wasn't kidding myself last year at this time. The band was going through a period of slump that had me worried more than I cared to admit. In addition, competition began to be noticed. At one time last year new bands were springing up so rapidly it was hard to keep track of them. The combination of events indicated that if we were to maintain our position as top band of the country we would have to do some fast work. . . . Speaking objectively as possible, I'm willing to be judged on the changes made. I think the band sounds better than it ever has in the past.

Looking back over the past year, Benny had good reason to be so pleased with what he'd managed to accomplish. He had survived the loss of star sidemen like Harry James and Teddy Wilson and completed the long, uncertain process of building a new band virtually from the ground up, fine-tuning it to the point where it finally met his exacting standards. He had also weathered the separation from Willard Alexander and the attendant difficulties with MCA, successfully negotiated the tricky transition from Victor to Columbia and faced the growing competition from Artie Shaw and Glenn Miller and the dozens of other up-and-coming swing bands with his popularity intact, all the while continuing to race along at full throttle through a relentless schedule of one-nighters, theater tours, hotel dates, record sessions and radio broadcasts. Surely the physical and emotional wear and tear all this exacted would have been entirely too much for anyone less fiercely driven by the desire for perfection and the need to succeed. But even Benny had his limits.

Benny had been having problems with his health all that summer, but it wasn't until the end of the year that he finally got around to doing something about it. After playing the final "Camel Caravan" show on December 30 and finishing up at the Waldorf on New Year's Day, he put the band on vacation and went down to Florida for what he described as "a couple of weeks of golf and relaxation." It all sounded quite casual, but this was the first extended time off the band as a whole had ever had, and the two-week hiatus forced the cancellation of a number of important bookings, including the birthday ball for President Roosevelt at Madison Square Garden, a swing concert at Town Hall, a date at the Paramount Theater and a return to the Victor Hugo in Los Angeles.

Benny was experiencing severe attacks of pain in his left leg, the result of what was provisionally diagnosed as sciatica, an inflammation of the sciatic nerve that runs from the lower spine down into the legs. Benny's physicians agreed the only way he could possibly hope to get some relief was through total and complete rest, yet after rejoining the band in New York City, he picked up his usual hectic pace, recording four sides on January 16, then taking off on a tour of one-nighters in upstate New York, New England and Washington, D.C. While playing a dance in Worcester, Massachusetts, he was floored with pain, and there were several nights it became so severe Ziggy had to front the band in his place. But Benny refused to let up. Following a marathon recording session in early February with the band and sextet and an all-star group of *Metronome* poll winners, he returned to the road for a series of theater dates in Pittsburgh, Indianapolis and Chicago.

By the time he arrived in Chicago on February 23, the pain had become constant and was now so excruciating it kept him doubled over the entire week, causing the doctors to immobilize the afflicted leg in a special orthopedic brace in the hope of providing some ease. Despite his miserable physical condition, Benny refused to miss any shows, smiled gamely when a photographer posed him next to two pretty jitterbugs ("I love 'em as long as they look as good as these") and honored his commitment to perform a free concert for the youngsters at Hull House. But once the engagement ended and he completed yet another recording session, he had no choice but to break up the band temporarily and fly down to the spa at Hot Springs, Arkansas, for more extensive treatment. "A couple of weeks of taking minerals baths and resting will fix me up in fast order," he insisted. Following Benny's lead, Leonard Vannerson assured the press that although a number of theater bookings had to be canceled, "I think we'll be in good shape again when we hit California," where the band was scheduled to open at the Cocoanut Grove on March 19.

When the band reassembled in Los Angeles, Benny claimed he was feeling "much improved" and gave himself over to another whirlwind burst of heavy activity. During his seven-week stay at the Grove he recorded a dozen more sides with the band and sextet. The night after he closed he performed the Mozart Clarinet Concerto at the Hollywood Bowl with Leopold Stokowski. The following week there was another record session featuring a guest appearance by Fred Astaire, and the week after that the recording of *Contrasts* with Béla Bartók and Joseph Szigeti. In the middle of May he left Los Angeles for a tour of one-nighters in Arizona and the Pacific Northwest, moved back down the coast to San Francisco for an engagement at the Mark Hopkins Hotel, then followed that up in June with a one-month stand at Catalina Island, a resort about forty miles west of Los Angeles. All this was bound to catch up with him eventually, and it finally did.

"The band was cooking at Catalina," Jerry Jerome remembers. "It was really good. We had a wonderful month there, and it was a great job, and everybody was happy. But Benny was in terrible shape. The pain had gotten so bad he had to play with his foot up on a barstool to get some relief, and he was very bent over. It was awful. That was the first time I ever saw him take a drink. Benny never drank, but one night he offered me a brandy between sets, and then he looked at me and said, 'Drinking with the leader, huh?' as if he couldn't believe what was happening. And there were so many old wives' tales about what to do. People would tell him to heat up bags of salt and put them on his leg or recommend chiropractors or masseurs. But nothing seemed to work. He was in constant pain. You couldn't tell it from his playing, though. There was nothing I could hear that was wrong. Forget about it, he was still blowing like a man possessed. Benny was almost a Christian Scientist when it came to his health. Some nights he'd be feeling so rotten, but then he'd just turn around and pass it off and start blowing. That was more important. By the same token, of course, he would not tolerate other people having their problems. He couldn't stand that. 'What do you mean, you don't feel well? Come on, come on, blow your horn and forget about it. You'll feel better.' "

According to one estimate, Benny had followed the prescriptions of no fewer than nineteen physicians from Hartford to Santa Catalina, but all to no avail. His left leg was almost totally paralyzed by now. Despite his efforts to obscure or at least minimize his condition, there was starting to be a lot of troublesome gossip that the band was falling apart and his playing days were over. This was given a certain amount of credibility when Benny's longtime manager Leonard Vannerson announced he had left the Goodman organization and taken a job with a public relations firm in Los Angeles so he could be with his new wife, Benny's former singing star Martha Tilton. Shortly after opening at Catalina, Benny sent a telegram to *Down Beat* imploring the magazine to set the record straight: "I am not retiring, nor is my band breaking up. Please make this clear and help dispel rumors appearing in other publications."

On July 10, five days before the Catalina stand came to an end, Benny left the band, not for a vacation in the Maine woods, as the press had been led to believe, but for the Mayo Clinic in Rochester, Minnesota, where he underwent surgery two days later. The underlying cause of Benny's problem had been diagnosed as a ruptured vertebral disk, one of the rings of cartilage interspersed between the bones of the spine. The nucleus pulposus, the soft substance in the center of the disk, had protruded through the surrounding cartilage and pressed upon the sciatic nerve emerging from the spinal cord, resulting in the agonizing pain and partial paralysis that had beset him over the past months. This condition, most commonly known as a slipped disk, was relatively rare and just beginning to be understood. Though it is now usually dealt with more conservatively through an extended period of rest, in Benny's case surgery was deemed necessary to bring about a permanent cure.

Kay Kyser, an old favorite of the Catalina crowd, and Ziggy Elman, shared fronting the band for the remainder of the engagement. MCA tried booking a national tour under Ziggy's leadership, but there wasn't much interest, and the plan to have Ziggy take over until Benny got back on his feet had to be abandoned. The last night of the Catalina engagement was the last night of the Benny Goodman orchestra. Lying in his hospital bed hundreds of miles away, Benny watched everything he had brought into being over the past year—the hard-won result of all those long months of worry, planning, unrelenting effort and stubborn refusal to be satisfied with anything less than the best—turn into ashes.

Had Benny picked up the current issue of *Metronome* from his night table and glanced at the record reviews, he would have seen an unintended testament to what he managed to accomplish:

At last a bunch of really good Goodman sides—all in one month! Plenty of musical excitement, most of it occasioned by Benny's brilliant blowing. Top ten inches are "The Hour of Parting," a wonderful arrangement that hits a perfect tempo. . . . Good figures help get the good beat on the reverse ("Coconut Grove"). . . . More brilliant bite, beat and Benny in "Can't You Tell." . . . Pianist Johnny Guarnieri plays some neat Basian piano in "Crazy Rhythm" and backs Helen Forrest's "Mr. Meadowlark" vocal tastefully, while there's more exciting Benny on both. . . . The entire band gets a wonderful lift on "Just Like Taking Candy from a Baby," which has a good Fred Astaire personality vocal. . . . Highlights of some ballad sides are Eddie Sauter's lovely arrangement of "The Moon Won't Talk" . . . and Toot's lead and hot alto on "I Can't Love You Anymore."

But all that now had suddenly become so much ancient history.

A core of key sidemen—Lionel Hampton, Charlie Christian, Ziggy Elman, Jimmy Maxwell, Artie Bernstein—were kept on salary so they'd be available whenever Benny was ready to come back. So were Eddie Sauter and Helen Forrest, but everyone else was let go. Benny's loss proved to be Artie Shaw's gain. After a few months lounging about in the Acapulco sun, "I began to feel an old familiar restlessness creeping up on me again," Artie recalled. To meet his commitment to Victor, that March he recorded half a dozen sides with a large orchestra of studio musicians in Los Angeles, including an attractive Latin melody that had caught his ear down in Mexico. When "Frenesi" turned into an immediate hit, he began putting together another band. Johnny Guarnieri had joined him a few weeks earlier, and now he also hired Jerry Jerome, Vernon Brown, Bus Bassey, Nick Fatool and Les Robinson. When Benny was asked the inevitable question, "Did Artie Shaw raid your band?" he answered, "Not at all. Artie did me a favor. All my band was on notice. Artie needed good musicians. So he offered to take some of my boys for his own outfit."

Benny remained at the Mayo Clinic until August 3, then flew to Banff, Canada, for a few weeks of rest. "He's happy up there," one of his brothers reported. "The other day he sent for his clarinet and a whole batch of records, so it looks as if he's really going to whip himself back into shape as soon as he can." Benny was said to be already making plans for a new band and claimed to be feeling "wonderful." But the operation was not wholly successful, and his problems with his back were never really cured.

Some twenty years later Jess Stacy joined Benny for an appearance on a Dinah Shore television show. "It was the last time I ever played with him, and as usual he wanted everything to be letter-perfect. We went over that damn tune so many times my fingers were swollen and I didn't ever want to hear it again. Well, I went down to his dressing room to talk to him about something, and he happened to have his shirt off. Do you know what a horse collar looks like? That's the kind of contraption he was wearing under his clothes so he'd be able to stand up from that back operation. God, it was awful. I felt so sorry for him."

"Benny never made any kind of reference to it at all," his friend Bill Savory tells us, "but he was frequently in a lot of very severe physical discomfort. Sometimes when I visited him, it would be transparent. He would start playing something, and then he'd suddenly stop because he was unable to concentrate any longer. He wouldn't talk about it. He'd just look up at the ceiling, move himself a little and say something like 'Let's have lunch.' Or he would take a couple pain-killers and muscle relaxants—he always had an assortment of pills around—and go off for a nap. The pills had to have their own effect, and along with the pain I think they accounted for a lot of his later rather idiosyncratic behavior.

"At times the pain would get so bad his playing would start to show it. One night when he was working with a small group, it had him so distracted he even went off on the basic structure of a tune that was very familiar to him, and one of the sidemen had to jump in and take over. Benny looked up in surprise, immediately heard what he'd done wrong, nodded at the guy and went on playing. The guy told me about it later and said, 'The pain must have been intense, or Benny would never have gotten that far off.'

"But he always tried to maintain an outward air of well-being. When an interviewer would ask him, 'Well, how's your back?' Benny wouldn't even answer him. He'd just stare out the window. It would have made him much more sympathetic if people realized what he was going through, but he didn't want there to be any excuses for his playing. Benny wanted the artistic judgment to be made solely on his performance, uncolored by any kind of sympathy they might have felt for him. In Benny's view, his physical condition was of absolutely no relevance to anyone who was interested in his music. Besides, he was the kind of person who would rather keep things like that quiet. Very quiet. The net upshot was that over the years there was a hell of a lot of misunderstanding of Benny's personality."

**The splendid Goodman band of 1941 with
Mel Powell, Peggy Lee, Vido Musso, Jimmy Maxwell and Billy Butterfield.**
Institute of Jazz Studies

Benny Rides Again

Despite assurances from John Hammond and other Goodman spokesmen that the surgery was completely successful and Benny would be back with a new band as soon as he completed his recuperation, the rumors persisted that at the age of thirty-one his playing days were over. When a reporter summoned up the nerve to question Benny himself about his future, he fluffed off the suggestion that he was planning to retire and, smiling gamely, answered, "My new band will be the greatest thing the dance band business has ever heard. That is, I hope it will be. My trouble is that I'm not even sure what I want. . . ."

Benny returned to New York in October 1940, three months after his operation, looking fairly fit, if still a little weak. He immediately began auditioning and rehearsing a great variety of musicians but did not yet have a very clear sense of direction about the kind of orchestra he wanted to put together. At least part of his uncertainty came from the fact that during his recuperation two of the key sidemen he had kept on salary had left. After what was reported as "a minor argument" with Benny, Ziggy Elman accepted an offer from Tommy Dorsey to replace the increasingly unreliable Bunny Berigan as Tommy's featured trumpet player. Then Lionel Hampton decided this was the opportune moment to take the big step forward he had been contemplating for some time and left to start his own orchestra, an inevitable move that received Benny's blessing and very possibly his financial support.

Ziggy and Lionel were, of course, both extremely strong soloists with a great deal of musical personality. Their presence had had a lot to do with shaping the character of Benny's music, and their departure left him with very little to draw on from the past. But if this created some formidable difficulties, it also gave him the opportunity to do some serious rethinking about how to proceed, and even while he was holding rehearsals, he was still weighing a number of very different options.

One possibility was scaling the band down to a much smaller size, which would both reduce his expenses and give him more of the musical flexibility and freedom he had found so gratifying with the sextet. At the other extreme, he was also exploring the possibility of augmenting a full-size big band with a double string quartet and had asked Eddie Sauter to write a number of arrangements for this instrumentation. The expanded personnel would make the band harder to book in hotels and ballrooms, but Benny was thinking about cutting back on this sort of work to concentrate on radio and records, which would be far less demanding on his still-fragile health, and he was close to signing a contract with one of the networks for a new weekly series. If the strings were likely to alienate some of the jitterbugs, Benny wasn't all that wedded to this part of his audience, and he was certainly aware of how successfully Artie Shaw had employed them on his recent hit record of "Frenesi."

Along with the commercial advantages they had to offer, strings also had their own strictly musical appeal. As Jimmy Maxwell points out, "Benny liked strings because of his penchant for classical music. I think he had the idea somewhere in the back of his mind that he was going to be the guy who finally brought together the marriage of classical music and jazz." Benny held several rehearsals with the string section, but according to Maxwell, Sauter's charts were disappointing. "Like most jazz arrangers, he didn't really know what to do with the strings, so they were just holding long chord notes while Benny noodled over them." Benny abandoned this experiment when the radio series fell through. Some twenty years later, though, Sauter demonstrated just how well he had learned to write for a string orchestra when he composed and arranged the magnificent *Focus* album for Stan Getz.

The most exciting and most radical possibility Benny had under consideration was a fully integrated big band composed of an equal number of black and white musicians. This sounds highly reminiscent of the all-star mixed band Hammond had tried to put together for Benny to take to Europe back in 1934, but this time around Benny himself seems to have been the energizing force. "I want to play for kicks instead of trying to please the mob," he had told friends while still recovering up in Canada, and by "playing for kicks" he meant working alongside black musicians of the caliber of Lester Young, Teddy Wilson, Earl Hines, Cozy Cole and Red Allen, all of whom were viewed as likely candidates for the new Goodman orchestra.

When the New York newspaper columnists discovered that Benny was seeking out black musicians, they wanted to play up the racial angle in their stories, but Benny's publicist was able to persuade them that this really wasn't all that important. MCA, however, was not so compliant and argued with Benny that a mixed band was simply not practical and would create too many booking problems. "It's possible that it would have been too hard," Jimmy Maxwell agrees, citing the kinds of hassles Benny had to contend with when he had only one or two black players with him: "The night we opened at the New Yorker there was trouble right from the start. I was sitting with Benny when the hotel manager came down and said, 'I don't want the colored musicians coming in the front door and walking through the ballroom.' Benny said, 'Look, you knew I had colored musicians when you hired me. If you don't like it, we can pack up and leave.' The manager said, 'Well, it doesn't look good. Just tell them I want them to come in through the kitchen.' Benny said, 'I don't think you want my band to play here. I think we better fold up right now. I'm not telling anybody to come in the back door.' I was surprised just how strongly he felt about it. He wouldn't take any nonsense at all."

Although Benny was finally pressured into giving up the idea of a fully integrated band, he continued considering individual black musicians, and around the middle of October he managed the extraordinary coup of luring the great Cootie Williams away from Duke Ellington. Cootie had taken part in the Ellington segment of Benny's 1938 Carnegie Hall concert and came away convinced the Goodman orchestra was "the greatest swing band I had ever heard." Benny was also impressed by the trumpet player's strong performance, but what really captured his attention and planted the seed for having Williams join him was the Ellington recording of "Concerto for Cootie," released shortly before Benny went off to the hospital in the summer of 1940.

"I used to carry around this windup phonograph and a cardboard box full of Louis Armstrong and Duke Ellington records," Jimmy Maxwell remembers. "Benny's brother Irving would sit with me on the bus, and we'd listen to them together. 'Concerto for Cootie' was one of the records we played all the time. One day Benny came back and asked us, 'Who is that trumpet player?' and Irving said, 'You've got to be kidding, Benny. That's Cootie Williams.' Benny just nodded and said, 'Yeah, that's a pretty good solo he plays there.' " The following October Benny had Irving call the creator of that "pretty good solo" and offer him a job. After negotiating Benny up to a two-hundred-dollar-a-week salary, more than Ellington could pay him, Cootie agreed to a one-year contract playing with the sextet, and he joined Benny in New York a few weeks later.

The 1940 Duke Ellington band was the finest of his long career, arguably the finest in the entire history of jazz, and Cootie Williams was one of its most glorious adornments. He had been the featured trumpet soloist with the Ellington orchestra for over a decade, and now that it had attained the very pinnacle of perfection, it was almost inconceivable that he would leave. Williams's departure was reported to be a terrible blow to Ellington, putting him at a complete loss for a replacement. Ellington fans were outraged. "I find [Benny Goodman's] action as contemptible as his clarinet playing," one of them wrote to *Down Beat* in "regret and disgust." "Evidently the 'King of Swing' has no artistic conscience whatsoever." An editorial in *Metronome* took Benny to task for absconding with "one of the brightest stars from the greatest aggregation jazz has ever known," and Cootie received hundreds of letters reproaching him for his defection. Raymond Scott even composed a lament commemorating this tragic event titled "When Cootie Left the Duke."

All this heavy emotionalism cast a lot more heat than light, and the following month Cootie tried to set the record straight by explaining that he had left Ellington not because of money but for the sake of his own musical self-fulfillment and continued artistic growth, "a grand opportunity to express myself more completely and freely than I ever have before." Nor was Cootie's departure as traumatic for Ellington as had generally been assumed. On the contrary, Cootie claimed that Ellington actually stage-managed his negotiations with Benny to make sure he would receive a suitable salary and be given the proper exposure. As for being left without an adequate replacement, the night after Williams handed in his notice Duke hired Ray Nance, a wonderful trumpet player who remained with him for many years and made his own distinctive contributions to Ellington's continuing greatness.

Cootie Williams was a highly disciplined musician who took great pride in his professionalism, and he always maintained that the year he spent with Benny was the happiest of his life. "Cootie swore up to the last time I saw him that Benny's band was the best band he ever played with," Jimmy Maxwell maintains. "I asked him how he could say that compared to Duke Ellington, and he told me, 'Because when Benny's band came in, they took care of business. They were on time. Their uniforms were neat. Everybody sat down and did what they were supposed to do.' I could see what he meant when I played with Duke for a while in 1962. All those years in a secret part of my heart I thought maybe I should have said to hell with my family and gone off with Duke Ellington, but when he finally offered me the job, I realized I couldn't have lasted a month with that band. It would have driven me crazy the way everyone showed up three hours late for rehearsal and all that casual anarchy. It's a prestige thing with some musicians. They think the later they come in, the bigger they are. Cootie had no tolerance for that, so he liked being with Benny's band." And Benny was delighted to have him there. In years to come he would say that Cootie Williams was the most able trumpet player who ever worked for him, surpassing even Harry James.

If there was one dissonant note, it was the pervasive racism that Cootie, like all the other black musicians who worked with white bands, had to contend with off the stand. "After Leonard Vannerson left, one of Benny's brothers became the road manager, and he did not really look out for the black musicians that well," Jimmy explains. "When we'd pull into a town, they often couldn't get into the white hotels and wouldn't have any place to stay. But Cootie and I did manage to room together. I would check in, sign 'Charles Melvin Williams' and 'James Davis Maxwell' on the hotel register, and then he'd come up to the room with me. He wanted to carry my bags so they'd think he was the bandboy, but I refused to go that far. I would try to get Cootie to come into the dining room with me, and I'd tell him, 'If they don't feed you, we'll bust up the place.' But he'd say, 'No, I don't make trouble.' It cost me a fortune with Cootie because I wouldn't eat in the dining room if he couldn't, so we both ended up getting room service. When there were black waiters, though, if you ordered a steak, they would bring you three of them."

Benny continued trying out musicians during the latter part of October, gradually hiring men like the fine Teagarden-influenced trombonist Lou McGarity and Artie Shaw's former saxophone star Georgie Auld. The one major change from his earlier instrumentation was the addition of a third alto player who doubled on baritone, and when the band started recording in November, Cootie usually sat in with the trumpet section, bringing the number of trumpets up to four for the first time.

Benny rehearsed most afternoons at the CBS studio, at first rather casually, frequently interrupting work on the arrangements to jam with his sidemen, but as the band started to coalesce, he stepped up the rehearsals to two a day and began to bear down in his old familiar manner. Not yet satisfied with its level of performance, he put off taking any long-term engagements in major hotels or ballrooms, preferring instead to play casual one-nighters a few nights a week around the New York area so he could woodshed the band on the job until it was ready to come to full public notice.

At the same time Benny was whipping the band into shape he was also working out the format and personnel for his new small group. By the end of October he had settled upon a seven-piece expanded "sextet" that included

Cootie on trumpet, Georgie Auld on tenor saxophone and a four-man rhythm section featuring Charlie Christian. Early in November Benny brought the group into the studio to make its debut recordings with Count Basie sitting in on piano. The results were remarkable, all the more so when one considers that Cootie had just come aboard and there had been virtually no time to break the group in over the course of rehearsals and live performances.

The four sides recorded that day—"Wholly Cats," "Royal Garden Blues," "As Long As I Live" and "Benny's Bugle"—are among the most successfully realized examples of small band swing ever made, in both conception and execution, perfectly balancing the sort of richly detailed ensemble work normally found only in big bands with the unconstrained improvising of impromptu jams. As befitting its larger size, the new seven-man Goodman Sextet is much more highly organized than were the trio and quartet or even the earlier sextet with Lionel Hampton. The three-horn front line provides a distinctively light, tightly voiced ensemble sound that is enormously pleasing, and when it masses its power, as in the final choruses of "Royal Garden Blues," it swings with the joyful ferocity of the entire Count Basie orchestra. If the sextet bears some resemblance to Duke Ellington's small group recordings in its careful blending of ensemble control and solo abandon, Benny's choice of hard-driving riff tunes to set its basic style suggests that the Basie band, along with Charlie Christian's guitar lines, gave him his primary inspiration and model. Benny and Charlie had sat in with the Basie band only two weeks earlier, and Basie's presence here, whether initiated by Hammond or Benny himself, certainly provided added assurance that the riffing would come out right. This particular edition of the sextet recorded just fourteen sides, a surprisingly small number considering the large place it occupies in the hearts and minds of all swing fans, and Basie appeared on more than half of them.

The ensemble playing on this first session is so varied and imaginative and beautifully executed it can be cherished for its own sake, but its immediate purpose is to frame and set off the soloists, and it is the exalted level of solo work here that ultimately makes these recordings so very memorable. The combination of Benny Goodman, Cootie Williams, Charlie Christian and Count Basie presented a formidable lineup of acknowledged masters, and if the young tenor saxophonist Georgie Auld had not yet attained quite the same degree of eminence, he had no trouble at all keeping up with them. As Cootie observed, "Each man could take care of himself. There was never a let down. Soon as one guy stopped playing, here comes another right in on top. With Benny no one could sit back—and *he* couldn't either." This last point is an important one and helps explain why, on all but "As Long As I Live," Benny ordered the sequence of solos so he was the last to come in, after the others had had their say and set the standard of performance he would have to match. And he rises to the challenge magnificently, playing with tremendous vitality and sense of excitement that surely had to dispel any lingering rumors about his being washed up.

Benny sounds just as invigorated on the debut recordings of the big band made one week later, soloing with bubbly good humor on "Nobody" and great warmth on "The Man I Love," then, after romping energetically through Fletcher's "Henderson Stomp," shifting to the concentrated lyricism of "Benny Rides Again." Like the recording date that introduced the re-vamped sextet, this session serves as a very clear notice that Benny is now off to something quite new and different. Three of the four sides are orchestrated by Eddie Sauter, and it is here that Eddie finally breaks free from the old swing band conventions that had constrained him in the past and is allowed to reveal the sort of highly original work he was capable of producing.

Starting with the brooding introduction that segues immediately and unexpectedly into Helen Forrest's superb vocal, "The Man I Love" is a radical rethinking of the fresh melodic and harmonic possibilities inherent in Gershwin's familiar standard, filled with unusual voicings and richly textured background figures. "Benny Rides Again" is even more startling. Eddie's first original composition for the Goodman orchestra, composed without the pres-sure of a deadline while Benny was still recuperating from his operation, it is an ambitious, extremely provocative piece of work, so filled with ideas it runs on for some four and a half minutes and had to be released on a twelve-inch disc. The composition celebrates Benny's return in substance as well as title. With great wit and style, it looks back with mock nostalgia at the last time he rode the range via riffs and a clarinet and tomtom duet that are unmistakable allusions to "Sing, Sing, Sing." Then, turning away from the bygone days of the old killer-diller routines, it presses onward into unexplored territory with a languorously sensual melody that, according to Gunther Schuller, was borrowed from Aleksandr Borodin's opera *Prince Igor*. Sauter recalled that Benny was so pleased with the result that a few days after the date he expressed his appreciation with a gift: "He sent me a case of wine; but my father drank it all."

Fletcher Henderson was still doing a certain amount of writing for the band, but the effort involved in grinding out one new arrangement after another had led to a serious impairment of his vision. During the previous summer, while Benny was convalescing, he was forced to seek medical help. "It was such a great strain, my eyes were affected to such an extent that my doctor ordered me to stop writing music and stop playing for at least a year," he explained. "Besides, it was killing me, for it was too much work. It was good money, but just too much for me to do." Toward the end of the year he told Benny he wanted to leave to start up his own band again. Benny not only encouraged him but put up the money to make that possible. The new

Henderson orchestra struggled along for a while, playing mostly one-nighters, and by 1943 it had reached the end of the road. Despite his deteriorating health, Fletcher was back writing for Benny in 1945.

Fletcher's departure left Eddie Sauter as Benny's principal arranger, the one who set the band's distinctive style, and it is fitting that the Goodman orchestra of this period has come to be known as "the Eddie Sauter band." For most Goodman fans, the Sauter band was one of the shining highlights of Benny's career, and there are those who feel it equaled or even surpassed the more celebrated Goodman orchestra of the mid-1930s. Benny himself was of several minds about it. "I quite liked that band," he maintained some two decades later. "It had a particular quality which was very interesting and very good." Yet Mel Tormé recalls that when he happened to mention to Benny just how much he loved the Goodman orchestra of that period, especially Eddie Sauter's "futuristic" charts, Benny "wrinkled his nose and looked at me as if I were crazy." He insisted: "Naw, I never really liked that band. Fletcher. He was *the* arranger. And my first band back in the thirties was the best I ever had."

Even as Benny stepped up his recordings in the early months of 1941, he continued experimenting with different sidemen. But despite the ongoing changes in personnel, the band was clearly coming into focus, and Benny was beginning to feel pleased enough with its progress to take on the sorts of jobs that would increase its exposure. In February he started a local thirteen-week radio series called "What's New?" that was broadcast live from the Manhattan Center over NBC's New York station WJZ. In April he returned to the Paramount, playing a mixture of familiar crowd pleasers like "One O'Clock Jump," "Don't Be That Way" and "Sing, Sing, Sing" and some of the newer Eddie Sauter charts like "Perfidia" and "The Man I Love." The *Metronome* review was ecstatic, claiming that "the band that brought Benny Goodman back is in many ways the best stage band that Benny Goodman has ever had."

Johnny Guarnieri had rejoined Benny briefly, but in the spring of 1941 he was replaced by a brilliant eighteen-year-old classically trained pianist who had been playing jazz for only about three years.

"I think at the time I was in Greenwich Village, playing with Bobby Hackett and Eddie Condon and that group—the Early Gospel," Mel Powell recalls. "Benny was seeking a new pianist, and George Simon, the *Metronome* writer, had recommended me to him, so Benny called and asked me to come uptown to audition. I went up there quite eagerly despite the fact that I was disappointing my good colleagues Zutty Singleton and Pee Wee Russell. They were all playing what they considered to be the Truth, while uptown were these guys who wore tuxedoes. Of course, they all knew Benny from Chicago, and I don't think there was much love lost between them.

"We met in some office in midtown, it might have been MCA, and along with Benny there was a young secretary, Muriel Zuckerman, who would go on to work with him for many, many years. I played for the two of them, and the way Benny told the tale, he wasn't sure how he felt about me, so he turned to Muriel and said, 'How about this fellow? Is he any good?' Benny loved to tell that story, and as time went by, he began to dress it up by adding that Muriel had a crush on me and answered, 'Oh, yeah, he's beautiful.' We all laughed about that years later. It might have happened that way. I don't really know. Benny could behave quite indecisively and muddled about these things, but I think all along he knew pretty well what he wanted. He would often come to me later and say, 'We've got to get somebody. What do you think about so-and-so?' Frankly I don't think it amounted to a hill of beans. I think his mind was already made up, and he just wanted to hear that others agreed with him.

"Benny started me off at a very handsome salary, probably three hundred and fifty dollars a week. He had the idea that I had a great deal of money, which happened not to be true—my parents were reasonably comfortable but certainly not affluent—so he did not diddle with me about money the way he did with some of the others. Apparently there were something about my behavior and the way that I dressed. I was so young and cavalier I must have given the impression that I didn't really need the job. Whether that's a technique I developed early in life from an observation that the rich get richer and the poor get poorer I really can't say, but Benny always believed that I had inherited money and he was dealing with landed gentry. I tried to persuade him later that it just wasn't so, but he remained convinced I had a fortune somewhere, so ironically, he would always pay me a great deal. Years later he would implore me to do things and I would name some outlandish figure because I was too busy to do them, and my God, he would meet the figure, and then I would be very embarrassed."

As young as he was, Powell already had a very substantial background in classical music, having trained as a pianist from the age of six, studied theory with a professor at Juilliard and composed his own chamber music. When he began playing jazz, he modeled his style on Earl Hines, Jess Stacy and Teddy Wilson and soon began working with traditional Chicago-style musicians like Brad Gowans, Pee Wee Russell and Eddie Condon. After the Second World War he studied composition with Paul Hindemith and became a professor of music at Yale, then provost of the California Institute of the Arts, where he currently teaches. He is probably best known now as a Pulitzer Prize-winning composer of nontonal classical music, but he was an absolutely phenomenal jazz pianist, playing with a taste and imagination and dazzling technique that provided Benny with much the same challenge and stimulation he had gotten from Teddy Wilson.

"I think part of the reason we were so compatible had to do with my background with the Chicagoans," Mel explains. "Even though he was an old man of thirty-two, which seemed ancient to me then, and I was a young whippersnapper of eighteen, Benny and I shared a secret patch of knowledge about the origins of what we were playing. Sometimes Benny would do an imitation of Pee Wee Russell, and I would answer him with Joe Sullivan, and we would look at one another and laugh. The rest of the band, many of them anyhow, didn't really understand what we were up to. There was also the fact that I was a great admirer of both Jess Stacy and Teddy Wilson and did a pretty good job of mimicking them, I think, so I was very comfortable for Benny both in the big band and the small groups. Johnny Guarnieri, who preceded me, was a wonderful pianist, but his playing at that time was still very surfacy. A little later on he got much better. But Benny and I could dig in together and take some chances, adding whatever slickness to the sort of style we both knew about in the past for updating."

The compatibility Mel and Benny shared on the bandstand carried over into their personal relationship. "Mel always amazed me," Jimmy Maxwell remembers. "He could talk to Benny as an equal. I was much too strata-conscious to see Benny as an equal, and I never could, but Mel didn't seem to have that problem." "I think that's quite true," Mel agrees. "Not that I was ever snippy with him. I always admired his performances. He was a wonderful player. But it probably had something to do with the fact, which is not widely known, that Benny began to study with me, harmony and things, because I came to jazz after formal training as a concert pianist.

"I'm sure that our shared Jewish background also contributed a great deal to the kind of friendship that developed. It often enabled us to talk in shorthand and code or even a gesture. There are Jewish gestures that commu-nicate so much information by a particular way of shrugging, a particular way of looking, as though you're carrying two thousand years of persecution on your shoulders. I remember with great amusement that when we were at the Paramount Theater and the singer was on, Benny would come over to the piano and stand there in the dark talking to me while I was playing. Interview-ers would ask me what we talked about at those moments, and I didn't tell them the truth at all. The truth was that we used to talk about annuities.

"Benny was always very paternal with me. I've never forgotten what happened the first time I went on the road with him. I was a novice. I hadn't yet established any sort of reputation. And not only was I with the prime band of the country, but I was also playing with all these sophisticates like Georgie Auld, and I didn't have an excess of self-confidence. Well, after the first one-nighter Popsi Randolph, the bandboy, was collecting the music and we were getting ready to climb back on the bus when someone came up and started playing the piano. And he played very well, something like Fats Waller or Earl Hines. This didn't bother me. I thought it sounded quite nice. But

Benny came over to me and said, 'I don't know who this guy is. Where did he come from?' His purpose was to reassure me that he wasn't looking for another piano player. He sensed I might be uncomfortable that a professional pianist was suddenly on the scene and probably thought I needed some harboring and protection. Then he just turned around and went back to his clarinet. I've always remembered this. I thought it was lovely.

"I wouldn't want to undo all of the legend that Benny was so wrapped up in himself and his music that he was incapable of thinking about anything else. Like anyone who is busy doing something, he had a focus for his attention, and the outside world often wasn't there. If the world is there too much, you really don't get anything done, so of course, Benny was self-obsessed, as many of us are. But at the same time, when he did pay attention, he was extremely vulnerable, extremely sensitive to others and their problems and their needs, perhaps overly so. But he was never verbal about it, and I think this may have caused a good bit of misunderstanding that has led some people to think he was a lot less sensitive than he was. I remember when his youngest brother Jerry was killed in a training accident during the war. That was shattering to Benny, as it would be, of course, to anyone, but from that time on he confronted the deaths of people he admired and in some cases loved with an absolutely closed mouth. One who knew him like I did could see the agony in his face and his body language, but he kept it all inside and never talked about it. He dealt with his own sometimes severe health problems in exactly the same fashion. He took his punishment and kept mum about it.

"Benny was a man of considerable style in his own strange way, considerable style and a sense of civility and good taste that were really remarkable, given, after all, his background. He would do what all of us would think of as very generous good deeds but then almost hide them by never being loud about it or trying to impress anyone."

Jimmy Maxwell's musical and personal relationships with Benny were not always that amiable. "Mel had no problems with Benny," he says. "Benny couldn't get on him at all. But he sometimes made me feel that I wasn't that good a player. When other leaders I'd worked for like Skinnay Ennis didn't like the way I played jazz, it didn't bother me because I figured, 'What the hell do they know?' But when Benny criticized me, I'd go home and cry because I believed him. He could hurt me because I thought he was a giant, and I still do. Benny was like a chicken that sees another chicken bleeding and will peck it to death. If he saw he had you down, he'd really go for the jugular. I asked him once, 'Why do you do those things?' And he said, 'I don't know. I just can't help it. I see a guy who's strong and stands up and says 'I'm the best,' and I respect that.' " Yet Jimmy also maintains that for all his self-centeredness Benny could at times be surprisingly sensitive and secretly quite generous.

"I wanted to borrow five hundred dollars from him once because I thought my sister needed an operation, and he said, 'How will you pay it back?' I said, 'I'll pay you back fifty dollars a week for ten weeks.' He said, 'How do you know you're going to be here another ten weeks?' I said, 'Well, I have to be here for eight weeks. You have to give me eight weeks' notice. We can start out with one-hundred-dollar payments and then go down to the fifty.' He said, 'No, I don't think it's a good idea.' Then a few weeks later, just after we'd been paid, my wallet was stolen out of my street coat backstage at the Chicago Theater. Benny went to the manager of the theater and raised bloody hell about it, then insisted on trying to give me another week's salary, which was three hundred and fifty dollars. A few weeks before he wouldn't *lend* me five hundred, but now he wanted to *give* me three fifty.

"When I left the band in 1942 for a job at CBS, I didn't have any money saved up, and Benny turned around and gave me a thousand dollars to live on while I put in for my union card. He said he would lend it to me at first, but when my birthday came around, he said, 'My birthday present to you is you don't have to pay it back.' As soon as I left the band, I came down with pneumonia and was in bed for a month, and after I got well, he sent me up to his home in the country to spend a few weeks recuperating.

"So Benny was funny that way. Nobody knows the good things he did. He kept Bunny Berigan on salary for years. Bunny's wife came and collected two hundred and fifty dollars a week all through the time he was in the hospital, and nobody knew about it. He kept Eddie Sauter on full salary when he got sick with tuberculosis, and he did the same thing with Charlie Christian. There were a lot of poor kids he kept in a music conservatory. I once said to him, 'People should know these things about you, Benny. They would have a much more sympathetic picture.' Benny's answer was, 'Well, if they knew about it, everybody in the country would be coming to me with their hands out.' He had a point, I guess. Famous people do get all kinds of letters from strangers asking for money, and he would have just gotten more of them. But for whatever reasons, he never wanted anyone to know about it."

The physical strain of keeping up with Benny's arduous schedule tested Charlie Christian's already fragile constitution, and all the late-night jam sessions and endless partying strained it even further. When Benny played Chicago in March 1940, Charlie had fallen ill, and Benny sent him to his own physician. The doctor discovered tuberculosis scars on Charlie's lungs, hospitalized him briefly for what was publicly described as "influenza" and advised him to get some rest and begin taking better care of himself. But Charlie refused to let up. During the band's lengthy stay in New York from October 1940 to June 1941, when he wasn't working with Benny, he was uptown in Harlem playing for his own pleasure. "We'd go to a basement room in the

Dewey Square Hotel, usually around ten in the morning," Mary Lou Williams recalled, "and sometimes we'd jam, just the two of us, until eleven at night. It smelled down there and the rats ran over our feet and only ten keys on the piano played, but we didn't pay any attention. . . . After we played a couple of hours he'd put down his pick and play classical guitar and things like 'Rhapsody in Blue.' It was beautiful."

In October 1940 the now-legendary Minton's Playhouse opened at the Hotel Cecil on 118th Street under the hospitable management of former bandleader Teddy Hill. The back room became the favorite meeting ground for a group of young, forward-thinking musicians like Dizzy Gillespie, Charlie Parker, Thelonious Monk and Kenny Clarke, who were hammering out the radical reformulations that within a few years became known as modern jazz. Charlie Christian found the lure of this new music irresistible and began sitting in almost nightly. "Charlie used to talk about the music at Minton's so much Benny Goodman even used to come," Clarke recalled. "He was all the rage at the time, and we always got a great deal of pleasure when he came in. We used to convert our style to coincide with his, so Benny played just the things he wanted to play." A Columbia undergraduate named Jerry Newman captured some of these all-night jams on his portable recording equipment, and we are fortunate to be left with a few examples of Charlie Christian at his untrammeled best, spinning out endless choruses of stunning improvisations alongside fellow innovators like Clarke and Monk. But all this took its toll.

In the middle of June, during a tour of the Midwest, Charlie collapsed and was rushed back to New York, where he was admitted to Bellevue Hospital. His condition was described as "fair, not dangerous," and it was said that he would probably rejoin the band within several months. But his health continued to worsen, and a short time later he was transferred to Seaview Hospital, a municipal sanitarium on Staten Island.

Charlie was anxious to leave Seaview and get back to Benny and the after-hours jamming at Minton's. But he was seriously, dangerously ill, and those who knew him well doubted he would ever return. "Our impression was that along with the tuberculosis he had syphilis and gonorrhea, the works," Jimmy Maxwell tells us. "And so-called friends would come by with an ounce of pot and some bottles and a couple of professional girls from uptown, thinking they were giving him a good time when they were only speeding him along on the way out. Of course, in those days if you were black and went to one of those big county hospitals, you weren't ever much likely to come back." Count Basie's physician began visiting Charlie weekly to supplement the hospital's rather lackadaisical care. It looked for a while as if he were starting to make some progress, but then he took a sudden turn for the worse, and on March 2, 1942, at the age of twenty-five, after only two brief years in the spotlight, one of the greatest jazz musicians who ever lived was gone.

Once Charlie Christian left the band, Cootie Williams took up full-time residence in the trumpet section, and the classic Goodman Sextet came to a natural end. Charlie had been the sextet's driving force, and rather than try to recapture the magic with a different, inevitably lesser guitar player, Benny turned to his new pianist and revived the older trio format, sometimes adding a bass player to make it a quartet.

"When it came to the small groups, the emphasis tended to be on the trio and quartet," Mel Powell explains, "partly because—how shall I say it?—we were, of course, also in show business, and Benny and I could fly, we could play as fast as anybody. For in-person performances you want to do sort of rousing stuff, and we were deft and light and fast and could really move. I don't think those qualities are bad, but they do add a certain glitz and glamour. We tended to do things like 'The Man I Love,' 'Body and Soul' and 'Runnin' Wild,' tunes that Benny had played with Teddy and Krupa. My recollection is that once in a while Benny would add a couple of the good players from the band, and we'd come out with a sextet and do some of the tunes from the sextet repertoire like 'Air Mail Special' and 'A Smooth One,' but the trio was the staple. Benny did form a new sextet in October, but I think he used the group primarily for recordings. He would just call some tunes, and we'd do them in one or two takes."

Benny did not record with the new trio, probably because its repertoire was still so very familiar from the Wilson-Krupa days. While the new, more casually organized sextet with trombonists Lou McGarity and Cutty Cutshall had its virtues and made several excellent recordings like "If I Had You" and "Limehouse Blues," it certainly never reached the same exalted heights as the Charlie Christian-Cootie Williams-Georgie Auld edition. Somewhat ironically, the prime Goodman small group performances of this period do not even carry Benny's name but were done under the leadership of Mel Powell.

On February 4, 1942, Mel recorded four sides for Milt Gabler's Commodore Music Shop label, using a front line of Goodman musicians that included Billy Butterfield, Lou McGarity, the tenor saxophonist George Berg and Benny himself, who appeared under the pseudonym "Shoeless John Jackson." Aside from a few Metronome All Star dates, this was the first time Benny consented to record as a sideman in more than five years, since his last Brunswick session with Teddy Wilson, which says a great deal about the esteem and affection he felt for his current pianist. The session turned out extraordinarily well, and Benny plays magnificently, especially on "The World Is Waiting for the Sunrise," the old favorite he used to perform nightly when he was just starting out with a band at Billy Rose's Music Hall.

Mel remembers the date with great fondness and humor. "I wanted a little sort of Chicago-style band, and I thought, 'Let's see, who's the best clarinet player I know?' and I came up with Benny. I said to him, 'Benny, I've been looking around for a clarinet player, and I think you'll have to do. I'm paying everybody scale. If you want to work for scale, you're on.' So he became one of the boys, and I was the bandleader and chose the tunes and the tempos and so on. 'The World Is Waiting for the Sunrise' was a pet of mine. I had learned 'When Did You Leave Heaven?' from Bobby Hackett down in the Village. Benny didn't know much about it." The other two tunes on the date were "Blue Skies" and an original blues Mel titled "Mood at Twilight." "It was such a relaxation for Benny not to have to front the band. He was like a kid again. He was having fun. It was the first time I had seen him out of a necktie, and I teased him about it. 'What makes you think I hire guys who wear open shirts?' I think it is some of the best playing he's ever done. He's so relaxed you can almost hear him smiling."

Was Benny pleased with the results? "The answer to that is that after the session we began playing 'The World Is Waiting for the Sunrise' with the trio, and about a month later he recorded it himself. He said, 'Hey, let's do that tune you did,' and I said, 'Okay, but you're going to louse me up because you'll sell more copies.' " Benny recorded two versions of "Sunrise" on his own date, one with the quartet and another with the sextet, and both turned out well, but on neither does he play with quite the same freedom and abandon he displayed on the Commodore session. "No, they're not the same," Mel agrees. "Now he was back in the responsible situation again."

Shortly after Mel joined the band, it took to the road, touring the Midwest in the middle of June, playing the Steel Pier in Atlantic City in early July, then going out to Chicago for the rest of the summer for an engagement at the Hotel Sherman. "We were working all the time," Mel recalls, "and Benny enjoyed a great deal of adulation from the public everywhere we went.

"We played an amalgam of the newer Eddie Sauter arrangements and a sufficient number of the older pieces to keep Benny in good spirits. I don't mean to imply that Benny wasn't fully committed to Sauter's writing. He admired Eddie professionally, and I think he was quite proud of the more advanced things we were playing. But I suspect Benny always had in the back of his mind the fact that his great success had come as the leader of a great dance band and without the dancers it wouldn't have happened. In his editing of Sauter's charts that was, perhaps, the uppermost consideration."

Around this time Mel also began writing for the Goodman orchestra. In the fifteen months he stayed with the band he contributed at least fifteen arrangements, ranging from pop tunes of the day like "Zoot Suit," "Kalamazoo" and "My Little Cousin" to rather commercial instrumentals like "Jersey

Bounce" and "String of Pearls" that any number of other bands were also playing to his own highly distinctive original compositions "The Earl" and "Mission to Moscow."

"Benny always gave me a great deal of freedom," he recalls. "Certainly he would suggest tunes. For example, he asked me to do 'Jersey Bounce' because he knew it was going to be a big hit. I looked at it and thought, 'Well, that's a pretty dinky thing,' but I did it, and it turned out to net him a fairly good royalty. But Benny did much less editing with me than he did with Eddie Sauter, probably because my writing was almost childish and playful compared to Eddie's, so it wasn't as necessary. On one occasion I did get very fancy, even going beyond Sauter to the kind of thing Stravinsky was writing at the time, and of course, that scared everyone. Oh, my God, nobody could even read it! But I must say Benny was awfully nice about it and even courteous, saying almost apologetically, 'Well, that's a little too fussy.' "

The first Mel Powell chart Benny recorded was his original composition "The Earl," a stunning tribute to Earl Hines that remains as fresh and inventive today as when it was first conceived. "I always admired Earl Hines," Mel explains. "Who hasn't? So I borrowed from him stylistically to some degree in my solos and also mimicked him with the orchestra by having them play, as it were, as though they were a grand piano, which made them a little more polyphonic than usual." One of the more remarkable things about the recording, which was done in New York about three weeks after the band returned from Chicago, is that it swings so relentlessly from beginning to end without benefit of a drummer. "Sid Catlett was our regular drummer then," Benny explained, "but he couldn't make the date for some reason. So we brought in another drummer—I believe it was Jo Jones. We had been rehearsing the number for some time before the date, and it must have been very difficult for a drummer to step right in and play the way we had rehearsed the number. Anyway, it didn't work out. So we just decided to go ahead without any drummer. As it turned out, we didn't really need one, did we?"

Mel Powell has a different account of what happened. "Sidney Catlett was one of the greatest percussionists who ever lived in any field. He was a magnificent drummer, and it's one of the grand mysteries of the world why Benny apparently became dissatisfied with him. Exactly what it was between Benny and Sidney I have no idea, but I do recall that on that very date there was a rupture between the two of them in the recording studio, and Sidney packed up his drums and left."

Russ Connor claims that Benny always denied he was disenchanted with Catlett and had refused to let him play on the session, insisting that he considered Big Sid "an excellent drummer." When Muggsy Spanier accused Benny of trying to steal away George Wettling, Benny laughed it off with a retort that suggests at least some of the time he did regard Catlett highly:

"What do I want with George Wettling or any other drummer when I've got Sid Catlett?" But though Sid drove the band magnificently—listen to the collection of air checks on the Honeysuckle Rose label issued under the title "Benny and Sid 'Roll 'Em' "—he was no more exempt from Benny's some-times withering criticisms than were Dave Tough, Buddy Schutz, Nick Fatool or, for that matter, Gene Krupa.

"Sid Catlett and Dave Tough were the best drummers I ever played with in my life," Jimmy Maxwell maintains. "It was like night and day for me when Sid came into the band and played behind my solos. He knew everything I was going to play before I played it, which I guess is likely since he had played with the people I copied. That band at the Sherman Hotel was the cookingest band we ever had. God, it was a pleasure to go to work every night. But then Benny began to get on Sid about tempos. Sid was literally a giant of a man. I used to see him on the train reach up and chin himself between the berths, pulling himself clear up to the ceiling. But he was also a very sensitive guy, and he would sit there with tears in his eyes he would be so upset. I told Benny once, 'You know, you're lucky he doesn't rip your head off. Instead he cries.' "

The bassist John Simmons, who joined the band that summer, recalled that Benny kept up the pressure on Catlett when they left Chicago for the Meadowbrook in New Jersey, but now Sid was no longer quite so passive. "Benny got on Sid's case. Well, he had a couple of vertebrae lacking in his spine, so naturally his wig was loose. So he'd give the downbeat and Sid would take it, and naturally he's supposed to hold the tempo there. But Benny started making Sid play faster and faster to try to make the band swing, and one night when they came off the stand Sid collared him. He said, 'Looky here, pops, you give me the downbeat and I'm supposed to keep that tempo. As long as you've been playing you know it's unprofessional to change the tempo once the dancers are on the floor. And all that rushing that you're giving me, that doesn't mean a thing to me as far as swinging the band. I'm going to swing, and if the band isn't swinging it isn't my fault.' " Benny remained silent, Simmons said, but a few weeks after "The Earl" was recorded, just before the band opened at the Hotel New Yorker, Catlett was replaced. As Mel Powell explains it, "Benny was not a follower, and neither was Sid. But Benny was the boss." Catlett was reported to have signed a one-year contract, but he lasted barely four months.

When Benny returned to New York in October 1941, he brought a new female vocalist with him. Unlike Mel Powell and some of the other Goodman musicians who had experienced the kinder, more sensitive side of Benny's nature, Helen Forrest had found him "a cold, inconsiderate character"—self-absorbed, rude, impossibly tightfisted—and working for him had turned out to be a thoroughly unpleasant experience. "The twenty or so months I spent with Benny felt like twenty years," she maintained. "[When I look] back, they seem like a life sentence." Forrest had threatened to quit a number of times, and on August 1, "after a night in which he noodled behind my meaningless vocals" at the Sherman Hotel in Chicago, she finally did, telling him, "This is it. Find another singer, and find her fast." There was some talk that Helen Ward might rejoin the band, but then Benny happened to drop by the club at the Ambassador Hotel where he was staying, and his attention was caught by an attractive but inexperienced nineteen-year-old not long removed from the plains of North Dakota.

Peggy Lee recalls that "Mel Powell would tell me later that when I came on stage and started singing, Benny mumbled, 'I guess we've got to get somebody for Helen.' Mel thinks he decided to hire me on the spot. It certainly didn't look that way to me. The musicians I was working with, The Four of Us, were excited that he was in the audience, but from where I stood it looked like he was just staring at me and chewing his tongue. I would learn that was just preoccupation, but at the time I was sure he didn't like me."

Benny hired Peggy the next day and put her to work that evening, even though Helen Forrest still had a month remaining on her contract. "He said, 'Stick until your contract runs out,'" Helen remembered. "I sat alongside Peggy on the bandstand and didn't sing a note for four weeks. She'd get up and sing, but I never got up. When people would ask me why I wasn't singing, I'd say, 'Ask Benny.' They'd ask him and he'd say, 'She's got laryngitis.' I was as healthy as a horse. That was the longest month of my life."

For Gunther Schuller, Helen Forrest was "with the possible exception of Jack Teagarden and Mildred Bailey—and until Sinatra came along—the finest white singer of the entire Swing Era." Peggy Lee, on the other hand, was just starting out and filled with the insecurities that beset any beginner. "I thought she had a terrific quality then," Benny said. "Unfortunately, when she came with the band she was so scared for about three or four months I don't think she got half the songs out of her mouth. She was very young then. But I persisted in any event, which I was glad I did, and so was she, and finally we came up with a couple of hit records." Her first recording with the band, made two weeks after she joined, was not one of them.

Peggy had been assigned a tricky novelty number called "Elmer's Tune" that Glenn Miller had recorded a few days earlier. John Hammond had flown into Chicago to supervise the date, and Bill Savory, who was in the control booth, recalls how the difficulties they were having with the session led to yet another in the growing number of bad flare-ups between Hammond and Benny: "Peggy was extremely nervous, and Benny kept calling take after take, trying to get one that was acceptable. It was a very tense situation. Then to make matters worse, John started hassling Benny about Peggy's deficiencies.

'Benny, she cahn't sing. She just cahn't sing.' Finally, out of exasperation, Benny picked up a chair and hurled it across the studio at him. John was amazed and very upset. 'What does one do?' he asked me. 'Does one fight?' 'Just forget it, John,' I told him. 'The sight of blood would probably make you faint.' "

The air checks recorded at the Meadowbrook that September reveal that Peggy still sounds strained and uncentered and very unsure of herself. But not too long after Benny opened at the New Yorker she began to settle down. In his review of the band in the December *Metronome* George T. Simon made a great point about how dramatically she had improved and claimed she was "slowly turning into one of the great singers in the field." Hammond, though, continued to hold fast to his disdain even after she had more than proved herself through such excellent recordings as "Let's Do It," "Where or When" and "Somebody Else Is Taking My Place," maintaining that "Miss Lee is a lady whose attractiveness occasionally makes the listener forget that she has no vocal or interpretive talent."

The Hotel New Yorker was an especially important engagement for Benny. He had done a week at the Paramount back in April and performed briefly at Monte Proser's ill-fated Dance Carnival in May, but this was his first extended appearance in New York since he had re-formed the band exactly one year earlier. Though he had done well at the Sherman in Chicago and the Meadowbrook in New Jersey, the real test of his current drawing power would be what happened when he returned to Manhattan. The prospects were not all that encouraging. Swing bands were not normally booked into the hotel's Terrace Room. Its patrons were more accustomed to straight commercial dance orchestras like Johnny Long, who had recently completed a very successful stand, and Benny would have to tone down the band's real strengths to adjust to their expectations. He would also have to share the stage with an elaborate ice show, not exactly the sort of attraction calculated to appeal to his regular fans.

Benny was also up against a lot of competition that autumn. Glenn Miller had emerged as the most popular band in the country, and he would be opening three nights earlier at the Cafe Rouge in the Hotel Pennsylvania, Benny's old stomping ground, for his third straight season. Harry James, now riding high on the success of "You Made Me Love You," was at the Hotel Lincoln. Any number of very popular sweet bands could also be heard at some of the other midtown hotels. Eddy Duchin was at the Waldorf, Vaughn Monroe at the Commodore, Sammy Kaye at the Essex House, Blue Barron at the Edison. Nearby nightclubs offered swing enthusiasts an enticing choice of Count Basie, Andy Kirk, Red Allen, Teddy Wilson and John Kirby.

Nor could Benny count on his current recordings to pull in the crowds. The record business had one of the best years it had ever seen in 1941, but it had been quite a while since Benny had scored a real hit. What was selling now, largely because of their vocals, were things like Glenn Miller's "Chattanooga Choo Choo" (Tex Beneke and the Modernaires), which would have one million copies in circulation by the end of the year. Other top sellers included Jimmy Dorsey's "Maria Elena" (Bob Eberly), "Green Eyes" and "Amapola" (both with Eberly and Helen O'Connell), and brother Tommy's "Yes, Indeed" (Jo Stafford and Sy Oliver), "This Love of Mine" (Frank Sinatra) and "Oh, Look at Me Now" (Sinatra, Connie Haines and the Pied Pipers).

It was beginning to look as if all those doom-laden prophets who had been wailing in the wilderness so long about swing's coming demise just might be on to something. Current recordings by Sammy Kaye, Wayne King and Freddy Martin were moving briskly on Victor and Bluebird. On Columbia, Benny's own label, the best-selling records for 1941 were Horace Heidt's dismal, "I Don't Want to Set the World on Fire" and Harry James's "You Made Me Love You." Certainly something was going on. A few weeks after Benny returned to New York, he was suddenly switched to Okeh, Columbia's less prestigious thirty-five-cent subsidiary, ostensibly to get into more juke-boxes and compete a little better with Bluebird artists like Glenn Miller. But it was the Mickey Mouse bands of Tommy Tucker and Dick Jurgens that gave Okeh its top-selling records for the year. No wonder an article published under Benny's by-line that August rather desperately wrapped swing in the flag and unashamedly equated it with good old-fashioned Americanism:

> Those who really "feel" swing—those who loved it for its own sake even before the fashionable word, "swing," made it acceptable to the public—will never let it die. They cannot conceive of American Democracy without it. Our music has grown out of our brand of government. A man who improvises with a musical instrument is using the same liberty exercised by an editorial writer who spouts his own opinions or an architect who throws over past ideas and builds the world a skyscraper. Improvisation is the application of an unhandcuffed-feeling to music. The same conditions that pioneered its birth will see its continuation in this country.

The band opened at the New Yorker on October 9. The *Variety* reviewer was unimpressed by Benny's efforts to accommodate himself to the Terrace Room's clientele. A few weeks later, though, *Metronome*'s George Simon gave Benny a solid rave, finding the band "both musically and commercially great. . . . It's a band that packs a tremendous punch; that plays brilliantly-scored arrangements; that reaches thrilling rhythmic heights, and that, contrary to what you might believe because of previous Goodman editions, can and does create wonderful, soft, mellow moods." The Terrace Room's customers seem to have shared Simon's opinion. Business started out strong and continued that way week after week, though it never quite matched what Glenn Miller was doing at the slightly larger Cafe Rouge. If the Terrace Room stand did not generate any of the excitement and high drama of the earlier triumphs at the Palomar and the Paramount, the five months Benny spent there certainly confirmed that he was still very much a musical force to be reckoned with and put an end to the speculation that both he and the sort of music he played were on the way out.

Admittedly, Benny's recordings during this period make a lot of concessions to the growing taste for pop singers doing current commercial tunes of no particular distinction. Almost two-thirds of the forty sides he recorded with the band and sextet during his stay at the New Yorker feature Peggy Lee or his new male vocalist Art Lund, then known as Art London. Yet Benny never stopped playing charts like "The Earl," "Clarinet a la King" and "Benny Rides Again" as well as a lot of the older instrumentals. And with men in the band like Mel Powell, Lou McGarity, Jimmy Maxwell and the recently returned Vido Musso, it couldn't help swinging.

Benny and Alice.

From the Benny Goodman Archives in the Music Library at Yale University

21

Alice

The band finished up at the New Yorker on March 12 and took a three-week vacation before going back on the road. This was Benny's first real time off since he returned from the Mayo Clinic a year and a half earlier, and he had his own very personal reasons to look forward to the break. On March 21, 1942, in Las Vegas, Nevada, he married Alice Hammond Duckworth, John Hammond's sister.

Alice and Benny met for the first time when Hammond took her to hear the new Goodman band perform at Billy Rose's Music Hall back in 1934. "It wasn't one of those love at first sight things," Benny later said. "It was just hello and goodbye." Three years older than Benny, Alice was then married to George Arthur Duckworth, a Conservative member of the British Parliament, whose ancestors numbered, in the inimitable words of the *New York Times* account of their elaborate wedding in 1927, "the Plantagenets and eleven other families who appear in Shakespeare's plays." Hammond described Alice as "the family rebel," the favorite of his four sisters. According to Spike Hughes, the English recording executive and jazz fan, she "was more like John in looks and temperament than any of the rest of her family."

There was a great spiritual affinity between brother and sister which, I suspect, often disconcerted Alice's English husband, who was plainly a little bewildered on returning from the House of Commons to his elegant house in Westminster on one occasion to find his wife entertaining Duke Ellington and me and playing us records of Bessie Smith. I think Alice enjoyed her life as an M.P.'s wife while it lasted, for she was a good hostess, with that rare gift of making all sorts and colors of people her immediate and devoted servants. But that "liberal-mindedness" which she shared with her brother must clearly have perplexed a typically Conservative and Old Etonian husband.

Benny and Alice came to know each other better during her later visits to New York. "I've been told that when she came 'round to the Hotel Pennsylvania, she would occasionally bring her knitting," Jim Maher remembers. "Alec Wilder used to call her Madame Defarge. Benny was always so tense whenever Alice was in the audience, the whole band felt it." By 1941 Alice's marriage was just about over. In November she filed for divorce in Reno, Nevada. Alice and Benny were keeping steady company by now. Peggy Lee recalls that she was with him the night he heard her sing for the first time at the Ambassador Hotel that summer. According to Mel Powell, Alice was always at the New Yorker, and they were staying together. "One thing I used to chuckle about all the time," he says, "is that Benny had this habit of walking very quickly, and therefore Alice was always bringing up the rear. I had a hunch that because she had just come through her marriage with Duckworth, the idea of this rather rude man with none of the British upper-class manners must have been absolutely exotic to her. I think this is part of what she loved about him."

The new couple honeymooned briefly in Phoenix, Arizona, but in the beginning of April Benny picked up his usual fast-moving pace. On April 2 the band did a week at the Center Theater in Passaic, New Jersey, then moved on to the Earle Theater in Philadelphia and the Stanley Theater in Camden. "Hardly anyone thought the marriage would work," Benny recalled. "Alice had been married to a rather staid Englishman and was used to a home life. We spent our first three months under seventy-three different roofs on the road."

It wasn't just the difference in life-styles that made the marriage seem so improbable, of course. There was also the vast difference in social backgrounds. Alice was born a Vanderbilt, and if her former husband was not titled nobility, as was commonly believed, he was from an old aristocratic family with manor houses and lands. Benny's great success in the music business had made him at thirty-four a very wealthy man, but he still had a lot of rough edges, and from the haughty perspective of the Protestant elite, there was no overlooking his immigrant Jewish origins. The differences in their personalities posed an even greater obstacle. Alice was, by all accounts, a gregarious, outgoing, extremely charming woman. Everyone adored her. Benny, on the other hand, was essentially the same withdrawn, sometimes prickly introvert he had always been, ill at ease in social situations and so wrapped up in his music there didn't seem to be room left over for anything else. Yet opposites have been known to attract.

"When Benny married Alice, it was a big surprise to everyone," the record producer George Avakian tells us, "including, I suspect, Benny himself. I don't think he ever expected to marry someone who came from such great wealth and social position. I couldn't imagine them falling in love, but they genuinely did. They really loved each other. You could feel it. I have the sense that on both sides they realized they were opposites and made a rather odd combination, but each of them was probably looking for something in the other that they found.

"Alice, I suppose, saw something that was refreshingly different from her own stodgy family. Her mother was a rather domineering sort of person. Alice resembled her physically. She was a tall, large-boned outdoorsy woman. Gardening was her great love. Whenever I went to the house, she would be down there on a knee pad digging in the dirt. And she was a strong person. It showed in her face. She was quite good-looking, but you could see the strength of character in the almost grim set of her jaw. Yet she was also very warm, unlike her brother, John, and she devoted herself to Benny. Benny was terribly self-conscious about the milieu Alice was raised in, but Alice was fantastic about that. I don't think she ever embarrassed him or forced any of her friends on him. I remember how she would interrupt Benny and me when we were listening to records or working together on something for too long and remind us it was time to eat. And from that moment on she became the focal point of attention and Benny would take a backseat. I was always very happy about that because I liked her so much. It was okay with Benny, too. He didn't mind in the least. She was just what he needed. They were very good for each other and very much in love."

"Alice was extremely astute about Benny's well-being," Bill Savory agrees. "And in ways that went beyond making sure he went to the doctor and dentist for a checkup. She was kind of like a protective hen in certain situations, particularly when Benny was going through periods of stress. Not that Benny was ever aware that he was being mothered. Alice would never want that. Then, when things would straighten out and Benny was flying again, she'd recede a little further into the background."

Marriage to Alice smoothed off a lot of Benny's rough edges and broadened his interests beyond music to give him a fuller, richer life. "Alice changed

him, and he changed himself," Avakian observes. "He was trying to live up
to something. That's what he wanted." "He became much more aware of the
social life that was always around him but which he previously ignored,"
Savory says. "Through Alice he came to appreciate art. She also broadened
Benny's view of, of all things, sports. When he was younger, he used to play
tennis once in a while, and he always enjoyed fishing because of the desire to
be alone. But then Alice got him into other things through a quietly subtle
left-field approach. For example, she piqued his interest in baseball by telling
him about Yogi Berra and his remarkable speech patterns, and Benny eventually came to enjoy it. I'm sure she also had something to do with his growing
interest in improving his physical appearance. She would never say to him,
'Hey, you look like a slob. Why don't you get a good suit?' It would be more
like 'John tells me that his tailor is about the best tailor there is,' and then
Benny would say, 'Well, I'm going to be down that way next week. Maybe I'll
drop by and see him.' "

In anticipation of his coming marriage Benny had bought a house near
New Canaan, Connecticut, an estate set back in the hills with a large swimming pool, vegetable and flower gardens and a grand view of the surrounding
countryside. In 1943 their daughter Rachel was born. Three years later they
had a second daughter, Benjie. Alice had three daughters by her first marriage, Gillian, Shirley and Sophia, so the house was filled with children.
"Benny was a very loving father," Avakian recalls. "I could see it in his
relationship with the kids. He was always extremely tolerant of their interruptions, and he spoke of them very often. He simply exuded being a good father.
Benny didn't have close friends. He never wanted to get too close to anyone.
But I think it was a close and loving family."

Hammond wrote about the marriage in his autobiography: "Mother and
Father liked Benny. They thought he was a marvelous musician and they gave
their blessing." Rather pointedly, he made no mention of how he himself felt
about it. The common impression was that he was none too pleased, and that
would be perfectly understandable, since during the months leading up to the
wedding his relationship with Benny had deteriorated badly.

There had always been a certain amount of tension and strain in their
friendship, even back in the mid-1930s, when the band was just starting out.
"Benny respected John's opinions and his conception of which musicians to
get for what," Helen Ward tells us. "John always meant well, and there were
times when he was one hundred percent right. But every now and then he
would stick in his oar just once too often—'Do it this way. Don't do that. Fire
this one. Hire him.'—and that would get under Benny's skin. Or Benny would
love something, and he'd sit there and knock it, so Benny would tell him off."

Hammond recalled that their first serious falling-out took place during the second "Spirituals to Swing" concert he produced in December 1939. Benny had agreed to close the show with his sextet, and "Without thinking too much about it, I sneaked Charlie Christian in ahead of Goodman to play with Buck Clayton and Lester Young in the Kansas City Six. . . . [Benny] was furious. I had used his star with another group, thus—he thought—weakening his own appearance in the finale." By March 1941 it was common knowledge that Benny and Hammond had quarreled over the band's current musical policy and Benny was no longer relying on Hammond's advice. During that summer and fall the quarreling became worse. There were flare-ups over the difficulties with Peggy Lee's first recording session, over Benny's firing of John Simmons, over his decision not to use Sid Catlett on "The Earl" recording date. "John had learned enough to consider himself an authority and did not like to be contradicted," Jimmy Maxwell explains. "And Benny was sick of John telling him what to do. Benny in many ways was indebted to John, and he resented it. John also rode on Benny's coattails a great deal, and *he* [John] resented that."

At the end of 1941 their formal working relationship came to an end when Hammond took what was described as "an indefinite leave of absence" from Columbia Records. Hammond had stopped writing for the music magazines during his tenure at Columbia "for fear that I would have to pull my punches," but now that he was free to say whatever he wished he joined the recently founded *Music and Rhythm* as coeditor and began a regular monthly column. In the first "John Hammond Says," published two months after Benny and Alice married, he had nothing but praise for his former employer, even though "I had to record plenty of stuff that was personally distasteful," but was scathingly critical of his new brother-in-law: "It was possible to respect the professional standards of a Dick Jurgens at the same time as looking with contempt at the gyrations Benny Goodman would go through to scale his music down to the taste of hotel managers and music operators. Better an unpretentious sweet group that played as well as it knew how than a sloppy, insincere swing band that ground out riff after riff of uninspired junk in the hope of catching public fancy."

The following month Hammond published a lengthy diatribe that blasted Benny unmercifully for his growing commercialism, alleged concessions to racial prejudice and overall lack of integrity:

> Benny is still a great musician, but he is no longer an innovator or a musical radical. Instead of forming popular tastes he is bowing to them and following the path laid down by his imitators. Rather than spend his time looking for unusual talent among sidemen, he takes what is easily available. He no longer defies convention by breaking down racial barriers, and thinks primarily of the commercial appeal of his music. . . .
> What caused Benny to change?

There are many reasons, among them pressure from booking agencies, coin machine operators, hotel managers and the like, but primarily it is the increasing conservatism of a man who has made his pile and who no longer wishes to buck popular prejudice. . . . Even in classical music he is not developing as he once gave promise of doing. . . . In the past years he has not been studying consistently, and although he has been playing more engagements, his own standard of performance has suffered.

Welcome to the family, Benny.

There is a grain of truth in some of Hammond's charges. Benny's records *were* becoming more commercial. Popular music was changing, and ever the survivor, Benny was changing along with it. Yet there had always been a strong commercial side to the Goodman band's music, even when it was swinging away at its hardest. And a few weeks after Hammond's article hit the stands Benny went into the studio to record "Six Flats Unfurnished" and "Mission to Moscow," certainly two of the band's more uncompromising instrumentals.

And yes, it was also true that there were no black musicians in the Goodman orchestra at the present moment. But maintaining a racially integrated band was never a cause for Benny as it was for John Hammond, and black musicians came and went like anyone else. Mel Powell insists, "Benny was one of the very, very few white people I've known who had not a fiber of racism in him. He was absolutely, authentically color-blind, and he thought all the fuss kicked up by the press whenever he hired a black musician was silly. One of the real giveaways to his outlook was that he could be as rude to a black man as to a white man. He did not get patronizing or suddenly gentle. Not at all. And I always found that admirable."

One could continue picking away at Hammond's charges, but there wouldn't be much point. The article is less a critical assessment than a barely disguised personal assault that reveals in almost every sentence the aggrieved bitterness of a friendship gone sour and the frustrated disappointment of a once trusted adviser whose advice is no longer valued. Hammond claimed that "Benny took my rap with good grace, in part perhaps because he was now my brother-in-law." One wonders. By Hammond's own account, when he returned from the army and met with Benny again after the war, his "often-unwelcome advice" was "even more unwelcome" than it had been before.

Wartime

n the early months of 1942 the big bands were riding higher than ever. Defense spending had pumped a flow of ready cash into the economy, and the tensions and uncertainties that followed fast upon America's active entry into the Second World War had led to a seize-the-day pursuit of a good time that was doing wonders for the entertainment business, especially for name orchestras like Benny Goodman and Glenn Miller and Tommy and Jimmy Dorsey.

"Dance bands playing in film theaters are the strongest box office items in American show business today," *Variety* announced in February in a front-page story that detailed how the uptrend of recent years had intensified to the point that the top orchestras were doubling and even tripling normal theater grosses. This did not go unnoticed by the Hollywood studios, and they, too, were now shelling out huge sums for token appearances in the musicals and comedies the wartime audiences were favoring. Jimmy Dorsey and Glenn Miller were able to command close to a hundred thousand dollars for the four to six weeks it took to shoot a movie, and even much less potent names were being paid about twenty thousand dollars. During 1942 Glenn Miller followed up the previous year's success of *Sun Valley Serenade* with *Orchestra Wives*, Jimmy

**Benny and Peggy Lee entertain the troops
in the 1943 movie *Stage Door Canteen*.**

Ken Whitten Collection

Dorsey appeared in *The Fleet's In* and his brother, Tommy, in *Ship Ahoy,* Harry James filmed *Private Buckaroo* and *Springtime in the Rockies* and Benny took part in *Syncopation, The Powers Girl* and *Stage Door Canteen.*

The war also created any number of frustrating problems for Benny and his fellow leaders. The supply of able sidemen, which had never been quite large enough to meet the demand, was made even smaller by enlistments and the draft. By August it was estimated that every name band had lost between one-quarter to one-half its personnel to the armed forces. Competition for the top section players and soloists who remained resulted in an unprecedented escalation of salaries. "Prices became astronomical," Jimmy Maxwell recalls. "After I left Benny to go into the studios, Woody Herman offered me seven hundred fifty dollars; then he offered me a thousand; then he asked me how much I wanted because no one could get any first trumpet players. All the bands were hungry for musicians. Everybody was offering me jobs. I couldn't believe it."

The bands had always made their biggest money touring the hinterlands and colleges on one-night stands, but now the rationing of tires and gasoline and the unavailability of chartered buses and railroad cars made road tours all but impossible, putting an end to this very lucrative part of their business. The musical instrument factories shifted over to producing war materials, causing a complete freeze on all new brass, woodwind and percussion instruments for civilian use. The shortage of shellac and copper also led the War Production Board to order a 30 percent cutback on the production of phonograph records. To make the most of their restricted output, the major companies stopped recording slow-selling jazz records, canceled many contracts and pressured their remaining bands to concentrate on surefire hit tunes rather than originals and standards. And then on August 1, 1942, the bands were forced to stop recording altogether.

James C. Petrillo, the autocratic head of the American Federation of Musicians, had announced at the union convention in June that the increasing use of phonograph records on radio and jukeboxes was ruining the livelihood of 60 percent of the membership; therefore, he was instituting a ban on all new recording until such time as the record companies agreed to pay a royalty to the AFM to compensate for the loss of jobs. This was a hugely unpopular decision that led to much public outrage and two congressional investigations. But Petrillo was supported by the union delegates, most of whom were older club date and local theater musicians with no great love for the younger traveling bands, and the ban went into effect that summer. It wasn't until September 1943 that Decca Records gave in to his demands, and Victor and Columbia did not come to terms until more than a year later. Meanwhile, no new big band music was commercially recorded, smoothing the way for the growing popularity of former band singers like Frank Sinatra and Dick

Haymes, who were able to continue to make records without instrumental accompaniment.

Benny came through the tumultuous early months of the war relatively unscathed. On May 15, 1942, he was called down to the army induction center at Fort Jay to take his physical examination for the draft and was classified 4-F because of his back condition. Artie Shaw had joined the navy in April, and Glenn Miller was to enlist in the Army Air Force that October, clearing the field of two of Benny's strongest rivals. The potential competition was reduced even further as other leaders like Bob Crosby, Eddy Duchin, Claude Thornhill and Ray McKinley entered the service and other orchestras like those led by Will Bradley, Red Norvo and Raymond Scott were forced to disband.

Harry James may now have been leading the most popular band in the country, but Benny was doing extraordinary business everywhere he appeared, drawing an enthusiastic audience of thirty-five hundred to Constitution Hall in Washington, D.C., for a joint swing and classical music concert with the National Symphony, lining up the crowds at daybreak at the Earle Theater in Philadelphia, where storefront windows were shattered and a policeman's horse killed in the mad rush for the box office, breaking all records when forty-five thousand swing fans jammed into Brooklyn's Prospect Park to hear him play a free dance. Benny's recordings continued to be issued with regularity despite the general cutback in releases. His last sessions before the recording ban went into effect produced "Why Don't You Do Right?," one of his biggest hits, and Mel Powell's "Mission to Moscow," one of his strongest instrumentals.

But around the end of July the Goodman band began to unravel. To the mystification of sympathetic observers, Benny replaced virtually his entire saxophone section, hired and fired and sometimes rehired any number of other sidemen and started to lose some of the key players who had contributed so much to his current success. Mel Powell left in August to join Raymond Scott's house band at CBS. Eddie Sauter also left following a flare-up of tuberculosis and a kind of nervous collapse brought on by strain and overwork that left him incapable of doing any further writing. A few months later Jimmy Maxwell and Lou McGarity, the band's star trombone player, handed in their notices and went off to the CBS studios. "Benny had me so buffaloed I didn't think anybody would hire me," Jimmy remembers. "And within a week of quitting the band Count Basie offered me a job. I said, 'Why didn't you ever ask me before, for God's sake?' He said, 'I couldn't afford to pay you.' And I said, 'You've offered me a hundred dollars a week more than Benny was paying me.' "

Benny restaffed the band with some excellent musicians like Hymie

Schertzer, who had been in and out of the Goodman saxophone section since 1934, and the seventeen-year-old drum prodigy Louis Bellson, the recent winner of a Gene Krupa amateur drum contest. But the ongoing changes in personnel took their inevitable toll. Writing about a November 17 broadcast from the Hotel New Yorker, *Metronome* gave Benny one of the worst reviews of his career: "Never before, in this reviewer's experience, has Benny's band sounded so bad. . . . Not one section played consistently together. . . . Soloists muffed notes, singers lost pitch and even such luminaries as Hymie Schertzer and the King himself played badly, the former flat, the latter with great squeaks."

Perhaps for the first time in his professional life Benny was having occasional problems with his own usually faultless musicianship. Two weeks earlier he had appeared with Arturo Toscanini and the NBC Symphony on their opening broadcast of the season, performing the clarinet solo on the *Rhapsody in Blue*. Coming off the famous glissando, Benny hit a huge, embarrassing clinker that had music lovers wincing from coast to coast. Jimmy Maxwell, who left the band a few weeks later, recalls, "I thought, 'We're really going to get it now. We're going to be dead.' We'd had enough hell the whole week he'd rehearsed it with the symphony. He would come back and rehearse the ass off us. 'You guys complain,' he'd say, 'but you don't know how Toscanini rehearses.' And after he hit that thing, there was no living with him."

Benny continued shifting around the band's personnel, bringing in the veteran trombonist Miff Mole and Lee Castle on trumpet, adding the bass saxophonist Joe Rushton to pump along with the rhythm section, somehow persuading Jess Stacy, who had sworn never to work for him again, to take back his old chair when Bob Crosby disbanded. Changes were being made every week and sometimes day to day, and when he returned to the Paramount on December 30, the orchestra's deficiencies were still apparent. But as *Variety* reported, "biz" was "big," and the following week MCA placed a full-page ad in the paper proclaiming that Benny had set "NEW ALL TIME RECORDS" for the theater, grossing a heady seventy-eight thousand dollars for his first four days. What the ad failed to mention was that the main reason for the turnout was not Benny Goodman but a last-minute "extra added attraction," Tommy Dorsey's former boy singer Frank Sinatra.

Sinatra had left Tommy Dorsey in September to strike out on his own. The recording of "There Are Such Things" he had made with the Dorsey band in July was getting a lot of play on the jukeboxes, and he had just come off his debut booking as a solo act at the Mosque Theater in Newark. But this was his first really major engagement, and as he stepped to the microphone during the opening show, he was greeted with a roar of anticipation from the teenage girls who packed the theater that was totally unexpected and fully matched the frenzied welcome Benny had received when he achieved his own dramatic breakthrough at the Paramount five years earlier. It is claimed that Benny had never heard of Sinatra before and was so taken aback by the uproar set off by his matter-of-fact introduction that he froze with his arms raised on the upbeat and muttered in disbelief, "What the fuck was that?"

What that was, of course, was the "proclamation of a new era" in popular music, as *Life* magazine was to call it, no less revolutionary than the advent of big band swing initiated by Benny's own earlier Paramount triumph. Within a few years it was the singers like Sinatra who dominated the record charts and radio shows and theater marquees, and big bands like Benny's went into a permanent decline. Perhaps it was some vague premonition of what lay in store that explains why Benny refused to share the stage with Sinatra on January 15, when they both were scheduled to be presented with awards from a fan magazine by the actress Madeleine Carroll.

Doubtlessly inspired by the behind-the-scenes maneuvering that had started the kids dancing in the aisles for Benny back in 1937, a few days after the opening Sinatra's press agent George Evans hired a dozen bobby-soxers to scream "Oh, Frankie!" and swoon in uncontrollable ecstasy at the appropriate moments, and like the dancing in the aisles, the screaming and swooning immediately took on a life of their own. Evans gave away hundreds of free tickets to make sure the theater stayed packed, but the precaution wasn't necessary. "Benny played as great as ever, I sang my songs and got some attention, but it was electric when Frank came on stage," Peggy Lee remembers. "We used to lean out the windows of the dressing room to see the crowd of swooners, like swarms of bees down there in the street, just waiting for the sight of Frankie."

Benny left New York at the end of January to film *The Gang's All Here* in Hollywood and play a six-week engagement at the Palladium. Still not satisfied with the way the band was shaping up, he continued hiring and firing musicians and also began changing around its basic instrumentation. At the Paramount he had used eight brass, five reeds and, counting Joe Rushton's bass saxophone, five rhythm. By the time he opened at the Palladium on February 23 he had cut back to three trumpets, two trombones and four saxophones. This was the same combination of instruments he had employed in the mid-1930s, when he achieved his greatest musical and commercial success, and now he also began reviving many of the classic charts from that period by Fletcher and Horace Henderson and Spud Murphy. This return to basics proved to be exactly what was needed, and after eight long months in the doldrums the band finally sprang back to life. "Benny's done it again," Leonard Feather raved about the Palladium appearance. "Coming out of a period of decline which . . . had critics wondering whether Goodman was at the beginning of the end, he's emerged with flying colors."

The band's morale was high, and Benny himself was in wonderful spirits, playing long, exuberant solos and even singing an occasional vocal on some current novelty items like "Rosie the Riveter" as well as Jack Teagarden's old standby "I Gotta Right to Sing the Blues." (Benny was no Teagarden when it came to singing, but his efforts made up in good-natured charm what they lacked in natural ability. "It was just kind of a gag," he explained, not to be taken all that seriously.) After marrying the band's guitarist Dave Barbour, Peggy Lee left in April, and Louis Bellson received his draft notice, but just about everything else that happened was positive. "Why Don't You Do Right?" had sold close to a million copies, turning it into one of the best selling records of 1942–1943, a period that produced such huge hits as Bing Crosby's "White Christmas," Jimmy Dorsey's "Green Eyes," Glenn Miller's "Chattanooga Choo Choo" and Harry James's "I've Heard That Song Before." Benny's recordings of "Taking a Chance on Love" and "Cabin in the Sky" were also doing well on the jukeboxes. And then on May 2, a few weeks after the Palladium closing, Alice gave birth to their daughter Rachel.

Over the next month or so Benny played some military bases on the West Coast, but he mostly stayed around the apartment he had rented in Los Angeles so he could be with his family. When he returned to New York for his July 28 opening at the Hotel Astor Roof, he brought along three of the veterans of his 1935 orchestra: Joe Harris on trombone, Ralph Muzzillo on trumpet and Allan Reuss on guitar. With Hymie Schertzer and Jess Stacy, this made five sidemen who had been with him when he made his original appearance at the Palomar. The emphasis, more than ever, was on the earlier style of music that Benny seemed to feel most comfortable playing and that his audiences seemed to want.

The Astor Roof engagement sustained the momentum Benny had built up at the Palladium. The room was packed with both younger and older fans who crowded around the bandstand. The reviews were filled with superlatives. If there were some slight misgivings about the heavy dependence upon the venerable Fletcher Henderson era arrangements, everyone agreed they still sounded fine and the band performed them beautifully. And Benny himself seemed happier than ever, content with his sidemen, less standoffish with the patrons and playing at the very top of his form.

Yet as *Down Beat* reported in August, "Just when everything seemed settled and the band [was] playing as it used to in the old days, the famous and familiar B.G. 'ray' went to work," and there was another major shake-up of personnel that saw the departure of Miff Mole and Joe Harris and a number of other important sidemen. There was much speculation about what Benny was up to, some of it sympathetic to his relentless pursuit of perfection, some of it faulting him for his "picayune criticism" and "cold indifference" to the musicians he hired, then fired with such nonchalance, all of it mystified by the seemingly pointless changes. Benny, as usual, kept his own counsel and continued moving ahead. One way or another the empty chairs were filled, and by the time the band returned to the Paramount on August 3 it was in good shape once again, riffing its way through "One O'Clock Jump" and "Henderson Stomp" to standing room only. And then on September 21 Benny brought back the old days at their fullest flowering by rehiring Gene Krupa.

Nineteen forty-three had been one long, unmitigated nightmare for this most amiable of men. There are widely varying accounts of what happened, but according to Anita O'Day, who had been singing with his orchestra, it all started when Gene's bandboy was drafted and gave him some high-grade marijuana as a going-away present. A federal narcotics officer got wind of the gift. "They were always hanging around the bands waiting for us to cough," Krupa recalled, and when a handful of joints were discovered in the new bandboy's pocket during a January theater appearance in San Francisco, Gene was placed under arrest and booked on a preliminary charge of contributing to the delinquency of a minor. On the assumption that admitting to this misdemeanor would lead to the dismissal of the far more serious felony charge that was pending, Gene's attorney had him plead guilty when the case came to trial in May, and he was sentenced to ninety days in the county jail. The felony charge, however, was not dropped, and at the end of June he was brought back to the courtroom, convicted on an obscure law prohibiting the use of a minor in transporting narcotics and sentenced to one to six years in the federal penitentiary at San Quentin. He remained there until August 9, when he was released on five thousand dollars' bail pending an appeal.

The appeal was eventually won close to a year later, but the damage had long since been done, leaving Gene's career in ruins. His arrest took place at a time when Harry Anslinger, the ambitious head of the Federal Narcotics Bureau, was mounting a vigorous public relations campaign against marijuana to enhance his own prestige and power, and swing band musicians were being singled out as a special target. Newspapers across the country played the case up in front-page headlines and screamed for Krupa's conviction. The district attorney conducted his prosecution with particular zeal, denouncing Gene as "the idol of foolish, swing-mad American youth—an idol who now shows feet of clay," and implored the jury to find him guilty as an object lesson to those misguided youngsters who might be tempted by this "deadly, dreadful, unpredictable drug." Gene did smoke grass occasionally. But he was hardly the reefer-crazed dope fiend depicted in the courtroom and press, a caricature so grotesquely distorted it might have seemed laughable if the general public, recalling his wild man antics on the drums, hadn't largely accepted it as accurate. Even before he was found guilty, bookers began canceling engagements, and he was forced to disband his orchestra. By the time he was released on bail he had lost his office in New York for nonpayment of rent, and his furniture and files had been thrown out on the sidewalk.

Benny was one of the very few powers in the business who stood by Gene unequivocally during this terrible ordeal. Despite their long-standing personal differences and the potentially harmful publicity, he visited Gene at the San Francisco county jail in June and told reporters, "He's a wonderful guy and a wonderful drummer. Anytime, anyplace, anywhere he wants his old job back, it's his." Krupa was completely demoralized when he left San Quentin in August and retreated to his home in Yonkers, certain he would never be allowed to perform in public again. Benny drove up to see him and, after they talked and played together awhile, asked him, as a personal favor, to join his orchestra on a short tour of service camps.

It *was* a favor in a way. Benny had fired his drummer after finishing at the Paramount and was having his usual problems finding a satisfactory replacement. Krupa's return fitted in perfectly with his current efforts to recapture the band's old excitement. But it also showed Gene that not everyone had turned his back on him and that he still might have some kind of future in music. Recordings of a radio broadcast from Ithaca, New York, early in the tour reveal just how well the reunion worked out for both of them. Propelled by Gene's inspired drumming, the band really digs in, playing with tremendous drive and spirit. And the roar of approval that greets Krupa's solo on "Three Little Words" certainly had to help relieve his misgivings about whether a return to the spotlight would be welcome.

Encouraged by this response, Gene accepted Benny's offer to continue playing with the band when it opened at the Terrace Room of the New Yorker on October 7. The hotel was afraid of bad publicity and tried to pressure Benny out of hiring him, but Benny was adamant and worked without a drummer until the management finally relented six nights later. Gene's name was omitted from the newspaper ads and broadcast announcements, but the critics and fans spread the word he was back and raising "the entire band to new emotional heights," as George T. Simon reported. "That Benny did a great thing for jazz, for Gene and for the cause of human kindness goes without saying," Simon observed. "And the reaction from New Yorker audiences proves that there still exists in this troubled world a goodly portion of tolerance."

Krupa remained with the Goodman band until the middle of December, when he left to join Tommy Dorsey at the Paramount. Benny was going off to California to film *Sweet and Lowdown,* and Gene felt uneasy about returning there so soon. There were also some rumors that the old strains in their relationship were beginning to resurface. Gene's appearance with Dorsey went unadvertised, but the crowd recognized him immediately and gave him such a warm, tumultuous greeting that he burst into tears. In the summer of 1944 he received a favorable ruling on his appeal and was able to start up his own orchestra again, though the scars from this experience never really healed.

A review of Benny's band at the Terrace Room called it "musically equal [to], if not greater than, the Goodman Gang that made swing history." This opinion is borne out by the radio broadcasts and V-discs, special recordings done for the armed services, it produced around this time. If the ban on commercial recordings hadn't limited its exposure, the 1943 Goodman orchestra, with or without Gene Krupa, would certainly be remembered as one of the best he ever led.

That October Benny had won both the Swing Band and Favorite Band categories in *Metronome*'s annual popularity poll. In January *Down Beat* readers also voted the Goodman orchestra the top swing band in the country, nearly doubling the number of ballots cast for him the year before, and named Benny their favorite soloist. Columbia had recently released some of the older recordings he had made before the ban took effect, and though they didn't reflect his current work, they were welcomed by the fans and universally praised by the critics. But then in March 1944, after finishing the movie, Benny suddenly put everyone on notice and made the startling announcement that he was disbanding his orchestra.

Over the past several years Benny had grown increasingly dissatisfied with the lax way MCA had been handling his bookings. "I think MCA or any agency should work for the bandleader. They think I'm working for them!" he complained. He had made repeated efforts to buy back his contract, which still had almost two years to run, reportedly offering as much as $50,000 for his release, and just before Christmas he appealed to the American Federation of Musicians to negotiate a settlement. But MCA saw no reason to release him, especially since it assumed he would probably sign with Willard Alexander at the rival William Morris agency. Furious at having lost control over his own career, Benny decided he would rather wait out the expiration of his contract without an orchestra than have the agency continue to represent him. The decision was made considerably easier by the whopping $150,000 he was said to have been paid for his work on *Sweet and Lowdown*. Under the current wartime income tax laws, he wouldn't have netted much more if he kept the band on the road the rest of the year.

Benny returned to New York with no particular plans in mind. "Why should I continue knocking myself out?" he explained with some bitterness.

"I'm tired of working hard, doing six shows a day in theaters and stuff like that. I'd like to take it easy for a while. You know, be a family man." During the spring and summer of 1944 he appeared on a few radio shows, made a number of V-discs, recorded two segments for Walt Disney's *Make Mine Music* and played some military hospitals in the area, none of which brought MCA any commissions. But compared with his usual nonstop pace, he was largely inactive. By autumn he had enough of "taking it easy" and was casting about for something to occupy his time more fully. A projected radio series for Chesterfield cigarettes fell through after the first rehearsal. An overseas tour of military bases was called off at the last minute when his doctor advised against it. Then, in October, he played a benefit in New Orleans for the National Jazz Foundation with Teddy Wilson, the drummer Morey Feld and the bassist Sid Weiss, and it went marvelously well, even prompting a rave review from John Hammond. Benny had been toying with the idea of starting up a big band again, but the success of this small group appearance gave him the sense of direction he needed. The following month he accepted Billy Rose's offer to take part in his latest theatrical venture, a revue called *The Seven Lively Arts,* and went into rehearsal with a quintet that added Red Norvo to the four musicians who had performed with him in New Orleans.

The Seven Lively Arts was a typical Billy Rose extravaganza, an old-fashioned star-studded entertainment designed to offer an evening's escape from the pressing cares of the war. Primed by Rose's aggressive ballyhoo, the show received a tremendous amount of publicity and generated record-breaking advance sales of more than half a million dollars. Yet it turned out to be considerably less than the sum of its very substantial parts.

There were serious problems backstage from the very beginning. Cole Porter's score was disappointing, producing only one memorable song, "Ev'ry Time We Say Goodbye." Benny's fellow headliners Bert Lahr and Beatrice Lillie were unhappy with the material they were called upon to perform and fought with Billy constantly. Billy was not pleased with the ballet he had commissioned from Igor Stravinsky to add a touch of high culture to the enterprise and tried to get his permission to have Robert Russell Bennett do some rescoring. ("Your music great success. Could be sensational," he wired the composer in California. "Satisfied with success," Stravinsky wired back.) Benny went along with the tinsel-bedecked dinner jackets Billy had picked out for the quintet's appearance at the end of the first act but absolutely refused to dress up in the eighteenth-century pastel costume he, along with the other stars, was required to wear for the curtain call. When he came out on opening night in the same set of tails he wore in his solo appearance in Act Two, Billy was heard to mutter, "That no-good son of a bitch!" and sent him an icy note saying no costume, no final bows. When Benny replied that was all right with him and he now had written permission to go home early, Billy had no choice but to let him wear whatever he wanted.

The revue opened at Billy's Ziegfeld Theater on December 7, the third anniversary of Pearl Harbor, a rather insensitively chosen date for such a frothy diversion. Most of the critics thought it failed to live up to the advance hype, but they had nothing but praise for the Goodman Quintet's spirited run-through of "After You've Gone" and "The World Is Waiting for the Sunrise." Benny's solo performance of Carl Maria von Weber's Concertino for Clarinet and Orchestra was seen as a great personal triumph and received the biggest hand of the evening. Everything considered, *The Seven Lively Arts* worked out well for Benny. It brought him back before a New York audience for the first time in a year. It gave him a good showcase for both the jazz and the classical sides of his playing. And as an added satisfaction, since performing in a Broadway show fell outside his MCA contract, the agency was not entitled to a piece of his salary.

In November 1944, while *The Seven Lively Arts* was still in rehearsal, the recording ban finally ended, and Benny rushed the quintet over to the Columbia studio to record "After You've Gone" and two of Cole Porter's tunes from the show. His striking opening cadenza on "Ev'ry Time We Say Goodbye" conveys just how happy he is to be back making records again, and though he gives the tune's lovely melodic line a fairly straight reading, he plays it with great feeling and beauty, satisfying both the music publisher and the jazz fans. That February he recorded again with a slightly revised and expanded personnel, adding Mike Bryan on guitar and replacing Sid Weiss with Slam Stewart, whose unique bowed bass and unison humming added another strong solo voice to the group.

Over the next months Benny did five more small group sessions, producing a total of thirteen issued sides, mostly old standards like "Tiger Rag" and "Shine," with an occasional original like "Slipped Disc" and "Rachel's Dream," which was named after his daughter and developed from a riff he had previously used as an introduction to "Three Little Words." In their totality they represent a unified body of work of a very high order, though they have never received the same attention as the more celebrated trio, quartet and sextet performances recorded some years earlier. Benny plays with tremendous fire and conviction throughout, and the other soloists—Red Norvo, Slam Stewart and either Teddy Wilson or Mel Powell, who returned from Glenn Miller's Army Air Force orchestra in August—seem inspired by his enthusiasm. Nothing especially new or adventuresome takes place, but the quality of the music provides its own justification and demonstrates the ongoing vitality of the basic swing idiom.

The same cannot be said of the new Goodman orchestra.

Despite the acclaim he received in *The Seven Lively Arts* Benny soon grew bored playing the same few numbers night after night, and in February 1945 he began making plans for another big band. The contract with MCA still remained in force, but Benny met with Bob Weitman, the manager of the Paramount, and negotiated his own deal over lunch to bring the sextet and a full orchestra into the theater for four weeks toward the end of March. To the consternation of the other bandleaders around New York, who were having enough problems holding on to their sidemen, Benny then began scouting the hotels, theaters and nightclubs for musicians. His previous band had been filled with Goodman veterans and employed the same instrumentation as his original orchestra, but this time around Benny decided to enlarge the personnel to four trumpets, three trombones and five saxophones, and aside from a few well-known players like the trombonist Trummy Young, who had starred with Jimmie Lunceford, he staffed the band with younger, less experienced musicians who did not yet have established reputations.

Danny Bank, who came in on baritone saxophone, an instrument Benny had used only sparingly in the past, recalls, "The band was made up of a swinging bunch of young guys from Brooklyn, Staten Island and the Bronx. There were five of us saxophone players who were old friends, and Popsi Randolph, Benny's bandboy, arranged to have us audition together as a section while Benny was still playing in *The Seven Lively Arts*. Benny hired all five of us and gave us a lot of section rehearsals and section recording playbacks before we sat in the band, before there even *was* a band.

"The band came together for the first time either at the Brunswick Studio on Seventh Avenue or in Carnegie Hall. Benny liked to rehearse at Carnegie Hall early in the morning. He loved the sound that came from that wooden stage. It was perfect. I had previously worked with Charlie Barnet, and Benny's approach to the orchestra was completely different. With Barnet, as with most other leaders, the lead trumpet, lead trombone and lead alto were not only the first voices; they were also the straw bosses and took responsibility for their sections. But nobody was responsible for the way Benny's sections played except Benny. Benny believed in the old symphony concept, which goes back hundreds of years. There was only one leader, the Kapellmeister, and that was him, just like with Toscanini. The period of organization lasted about a month; then we quickly got into weekends and club dates and signed contracts with him. The contracts meant nothing. If he didn't like you, you were gone. But he always made them anyhow. I guess he liked to write his name."

After leaving *The Seven Likely Arts* the middle of March, Benny focused all his attention on whipping the band into shape. To prepare for the Paramount opening, he took it on the road for two weeks of one-nighters at nearby military bases and East Coast ballrooms. The dates were booked by MCA, and the bad feelings between Benny and the agency were exacerbated when he backed out of several engagements at the last minute, claiming they had been set without his approval. A broadcast from Camp Kilmer, New Jersey, on March 15 was disappointing. The band plays without much assurance and sounds far from ready. Benny's own solo work is only fair. The updated Henderson chart of "King Porter Stomp" still seems rather old-fashioned, and his arrangement of "Frenesi," originally written back in 1940, also shows its age. Two days later the band made its first records. None of the four sides was deemed fit for commercial release.

On March 28 the new Goodman orchestra followed Ella Fitzgerald, Cootie Williams and the Ink Spots into the Paramount. Business was good, grossing an impressive eighty-eight thousand dollars for the first week. But *Variety* judged the band "not in the same league with orchestras Goodman had fielded in the past" and was puzzled by the way he diluted its impact with comedy bits and a hokey black light-phosphorescent gloves routine on the old Zez Confrey finger buster "Dizzy Fingers."

"The impression you were supposed to get was of two disembodied hands playing the clarinet in the dark"—Danny Bank laughs—"but of course, the clarinet is black, so all you saw was the phosphorescent gloves and very often you didn't even see that. Being the absentminded man that he was, Benny was always forgetting to put them on or would lose them in the piano. The arrangement had the baritone answering Benny, and one time when he forgot to wear them, I put them on myself, so Benny was left in the dark and the gloves were playing the baritone.

"Some funny things happened on that job. We had to sit on hard wooden stools for four and five shows a day, which made it awfully tough on your rear end. My friend Al Epstein, a darling guy who played tenor in the band, had bleeding piles, and to get some relief, he went to the drugstore and bought an inflatable rubber ring to use as a cushion. Well, Benny came out to the pit early while the coming attractions were still on, and he saw this thing on top of Epstein's stool. It wasn't orderly—everybody had a white painted stool, and there's this one red rubber ring—so Benny reached into his pocket, pulled out a safety pin and punctured a hole in it. When Epstein sat down and the ring collapsed, he realized there had been some foul play, so after the show he bought a tire repair kit and patched it up. But Benny still had the safety pin and punctured it again. And it went on that way until Epstein ran out of patches. Benny never said a word to him about it. I think he saw it as a game."

President Roosevelt died during the third week of the Paramount engagement, but the fans continued to crowd the theater during the period of national mourning, and when Benny opened at Manhattan's 400 Club on May 2, they jammed the spacious room to capacity. Yet once again there was the feeling that the band was not living up to expectations. "It seems apparent that Goodman has no intention of embarking on anything new this time out of the barn," the *Variety* review concluded. "He knows what has been earned by a solid, orthodox swing band in the past and evidently sees no reason to do any experimenting."

Benny was hardly that complacent. He was experimenting constantly to bring the new orchestra to life, though hardly any of his efforts bore fruit. Just the week before he had put the band through a grueling session in the recording studio, doing take after take of "June Is Busting Out All Over" in a vain attempt to come up with something he found acceptable. "We were there all day," Danny Bank recalls. "Benny tried different arrangements and different tempos and different approaches, but he just couldn't get that tune set in his mind. He had more than one arranger on it, and first he had the idea of doing it with a big band, then maybe with a smaller band, then maybe with a quartet. He tried everything. We were like prisoners in that studio. Eventually he did get something good out of it on a later date."

Benny was also looking around for new arrangements to impart some freshness to the band, commissioning charts from Alec Wilder, Turk Van Lake, Ellis Larkins and George Siravo among many others. "He tried everybody," Danny tells us, "but it would always end up with the red pencil. If it was too complicated for his taste, the red pencil came out, and the poor guy would go home biting his teeth." Benny did add a few interesting charts by Mel Powell and Eddie Sauter, who had recuperated sufficiently to send in an occasional arrangement, but it was the old veterans like Edgar Sampson and Fletcher Henderson, Fletcher especially, who gave him the kind of simple, direct orchestrations he still preferred, even though this sort of writing had become overly familiar by now and was beginning to seem passé. A few days after the 400 Club opening Benny paid Fletcher two thousand dollars to deliver fifteen arrangements during the next three months, and as this material entered Benny's library, joining the scores Henderson had provided over the past decade, the band took on an increasingly conservative cast.

Nor was Benny satisfied with the band's level of performance or its failure to come into focus. "Benny hired and fired relentlessly," Danny says. "He kept looking for the band and couldn't find it. During the year and a half I was with him I must have met forty saxophone players. They passed through the band like a parade. I rehearsed them, played their auditions, and then I saw them leave. And there were about the same number of brass players. Benny would hire a trumpet player and have him sit next to the drummer in the Harry James chair, then after a while move him over one spot to the first trumpet chair, then down the line to second trumpet, and then I'd see him on the end and tell him, 'Hey, you better pack your bag because you're on the way out.' We would have one band for as long as three or four weeks; then there would be a new body, and everyone had to get used to each other all over again."

Benny finally negotiated a settlement with MCA whereby the agency would continue to collect full commissions until his contract expired in July in exchange for allowing him the freedom to handle his own bookings. When the 400 Club engagement ended in June, Benny took the band on tour for the summer and continued to pull in the crowds, even breaking Glenn Miller's old box-office record in Detroit. But unlike his current small group recordings, which were universally praised, the Goodman orchestra's new records were found seriously wanting. To *Down Beat,* the band sounded "listless" and Benny "uninspired" on "It's Only a Paper Moon" and "I'm Gonna Love That Guy," released early that fall, and the orchestrations distressingly "ordinary." "Such stuff doesn't help the 'King of Swing' stay king," it cautioned. *Metronome* was equally critical: "The arrangements smack of the mid 1930s and are no more than passable in the light of what the Hermans and Raeburns are producing on pop songs nowadays."

Comparisons with the new, forward-thinking orchestras of Woody Herman and Boyd Raeburn were inevitable, especially with Woody Herman, whose formidable big band was now wailing away with the same kind of spirit and excitement and sense of involvement that had brought Benny to the fore a decade earlier. Herman had led an adequate second-tier big band since 1936, playing a modified Dixieland style with an occasional touch of Duke Ellington and achieving a certain amount of success as "The Band That Plays The Blues." By 1945 its approach had changed radically to incorporate some of the innovations recently introduced by musicians like Charlie Parker and Dizzy Gillespie.

By 1945 the modern jazz revolution had completed its early period of experimentation at Minton's Playhouse and the other after-hours clubs up-town and moved down to Fifty-second Street and into the recording studios. Over the course of the year Gillespie and Parker recorded the first sides under their own names for small independent companies like Manor, Guild and Savoy, disseminating this new music, now known as bebop, to a fairly large audience. The jagged, shifting rhythms, extended harmonies and long, angular melodic lines, often delivered at lightning-fast speed, that characterized most of these performances seemed at the time to be a deliberate, even belligerent repudiation of the jazz of the past and generated fierce controversy. Many older listeners whose tastes were formed by traditional jazz and swing found what they heard harsh and discordant and totally unacceptable. At their most adamant, they denied it was jazz at all or even music. Its proponents argued that the swing style of the 1930s had played itself out by now and was languishing in a dead end of repetition and cliché and that the infusion of new ideas was absolutely necessary to keep the music alive as something more than mere commercial entertainment.

The Herman orchestra was not, strictly speaking, a bop band. Its main soloists, the tenor player Flip Phillips and Benny's former trombonist Bill Harris, were, like the band itself, firmly rooted in the Swing Era, and the drummer was another Goodman veteran, Dave Tough, who had finally found a leader appreciative of his talents. But its ranks were filled with young bop-oriented musicians fed into the band by the bass player Chubby Jackson, and their influence was apparent in the orchestra's tonal qualities and rhythms and the hard-driving, communally generated head arrangements like "Apple Honey" and "Northwest Passage" that formed the core of its repertoire. Thanks to the modern young arranger Ralph Burns, even the obligatory pop tunes like "Gee, It's Good to Hold You" and "Put That Ring on My Finger" had a more contemporary cast than Benny's comparable efforts, and their musical interest was sustained by the marvelous vocals of Frances Wayne and Woody's own very attractive singing.

Herman began recording for Columbia, Benny's own label, in February 1945, and the first side to be issued, the future standard "Laura," turned out to be a hit. Columbia promoted the orchestra vigorously, a weekly radio series for Wildroot hair tonic gave it further exposure and it emerged as the musical sensation of the year. *Down Beat* and *Metronome* readers voted it first place in the magazines' annual polls, relegating Benny to a distant third and fourth. "There is no band today that can top this Herman Herd," *Down Beat* raved in its review of "Apple Honey" and "Out of This World." "Woody's six sides for Columbia released within the last six weeks prove this point. And they also prove just how far and to what advantage swing music has advanced since . . . Benny Goodman brought big band swing upon the scene almost ten years ago."

Benny also had his share of young bop-inclined sidemen, but unlike Woody Herman, who was noted for his musical flexibility and openness to fresh ideas, he did not allow them to influence the direction of his orchestra. Danny Bank remembers, "The band had a number of youngsters like Kai Winding and Stan Getz who carried Charlie Parker records with them on the road and practiced playing bebop together in the closet very secretly. They were like a closed society. It was a great honor to be working for Benny Goodman, and I'm sure they played his music as best they could, but they were growing in another direction. Stan Getz was growing constantly. He was only about seventeen years old and already a terrific talent. Sometimes Benny would poke his nose in the dressing room and listen to what they were doing; then he'd go 'Tsk, tsk, tsk' and walk away. He probably went out and bought some records, but it wasn't his métier at all. It's not easy to find a language on the clarinet, and it's very difficult to change your language in the middle of your life."

A few of Benny's contemporaries in the band welcomed this new music with open arms. The trombonist Trummy Young had taken part in Dizzy

Gillespie's first recording session as a leader at the beginning of 1945 and served as a kind of mentor to the younger Goodman musicians, teaching them the chord substitutions and other bop devices they practiced in the dressing room. That June Red Norvo hired Dizzy and Charlie Parker for a record date otherwise composed of Swing Era veterans like Teddy Wilson and Slam Stewart from the current Goodman Sextet and Woody Herman's Flip Phillips. "Bird and Diz were dirty words for musicians of my generation," Norvo explained. "But jazz had always gone through changes, and in 1945 we were in the middle of another one. Bird and Diz were saying new things in an exciting way. I had a free hand, so I gambled." The gamble paid off spectacularly well despite the apparently incongruous mix of styles, producing four classic sides—"Congo Blues," "Get Happy," "Slam Slam Blues" and "Hallelujah!"—that transcended stylistic boundaries and made a lot of the more conservative jazz fans realize that bop was nowhere near as alien as they had thought. *Metronome* called it "probably the top date of the year." Norvo remembers that everyone in the Goodman band played the records constantly, but he was never able to tell whether Benny liked or disliked them. "He was noncommittal."

In January 1946 Red switched over to Woody Herman's musically more congenial orchestra, where he was given more solo space and allowed to develop his interest in bebop as director of the Woodchoppers, Woody's very advanced small band within the band. Trummy Young and Benny had parted company the previous September after an argument in Atlantic City had become so heated Trummy threatened to toss him off the pier. "Benny was nitpicking," Danny recalls, "telling Trummy to play a certain note a little shorter or a little longer or maybe getting on him about his volume. The music had to be absolutely right for Benny, and he had to have control. As soon as he felt the band slipping away from him or going in another direction, he became very upset."

Benny continued to do exceptional business everywhere he appeared. He jammed Newark's Terrace Room to capacity toward the end of 1945 despite terrible weather. Broke all records at the Meadowbrook Gardens in Culver City, California, in January. Set a new all-time high at the Paramount when he returned to New York in March, grossing an extraordinary $135,000 his opening week for an unprecedented forty-three shows. But critical opinion was turning against him, and he was getting it from all sides.

The traditionalist critics, the so-called Moldy Figs, who championed recently rediscovered New Orleans old-timers like Bunk Johnson and George Lewis as the only true keepers of the flame, saw Benny as the symbol of everything that had gone wrong with jazz since it abandoned its delta roots and excoriated him in the harshest, most irrational terms. Reviewing Benny's

wonderful performance with the quintet at an *Esquire* jazz concert, Rudi Blesh
dismissed "the flashy virtuosity which has fooled so many into thinking him
a great player and a creative personality [when] in spite of great commercial
and popular success, he is, of course, neither." *Jazz Session* magazine went
even further, calling Benny "probably the poorest musician in America, an
uncreative riffster trying desperately to copy even the poorest of Negro musicians, and failing miserably." Proponents of bebop like Barry Ulanov still
respected his small group work but found the current big band sadly dated.
Its March appearance at the Paramount "would have been sensational in
1935," Ulanov wrote. "As late as 1941 it would have been interesting. But by
1946 it was a good deal less than either of these qualities." And even long-term
advocates of big band swing like George T. Simon were taking Benny to task
for his ongoing reliance upon Fletcher Henderson's arrangements to the
exclusion of fresher, more varied writing and more interesting material.

In response to the charge that the band was playing "1937 music,"
Benny answered, "Yeah, but it attracts 1937 crowds!" To the complaint that
Fletcher's charts sounded awfully old hat compared with what other bands
were now playing, he replied, "I like them. And I guess I've got a right to like
them, haven't I? . . . I will [try something new] as soon as I find something
new that I think is worthwhile." Benny did record Jack Pleis's very modern
original "Fly by Night," but the side was withheld from release. A few boppish
figures sneak into Johnny Thompson's arrangement of "All the Cats Join In,"
recorded in February 1946, and Mel Powell's "Oh Baby!," recorded that
May. "Oh Baby!" even contains a passing reference to Dizzy Gillespie's
bebop anthem "Salt Peanuts." But these are just momentary allusions that
have no real bearing upon the predominantly Swing Era style of the writing.
For all intents and purposes, Benny had, as his critics maintained, "stopped
going forward." When he began a weekly radio show in July as a summer
replacement for "Information Please," he played vintage numbers almost
exclusively and frequently brought back some of his old stars to reprise their
old hits. *Metronome* judged the opening broadcast "dreary" and reported that
the band "sounded more like ten years ago than at almost any place or time,
even ten years ago."

It wasn't only Benny's conservatism that troubled the critics. There were
also complaints that the band sounded lethargic and underrehearsed and that
Benny's usually faultless playing often sounded tired and sometimes even
slipshod, "more like a Goodman imitator than the great man himself," as one
critic put it. All this led some observers to conclude that now that Benny had
reached his middle thirties and piled up enough money to last him a lifetime
he simply didn't care very much anymore and was rapidly losing interest in
what he was doing.

That may well have been the case. Charlie Barnet recalls that he fronted
the Goodman band for a few days at the Paramount because Benny "just

didn't feel like working." (He also remembers that for this very substantial favor "Benny gave me a Dunhill lighter that someone had given him, but he had the engraving changed to make it look as though it were a present from *him*. . . . Besides which, the damn thing never worked.") It was perfectly understandable that Benny would cut back on his schedule after his second daughter, Benjie, was born in April to spend more time with the family at his Bedford Hills estate. But nowadays, so it was said, he also preferred keeping company with the local gentry to expending the effort it would take to have a band that was worthy of him.

"I'm sick and tired of rehearsing," Benny admitted in the fall of 1946 in an interview that addressed some of the current criticism. "I've had enough of that stuff. I guess I've just passed the stage where I want to knock myself out. What for? If [I] wanted to have everything just the way I want it, I'd have to rehearse all the time, and even then I'm not sure that I'd get it." As for his refusal to keep up with the changing times, "I've been listening to some of the rebop or bebop musicians," he said. "You know, some of them can't even hold a tone! They're just faking. They're not real musicians. . . . Bebop reminds me of guys who refuse to write a major chord even if it's going to sound good. A lot of things they do are too pretentious. They're just writing or playing for effect, and a lot of it doesn't swing. . . . I could play a lot of weird notes if I wanted to. But I don't want to."

Benny returned to the 400 Club on October 31 for a six-week engagement. The opening night turnout was "not good enough," *Variety* reported, and attendance continued to be down during the weeks that followed. Benny had just come off the road and done surprisingly poor business at several locations, and he was said to be upset. Yet all this had less to do with a sudden decline in his personal drawing power than with a more general box-office slump that hit the big swing bands toward the end of the year.

The dollars had been flowing freely during the war, and the more popular leaders had been able to pay top salaries and demand unprecedented prices. But the wartime boom was now over. The fans were no longer so willing to meet the high costs of an evening's entertainment. The ballroom, theater and nightclub operators could no longer come up with the same guarantees. The leaders were finding it difficult to meet their top-heavy payrolls and heavy travel expenses. The sidemen argued that they couldn't afford the inflated cost of life on the road for much less than they'd been earning. Tastes and priorities were changing, too. Veterans returning from the war were more interested in raising families and buying homes than going out for a big night on the town. Romantic singers like Frank Sinatra, Dick Haymes and Perry Como most suited the current mood and were taking over the radio shows and record charts. It all came to a head during the closing months of 1946. Within a matter of weeks more than half a dozen leaders, including Harry James, Tommy Dorsey and Les Brown, decided to disband for the time being until they could find some way out of the current impasse. "The future of swing music is uncertain," an end-of-the-year report concluded. "If it continues at its present speedy rate of commercial disintegration, it may soon become another of the transient musical forms, remembered by its fans with nostalgia but little more."

During the 400 Club engagement critics continued to fault Benny for "the miserable staleness of many arrangements, the insistence on tunes [he] had been driving into the ground for umpteen years, and a general lack of guts, drive and spirit." Benny himself was finding it difficult to muster up much enthusiasm. The owner of the club complained bitterly that he kept showing up late and leaving early and filed charges against him with the union. But if this uncharacteristic breach of professionalism suggests that Benny was fast running out of interest in the band, his enthusiasm for classical music remained undiminished. He was taking lessons from Simeon Bellison, first clarinetist with the New York Philharmonic, whom he extolled as "a complete master of the instrument" and "tops on my list" of favorite clarinet players. Over the past year he had made numerous guest appearances with symphony orchestras around the country and recorded the Brahms Sonata No. 2 in E-Flat Major for Clarinet and Piano with Nadia Reisenberg. Reisenberg's son remembers that he spent many hours at their home playing duets with the eminent pianist and teacher, and that Benny "in later years told me that making music with Mother was a joy."

On November 18, halfway through the 400 Club stand, Benny appeared with Leonard Bernstein and the New York Symphony, performing the Revue for Clarinet and Orchestra, a new work he had commissioned from Alex North. The concert was very favorably reviewed and brought him the best notices he had received in several years. The following week Benny announced that he had decided to break up the band at the end of the engagement so he could devote himself more fully to the classics. When he moved to Los Angeles to continue his current radio show with Victor Borge, he planned to use studio musicians for his broadcasts and recordings, and he intended, so he said, never again to play one-nighters or location dates if he could possibly help it. Benny seems to have been energized by this decision and immediately began making plans to step up his involvement with classical music. On December 10 he commissioned Paul Hindemith to write a composition for clarinet and small symphony orchestra, paying him two thousand dollars for a work to be delivered that fall. Three weeks later he entered into a similar arrangement with Aaron Copland.

Benny, Teddy Wilson, and Eddie Sauter, c. 1948. Ken Whitten Collection

"A/C-D/C Current": The Benny Goodman Sextet with Charlie Christian and Lionel Hampton, 1939. From the Benny Goodman Archives in the Music Library at Yale University

Benny and Mel Powell share a moment onstage, 1941. Ken Whitten Collection

"Wholly Cats": The revamped seven-man Goodman Sextet with Georgie Auld, Charlie Christian and Cootie Williams, c. 1941. Institute of Jazz Studies

Benny and Alice with daughters, Rachel and Benjie.

From the Benny Goodman Archives in the Music Library at Yale University

23

Benny's Bop

In December 1946 Benny moved to Los Angeles with Alice and the children, taking up residence at the large, comfortable house in Westwood Village he had owned for three years but had yet to spend more than a few nights in. George Hill, the orchestra manager for his radio show, put together a big band for Benny to use on the air, filled with Goodman veterans like Jess Stacy, Nate Kazebier, Lou McGarity and Babe Russin, most of whom were now regularly employed in the radio and film studios. The work was not terribly demanding. Much of the half hour broadcast was taken up by Victor Borge's comedy and the guest star of the week, and Benny's portion of the show required him only to run through a couple of numbers. He practiced the clarinet several hours a day but still had plenty of time left over to laze about the house, putter in the garden and be a father to Rachel and Benjie. "This is what I've dreamed of for years," he said.

In the middle of January Benny ended his eight-year association with Columbia Records and switched over to Capitol, a relatively new company based in Los Angeles. According to the record producer George Avakian, who was working at Columbia at the time, Benny and his old label had run out of

**Benny bops (with mixed feelings) at the Hollywood Palladium
with Buddy Greco and Wardell Gray, 1949.**

From the Benny Goodman Archives in the Music Library at Yale University

enthusiasm for each other and were both ready for a change.

"Benny was very unhappy with the sort of material he was being given to record," Avakian says, "and complained to me about how he was still having to do the same kind of terrible tunes he had to do at Victor. The feeling at Columbia was that the big bands were over and it had gotten to be another time. Their main emphasis now was on singers like Frank Sinatra, Dinah Shore, Doris Day and Buddy Clark. They were the company's big stars, and Benny was kind of kept on without meaning much in terms of sales just because he was Benny. He received much more exposure at Capitol because he didn't have to compete with so many name artists who were considered more important—and I hate to say this, but that included almost everyone on the Columbia roster. Benny also had a freer hand at Capitol and got the chance to do some experimenting because they didn't want the same old straight-ahead stuff. Nobody at Columbia said, 'Benny, you can't experiment,' but he was expected to do Benny Goodman, and that was fine for what it was. The chances are Capitol also offered him more money."

Benny negotiated his own contract with Johnny Mercer, an old friend who had sung with the Goodman band on recordings and the "Camel Caravan" show in the 1930s and was now one of the principal owners of the company. Benny's first few recording dates do suggest that he was allowed greater freedom than he had at Columbia and was encouraged to try a variety of different approaches, some of them quite new and unexpected. For his debut session on January 28 he recorded four sides with his radio orchestra: a pair of vocals with Johnny Mercer and Matt Dennis to satisfy the pop market and, more promisingly, two original instrumentals, "Lonely Moments" and "Whistle Blues," by Mary Lou Williams, who had written the marvelous arrangement of "Roll 'Em" back in 1937 and had now moved into the camp of the modernists without completely abandoning her old Swing Era loyalties. A few weeks later, on February 19, Benny inaugurated Capitol's classical division by recording Carl Maria von Weber's Grand Duo Concertant for Piano and Clarinet with Nadia Reisenberg. Over the course of the month he also produced a number of small group sides featuring, of all things, the accordion of Ernie Felice.

The records were largely disappointing. Of the four big band sides, only the boppish "Lonely Moments" lived up to expectations. Benny had scoffed, "Oh, bebop!" when Mary Lou first showed him the chart and insisted she simplify some of the more harmonically complex passages. Though the arrangement falls back on the old clarinet and tomtom routine left over from "Sing, Sing, Sing," it is still fresher and more adventurous than anything Benny had tried in some time, and he even interjects a few bebop embellishments into his own solo. The performance of the von Weber seems to have gone badly. Capitol withheld it from release, and Benny did not make any further attempts to record classical music during the three years he remained with the label. As for the small group recordings, though Ernie Felice was a skillful player, he had very little aptitude for jazz improvisation, and the performances suffered accordingly. For *Metronome*, "Fine and Dandy" and "The Lonesome Road," the first pair of sides to be issued, sounded "like a fairly clean small radio station's swing band's idea of Jazz Music" and concluded its review, "For shame, Mr. G." *Down Beat* found them "shocking, possibly the worst jazz side[s] ever released under Benny's name."

Benny's reputation continued to slip among both the critics and the fans. His own playing was still given its due, but at the beginning of 1947 the Goodman band received a meager 317 votes in *Down Beat*'s annual readers' poll, and it fared even worse in *Metronome*'s comparable survey. A disgruntled listener complained to *Down Beat* that spring, "No matter what a musician may have accomplished before, as long as he plays or leads a band he owes it to music and himself to put forth all that his talent allows. Benny Goodman has failed miserably in this respect." Though Benny had his defenders, even some of them seemed to think that "the great man is now at the sunset of a brilliant career" and asked no more than "the King be allowed to descend gently from his throne [without being] harassed into oblivion."

Benny's NBC radio series went off the air in June, and in July he was signed by Samuel Goldwyn to perform and play an acting role in the Danny Kaye musical *A Song Is Born*. Tommy Dorsey, Louis Armstrong, Lionel Hampton and Charlie Barnet also appeared in the film, but the most notable thing about it was the scuffle with Dorsey that took place off camera when Benny showed up almost four hours late to shoot the jam session scene. "Nobody landed a punch," Barnet recalled. "All they did was knock over a bunch of music stands." But the following morning the *Los Angeles Herald-Examiner* ran a screaming eight-column headline across the front page, TOMMY DORSEY KNOCKS DOWN BENNY GOODMAN IN FIST FIGHT, and the story was picked up by newspapers around the country.

Benny continued to record extensively for Capitol over 1947, mostly with small groups, occasionally with a big band temporarily assembled for that purpose. The Capitol engineers filtered Benny's clarinet through an echo chamber that reproduced it with great clarity and precision but failed to capture the warmth that was one of its most appealing characteristics. This has led some later observers to complain about the "chilly perfectionism" of Benny's playing during this period and to attribute it to a deeper immersion in classical music that, in fact, had not yet taken place.

Benny continued to play some classical engagements during this period, but he did not radically change the direction of his career as he announced he would do at the end of 1946. Paul Hindemith met the deadline Benny had set in his contract and completed the Concerto for Clarinet and Orchestra in September 1947. Aaron Copland was diverted by a lucrative offer from Hollywood to score the film of John Steinbeck's *The Red Pony* and did not finish his Clarinet Concerto until a year later. Benny had been extremely encouraging to both composers—assuring Hindemith that he was "studying his part" and "only waiting to let loose," writing Copland that he was "looking forward in great anticipation for this piece"—and both of them assumed he would premiere their new works shortly after they were delivered. But to their disappointment it wasn't until November 1950, four years after the compositions had been commissioned and just before Benny's right to perform them exclusively expired, that he finally got around to giving them their first public hearing.

During the spring of 1947 Benny stopped using Ernie Felice on his small group dates and returned to former sidemen like Red Norvo and Mel Powell, known quantities that had collaborated with him successfully in the past and proved to be his musical peers. Some of these sessions yielded only perfunctory run-throughs of overly familiar material, but some marvelous records were also produced: Mel Powell's "Hi 'Ya Sophia" and "Shirley Steps Out," his slightly boppish recasting of "How High the Moon," for example, both of them named after Benny's stepdaughters, and the gorgeous adaptation of Delibes's *The Maids of Cadiz* with Norvo and Jimmy Rowles. The critical attitude toward Benny, though, had become so reflexively negative by now that even they were largely overlooked and undervalued. Peculiarly enough, one of the few people not to go along with the prevailing opinion about Benny's current work was the unimpeachably hip bebop eminence Charlie Parker. "That's typical Goodman," Parker said upon hearing the recent sextet recording of "Nagasaki" during one of Leonard Feather's Blindfold Tests. "And Benny's always superb, that's natural. He's one of the few that never retards. I don't agree with people who think Benny's old-fashioned."

Benny's big band recordings had much less to recommend them and were largely, as the critics charged, mired in the past. Many of them were arranged by Fletcher Henderson, who was no fan of modernism. "Of all the cruelties in the world, bebop is the most phenomenal," he grumbled. "It isn't music to me." Unlike Mary Lou Williams, Fletcher did not update his writing style to make it more contemporary, and a hastily assembled orchestra with no existence outside the recording studio could not possibly perform his arrangements with the same spirit and authority the Goodman band had brought to similar material a decade earlier.

When Benny did break away from the old format and try something different, he tended to resort to things like "Give Me the Good Old Days," a deliberately corny novelty item with a vocal quartet, or the syrupy violin-laden rendition of Charles Trenet's "La Mer," which had more in common with easy-listening elevator music than anything that could remotely be called jazz. Such efforts incensed the critics even further and only confused Benny's fans. As George Avakian observed, "There was no direction in Benny's music at Capitol. It was all over the place, whereas before you could depend on a Goodman record. Even if it was a lousy pop tune, you knew you'd get a good Benny solo."

That October two albums of Goodman recordings appeared in the record shops: one a reissue of some of the classic sides like "King Porter Stomp" and "Sometimes I'm Happy" Benny had done for Victor between 1935 and 1937, the other a sampling of his recent small group and big band work that Capitol saddled with the asking-for-trouble title *Benny Rides Again.* Comparisons between the two albums were inevitable, and reviewers made a great point about just how far Benny had fallen from "the glory that once was Goodman." An especially exasperated critic complained about the Capitol set: "For Goodman, this is cheap shoddy. If he doesn't want to have a band and [wants to] live a comfortable life, wonderful. But when he makes records he should forget to be comfortable and play."

Toward the end of 1947 a dispute between the American Federation of Musicians and the record companies about the union's unilateral control of the royalty fund set up after the 1942 musicians' strike led to a second ban on recordings. It took a full year to hammer out a mutually acceptable arrangement for administering the fund. Meanwhile, no new records were made other than by singers working without instrumental accompaniment. In a way the ban brought Benny some unexpected benefits. Freed from the pressure of having to grind out records for Capitol that pleased no one, including himself, he was given a chance to step back and gain some perspective on the kind of music he'd been playing and try to find a way to redeem his reputation and reenergize his career.

On April 29, 1947, Benny had made one of his increasingly rare public appearances playing at a Just Jazz concert in Pasadena with a small group featuring Red Norvo and Jimmy Rowles. The other headliners included Benny Carter, Peggy Lee, Charlie Barnet, Erroll Garner and a bop band led by Howard McGee with the young tenor saxophonist Wardell Gray. The concert had gone well, filling every one of the almost three thousand seats in the large municipal auditorium, and Benny was in excellent form, "a treat for those who had decided on the basis of his work on the air that he had run out of everything except shakes and trills," as one review reported. But the real star of the evening was the relatively obscure Wardell Gray, who had been working in Billy Eckstine's backup band at Billy Berg's nightclub in Los

Angeles and was just beginning to gain a reputation among the more aware jazz fans.

The twenty-six-year old tenor man was an unusually accomplished and versatile musician. Influenced by both Benny's old favorite Lester Young and Charlie Parker, with whom he had recorded a few months earlier, he combined Lester's characteristic sound and phrasing with Parker's advanced conception, bridging the gap between the old jazz and the new with long-lined, loose-limbed solos notable for their warmth, lucidity and unfaltering sense of swing. Over the course of the evening he proved equally adept playing high-powered pressure cooker bebop with Howard McGee and more relaxed swing-oriented jazz with Erroll Garner. The recording of "Blue Lou" made with Garner at the concert contains what is widely regarded as one of his finest solos and was awarded the French Grand Prix du Disque the following year. Benny was also impressed with Wardell's playing. "If he's bop, that's great," he enthused. "He's wonderful." When Benny took part in another Just Jazz concert that December, he invited Wardell to join him onstage for several numbers, laying the groundwork for an experiment that was to free him from his heavy dependence upon the past.

Two months later Benny stopped by a jam session at the Club 47 in Los Angeles and heard another young modernist who also played a key role in redirecting the course of his music. Ake ("Stan") Hasselgard was a twenty-five-year-old clarinetist who had arrived in the United States from his native Sweden the previous July to do graduate work in art history and English at Columbia University. Though he had led his own dance band in college and made some recordings back in Sweden, Hasselgard had no intention of becoming a professional musician, but after sitting in with Jack Teagarden and experiencing some of the other musical riches New York had to offer, he decided to withdraw from graduate school and try to make jazz his career. Moving to California, he took out a union card and quickly came to the notice of established players like Red Norvo and the guitarist Barney Kessel, both of whom spread the word about his talent and took part in his first American recording date when he secured a contract with Capitol for four sides toward the end of 1947.

Benny had been Stan's original inspiration and model. "I've been buying American records since I was a child," he said, "and Benny Goodman was always my favorite." His Swedish recordings all were "in the traditional Goodman style," he recalled, and Benny remained an important, much-venerated influence, so much so that he managed to talk his way into several Goodman recording sessions and even struck up a casual friendship with his normally standoffish hero. But under the guidance of Barney Kessel, Hasselgard also became attracted to the recent developments in jazz and soon incorporated them into his playing. What Benny heard at the Club 47 that night was a synthesis of his own style and a more modern approach that meshed with it so seamlessly it seemed like a natural extension. Like Wardell Gray, Hasselgard straddled both bebop and swing, and like Wardell, he was an exceptional soloist—warm, inventive, tasteful and always hard-swinging. According to Kessel, he did not read music and, because he was completely self-taught, played many incorrect fingerings, limitations that might be expected to offend Benny's inflexibly high standards of musicianship. Yet Benny was so impressed by his performance he invited Stan to his home the next day. Benny had by now rethought his earlier decision to limit his jazz activities to radio and recordings, and he asked Hasselgard to join Wardell Gray in the new seven-piece group he was in the process of forming to play some live engagements back east.

This was the only time Benny ever featured another clarinetist, and his motives remain obscure. Certainly he admired Hasselgard greatly. "He's the first clarinet player in a long time I thought was good," Benny maintained, and he claimed to feel so strongly about his abilities that he was making him part of his band just "to show him off" and help promote his career. Yet it also seems likely that Benny felt he had something to learn from how his young disciple had adapted the new music of Charlie Parker and Dizzy Gillespie to the clarinet, which hardly anyone else had managed to do so effectively, and there was no better way to learn that than by playing next to him every night.

Benny brought Hasselgard and Gray to New York in the spring of 1948 and put together a rhythm section composed of Teddy Wilson on piano and three bop-oriented musicians with solid swing band credentials: Woody Herman's former guitarist Billy Bauer, the bassist Arnold Fishkind, who had worked with Bunny Berigan and Jack Teagarden, and Mel Zelnick on drums. Benny commissioned Mary Lou Williams and Mel Powell to sketch out some charts and went into rehearsal in early May. The new Goodman Septet was scheduled to debut at Carnegie Hall on May 10. Jazz concerts were no longer such a novelty in this once-exclusive bastion of high culture, and recent appearances by Louis Armstrong, Kid Ory's Creole Jazz Band and Dizzy Gillespie had drawn disappointing crowds. Nor was Benny's current appeal strong enough to lure the fans away from their newly acquired television sets. Advance ticket sales were so poor that four days before it was due to take place the concert was cancelled.

On May 24 the septet began a two-week engagement at the Click nightclub in Philadelphia. Bootleg recordings of broadcasts from the club reveal that this was easily the freshest and most interesting band Benny had led in years. The unusual front line of tenor saxophone and two clarinets gave the group a distinctive, wonderfully reedy sound. The arrangements featured long-lined, tightly voiced ensemble passages startlingly like the sort of thing

the very advanced pianist Lennie Tristano was now doing with the saxophonists Lee Konitz and Warne March. (Bauer, Fishkind and Zelnick were all
closely associated with Tristano and may have played some part in bringing
their mentor to Benny's attention.) Along with the obligatory trio numbers
with Teddy Wilson and an occasional vocal by Patti Page, the repertoire
included some unexpectedly modern originals and boppish reworkings of
familiar standards like "Limehouse Blues," "Bye Bye Blues" and Charlie
Parker's variations on "Indiana." Wardell Gray and Stan Hasselgard provided the sort of stimulation Benny always welcomed, challenging him with
their modernity without being too modern for his taste, and Teddy Wilson
served as a reassuring presence that kept everything in balance. Benny's solo
work exhibits some slight bebop tendencies but remains rooted in the familiar
Goodman style, and he sounds comfortable and happy playing in this artfully
constructed blending of older and newer conceptions and much more involved than on most of his recent Capitol efforts.

Unfortunately this was not the sort of music Goodman fans wanted to
hear. Boppish numbers like "Bye Bye Blues" received only perfunctory applause, while Patti Page's rather ordinary vocals were greeted with great
enthusiasm. The septet did very poor business, and halfway through the
engagement the owner of the club tried to renegotiate Benny's contract,
claiming that the receipts simply didn't justify the forty-five hundred dollars
a week he was being paid.

Even before the money hassles with the Click Benny had decided to take
full financial control over his own personal appearances and had booked
himself into the Westchester County Center in White Plains for the summer
weekends. He rented the hall, paid for the advertising, hired a local big band
to alternate with the septet, and with the young bopper Red Rodney added
on trumpet, kicked off a series of dances on June 26. To appeal to the widest
possible audience, Benny played a mix of familiar Goodman favorites and
more modern material, yet the band fared no better than it had in Philadelphia. The huge County Center held six thousand people, but only about
fifteen hundred tickets were purchased. Attendance fell even lower the following week. After a third money-losing weekend Benny had enough of the
venture and canceled the remainder of the dates, which would have kept the
band working into September.

Benny told an interviewer that he thought his new group was contributing something to jazz and he very much wanted to hold it together. And he
felt bad, he said, that one of the reasons it failed to draw much of a crowd was
that his policy of welcoming black patrons had kept many white fans away.
Benny denied that he was trying to adapt his clarinet style to a more modern
conception. ("I'm not changing at all. I couldn't. What for? It would be silly.")
But he also bristled at the charge that he was as reactionary as he was often

made out to be, citing his past involvement with Belá Bartók, Eddie Sauter and Charlie Christian. As for bebop itself, Benny had decidedly mixed feelings. "It certainly deserves to be encouraged. They're doing something different, not copying. I like some bop. I like some of Dizzy's stuff, 'Emanon' especially. And of course I like Charlie Parker. But I don't like to listen to a lot of bop. It seems that everybody is trying to see just how much he can put in. It's nervous music more than exciting music. If some of them would just try to simplify their arrangements and solos, they'd come off much better. It seems that they're all trying to outdo and outstartle each other. And yet, you know, I think something good will come out of all this."

Benny was eager for the recording ban to end so he could bring his new group before a larger public. That July he did make a few V-discs and radio transcriptions for the armed forces, including "Limehouse Blues," which he retitled "Benny's Bop" as a sign that his interest in modern jazz was continuing unabated. In September the union allowed him permission to record one side, "Stealin' Apples," for a special album benefiting the Damon Runyon Cancer Fund that was largely comprised of sound tracks from *A Song Is Born* made before the ban went into effect. "Stealin' Apples" is notable for the addition of Fats Navarro, one of the preeminent bebop trumpet players, who was working in Tadd Dameron's band at the Royal Roost. Wardell Gray frequently sat in with Dameron during the septet's layoff, and it was probably this connection that brought Navarro into the Goodman fold. In no small part because of Navarro's masterful solo and ensemble work, the date came off exceptionally well and was included in *Metronome*'s list of the year's best releases.

Hasselgard did not take part in any of these sessions. As much as Benny liked and admired him, he seems to have had a lot of ambivalence about sharing the spotlight with his young protégé. During the Philadelphia engagement he varied Stan's role from one night to the next, sometimes giving him a generous amount of solo space, sometimes hardly allowing him to solo at all. Jim Maher recalls that during the first weekend at the Westchester County Center Hasselgard was playing a solo that had the audience up on its feet cheering when Benny walked over, planted himself in front of the microphone and cut him off in mid-chorus. "I asked Benny years later if he remembered that night in White Plains. Benny did remember, and we started to talk about it. I didn't quite say, 'Why did you take Stan's solo away from him?' I said, 'Stan was really wailing that night.' And Benny said, 'Yeah . . . He was . . . wasn't he?' I knew him well enough to recognize that the sudden shift in his tone of voice and the way he said 'Wasn't he?' were a little signal to me that we weren't going to discuss it any further." Benny had spoken to Hasselgard about backing him in his own group, but when Stan pursued the subject while visiting Benny at home, he grew vague about the details, and nothing ever came of it. On November 22, 1948, a month after his twenty-sixth birthday, Hasselgard was on his way to Mexico to renew his visa when he was killed in an automobile accident, putting an end to a brief career that had barely begun to fulfill its early promise.

By October Benny had given up on the septet and was starting to rehearse a new big band to take out on the road. Though the band business had not really recovered from the slump that took place toward the end of 1946, Benny thought it still might be possible for the right kind of orchestra to attain the sort of widespread popular acceptance Harry James had managed to achieve a few years earlier. The Stan Kenton band currently had an enthusiastic following in the colleges, but the way Benny saw it, its strident "progressive jazz" was too specialized a taste to appeal to a broader, more mainstream audience. "As for me, personally," he said, "I wouldn't go out of my way to hear the band, though I must admit that what they're doing, they're doing violently."

Benny wanted a young band filled with modern soloists who still knew how to swing, and this time around he did not call upon any of the older Goodman veterans who had staffed most of his recent orchestras. Wardell Gray came aboard as featured saxophonist. Fats Navarro was hired for the solo trumpet chair but occupied it only briefly. After he kept showing up late for rehearsal, Benny let him go and brought in Doug Mettome, a brilliant twenty-three-year-old who had replaced Navarro in the Billy Eckstine band in 1946. The trombonists Eddie Bert and Milt Bernhart had recently worked with Stan Kenton. For his pianist and boy singer, he hired Buddy Greco, a young classically trained musician who was currently riding a big hit record with his own trio of "Oooh! Look-a There, Ain't She Pretty?"

"After 'Ain't She Pretty?' became a million seller, a lot of leaders asked me to join their bands, but I wasn't interested," Buddy recalls. "But I always wanted to work for Benny Goodman. I wanted to learn my profession the best way possible, and I gave up a lot of money to go with him. For some reason, Benny took a real liking to me. He knew I had come from a very poor background in South Philadelphia and had won a scholarship to Curtis Institute when I was fourteen, and I think that impressed him. The first thing he had me play at my audition was a very heavy classical piece; it may have been by Delius. He just threw it in front of me, and I played it, and that afternoon he took me to meet Igor Stravinsky, of all people.

"I think one of the things Benny liked about me was that I have perfect pitch, even though there were times I would get him upset by using it to play a little trick on him. I would change the keys on the introductions to certain songs, and he wouldn't be able to hear it right away, so he'd come in the original key, then look over his glasses and give me the Ray. He must have fired me ten times during the year and a half I was with him, then hired me right back with a raise.

"But my relationship with Benny was fabulous. At the time I joined him I was still living in Philadelphia, and he invited me to stay with him and Mrs. Goodman and the kids at their home in New York. He also sent money back to my parents. That was not at all typical of Benny Goodman. As everyone knows, he was a very odd person. But to me he was always extremely kind and generous."

Benny immersed himself in modern jazz while the band was coming together. He spent many evenings at the Royal Roost and listened to a lot of recordings, familiarizing himself with the different players and becoming comfortable enough with what they were doing to be able to form judgments about particular performances. When Leonard Feather played him some bebop records on one of his Blindfold Tests, Benny had no difficulty at all identifying Navarro and Dameron, praised Dizzy Gillespie's "Shaw 'Nuff" ("That's a very good record, and it's one of the cleaner ones, too—good execution") and was surprisingly receptive to Thelonious Monk, whose idiosyncratic approach to the piano still seemed too strange and forbidding to all but the hippest bop fans. "Changed my opinion? Well, yes, I suppose I have really," Benny reflected. "I think the important thing about bop is that it's bringing something new to jazz melodically. It's very interesting. Of course, some of the old things, some of my older records, still sound great to me, but it's a different age."

As intrigued as Benny had become with some of the newer developments, he was far from ready to put "the old things" behind him. "We had two books," Buddy remembers. "We had the old Fletcher Henderson-style book made up of all his big hits, and we had the much smaller bop book by Chico O'Farrill, Tadd Dameron and a number of other modern writers, including myself. When we went out on one-nighters, Benny would start off playing 'Jersey Bounce' and 'A String of Pearls' and his other hits; then toward the end of the evening he'd turn over the band to me and leave the stage, and we'd take out the bop book and play that. I adjusted my own playing to whatever we were doing. When I had my Benny Goodman hat on, I played Benny Goodman music. When we turned into a bop band, I tried to play like Bud Powell. Wardell and Doug Mettome did the same sort of thing. When Benny was fronting the band, Doug got into a Roy Eldridge bag; then later on in the evening he switched over to Dizzy or Miles. Doug was a genius player, and Benny was very, very hot on him. In fact, at one point he wanted to send him out on his own doing a more commercial kind of thing a la Harry James. Unfortunately Doug had some personal problems, but he was some talent."

Benny was almost forty years old and, understandably enough, not very comfortable surrounded by a band full of young boppers mostly in their early twenties. "I think he felt very alien in that band," Chico O'Farrill recalled. "I used to bring in arrangements and guys like Doug Mettome, Wardell Gray, Eddie Bert, Buddy Greco—they would cut the chords with me, and they would know what was happening, [but when] Benny would get to [his] solo, he would be completely detached from what was happening within the rest of the band. I think he actually felt embarrassed, if there's such a thing as embarrassment in Benny. When Benny's solo turn came about, I tried to simplify the harmonies a little bit without making it too incongruous all of a sudden. I remember one time I wrote an arrangement for the band on 'Goodnight, Sweetheart,' and I really went pretty far out. So one day we ran through it once, and Benny said, 'What is this, Chico, you trying to give us harmony lessons?' "

The band's peculiarly double-sided musical personality was to a certain extent unavoidable. Toward the end of 1948 Charlie Barnet also returned to the business with a new, much more modern orchestra, and though he was far less ambivalent about bebop than Benny, he, too, found himself having to perform many of his old tried and true crowd pleasers. "We have no choice," he explained. "The kids keep asking for the old ones that *made* us on records and around the ballrooms, so we give 'em what they want." And from a strictly business point of view, the mixture seemed to work, at least at the beginning. During the Goodman band's break-in tour of the Northeast that autumn it drew large and enthusiastic audiences composed of both Swing Era diehards who expected to hear "Don't Be That Way" and young boppers who had come to check out Wardell Gray and Chico O'Farrill's arrangements.

But Benny's efforts to satisfy everyone, including those who just wanted to dance to the latest pop ballads, gave the band a disconcerting lack of focus that ultimately worked against it. And this indecision was reflected in Benny's own playing. "When playing ideas written for him to play with the Sextet or the slow figures designed for his work with the band, he moves a little too ostentatiously through elementary bop," a reviewer observed. "But at an up-tempo over an ad-lib solo of any length, he goes right back to the essential Chicago style he always has used, garnished with his usual display of technical ease. It gives a confused result."

"Benny respected boppers like Fats Navarro as the musicians they were, but I don't believe he understood bop or ever really liked it," Buddy Greco maintains. "I *know* he didn't like it. He had a habit of putting us on a little bit, making musical fun of what we were doing. Sometimes he did try to stretch out a little and play more modern, but he was so good at what he did that when he soloed on the new charts in his usual style, to my way of thinking he fit in just fine. It would have been a shame for him to change. It was a very

happy band when we started out, and of course, we all loved being with Benny
Goodman. And Benny seemed fairly happy, too, as happy as he could be
without really knowing where we were going. I think he did have a lot of
uncertainty and confusion about the band's direction. When we started recording, one day we would do Chico O'Farrill's 'Undercurrent Blues' and
another day do 'That Wonderful Girl of Mine,' which is an old Yiddish song.
The records were such a mixture I don't believe they did very well. If you
don't have a fix on what you're doing, people don't know what to expect.
That's probably one reason why the writers came down so hard on him. They
were confused, too. But Benny was so pressured by the record company he
had to get into the bop thing even if he wasn't very comfortable with it."

The part Capitol Records played in Benny's decision to experiment with
big band bebop shouldn't be underestimated. At the time the recording ban
was lifted at the end of 1948 bebop was receiving a great deal of attention in
the popular press, and for a brief moment it looked as if it might become the
next big musical fad. Capitol had been formed too late to benefit from the
earlier swing craze, but it was determined to get in on the bottom floor of this
latest musical vogue. "Bebop performers who have aroused wildly fanatical
followings in the New York area are being signed almost daily to exclusive
contracts," the president of the company announced, and though this was
something of an overstatement, Capitol did take a much more aggressive
position than the other major labels, signing up Miles Davis, Tadd Dameron,
Lennie Tristano and the bop singers Dave Lambert and Babs Gonzales along
with a number of others. Stan Kenton had been the company's best-selling
modernist, but when he disbanded his orchestra for personal reasons toward
the end of the year, it needed another modern big band to fill the void. Woody
Herman and Charlie Barnet were two likely candidates. Benny Goodman was
another. When "Undercurrent Blues" was issued, it carried the words "Bop
Instrumental" on the label, and Benny's small band recordings of "Blue Lou"
and "There's a Small Hotel" were advertised along with the latest releases by
Miles Davis and Lennie Tristano as "Tops in Bop and Progressive Jazz; Solid
Sides from Capitol's Bop Shop."

After completing its tour of the Northeast, the Goodman orchestra made its
New York debut at the Paramount Theater on December 15, 1948. Benny
had thought for some time that big bands could no longer get by just coming
out onstage and playing some tunes, and to make the most of this important
engagement, he hired the radio writer Sherman Marks to devise an elaborate
theatrical production that would present the orchestra in a novel, more
broadly entertaining setting. Expanding upon the "Twenty Years of Jazz"
idea Benny had used in his 1938 Carnegie Hall concert, "The Benny Good-

man Jazz Cavalcade" was both an up-the-river-from-New Orleans capsule history of jazz and an autobiographical account of Benny's own musical progress. The show offered a fully scripted running commentary by Benny, a team of lindy hoppers, dramatic lighting effects and a large screen slide show display of some of his more famous alumni. It was a very shrewdly conceived presentation, allowing Benny to run the gamut from "Bugle Call Rag" and "Sing, Sing, Sing" to "Undercurrent Blues" without losing either the youngsters in the audience who had never heard of the Swing Era or the older fans still intimidated by bop.

The bebop holdouts were eased into the new music with a piece of special material that had Buddy Greco introduce a reluctant Benny to modern jazz through some comic back-and-forth patter set to the tune of "There'll Be Some Changes Made." When the columnist Earl Wilson came backstage and questioned Benny about whether or not he was actually playing bebop these days, Benny was evasive. "Uh, well, I got a new band. There are some kids in it. Some of them are nuts about bop. If I like the way they play, I don't care what the hell they call it. I don't know [if I play bop]. You'd have to ask them. I've probably been doing it for years. Any kind of good bebop is swing."

The show was praised as a "well-rounded musical entertainment" and, helped along by the strong Bob Hope-Jane Russell movie *Pale Face,* did excellent business. Overcoming unusually severe December weather and the normal Christmas season slump, it grossed an impressive eighty thousand dollars the first week, ninety thousand the second and ninety-two thousand the third and final week of the engagement. But then, on the Saturday night before he closed, Benny suddenly walked off the bandstand in the middle of a performance, and Gene Krupa had to be called in to take over fronting the orchestra for the last three days. *Variety* reported the story on its front page, speculating that Benny's disappearance might have been caused by the friction he'd been having with the Paramount staging executives and raised the question whether he was abandoning his new orchestra. The following week a sternly worded letter from Benny's attorney stated that he had been under a doctor's care for "a severe sore throat and bad cold" and had left the theater only because "he was on the verge of a collapse." He was currently recuperating at home in California, the lawyer asserted, and "has never been more pleased with any band than he is with the present one." According to Buddy Greco, Benny *was* seriously ill, but it was because his old back problem had flared up again, leaving him too racked with pain to go on. It was completely in character for Benny to conceal the true nature of his illness, and a quarter century in show business had taught him that future bookings could be jeopardized if word got around he was still suffering from a chronic, sometimes debilitating health problem.

Benny flew back to New York to prepare the band for its first recording session for Capitol but collapsed during a rehearsal. Against his doctor's advice he played President Truman's Inaugural Ball in Washington with Guy Lombardo and Xavier Cugat on January 20, 1949, then immediately returned to California to complete his recuperation. The band was booked into the Hollywood Palladium for four weeks at the beginning of March, and Buddy Greco took over front man duties as it worked its way west. Still showing the effects of his illness, Benny rejoined the band shortly before the Palladium opening on March 1. It was reported that "Goodman's Palladium engagement was one of the most spectacular and profitable runs the dancery had enjoyed in years." What Buddy remembers best about it was what took place one afternoon while Benny was auditioning female singers. "One of the girls who showed up introduced herself as Norma Jean Baker and asked me to back her on 'How Deep Is the Ocean?' She wasn't Marilyn Monroe yet, and she wasn't a blonde, but she was absolutely gorgeous, and all the guys in the band went nuts. Benny looked at her, and when she finally finished, he said, 'I think you're very pretty, but you'll never really get anywhere in show business. I think you ought to go home.' "

The band remained around Los Angeles until the middle of April and did a lot of recording. It produced a handful of boppish instrumentals during its California stay—"Bop Hop," Buddy Greco's "Dreazag," Chico O'Farrill's "Undercurrent Blues" and "Shishkabop"—but most of its output consisted of pop ballads and novelty numbers that were trounced by the critics. Capitol was disappointed by the sessions and withheld half the sides from release. A small group date done just before the band left for a tour of the Midwest yielded Benny's most successful excursions into bebop, but even the septet's sizzling performance of Wardell Gray's "Bedlam" received only begrudging approval from most of the reviewers and failed to win over the hard-core boppers.

Benny planned to take the band to Europe for the summer, starting off with two weeks at the London Palladium, then moving on to France, Belgium, Holland and the Scandinavian countries in what would have been the first extended postwar tour by a major American orchestra. The British musicians' union, however, would not grant the full Goodman band permission to work in England and allowed Benny to bring along only Buddy Greco and Marcy Lutes, his current female singer. Benny opened at the Palladium on July 18, fronting the English Skyrockets stage band, augmented by some strong British soloists like Johnny Dankworth on alto saxophone and Kenny Baker on trumpet. Benny used the same revue format he had introduced at the Paramount and met with a similar success. The London critics were hungry to hear American jazzmen of Benny's stature in person and gave him the kinds of reviews he hardly ever received anymore back in the United States. "Goodman himself is as great as we expected him to be, and as well as we know his ability, his clarinet playing in the flesh is still a revelation," the *Melody Maker* raved. The reviewer for the *Daily Worker* reported, "I came out reeling."

Benny dropped his plan to meet up with the band in Oslo and go on with the tour of the Continent when he discovered that currency restrictions made it impossible to take any money back home with him. After vacationing briefly with Alice on the Riviera, he returned to New York in the middle of August. On October 15 he brought his jazz revue into the Roxy Theater in Manhattan, the first time he had played somewhere other than the Paramount since his triumphant debut there back in 1937. The Roxy was one of the largest houses on Broadway with over two thousand more seats than the Paramount, but the Goodman name was no longer a strong enough attraction to come anywhere near filling them. The band took in a very disappointing sixty-six thousand dollars the first week and slipped down to a dismal forty-six thousand the second.

Benny was hardly the only leader suffering from such a precipitous decline in drawing power. By the middle of 1949 the bottom had dropped out of the band business. Orchestras ranging in style from Tommy Dorsey to Sammy Kaye were equally cold at the box office. Even the perennially popular Guy Lombardo had lost money on his recent southern tour. And the big bop fad that was expected to instill some new life into the business had never really materialized. "Bop is a flop—commercially," *Variety* reported. "The musical style is dying almost as fast as it began, according to maestros who employ it, agents who book it and recording companies which grabbed fast a few months ago to corral its exponents."

Charlie Barnet was forced to give up his orchestra in October. "Out of fifteen one-nighters we were lucky if we got a warm reception at one," he explained. "People wanted things corned up. They wanted 'Hop Scotch Polka.' They didn't care what you stood for in music. I was very unhappy. Actually, the music being played today by bands like mine and Woody's is not particularly good for dancing, and in that respect the customers have a legitimate beef." Two months later Woody Herman also disbanded. "I felt strongly about the music we were playing, and I couldn't accept the fact that we didn't have a wider audience," he recalled. "When I found that I was $175,000 in the hole, I became very much aware. We kept trying to make a go of the Second Herd. But it appeared that the ballgame was over, not only for us, but for big bands in general."

Benny did a short concert tour of the Philippines in November, performing a mixed program of classical music with the Manila Little Symphony and jazz with his own quartet. By the time he returned to New York in December he had arrived at the painful decision to close the band down. "We were very disappointed, of course," Buddy Greco remembers. "But the business was dying, and he didn't feel there was any use going on. It just wasn't happening anymore. We had lost a lot of players, too, including Wardell Gray. As the only black guy in the band Wardell had to put up with a lot of racism. There were times he couldn't check into the hotel or eat in the restaurants. And then, when we worked down in Virginia, some Ku Klux Klanners burst into the little apartment Doug Mettome and I shared with him and threatened to lynch him. Being Italian, I get very, very dark, and the only reason they left me alone was when I was getting dressed, they saw that my backside was white. We had a lot of problems with racial situations, and Wardell finally had enough."

In years to come Benny now and then assembled a big band for a specific occasion—a concert, a tour, a series of recordings—but this was the last Benny Goodman orchestra that was intended to have some degree of permanence, and as such it represents the end of an era. And once he put it behind him, Benny also turned away from virtually all the young modernists who helped bring it into being. "I never worked with Benny again," Buddy recalls, still a little disturbed that such a close personal and musical association could end so abruptly. "I think he came to hear me one time at Basin Street, but other than that I never saw the man again. I don't know what to make of it. He was around. Sometimes he would take a band out. And I really felt kind of hurt he never asked me to go with him. Maybe he thought I'd turn him down because I was starting to make a lot of noise as a singer. But he never even tried. And I probably would have said yes if he had."

The demise of the 1949 band put an end to Benny's uneasy flirtation with bebop. In the fall of that year Benny claimed he had developed a liking for modern jazz and was regretful it wasn't taking hold with the general public the way swing did in the thirties. "It's too confusing to me. I don't know why they don't like it more. The bop musicians I've known have been fine musicians. They can read anything." By 1953 he had done a complete about-face and was reviling it in terms worthy of the most reactionary Moldy Fig. "Maybe bop has done more to set music back for years than anything," he complained to the *New York Times*. "Basically, it's all wrong. It's not even knowing the scales. The results have got to be bad. What you hear in bop is a lot of noise—the wrong kind of noise. They can't play their horns. No tone, no phrasing, no technique. And they can't take direction. That's not any kind of music. The damn monotony of it got to me. Bop was mostly publicity and people figuring angles."

The Kell
Interlude

hen Benny disbanded his orchestra at the end of 1949, he moved back east and announced, once again, that he intended to devote most of his time to classical music. Benny's involvement with the classics had continued to deepen over the years, and he had by now more than proved the seriousness of his commitment through a large number of recordings, concert appearances and commissions. The critics treated Benny's classical work respectfully, but once it moved past the novelty stage of the rough-and-ready Chicago jazzman taking on Mozart, they also began to subject it to the same sort of scrutiny they brought to bear on any concert artist.

As far back as 1938 the music critic B. H. Haggin observed that though Benny had come to love Mozart's music, "its language was not the one he had grown up with and that he could himself speak, as a performer, with the naturalness, the richness and potency of inflection with which he spoke the language of popular music." In Haggin's view, Benny's playing improved dramatically over the next few years, but in assessing a 1940 performance of Mozart's Clarinet Concerto with the New York Philharmonic, he offered the opinion that Benny's phrasing, "though beautiful," still sounded "studied"

Benny and Reginald Kell, c. 1950.

and "he has yet to reach the point where it will be done with the relaxed ease, the freedom and spontaneity that are the necessary conditions for it to acquire the sharpened contours of style."

"Relaxed ease," "freedom," "spontaneity"—Benny's jazz playing possessed these qualities in abundance, and they helped make him one of the most vivacious jazz soloists of his generation. But over the course of the decade it continued to be noted that they were frequently missing when he turned to the classics. "He seems hesitant, stiff, more like a student than a finished clarinetist," one reviewer wrote about his 1945 recording of the Second Brahms Clarinet Sonata with Nadia Reisenberg. A 1947 concert appearance at New York's Town Hall drew similar criticism: "The performance lacked spontaneity and was along monochrome lines dynamically. Mr. Goodman was too self-effacing for the good of the music and unbelievably so for the 'King of Swing.' He gave the impression of a rich musical talent and superb technical equipment but of timid personality. Mr. Goodman is not subdued at the Paramount. Why give less vitality to performances at Town Hall?"

Benny was his own severest critic, especially when it came to his efforts to master the challenge of classical music. He was reported to have dismissed his 1938 recording of the Mozart Clarinet Quintet with the comment that he was "still just reading notes" rather than giving the composition the expressive interpretation it called for, and he did not disagree with those critics who found his overall approach too studied and constrained. In a 1944 interview he freely acknowledged this problem as well as the need to find some way out of it if he was to reach the same level of proficiency in the concert hall he had long since attained on the bandstand. "The thing that appeals to an audience when you play clarinet with a swing band is the ease with which you do it. The same thing is essentially what appeals to an audience at a serious concert. This ease, this relaxation for the player, is what is important in playing either kind of music. That's the difficulty for me. The relaxation I know in jazz comes harder in serious music." Then, in December 1949, just after he disbanded his orchestra and had reached the decision to bear down on the classical side of his career, Benny formed an association with the one person uniquely qualified to help him work his way past this troubling limitation.

Reginald Kell had arrived in the United States from his native England the previous year, carrying with him the reputation as one of the world's most accomplished classical clarinetists. The tall, tweedy, seemingly stolid Yorkshireman had revolutionized the approach to the clarinet fifteen years earlier, when, at the age of twenty-five, he rejected the rather prim and colorless manner of playing then deemed acceptable and introduced the same sort of passion and expressive freedom taken for granted by singers like Kirsten

Flagstad and soloists on other instruments like Jascha Heifetz.

Kell stated his musical position in *Woodwind Magazine* shortly after his arrival:

> I do not play the clarinet, I play music on it. I use it to express my personal feelings in sound. Purity of sound should not be the beginning and end of music. Can you imagine Fritz Kreisler, Casals or any of the finest singers in the world performing on their chosen instruments without that warmth which listeners and players alike so loosely call "vibrato," that same personal expression and vibrant glow so readily disregarded by the majority of clarinetists? . . . An instrument is just a heap of dimensions with no life or intelligence. How different this can become in the hands of someone who has mastered the technical difficulties and uses it as a means to transfer both the composer's and his own thoughts into sound. It is no longer lifeless and dull, it lives and reflects the message of the music no matter how sad or cheerful it may be. If you are going to play, then play with character: try to make the different characteristics of the music come to life.

Kell's innovations had generated a great deal of controversy back in Britain (as did his recent remarks in *Woodwind Magazine* to the community of clarinetists in the United States). "I nearly lost all my friends," he recalled. "They thought I'd gone off my head." But the impassioned brilliance of his playing could not be denied, and by the time he landed in New York and announced his intention to become an American citizen he had occupied the first clarinet chair in virtually every major symphony orchestra in Great Britain and established himself as a solo recording artist whose records were much prized by a coterie of connoisseurs.

Kell's American debut at Town Hall on December 19, 1948, was praised for its "wealth of expressiveness" as well as for its "sensitiveness of phrase," "extraordinary beauty of tone" and "technical proficiency." Critics compared him to Arthur Rubinstein and Pablo Casals. Winthrop Sargeant called him "one of the most truly musical minds I have come across among players of any instrument." But there was very little market for classical clarinet in the United States, and he was booked by the Henry Colbert agency as "a musical attraction for anybody's budget" at the less than Rubinsteinian fee of $375 a performance, which included the cost of two assisting artists. "This was about average for classical clarinetists giving chamber music concerts," Mrs. Colbert explains. "Pianists received more, but clarinetists were not in such great demand. Nor was chamber music at that time." To supplement his income, Kell took on a number of students. His pupils included other professionals who wanted to add more "vibrato" to their playing, a few ardent beginners like the writer Lillian Ross, who had interviewed him for *The New Yorker*, and the photographer Leonard McCombe, who had taken his picture for *Life* magazine, and then, at the end of 1949, Benny Goodman.

Benny had been aware of Kell for at least a decade and had expressed admiration for the "very relaxed style" he brought to the instrument. Kell did not play jazz himself ("In a jam session I'm like a rabbit at a stoat's tea party"), but he liked jazz for its warmth and sense of freedom and was especially fond of the jazz clarinetists: "In classical music, for some reason, the clarinet is usually played cold and straight. I prefer the jazz boys' approach to it. Their vibrato may be wild, but at least it's there." And of all the jazz clarinetists, Benny seemed to him easily the best. "Fundamentally, Benny can *play* the clarinet," he stated, no small compliment from a clarinet player of Kell's exalted virtuosity.

On two separate occasions Kell had written letters to Benny late in the evening thanking him for some kind remarks Benny had made about him in the press but had torn them up the next morning. "I thought, why bother," he explained to Irving Kolodin. "He'd never answer." Benny, for his part, had several times been at the point of sailing to England to make Kell's acquaintance but had changed his mind at the last minute. Though he was eager to meet with Kell immediately after he arrived in New York, he put that off, too, until Kolodin brought them together over lunch at the Stork Club. "I told him I'd always been afraid he'd turn out to be a stinker," Benny recalled, "and he told me he'd always been afraid I'd turn out to be a stinker. We got along fine."

Kell began giving Benny lessons once or twice a week at the Goodman apartment on Park Avenue. Benny's main goal was to try to learn to incorporate some of Kell's ease and expressiveness into his own playing, and they worked their way through the standard clarinet repertoire by Mozart, Brahms, von Weber and the like, addressing specific technical problems of intonation and execution as they arose but keeping the primary focus on the overall quality of interpretation. Lillian Ross was allowed into one of their early sessions and found Benny in shirt sleeves and bedroom slippers, his face flushed, his hair tousled, full of worry and self-reproach as he struggled to master an arpeggio in von Weber's Clarinet Concerto No. 1 in F Minor under Kell's stern but encouraging guidance. "He's doing fine," Kell remarked as Benny took a short break and lit up a cigarette. "His playing has developed character, which it didn't have at the beginning."

During the first few months of studying with Kell Benny moved away from the standard single-lip embouchure, playing with his teeth on top of the mouthpiece, that he had used up to now and began experimenting with the double-lip embouchure employed by Kell and some of the other classical clarinetists. This was a radical and potentially hazardous alteration in basic technique for someone who had played the instrument a certain way for over a quarter of a century, and Kell may or may not have recommended it. But according to Jim Maher, who was one of Kell's amateur students, if Benny wanted to achieve Kell's characteristically warm sound in his own classical endeavors, it was almost inevitable that he try it out since the double-lip embouchure creates a slightly larger sound chamber that affects the overall tonal quality. What is a good bit more certain is that Kell did not approve of Benny's decision to maintain his old single-lip embouchure for his jazz work, switching back and forth between the two as the musical occasion warranted. When Benny told Lillian Ross, "A lot of people I know play both ways," Kell interjected, "They may be good players, playing both ways, but they'd be better players if they didn't," a warning that anticipated the upsetting difficulties Benny occasionally encountered in the years to come when he momentarily lost track of which embouchure he was using.

Benny's enthusiasm about playing with Kell led him in the summer of 1950 to commission a concerto for two clarinets from the young Swedish composer Ingolf Dahl. "[Reg will] play his part straight, and [I'll] jazz mine up a little," Benny joked with the press, yet Maher recalls that when he heard the two of them rehearse a preliminary draft of the piece, "Kell sounded so good and Benny sounded so stiff," without any of the looseness and ease he had in his jazz playing. Dahl ran into problems completing the composition and withdrew from the project, so there is no way of knowing whether Benny might have eventually raised his performance level to the point where it could have withstood side-by-side comparison with his mentor. But it seems fairly clear that his studies with Kell did not ultimately accomplish all that he had hoped for.

The two and a half years or so that Benny studied with Kell did help him improve his interpretive abilities. Mel Powell makes the important point that they almost certainly also helped extend the life of his career. "Benny always had this extraordinary technique. I think it was there in his DNA. He was like a two-fingered typist who can type as fast as anybody without really knowing how to type. But as he grew older, I think he would not have been able to sustain the kind of technique he had as a young man if he had not studied with Kell. His embouchure would have weakened because he was not playing in the most efficient way. I am not a clarinetist, but it is my informed guess that the so-called proper technique he began to acquire from his studies with Kell helped him sustain the musculature he was using over a vastly long period of time. That's what proper technique means: using the proper muscles in the proper way. When you think about it, there have been so many singers and players blessed with enormous technical gifts who fell apart, but Benny continued to play in a masterful fashion almost to the day he died, and I don't believe he would have been able to do that otherwise."

Yet the criticism continued to be made that Benny still seemed intimidated by classical music, and his performances lacked the sort of relaxation and expressiveness that he had come to Kell to find. When Gertrud Hindemith attended the final rehearsal for the premiere of her husband's Clarinet Concerto in December 1950, she observed that though Benny "played marvelously and with flawless technique, unfortunately, he seemed to be rather academic, and I was astonished to detect a certain dryness in his playing." A review of his 1951 rerecording of the Mozart Clarinet Quintet also faulted Benny for being too stiff and literalistic, "so intent on doing justice to the letter of Mozart that he misses out on the flexibility of phrasing, buoyancy of melodic line and delicate variety of tone-coloring which are the quintessence of the Mozartian spirit." The composer-pianist Harold Shapero recalls that when he played the Copland Clarinet Concerto with Benny in Rome, "I remember telling Benny when he got to the interlude, 'You're supposed to swing it. It's written for you, you know.' So he said, 'Yeah? You think so?' Benny was very resistant to criticism of any kind. He did loosen it up. When he got done with the performance, he said, 'Okay, kid, now tell me how to play jazz.' "

Curiously, although the whole thrust of Benny's involvement with Kell was to learn how to "loosen it up" and play with greater emotion and abandon, his classical studies were frequently blamed for producing just the opposite effect on his jazz work during this period. Reviewing Benny's 1953 jazz concert at Carnegie Hall, one critic maintained that he "startled careful listeners with an almost completely pure classical tone" and "sounded like a classically-trained studio musician reading someone else's solo." A nightclub appearance at New York's Basin Street the following year brought forth the complaint that as a result of "studying in longhair circles" Benny "didn't sail off the way he used to" and "somehow appears to be ashamed of where he is and what he's doing." These opinions, though common, are not universally shared and do not seem borne out by the jazz records he made during the 1950s. Mel Powell, who worked the Basin Street engagement, adamantly denies that Benny's jazz playing suffered as a result of the Kell association. "When people say he didn't play jazz just as well, I don't know what they're talking about. What's commonly said is commonly wrong."

Benny continued recording and performing classical music with various symphony orchestras and chamber groups around the country, but he acknowledged he still had a long way to go before he attained the sort of mastery he was after. "In classical music the performer must try to look into the composer's mind, to play like the composer meant the work to be played," he stated in 1956. "To do this in a natural manner calls for endless preparation and practice. I don't think you're ever through learning an instrument."

The eminent classical clarinet teacher Leon Russianoff, who held half a dozen or so sessions with Benny in 1971 mainly devoted to exploring the fine points of different kinds of reeds and mouthpieces, recalls, "He always wanted to learn. The clarinet was the central thing in his life. One evening he invited me to his home to see his very famous Vlaminck. I waited at the door a long time, and when he finally let me in, he had a Benny Goodman record under one arm, his clarinet under the other and was holding up his trousers with his hands. Even in the bathroom he couldn't forget about it for a few minutes. And by the time we got together he had been to just about every leading clarinet teacher in the world."

In Russianoff's opinion, most of the instruction Benny received was of doubtful benefit. "I had enormous respect for his talent like many of us did. One of our greatest players is Elsa Ludwig Bergere, who is a distinguished professor at Michigan State. But when Benny came to hear her perform Bartók's *Contrasts* at a concert in Merkin Hall, she was so overwhelmed when she saw him walk in that she wasn't able to play. That's the effect he had on a lot of us. But most of his teachers had a stuffy attitude toward jazz and were rather contemptuous of anybody who played it. They called him a 'jazznik' and figured, 'What's the use? Just give him a lesson and take his money.' They didn't understand the man's genius and how that could have been used to make him a great classical clarinetist. He had a very good foundation. His fingers were gorgeous. His time was impeccable. He told me once when we were playing together, 'You're rushing,' and here I am supposed to be helping him. And it was true. I do have a tendency to rush. I think the main thing that held him back was their lack of respect for his basic ability. They didn't understand the closeness of classical playing to jazz. It's not a whole different world. It's not a million miles away.

"Benny was very close to being a great player. A couple of little things would have taken him there. His biggest limitation was that he couldn't let go. The best way to play any instrument is to stick it in your mouth, forget about any teaching you had and just play. I think the best classical record he made was before he started to study: that recording of the Debussy Rhapsody done with Barbirolli back in 1940. He saw the notes and nobody told him how to phrase them, and he played them cleanly and accurately and beautifully. In my view, it's probably the best recording of the Debussy ever done.

"Benny didn't allow himself to use his own style and get it from the music rather than from the printed page. You can no more get classical music from the page than you can get jazz from the page. He wouldn't admit it, but he was intimidated. We're all taught that we're expected to observe the markings—play this fast, play this slow—but the markings are the composer's absence, and if you pay too much attention to them, it's like a director telling an actor on stage, 'Smile now. Now walk a little faster,' and the movements are all jerky and spasmodic. It's not your soul playing.

"I found it impossible to move him in that direction. One night when he had invited me out to dinner, I had a couple drinks at his apartment beforehand and loosened up enough to try to talk to him about it. I said, 'Benny, I have this dream that you should be to the classical world what you are to jazz.' He became very defensive and said, 'Well, I am.' Then he suddenly developed laryngitis, the dinner was off and I felt like I was being ushered out the door."

Benny seems to have been aware of the inhibiting effects of his studies and that if something was gained from them, something was also lost. Looking back at his earliest attempts at the classics in the 1930s two decades later, he reminisced, "I made some mistakes, but they were interesting mistakes. The playing was innocent; and sort of the way Mozart's music is—strong and clear and pure. Now I know a lot more about Mozart, which makes him a lot harder to play. In music, it sometimes happens that the less you know, the better off you are. Still, you've got to keep moving." Then he shrugged his shoulders and laughed.

Benny and an ailing Fletcher Henderson in October 1952, two months before Fletcher's death.

From the Benny Goodman Archives in the Music Library at Yale University

25

Carnegie Hall Revisited

On July 19, 1950, a press release from Columbia Records announced that Benny Goodman, "famous clarinetist and swing band leader," was returning to the label after a three-and-a-half-year absence and bringing with him "the master records cut at the band's historic 1938 Carnegie Hall appearance, the first swing concert ever presented there." Mitch Miller, the head of Columbia's popular record division, stated: "We feel that there will be a tremendous interest in Benny Goodman's Carnegie Hall recordings. Columbia will make it possible to hear on two twelve-inch Long Playing records nearly an hour and a half of one of the most memorable jazz concerts ever given anywhere."

At the time of the announcement Benny's original contract with Capitol still had several months to run, but both parties had become unhappy with the relationship and were eager to bring it to an end. George Avakian, who became Benny's producer at Columbia, recalls, "After Benny got rolling on Capitol, there was a resurgence of sales and then a big dropoff. I have the feeling Capitol may have dropped him. Benny was certainly enthusiastic about returning to Columbia. He may not have used the phrase 'Well, it's good to be home again,' but that was his general attitude. He seemed very much at ease and was obviously glad to be back among old friends. One of the inducements for Benny to return to Columbia was that he would be allowed to record classical music, which he always wanted to do. And one of the big inducements for Columbia was that it would have the rights to put out the Carnegie Hall concert."

Benny's recording schedule was fairly active during his early months with Columbia. On November 15, ten days after he gave it its world premiere on NBC's "Symphony Hour," Benny recorded Aaron Copland's Concerto for Clarinet with Copland himself conducting. Two months later he rerecorded the Mozart Quintet for Clarinet and Strings in A Major with the American String Quartet, and that spring he took part, without featured billing, in Leonard Bernstein's recording of Milhaud's *La Création du Monde*. Though Benny had virtually stopped performing jazz in public, he also recorded a few small group dates with a sextet that included Teddy Wilson and the young vibes player Terry Gibbs that he had put together for his weekly appearances on the Dumont network's "Star Time" television series. But Columbia was less interested in Benny's current output than in preparing for release the material he had played at the height of his popularity more than a decade earlier.

The idea for recording the Carnegie Hall concert had come from Albert Marx, a well-to-do friend of Benny's then married to Helen Ward. Marx arranged for two sets of twelve-inch 78 rpm acetates to be made, then presented one to Helen as a special anniversary gift and gave the other to Benny as a souvenir. Benny recalled with a smile:

> I kept them as a sort of heirloom, but I never knew where they were. They used to show up at the office and then at the apartment, or if I moved they would show up in the place I moved to. So about twelve years later I moved out of a place we lived in New York on 92nd Street, and my sister-in-law Mrs. Rachel Speiden, who was going to take the apartment over after I left, called me and *again* told me that these records were at her apartment and unless I came to take 'em, her son Dougie would get ahold of them and that would be the end of them.

Benny took the acetates home and put them on his turntable, thinking he might hear something faintly amusing. But when the music came blasting out of the speaker, he was shocked to discover just how good it was and how unexpectedly well recorded and how different from the commercially issued versions of the same tunes he had made for Victor. He also realized that he had something of real value in his hands that could, at the very least, give him the leverage he needed to land a favorable recording contract with another company.

"Benny went directly to Ted Wallerstein, and Wallerstein liked the idea," George Avakian remembers. "When I heard about it, I was flabbergasted. I couldn't believe anybody had managed to save acetates from that period because they are so perishable. Ted's first concern was whether the sound quality was any good, and he had already spoken to Bill Bachman, the head of Columbia's research and engineering departments. Bachman turned them over to Bill Savory, who was the assistant head of research and development. I knew Bill had listened to them by now and was already working on them, so one afternoon, when I had a free twenty minutes, I went upstairs, and there was Bill playing this stuff. His eyes lit up when I walked in, and he said, 'Man, wait till you hear this.' I said, 'Is it any good?' He said, 'Listen.' I think the first thing I heard was 'Blue Lou,' and I said, 'Jesus Christ! They really are swinging!' And Bill said, 'You haven't heard anything. The whole thing is this good!'

"Bill continued working on the sound, and there was a great deal of work to be done. The acetates had deteriorated. A lot of the sound was poor. But Bill was a brilliant engineer, absolutely the best guy for getting the best possible sound out of whatever he had to work with. And he was very inventive. He probably invented methods of transferring acetates to tape that hadn't even been dreamed of yet, and he did a wonderful job."

Bill Savory is a Harvard-educated physicist and a trained musician who gained a solid background in audio engineering from building and testing equipment for the various recording studios around New York. Extremely knowledgeable about jazz, he had been friendly with Benny since the mid-1930s, when he recorded some of the air checks Benny ordered up to monitor the band's progress.

"Benny had told me about the records shortly after he recovered them from his sister-in-law's closet," Savory recalls. "He was really turned on by the music and was playing the acetates around the house. He'd put the needle down casually and say, 'Oh, that's not the beginning,' and drag the arm across the record. On 'Dizzy Spells' he had made a mistake, coming in sixteen bars too early in one place, and that apparently amused him. He kept playing that part over and over again with that wide-open silent laugh on his face. I said, 'Benny, don't do that because these things are not going to last forever,' so he went to a studio and had them copied off on seven-and-a-half-inch tape, which he then proceeded to use as kind of a sales number. Benny got in touch with me again and asked me to meet him at Columbia when he was going to play them for Ted Wallerstein. Ted got very enthusiastic, and within a short time they had come to a financial arrangement and made a contract. Then Benny came back with the tin box with the original recordings. I don't know whether or not he told Ted he wanted me to work on them, but that's what I ended up doing for the next six weeks.

"The concert had been recorded in parallel in two places: Harry Smith's Artists Recording Studio on West Forty-sixth Street and Universal Recording Studios, which was run by Raymond Scott. Albert Marx presumably ordered two sets from Harry Smith, which meant that Harry would have needed four turntables, two for each set. You can't just record a selection to the end of the record, then lift the cutting head, turn it over and start recording again. You'd miss too much, so you have to switch over to a second turntable. To record two sets at once, you'd have to be pretty agile turning over the records on four turntables in sequence. It would be like flipping flapjacks. So Harry farmed the second set out to Raymond Scott's outfit, and that was the one that was given to Benny.

"The recording was probably done in the following manner: There was one forty-four-BX microphone, the famous RCA diamond-shaped thing, that was hung up above where the conductor's podium would normally be. Benny believed almost to the day he died that that was the only microphone there, but there were at least three others. All of them were connected to a mixing console backstage used for recording setups and broadcasts from Carnegie Hall, which was connected by class A broadcast-quality telephone lines via some nearby central exchange to CBS master control. Master control then picked up the incoming feed from Carnegie and patched it in to Harry Smith and Raymond Scott. So they were able to get a very fine noise-free, distortion-free connection.

"But no one seems to have been running the console backstage the night of Benny's concert. The CBS guy or the designated Carnegie Hall grip may have been asked to turn it on but not fool with the knobs. That involved another union. The fact that the sound was as good as it was was remarkable, considering, but some of it I knew very quickly was never going to fly because the sound level was much too low or there wasn't a microphone cranked up or placed near enough a particular instrument. That meant that some sections of certain selections had to be excised. You couldn't hear Walter Page's bass solo on 'Honeysuckle Rose,' for example. Harry Goodman's bass was also a little weak on the big band numbers. From time to time I was able to bring that up, but if I brought it up too high, all you got was Krupa's foot.

"There were a lot of technical problems. They could only get about three minutes and forty-eight seconds on a twelve-inch seventy-eight rpm disc before having to switch over to the second turntable, so there were all these breaks in the middle of the various numbers. Only one record in that whole complete set of seventy-eights ended with applause at the end of the selection. The rest had to be spliced together, which created quite a problem because one of the recording turntables ran faster than the other and the pitch varied noticeably when I picked up the second part of the tune. So I had to fool around with that, which was a lot of fun. By that time they didn't make turntables with adjustable speeds anymore. But I finally got that down.

"There was also a good bit of editing to be done inside the tunes. On some of them I had to cut out a whole chorus, then patch it up so it made sense musically and came out at the right place. There were a lot of clicks and pops. There were also some problems with the material itself. In the long jam session on 'Honeysuckle Rose' the tempo slowed down toward the end because everyone had gotten tired. The 'Twenty Years of Jazz' thing worked okay on the stage but didn't really fly when you listened to it. Benny and I had a big discussion about that, but he insisted I do it. I also had to fool around with some equalizers to get it to sound. It took about six weeks of steady work to straighten all that out and get it to the point where Benny said, 'Okay, let's go.' "

A number of legal complications also had to be ironed out before the album could be released, but despite the expenditure of all this time and money and effort, Columbia's enthusiasm for the project continued undiminished. The company originally planned to issue the concert through its popular record division, which would have been the normal thing to do with a jazz recording, but soon decided to switch it over to the more prestigious Masterworks label usually reserved for classical music. "From the very beginning the sales department saw it as something special, so it was treated in a first-class fashion," George Avakian explains. "Releasing the concert on Masterworks allowed them to charge a dollar more a record, but they also felt that would put it in a special category and give it a cachet of extra dignity and permanence. There was a sense right at the beginning that the album was going to be a blockbuster. The advertising and sales promotion people and distributors all had the feeling that this was going to be really important, and they gave it one of the best all-out efforts I had ever seen."

As much as Columbia had riding on the outcome, Benny had even more. It had been a long time between hits. His popularity had waned. His career was floundering. For all his apparent confidence, he was full of self-doubts and badly in need of some sort of personal validation. "The records they made of that Carnegie Hall concert, I had to be an egomaniac about that," he said a few years later. "I had to see that swing wasn't just a fad. I told myself, if that doesn't sell, then my whole life's work is worth nothing."

The Famous 1938 Carnegie Hall Jazz Concert, as it was called, was released as a deluxe two-record set on November 13, 1950, just as the Christmas shopping season was getting under way. The timing was ideal in several other respects as well. Earlier in the year the 33⅓ rpm long-playing microgroove record, which Columbia introduced in 1948, had won the "battle of the speeds" with RCA's competing seven-inch 45 rpm alternative and was now established in the marketplace as the standard record album format. Able to deliver up to twenty-three minutes of music on a single twelve-inch side, it was the perfect medium for presenting a performance the length of the Carnegie Hall concert and made it possible to reproduce the more extended selections without distracting breaks that would have diluted their impact. Had Benny retrieved the recordings from his sister-in-law's closet a few years earlier, before the LP existed, it is doubtful if they would have made their way out of his music room.

Nor is it likely they would have found much of an audience if they had, since big band swing had fallen so out of favor with both the critics and the general public. By 1950, though, the short-lived bop fad was over, critical tempers had cooled and though bebop was still very much alive, it was now being perceived as a continuation, rather than a rejection, of the jazz tradition. Modernist critics who previously scorned the sort of music Benny played were now showing a new respect for earlier styles of jazz and no longer taking Benny to task for his musical conservatism. This turnabout was paralleled in the changing tastes of the general public. Popular singers still held the top of the record charts, but there was a growing nostalgia for the big bands that led many observers to believe that the stage was being set for a full-scale revival.

The *Carnegie Hall* album was an immediate hit. "It just jumped right out," George Avakian remembers. "The sales even surprised us." By 1953 it had sold some 220,000 copies, more than any other jazz album up to that time. By the end of the decade sales had climbed to more than a million. "And an interesting thing happened," Avakian points out. "That album brought Benny back to young kids. When he began doing some personal appearances, his audience started getting younger again, and they all knew the Carnegie Hall recordings. So it was not just a nostalgia item. It was a very live thing."

Thanks to Bill Savory, another album of vintage live recordings soon went into production to follow up the Carnegie Hall concert's success. During 1937 and 1938, when the band was at the very height of its power, Savory had recorded dozens of Goodman broadcasts late at night while working on equipment in the New York recording studios. No one at Columbia even knew this material existed until Savory sprang it on Benny one afternoon while they were listening to the playback tapes of the Copland Clarinet Concerto recorded a few days after the *Carnegie Hall* album was released.

"Benny was trying to make some decisions about how the tapes should be edited," Savory recalls, "and when he got to the second movement, he discovered something had gone wrong, that his part and the conductor's score didn't match. We searched around and found out that a cut had been made and nobody had bothered to tell him about it. By that time Benny was getting a bit too annoyed about a lot of things, and he said, 'Well, all right, we'll get back to this later.' I said to him, 'You want to hear something good, Benny?'

He said, 'Yeah, that would be a change!' So I pulled out some of these air checks I had quietly been putting on tape, and I played a couple for him. He became unglued immediately. He went flying off the chair and said, 'What the hell is that?' I had them all dolled up. I had put them through an echo chamber and equalized them so they didn't sound like air checks until you got to the end and heard the applause. I said, 'They're air checks, Benny. That one's from November seventh, 1937.' 'Holy cow! You got some more of those?' 'Yeah, I've got a whole bunch of them.' So that's how that got started."

The original broadcast engineers had given the band a much better microphone balance than had been possible with the Carnegie Hall recordings. The musicians were playing in familiar venues like the Hotel Pennsylvania and the Palomar Ballroom and were much more relaxed. And unlike the Carnegie Hall concert, there was a wealth of material to choose from. Savory had acetates of over one hundred selections, including up to half a dozen run-throughs of certain arrangements, radically different versions of familiar numbers issued by Victor, as well as a lot of material Benny had never recorded commercially. The final result was a superb collection of thirty-seven performances that put the emphasis where it belonged: on the jazz rather than the pop music side of Benny's repertoire. There were only three vocals, and sixteen of the numbers were by the trio or quartet. Fifteen of the tunes had never appeared on record, and five that had were substantially different. It was a very exciting package, superior in just about every respect to the *Carnegie Hall* album.

The air checks were issued on two twelve-inch LPs in the fall of 1952 under the cumbersome and misleading title *Benny Goodman Jazz Concert 1937– 1938 No. 2*. George Avakian, who supervised the production and contributed a five-thousand-word set of liner notes, explains, "The vice-president in charge of sales absolutely insisted on that title, and I fought it down the line. God, I hated it so much I still have trouble saying it." The album itself, though, was universally hailed as "the definitive reproduction of the Goodman band at its technical and emotional height." Even Benny was pleased with it:

One of the great things about these LPs is how much looser the band played and because of that how much more exciting the music sounds. There are many reasons for this. One of these is one that many people overlook, and that is that we really knew and felt these numbers when we played them on the air. Most of our arrangements, on the other hand, were new, or almost new, when we recorded them, and we cut the sides before we really felt the things. . . . The sound, too, is different. The recording studio had that tight sound, which is great as far as guys hearing each other is concerned. But it doesn't have the excitement that these sides have. . . . And then, of course, there were those crowds. They really made you play, whether you felt like it or not, with their contagious enthusiasm. . . . I can remember many times after we'd done a particular number especially well, or after we had played a good job, how Harry or Gene or Hymie would remark, 'If we could only play like that when we're making records!' . . . And also on some of those dates, the whiskey flowed a little, shall I say, more freely.

"Columbia gave the broadcast album the same kind of strong effort it put behind the Carnegie Hall concert," Avakian recalls. "There was the feeling that it was going to happen all over again, and it did. Sales never quite reached the same volume because there was no competition at all for the *Carnegie Hall* album—it was the first of its kind—but they were still huge."

The success of the *Carnegie Hall* album was heralded by some critics and fans as certain proof that the anticipated swing band revival was now very much under way. In the long run this amounted to so much wishful thinking, but there was a certain amount of evidence at the time to suggest it might be so. Established leaders like Duke Ellington, Count Basie, Woody Herman and Stan Kenton had cut their prices and were getting more bookings and drawing better crowds. The new, more commercially oriented dance bands started up by Ray Anthony, Ralph Flanagan and Jerry Gray, all modeled on the old Glenn Miller orchestra, were selling a lot of records and beginning to tour the country with considerable success. Influential disc jockeys like Martin Block and Art Ford were helping the effort along by proselytizing for the return of the big bands on their daily radio shows.

Many swing fans looked to Benny to take the lead by coming out of semiretirement and returning to the fray, but Benny himself resisted the idea. "For one thing, it would take a little digging to find a band like that today," was his cautious reply when *Time* magazine asked him whether he had any plans to form a new orchestra like the one that had played Carnegie Hall. "To get Harry James, you'd have to call him from Hollywood. Gene Krupa used to make our tops—$165 a week. Now he has his own band. [Chris Griffin] is probably making $600 a week. . . . Besides, it was a different era of jazz." Benny was also forty-one years old and had settled into the comfortable life of a country gentleman on his Connecticut estate.

Yet the response to the *Carnegie Hall* album had certainly rekindled Benny's interest in the old days, as had Bill Savory's air checks and the hourlong reunion of the original Goodman Trio on Martin Block's "Make Believe Ballroom" radio show on April 1, 1951, a few months after the album was released. Block had organized the event as a tribute to Fletcher Henderson, who had suffered a cerebral hemorrhage in December while leading a six-piece band at Café Society in New York. The left side of Fletcher's body was almost completely paralyzed, and it seemed unlikely he would ever work again. To help meet his expenses, he was given the full proceeds from the recordings of the broadcast, which were privately issued in a limited edition of twenty-five hundred copies and sold through the radio station at a premium price of seven dollars. If Fletcher's illness carried with it some intimations of mortality, the splendid music performed in his honor that Sunday afternoon also suggested the possibility that the past could be recaptured and time brought to a stop. As Leonard Feather observed from the studio audience, "Though they hadn't played together in years, nothing actually sounded different. It was as though time had stood still, except for the few gray hairs on Teddy's temple and the slight paunch on Benny and a few more lines on Gene's frantic face as he gesticulated his way wildly through a solo."

Despite the considerable difficulties it would entail, the possibility of going back out on the road with another big band like the one that had brought him his initial success was not totally out of the question. Benny explored the idea quietly, then put it aside for the time being when one of his former stars said he wasn't interested. But to test it out a bit further, toward the end of April Benny scheduled two recording sessions for Columbia and assembled a fifteen-piece orchestra filled with Swing Era veterans, including some Goodman alumni like Chris Griffin, Hymie Schertzer, Lou McGarity and Jimmy Maxwell, most of whom were now profitably employed in the network studios.

For the first date on April 26 Benny pulled out Fletcher's old arrangement of "Down South Camp Meeting," originally recorded for Victor back in 1936, and three somewhat more recent Henderson charts in the familiar vintage style he had not previously put on record. For the second date three days later he revived three more Henderson classics from the mid-1930s— "Star Dust," "Wrappin' It Up" and "King Porter Stomp"—along with an unrecorded arrangement of "Lulu's Back in Town" Fletcher had written in 1946. The reviews were generally positive, if somewhat mixed. Some critics were wildly enthusiastic. Others thought that though these were good, solid records, the remakes did not compare with the original Victor versions and that both sessions would have been much better had Benny soloed with the same fire and drive that characterized his playing fifteen years earlier. Benny himself, though, was pleased and claimed, "This was more fun than I've had in three years!"

Over the next two years, between occasional recordings and personal appearances with a casually assembled sextet and some classical concertizing, Benny held four more recording dates with a big swing band, using many of the same musicians and drawing heavily upon Fletcher Henderson's arrangements. But his enthusiasm was often tempered now by a growing sense of dissatisfaction that suggests some strong misgivings about whether he should move ahead in this direction.

Sometimes it had to do with the band's level of performance. Jim Maher recalls, "I was at a session he did in the spring of 1952. Mel Powell was playing piano and had brought in an arrangement of 'Love Me or Leave Me,' I believe it was, that sounded absolutely marvelous. Benny ran through it a couple times, and then he suddenly picked up the parts and packed them away. The guys were not cutting it to his satisfaction, and he obviously felt it wasn't going to happen, though he hadn't really given them enough time to get it in hand." Sometimes it had to do with his own playing. "Benny had some difficulties with himself," Bill Savory remembers. "He told me privately, 'It's not easy to switch over from this double embouchure to the way you have to handle a horn when you're playing Fletcher.' And in truth, he did have to struggle." Most often the problem was with Columbia's method of recording, especially its use of multiple microphones, which captured the band's sound with much greater clarity and brilliance than had been possible in the old Victor days but to Benny's way of hearing lost something essential in reproducing the quality of its music.

Maher recalls the session that took place on February 23, 1953. "At a quarter past one in the morning we were all sitting around listening to a playback of 'What a Little Moonlight Can Do,' which featured a terrific vocal by Helen Ward. When it was over, the band gave her a big hand, but in a way they were also applauding themselves. I was sitting next to Benny on one of the movable platforms used to hold those huge Altec Lansing speakers, and everybody kept coming over to tell him how much they liked the playback and how marvelous they thought the band sounded. There was a moment of quiet, and Benny turned to me and said rather sadly, 'Yeah, but it doesn't sound like *the* band.' The enthusiasm of everyone else in the studio made it an especially poignant moment. It was as though Benny realized his youth had passed and wasn't ever going to come back, and he was never going to hear the glorious Benny Goodman band of the 1930s again."

The irretrievable losses of time had been driven home with particular force by the recent death of Fletcher Henderson. While convalescing from his cerebral hemorrhage, Fletcher had been felled by a heart attack the previous April. Benny quietly paid his hospital bills and arranged to have Columbia reissue the trio reunion broadcast album to generate further income for him. Though Fletcher could get around only with great difficulty, he managed to attend the party of Goodman alumni held in October to celebrate the release of *Jazz Concert No. 2*. One of the photographs taken that evening shows Benny bending over him solicitously, almost like a son tending to the needs of an ailing father. A faint trace of a smile plays over both their faces, as if they had just finished laughing at some shared recollection and were now fading into their private reveries. Fletcher looks frail and ill and very, very old. He had not yet quite reached his fifty-fourth birthday. It was the last time they were together. Two months later Fletcher suffered a final heart seizure. Benny served as one of the honorary pallbearers.

Whatever the problems with re-creating on record the precise character and sound of the original Goodman orchestra, the success of *Jazz Concert No. 2* and the ongoing popularity of the Carnegie Hall album made it evident that there continued to be a very substantial audience for this kind of music. Encouraged by the strongest record sales he'd had in years, at the beginning of 1953 Benny revived his earlier plan to dust off the old Fletcher Henderson era library, put together a big band of veteran sidemen and go out on tour.

Alice was not happy with this decision and argued against it. Benny was still having trouble with his back. The physical strain might be too much for him. But Benny overrode her objections and arranged with Joe Glaser's Associated Booking to set up six weeks of concerts for the spring that would take him across the country into a different town every night. Glaser had been Louis Armstrong's personal manager for many years. According to George Avakian, he thought Louis's career "needed a good shot in the arm" just then, so he persuaded Benny to have Louis and his All Stars included on the bill as the opening act. This was an unusually strong booking, and it was heralded in the press as "one of the most exciting combinations in the history of jazz," "a perfect climax to the career of two musicians who must go down in jazz history as the two greatest instrumentalists jazz has ever known."

Benny claimed to be "thrilled and delighted" about sharing the stage with Louis, who had been one of his boyhood idols, and he looked forward to the start of the tour with great eagerness. "He was very enthusiastic," Avakian recalls. "He considered it a very important event and was happy to be coming back before the public on what he saw as his own terms. He thought about the return to his Fletcher Henderson roots as 'being himself,' and I did, too. There was no sense of going out with a nostalgia act as we think of it today. Benny felt he had a personal audience that was hungry for him, and Joe Glaser also sensed that, more than any of the other bookers. I was surprised when Benny had him handle the tour because he had never worked with Joe Glaser before."

Benny wanted to take along as many of his original sidemen as possible, and to help with this considerable task, he reached back to another old associate, his brother-in-law John Hammond. Benny and Hammond had not had much to do with each other in more than a decade, not since the estrangement that took place about the time Benny married John's sister. But

Fletcher's illness and death seem to have canceled out at least some of the bad feelings that remained and got them to start seeing each other again beyond the unavoidable family gatherings. They had met to talk about putting on a benefit concert for Fletcher after his cerebral hemorrhage. Hammond had attended the "Make Believe Ballroom" reunion of the Goodman Trio honoring Fletcher. He had also been one of Fletcher's pallbearers. Nevertheless, he was extremely reluctant to accept Benny's proposal that he manage the tour. "I had not wanted to become involved with him again, either musically or in a business way. Our relations in the past had often been strained, and my contributions and suggestions, once so welcome, now struck Benny as interference." But the offer included an advance of three hundred dollars a week in expenses against 20 percent of Benny's net profits, and Hammond needed the money. He had recently divorced and remarried, and what with alimony payments, child support and the expenses of starting a new family, he was under considerable financial pressure. The prospect of bringing the original Goodman band back together again also had its appeal.

Hammond had his work cut out for him. Many of Benny's old sidemen were no longer available. Harry James and Lionel Hampton were leading their own orchestras. Chris Griffin, Hymie Schertzer and Babe Russin were busy with studio work. Jess Stacy was committed to playing some solo dates on the West Coast. Others like Gene Krupa, Teddy Wilson and Ziggy Elman had become high-priced stars in their own right and expected to be paid accordingly. Many Goodman veterans felt Benny had taken advantage of them in the old days and were determined to make up for it now. (The payroll, Hammond recalled, was enormous.) Yet others had less than pleasant memories of Benny and had to be persuaded to return. But by early in the spring a very good band had been assembled. Though it was not the "original" Goodman orchestra, it included such alumni as Teddy, Gene, Ziggy, Georgie Auld, Vernon Brown and Helen Ward, along with a number of stand-ins who had not worked with Benny before, including Charlie Shavers on trumpet, Willie Smith on alto saxophone and Steve Jordan on guitar.

"We rehearsed for a couple of weeks," Jordan recalls. "It was a happy band. Everyone was glad to be back together, and we were all very familiar with those Fletcher Henderson charts. Benny was nice, sometimes almost one of the boys, but sometimes he was also kind of strange. One afternoon he pulled a half dollar out of his pocket and sent the bandboy out to get him a package of Ritz crackers and a Coke. The half dollar slipped through his fingers and went rolling under the piano and over near the radiator. Benny turned to me and said, 'Take a look under the radiator and see if it's over there.' It was filthy dirty, and I had to get down on my knees. I said, 'Benny, I can't see the half dollar.' He said, 'Well, it must be somewhere. I just dropped it.' It went on to the point where I wanted to say to him, 'Look,

Benny, let me give you a half dollar. Come on, let's play.' When I told Mel Powell what happened, he said, 'If you had done that, he probably would have taken it, had his Coke and crackers, then, when the rehearsal was over, come back and looked for the one he dropped. Once poor, always poor in spirit.'

"Benny didn't have any problems with any of the musicians in the band," Steve maintains. "All of them had their own names and reputations, and if he'd given anyone the Ray, they would have said good-bye or given it right back to him. At one time they might have gotten upset, but they were twelve or fifteen years older now. And Benny was older, too, and seemed to have mellowed." But as the date of the first concert approached, Benny became increasingly uneasy and on edge. Jim Maher attended several rehearsals with Reginald Kell and found him "very tight, apprehensive almost, and a bit truculent." Steve remembers, "A couple times Benny got mixed up and switched back to the double embouchure he used to play classical music, and nothing came out of his horn. He'd just say, 'Let's try that again,' and then he'd remember, but he seemed quite upset. I think he had it in the back of his mind that when the chips were down and he was up there before a big audience, he was going to forget again and then he wouldn't be Benny Goodman anymore."

John Hammond recalled, "About a week before the tour was to begin Benny became alarmed about starting the show without a couple of break-in engagements far enough out of town so none of the New York critics would hear the band before it was ready." Hammond quickly set up two dance dates in New England for the weekend of April 10 and 11. The first at the small Carousel Ballroom in Manchester, New Hampshire, drew a huge crowd of twenty-three hundred despite a driving rainstorm. George Avakian had arranged for Columbia to record the band on tour once it hit its stride and had driven up to Manchester with Bill Savory to check out its repertoire and do some preliminary taping. "That first night was just so-so," he remembers, "though some of it was okay. Benny reassured me, 'I know you didn't get much, but it's going to be all right. The band is still just breaking in.' " The following night at the South Portland Armory in Portland, Maine, went much better. The crowd was even larger, and according to Hammond, "Benny relaxed and played as I had not heard him play for years. The band was like a bunch of kids, happy to know that the old music still had a public, that they had not been forgotten."

Benny had not yet met with Louis Armstrong to discuss the details of the tour and work out their routine for the finale. It wasn't until two days before they opened in New Haven that they finally got together at the rehearsal hall in New York. By now Benny was having serious second thoughts about having to share both the spotlight and the profits with Armstrong, who was an unexcelled crowd pleaser and scene stealer. Never a master of tact, he seems to have gone out of his way to make his reluctance apparent.

There are several different versions of what happened, but this is how Steve Jordan remembers it: "Benny called a rehearsal for ten o'clock in the morning, and Louis and his band were all there. Louis hadn't finished work until two A.M. the previous night and was very tired, but Benny kept him waiting around for two or two and a half hours while he ran us through our numbers. Louis finally said to him, 'Come on, Benny, let's go through this thing, so we can get back to our hotels and get some sleep.' Benny said, 'Well, I've got to finish my stuff first.' Louis said, 'I don't really need this,' but Benny just stood there chewing on his tongue. Louis's feelings were so hurt he actually started to cry. Georgie Auld went over and patted him on the back, and Louis said, 'That son of a bitch! When he was a little boy in short pants, I used to let him sit in with my band to learn how to play, and now he lets me hang around and wait like I'm nobody.' Louis was the nicest man in the world, but he had an ego, too, and there was bad blood between them from then on."

Louis did not show up for rehearsal the next day. At the kickoff performance in New Haven the following night he stayed on stage a full hour and twenty minutes instead of the scheduled forty, making his part of the show equal to Benny's, and brought down the house with what Hammond described as "his regular vaudeville act." When Benny called him back on for the finale, he refused to leave his dressing room. The situation continued to deteriorate at the Mosque Theater in Newark the next evening. Very uncharacteristically Louis arrived at the theater late, forcing Benny to play the first set himself, in effect opening for his own supporting act. During the intermission there was a fierce altercation backstage in Louis's dressing room.

"The first night of the tour Benny started telling Louis what to do," Georgie Auld recalled. " 'I want you to play such-and-such a tune' and stuff like that. So Louis called Joe Glaser, and Joe laced into Benny the next night at the Mosque Theater. 'Where do you come off? Who the fuck do you think you are? When this man lands in Europe there are 35,000 people waiting for him. Can you do that? How dare you tell him what to do! He's a legend! He's bigger than you!' He screamed and screamed at him."

Benny was shaken by Glaser's assault and furious that what was to have been his triumphant comeback tour was now falling apart before his eyes. He left Louis's dressing room with a drink in his hand and then, as if to lash out at everything that was going wrong, hurled the glass violently against the cement wall. "Everybody was afraid to take a deep breath," Auld remembered, and to try to ease the tension, he blurted out the line, "Look, the Jewish Marlon Brando!" The tension did dissipate, but only for the moment. The following night they were booked into Carnegie Hall.

The return to Carnegie Hall on April 17 brought Benny back full circle to the scene of his original triumph some fifteen years earlier and was to have been the culminating event in the series of comeback moves set off by the spectacular success of the 1938 concert album. The demand for tickets was so great that a second show had to be added on at midnight. Both quickly sold out, setting a new box-office record of twenty-four thousand dollars. Louis opened with his All Stars playing a set that was as much comedy act as music, full of bawdy jokes and old-time vaudeville shenanigans, including some death-defying splits by his oversize vocalist, Velma Middleton. Benny was appalled, but the audience ate it up, and when the Goodman band finally took the stage, it was almost like an added attraction.

The classical music critics for the *New York Times* and *Herald Tribune* were not very knowledgeable about jazz and reviewed Benny's performance in favorable, if very generalized, terms as a nostalgic return to the glory days of the Swing Era. Those who knew better were dismayed by what they heard. For John Hammond, Benny played "atrociously." For Bobby Hackett, who had performed the Bix Beiderbecke solo at the original 1938 concert, "He sounded terrible. He just couldn't do anything. It was embarrassing. Jesus, if I'd been able to do so I'd have stopped the show." To try to calm his shattered nerves, Benny had been drinking heavily backstage, something he never did before, and by the time he came on for the second show the cognac had taken effect. "To veteran Goodman fans, something was wrong with the great clarinetist at the midnight Carnegie Hall concert Friday," the mystified reviewer from the *Daily News* reported. "He played very little, seemed annoyed at his audience, missed cues and was otherwise offbeat. At one point, during his famed 'One O'Clock Jump' number, he broke off his clarinet solo in the middle of a phrase. Later he turned his horn around, put the bell over his nose and made a pretense of playing it backward. Long established as a stern disciplinarian as well as a great soloist, such antics were unbelievable to his fans."

Benny's behavior was equally strange the following night, when the tour moved on to Providence, Rhode Island. "Benny just wasn't himself," Helen Ward recalls. "He never drank, but he was guzzling brandy. He got into a peculiar argument onstage with some guy in one of the boxes who said something he thought was out of line. 'Who do you think you are? Bottles?' he shouted up at him. I have no idea what he was talking about. For our opening number Frank Loesser had written a terrific piece of special material for Benny and me, and I must have missed a word or a cue. Normally Benny would have just let it go and kept right on playing. But he stopped the band in the middle of the number, and right there on the stage of the packed theater he turned to me and said, 'Maybe we didn't rehearse this enough. Now let's start over again.' I was standing there with egg on my face. I tell you I wanted to die. After the show I said to him, 'If you do anything like that to me again,

Benny, that's it, I'm leaving!' It was such a hideous thing to do and so completely unlike him."

After finishing in Providence, Benny drove to Boston, where he was scheduled to play two concerts the next day at Symphony Hall. About two in the morning he collapsed in his hotel room at the Ritz-Carlton. A fire department rescue team worked over an hour to revive him with an inhalator. Gene Krupa took over fronting the band, and Georgie Auld and Willie Smith divided up his solo spots. Later that evening Benny suffered a relapse while resting in his room and was put under an oxygen tent. The doctor refused to comment on the specific nature of his illness but said it was not severe enough to warrant immediate hospitalization. Benny's spokesman described it as an "acute respiratory ailment," but rumors continued to circulate that it was really a heart attack. It was unclear whether Benny would be rejoining the band or what effect his absence might have on the rest of the bookings.

Benny's secretary stated the following day that though he was still too weak to be moved to New York in an ambulance, as planned, Benny was "feeling better" and the outlook was "good" that he would be ready to come back in "about two weeks." The future of the tour, though, remained uncertain. When it played Reading, Pennsylvania, that Wednesday, the house was half empty. Many reserved tickets were not picked up, and some irate fans demanded their money back because Benny was absent. By the end of the week Benny was resting at home in Stamford, Connecticut, and it was officially announced that because his doctor advised against it, he would not be returning. The band would continue to tour without him under Gene Krupa's leadership.

Benny's claim that he was forced to withdraw from the tour because of his health was greeted with a great deal of skepticism and in some cases strong anger. Norman Granz, who had booked a number of upcoming dates, maintained that Benny was not sick at all but quit because he felt he could not play jazz anymore and said he might take him up before the union. Joe Glaser threatened to sue him. John Hammond, who was unceremoniously dismissed from his post when he was caught in the crossfire between Benny and Glaser and vowed never to work for his brother-in-law again, said that Benny wanted to get Louis off the tour before he fell ill and exaggerated his illness as a way to put pressure on Glaser, then sabotage the entire enterprise.

Whatever the truth of the matter—and the tangled trail of recriminations, counteraccusations, confusion and bad feelings it left in its wake makes it impossible to know for certain—the evidence seems overwhelming that Benny did suffer some kind of real and very serious physical and psychological breakdown. The tension had started building from the time he began having problems rerecording the old Fletcher Henderson charts two years before. It was exacerbated by the strain and exhaustion of getting the band together again and going back on the road and by how much was riding on each and every performance. And it was all brought to a head by the distressing rift with Louis Armstrong, which put him into contention with one of the heroes of his youth, the most universally beloved figure in the entire history of jazz.

"Louis was so hugely successful playing the first half of the show that the audiences treated Benny as kind of an afterthought," George Avakian recalls. "Benny felt that and resented it bitterly. It didn't take much to upset Benny when he took something seriously. If something went wrong, it was like the world was coming to an end. And he took that tour very, very seriously, maybe too much so. That's why Louis's enormous popularity was such a huge shock to him. Benny was very competitive. He never wanted to be upstaged by anybody. And his reactions were overreactions."

The tour continued without him. After a few shaky engagements it picked up momentum and did very well. "The band sounded the same," Steve Jordan remembers. "It was just as good. And the houses were packed. At one of the concerts Norman Granz looked out at the audience and said, 'Benny ought to be here.' I asked him, 'Where would you put all the extra people?' " Benny withdrew into the seclusion of his home, seeing no one outside his family. He did not play in public again for another full year. The Carnegie Hall and broadcast albums continued to sell, but when his three-year contract with Columbia expired, it was not renewed. The long-anticipated comeback did not take place. Neither did the big swing band revival that was expected to come with it.

Alice, Benny, Steve Allen and his wife, Jayne Meadows,
at the premiere of *The Benny Goodman Story*, 1956.

From the Benny Goodman Archives in the Music Library at Yale University

26

The Benny Goodman Story

On March 31, 1954, Universal-International Pictures announced it had acquired the rights to film the life story of Benny Goodman. Universal's current movie about Glenn Miller had turned out to be a runaway hit that promised to become one of the top-grossing films of all time, and a similar "bio-pic" about Benny Goodman seemed like a natural follow-up. To ensure a similar success, the studio had already assigned the same producer, Aaron Rosenberg, to oversee the production and chosen Valentine Davies, who coauthored *The Glenn Miller Story*, to write the script and direct.

It had taken a lot of doing to transform the prosaic facts of Glenn Miller's biography into the stuff that Hollywood hits are made of. He was by all accounts a rather cold and colorless individual, a hard-driving, ambitious disciplinarian who was respected for his musicianship but not especially well liked by most of those who knew him. After plugging along for a number of years, he eventually achieved great popularity and financial success, but the only really dramatic event in his life was his death when his plane went down over the English Channel during the Second World War.

Universal overcame the first obstacle by simply ignoring the realities of

Miller's less than engaging personality and casting the enormously appealing actor James Stewart in the title role. It got around the second by concentrating on the love affair between Miller and his wife, Helen, and turning the Miller band's trademark clarinet-lead sax section voicing into something tantamount to the search for the Lost Chord. ("It's hard to explain, but a band ought to have a sound all of its own. I haven't found it yet, but someday I'm going to find it. And when I do . . ."). The strategy worked. Under the skillful direction of Anthony Mann, who had recently directed him in two superior westerns, Stewart gave one of his most relaxed and ingratiating performances. June Allyson provided a suitable love interest, now perky, now moist-eyed as the twists and turns of the plot demanded, just as she had when they were paired together in the film about the baseball player Monty Stratton a few years earlier. The search for "the Miller sound" seems terribly contrived and overblown. ("I think he's got it!" "No doubt about it! It's the sound!") But it did give a dramatic focus to the music. And the music itself was effectively presented and very well played.

Benny was impressed. He had been interested in having a movie made about his life at least as far back as 1942, when he commissioned a screenplay and attempted to peddle it along with the band and himself to the Hollywood studios. When nothing came of his efforts, his interest had waned, and though he was approached every few years by someone with a film treatment, he always turned the offers down. But he liked what Universal had managed to accomplish and decided to give it the go-ahead. "I knew Glenn very well, and I knew his story well, and when I saw what they could make out of his 'search for the sound,' I realized I didn't know anything about making pictures," he explained. "They could build a whole movie around a stupid little saxophone sound. I wouldn't have believed it if you had shown me the script, but they did it very well. In Glenn's life, this was too minor a thing to make into something tremendous, but it still made sense, because all the time I was sitting there watching it, thinking it was ridiculous, I believed it. So after I met the producer and found him to be a very sincere guy, I just put it in his hands."

The Benny Goodman Story was not to go into production for another year, but Benny's optimism about the project restored some of his badly battered self-confidence and brought him out of the seclusion that had kept him from performing in public since the disastrous tour with Louis Armstrong the previous April. Two weeks after the contract with Universal was signed he was back in his hometown of Chicago playing a two-week engagement at the Blue Note with a sextet that included Mel Powell and the formidable Charlie Shavers on trumpet. After some classical concerts in Toronto and Birmingham, Alabama, and a benefit for the NAACP in New York that reunited him with his original quartet, he brought his new group into Manhattan's Basin Street for three weeks for his first extended local appearance in several years. Some reviewers were disappointed by the overly familiar repertoire and approach and the general lack of excitement in Benny's solo work. But his playing was warm and relaxed without any of the distressing peculiarities that had marred his appearance at Carnegie Hall, and there were moments when the old fire and drive returned in full force.

Benny continued his busy schedule of activities into the fall. He played the Hollywood Bowl with a symphony orchestra and Las Vegas with a sextet and participated in a memorial benefit for the great trumpet player Hot Lips Page at the raucous Central Plaza in New York. Early in November he invited the CBS television cameras into his home in Stamford, Connecticut, for a visit with Edward R. Murrow's "Person to Person." Introduced as "a legend in his lifetime" whose records "were selling better than ever," Benny showed off his eighteenth-century music stand and the mounted tarpon he caught in Florida, introduced Murrow to Alice and the children, played a bit of Mozart with Rachel and took Benjie for a stroll down to his private trout pond. Though he gave the impression he was now very much the leisured country gentleman and family man, a few days later he sprang back into action with a marathon series of recording dates for a one-shot album for Capitol that yielded some nineteen big band and small group sides in a little over a week.

Benny drew heavily upon the cadre of ex-swing band musicians now working in the New York studios and largely limited himself to familiar material arranged in the old Fletcher Henderson mode. *B.G. in Hi-Fi*, as the album was called, was crisply performed and very well recorded, but Benny's playing is not notably inspired and the overall conception seems dated. The only real excitement comes from the young trumpet player Ruby Braff, who is prominently showcased on most of the numbers.

The high point of Benny's varied activities that winter, which ranged from a promotional short for the March of Dimes with the original Goodman Trio to a performance of the Hindemith Clarinet Concerto with Leonard Bernstein at Carnegie Hall, was a series of ten weekend engagements at Basin Street that began toward the end of February. Benny assembled an exceptionally strong eight-piece band full of commanding soloists like Teddy Wilson, Ruby Braff, the phenomenal young trombonist Urbie Green and the former Basie tenor saxophonist Paul Quinichette. It was probably the best group he'd had since the small bop band with Wardell Gray and Stan Hasselgard back in 1948. There were some lightly sketched arrangements, but the emphasis was almost entirely on the solo work, and Benny allowed everyone his turn in the spotlight. Having to keep up with such high-powered, mostly younger sidemen gave Benny the stimulation he needed, and even on the old Goodman warhorses that served as the bulk of the band's repertoire they had him blowing with more energy and invention than he'd displayed in years.

When *The New Yorker*'s Lillian Ross visited Benny backstage, she found him as joyously enthusiastic as the audiences out front that had been packing the club every weekend. "Maybe I've been rejuvenated," Benny reflected. "When I was playing here last summer, I was just trying to get *back* to something I used to do, but now it's a new thing that grows out of the past but is new and alive." Fortunately Benny had some recording equipment brought into the club to preserve several evenings' worth of performances. Unfortunately the recordings were not released for another twelve years and then only in a blandly titled and not readily available three-record set, *Benny Goodman Plays an Album of Swing Classics.*

By the spring of 1955 preproduction had been completed, and *The Benny Goodman Story* was ready to start shooting. Benny had some doubts about the script but overcame his misgivings after showing it to the Broadway director Joshua Logan. "Logan was noncommittal," Jim Maher remembers, "telling Benny it was all right and would probably make a pretty decent movie. Benny leaped on his response as if it were a lot more positive than it really was. He had to believe it was going to be good."

John Hammond had his own very different opinion. He had insisted upon seeing the script before allowing himself to be represented on-screen and was outraged by how his considerable contribution to Benny's success had been distorted and diminished. The memory of being fired from the tour with Louis Armstrong still rankled, and he refused to sign the release unless Universal paid him fifty thousand dollars instead of the three thousand it had offered, just recompense, his lawyer argued, for being treated so shabbily. The studio tried writing him out of the movie by reassigning his part in Benny's story to Willard Alexander, but Willard objected strongly to this further distortion and insisted Hammond be given the credit due him. The impasse created even more bad blood between Benny and his brother-in-law and threatened to provoke a serious family crisis. It was finally resolved when Hammond reluctantly accepted Universal's revised offer of five thousand dollars. His demand that he also be made musical supervisor of the film had to be abandoned when "Benny would not hear of my having anything to do with the picture."

Universal had an established policy of casting only top movie stars in the leads of its big-budget productions, a sensible form of box-office insurance that had always paid off well in the past. Benny suggested to Aaron Rosenberg that he think about getting Tony Curtis. But this time the studio broke with its usual practice and gave the title role to Steve Allen, a television personality who hosted NBC's "Tonight" show. The decision was greeted with widespread astonishment in Hollywood movie circles, though it did have a certain logic. Allen bore a slight physical resemblance to Benny. More important, he was closely associated with jazz and had a rare ability to make the music acceptable to the general public. A passable pianist himself, he had presented a great many jazz musicians on his late-night television program, ranging from Eddie Condon to Lester Young and Billie Holiday to Gerry Mulligan and Chet Baker, and had managed to do so with a minimal number of complaints from viewers and network executives. Allen took his acting role seriously, even studying clarinet for three months with Goodman clone Sol Yaged so he could look plausible handling the instrument on-screen. But though he had made a few brief movie appearances in the past, he had no significant background of training and experience as an actor, which made it extremely unlikely that he would be able to carry off a part of this size and dimension.

Benny had reserved the right to select the musicians he would use to reproduce his old hits on the sound track. Teddy Wilson and Gene Krupa were among the first to be signed, and they were soon followed by Lionel Hampton, Ziggy Elman, Martha Tilton, Harry James and a number of other veterans. Benny filled out their ranks with several more recent associates like Stan Getz and Urbie Green and some good Hollywood session players. For some reason he also brought in from New York the former Basie trumpet star Buck Clayton, who had never been part of his orchestra. Vido Musso and Jess Stacy were conspicuous by their absence. "I didn't do the movie because Benny just wanted me for one thing: to try to re-create the solo I did at Carnegie Hall," Jess explains. "And they were only going to pay me scale while all those other guys were getting big money. So I figured, what the hell, who needs it? I didn't want any part of it. Besides, who can ever really re-create anything that they did? That was just a moment that happened."

Benny arrived in Hollywood toward the end of June to watch over the filming and record his part of the sound track. As the weeks went by, it became increasingly apparent that the inadequacies of Valentine Davies's script were not being overcome by his even more inadequate direction or the perform-ances by Steve Allen and the other actors, and the high-spirited optimism Benny had felt during the Basin Street engagement a few months earlier now gave way to a darker, far less affable frame of mind. "Benny had a continuous fight going on nearly all the time with different musicians on the set," Buck Clayton remembers. When he recorded "Sing, Sing, Sing" for the Carnegie Hall concert sequence that would serve as the dramatic climax of the film, Benny ran into trouble with his own solo and, to everyone's embarrassment, had to keep doing it over and over again until he came up with an acceptable take. And the cold, hard grins exchanged with Gene Krupa during the session made it clear that the old frictions that had led to Gene's departure shortly after the number was performed at the actual concert had resurfaced. It was reported that they didn't start speaking again until Lionel Hampton arrived in town some days later and propelled the quartet through a sizzling rendition of "Avalon" that turned out to be the only really effective piece of music in the picture.

Benny's relations with Universal were no less strained. It was understood from the beginning that Benny would not be seen on camera, but he eventually came to feel this would leave audiences with the impression that he was a relic from the past who was no longer actively involved in music. He prevailed upon Rosenberg to add a prologue and epilogue showing him playing with the sound track orchestra, but the studio overruled this decision, arguing it would detract from the illusion of Steve Allen's impersonation. From that point on Benny and the front office were in conflict.

Filming was completed in August. The picture was rushed into editing so it could be released as quickly as possible to take advantage of the interest aroused by Jack Webb's competing jazz film *Pete Kelly's Blues*. As the February release date approached, feature stories about Benny and the movie began appearing in national magazines like *Life*, *Look*, *Collier's* and *Ebony*. *Down Beat* and *Metronome* both published special Benny Goodman issues. The record companies also jumped in on the action, and there was a massive release of Benny Goodman recordings that put more of his music before the public than at any time in his career.

Decca issued a two-record set from the sound track that offered perfunctory replays of early Goodman hits like "Bugle Call Rag" and "King Porter Stomp" that failed to recapture any of the freshness and excitement of the originals. Benny's newly recorded versions of many of the same tunes for Capitol, *Mr. Benny Goodman*, turned out somewhat better, thanks to the spirited solo work of Ruby Braff and Mel Powell, but was also largely an exercise in déjà vu. Victor virtually emptied its vaults of classic Goodman material from the 1930s, putting out a deluxe five-record package, *The Golden Age of Swing*, as well as a separate LP, *The Benny Goodman Story*, devoted to selections featured in the movie. Not to be outdone, Columbia reissued the Carnegie Hall and broadcast albums, along with a sampler of tunes from the film, a superb compilation of sides done in the early thirties with colleagues like Jack Teagarden and Billie Holiday and several budget-priced ten-inch LPs by more recent Goodman big bands and small groups. Coral, a Decca subsidiary, issued another album of re-creations with Steve Allen playing most of the solos on piano. Decca's Brunswick label returned to the original source with a fine anthology of vintage performances, *B.G. 1927–1934*, Benny had recorded early in his career with the likes of Joe Venuti, Eddie Lang and Red Nichols. Clef offered Gene Krupa, Lionel Hampton and Teddy Wilson jamming at length on some of the numbers from the picture. Atlantic released *A Tribute to Benny Goodman* with Jess Stacy and a scaled-down big band that included Ziggy Elman, who played with his customary fire despite a bleeding lip that had kept him from performing in the movie though he was seen on the screen. No other jazz musician had ever before been accorded such a full retrospective, and the record stores were filled with Goodman and Goodman-related albums.

If *The Benny Goodman Story* accomplished nothing else, at least it brought Benny back to public consciousness through the sheer quantity of recordings and press coverage that accompanied its release. The picture itself, though, was absolutely dreadful. The story was patently false, no more so, perhaps, than the Glenn Miller movie, but the stilted dialogue and blatantly contrived situations made it seem even more artificial. (Benny hears jazz for the first time as a teenager and without a moment's hesitation immediately starts playing it like, well, Benny Goodman. Lionel Hampton is discovered working in a diner as a jack-of-all-trades bartender, waiter, chef and one-man floor show.) Rather than try to convey some of the truly dramatic realities of Benny's biography—the abysmal poverty of his youth, his precedent-breaking assault on racial barriers, the driving ambition and perfectionism that often estranged him from his peers—Davies's script follows the same well-trodden path that led to the pot of gold with the Glenn Miller picture. Benny pursues a musical vision much like Miller's romanticized search for "the sound." ("I want a band that plays hot music. That really takes off. I have a few ideas. I don't know if they're crazy. Maybe if we played our kind of music so they could dance and not just listen.") The main emphasis is not on music at all but on a largely fictionalized account of Benny's across-the-tracks romance with Alice that completely ignores the inconvenient fact she was married and the mother of three children at the time they were supposed to be courting. Steve Allen's inexperience as an actor results in a stiff, awkward performance that may be charitably viewed as an attempt to convey something of Benny's own introverted personality, but his scenes with Donna Reed, who had her own problems playing Alice, lack any of the chemistry that Jimmy Stewart and June Allyson had been able to generate. Nor are they helped very much by the particularly sappy dialogue they are required to regurgitate: "Alice, you're wonderful." "You're the wonderful one, Benny. Unbelievably, hopelessly wonderful."

The rest of the picture is just as unbelievable, just as hopeless. John Hammond is portrayed as an upper-class nonentity with nothing better to do than squire Alice around to Benny's gigs. Fletcher Henderson shows up at the "Let's Dance" show to offer Benny his help, which seems mainly to consist of holding his clarinet for him when he comes off the stand. Mrs. Goodman, badly overplayed by Berta Gersten, is a grossly caricatured Jewish mother who at first is against the romance between Alice and her son ("You don't mix caviar with bagels"), then is suddenly for it for no other reason than to expedite the obligatory happy ending. Gene Krupa and Teddy Wilson recite their "hepcat" lines as Benny's stooges—"You were really in the groove tonight." "Yeah, he's a mean man with a licorice stick"—with no more conviction than such fatuous dialogue merits. Much of this might have been redeemed had some of the original excitement of the Swing Era been recaptured, but most of the music lacks any real passion, and like everything else in the movie, it is filmed in a static, lifeless manner that reveals all too clearly that this was the first motion picture Valentine Davies had ever directed.

The Benny Goodman Story opened in February 1956 to mixed reviews, ranging from mildly favorable to vehemently negative. It did fairly good business for a few weeks but came nowhere near matching the box-office success of the Glenn Miller movie. When reporters asked Benny how he felt seeing his life up on the screen, he tried to say something positive but wasn't able to muster much enthusiasm. "They did a lot better with it than I thought they could," he equivocated with *The New Yorker.* "My mother is eighty, and when she saw a preview of the movie, all she said was, 'Benny, it's beautiful.' So I guess it must be pretty good." Jim Maher recalls: "Benny knew it was awful, an absolute piece of trash almost as soon as it was finished. He could kid around about it occasionally. One day, laughing like hell, he said to me, 'You know what would have made a good scene? We're backstage at the Paramount and I'm wiping the sweat off with a towel when all of a sudden there's a knock on the door and Alice walks in. She looks around and says, 'Benny, why don't you just get rid of these bums and let's go to the south of France?' That would have made a hell of a scene, wouldn't it?' But I think he was sorry about it the rest of his life."

27

On the Road Again

 few weeks before *The Benny Goodman Story* opened in New York, Benny brought a thirteen-piece big band into the Waldorf-Astoria. This was the first full-size orchestra he had led outside the recording studio since the 1953 tour with Louis Armstrong and his first appearance at the Waldorf in seventeen years. "Part of the idea of re-forming the band has to do with the film," Benny explained, "but I'm also quite enthusiastic about playing again, so we're going to keep it working."

When Benny appeared at the Waldorf back in 1939, he played some of Eddie Sauter's advanced arrangements and featured the very modern guitar work of Charlie Christian. This time around he was much less adventurous and relied almost exclusively on the earlier contributions of Fletcher Henderson, Jimmy Mundy and Spud Murphy that had brought him his original popularity. "Those arrangements amaze me," he maintained. "They're ageless." In a way they were, but the music had undergone a lot of changes in the intervening years, and Benny had considerable difficulty locating younger sidemen who could play them with some degree of authenticity and conviction. "It's been a real hassle digging up new talent," he admitted, "but you have to find it." Several of the band's soloists were closely associated with the modern jazz movement that Benny now scorned unequivocally. The pianist

Benny and band en route to the Far East, 1956.

From the Benny Goodman Archives in the Music Library at Yale University

Hank Jones had been influenced by Bud Powell. The tenor saxophonist Budd Johnson had been part of the first organized small bop band with Dizzy Gillespie. But they were versatile musicians and kept their modernity under wraps, adapting themselves to what was, in effect, yet another re-creation of the Benny Goodman orchestra of the mid-1930s.

Resembling "a well-rounded, balding businessman in spectacles," as one reviewer described him, Benny seemed pleased with the way the orchestra was shaping up and was particularly happy to be back in front of a dance band again. "I get a kick out of playing for dancers," he said. "It's more *fun.*" Middle-aged swing fans polished up their old lindy routines and filled the Waldorf's dance floor to capacity. There was much nostalgic talk in the press about how the clock had been turned back twenty years and that even without Gene Krupa, Harry James and the other idols of their youth the old killer-dillers were still as stirring as ever. Less misty-eyed observers, though, found all this living in the past unworthy of Benny and ultimately self-defeating. "This new Goodman incarnation neither sets new jazz criteria nor meets old," *Variety* reported. "Comparisons are inevitable, however invidious. To look backward so consistently as does Goodman invites others to look backward too. He reprised history and in the process failed to make any. Those who had come to honor a jazz prophet were asked only to share some jazz memories. Nothing of tomorrow was suggested. Goodman himself, over many years, has educated people to expect more of Goodman."

The band continued at the Waldorf into the spring, then took to the road for a series of college and ballroom engagements. Appearances at Milwaukee's Million Dollar Ballroom, the University of Detroit and Pottstown, Pennsylvania, all drew well, thanks to the publicity generated by the film. There were rumors that Benny's health was bothering him again, but he kept the band working until the middle of July. After taking the rest of the summer off, he reassembled it in November for a tour of the Far East that cast him in a new role as official representative of the United States government.

Five months earlier public affairs officers responsible for running the American propaganda machine in Southeast Asia had complained to the *New York Times* that they were fighting the cold war "with their hands tied behind their backs" by being deprived of the United States' two most potent weapons, its motion pictures and its jazz. "American jazz has as great a grip on Southeast Asia as it has over Europe," they argued, but though the government had shipped them tennis players and track stars, symphony orchestras and harpsichordists, it continued to refuse their requests to send over some jazz musicians. The previous year Dizzy Gillespie had conducted a very successful tour of the Middle East for the State Department, yet a number of influential members of Congress still thought that jazz was not a suitable representation of American culture. But the *Times* article seems to have been persuasive. That October it was announced that under the auspices of the international exchange program of the American National Theater and Academy, the State Department would be sponsoring Benny on a tour of eight Far Eastern nations.

The band left for the Orient on December 2, 1956. After a thirty-hour flight it landed in Bangkok. "We got off the plane and were supposed to rest for a day before playing a command performance for the king of Thailand," Steve Jordan remembers. "But the contractor forgot that we lost twenty-four hours when we crossed the international date line, and we were due at the palace immediately after we landed. Holy smoke! Benny's secretary, Muriel Zuckerman, ran around and got everybody's jackets and had them pressed real quick, and off we went to do the concert."

Bhumibol Adulyadej, the twenty-nine-year-old king of Thailand, was in some ways a traditional protocol-bound Oriental monarch. "He and the queen sat in these high thronelike chairs in front of the stage," Steve recalls. "No one's head is supposed to be higher than the king's, so whenever somebody went over to say something to him or offer him a drink, he had to get down on his hands and knees." But His Majesty had been born in Cambridge, Massachusetts, while his father was attending Harvard Medical School, and he was also an avid jazz fan, an amateur Dixieland clarinetist and saxophonist who had led his own seven-piece band while studying in Switzerland and held weekly jam sessions at the palace every Friday night that sometimes went on until seven the next morning. The ninth monarch of the Chakri dynasty listened with obvious pleasure as the Goodman band had the walls of the palace shaking, keeping time with his royal foot and applauding long and loud between selections. After a buffet supper in the huge banquet hall he joined Benny for some impromptu duets that went on for the next hour. It was the first time, his retainers noted with astonishment, that His Majesty had played side by side with a foreigner in his native land. "He was quite a good player," Benny recalled, "considering his rank."

The next night the band began a two-week engagement at the Thailand International Trade Fair. Word had gotten around that *"Benny ma lao"* ("Benny is here"), and Bangkok's Lumphani Park was packed solid with thousands of Thai jazz fans. The band played two shows a day, drawing over a million listeners. It was easily the top attraction of the eleven-nation exposition, surpassing Japan's nightly beauty contest and even the main U.S. exhibit of an appliance-laden American home. Audiences were delighted when Benny added a number of Thai songs to the band's repertoire, including several by the king. Singer Dottie Reid's valiant struggle to master the words of a Thai ballad brought down the house. But it was offstage that the band had its greatest impact. Every night after their regular performance the Goodman sidemen made the rounds of Bangkok's nightclubs and dance halls and sat in with the local musicians. During the day they hung out with the fans and gave informal lessons to their Asian counterparts. And there were frequent return visits to the palace. The king was normally confined to playing with members of the royal family and other high-ranking dignitaries and wasn't about to pass up the unprecedented opportunity to jam with some really good American professionals. "We've been spending so much time at the palace we might as well be living there," Benny's drummer, Mousey Alexander, remarked.

"The first time he asked I went there with Budd Johnson, our trumpet player Mel Davis, Mousey Alexander, Hank Jones and Israel Crosby," Steve Jordan remembers. "The king had his own recording studio, and we made some tapes, then had lunch on the veranda. It was beautiful. The second time he asked for Benny. An emissary came to the hotel and told Benny, 'The king would like to see you this afternoon and play a little.' I heard Benny say to him, 'Well, gee, tell him that's awfully nice, but I'm expecting some very important telephone calls from the United States.' The guy said, 'You don't understand, Mr. Goodman. When the king says he would like to see you, you don't expect nothing except to go to the king.' Benny got the idea and grabbed his jacket. On their way out the door I told him he ought to make a tape and call it *The King and I*."

When the fair closed on December 22, it was reported that "Goodman had seen more of the King, and on closer terms, than any other visiting American." The king's intimates said they had "never seen him so happy." Benny recalled with a laugh: "His enthusiasm for music was just unbelievable. He sat and played for as many as five and six hours at a time. I must say he really wore me out as far as endurance was concerned."

The rest of the seven-week tour was just as successful. In Phnom Penh, Cambodia, the band played before a huge crowd of twenty-five thousand, then gave a command performance at the royal palace, where the king requested "Blue Skies" and "Bugle Call Rag." In Rangoon Benny came onstage after the intermission dressed in the traditional Burmese costume of pink *gaungbaung* headgear, black alpaca jacket and checked sarong, and everyone in the audience, including the Soviet ambassador, broke out in wild applause. At Kuala Lumpur, Malaya, the three-thousand-seat house was sold out weeks before the concert, and the demand for tickets created a brisk business on the black market. In Tokyo, where Benny also performed a recital with a Japanese string quartet, he was besieged with requests for "Sing, Sing, Sing" and asked to sign countless autographs. "It isn't just me," Benny explained upon his return. "It's jazz. American jazz doesn't need any hard sell in Asia. They've bought it. They know all the big bands. They have all the records. All the latest things. I even heard Elvis Presley records in Bangkok, Singapore and Tokyo."

The tour achieved its political purpose admirably, leaving behind a wake of good feeling toward the United States and an impression that "America is not only great in modern plumbing and fancy cars," as one American official put it, "but in things of the spirit and the arts." The Goodman band included several black musicians, and that also made a strong impression. The world was watching the civil rights struggle in the United States gather force and saw how it was being met with harsh, often violent attempts at suppression. "I was constantly asked by the press over there about the colored people here," Benny said. "They were quite concerned. I didn't really have anything particular to say, other than we've had colored musicians in the band for twenty-five years. That was probably more than enough to offset what they had been hearing from the other side."

Though illness had kept Benny from performing on several dates, the tumultuous reception he received throughout the tour encouraged and energized him. After resting a few weeks, he put together another big band with a substantially different personnel, played some concerts and dances on the East Coast, then returned to the Waldorf-Astoria on March 11 for a four-week engagement. Now that he was back home performing before a rather less impressionable audience, the criticism that he was still living too much in the past began to resurface. Even *The New Yorker,* which had been so enthusiastic about his previous appearance at the Waldorf the year before, took issue with his musical conservativism: "There have been no new developments; for the most part, the band plays the same old arrangements of the same old numbers."

Benny disbanded at the end of the engagement and limited his activities over the rest of the spring and summer to a few television appearances and some private recordings for his own Park Recording Company. (For the first time in close to a quarter century he was no longer under contract to a major label.) That fall he assembled another orchestra and sent it out on the road under the leadership of Urbie Green. "I'm still enthused about my band," Benny maintained, but he joined it only for an occasional date. Without his presence it failed to develop into much of an attraction and folded after a New Year's Eve job in Chicago.

Benny resurfaced in April as the star of the NBC television special "Swing into Spring." Galvanized by the enormous popularity of Elvis Presley, rock 'n' roll had become the latest musical craze ("It's here to stay," Benny observed glumly), but the hourlong show was an unashamed exercise in nostalgia for the long-departed Swing Era. "Ever noticed how some things don't really change very much?" the host Dave Garroway remarked in his opening comments, probably not realizing the full import of what he was saying. "Well, that's really what this show is about tonight. Things that never change. Like spring or swing or the King of Swing, Benny Goodman."

Though its musical content couldn't compare with CBS's extraordinary

"The Sound of Jazz" aired earlier that season, which brought Billie Holiday, Thelonious Monk, Lester Young and a host of other great jazz musicians to a Sunday afternoon audience, this stroll down memory lane was really quite good for what it was. The emphasis was almost entirely on music, a rarity for prime-time television of that day. The supporting cast featured former band singers Ella Fitzgerald, Jo Stafford and Ray Eberle, but the spotlight stayed mainly on Benny. Reunited with some of his more illustrious alumni like Teddy Wilson, Red Norvo and Harry James, performing both in a small group format and in front of a kicking big band filled with ex-sidemen, Benny sounded alert and alive and very much involved with what he was doing as he once again trotted out some of the old war-horses like "Don't Be That Way" and "King Porter Stomp." Television critics happy to relive their youths for an hour gave the show glowing reviews. Texaco was pleased enough by the ratings to sponsor a second special with Benny the following April.

At the time of the broadcast Benny was completing preparations to return overseas, where there continued to be a sizable market for his music. On May 2 he flew to Europe with a new big band for a monthlong tour of the Continent that was to take him on a strenuous itinerary of one-nighters through Sweden, Denmark, Norway, Germany, Austria, Switzerland and Holland before settling down for a week at the 1958 World's Fair in Brussels.

The Brussels exposition was promoted with the usual high-minded rhetoric about advancing world peace and understanding, but for the United States and the Soviet Union it was another skirmish in the ongoing cold war between them. The USSR took its appearance at the fair very seriously, spending about sixty million dollars on its exhibition and another ten million on publicity. Hobbled by a few influential members of Congress who believed that exporting American culture was a waste of money, the U.S. exhibit had to make do with a small fraction of this amount, and the prospects for winning the hearts and minds of the expected sixty million visitors were not encouraging. Several months before the official opening in the middle of April the *New York Times* lamented, "It is now a notorious and unhappy fact that the Soviet Union is going to put on a display of culture and science at Brussels which will make the United States look like a second-rate power." Two weeks later the Westinghouse Broadcasting Company announced that as "a public service" it would strengthen the almost nonexistent performing arts program at the American pavilion by underwriting a week of concerts by "the great Benny Goodman orchestra." Westinghouse's president explained: "In sponsoring these performances of American jazz, we will add a dimension to the Brussels Fair in which the Soviet Union cannot compete. American jazz has been shown to be a great force for good will abroad."

The Goodman band opened at the Brussels fair on May 25, 1958. It was the first live presentation at the American theater, which up to now had only been used to screen the film of *South Pacific* twice a day to small and unenthusiastic audiences. The rest of the U.S. exhibit had fared just as poorly. According to the humorist Art Buchwald, "The main attraction has been our free washrooms." But Benny filled the eleven-hundred-seat house to capacity and brought a sedate first-night audience of diplomats and officials to their feet whistling and screaming. The performance "shook the United States world fair cultural effort out of the doldrums," the *Times* reported the next morning. Lured by the chance to hear Benny Goodman in person, visitors from around the world jammed the American pavilion the rest of the week. And radio and television brought the performances to millions of others. On the band's closing night it played an outdoor concert at Brussels's nine-century-old marketplace to mark Benny's forty-ninth birthday. A capacity crowd of ten thousand gave him and the orchestra a tumultuous reception, interrupting almost every number with frenzied applause.

The week in Brussels was an unqualified personal and political triumph, but the music itself was largely disappointing. The band Benny assembled for the occasion certainly had the potential to be something more than another pallid re-creation of the past. It included a number of outstanding younger soloists like the saxophonist Zoot Sims and the marvelous pianist Roland Hanna, and instead of the nondescript singers he had been using in recent years, Benny brought along Ethel Ennis and the great Jimmy Rushing, who had starred with Count Basie. Though Benny said he planned to restrict himself to playing swing because "bop and progressive jazz are not our cup of tea," he had, in fact, commissioned some interesting new arrangements by more contemporary writers like Gil Evans and Bobby Gutesha. But to judge from live recordings issued by Columbia and Westinghouse, very little of this potential was realized in performance.

The band had its moments. The strong array of soloists and the hard-driving drumming of the twenty-two-year-old Roy Burnes built up an impressive head of steam on the extended, slightly revamped versions of "One O'Clock Jump," "Bugle Call Rag" and "Roll 'Em." Yet for the most part it was, as a review of the Columbia albums put it, "familiar scores . . . played without much conviction or life." The trumpet man Taft Jordan explained: "Benny wouldn't let the band go. One night his sacroiliac condition was acting up very bad, and he had to leave the bandstand. When Jimmy Rushing came on, the band started to let it go, to sound like a big band should. . . . Benny couldn't stand that, and he soon came back from the dressing room." It is probably the recurrence of Benny's painful and debilitating sciatica that accounts for the major disappointment on these recordings, the shocking unevenness of his own playing that has him sounding at times weak and strained and so unfocused that he seems at a loss for ideas.

Benny rested at home during the month of June. By the Fourth of July he was feeling well enough to take a big band to the Newport Jazz Festival for a special "Benny Goodman Night" that would celebrate his contribution to American music. Benny rehired half a dozen of the sidemen who had toured with him in Europe and filled out the sections with some good New York session players. He rehearsed the band diligently for three days before traveling up to Rhode Island, but this was hardly enough time to reach an adequate performance level, and he was further hampered by the antipathy most of his musicians felt for the old Swing Era numbers that formed the bulk of the evening's program. "You always played the same things with him," one sideman complained. "We wanted to play something different, but it didn't work out that way. It wasn't really a set band. We weren't working for him every week, you know. Who cared? The band was well juiced by the time it got on the stand."

The trumpet section fell apart on the opening number. Other mistakes followed. Benny's annoyance was apparent as the band plodded listlessly through the arrangements that earlier generations of Goodman musicians had brought so brilliantly to life with their enthusiasm and commitment. It was an important appearance for Benny, and he had taken the stage in excellent spirits. But the anger and frustration he experienced as the ragged, dispirited orchestra turned the evening into a shambles inevitably affected his own performance. Critics observed that they had seldom seen him so anxious, that his sound was erratic, that he seemed to be having trouble with his instrument and was playing "nervously and off pitch." Columbia recorded the concert but canceled its plans to release it.

During the months following the Newport fiasco Benny made some efforts to adapt himself to a somewhat more contemporary musical conception. He recorded several small group dates for his own production company, using modern musicians like Russ Freeman and André Previn on piano, Red Mitchell on bass and Shelly Manne on drums. "What [style musicians] play is not nearly as important as how well they play it," he maintained, softening his recent hard-line stand against modern jazz. "I don't care what school they're from as long as they are musical." The big band he assembled to tour the East Coast that fall included boppers like the saxophonists Herb Geller and Pepper Adams, and it performed a number of Bobby Gutesha's harmonically advanced arrangements as well as the old standbys his original fans still demanded. ("Sing, Sing, Sing," Benny said with a laugh, "is like 'The Star-Spangled Banner.' It's always in the program.") A review of the October 18 concert at Boston's Symphony Hall found that "the band swung more on the newer and more modern arrangements, probably because they meant more to the musicians." When Benny recorded the band upon its return to New York, he concentrated on the recent arrangements by Gutesha and André

Previn. Though he did some reaching back to the past, it was not to the usual Fletcher Henderson era numbers of the mid-1930s but to the later and much more contemporary-sounding charts of Mel Powell and Eddie Sauter, whose "Clarinet a la King" and "Benny Rides Again," both rerecorded that November, Benny proudly cited as early examples of "progressive jazz."

The commercial failure of his bop band back in 1949 gave Benny good reason to be cautious, but he continued to experiment with more modern writing when he put together another orchestra in the spring of 1959 for a three-week tour of the United States and Canada with Ahmad Jamal and singer Dakota Staton. He "was intrigued with the new arrangements he had commissioned from Bill Holman, Shorty Rogers and Gil Evans," the saxophonist Bob Wilber recalls. "Bill had done a chart on 'After You've Gone' which sounded more like Kenton than Goodman. Nevertheless, Benny enjoyed the new sounds and worked hard to get the charts right." Benny's old fans, however, did not share his appreciation. On opening night the arrangements "were received with polite applause, if not wild enthusiasm," Wilber remembers. The second night "the audience was absolutely stunned—they were expecting the Fletcher Henderson sound and what they heard was so totally different. The applause was lukewarm at best. Benny was obviously upset and when he came offstage he growled, 'These goddamned modern arrangements. That's what's killing the music.' He ordered [his manager] Jay Feingold to take them all out of the book and we opened the second half with 'Don't Be That Way.' The applause was deafening and Benny was happy once more. All those expensive new arrangements we had rehearsed so carefully were never to be played again."

For Wilber, Benny's reaction indicated "how important the roar of the crowd could be to a big star." But Benny's recent recordings suggest that quite apart from the audience's acceptance or rejection, he was extremely uncomfortable trying to adapt himself to a more contemporary musical idiom. Benny leased Columbia and Chess records some of the material he had recorded for his own production company a few months earlier, and on both of these albums, *Happy Session* and *Benny Goodman Rides Again,* he seems to be making a conscious effort to update his style to fit in with his younger sidemen and the more modern cast of most of the writing. The results are distressingly unsuccessful. Chirping along in the upper register favored by the few clarinetists like Buddy DeFranco and Tony Scott who had managed to coax some credible bebop out of an instrument that did not readily lend itself to this kind of playing, Benny sounds strident and strained and thoroughly ill at ease, so uncentered he is unable to settle into a proper groove even on familiar standards like "Whispering" and the older Eddie Sauter and Mel Powell arrangements. One has to assume the only reason he allowed these albums to be released was that he thought it was time to get some new product on the market.

That October Benny returned to Europe for a monthlong tour of Germany, Sweden, France, Switzerland and Austria. Rather than put together his own band, he fronted Red Norvo's excellent nine-piece group, which was filled with strong soloists like Bill Harris, Russ Freeman, the trumpet player Jack Sheldon and saxophonists Flip Phillips and Jerry Dodgion. For his vocalist he hired Anita O'Day, who had been one of the big hits of the Newport Jazz Festival the previous summer. Anita remembered the experience with considerable bitterness: "I began singing five numbers which went over well. Too well. That's when I began experiencing some of the much talked about Benny Goodman competitiveness. Benny doesn't want anyone or anything to stand out above him and his orchestra. If it does, he doesn't just compete, he undercuts the competition." A few days into the tour, she claims, Benny cut her portion of the program down to two numbers.

Despite the bad moments with Anita O'Day, the tour went extremely well. Norvo was an old friend. The band accommodated itself gracefully to the basic Goodman style. There were a few excellent new charts by the young arranger Fred Karlin, but the repertoire largely consisted of old Goodman Sextet numbers like "Breakfast Feud," "Slipped Disc" and "Rachel's Dream" that Benny hadn't played for a while and found stimulating to revisit. A bootleg recording of the October 28 concert at Basel reveals that Benny was back on firm footing, soloing with the self-assurance and conviction that had been sadly lacking in his recent performances.

He repeated his European success when he returned home in November and took the band into Basin Street East for three weeks. It was his first New York nightclub appearance in more than three years, and the fans lined up outside the club by the hundreds. Inside, the room was "seething, writhing with excitement," one review noted. The middle-aged audience snapped their fingers, clapped their hands and bobbed their heads as old favorites were brought to life once again, then shouted and cheered, stood up and applauded wildly as Benny charged through an up-tempo rendition of "After You've Gone."

What better evidence could there be that there was no longer any need to try to keep up with the changing times? Asked to comment on the criticism that he was back to playing the way he had in the 1930s, Benny replied, "Well, that's absolutely what I'd like to do. I don't think anything much has been discovered since then. I think that bit about the '30s is a compliment." As if to underscore this embrace of the past, a few weeks later MGM Records released *The Benny Goodman Treasure Chest,* a three-volume set of broadcast recordings from the 1930s, when Benny was at the height of his power and popularity and able to soar above such mundane concerns as the carping of the critics and the disaffection of his own sidemen.

Benny with Stan Hasselgard and Wardell Gray, 1948.
Ken Whitten Collection

Benny and Louis Armstrong
before tempers flared on their ill-fated 1953 tour.
From the Benny Goodman Archives in the Music Library at Yale University

Benny sitting in with local musicians during his 1956 sweep through the Far East. From the Benny Goodman Archives in the Music Library at Yale University

Peggy Lee, Lionel Hampton and Ella Fitzgerald help Benny celebrate his twenty-fifth year as a bandleader, 1959. Institute of Jazz Studies

A reflective Benny confronts the future, c. 1953.

From the Benny Goodman Archives in the Music Library at Yale University

Mission to
Moscow

Benny had a long-standing senti-
mental attachment to Russia as his parents' homeland and had been trying
for many years to take a band to the Soviet Union. By 1961 this desire had
become, in his own words, a "near obsession."

As far back as 1946 Benny had made an unsuccessful attempt to set up
a nonprofit "goodwill" tour with a jazz trio that would also include some
classical performances with the Moscow Symphony. In the mid-1950s he
stepped up his campaign, appealing to the American ambassador to use his
influence, sending several hundred dollars' worth of jazz records to the Soviet
Ministry of Culture, then pressing the U.S. State Department to sponsor a
visit as part of the current cultural exchange program. In 1958 he applied
directly for a visa to enter Russia with his band while he was appearing at the
Brussels World's Fair but was turned down once again, this time on the
ground that the Russian people were simply not interested in jazz.

Nothing could have been farther from the case. A member of the Phila-
delphia Symphony, fresh from a tour of the Soviet Union, reported that
"Every Russian youth I met listened to the Voice of America's jazz show" and
"Everyone in Russia is crazy about Benny Goodman." Other travelers told

Benny in Moscow, 1962.

From the Benny Goodman Archives in the Music Library at Yale University

of dedicated young jazz musicians in every major Russian city who were struggling to keep up with the latest developments and how there was such a hunger for American jazz records they were being copied onto discarded X-ray plates. If anything, jazz was *too* popular for the official guardians of Soviet culture, who excoriated it as culturally decadent, an incitement to hooliganism and an instrument of capitalist propaganda. Given the Voice of America's exploitation of jazz's appeal and all the talk in the American press about jazz as "America's secret weapon," this last charge did have a certain amount of merit.

In the fall of 1959 a group of Soviet composers visited the United States to survey the current state of American music. Benny had had some contact with Dmitri Shostakovich and Tikhon Khrennikov, the politically influential head of the composers' union, while serving as honorary chairman of the popular music division of Russian War Relief back in 1942, and he invited the group to hear him perform at Basin Street East. "We had a wonderful feast for them," he recalled with a sly smile. "They sat at a big table right in front of us [and] came to the dressing room to pay their respects." Upon his return home Khrennikov stated that Benny Goodman played the best jazz they had heard in America, but even this nod of approval wasn't enough to open the doors.

Benny's frustration was very much in evidence when two Soviet musicologists visited him backstage at Basin Street East in the spring of 1961. When they politely remarked that his records were quite popular in the Soviet Union, he undiplomatically snapped back, "If I'm so popular, why can't I get in to play there?" and he was sick and tired of "being put off." Benny's fit of bad temper made it an extremely uncomfortable half hour and did nothing to advance his cause. Yet some observers believed the very fact these Soviet scholars had come to hear him play and were seen applauding from their ringside table after the exchange suggested something of a softening in the official Soviet attitude toward jazz. And in fact, the ever-shifting party line was in the process of undergoing a radical revision.

The previous month Leonid Osipovich Utyosov, a popular Russian orchestra leader, had published a strongly worded defense of Western jazz in *Sovietskaya Kultura*, the official organ of the Soviet Ministry of Culture. Assailing those who made a "forbidden fruit" of the music, Utyosov declared categorically that "good jazz is good art, not a synonym for imperialism," arguing that it had its roots "not in the bankers' safes but in the poor Negro quarters." ("In Odessa long ago, musicians always improvised at weddings," he added, "and this gives me grounds to say that so-called Dixieland existed in Odessa before New Orleans.") "We need jazz," this highly credentialed people's artist of the Russian Federation concluded. "There is a demand for it." Two months later *Komsomolskaya Pravda*, the official newspaper of Soviet youth, which had been attacking jazz for years as a capitalist evil, called for a nationwide network of jazz nightclubs to be staffed by student jazz bands.

This shift in the official attitude was apparent when George Avakian met with Soviet bureaucrats in Moscow that August to arrange a concert appearance by his sister-in-law Maro Ajemian, the classical pianist who had introduced Aram Khachaturian's music in the United States two decades earlier. "In the course of trying to set this up, I also began talking to them about inviting some American jazz musicians to the Soviet Union," Avakian remembers, "and by golly, they were interested. They asked me who I thought should be invited, and three names immediately came to mind: Louis Armstrong, Duke Ellington and Benny Goodman. I pushed Louis Armstrong the hardest because I knew his warm, outgoing personality would make him an absolute smash, but they told me Louis would not be acceptable because he would arouse people too much. 'We'd rather have Mr. Goodman,' they said. 'His music is more organized, and our people are more used to organized music.' "

On March 8, 1962, Benny's years of perseverance finally paid off when the United States and the Soviet Union signed a new two-year agreement expanding cultural, scientific, technical and educational exchanges between the two nations. As part of the thirty-three-page pact it was agreed that Benny Goodman would be allowed to take a big band on a six-week tour of Soviet cities in return for a comparable tour of the United States by the Ukrainian Dance Ensemble. Though this would not be the first appearance of an American jazz musician in the Soviet Union, as was frequently reported, nothing on this grand a scale had ever been attempted before, and as such it was considered a major breakthrough, meriting front-page coverage in the *New York Times*.

Benny, of course, was elated. The dream had been haunting him for years, he said, and he had never looked forward to a trip with so much enthusiasm and interest. The tour would get started in May, and he immediately began lining up the musicians he wanted to take with him. Benny's involvement with the classics had played a part in the Russians' decision to grant him admission, and he also began selecting the compositions he planned to perform with Soviet symphonies and chamber groups over the course of his visit. When Avakian, who was now running the popular music division of RCA Victor, approached him about recording the tour, he found him unusually receptive. "Normally when you proposed something to Benny, he would react very coolly and say, 'Well-ll, you know . . . Not bad . . . We'll think about it.' But this time he was wildly excited. The tour was very important to him, and he had a full understanding of its historical significance."

The one dissonant note was the unexpectedly negative response from the jazz community. A number of prominent modernists, including Dizzy Gillespie and George Shearing, objected that Benny's brand of swing was too limited and no longer represented the sort of jazz being played in the United States. Some critics dismissed Benny as "a retired, commercial exponent of jazz" or not a real jazzman at all and argued that Duke Ellington or Louis Armstrong or one of the other "jazz founders" ought to have been sent in his place. One black publication strongly intimated that the only reason Benny was selected over Duke Ellington was that he was white.

Rather uncharacteristically, Benny took these complaints to heart and made a real effort to accommodate them. He invited Duke Ellington to join him as a guest star for a couple of weeks and take over part of the program, but Ellington rejected the offer, saying he was "a band guy" who liked to keep his own orchestra working "fifty-two weeks a year." Benny also talked to Jack Teagarden and Lionel Hampton about appearing as special guest soloists, but the State Department vetoed the suggestion. To present the broadest possible spectrum of jazz styles, Benny ended up reviving the old jazz anthology idea he first used in his original Carnegie Hall concert and had Bob Prince write a half hour survey of jazz history that ran the gamut from New Orleans funeral marches to Charlie Parker and Miles Davis. In response to the charge that his music was dated, he largely staffed the band with younger sidemen and commissioned a stack of new charts by contemporary arrangers like Tadd Dameron, Johnny Carisi, Oliver Nelson and Gary McFarland to supplement the Fletcher Henderson era standbys. "We'll play some of the things they expect and some new things," Benny promised. "I'll give the audiences anything I think is good."

Benny's enthusiasm about the tour led him to assemble what was, man for man, one of the strongest bands of his career, filled with exceptional soloists who had their own reputations. The saxophone section included Zoot Sims, Phil Woods, Jerry Dodgion, Gene Allen and Tommy Newsom, who also provided some of the new arrangements. On trumpets there were former Basieites Joe Newman and Joe Wilder, along with John Frosk and Jimmy Maxwell. Jimmy Knepper, Willie Dennis and Wayne Andre made up the very modern trombone section. The rhythm section consisted of John Bunch on piano, Turk Van Lake on guitar, Bill Crow on bass and Mel Lewis on drums. Teddy Wilson and the vibraphonist Vic Feldman were to be featured on the small group numbers. The superb Joya Sherrill, who had starred with Duke Ellington, gave up the chance to appear in a Broadway musical to come along as the singer.

Benny was so intent upon getting the musicians he wanted that when Jimmy Maxwell was reluctant to leave his studio post to take over the first trumpet chair, he kept raising his offer until it reached a thousand dollars a

410 THE LIFE & TIMES OF BENNY GOODMAN

week, and as an added inducement he hired Jimmy's teenaged son as his bandboy. "I was getting far more money than any of the other sidemen," Jimmy recalls with a smile. "The next highest was Teddy Wilson, who was getting six hundred. The funny thing was that Benny then decided not to have me play lead. He said I was getting old like him and should just sit back and take it easy. There was a joke in the band that I was the highest-paid fourth trumpet in the world."

The band began rehearsing in New York the middle of April before the final personnel was quite set. According to Bill Crow, who has published a long, fascinating account of the tour, though Benny "was a little patronizing and would get on different guys about inconsequential things—he kept trying to get Joe Newman to sit up straighter," the morale of the band was high and everyone was proud to be part of it. Only a few weeks later, however, while they were playing some break-in engagements on the West Coast, their spirits had already begun to deteriorate. Crow writes:

> Benny had become the bandleader I'd heard all the stories about. His manner became severe—the hard taskmaster. He started fixing things that weren't broken, moving parts around, changing tempos, changing soloists, glaring and snapping at us. . . . His general demeanor indicated that he thought he was, by virtue of being The Great Benny Goodman, superior to us mere mortals. . . . And the band didn't subscribe to Benny's special view of himself. We gave him credit for his achievements, and respected his musicianship, but we also respected our own. We wanted to be treated as adults and professionals.

By the time the band finished a six-night engagement at the Seattle World's Fair, half a dozen of the musicians were so disaffected they were threatening to quit, and the State Department, which already had enough problems working out the last-minute arrangements with the Russians, had to prevail upon them not to leave.

The band arrived in Moscow on May 28, 1962. Soviet advance publicity had made a great point of an editorial in the *New York Daily News* urging that spies be planted in the orchestra, and though Benny dismissed the bizarre suggestion with a laugh, the suspicions it generated clearly upset him. At rehearsal the next morning he seemed unusually on edge. And the distance between Benny and his musicians continued to widen. On the flight over they had discovered that a clause in their contracts gave Benny a week-to-week option on their services for several months after they returned to the United States, tying up their ability to take other work without obligating Benny to hire them, and most of the men refused to sign. Nor did they hide their displeasure that Benny was shying away from the new arrangements in favor of the old tried and true Goodman standards. "This band doesn't think big; it thinks back," Joe Wilder commented, summing up their growing disenchantment.

The band gave its premiere performance on May 30, the evening of Benny's fifty-third birthday. It was the social event of the season, and the forty-six-hundred-seat arena of the Central Army Sports Club was packed with Moscow elite and high-ranking party officials. About a thousand youngsters who had been unable to buy tickets mulled around outside the gates of the large hall. A few minutes before the music got under way, Nikita Khrushchev, the Soviet premier, appeared unexpectedly with his wife and three other members of the ruling Presidium. The premier's associates looked puzzled as the band launched into "Let's Dance," but Khrushchev, who had just come from denouncing the United States at a meeting at the Great Kremlin Palace, chuckled and smiled broadly. Benny seemed unsettled, taking a long, awkward pause with his back to the audience before kicking off the next number. When asked what he did during these mystifying lulls, which were repeated over the course of the concert, one of his sidemen answered, "Nothing; just stares into space and gets everyone nervous."

The applause was polite but restrained. There were very few jazz fans in the audience, and everyone was a bit intimidated by Khrushchev's formidable presence. It took Joya Sherrill to loosen the crowd up, and she provided the only showstopping moments of the evening. Khrushchev sent her a note backstage complimenting her on performing in such "a warm, wonderful manner." ("From that moment on Joya was dead," Jimmy Maxwell remembers. "Benny just didn't want the competition.") Khrushchev left during the intermission, saying, "I don't dance myself, so I don't understand these things too well, but I enjoyed it." The fact that he had shown up at all, however, was considered to have given a further stamp of approval to American jazz that made it almost respectable.

The next night went much better. The audience was younger and far more demonstrative, applauding Joya wildly, rushing the stage when the band broke into a swing rendition of the old Soviet favorite "Meadowlands," calling it back at the end of the concert with a long standing ovation for twenty-five minutes of encores. "I think we're beginning to get through," Benny told the American reporters with obvious relief. The evening was an unqualified success, and after all the years of planning and waiting, Benny had every reason to feel jubilant. Yet when George Avakian met with him a few hours later, he found him strangely distraught.

"The Soviets didn't want the tour to be too successful, and they threw a number of roadblocks in the way," Avakian recalls. "They were not at all cooperative about my recording the concerts and had held back my visa to make sure I missed the opening performance. The first time I was able to get together with Benny was when we went out for something to eat after the second night. Benny was extremely uptight, in some kind of agitated state unlike anything I had ever seen. For some reason he wouldn't explain, he seemed to feel the tour was not going to go well. Maybe he already sensed that he had a kind of revolution on his hands with his musicians. Maybe the tensions from the tremendous importance he placed on the visit were finally getting to him. But he was so nervous and jumpy he kept moving around from one subject to another and wouldn't let me talk to him about the recording setups and all the other arrangements we had to get straight. Finally he looked at me and said, 'I don't really know why you came here, George.' I said, 'Benny, what are you talking about? We planned this together months ago. You were full of enthusiasm. We're going to make history. That's what this is about.' He said, 'Oh, I don't know. Maybe we ought to forget the whole thing. I think maybe you ought to go home.' I managed to talk him out of it fairly easily. I think he just wanted some reassurance that everything was going to be all right. Benny had a way of begging you for help without your realizing it until later. But he sure set me back on my heels. I knew him quite well by now, and I had never seen him behave so irrationally."

"It was the pills," Jimmy Maxwell maintains. "Benny told me, 'This tour is the most important thing in my life.' He was really hysterical about it. Benny was not a drinker, and he was not a drugger. He once threatened to fire anybody in his band who smoked pot, and his brother Irving had a big fight with him because he was going to get rid of Georgie Auld. But he began taking these giant uppers and downers because he thought they would settle his nerves. I think he started taking something to make it through the night and get some sleep, but they were so powerful he needed something else to wake him up the next day, and the combination just made a wreck out of him. He told me himself he was completely confused during that whole trip.

"Benny was always a little unpredictable to begin with, but he became very unpredictable in the Soviet Union. Before we left the United States, he hired my son David as his bandboy; then once we got over there, he completely denied he ever did anything like that and insisted I pay for David's airfare and living expenses. Benny was a close guy with a buck and would scrounge you out of anything he could, but he never lied, and he never cheated, and he never went back on his word; he was very honest. But in the Soviet Union he was truly not himself at all. Sometimes it got so bad he would stand on the side of the stage with his tongue hanging out of his mouth and saliva running down his chin like somebody in an institution. I really felt sorry for him."

The band played to another capacity house the next night. The concert was warmly applauded, and hundreds of jazz fans swarmed down to the foot of the stage to get a closer look at Benny and his musicians before they disappeared into the wings. The following day the first official review appeared in *Sovietskaya Kultura*. Benny was hailed as a "genuine poet of the clarinet who enlarges the expressive possibilities of the instrument to literally impossible limits" and his orchestra praised as an ensemble of master virtuosos. The review also took issue with those Soviet jazz experts who privately criticized Benny for being too old-fashioned, denouncing them as musical illiterates who "think jazz must be reduced to extravagant cacophony and sounds that excite the nerves."

That afternoon Benny and the band, along with a large entourage that included Benny's wife and daughters, flew to Sochi, a resort on the Black Sea, for the second leg of their journey. Over the next five nights they packed the fifteen-hundred-seat outdoor amphitheater with a mixture of middle-aged party functionaries and youngsters who somehow had gotten hold of the expensive and hard-to-find tickets. The response was warm but a bit uncertain. The older members of the audience listened carefully but weren't quite sure what they were hearing. The younger jazz fans were surprisingly knowledgeable, shouting out the first names of Zoot Sims, Phil Woods and the other soloists, but some of them dismissed Benny's music as passé. "Why, the latest number he plays was written twenty years ago," one complained. When asked why he wasn't playing more modern jazz, Benny bristled: "A vocal minority screams for progressive jazz in both the U.S. and Russia. Then there are the music lovers."

The Sochi officials tried to keep the band under wraps, cutting short an after-hours jam session, preventing the musicians from passing out buttons commemorating the tour, arresting a fan who was caught fraternizing, obstructing Avakian and an NBC television crew from taping the concerts. Tensions were exacerbated by the bad food, the frequent bouts of dysentery, the language barrier and the growing animosity between Benny and his sidemen. "With such a good band, we couldn't understand why Benny didn't just let us play," Bill Crow recalls. "If he had let us alone, played his solos and taken the bows, the tour would have been a piece of cake for him. Instead, he seemed to be always on his guard against us, as if we had been shanghaied and had to be watched for signs of mutiny. . . . We were proud of the band, and couldn't understand why Benny didn't seem to feel that way too."

Benny threw a champagne party for the band after the Sochi opening and apologized for being so hard on everyone. "But it might happen again," he added as a halfway humorous afterthought. The next night it did. "He snapped at Mel [Lewis] and Jimmy Knepper about their playing, glared at us and generally made us miserable on stage," Crow remembers. "He tried to give Zoot one of Phil's solos, but Phil was a little loaded and feeling aggressive. Before Zoot could get his horn in his mouth, Phil jumped up and took his solo anyway." A few nights later Phil delivered an equally impassioned tirade against Benny at a get-together in one of the musicians' hotel rooms, stepping out on the balcony to end his chorus of invectives with the culminating malediction "Fuck you, King!" Benny was standing on his own balcony one floor below and overheard every word that was uttered. The next morning he called a special rehearsal, which forced everyone to cancel his plans to spend the afternoon at the beach, and in a particularly foul mood drilled them on all the arrangements in the book they weren't using.

From Sochi the band flew to Tiflis, the capital of Georgia, where it played five concerts in the eight-thousand-seat Sports Palace. The fiercely nationalistic Georgians, who spoke Russian only unwillingly, hooted down Joya Sherrill when she sang the Russian folk song "Katyusha" in the original language, but then applauded her warmly when she moved on to "I'm Beginning to See the Light." *Zaraya Vostoka,* the official publication of the Georgian Communist party, had given the Goodman band its biggest advance buildup so far, saying, "Our jazz fans are awaiting with impatience their meeting with this well-known musical collective." Though the overall response was good, it was not as enthusiastic as expected. Following a closing night banquet thrown by the Georgian Philharmonia, which left everyone with serious hangovers, the band flew to the remote city of Tashkent in Uzbekistan, two thousand miles east of Moscow. "The Tashkent concerts weren't great successes," Bill Crow recalls. "The hall was hot, the audiences cool." Benny had grown increasingly uncommunicative with both his musicians and his audiences. He arbitrarily cut off solos and encores and called for unscheduled numbers in the middle of a performance, destroying the momentum of the concert while the men dug out the scores. At the final performance he abruptly moved into the closing theme after a mere sixty-five minutes of music, then walked off the stage.

The band scored its most resounding success when it opened in Leningrad on June 20. Leningrad was the most cosmopolitan and culturally aware of Russian cities, and for the first time on the tour the tickets were not largely appropriated by Communist party officials. Close to six thousand fans, mostly teenagers, jammed the Winter Garden Stadium and cheered every number wildly, not letting up until they were given forty minutes of encores. "It was like the Paramount in the old days," an exhausted but satisfied Benny remarked as he rested backstage. The next day, however, he reverted back to the same mystifying, ultimately self-defeating behavior that had confused and alienated his musicians from the time they left New York.

Benny had backed out of his original plan to appear with the Moscow Philharmonic, and to make good on his promise to perform some classical music, which had been one of his big selling points to the Russians, he had scheduled a performance of the *Rhapsody in Blue* with the American pianist Byron Janis, just then completing his own very successful tour of the Soviet Union. Benny resurrected an old dance band arrangement and met with Janis for the first of two rehearsals the day before the concert. Inexplicably he refused to conduct the band through the tricky tempo changes and insisted on standing where Janis's view of him was blocked by the lid of the grand piano. Janis was understandably upset, but Benny reassured him they would work out the problems at the second rehearsal the next day. When Benny canceled the rehearsal at the last minute, Janis was ready to call off the appearance, and the American Embassy had to plead with him not to leave. Predictably enough, the performance was a fiasco. Benny ran into reed problems with the clarinet introduction and made two false starts. The band was hesitant and ragged. Left no choice but to conduct the piece at the same time he was playing, Janis was way off his mark and had turned into a nervous wreck by the time he finished struggling through it. "The man has incredible vanity," he complained to *Time* magazine, furious at "Mr. Goodman's obvious lack of interest in making this performance of the *Rhapsody* a success."

Byron Janis and the Goodman musicians were not the only ones put on edge by Benny's increasingly peculiar behavior. "One morning in Leningrad I came downstairs and saw Alice at the front desk with her bags," Jimmy Maxwell recalls. "When she told me she was flying back to New York, I asked what was wrong, and she said, 'I'm suffering from the same thing as everybody else.' I said, 'You mean stomach virus?' She says, 'No. I mean Benny Goodman.' At that point Benny came down and said, 'Hi, Alice, where are you going?' She told him she was going home. All he said was, 'Oh,' and then he went in to breakfast. I found it shocking and a little sad that he could let his wife leave like that without even offering to take her to the airport. When Benny went into the dining room, he sat down with one of the guys in the band and started making a play for his girl friend. The guy was a vital young stud, and there was Benny, a tired old man thinking he was going to make out with her. It was pathetic."

After five concerts in Kiev, where police cordons lined the front of the stage to block off any contact with the musicians, the band returned to Moscow for its final half dozen performances. The opening night crowd jammed the huge fifteen-thousand-seat Sports Palace and kept the band playing encore after encore, continuing to roar for more even after the curtain was lowered. The next afternoon Khrushchev paid a surprise visit to the American Embassy's Fourth of July reception and, after shaking hands with each of the Goodman musicians, engaged Benny in a friendly argument about the merits of jazz and modern art. "I am not a jazz fan," the premier maintained. "I like real music. I don't understand jazz. I don't mean just yours. I don't even understand our own." When Benny explained it took some getting used to, Khrushchev replied, "Good music should appeal at once; it shouldn't take time." But both of them agreed they liked Mozart.

Benny broke out some of the modern arrangements the last three nights in Moscow so he would be able to include them on his album, but they came too late to raise the morale of his dispirited sidemen. When the band was invited to do a week in Warsaw on the way home, nobody was willing to go. Most of the men still hadn't signed their contracts, and when Benny's chief of staff, Muriel Zuckerman, threatened to withhold their final paychecks, they refused to take the stage for the closing concert, causing a twenty-minute delay until the checks were delivered into their hands. Joe Wilder was outraged that about sixty dollars had been deducted for excess baggage charges and refused to play at all. The concert itself was nothing to be proud of. There were harsh words between Benny and the musicians. One number was so untogether it had to be started over again.

After resting a week in London, Benny returned to New York. Upon landing at Idlewild Airport, he praised the Russian audiences and denied there had been any friction with his sidemen. "They behaved beautifully, they played beautifully and I think they were wonderful." The musicians were much less diplomatic, and a good bit of press coverage was given to their grievances. "Benny wanted to play all of his old Carnegie Hall things— arrangements of the '30s—while we wanted to play good modern music," trumpeter John Frosk complained, accounting for the frosty cold war atmosphere that pervaded the tour. The vibes player Vic Feldman accused Benny of undermining his sidemen while they were performing onstage. "During the concerts he'd noodle during solos, or hum while Joya Sherrill was singing. He has so many different ways of getting people tense and upset." Drummer Mel Lewis faulted him for his competitiveness. "After I got a big hand on my 'Sing, Sing, Sing' solo, he took the solo away. After Phil Woods took a solo one night on 'Greetings to Moscow' and got a great hand, the same thing happened."

Benny had his defenders. Some of the Goodman veterans in the orchestra pointed out that Benny was, as he well should have been, extremely conscious of the audiences' reactions and used them to guide his decisions about what to play. And after all, it was *his* band. Sympathetic critics like Dan Morgenstern argued that Benny "has long since earned the right to be bossy, eccentric and opinionated" and thanked him "for helping the cause of jazz once more." But everyone agreed that what should have been the culminating achievement in a long and distinguished career had turned out to be considerably less than that.

George Avakian had his hands full putting the album together. It was produced through Benny's Park Recording Company, and rather than pay RCA recording engineers their going salaries, Benny had brought along his own relatively inexperienced engineer. "The guy was not really a professional, and the balance came out different every night," Avakian recalls. "Some nights nothing was usable no matter how well it was played. Certain numbers had to be spliced together from two or three different performances recorded in different cities, and I had to work for days with the RCA engineers in New York to get a proper equalization and force the stereo split to sound reasonably correct. I also had to fake a couple of things. I wanted to catch the cheering for Zoot Sims on 'Titter Pipes,' which didn't come through clearly on the tape, so I talked to the engineers about it, and they said, 'Well, we'll just record some shouts here in the studio and figure out where to put them in.' I auditioned the engineers, and a couple of them captured exactly the sound of the Russian audience I had in my head.

"It had been Benny's idea to get a modern band together and commission charts from arrangers like Tadd Dameron, so it wouldn't be just another Benny Goodman nostalgia album. He made a point of telling me both before and after I arrived in Moscow, 'Now be sure to record those arrangements because we should have a good across-the-board selection.' But he played them very infrequently, and some he didn't play at all. I really had to stretch to get some on the album, but I tried very hard to include as many as I could. Benny could be so self-destructive. The problems he caused himself by upsetting the other musicians! But there were enough times they managed to save themselves so that we did get a hell of a good album out of it.

"Once Benny returned from the Soviet Union, he went back to the attitude that this was a very important project that he wanted to be an all-time document. It was as if none of that weirdness had ever happened. The one thing he insisted upon was that he didn't want Joya Sherrill on the album or even mentioned in the notes, and he was very specific about that. I think he resented her success. The audiences really loved her. I was extremely annoyed with him for that, and I felt badly for Joya. It really hurt her. She was a wonderful singer, and her songs were one of the high points of the tour."

The two-record set was released in September. Though it was pieced together from performances recorded over the course of the six-week visit, RCA insisted on the title *Benny Goodman in Moscow* and claimed in the press release that everything was taken from Benny's farewell concert. Thanks to Avakian's perseverance in the editing room and careful selection of material, it turned out surprisingly well. It is easily the freshest, most interesting album issued under Benny's name in a number of years. Though Benny had his good and bad nights on the tour, everything he plays here shows him in consistently excellent form.

Despite its strong musical content, the album had a disappointingly brief shelf life and soon went permanently out of print. According to Avakian, "When the sales fell below a certain figure, RCA had to give Benny back the rights, and for some reason he wouldn't explain, he would never okay a reissue. Time and time again I told him, 'Benny, we should bring this out again. There's at least another LP's worth of material. We could make it a three-record set.' But Benny was very weird about that. He'd say, 'Yeah, it's a good idea. We must do that sometime,' and then he'd change the subject. Once I said to him, 'You know, I wish you had let me include some of Joya's songs because she was so good and the arrangements were so interesting,' and he looked at me kind of blankly and answered, 'Oh, they're not in there?' I said, 'No, you didn't want them,' and he said, 'Oh, really?' in that way that he had when he didn't want to discuss something, in effect denying he had ever made such a statement."

To capitalize on the new visibility the Soviet visit had brought him, Benny set up an extensive summer tour of the United States. Only four veterans of the Russian campaign were rehired, and the rest of the band had to be hastily assembled from the pool of available free-lancers around New York. The orchestra's August appearance at the Freedomland entertainment park in the Bronx was criticized for its "lack of fire and drive." Benny's back began giving him trouble again, and early in September he was forced to disband. Much of October was spent in the hospital.

Following Khrushchev's humiliation during the October Cuban missile crisis, there was a sudden return to the earlier hard-line policy that regarded jazz and modern painting as unsavory foreign influences unfit for Soviet consumption. In December *Pravda* printed a sweeping condemnation of "the peculiar jazzomania that has lately seized many fields of our musical life" that castigated "the screeching and crashing" that "has unfortunately been sounding too often in youth clubs and cafés and sometimes even deafens large audiences in our major concert halls." In February the Soviet government completely ruled out American jazz as part of its 1963 cultural exchange program with the United States, rejecting proposed tours by Duke Ellington and Count Basie. To underscore the perils of allowing American jazz musicians on Russian soil, the following year *Izvestia* revived the accusation that had greeted Benny when he first landed in Moscow and charged that four of his musicians were actually secret agents planted by the CIA.

29

September Song

Ⓣhe Russian tour added a fresh supply of anecdotes to the stockpile of Benny Goodman stories former sidemen always ended up swapping with one another whenever they got together over a few drinks. Over the years Benny's idiosyncratic, often inexplicable behavior had given birth to endless tales about such matters as his obsessive quest for the perfect reed, the soul-shattering effects of the notorious Goodman "Ray" and the almost comical penny-pinching that could bring him to cadge a cigarette from one of his musicians, then walk off with the rest of the pack or stick unsuspecting sidemen with the tab whenever he deigned to join them for dinner. Benny's abiding self-absorption was a favorite topic of conversation and yielded a wealth of cherished anecdotes that were passed down from one generation of Goodman veterans to the next. There was the famous taxicab story: Benny gets into a cab and sits there silently while the driver waits to be given a destination. When finally asked, "Well, what about it?" he reaches for his wallet and asks, "Oh, how much do I owe you?" as he prepares to step back out on the street. There was the ketchup bottle story, another favorite: Benny is sitting in a coffee shop reading the sports page, as he usually did whether someone was with him or not. When the waitress delivers his scram-

The original Benny Goodman Quartet—Benny, Gene Krupa, Lionel Hampton and Teddy Wilson—together again for a final recording session, 1963.

From the Benny Goodman Archives in the Music Library at Yale University

bled eggs, he gives the ketchup bottle a good shake and the cap falls off onto the middle of his plate. Benny glances down, shrugs and goes back to his paper, letting the cap just lie there while he eats around it. And the story about the time Benny was rehearsing a group of musicians up in Stamford: The unheated studio is extremely uncomfortable, and when someone finally gets up the nerve to bring this to Benny's attention, he mumbles a terse acknowledgment that yes, it is a little chilly and disappears, then returns five minutes later wearing a heavy sweater.

The stories went on and on. For some battle-bruised veterans they demonstrated Benny's appalling egocentrism that made him oblivious of everyone else on the planet. For more sympathetic alumni, well, that was just Benny, and they retold the old tales with a good-humored tolerance and even a certain amount of affection.

Benny was back on his feet by November 1962 and spent the next year engaged in a wide variety of musical activities. He recorded the Copland Concerto, Morton Gould's *Derivations for Clarinet and Band* and Leonard Bernstein's *Prelude, Fugue and Riffs* for Columbia and appeared with Bernstein at Carnegie Hall at a memorial concert for Francis Poulenc. He toured with the Berkshire String Quartet and a small jazz group featuring Bobby Hackett and John Bunch and played several weeks at Basin Street East opposite the up-and-coming young singer Barbra Streisand. During the summer he produced the first of what would be an annual series of "Benny Goodman Presents" music festivals in Stamford, four evenings benefiting the Stamford Museum and Nature Center that brought performers like Rudolf and Peter Serkin, Isaac Stern and Dave Brubeck to overflow audiences at the local high school. That fall he performed with his daughter Rachel at the Shakespeare Festival in Stratford, Connecticut. And in what certainly had to be one of the high points of his year he reassembled the original Goodman Quartet to record a memorable album for RCA Victor.

Aside from a brief promotional appearance at Macy's department store three years earlier, this was the first time Benny, Lionel Hampton, Teddy Wilson and Gene Krupa had played together since they filmed *The Benny Goodman Story* back in 1955. The reunion was Benny's idea, and after all the animosity he'd encountered on the Soviet tour, it was something he looked forward to with particular enthusiasm. Lionel, Teddy and Gene could always be counted on to provide a supportive yet stimulating musical environment that allowed Benny to be himself without having to fight his way past obstructive sidemen who felt his whole approach was outmoded and he no longer had anything much to say. But if this was to be a return to the past, it was a return with a difference.

"When Benny sounded me about bringing the original quartet back for a recording date, I immediately said, 'Okay, let's do it!' " George Avakian recalls. "My one reservation was that I didn't want to remake a lot of the old Goodman Quartet numbers and turn it into a nostalgia album. But when I mentioned this to Benny, I saw right away he had the same idea and had already decided to record fresh material they hadn't played to death in the old days."

When the quartet reconvened at the Victor studio for the first session on February 13, Benny brought along an unusual list of tunes that ranged from ancient obscurities like "Love Sends a Little Gift of Roses," a 1919 ballad recorded by the Irish tenor John McCormack, to the relatively recent jam session favorite "Bernie's Tune" introduced by Gerry Mulligan in the 1950s. The other titles on his list included a number of older Broadway show tunes not part of his standard repertoire like Kurt Weill's "September Song," which may well have come to mind from Benny's awareness that more than a quarter century had gone by since the four of them made their first recordings together and they all were by now approaching their own autumnal years.

"The date started very, very slowly," Avakian remembers, "mostly because everyone had to feel their way through the unfamiliar material. I don't believe Benny came in with any music, and every so often there was a little puzzlement about how the chord changes ought to go. There were long waits between takes. Benny would start changing reeds and make everyone nervous, but the four of them seemed to get along just fine. Once or twice there was a bit of roughness between Benny and Hampton when Benny wouldn't accept some of Hamp's suggestions about background figures. Benny was definitely in charge, and he wanted to use his own ideas. But then the frown would leave Hamp's face, and he'd give that little giggle of his and laugh it off.

"With all this going on, the first date was rather pedestrian, and we got only one take we could use. The same thing happened the next day. Benny's attitude was: 'Don't worry. It'll jell. It's going to be all right.' But then he decided to stop recording and let it sit for a while, and I didn't push him on it. You didn't push Benny."

The quartet did not resume recording until six months later, on August 26. This time, through whatever mysterious concatenation of circumstances that makes the act of creative collaboration so utterly unpredictable, everything came together in a white-hot frenzy of give-and-take that recaptured all the driving excitement and joyful high spirits that had made the original Goodman Quartet such a heart-thumping phenomenon twenty-five years before. In more recent years Hampton had veered dangerously close to letting his knack for crowd-pleasing showmanship take precedence over his playing, but that afternoon he became once again the great straight-ahead jazz musician he still had it in him to be. Avakian recalls that Teddy was unusually withdrawn and looked a bit under the weather, as if something might be wrong with his health, but none of that came through in his playing, which flowed with the same effortless elegance and controlled emotion one had come to expect of him. Gene, for some reason, sounded even better than he had in the old days, playing with more subtlety and far more swing. And Benny seemed absolutely rejuvenated, soloing with the passionate involvement of a teenager rejoicing in the strength of his new found powers.

One good take followed another as the four of them swung their way masterfully through the old Charlie Christian riff "Seven Come Eleven," "I've Found a New Baby," "Somebody Loves Me," "I'll Get By," "Say It Isn't So" and the original blues "Four Once More." Caught up in the spirit of the moment, Benny called for a redo of "Runnin' Wild," one of the quartet's most exciting numbers back in 1937, and the result does not compare unfavorably with the original. By the end of the date seven of the ten tracks that made their way to the finished album had been laid down to Benny's satisfaction.

Together Again! surprised a lot of listeners who had written Benny off as a once-great jazz musician now coasting on his reputation. And in truth, much of Benny's current work did little to dispel this impression. His playing on *Made in Japan,* recorded at a concert in Tokyo in February 1964, is distressingly perfunctory. Benny sounds weak and uninspired and fails to establish any discernible rapport with the much younger sidemen he'd brought along for the eight-city tour. *Hello, Benny!,* a big band run-through of some recent pop hits and a few vintage Fletcher Henderson charts recorded in California four months later, is equally undistinguished and has little to recommend it other than Tommy Newsom's Eddie Sauter-like arrangements. But when the circumstances were right and the spirit moved him, the years fell away, Benny shook off the torpor of middle age and stepped out swinging once again with all of "the old pepper," as he called it, very much intact. "I don't agree with a lot of the people who put him down," John Bunch maintained in a 1964 interview. "When he's really playing—forget about it, he'll scare you to death! Anybody that says he can't play—well, they just aren't around when he *is* playing."

Bunch worked with Benny frequently after he returned from Russia and found it "amazing how he seems to have changed since then. He's more relaxed, remembers everybody's name and is generally easier to get along with." In the months following the Soviet tour Benny performed almost exclusively with loosely organized small groups, where the emphasis was largely on improvisation. Now that he no longer had to contend with all the pressures it took to forge over a dozen musicians into a cohesive unit, he could allow himself to become a good bit more tolerant and easygoing. On those few occasions when he did put a big band together for a personal appearance or recording date his behavior could still be as perplexing as ever. "Doing the *Hello, Benny!* album was a crazy experience," the saxophonist Skeets Herfurt remembered. "One session I'd play the lead sax, the next Benny would have somebody else take it. He was continually taking parts away from the lead men and having others do it. It was quite confusing." And however much he may have mellowed after the Russian campaign, even when he went out with a small group, he could still be at times an exceedingly difficult man to work for. Certainly that was the experience of Marian McPartland when she toured with him for several months toward the end of 1963.

Married to Benny's boyhood chum Jimmy McPartland, Marian had established her own reputation as a fine modern pianist and achieved considerable success leading her own trio. "I think Benny hired me because I was starting to make a little name for myself," she recalls. "I went with him because I hadn't had much experience working as a sideman in someone else's group and thought it would add another facet to my career. I thought it would be interesting, and it was interesting, though not in the way I expected.

"It started out with Benny calling me on the phone and saying in that very proper way of his, 'I'm putting this little band together, and I'd like to ask you if you're interested.' I was really quite thrilled. I had known Benny for years through Jimmy, though not very well, and assumed that because *I* had my own group, *I* would be perfectly fine with him and wouldn't be subject to all those terrible things he was known for. After that conversation Benny had me come up to the house a number of times to play with him. One afternoon he walked out of the room without saying anything, and I just sat there fiddling around at the piano until I suddenly realized a couple of hours had gone by. I searched through the house and finally found him picking out reeds and doing some work on his horn. He said, 'Oh, are you still here?' I said, 'I thought . . .' He said, 'Oh, no. We're all through. You can leave.' I must have been eager to have the job because that should have been enough right there.

"When Benny eventually asked me to join him, he offered me a very small salary, and I had to haggle with him about money. I wanted something like six or seven hundred dollars a week, which didn't seem all that much to me, but it was more than he wanted to pay. He said, 'All you guys go down to the Half Note and sit in for free, then you expect me to pay you a big salary.' But I stuck to my guns, and that's how it wound up.

"We started out doing some trio dates in places like York, Pennsylvania. I was very anxious not to play any wrong chords or do anything that would cause Benny to give me that funny look, and I thought the dates went quite well. But then we went back to New York and started rehearsing the full group with Red Norvo, Bobby Hackett and Modesto Brisano, an albino saxophone player Benny liked very much and had taken under his wing. Right there at that first rehearsal I began to get the feeling that he wasn't all that pleased with what I was doing. Nothing was said, but later that night Bobby Hackett called me and mentioned that Benny didn't like the way I voiced certain chords on some tune like 'Body and Soul.' I guess I was slipping in flatted fifths, and Benny didn't care for those kind of extended modern harmonies, but even Hackett couldn't explain very clearly what was bothering him. I asked Bobby, 'Why doesn't Benny tell me himself?' and he said, 'Well, you know how he is. Benny's so into the music it's hard for him to say what he wants. It's nothing really. I just figured I'd mention it to you.' I had been trying to do everything I thought Benny wanted, and I found the whole conversation extremely unnerving.

"We went out on tour with a small chamber group, and Benny divided the program between jazz and the classics. The tour lasted two months but seemed much longer. I always tried to act very confident, but I really wasn't, and Benny innately knew when somebody was intimidated by him. Sometimes he would hunch his shoulders and wince and look around at me as if he were in great pain from what he heard me playing behind him. Sometimes he would give me a kind of satirical grin, as if to say, 'What did you just play? Haven't you heard that tune before?' It was devastating, and what made it even more upsetting is that he never really told me what he didn't like. It was always left vague. Benny was so distant and elusive. And I was too scared or too naïve to ask him—maybe because I was afraid what the answer might be. When Russ Freeman went with Benny, he didn't kowtow to him about playing certain chords. He played whatever chords he wanted to play, and if Benny gave him any funny looks, he just ignored them. It might have gone better if I had done the same thing. I was probably too sensitive. But every night before the show I began to feel queasy and would ask myself whether I would get through it without getting the look or the feeling that Benny hated me.

"One night we were at a party, and Benny and I wound up sitting together on a couch. I'd had a few drinks by then. Otherwise I never would have been able to say this. But I told him, 'Benny, I know you're really not happy with my playing, and if you don't like the way I play, why did you hire me?' Benny looked at me very innocently and said, 'Damn if I know.' So I said, 'Well, why don't you get somebody else for the rest of the tour?' Benny sort of perked up and said, 'Would you mind?' I told him, 'Not at all. As a matter of fact, I'd be a lot happier.' Benny said, 'Well, I'll get John Bunch, and you can continue to do your featured spot,' and I said that would be great.

"John felt Benny had treated me badly and was quite embarrassed about taking over, but I told him I was glad he was there and delighted that all I had to do now was play my spot with the rhythm section, then disappear. But the day he arrived Benny said to him, 'Oh, John, let Marian play the show tonight'; then afterwards he told him, 'Gee, Marian sounded good. Why did I get you down here?' John, who was used to Benny by now and not as insecure as me, just laughed. The next night Benny had John play with the group, and at the end of the show he asked us to do a number together. It turned out to be sensational. It broke the place up. I think he let us do it one more time and then dropped it from the program. John said, 'Well, I guess we were too big a hit.'

"We ended the tour shortly after President Kennedy was assassinated. We were on our way to Dallas when that happened. The last date was in Topeka, Kansas, the home of the Menninger Clinic. I was in such a miserable state by now I decided I could use some psychiatric help and went over to the clinic to see if they could recommend someone. When I mentioned this to Benny, he said in total surprise, 'Oh, you seem very normal to me,' and I had to tell him he was the reason that was driving me there. I spent a couple weeks at the Menninger Clinic, then went into therapy back home in Long Island. I think it did me a great deal of good. As a result of being able to spell out this whole experience to someone, I leaped forward musically and generally became a lot more confident about myself. So in a sense you could say that Benny ended up doing me a favor."

Benny's income from record royalties, Wall Street investments and the like was said to be in the neighborhood of three hundred thousand dollars a year. He had the house in Stamford, Connecticut, an apartment and office on the East Side of Manhattan, and in 1966 he built a third home on the Caribbean island of St. Martin in the Dutch West Indies, where he vacationed frequently with Alice and indulged his passion for fishing. During the latter part of the decade he began to receive the sort of honors and awards commonly bestowed upon eminent public figures who have reached the twilight of their careers. Yet he still practiced the clarinet several hours a day, and he bristled at the suggestion that his interest in performing had waned and he was about ready to retire. "You take a fellow like Isaac Stern. He doesn't tour fifty weeks a year. That's the nature of our business now. Being that this business has become a concert business, we use the same procedures. At the time that we used to work fifty weeks a year, people asked us how we could stand the pace. Now they ask why we don't work more."

But if Benny had no intention of withdrawing completely from the fray, neither was he any longer really a full-time participant. He was no longer under contract to a major label and recorded only sporadically. He kept no musicians permanently on the payroll but would put together a group for this or that engagement, usually drawing on New York-based players like Doc

Cheatham, Hank Jones, Joe Newman, Zoot Sims and the guitarist Bucky Pizzarelli, who had their own strong solo voices and knew how to adapt themselves gracefully to the basic Goodman approach. By the middle of the decade he had also severed his ties with the booking agencies and was handling his own bookings with the aid of a small staff headed by Muriel Zuckerman, who screened the offers, took care of the contracts, made the travel arrangements and watched over the money.

Over the course of the 1960s jazz and popular music both underwent major transformations. Thanks initially to the extraordinary mass appeal of the Beatles, popular music became dominated by rock 'n' roll. And the free jazz experimentations of Ornette Coleman, John Coltrane and Cecil Taylor led to the second radical disruption of the established jazz tradition. Benny was fully aware of both these developments. He always made a point of keeping abreast of the latest musical trends, and albums by John Coltrane and rock groups like the Grateful Dead found their way onto his record shelves. Benny had little to say about the free jazz revolution but was surprisingly tolerant about the advent of rock 'n' roll. "I have no quarrel with it," he maintained in 1966. "Today's youngsters want to discover their own music. They're receptive to rock 'n' roll because it's simple. They like the beat, and the lyrics are straight to the point. It's encouraging that they get so excited about the music, and I think they'll graduate from it."

(A few years later, after it was apparent that this graduation was not going to take place, he became considerably more critical. "I hate all that amplification. I don't know what it's all about," he grumbled, dismissing rock as "a very immature musical form.")

Benny occasionally tried his hand at the odd Beatles tune like "Yesterday" and recorded a few numbers done by Blood, Sweat and Tears, but rock 'n' roll had no significant impact on the sort of music he played, and neither did the free jazz innovations of John Coltrane and his disciples. Benny's indifference to keeping up with the changing times distanced him even further from contemporary audiences. He still had his following, and reviewers continued to be enthusiastic about his personal appearances, but now the word *nostalgia* began to show up regularly in his reviews. Benny disliked the implication that he was living in the past. *"These* are the good old days," he insisted. But since he continued to play the old familiar standbys in the old familiar manner, largely for middle-aged swing fans who remembered him when, there was no way to avoid this perception.

In 1966 Benny confronted a medical crisis that put his life as well as his career in serious jeopardy. His back had started bothering him again, and when he went to see a physician, a rectal examination revealed that the cause of his distress was not a flare-up of the old sciatica but a far more serious carcinoma of the bowel. Benny was rushed to New York University Hospital, where a colostomy was performed by the surgeon Arthur Localio. The operation was successful, but according to Dr. Localio, who became a close personal friend, it was Benny's ferociously positive attitude that led to his swift recuperation.

The cancer was not totally cured. There were recurrent problems the rest of his life. But Benny responded with the same focused determination that had always been the driving force in his personality and refused to let them get in the way of his playing. "He went right past it," says Dr. William J. Welch, another personal friend who treated him medically on numerous occasions. "It didn't affect his ability to work or perform at all." Benny kept the condition hidden from everyone but his family and a few members of his inner circle. If his infirmity had been more widely known, it would have made him a more sympathetic figure, certainly to those sidemen who felt the brunt of his sometimes inexplicably abrasive behavior. Yet there was something almost heroic about the way he chose to deal with it.

Perhaps because of the aftereffects of the surgery, Benny cut back on his activities during the first nine months of 1969, limiting himself to a handful of classical concerts and small group jazz dates. Then early in October he recorded a series of sessions for a *Reader's Digest* record division project involving big swing band renditions of current pop hits. He was not especially pleased with the results, but this was the first time he had done any substantial work with a big band in almost four years, and it whetted his appetite for more.

Benny had scheduled a vacation in London at the end of the month and put in a call to the English saxophonist Frank Reidy, an old friend who had been telling him for years about the merits of the British big band musicians. "I'd like to play with an English band, Frank," Reidy remembered his saying. "Can you get one together for me?" "I said, 'What's it for?' He said, 'Oh, I just want to see how the English boys play.' I told him I thought it was rather a waste of money: 'If I've got to book a band, obviously they've got to be paid.' 'Oh, yes, fine—I'll pay. No trouble. Get me a hall—anywhere will do.' Later I phoned him back and said, 'Rather than waste the money, why don't you make an album?' "

Benny was receptive to the idea, and Reidy contacted an executive at Philips Records, commissioned some new arrangements and assembled a big band of top session musicians. The men worked together regularly in Jack Parnell's studio orchestra, so they were already a cohesive unit, and they were thrilled at the chance to take a break from their usual routine backing acts like Tom Jones to play with an American jazzman of Benny's stature. Benny, for his part, "was more than pleasantly surprised," Reidy recalled. "He was absolutely knocked out."

Benny flew back to London in November to complete the album, bringing with him some vintage Fletcher Henderson charts to balance the selection of contemporary standards supplied by the British arrangers. Considering the short rehearsal time and the fact that he had never worked with any of these musicians before, the *London Date* album turned out amazingly well. The new writing is fresh and consistently interesting. The band is tight and strong and impressively hard-swinging. And spurred on by his sidemen's enthusiasm, Benny really digs in, playing with the sort of passionate involvement not commonly found in jazz musicians who have passed their sixtieth birthdays.

Benny was so delighted with the recording he decided to take the band on the road and began making plans for a European tour. He returned to London the beginning of February with Muriel Zuckerman, Bucky Pizzarelli and a stack of arrangements from his original library and spent the next four afternoons rehearsing the orchestra at a pub in Acton. This was considerably less time than Benny normally required to bring a band up to performance level, but these were extremely proficient musicians who had been listening to Benny Goodman all their lives and knew what was expected of them. "The band swung its arse off, as we say in the trade," Reidy reported after the first rehearsal. "The Master was pleased."

The tour kicked off in Zurich on February 5, then moved through a rigorous itinerary of one-nighters that had Benny playing fifteen concerts in eight countries in less than a month. During the day he rested in his hotel room, conserving his strength. By the time the first sideman arrived at the concert hall he was already in his dressing room, warming up with some Mozart or von Weber. The musicians found his playing inspiring. "I think Benny's playing *better* now than in earlier years," the pianist Bill McGuffie insisted. "And when you start to play with him, it puts something into *you*. You find yourself doing things you never knew you could do. He's egging you on all the time." And according to Reidy, "The better the band played, the better *he* played. He wasn't afraid of a challenge at all." There was none of the acrimony that had marred the tour of Russia eight years earlier. "Nobody battled him this time," Muriel Zuckerman observed. "Maybe that's why it was so great." And from Geneva to Milan on to Bucharest and Hamburg, the audience reaction was unrelentingly ecstatic. The drummer Bobby Orr recalled that at the final concert in Berlin, "There were seven or eight thousand people demanding encore after encore. As soon as Benny walked onstage, they were shouting, 'Benny, Benny Benny!' "

During a night off in Copenhagen halfway through the tour Benny casually mentioned to his old friend the Danish violinist Svend Asmussen that "the band's just about cooking nicely now" and he was thinking about doing a record. Asmussen recommended an engineer in Stockholm, where Benny was appearing the next day, and arrangements were quickly made to record that performance. According to Bill McGuffie, the Stockholm concert did not reach the same exalted heights as some of the other dates on the tour, but despite a few disappointing numbers, like a fourteen-minute rendition of "Sing, Sing Sing" that fails to come into focus, the resulting two-record set *Benny Goodman Today* impressively documents what a good band this was and just how well Benny could still play. Though it was largely overlooked by all but the most devoted Goodman fans, Benny was enormously pleased with the album and considered it his best release in years.

Despite the bad weather and occasional mishap and some annoying problems with the procession of incompetent photographers he hired and fired, Benny called the tour "one of the most pleasurable I've ever taken" and said he would more than likely want to try it again. Five months later he did, calling the band back together for a two-week tour of Italy and Switzerland. That March he set up another string of engagements that was scheduled to take him to eleven cities in Germany, then on to Stockholm, Gothenburg, Copenhagen, Brussels, Paris and London. The tour had to be cut short when Benny injured his back in a dressing room accident in Düsseldorf, and he spent the next month recuperating in St. Martin. By September he was feeling good enough to return to England once more for a pair of concerts in Brighton and London's Royal Albert Hall.

The Albert Hall concert marked Benny's final appearance with his British orchestra, ending a mutually satisfying collaboration that had led to four tours of Europe and Great Britain within a year and a half. Certainly the main reason for such an extended involvement was the ongoing pleasure Benny took working with a group of highly skilled, personally congenial musicians who shared his enthusiasm for the old Goodman arrangements and enabled him to breathe new life into material he had been playing for more than three decades. It was, as he said, "a hell of a band." But the accompanying roar of the crowd also had its appeal. European audiences were still hungry for the kind of music he had to offer, and Benny was gratified by the appreciative reception he received everywhere he appeared. "It might be easier and more profitable to play four weeks in Vegas," he explained, "but who wants to travel 2,500 miles to be brought down by people who are straining to get back to the crap tables? Over there, they listen."

Benny returned to Europe half a dozen times over the next four years and also traveled to Australia. Before embarking on a 1972 tour of England and the Continent, he said he intended to hold himself down to a "civilized pace" but ended up playing sixteen cities in twenty-five days. The fatigue began to take its toll toward the end of the tour, causing him to pass up some press conferences and diplomatic receptions, and a live recording of the concert in Copenhagen, *On Stage with Benny Goodman and His Sextet,* fails to generate much excitement. Though his playing has its moments, Benny largely coasts through his standard repertoire, sticking close to the melody on several tunes and limiting himself to a single perfunctory chorus.

Benny continued to profess disdain for "this nostalgia business that's going on." And he curtly dismissed the suggestion that he was catering to his older fans: "I just cater to myself." But it was mainly the older fans who turned out to see him in such profusion, packing the concert halls from London and Paris to Melbourne and Prague, and it was unquestionably nostalgia for the music of their youth that was bringing them there. Yet the foot-stomping enthusiasm of the European and Australian audiences was contagious, and the reviews make it clear that Benny usually delivered a lot more than the stroll down memory lane they expected.

Benny's recurrent back problems became especially severe during the early 1970s. Observers frequently noted that he performed half seated on the edge of a stool, without making any particular point of it. According to John Hammond, though, Benny's back pain had become "the focal thing in his life," and it was just too painful for him to stand. The pain forced Benny to spend his sixty-fifth birthday at home in bed, yet the following night he opened at the Rainbow Grill as scheduled before a packed house that hadn't the slightest notion that anything was bothering him. The *Variety* reviewer found that evening's performance "as ageless and youthful as ever."

For all his remarkable willpower, Benny was not always able to rise above the debilitating effects of his infirmities. A few weeks later, on June 29, he played the 1973 Newport Jazz Festival in New York with the original Goodman Quartet, and the sold-out audience was stunned by his strangely distracted behavior. He shifted his stool around from one part of the stage to another. He fooled with his reed and stared into space for long moments between numbers while the puzzled fans grew increasingly restless. For some inexplicable reason he broke into a bizarre impression of Groucho Marx, mugging and leering and wiggling his eyebrows. The performance suffered accordingly, and the opening group led by his former trumpet player Ruby Braff and the guitarist George Barnes walked away with the musical honors.

Benny's frame of mind certainly wasn't helped by his lack of enthusiasm about bringing the quartet back together. A decade had passed since the reunion album for Victor, and in the intervening years the distance between Benny and his former sidemen had continued to widen. When the Timex Corporation approached him the previous fall about reassembling the quartet for a nostalgia-laden television special that would also have Count Basie, Duke Ellington and Dave Brubeck reprise some of their old hits, Benny had resisted the idea and tried to talk the producers into letting him do the show with his current musicians. Though the quartet performed brilliantly on camera, the rehearsal was marred by a flare-up between Krupa and Benny, who seemed to forget that Gene was no longer working for him and subject to his commands. The Newport rehearsal was also filled with tensions. Gene was suffering from leukemia and had just gotten out of the hospital, and there was some question about whether he would be well enough to play. Lionel had become a big businessman by now and seemed to have his mind on other matters. Teddy wanted to leave early and brusquely rejected Benny's appeals to stick around for a few more run-throughs. But despite the lack of rapport and the disappointing performance, the original Goodman Quartet was such a strong commercial attraction Benny agreed to several further bookings over that summer.

"I don't think they recaptured anything," he said a few years later. "You can't expect people to come together and pick up right where they left off. That's impossible. In 1937 it was 'The Benny Goodman Quartet.' In 1973 we were all leaders. Leaders don't want to become sidemen again, do they? The concerts went well to the extent that we were all good musicians and played well together. But it wasn't like it was before. . . . And there were all these personality problems."

The quartet's appearance at Saratoga Springs, New York, on August 18 was its final performance. Two months later, on October 16, Gene Krupa died at the age of sixty-four. Time was also starting to run out on a lot of Benny's other old associates. Jack Teagarden and Artie Bernstein had died in 1964, and Ziggy Elman and Cutty Cutshall four years later. Nineteen seventy-one saw the deaths of Ben Pollack and Lou McGarity. Edgar Sampson died in 1972. Within a few years Gil Rodin, Hymie Schertzer, Bobby Hackett and Johnny Mercer would also be gone.

During the mid-1970s Benny finally began to feel his own years catching up with him. "I don't have the stamina I used to," he admitted. "I used to rehearse all day, play five or six shows a night and then go out afterwards. I find that unthinkable today—I pace myself today." Rehearsals and airplane travel had become "grueling." He gave up extended road tours and club engagements. "I'm not interested in knocking myself out when there are good fish to be caught and other interesting things to do," he maintained. Yet he practiced regularly several hours every day and still played the jobs he wanted to play, crisscrossing the country once or twice a week for a jazz concert or guest appearance with a symphony orchestra. For the most part Benny worked with loosely organized small groups made up of Goodman regulars like Zoot Sims, Urbie Green, Bucky Pizzarelli, Hank Jones and the vibraphonist Peter Appleyard. To conserve his energy, he often turned the first half of the program over to his sidemen and further paced himself when he joined them by keeping his own solos short and giving everyone his own featured number or two.

Largely performing the same well-worn melodies he had played count-less times before in an informal, relatively undemanding musical setting, Benny often coasted along, revisiting familiar territory in a low-keyed, easygoing manner, failing to light any fires but receiving standing ovations anyhow just for still being there. The 1970s brought a new appreciation for Benny and the other jazz musicians of his generation. As Dan Morgenstern observed in a look back at the decade published in 1980, following the death of John Coltrane in 1967 jazz was no longer dominated by a single innovative force pointing the way into the future, and the old debates between generations and styles gave way at an acceptance of musical diversity and a rediscovery of the jazz tradition. Surviving veterans of earlier eras, ranging from ragtime's Eubie Blake to bebop's Dexter Gordon, were now venerated as heroic figures from the music's illustrious past, living proof of the ongoing vitality of a cherished heritage. And Benny was one of jazz's most eminent elders.

Yet Benny still possessed the ability to startle, and there were times in the middle of a comfortably familiar solo or background riff when he would be caught up in the inspiration of the moment and suddenly spring to life. Discovering there were still new things to be revealed in this or that old standard, he would forget about "pacing himself" and bear down on the business at hand with the emotional intensity of a man half his age, amazing his musicians, his audiences and sometimes even himself as he soared above the predictably routine in pursuit of the untrammeled spontaneity of his youth. This is precisely what television audiences witnessed during a 1975 tribute to John Hammond.

Hammond had been working as director of talent acquisition for Co-lumbia Records since 1958 and had now reached the mandatory retirement age of sixty-five. During his tenure he continued to demonstrate his knack for unearthing important new artists, bringing into the company such future names to be reckoned with as Aretha Franklin, George Benson, Bob Dylan and Bruce Springsteen. (Dylan's virtues were so obscure to most Columbia executives that when Hammond insisted on signing him, he was known around the office as "Hammond's Folly.") The three-hour television special, produced by the Public Broadcasting System as part of the estimable "Sound Stage" series, was to honor Hammond's lifelong contribution to American music by presenting a sample of the many performers whose careers he had abetted. Benny seemed like a natural enough choice, but relations between them were still strained, and Benny would not commit himself or even discuss the matter with Hammond when they met for dinner. Benny finally consented several weeks later, yet when the associate producer John McDonough asked him to join George Benson in a salute to Charlie Christian, he once again became evasive. Though Benson was a formidable jazz guitarist in his own right, he was best known for the very commercial pop fusion music he recorded for CTI after leaving Columbia, and Benny had not been impressed with what he'd heard.

After rehearsing with Benson the day of the taping, Benny revised his opinion and decided to go along with McDonough's suggestion that they share the spotlight on Christian's "Seven Come Eleven." Benny started off his segment of the show playing three numbers backed by Red Norvo and a rhythm section that included Benson and Teddy Wilson. The results were pleasant but hardly spectacular. Then he brought Benson out front and moved on to the Charlie Christian tribute. The performance began tentatively, with some confusion about keys and missed cues, but then, almost miraculously, toward the end of Benson's solo everything snapped into place. McDonough recalled:

> Benny started to feed him a single high note riff. Benson began picking it up, and suddenly they were in unison. Then each leaped together into a collective ensemble that was completely spontaneous and electrifying. Benson ran off long sweeping lines, and Goodman fought harder than ever to hold his own. I hadn't seen Benny play with such desperate brilliance in years. It was perhaps the most invigorating musical explosion I had ever witnessed. The crowd leaped to its feet in the only standing ovation of the night. John Hammond declared that he saw forty years drop off Benny during that number and that he had not seen him react that way to another musician since the first meeting with Charlie Christian.

The dangers inherent in trying to recapture one's earlier triumphs were driven home with particular force when Benny returned to Carnegie Hall on January 17, 1978, to celebrate the fortieth anniversary of his now-legendary 1938 concert. Benny seemed aware of the potential hazards. "You can't go back forty years musically any more than you can put together the New York Yankees of Joe DiMaggio and Lou Gehrig," he told *The New Yorker* in an interview promoting the appearance. And at a November 1 press conference he said that though he planned to include "some of the old material," he had no intention of re-creating the original program. It should just be "a fun night," he said, "done as easily as possible." But the very fact that a press conference was called singled out the occasion. And the disclosure that he was trying to round up some of the original participants—Harry James, Teddy Wilson, Lionel Hampton, Jess Stacy—inevitably created certain nostalgic expectations in the minds of his fans.

This was an important appearance for Benny. It was being recorded by London Records. Television cameras were covering it for the network news. The tickets completely sold out a few hours after they went on sale, and the house was packed with celebrities and journalists from around the world. But as with the 1953 tour with Louis Armstrong and the Russian sojourn nine years later, Benny seemed to buckle under the pressure, and through a series of self-defeating miscalculations he turned the evening into a shambles.

The band was woefully underrehearsed and for the most part stumbled its way uncertainly through the Goodman standbys. Inexplicably, Benny brought out Jack Sheldon, a good trumpet player, for a Las Vegas-style comedy turn that was completely inappropriate and wasted more valuable stage time on an inexperienced and frightened young singer he had heard only a few days before. The wait between numbers was interminable, destroying whatever momentum the evening might have been able to gather. And Benny's own playing was distressingly off, tense and unfocused and frequently at such a loss for ideas his solos consisted of little more than a string of repeated riffs. Some excitement was generated by featured guests Mary Lou Williams and Lionel Hampton, who, along with Martha Tilton, was the only returning veterans of the original concert. But this was not nearly enough to rescue the evening from the abiding aimlessness and confusion that began to empty the hall well before it came to a close.

The reviewers shared the audience's disappointment, writing the concert off as "a disaster," "an embarrassing and insulting performance" and "one of the oddest chapters in the Benny Goodman story." Making the unavoidable comparison with the 1938 triumph it was meant to commemorate, the *New York Times* concluded, "Despite [his] work[ing] in an aura of nostalgia for the last thirty years, the past seems to have slipped away from Benny Goodman."

Benny in 1986, the year of his death.
Ken Whitten Collection

30

Good-bye

On February 4, 1978, two and a half weeks after the Carnegie Hall concert, Alice Goodman died of a heart attack while vacationing in St. Martin. She had been ill for only a few days, and Benny had been told it wasn't anything very serious. He was playing a job in Youngstown, Ohio, when the news reached him. The funeral was held on February 9 at St. Francis Church in North Stamford, Connecticut.

Benny and Alice would have celebrated their thirty-sixth wedding anniversary that March. Though Benny's work kept them frequently apart and, like most long-term marriages, it had its share of stresses and strains, it was a close and loving relationship, and the loss affected Benny deeply.

Benny filled the void the only way he knew how: by keeping himself busy performing. He had been booked to play a benefit for a hospital in New Jersey the day after Alice was cremated and decided to go ahead with it as scheduled. Later that week he appeared at another benefit for Hymie Schertzer at the Rainbow Room. Benny still drew large audiences, and there were constant phone calls from bookers and promoters. After Alice died, he began to accept more of these offers, and the late 1970s and early 1980s saw him become increasingly active, guesting with symphony orchestras in the United States and Europe and playing jazz with small pickup groups that included musicians like John Bunch, Warren Vaché and the saxophonists Buddy Tate and Scott Hamilton.

Though Benny confided to his friend and discographer Russ Connor that he thought he was performing "cocktail lounge music" now and found little enjoyment in it, at other moments he seemed as enthusiastic as ever and continued to challenge himself with the same high standards of performance he had always done his best to live up to. "I always try to play well," he maintained in an interview published on his seventieth birthday. "I think you're always striving for something, whatever it is. I do simply because one has to. When you give up, then you've had it." And in typical Goodman fashion, what he demanded of himself he also demanded of his musical associates.

"He used to poke fun at Teddy Wilson because of what he felt was Teddy's deterioration into a much more simple, cocktaily kind of player than he had been at one time," recalls Loren Schoenberg, the saxophonist who began working in the Goodman office in 1980. "I remember being in a limousine with Benny riding to a concert they did together in Carnegie Hall in 1982 and Benny telling me how he was going to light a fire under Teddy's ass to goose him. During the rehearsal he tried to get Teddy to play some different tunes than they usually did when they got back together. Benny and Teddy weren't speaking at that point, so Benny said to me while the three of us were sitting backstage, 'Loren, ask Teddy if he wants to play "China Boy,"' and Teddy turned to me and said, 'Tell Benny I don't play "China Boy" anymore.' It was really nuts. During the rehearsal Benny called 'You Go to My Head,' which Teddy had recorded back in 1938 and Benny had played on broadcasts. It's a difficult tune, and Teddy was having a hard time with it. But what resulted was a fresh Teddy Wilson. Some real stuff came out. Of course, by the time of the concert they forgot all about it and went back to doing all the usual things.

"I think this sort of experience had something to do with the ennui Benny occasionally felt. I also think Benny was a little mixed up about who he was, whether he was an English country gentleman or the Chicago kid. And coupled with his deep involvement with classical music, all of this translated into a little bit of condescension about jazz that was tempered by the realization that a jazz player is what he was and jazz was what had made him great. It was a fascinating mixture of attitudes."

Toward the end of 1982 Benny met Carol Phillips, a dynamic, strikingly attractive woman who ran the highly successful Clinique cosmetics and skin care products company, and they began a close personal relationship that continued to the end of his life. "I had danced to Benny's music as a young girl when he was at the Pennsylvania Hotel," she recalls. "But we met for the first time at a party at the house of an old friend who had been a great friend of Alice's, and we immediately took to one another. Benny was lonely. His beloved family was elsewhere, and we began to spend a lot of time together." Though he was now in his early seventies, Benny continued to be attractive to women, and after one of his concerts there would frequently be a procession of older female admirers visiting him backstage in his dressing room. "But Carol was different," Loren remembers. "She was vital and vibrant and a superexecutive, and she didn't take any stuff from him. She was a very big influence on Benny and deserves a lot of credit for bringing him back to life."

"Benny had a certain confidence in me because, for one thing, he knew I wasn't after his money, and that mattered to him terribly." Carol laughs. "I remember when he telephoned his daughter Benjie and told her, 'I've got a new girl—and she's a tycoon in her own right!' It was hilarious. My refusal to marry him was also very helpful. At some point he said to me, 'I suppose we should talk about getting married,' and I said, 'Listen, as far as I'm concerned, we *are* married, but I hate paper work.' And Benny said, 'Oh, I think that's wonderful.' I didn't want to get mixed up with his money and his family. I had my own family and my own obligations, and knowing how Benny was, I could see nothing but strain coming out of it."

As Benny moved into his seventies, the honors and awards became even more plentiful than before. He was inducted into the National Broadcasters Hall of Fame in 1980 and honored along with David Rockefeller by the ICD Rehabilitation and Research Center, invited to play a White House banquet for Jordan's King Hussein in 1981 and in 1982 received both an honorary Doctor of Music from Yale and a Lifetime Achievement Award from the Kennedy Center in Washington for his contribution to the performing arts.

The other recipients of the Kennedy Center honors that year included Gene Kelly, Eugene Ormandy, the eighty-six-year-old actress Lillian Gish and the ninety-five-year-old Broadway director George Abbott, almost all of whom had long since retired. Whether Benny was beginning to think about retiring had become a standard item on an interviewer's list of questions and was always answered with a resounding no. "I think a lot of people nowadays feel as if they're in good shape and they might as well do what they can do," he explained. "You give a lot of people pleasure, and that's always desirable." Benny remained active and continued to impart a great deal of pleasure to his fans, but his health continued to decline, and that was starting to have a noticeable effect on what he was able to accomplish.

A 1982 tour of the European summer jazz festival circuit fronting Scott

Hamilton's band was marked by the last-minute cancellation of a concert in London and a substandard performance in Bad Segeberg that was trounced by the German press. "The agents were calling the office from Europe wanting to know what was going on," Loren remembers. "Benny was in a bad mood and acting strange. He wouldn't play with the band half the time. He'd wave them out and just play duets with the guitarist Chris Flory. He started screwing with Mel Lewis, putting him at the other end of the bandstand. The guys were so angry with him they ignored him at the restaurant at the airport while he waited to be asked to join them. Then Muriel Zuckerman and I suddenly got word we were fired."

Benny returned home the end of July and cut back drastically on his bookings. Over the next ten months he played only sixteen engagements, the last a combined classical and jazz concert with André Previn and the Pittsburgh Symphony on May 3, 1983. A June chamber music recital at Manhattanville College was canceled because of an aching shoulder. Benny was unable to appear at a private party he had scheduled for August. Plans for a tour of Japan were abandoned. Health problems also caused him to cancel dates in Pennsylvania and Florida that fall.

He was having trouble with one of his knees. Arthritis afflicted his hands, and though he exercised them constantly, the stiffness interfered with his ability to finger the clarinet. And his back condition was acting up again, making it impossible for him to sleep more than a few hours at a stretch.

"It was a particularly bad period," Carol Phillips remembers. "He was in pain all the time. Benny was always in search of some relief from his difficulties, and if he heard about some new kind of orthopedic or rheumatoid person, he would entertain the possibility of a new sort of treatment. I don't know how many different treatments I saw him through. While he was up in Stamford, he went to see a new physician who X-rayed his spine and found a small strange bubble lodged in his aorta. It was fantastic luck that he happened to go to that doctor and that doctor happened to X-ray him because otherwise the bubble would have exploded and he would have died. Benny knew I was having dinner with my sister that evening, and it was so typical of his character that when he called me from Connecticut, he simply said very calmly, 'Well, in a few days I'll be having surgery for that little thing they found.' I had no idea how serious it really was."

Benny was admitted to New York University Hospital on November 23, 1983. "We stayed in the hospital for four days while he was being prepped," Carol recalls. "Benny was a very good patient, but he didn't want anybody to know about it. He didn't tell his sisters. He didn't tell his daughters. And he said, 'I don't want it in the papers.' It was a very long surgery that lasted about six hours; then he was in intensive care for several weeks. One of his friends had tipped the press, and there were flowers and phone calls and suitcases full of mail. Frank Sinatra called. Some of the letters were simply addressed to 'The King of Swing, New York City.' Benny was funny about attention. You never knew how he was going to respond to strangers coming up to him in public. Sometimes it was with great warmth, and sometimes it was with cold fury. But his friend probably did the right thing because all this attention came at a pretty good time. It was kind of a balm for him. However, there were also some fans who laid siege at the door and insisted on trying to get in to see him. They thought they owned him. After several weeks in intensive care his wonderful friend Dr. Arthur Localio and his wife took him from the hospital to their farm in Deerfield, Massachusetts, where it was peaceful and beautiful, and kept him quietly there for two weeks, and then he came home for Christmas."

That January there was a second operation to implant a pacemaker. Then Benny continued the long period of recuperation. "We spent the weekends in the country," Carol remembers. "There were frequent visits to St. Martin, sometimes long weekends, sometimes a week, sometimes a fortnight. Benny saw his friends, good buddies like Bob Peary, who was head of the Rothschild Bank, the rare book dealer John Fleming and Charles Ryskamp, who was head of the Morgan Library. He talked on the telephone. Benny was a big phone talker early in the morning. He must have spoken with Morton Gould every other day. He did various things with various people. He loved to go salmon fishing. He was nuts about sports, and it was a real date for him when the Mets or the Red Sox were playing. He also loved tennis and boxing. He was so crazy about prizefighting I would forbid him to watch it because he got too excited. He went in the ring with them, and he did the same thing with baseball. He was the coach, and he told them how to do it. I used to say to him, 'Is Davey Johnson or you the manager? Where's the salary if you're the manager? Where is it, Benny?' He shuffled around his office. For reasons of his health he also swam every day. That was important to him and took up a lot of time. And of course, he also played every day. He wasn't performing, but he continued to do his scales. Benny didn't have respect for musicians who didn't do their scales every day. He thought it was a crime that Artie Shaw had stopped doing his scales. So the days went very fast."

By the spring of 1984 Benny was feeling good enough to make a few public appearances without his clarinet. He attended a ceremony at the Waldorf-Astoria to receive an award from the Songwriters Hall of Fame and was greeted with a standing ovation. Following the death of Count Basie on April 26, he taped some brief reminiscences for CBS television. On June 7 he attended the Harvard University commencement to receive an honorary degree along with King Juan Carlos of Spain and Teddy Kollek, the mayor of Jerusalem.

Though Benny was not yet ready to perform in public, occasionally, when he was feeling up to it, he would invite someone over to play with him for a few hours. But his health was still fragile, and sometimes even this got to be more than he could handle. "One day after lunch Benny was telling me how they discovered he had a heart condition, and I said, 'My God, you're not trying to play, are you?' " Jim Maher recalls. "The possibility that he was alarmed me greatly because playing the clarinet isn't like going for a walk. The pressure puts an enormous amount of exertion on the lungs and on the heart. Benny answered, 'Well, you know, some days I feel pretty good. Bob Wilber came up about a week ago, and we played some duets.' But then he said, and I still remember how it scared the hell out of me, 'And that night I almost died.' So any kind of playing was a very risky piece of business for him."

Despite the serious risks, Benny was starting to think about going back to work. Loren Schoenberg, who returned to the Goodman office about this time, remembers: "His spirits were up. The combination of the pacemaker and his relationship with Carol Phillips had gotten everything moving in a positive direction. Though Benny had never completely stopped practicing and playing, I think that after the heart surgery he was scared that the pressure of performing in public would be too much for him. For Benny, playing in public was like an athletic endeavor. There was a lot of physical and psychological stress, and he knew that he would never be able to hold himself in check. By the time I came back into the picture, Benny had already made up his mind that he was going to get past that fear and start performing again, and he went at it like an athlete getting into shape. Then, like a prizefighter doing his preliminaries, he began to do some sitting in."

On February 15, 1985, while attending a dinner given by the Chicago Historical Society to mark the opening of an exhibit about the city's musical history, Benny borrowed a clarinet, pulled a mouthpiece out of his pocket and joined the house band on "Sweet Georgia Brown." "I guess it sounds as if I'm disabled, doesn't it?" he confided to John McDonough the next morning. "Well, I'm not. In fact, I feel a hell of a lot better. I've just taken my time. But I am anxious to get back to work." Three weeks later, to everyone's surprise, he accepted an offer to play the wedding reception of a friend's daughter in New Jersey. "His playing is brilliant," Russ Connor writes of the videotape of the forty-five-minute performance, "effortless, faultless, inspiring. He takes blazing, extended choruses in the uptempo tunes, emotional soli in the ballads; the sidemen are visibly impressed. . . . In [my] view, Benny had not played this well . . . through the late '70s and early '80s."

That spring the producer George Wein encouraged Benny to take part in the tribute to John Hammond he was putting together for the 1985 Kool Jazz Festival in New York. "Benny kept putting Wein off and changing his mind," Loren remembers. "He was going in and out of the hospital all the time at this point. Nobody knew what was wrong with him, but he kept getting sick. But then the night of the concert he decided to do it.

"There had been a serious estrangement between Benny and Hammond after John published his autobiography, *John Hammond on the Record,* in 1977 and gave his side of what happened on the 1953 tour with Louis Armstrong. There might have been a bit of a rapprochement between them when Alice died the next year. I would see John and he would ask how Benny was, and I would mention this to Benny, but there was no real contact. Then I remember one day Benny was opening his mail and John or his wife, Esme, had sent him some photographs of the two of them with Alice, and that was kind of a peace offering. And then, as John's own health began to fail, they would talk on the telephone. I don't believe they saw each other very much, hardly at all, but by the time of the concert at least they were communicating. Without a doubt the fact that this was a tribute to John had something to do with Benny's decision to put in an appearance. It was a confluence of things. Benny *was* going to appear somewhere, and here was this tribute to John Hammond, and that was the perfect place to do it."

The June 25 concert at Avery Fisher Hall was Benny's first real public performance in over two years. Sadly and rather ironically, Hammond had suffered a stroke two weeks before and was unable to attend. The audience had not been told Benny would be playing, and when he walked onstage with his clarinet at the end of the first half of the program, he was greeted, the *New York Times* reported, "with the kind of cheers he was accustomed to when he was leading his band in the 1930's and 40's and was 'The King of Swing.'" Backed by a strong rhythm section that included George Benson and the pianist Dick Hyman, he moved softly and somewhat tentatively through "Lady Be Good" and "Body and Soul." Then he was joined by Scott Hamilton and the trumpet player Harry Edison and began heating things up a bit with "Back Home in Indiana." The cheers grew even stronger as he swung the group into "Don't Be That Way" and, introducing "Stompin' at the Savoy" as a countermelody, built to a killer-diller climax that was the dramatic high point of the evening. "Benny played well, not extraordinarily well, but it was a watershed moment," Loren recalls. "He was on the mend and he was happy to be back out there again, just like an athlete who had been written off because of bad health and makes a successful return."

Shortly after the Hammond tribute Harvey Sampson, a close friend of Benny's who thought he needed to get back to work, arranged a dinner at the Four Seasons with Sol Linowitz, the former chairman of the Xerox Corporation and a major benefactor of the Public Broadcasting System. "At some point Sol moved his chair back and asked me, 'Is Benny well enough to do a PBS special?'" Carol Phillips recalls. "I said, 'Well, PBS in San Francisco has been wanting him to do something, and that didn't pan out, so I don't know. There's no reason why he can't if he feels like it.' The doctors hadn't told Benny that he couldn't play. What they did tell him was that an aneurysm results from the thinning of the wall of the heart, and obviously additional strain is additional risk, but then so is life. And Sol said, 'Well, if it isn't medically incorrect, I'm going to see if we can do this.' A wonderful guy at PBS named Jack Samath got together with Benny, and they began to work up an outline for a one-hour program that would be used as a PBS fund raiser. Jack was so responsive to everything they discussed, and the whole thing evolved very quickly."

There would be a few small group performances, they decided, and several guest artists, but most of the program would be devoted to Benny leading a big band through some of the vintage arrangements that had established his original popularity. The show would be shot before a live audience, and in a further return to his Swing Era roots, Benny insisted that provisions be made for dancing. Since putting in a dance floor meant cutting back on the number of tables available for the corporate underwriters of the show, this eventually caused some serious logistical problems. "Rationing those tickets was murder." Carol laughs. "And then Benny kept thinking of people he wanted to invite, and he could never understand why a table meant for eight couldn't seat sixteen." The most immediate problem, though, was how to get a good big band together on such short notice for this extremely important and highly visible event.

"Dick Hyman started hiring a band with Walt Levinsky and Al Klink and Bernie Privin and all those great studio guys who used to work for Benny," Loren remembers. "And because everyone knew him, all he had to do was come down and do a rehearsal or two and they'd have an orchestra for the show. But Benny kept saying he didn't want to play with them. He felt that studio musicians are always looking at their watches and wouldn't want to put in the time to make it more than a cursory thing. On top of which there were these whole multilayered psychodramas he had been through with every one of them.

"Benny once said something very revealing to me. He had been asked to appear with a big band and wasn't interested, and he said, 'Well, you know, it's so much work getting a band together. You've got to get all the musicians. You've got to rent a rehearsal hall. . . .' And then in the middle of this list of things, he said, 'You've got to get everybody mad at you.' He felt he had to get everybody mad at him. He really did. And they did get mad at him. I wouldn't say Benny wanted it that way, though all his bands were tense and a certain amount of tension does put everyone on their toes. It was more a matter of being resigned to the fact that when he took a band through the ropes and drilled them and put them through the incredible kind of intensive rehearsal procedure he insisted upon, of course, they were going to get angry at him. It had to happen. That's the way it had always been and the way it was always going to be. It was an offshoot of the same perfectionism he brought to the clarinet."

Though Loren was still in his twenties, he felt a strong affinity for the music of the Swing Era and had been leading his own part-time swing band for several years, playing some of the scores from the Goodman library Benny had lent him along with other arrangements from the period. The band included a few Goodman alumni like Eddie Bert, Danny Bank and Mel Lewis but largely consisted of talented younger musicians like Ken Peplowski and Randy Sandke who also shared a love for the idiom. Loren had tried repeatedly to get Benny to come hear the band, but Benny was unresponsive. When he recorded an album for the small Aviva label, he included two Goodman selections and gave Benny a copy. "He made a few very good comments," Loren recalls. "He said 'Wrappin' It Up' was too fast and the title tune 'That's The Way It Goes' was too slow, and he was right. But that was it. He never mentioned it again.

"Benny kept telling me he wasn't interested in playing with the musicians Dick Hyman was putting together for the show and was thinking about squelching the whole thing. Of course, I'm dying to say to him, 'Well, *I've* got a band!'—and of course, he knew it. We would play these games with each other. A big part of Benny would be the games. But I had learned that you never asked Benny for anything and you never volunteered an opinion, so I didn't say a word. Then Benny started calling me at the office from his apartment, and my record would be playing in the background. 'I don't know what to do,' he would say. 'I wonder what I should do.' I could hear 'Wrappin' It Up' in the background, but I didn't say a word. I wasn't going to give him the satisfaction. Then Benny would tell me to come up to the apartment, and the record wouldn't be playing, but I'd see it prominently displayed somewhere in the room. And then he started asking me questions about the people in the band without ever indicating he was interested in using them. 'You have a girl trumpet player? Who's this Chuck Wilson? Who's Ken Peplowski? Are they any good?'

"Finally Benny asked me, 'Are you guys rehearsing?' The truth was we weren't rehearsing. We weren't working. But I called everyone on the phone and said, '*Benny* wants to hear the band!' Nobody could really believe he was going to show up. And he had been in and out of the hospital again. He was very mysterious about it, but I'd hear what was going on from his housekeeper. He was back in the hospital the day before we were supposed to hold the rehearsal, but I didn't tell anybody and went ahead with it as planned. We were playing 'Down South Camp Meeting' when like a scene from a movie, he came walking through the door. I was a professional musician, and I had been around Benny a lot, but I have to tell you my knees started shaking. It was an unbelievable experience for everyone. Benny was very nice, very friendly, and he took out his clarinet and started playing along with us. There were several more rehearsals over the next week, which Benny recorded on his ancient Nagra. At one point he put on a tape of my band playing 'Don't Be That Way' and A and B'd it with the 1938 Carnegie Hall concert version. 'Now listen to this. Now listen to your band.' What could I say? We couldn't come near it.

"Benny still hadn't committed himself to anything, and I wasn't going to ask him. The next Friday he asked me to drive him and Carol up to Stamford in his Mercedes, have lunch, then bring the car back. He was in a weird mood by the time we got up there and wasn't talking to either of us. Carol got called away to the telephone during lunch, and then Benny disappeared from the table. I was very uncomfortable and didn't know what to do, so after waiting twenty minutes, I walked back toward the kitchen and found him on his tiptoes in the pantry, eating cookies out of a bakery box. Finally Carol gets off the phone, and we go back out to the porch to have dessert. Dorothy, the housekeeper, brings out the stuff, and Carol says, 'Benny, what happened to the cookies? There's only half of them here.' Benny says, 'Loren ate them.' I just nodded my head. Benny disappeared again, then came back walking his dog, a little poodle named Shimu. He's still not talking to us, but now he begins talking to the dog: 'Hello. How are you? How's your week? My week was fine. Isn't it nice to have everybody here?' Eventually he asks us if we'd like to go swimming, so we change and jump into the pool. And in the course of swimming in Stamford that hot summer afternoon, as he was coming up from the water to get some air, he told me, 'Oh, by the way, I'm going to use your band on the TV show.' "

Now that he had made his decision, Benny hunkered down and began putting the band through a grueling regimen of long and demanding rehearsals. Certainly he wanted to avoid the lack of preparation that had turned the fortieth anniversary Carnegie Hall concert into such a shambles the last time he appeared in New York with a big band. And he may have already been thinking about keeping the band working after the PBS telecast. But something more was also at stake. "I'm convinced Benny knew this would be his swan song, his last big television special," Loren maintains. "It was so important to him that it be done right, not with a studio band or guys he didn't like or not enough rehearsal time." Carol Phillips remembers: "Benny was nervous. He had not had a standing band in many years, nor with one exception had he performed in New York. And he was in questionable health. The whole thing was very, very risky." Yet he was adamant about pushing both the band and himself to the very limit of their endurance.

"We had always talked about those Fletcher Henderson arrangements," Loren recalls, "but once we started rehearsing them, I really began to understand Benny's stature as a bandleader and the real worth of those arrangements, what they really mean. Playing those charts with Benny Goodman was almost like playing a Mozart quintet with Mozart there. The care and precision with which he could dissect them and put them back together again was truly remarkable. He had an intimate knowledge of every note of every part, and he insisted they be played in a very specific way. Take an arrangement like 'Blue Skies,' which was probably his all-time Fletcher Henderson favorite. He made us keep going over and over those opening figures a countless number of times. It wasn't that the band wasn't playing the right notes, but it wasn't playing them precisely the way he wanted them played, with the exact nuances of phrasing. There's a little pickup note in the introduction to 'Don't Be That Way,' a little sixteenth grace note that most people don't even know is there. We spent an entire day on it.

"Now it had the effect of killing us, taking away all our enthusiasm and spontaneity, and as Benny's odd personality quirks began to emerge, the rehearsals turned into little daily psychodramas. But it really got us inside the music. The background figures of 'Blue Room,' for example. Yes, they're simple, but they're so well constructed and melodic and straight to the point that once we got them right, I couldn't get them out of my head and walked around singing and thinking about them. When I mentioned this to Benny, he said, 'Well, genius consists of an infinite patience for detail.' And that's how it was with Benny with everything where he was strong and great. It was in his clarinet playing and the way he led a band and the way he rehearsed. He had that geniuslike capacity for monotonous, repetitive attention to the most minute detail that resulted in all those incredible performances."

Whipping the band into shape placed an enormous amount of strain on Benny himself as well as his sidemen, and there were moments when it was more than his precariously balanced health could tolerate. "There was one rehearsal where we all thought he was going to drop dead," Loren remembers. "He was pushing and pushing and kind of angry and frustrated when he suddenly turned white and looked like he was about to die. At that point it became obvious to us that he was a very sick man. But he looked great the next day, and we forgot about it."

A week before the taping Benny played a warm-up concert at Waterloo Village in Stanhope, New Jersey. It was the first time in seven years he had appeared with a big band, and when he walked out onstage, three thousand fans greeted him with a thunderous standing ovation. Benny was in a wonderful mood, joking with his musicians and smiling broadly at the audience as he put the band through its paces on "King Porter Stomp," "Sometimes I'm Happy" and many of the other Fletcher Henderson classics. As for his own playing, "From his very first notes in his opening theme—so easy, so effortless, so full of grace—it was evident he was still in excellent form [and] remains a model clarinet soloist," one enthralled reviewer reported. Benny was clearly happy to be back and delighted that everything was going so well, and he played one encore after another, not calling it a night until 11:00 P.M., long past the scheduled closing.

"Benny Goodman: Let's Dance, a Musical Tribute," as it was called, was taped on October 7, 1985, at the Marriott Marquis Hotel, a short walk down Broadway from the site of the old Billy Rose Music Hall, where Benny had led his first orchestra. Along with performances by the band, the show offered a warmhearted retrospective of Benny's career. Film clips and still photographs traced his rise to eminence from his impoverished beginnings. Morton Gould, Bobby Short, Frank Sinatra and Bartlett Giamatti, the president of Yale, praised his accomplishments and told some good-humored anecdotes. Rosemary Clooney sang a medley of songs associated with Helen Ward, Martha Tilton and Peggy Lee. A sadly impaired Teddy Wilson, who was dying of stomach cancer, was brought out for a solo. Red Norvo, who had injured his back on the flight in from California and had to come onstage in a wheelchair, also had a featured number. In keeping with the elegiac tone of the evening, Benny dedicated the show to Fletcher Henderson. "Fletcher was one of the great orchestrators of the twenties and early thirties," he explained to the audience, implicitly acknowledging his indebtedness. "The fascination with his arrangements was endless. What I mean is, you heard [one] for the first time and [then when] you'd hear it again, you'd always hear something different. That's why I really thought he was a genius. And that's the reason I'm really dedicating this program to [him]."

Perhaps it was because he had just gotten out of a sickbed the day before. Or maybe the thought lay heavily that this was probably his last appearance before a large national audience. But for all the nostalgic good feeling that suffused the evening, Benny was in an especially bad frame of mind. "As full of fun and life as he had been at the Waterloo concert, now he was morose," Loren recalls. "He was in one of his moods, one of his funks, and was acting strange. He sequestered himself in his dressing room and didn't want to see anybody. He told me not to play and had Danny Bank take over my part on baritone. He was kind of mean to the guys in the band. When he walked out onstage, he turned to one of the trumpet players and said, 'Hey, fat face!' before stomping off 'Don't Be That Way.' So what you saw on that TV show was not a smiling band as it was at Waterloo. We were all kind of angry and upset." It had been arranged beforehand that after saying a few words about Benny, Frank Sinatra would join him on "All of Me." But when Benny fed him his cue line, "Oh, say, Frank, why don't we do something?" for some reason or other Sinatra looked at his watch and answered, 'No, I'm sorry. I've got a dinner date, Benny," and headed toward the exit, hitting a note on the piano as he disappeared and telling the band, "Tune up, guys." "We all just put our heads down," Loren says. "Benny had been in a bad mood before, and now this. It put a pall on the evening, and the rest of the night, as I remember it, was an emotional downer."

Despite all the tension and Benny's last-minute substitution of Bob Haggart and Louis Bellson for the regular bass player and drummer, the band gave an excellent account of itself. And if Benny's solos failed to reach the heights one might have hoped for, their energy and enthusiasm were more than one had a right to expect in a man who had passed his seventy-sixth birthday. By the end of the evening Benny was exhausted and soaked in perspiration. But everything considered, the show had gone well, and now that the pressure was off, he recovered his good spirits. After resting for an hour, he and Carol went off to the "small" dinner party he had asked her to arrange at Hubert's restaurant. "By the time he finished inviting the families and a few of the people who had helped out at the office and some old pals and people he ran into on the street, his doctor, his dentist, his lawyer, there must have been forty or fifty names on the guest list," Carol recalls. "When we walked into the restaurant, there was such a marvelous, warming, excited, appreciative reception. Benny was so happy."

Benny was pleased with the show, satisfied with the band and delighted to be back in action again. Encouraged and energized by all the positive things that were happening, he looked at the offers that were starting to come in and began making plans to step up his activities. By way of preparation, over the next few weeks he made several major changes. Before playing his next engagement on December 8, a benefit to raise money for Yale School of Music Scholarship Fund, he eased out Loren Schoenberg, in effect firing him from his own orchestra. "It could have been because the guys still looked to me as the leader, which made it a difficult situation for everyone," Loren speculates. "Or maybe he had just become dissatisfied with my playing, in which case I was in some very good company." Shortly after the concert he also pared the band down to the original instrumentation he had used back in the mid-1930s, dropping the fourth trumpet, third trombone and baritone saxophone. "We had spoken about that," Loren explains. "He wanted to concentrate on the Fletcher Henderson book, which was written for five brass and four reeds, and he felt the added instruments were 'deadwood,' that was the phrase he used." Benny had never much cared for the baritone saxophone anyway. "When he called me up and said he wouldn't be using the baritone anymore, I told him, 'Benny, I've been expecting your call,' " Danny Bank recalls with a smile.

As the bookings began to pile up, those close to Benny became concerned he was taking on more than he could safely handle. "People would ask me, 'Should he be doing all this?' " Carol remembers, "and I would give them the same answer I had learned from him: He had tried the rocking chair, and he didn't like it. Benny really did not have the strength and the stamina and the health to be working that hard. It was obvious to me. And it was obvious to him. He knew he would pay a price, but he didn't care. He knew what he was doing. There was nothing about it he didn't know."

"Years earlier we had been going down the corridor of his apartment house and came across this senile old guy with a cane who was repeatedly walking into the wall," Loren recalls. "Benny said, 'You know who that is?' and told me he used to be president of some big insurance company. And then he said, 'Poor bastard. I'll never wind up like him.' It seemed at the time like a weird thing to say, but he had already made up his mind that he would never become Benny Goodman who couldn't play the clarinet, Benny Goodman who couldn't have a band, Benny Goodman who was too old and sick to do anything anymore. He was not going to wind up like that, and he didn't. He was determined to go out with his boots on, exactly the way he wanted to go, and that's what he did."

There were recurrent health problems, and Benny was frequently out of sorts. Jeff Nissim, who had issued some of Benny's classical recordings and the sound track of the PBS special on his Musicmasters label, remembers that during a recording date with the band in January 1986, "He was having trouble with his back but wasn't taking his pain-killers because he wanted to be sharp, and he was in such pain my wife had to give him massages." Carol Phillips recalls: "Sometimes at dinner parties he was in such severe pain we would have to leave early, slipping out without excusing ourselves, which is why a lot of people never understood his manners." But Benny was doing what he wanted to do and doing it well, and the contentment he derived from that gave him the strength, for the time being at least, to overcome his physical debilitations.

"He looked so well the last year of his life," Carol says. "He was much more handsome than he had ever been before. And he was on top of everything. He was happy and funny and could laugh at himself. As everyone knows, Benny could be such a son of a gun, but he was trying very hard to be a better fellow. It was so attractive. Even John Hammond had to acknowledge the change. The last time I spoke to him before Benny died he said, 'You know, Benny is a lot better fellow now than he used to be.' "

For Danny Bank, Benny had become a much warmer and more accessible human being than when he had played with his band back in the 1940s. "When I began driving him home after the rehearsals, we struck up a very genuine friendship. He took me swimming at his health club across the street from his apartment. He invited me up for duets. Sometimes we stopped off for dinner at an Italian restaurant. I got to know him for the first time, really, as a person, as a man. We talked politics. We talked people. We talked about music. Oh, he had to do his stretching every day, his calisthenics and his swimming. He had to do things to stay alive. But we came to know each other pretty well, and I found him perfect, just right, a mellow old man."

Jess Stacy, who had had a rather stormy relationship with Benny over the years, also noticed the change and reached a kind of rapprochement that put the personal differences of the past to rest. "I talked with Benny for the last time right before he did the PBS show. He wanted me to come back for that, and I told him, 'Benny, I haven't played in so long. I'm too rusty. Thank you very much.' But we reminisced a long time. I said, 'Remember that chorus you took on "Pagan Love Song"? That should be put in a gold frame and hung in the Louvre.' He liked painting, you know, so that meant something to him. We talked for about half an hour, just reminiscing. And he sounded just great. You know, you could never just hate him."

For Jim Maher, Benny grew increasingly contemplative and introspective as he approached his final days. "He began to go more inward than he ever had before in our many conversations. He talked about his childhood. He began to talk about his father. And then, during the last months of his life, he began dropping some hints that he was thinking about doing his autobiography, which surprised the hell out of me. Benny had always said, 'Oh, God, I couldn't stand sitting here hour after hour looking at some guy with a tape recorder in his lap asking me questions.' But one day he mentioned in a rather offhanded way that he wanted to set the record straight. I think he had gotten awfully tired of the image that he was merely a puppet dancing around while John Hammond pulled the strings, and he was right on the threshold of making the decision that the time had come for a summing-up, the equivalent of the sort of summing-up he was also coming to in his life as a musician.

"Sometimes when I went up to his apartment to have lunch, I'd hear him playing behind the door. The last time that happened, which was probably only about a month before his death, I got off the elevator and was about to turn the doorknob when I heard him playing one of the Brahms clarinet and piano sonatas. These are pieces that are especially evocative of the autumnal sense you get in Brahms's music of that period, so much so that I have friends in their sixties and seventies who can't bring themselves to listen to them although they love them. I stood at the door and thought, 'I'm not going to break in on this. I just want to listen.' And I heard Benny playing that music in a way I had never quite heard him play it before. He was not playing for an audience. He was playing for himself. And the music sounded so contemplative—that's the only word I can use—so thoughtful and full of emotion. Benny wasn't just playing Brahms anymore. They were visiting. I swear to God it was that kind of feeling. I was listening to a man who was thinking his way into that time of his life, and the music was so appropriate. It was very poignant and very touching, and Benny played so beautifully."

The sound track album of the PBS special was released in March 1986, the same month the show was aired, and Benny agreed to accompany Jeff Nissim to the National Association of Recording Merchandisers convention in Los Angeles to help promote it. "When Benny appeared at the little booth where our record was displayed, nobody came over, and I was scared to death nothing was going to happen," Nissim remembers. "As it turned out, no one could believe it was really Benny Goodman, but about ten minutes later the crowd was twenty people deep. All the heads of the record companies, all the top people dropped what they were doing and lined up to get his autograph. Benny signed every record, and by now the crowd was so huge we had to have him escorted out.

"NARM presented Benny with a special award at the banquet that evening. He had said he would play something at the ceremony, but he was unhappy with the guitarist who was supposed to back him up and decided at the last minute to go ahead and do it without any accompaniment. He played Charlie Chaplin's ballad 'Smile.' The audience response was respectful but quiet, which was unusual for this crowd. Then he said, 'Well, let me play one other thing for you,' and tore into 'After You've Gone.' He did about six choruses at about a hundred miles an hour. There was a stunned silence when he finished; then everyone literally jumped to their feet and gave him a standing ovation. The people from NARM wrote me it was one of the most unforgettable moments in the entire history of that convention. When I got off the plane in New York, there were all these rock 'n' rollers and heavy metal PR people standing around the carousel, waiting for their luggage. Someone goes up to this kid in an RCA Record jacket and asks him, 'Hey, did you hear any good music?' and he says, 'You won't believe who we heard. We heard Benny Goodman!' Benny would have loved it. Here were these twenty-two-year-old kids who had seen all the big rock acts, and he was the one who knocked them out."

Later that month, a week after doing a show with Frank Sinatra at Radio City Music Hall, Benny flew the band to Ann Arbor for a concert at the University of Michigan. "We both were sick with the flu," Carol recalls. "Benny had no business going out. He was not well enough at all. But he had a date, and he was going to play it." Most of the concert went fairly smoothly, but then toward the end Benny suddenly fell apart and was unable to continue. After calling for "Good-bye," his closing theme, he just stood there in a daze, and the band's singer, Carrie Smith, had to help him offstage. The police and fire department medics were summoned. A half hour later he seemed to come to himself and was taken back to his hotel room, where he fell into a deep sleep. "I never knew whether it was plain exhaustion or because he had the flu and wasn't supposed to fly," Carol says. "But it was a very bad thing and the beginning of the wrong thing."

Benny recuperated in St. Martin for ten days, and by the middle of April he was back in New York, jamming at his apartment, pitching Jeff Nissim about doing a series of small group recordings spotlighting some of the younger soloists in the band, making plans for a growing number of upcoming bookings including an August appearance at the prestigious Mostly Mozart Festival at Manhattan's Avery Fisher Hall. In an interview with the rock-oriented *Pulse* magazine Benny bristled at the insinuation that his music had become passé. "Contemporary, shmentemporary. It doesn't mean a God damn thing. I think I'm a pretty good musician, always have been, and I don't have to change anything. . . . Look, what are you trying to ask me? What is this interview about?" He was similarly short-tempered when the *Wall Street Journal* solicited his comments on the current popularity of so-called ghost bands, orchestras that continued to operate under the names of deceased leaders like Glenn Miller, Count Basie and Duke Ellington. Following a burst of profanity he answered, "I absolutely don't want it. Anything under my name should be me. I'm the product."

That May Benny received honorary degrees from Bard College, Brandeis and Columbia University, whose president extolled him for bringing "distinction and world recognition to American music and musicians." On May 30 he celebrated his seventy-seventh birthday with his family in Stamford. Unlike the birthday party two years before, which had been a large and fun-filled occasion, it was a very small gathering, Carol remembers. "The girls were there, all his daughters and stepdaughters, and maybe their husbands. Benny was not in great shape physically. I had to go off to a sales meeting in California and could only stay a few minutes, and I was worried about leaving him. I knew he was very tired. I knew he was emotionally exhausted. And I knew he was going to overdo it. Maybe he already had some warnings that were right there on his face to read."

The following week, on June 7, Benny played a concert with the band at Wolf Trap in Vienna, Virginia. He was enthusiastic about the date and tried to talk Jeff Nissim into recording it, but toward the end of the performance he once again ran into trouble.

"When I had lunch with Benny four days later he told me that Wolf Trap had been extremely difficult for him," Jim Maher recalls. "He said he had trouble breathing, and by the end of the concert he was faking it, moving his fingers on the keys but not producing a sound. He said he simply could not get his breath. I asked him to start thinking about canceling some of the many concerts he had coming up. He had bookings all the way into the spring of the following year. But he ignored my concern and talked instead about his upcoming appearance at the Mostly Mozart Festival, which he was looking forward to with great enthusiasm. Mostly Mozart was becoming something very special in the world of classical music, a focal point for outstanding musicians, and it had a kind of youthful aura that appealed to Benny. I think it gave him that marvelous sense of being part of the present moment."

Upon returning from California shortly after the Wolf Trap concert, Carol Phillips joined Benny in Stamford and found him "not himself but very peaceful. My birthday was coming up and we had lunch out and it was magnificent weather and the Mets were winning, which was the most important thing that happened that week as far as Benny was concerned."

On June 10, three days after Wolf Trap, Benny drove to New Haven with his lawyer, Bill Hyland, to have lunch with Harold Samuel, director of the Yale University Music Library. "He had already given us some arrangements, and we'd had some conversation about forming a Benny Goodman archive," Samuel recalls, "but Benny had never told me outright that he was going to leave us more material, and I assumed he wanted to come up to talk turkey. But when Hyland called to make the date, he said, 'No, it's just a social visit. Benny has never seen the music library before.' As it turned out, he had already added a codicil to his will in April bequeathing us fifteen hundred arrangements, master tapes of his unissued recordings, about forty scrapbooks and about five thousand photographs.

"We had lunch at Morey's in a private dining room on the second floor I had reserved so Benny wouldn't be bothered by strangers. But as soon as the waiters found out he was there, they went home to get their Benny Goodman records so he could autograph them. Benny was in good spirits, very congenial and very pleasant. We didn't talk about the archive at all or any of his career activities. Most of the conversation was about fishing. That morning the *New York Times* had reported that the Yale president, Bartlett Giamatti, had accepted an offer to become commissioner of the National League, and I went into a long diatribe about how if he was going to leave Yale, at least he should be doing it to become head of the Carnegie or Ford Foundation, where he could continue to be a spokesman for higher education. Benny laughed and said, 'Aw, anyone can do that. It takes a special person to be a baseball commissioner.' After lunch we came back to my office, and I showed him some photographs taken of him in the recording studio in the 1940s or '50s. He enjoyed that tremendously, going through them piece by piece and having an awfully good time reminiscing. Benny had to walk slowly because of his chronic back problem, but other than for that there was no sign of any illness, no indication whatsoever that in a couple of days he would pass away."

Russ Connor spoke to Benny that evening and found his speech distressingly thick and hesitant. Benny admitted it had been a very long day and he was tired but dismissed Connor's concern that maybe he was pushing himself too hard. By the next morning he seemed to have recovered. He agreed to do a ten- or fifteen-minute radio interview from his office and ended up answering questions from the call-in audience for almost three-quarters of an hour. The following morning he had a long talk on the telephone with Jim Maher about a major piece the *New York Times Magazine* wanted to commission as part of a series on seminal American artists and called Jeff Nissim with some good news about the Mostly Mozart Festival. "Get this!" Nissim remembers his saying. "I'm the first concert to sell out. In all my years I've never had this kind of thing happen to me in classical music. There's such a demand for tickets they want me to do an extra show." "He was like a kid," Nissim recalls.

That night Benny took Carol and some friends out to dinner to celebrate her birthday, going to a new supper club called Mr. Sam's so he could check out the singer Marlene VerPlanck as a possible substitute for Carrie Smith for his upcoming concert in Chattanooga. "It was a terribly rainy night," Carol remembers, "and the club was near the apartment I kept, though I lived with Benny on Sixty-sixth Street. I said to him, 'It's so wet out, don't you just want to go back to my place?' but he said, 'No, I want to go home.' I could see things were not right.

"The next day was Friday, and we planned to spend the weekend in the country. When Benny got up that morning, he said rather calmly, 'You know, I have quite a pain in my back. Would you rub it for me?' I asked him if he thought he ought to see a doctor, but he didn't want to. Benny's habit was to do his scales, eat breakfast and then rest awhile. I said I would go to the office and touch bases, get the car and the groceries for the country, then pick him up around two o'clock. I hurried through my work, bought a bunch of groceries and was picking up the car at my apartment house when the doorman told me, 'Mr. Goodman's housekeeper is trying to reach you.' I said, 'Is there trouble?' He said, 'Something bad.' I left the groceries in the lobby and ran the blocks to his home.

"Benny was still alive when I got there, but he was pretty far gone. His eyes were already glazed. He was sitting on the sofa in his study. He had been playing Mozart. He was still holding his clarinet. I called nine-one-one and the doctor downstairs, and everybody showed up at once. But it was too late."

At approximately two thirty-five on the afternoon of June 13, 1986, two weeks past his seventy-seventh birthday, Benny Goodman died of a heart attack.

"I'm sure he knew he was having the attack that morning when he asked me to rub his back," Carol maintains. "But he had lived with symptoms so profound and implicit of trouble for so long that he didn't make much of a fuss about them when they came along in order. There was such a stoicism about Benny and such a courtesy, too. He never wanted to load it up on you. It happened so suddenly, and it was sad, sad, sad to see it was over and to know that the live music wouldn't be played anymore. But when you think about it, he had such a fabulous life. And despite all the pain, everything had been going his way those last two years and he was having such a wonderful time.

"Benny did not believe in an afterlife. He felt you're here and that's it. Churches were of architectural or acoustical interest for him, but that was all. He had long since told me he wanted to be buried quickly without a big formal funeral."

On the afternoon of June 15 Benny was buried at Long Ridge Cemetery in Stamford. About forty family members and close friends attended the private ceremony. There was a twenty-minute nonsectarian service at the graveside. His daughters and stepdaughters read short passages from the Bible, and his attorney and good friend Bill Hyland delivered a brief eulogy. Then Benny was lowered into the ground in a plain wooden casket and laid to rest beside his wife, Alice.

The family discouraged requests to hold a public memorial service. But the Mostly Mozart concert Benny was to have played on August 18 was dedicated to his memory. And on October 31 the American Jazz Orchestra, a repertory orchestra of top New York musicians, including a number of Goodman veterans, played an evening of his music at Cooper Union and a new composition written in his honor. On November 8, 150 friends and relatives gathered at the Century Club in New York to celebrate his memory with cocktails and dinner and some warm personal reminiscences. There were also film clips of Benny in performance and excerpts of an interview with André Previn. Questioned about the ongoing appeal of his music, Benny reflected, "Sometimes I think it is nostalgia, and then I listen to the records and say, 'No, it isn't—absolutely not.' "

All the recordings Benny made for Victor during the glory days of the Swing Era still remain in print. Much of the Columbia material is also still available. The many hours of unreleased performances Benny bequeathed to Yale are being commercially issued on Musicmasters to help finance the Benny Goodman archive. On January 16, 1988, fifty years to the day after his historic Carnegie Hall concert, Bob Wilber led a big band through a re-creation of the original program before a sold-out audience that overflowed onto the Carnegie stage. A lifetime of music making that spanned close to seven decades—that began in the Chicago slums, reached its peak in the Swing Era frenzy of the 1930s and continued to forge ahead during the many years that followed, surviving every musical revolution and shift in popular taste and all the waxing and waning of critical opinion—isn't over yet. The music itself lives on.

Sources

CHAPTER ONE: The Kid in Short Pants

Balliett, Whitney. *American Musicians*. New York: Oxford University Press, 1968.
Berkow, Ira. *Maxwell Street*. Garden City, N.Y.: Doubleday & Company, 1977.
————. Author's interview, August 1, 1989.
Britton, Gertrude Howe. *The Boy Problem in the 19th Ward*. Chicago: h.p., 1920.
————. Letter to William C. Graves, December 4, 1925.
————. Letter to William Graves, December 22, 1925.
————. Letter to Julius Rosenwald, November 18, 1929.
————. Letter to Raymond S. Rubinow, December 27, 1929.
Condon, Eddie, with Thomas Sugrue. *We Called It Music*. New York: Henry Holt and Company, 1947.
Dance, Stanley. "Freddy Goodman." *The World of Earl Hines*. New York: Charles Scribner's Sons, 1977.
————. *Buster Bailey: All about Memphis*. Felsted Records, 1958.
————. "Conversation with Benny Goodman." *Jazz* (November–December 1963).
Davis, Allen F., and Mary Lynn McCree, eds. *Eighty Years at Hull House*. Chicago: Quadrangle Books, 1969.
Deffaa, Chip. "Jimmy McPartland's Story. Part One." *Mississippi Rag* (July 1987).
Feather, Leonard. *The Encyclopedia of Jazz*. New York: Bonanza Books, 1960.
Freeman, Bud, with Robert Wolf. *Crazeology*. Urbana and Chicago: University of Illinois Press, 1989.

————. *You Don't Look Like a Musician.* Detroit: Belamp Publishing, 1974.

————. Interview with Helen Oakley Dance, Smithsonian Jazz Oral History Project, n.d.

Gayer, Dixon. " 'Chicago Style All Bunk,' Bud Freeman Asserts, 'Ain't No Such Animal.' " *Down Beat* (December 1, 1942).

Goodman, Benny, with Irving Kolodin. *The Kingdom of Swing.* New York: Stackpole Sons, 1939.

————. "My Ten Favorite Clarinetists." *Music and Rhythm* (October 6, 1941).

————. Interview for *First Person Singular*, 1962.

Hadlock, Richard. *Jazz Masters of the Twenties.* New York: Collier Macmillan, 1965.

Hinton, Milt, and David G. Berger. *Bass Line: The Stories and Photographs of Milt Hinton.* Philadelphia: Temple University Press, 1988.

Hodes, Art. Interview with Don De Michael. Smithsonian Jazz Oral History Project, February 1979.

Hovde, Jane. *Jane Addams.* New York: Facts on File, 1989.

Howe, Irving. *World of Our Fathers.* New York: Harcourt Brace Jovanovich, 1976.

Hull House. Letter of appeal, July 18, 1922.

Hull-House Maps and Papers. New York: Thomas Y. Crowell & Company, 1895.

Kalma, Vic. "King of Swing Still Reigns." *Newark* (N.J.) *Sunday Star-Ledger,* September 15, 1985.

Knauss, Zane. *Conversations with Jazz Musicians.* Detroit: Gale Research Company, 1977.

Koval, Patricia O'Brien. "School Board Forced to Face the Music." *Chicago Sun-Times,* May 18, 1972.

Maher, James T. Author's interview, August 11, 1989.

Mares, Paul. "Leon Rappolo as I Knew Him." *Jazz Quarterly,* n.d.

McCarthy, Albert, and Alun Morgan, Paul Oliver, and Max Harrison. *Jazz on Record.* London: Hanover Books Ltd., 1968.

McPartland, Jimmy. Author's interview, August 31, 1987.

Metronome. "Freeman—A Market Report." March 1956.

Piazza, Tom. Interview with Benny Goodman, n.d.

Pollack, Ben. " 'Ten Years of Good Bands and Bad Breaks!" *Down Beat* (October 1936).

Rodin, Gil. "Rodin Tells of Goodman's Short-Pants Days & The Louie-Oliver Duets." *Down Beat* (November 1937).

Rust, Brian. *Jazz Records 1897–1942.* New Rochelle, N.Y.: Arlington House, 1978.

Shapiro, Nat, and Nat Hentoff. *Hear Me Talkin' to Ya.* New York: Rinehart and Company, Inc., 1955.

Simon, George T. *The Big Bands.* New York: Macmillan Company, 1967.

————. *Glenn Miller and His Orchestra.* New York: Thomas Y. Crowell, 1974.

Smith, Charles Edward. "The Austin High Gang." In *Jazzmen*, ed. Frederic Ramsey, Jr., and Charles Edward Smith. New York: Harcourt, Brace & Company, 1939.

Stearns, Marshall W. *The Story of Jazz.* New York: Oxford University Press, 1956.

Steiner, John. *Jazz Odyssey,* Vol. II, *The Sound of Chicago (1923–1940).* Columbia Records, 1964.

Sudhalter, Richard. "Benny Goodman: An Interview with the King of Swing." *American Heritage* (November 1981).

————. and Philip R. Evans. *Bix: Man and Legend.* New Rochelle, N.Y.: Arlington House, 1974.

Tobin, Paul. Letter to the author, July 31, 1987.

————. Author's interview, July 1987.

Travis, Dempsey J. *An Autobiography of Black Jazz.* Chicago: Urban Research Institute, 1983.

West, Hollie I. "Benny Goodman: The Jazzman Remembers." *Washington Post,* September 15, 1974.

Williams, Martin. *Jazz Masters of New Orleans*. New York and London: Macmillan Company, 1967.

Winer, Linda. "Benny Toots Music Horn." *Chicago Tribune*, May 18, 1972.

CHAPTER TWO: The Two Bennys

Atkinson, J. Brooks. "The Play." *New York Times*, December 27, 1928.

Avakian, George. *Chicago Style Jazz*. Columbia Records, 1955.

Balliett, Whitney. *American Musicians*. New York: Oxford University Press, 1968.

Barnes, Anthony. *Woodwind Instruments and Their History*, rev. ed. New York: W. W. Norton & Company, Inc., 1962.

Barnet, Charlie, with Stanley Dance. *Those Swinging Years*. Baton Rouge: University of Louisiana Press. 1984.

Blesh, Rudi. *Combo: USA: Eight Lives in Jazz*. Philadelphia, New York and London: Chilton Book Co., 1971.

Carse, Adam. *Musical Wind Instruments*. New York: Da Capo Press, 1965.

Charters, Samuel B., and Leonard Kunstadt. *Jazz: A History of the New York Scene*. New York: Doubleday & Company, 1962.

Chicago Tribune. "Sues Band Leader," n.d.

Chilton, John. *Stomp Off, Let's Go: The Story of Bob Crosby's Bob Cats and Big Band*. London: Jazz Book Service, 1983.

Condon, Eddie, with Thomas Sugrue. *We Called It Music*. New York: Henry Holt and Company, 1947.

Connor, D. Russell. *The Record of a Legend*. Let's Dance Corporation, 1984.

Dance, Stanley. *The World of Earl Hines*. New York: Charles Scribner's Sons, 1977.

———. "Conversation with Benny Goodman." *Jazz* (November–December 1963).

Deffaa, Chip. "Jimmy McPartland's Story. Part One." *Mississippi Rag* (July 1987).

———. "Jimmy McPartland's Story. Part Two." *Mississippi Rag* (August 1987).

Down Beat. "Ben Pollack Suing 7 Leaders?" (November 1, 1939).

———. "An Epic Page from the History of Jazz" (1942).

Emge, Charles. "Bouquets To Ben Pollack, Top Leader-Organizer." *Down Beat* (October 6, 1950).

Ervine, St. John. "The New Play." *New York World*, December 27, 1928.

Feather, Leonard. *The Book of Jazz*. New York: Horizon Press, 1965.

———. *The Encyclopedia of Jazz*. New York: Bonanza Books, 1960.

———. "Jack Teagarden Blindfold Test." *Down Beat* (August 20, 1959).

———. "Ben Pollack Blindfold Test." *Down Beat* (February 14, 1963).

Freeman, Bud, with Robert Wolf. *Crazeology*. Urbana and Chicago: University of Illinois Press, 1989.

———. *You Don't Look Like a Musician*. Detroit: Belamp Publishing, 1974.

———. Interview with Helen Oakley Dance. Smithsonian Jazz Oral History Project, n.d.

Gabriel, Gilbert W. "Gabriel Appraises Piece That Brings Lew Fields Back." *New York American*, December 27, 1928.

Goodman, Benny, with Irving Kolodin. *The Kingdom of Swing*. New York: Stackpole Sons, 1939.

———. Interview for *First Person Singular*, 1962.

Guttridge, Leonard E., and John S. Wilson. *Giants of Jazz: Jack Teagarden*. Time-Life Records, 1979.

Hadlock, Richard. *Jazz Masters of the Twenties*. New York: Collier Macmillan, 1965.

Hammond, Percy. "The Theaters." *New York Tribune*, December 27, 1928.

Jones, Max. *Talking Jazz*. New York: W. W. Norton & Company, Inc., 1988.

Kalman, Vic. "King of Swing Still Reigns." *Newark* (N.J.) *Sunday Star-Ledger*, September 15, 1985.

Kaminsky, Max, with V. E. Hughes. *My Life in Jazz*. New York: Harper & Row, 1963.

Kappler, Frank K., and George T. Simon. *Giants of Jazz: Benny Goodman*. Time-Life Records, 1979.

Kincaide, Deane. Interviews with James T. Maher, August 8 and August 19, 1961.

Knauss, Zane. *Conversations with Jazz Musicians*. Detroit: Gale Research Company, 1977.

Knefler, Joe. "Ben Pollack: From New Orleans to Bop." *Escapade* (n.d).

Littell, Robert. "The Play." *New York Post*, December 27, 1928.

Lockridge, Richard. " 'Hello Daddy' Opens." *New York Sun*, December 27, 1928.

Maher, James T. Author's interview, August 11, 1989.

McCarthy, Albert. *Big Band Jazz*. New York: G. P. Putnam's Sons, 1974.

———, and Alun Morgan, Paul Oliver, and Max Harrison. *Jazz on Record*. London: Hanover Books Ltd., 1968.

McPartland, Jimmy. Author's interview, August 31, 1987.

Melody News. "The Playback." October 1, 1934.

Mezzrow, Milton "Mezz," and Bernard Wolfe. *Really the Blues*. New York: Random House, 1946.

Napoleon, Art. "May It Please You—Thoughts on Ben Pollack." *Jazz Journal* (September 1971).

Piazza, Tom. Interview with Benny Goodman. n.d.

Pollack, Ben. " 'Ten Years of Good Bands and Bad Breaks!' " *Down Beat* (October 1936).

———. " 'Long-Hair' Stumps Rhythm Kings." *Down Beat* (November 1936).

———. " 'Throw Out the Women or We Break Contract!' Mgr. Threatens." *Down Beat* (January 1937).

———. "Love, Money and Drink Split up Pollack's Band of Swing Stars." *Down Beat* (February 1937).

———. "Band Ribs Pollack about $12 Chauffeur." *Down Beat* (March 1937).

Ramsey, Frederick, Jr., and Charles Edward Smith. *Jazzmen*. New York: Harcourt, Brace and Company, 1939.

Rodin, Gil. "Rodin Tells of Goodman's Short-Pants Days & the Louie-Oliver Duets." *Down Beat* (November 1937).

———. "Teagarden's 'Glass & Half' Trombone Was a Killer!" *Down Beat* (December 1937).

———. "Rodin Clears Up a Few Silly Accusations." *Down Beat* (January 1938).

Rollini, Arthur. *Thirty Years with the Big Bands*. Urbana and Chicago: University of Illinois Press, 1987.

Rust, Brian. *Jazz Records 1897–1942*. New Rochelle, N.Y.: Arlington House, 1978.

Shapiro, Nat, and Nat Hentoff. *Hear Me Talkin' to Ya*. New York: Rinehart and Company, Inc., 1955.

Simon, George T. *The Big Bands*. New York: Macmillan Company, 1967.

———. *Glenn Miller and His Orchestra*. New York: Thomas Y. Crowell, 1974.

———. *Simon Says: The Sights and Sounds of the Swing Era 1935–1955*. New Rochelle, N.Y.: Arlington House, 1971.

Smith, Jay D., and Len Guttridge. *Jack Teagarden: The Story of a Jazz Maverick*. London: Cassell, 1960.

Standard Certificate of Death: David Goodman, December 10, 1926.

Stearns, Marshall W. *The Story of Jazz*. New York: Oxford University Press, 1956.

Sudhalter, Richard. "Benny Goodman: An Interview with the King of Swing." *American Heritage* (November 1981).

Teagarden, Jack. "Blue Notes." *Record Changer*. (August 1946).

Variety. "Little Club," May 2, 1928.

———. "Pollack and Weiss Differ," May 9, 1928.

———. "Park Central Hotel," October 3, 1928.

Waters, Howard J., Jr. *Jack Teagarden's Music.* Stanhope, N.J.: Walter C. Allen, 1960.

West, Hollie I. "Benny Goodman: The Jazzman Remembers." *Washington Post,* September 15, 1974.

Chapter Three: The Free-lance Years

The Annals of America, vol. XV, *1929–1939 The Great Depression.* Chicago: Encyclopaedia Britannica, Inc., 1968.

Atkinson, J. Brooks. "The Play." *New York Times,* January 17, 1930.

Boardman, Gerald. *American Musical Theatre: A Chronicle.* New York: Oxford University Press, 1978.

Bolitho, William. "Strike Up the Band." *New York World,* March 29, 1930.

Brooklyn Daily Eagle. " 'The 9:15,' " February 13, 1930.

———. " 'Girl Crazy,' " October 15, 1930.

———. " 'Free for All,' " September 9, 1931.

Brown, John Mason. "The Play," *New York Evening Post,* January 17, 1930.

———. "The Play." *New York Evening Post,* September 9, 1931.

Carmichael, Hoagy, with Stephen Longstreet. *Sometimes I Wonder: The Story of Hoagy Carmichael.* New York: Farrar, Straus & Giroux, 1965.

Carr, Ian, and Digby Fairweather and Brian Priestley. *Jazz: The Essential Companion.* New York: Prentice Hall Press, 1987.

Charters, Samuel B., and Leonard Kunstadt. *Jazz: A History of the New York Scene.* New York: Doubleday & Company, 1962.

Condon, Eddie, with Thomas Sugrue. *We Called It Music.* New York: Henry Holt and Company, 1947.

Connor, D. Russell. *The Record of a Legend.* Let's Dance Corporation, 1984.

Dance, Stanley. *The World of Earl Hines.* New York: Charles Scribner's Sons, 1977.

Dapogny, James. "Red Nichols." In *The New Grove Encyclopedia of Jazz.* London: Macmillan Press Limited, 1988.

Dudley, Bide. " 'The Nine Fifteen Revue.' " *New York Evening World,* February 12, 1930.

Dunning, John. *Tune In Yesterday: The Ultimate Encyclopedia of Old-Time Radio 1925–1976.* Englewood Cliffs, N.J.: Prentice-Hall, Inc., 1976.

Ewen, David. *George Gershwin: His Journey to Greatness.* Englewood Cliffs, N.J.: Prentice-Hall, Inc., 1970.

Feather, Leonard. *The Encyclopedia of Jazz.* New York: Bonanza Books, 1960.

Ferguson, Otis. "The Five Pennies." In *Jazzmen,* ed. Frederick Ramsey, Jr., and Charles Edward Smith. New York: Harcourt, Brace and Company, 1939.

Freeman, Bud, with Robert Wolf. *Crazeology.* Urbana and Chicago: University of Illinois Press, 1989.

Gabriel, Gilbert W. " 'Strike Up the Band.' " *New York American,* January 15, 1930.

———. " 'Free for All.' " *New York American,* September 9, 1931.

Gelatt, Roland. *The Fabulous Phonograph: 1877–1977.* New York: Macmillan Publishing Company, Inc., 1977.

Goodman, Benny, with Irving Kolodin. *The Kingdom of Swing.* New York: Stackpole Sons, 1939.

———. Interview for *First Person Singular,* 1962.

Guttridge, Leonard E., and John S. Wilson. *Giants of Jazz: Jack Teagarden.* Time-Life Records, 1979.

Hadlock, Richard. *Jazz Masters of the Twenties*. New York: Collier Macmillan, 1965.

Hammond, John, with Irving Townsend. *John Hammond on Record*. New York: Ridge Press/Summit Books. 1977.

Hammond, Percy. " 'Free for All.' " *New York Herald Tribune*, September 9, 1931.

Johnson, Grady. *The Five Pennies*. New York: Dell Publishing Company, 1959.

Kaminsky, Max, with V. E. Hughes. *My Life in Jazz*. New York: Harper & Row, 1963.

Kappler, Frank K., and George T. Simon. *Giants of Jazz: Benny Goodman*. Time-Life Records, 1979.

Kemp, Steve. "How to Make Money as a Musician." *Metronome* (October 1934).

Knauss, Zane. *Conversations with Jazz Musicians*. Detroit: Gale Research Company, 1977.

Koszarski, Richard. *The Astoria Studio and Its Fabulous Films*. New York: Dover Publications, Inc., 1983.

Krupa, Gene. "Drummer's Dope." *Metronome* (March 1938).

Littell, Robert. "The New Play." *New York World*, January 15, 1930.

Lockridge, Richard. "Tentative Travesty." *New York Sun*, January 15, 1930.

Mezzrow, Milton "Mezz," and Bernard Wolfe. *Really the Blues*. New York: Random House, 1946.

New York American. " '9:15 Revue; Bright in Music, Sketches," February 12, 1930.

New York Times. " 'Nine Fifteen Review' Is Noisy and Speedy," February 12, 1930.

———. " 'Girl Crazy' a Lively and Melodious Show," October 15, 1930.

———. " 'Girl Crazy,' " December 28, 1930.

———. "Communism with Music," September 9, 1931.

———. "Benjamin B. Selvin, 82; Longtime Band Leader," July 16, 1980.

Pollack, Arthur. "The Theater." *Brooklyn Daily Eagle*, January 15, 1930.

Pollack, Ben. "Love, Money and Drink Split Up Pollack's Band of Swing Stars." *Down Beat* (February 1937).

Rathbun, Stephen. " 'Nine Fifteen Revue.' " *New York Sun*, February 12, 1930.

———. " 'Free for All' Opens." *New York Sun*, September 9, 1931.

Record Research. "It's a Fact—Mac." April–May, 1957.

Ruhl, Arthur. "The Theaters." *New York Herald Tribune*, January 15, 1930.

———. "Girl Crazy." *New York Herald Tribune*, October 15, 1930.

Rust, Brian. *Jazz Records 1897–1942*. New Rochelle, N.Y.: Arlington House, 1978.

Sanford, Herb. *Tommy and Jimmy: The Dorsey Years*. New Rochelle, N.Y.: Arlington House, 1972.

Sanjek, Russell. *American Popular Music and Its Business*, vol. III, FROM 1900 TO 1984. New York: Oxford University Press, 1988.

Schoenberg, Loren. Author's interview, July 8, 1991.

Schwartz, Charles. *Gershwin: His Life and Music*. Indianapolis: Bobbs-Merrill, 1973.

Shapiro, Nat, and Nat Hentoff. *Hear Me Talkin' to Ya*. New York: Rinehart and Company, Inc., 1955.

Simon, George T. *The Big Bands*. New York: Macmillan Company, 1967.

———. *Glenn Miller and His Orchestra*. New York: Thomas Y. Crowell, 1974.

———. "The Jazz Beat: Red Nichols' Memory Book." *New York Herald Tribune*, August 5, 1962.

Smith, Alison. " 'Nine Fifteen Revue.' " *New York World*, February 12, 1930.

———. " 'Girl Crazy.' " *New York World*, October 15, 1930.

Stearns, Marshall W. *The Story of Jazz*. New York: Oxford University Press, 1956.

Sudhalter, Richard, and Philip R. Evans. *Bix: Man and Legend*. New Rochelle, N.Y.: Arlington House, 1974.

———. "Benny Goodman: An Interview with the King of Swing." *American Heritage* (November 1981).

Teagarden, Jack. "Blue Notes." *Record Changer* (August 1946).

Ulanov, Barry. *A History of Jazz in America.* New York: Viking Press, 1952.

Vance, Joel. *Fats Waller: His Life and Times.* Chicago: Contemporary Books, Inc., 1977.

Variety. "Wall Street Lays an Egg," October 30, 1929.

———. "Woodmansten Inn," May 10, 1932.

"Voorhees, Donald." *Current Biography 1950.* New York: H.W. Wilson Company, 1950.

Waldorf, Witella. " 'Nine Fifteen Revue.' " *New York Evening Post,* February 12, 1930.

Waller, Maurice, and Anthony Calabrese. *Fats Waller.* New York: Schirmer Books, 1977.

Washer, Ben. " 'Free for All.' " *New York World-Telegram,* September 9, 1931.

Watts, Richard Jr. "Sight and Sound." *New York Herald Tribune,* January 22, 1930.

———. " 'Nine Fifteen Review.' " *New York Herald Tribune,* February 12, 1930.

Chapter Four: Ain'tcha Glad?

Albertson, Chris. *Bessie.* New York: Stein and Day, 1972.

Altshuler, Bob. Author's Interview, October 30, 1987.

Berger, Morroe; Edward Berger; and James Patrick. *Benny Carter: A Life in American Music.* Metuchen, N.J.: Scarecrow Press, 1982.

Connor, D. Russell. *The Record of a Legend.* Let's Dance Corporation, 1984.

Feather, Leonard. *The Book of Jazz.* New York: Horizon Press, 1957.

Gehman, Richard. "A Triumph of Enthusiasm." *Esquire* (January 1959).

Goodman, Benny, with Irving Kolodin. *The Kingdom of Swing.* New York: Stackpole Sons, 1939.

———, with Richard Gehman. "That Old Gang of Mine." *Collier's* (January 20, 1956).

Griffin, Chris. Author's interview, August 27, 1987.

Hammond, John, with Irving Townsend. *John Hammond on Record.* New York: Ridge Press/Summit Books. 1977.

———. "The Negro Theatre Flops." *Melody Maker* (June 1932).

———. "John Hammond's New York Letter." *Melody Maker* (November 11, 1933).

———. "BG: Part One." *Down Beat* (February 8, 1956).

Holiday, Billie, with William Dufty. *Lady Sings the Blues.* Garden City, N.Y.: Doubleday & Co., Inc., 1956.

Hughes, Spike. *Second Movement.* London: Museum Press, 1951.

Maher, James T. Author's interview, October 13, 1987.

Shaw, Arnold. *The Street That Never Slept.* New York: Coward, McCann & Geoghegan, 1971.

Chapter Five: Music Hall Rag

Barnet, Charlie. Interview with Patricia Willard. Smithsonian Jazz Oral History Project, April 23, 1978.

Baron, Stanley. Introduction to *Benny: King of Swing.* New York: William Morrow & Co., Inc., 1979.

Berger, Morroe; Edward Berger; and James Patrick. *Benny Carter: A Life in American Music.* Metuchen, N.J.: Scarecrow Press, 1982.

Connor, D. Russell. *The Record of a Legend.* Let's Dance Corporation, 1984.

Down Beat. "Benny Goodman and Orch. Big Success on Broadway" (September 1934).

———. "Dorsey Brothers Picked for NBC Build-Up." (October 1934).

———. "Trip to England for Black and White Orch. Is Off." October 1934.

———. "Dorsey Brothers Have Fast Climb to Fame" (January 1935).

———. "Black and White Band Blocked by English Bookers." (April–May 1935).

Goodman, Benny, with Irving Kolodin. *The Kingdom of Swing.* New York: Stackpole Sons, 1939.

————. with Richard Gehman. "That Old Gang of Mine." *Collier's* (January 20, 1956).

Gottlieb, Polly Rose. *The Nine Lives of Billy Rose: An Intimate Portrait.* New York: Crown Publishing, 1968.

Green, Abel, and Joe Laurie, Jr. *Show Biz from Vaude to Video.* New York: Henry Holt & Co., 1951.

Guttridge, Leonard F. *Giants of Jazz: Jack Teagarden.* Time-Life Records, 1979.

Hammond, John, with Irving Townsend. *John Hammond on Record.* New York: Ridge Press/Summit Books, 1977.

————. "John Hammond's New York Uptown Lowdown." *Melody Maker* (June 16, 1934).

————. "John Hammond's New York Notes." *Melody Maker* (July 14, 1934).

————. "The Black-and-White Band: Its Latest Developments." *Melody Maker* (August 25, 1934).

————. Untitled article. *Melody Maker* (September 29, 1934).

————. "BG: Part Two." *Down Beat* (February 22, 1956).

Levant, Oscar. *The Unimportance of Being Oscar.* New York: G. P. Putnam's Sons, 1968.

Maher, James T. Author's interview, October 13, 1987.

————. Author's interview, October 16, 1987.

————. *The Essential Benny Goodman.* Verve Records, 1964.

Melody Maker. "Dorseys Form Own Band." (June 30, 1934).

————. "Fantastic Band Offered Hylton" (July 7, 1934).

————. "Benny Goodman Black and White Band Offered Contract" (July 21, 1934).

————. "Goodman Fantasy Band nearer England" (August 4, 1934).

————. "Hammond Rubs Salt in Yankee Sores" (May 8, 1935).

Michaud, Arthur. Letter to James T. Maher, February 22, 1960.

Rollini, Arthur. *Thirty Years with the Big Bands.* Urbana and Chicago: University of Illinois Press, 1987.

Rose, Billy. *Wine, Women and Words.* New York: Simon & Schuster, 1968.

"Rose, Billy." *Current Biography 1940.* New York: H. W. Wilson Co., 1940.

Simon, George T. *The Big Bands.* New York: Macmillan Company, 1967.

————. *Glenn Miller and His Orchestra.* New York: Thomas Y. Crowell Co., 1967.

————. *Simon Says: The Sights and Sounds of the Swing Era 1935–1955.* New Rochelle, N.Y.: Arlington House, 1971.

Stearns, Marshall W. *The Story of Jazz.* New York: Oxford University Press, 1956.

Variety. "Jersey Wonder Bar Beats Billy Rose into Cheap Field," April 10, 1934.

————. "Cafes May Use 500 Acts. Route Will Run Coast to Coast," April 24, 1934.

————. "B'Way Niteries Praying for Good Ol' Prohi' Days; Ain't No Drinkin'," May 8, 1934.

————. Advertisement for the Casa Loma band, June 5, 1934.

————. "Billy Rose's Music Hall Is Another New Phase of Show Biz," June 26, 1934.

————. "September Music Survey," October 9, 1934.

————. "October Music Survey," November 13, 1934.

Ward, Helen. Author's interview, April 29, 1987.

————. Author's interview, November 13, 1987.

CHAPTER SIX: Let's Dance: 1

Allen, Walter C. *Hendersonia: The Music of Fletcher Henderson and His Musicians.* Highland Park, N.J.. Walter C. Allen, 1973.

Armistad Log. "Papers of the Fletcher Hamilton Henderson Family." February 1985.

Balliett, Whitney. "Mechanic." *The New Yorker,* (May 26, 1962).

Baron, Stanley. Introduction to *Benny: King of Swing.* New York: William Morrow & Co., Inc., 1979.

Billboard. "Films, Radio Rank High in Survey of Leisure Activity," November 3, 1934.
———. "Research Activities Reveal No Letdown in Radio Homes," December 1, 1934.
Charters, Samuel B., and Leonard Kunstadt. *Jazz: A History of the New York Scene.* Garden City, N.Y.: Doubleday & Co., Inc., 1962.
Connor, D. Russell. *The Record of a Legend.* Let's Dance Corporation, 1984.
Cugat, Xavier. *Rumba Is My Life.* New York: Didier Publishers, 1948.
"Cugar, Xavier." *Current Biography 1934.* New York: H. W. Wilson Co., 1934.
Driggs, Frank. *A Study in Frustration: The Fletcher Henderson Story.* Columbia Records, 1962.
———. "Don Redman, Jazz Composer-Arranger." *Jazz Panorama,* ed. Martin Williams. New York: Collier Books, 1964.
Ellington, Duke. "Jazz as I Have Seen It: Part V." *Swing* (July 1940).
———. "Jazz as I Have Seen It: Part VI." *Swing* (August 1940).
Erwin, Pee Wee, with Warren W. Vache, Sr., *This Horn for Hire.* Metuchen, N.J., and London: Scarecrow Press and Institute of Jazz Studies, Rutgers University. 1987.
Goodman, Benny, with Irving Kolodin. *The Kingdom of Swing.* New York: Stackpole Sons, 1939.
———, with Richard Gehman. "That Old Gang of Mine." *Collier's* (January 20, 1956).
Hadlock, Richard. *Jazz Masters of the Twenties.* New York: Collier Macmillan, 1965.
Hammond, John, with Irving Townsend. *John Hammond on Record.* New York: Ridge Press/Summit Books, 1977.
———. "Negro Theatre Flops." *Melody Maker* (June 1932).
———. " 'Blue Rhythm Band Or Else—!" *Melody Maker* (July 14, 1934).
———. "Smack: A Big Figure in Jazz History." *Down Beat* (March 23, 1951).
———. "BG: Part Two." *Down Beat* (February 22, 1956).
———. *A Study in Frustration: The Fletcher Henderson Story.* Columbia Records, 1962.
Henderson, Horace. Interview with Tom MacCluskey. Smithsonian Jazz Oral History Project, April 9–12, 1975.
Maher, James T. Author's interview, October 13, 1987.
———. Author's interview, October 16, 1987.
———. Author's interview, November, 1987.
———. *The Essential Benny Goodman.* Verve Records, 1963.
———. *The Essential Gene Krupa.* Verve Records, 1964.
McCarthy, Albert. *Big Band Jazz.* New York: G. P. Putnam's Sons, 1974.
Merz, Charles. *The Great American Band Wagon: A Study of Exaggerations.* New York: John Day Co., 1928.
Metronome. Untitled article. August 1934.
Mondello, Toots. Author's interview, September 1, 1987.
Shapiro, Nat, and Nat Hentoff. *Hear Me Talkin' to Ya.* New York: Rinehart and Company, Inc., 1955.
Simon, George T. *The Big Bands.* New York: Macmillan Company, 1967.
———. *Simon Says: The Sights and Sounds of the Big Bands.* New Rochelle, N.Y.: Arlington House, 1971.
Stearns, Marshall W. *The Story of Jazz.* New York: Oxford University Press, 1956.
Ward, Helen. Author's interview, April 29, 1987.
———. Author's interview, November 13, 1987.
Waters, Ethel, with Charles Samuels. *His Eye Is on the Sparrow.* Garden City, N.Y.: Doubleday & Co., Inc., 1951.
West, Hollie I. "Benny Goodman: The Jazzman Remembers." *Washington Post,* September 15, 1974.
Wilson, John S. "Fletcher Henderson." *The Jazz Makers,* ed. Nat Shapiro and Nat Hentoff. New York: Rinehart & Co., 1957.

CHAPTER SEVEN: Let's Dance: 2

Alexander, Willard. Interview with James T. Maher, August 4, 1961.
———. Letter to James T. Maher, August 9, 1961.
———. Program for Memorial Service, St. Peter's Church, September 13, 1984.
Billboard. "Let's Dance," December 15, 1934.
Blesh, Rudi. *Combo: U.S.A.: Eight Lives in Jazz.* Philadelphia, New York, London: Chilton Book Co., 1971.
Connor, D. Russell. *The Record of a Legend.* Let's Dance Corporation, 1984.
Conover, Willis. "Gene Krupa and Buddy Rich." *Metronome* (April 1956).
Crowther, Bruce. *Gene Krupa: His Life & Times.* New York: Universe Books, 1987.
Cugat, Xavier. *Rumba Is My Life.* New York: Didier Publishers, 1948.
Down Beat. "Benny Goodman on Air in Amazing Program" (January 1935).
Erwin, Pee Wee, with Warren W. Vache, Sr. *This Horn for Hire.* Metuchen, N.J., and London: Scarecrow Press and Institute of Jazz Studies, Rutgers University, 1987.
Feather, Leonard. *The Encyclopedia of Jazz.* New York: Bonanza Books, 1960.
Goode, Mort. *Benny Goodman—The RCA Years.* RCA Victor Records, 1987.
Goodman, Benny, with Irving Kolodin. *The Kingdom of Swing.* New York: Stackpole Sons., 1939.
———, with Richard Gehman. "That Old Gang of Mine." *Collier's* (January 20, 1956).
Griffin, Chris. Author's interview, August 27, 1987.
Hammond, John, with Irving Townsend. *John Hammond on Record.* New York: Ridge Press/Summit Books, 1977.
———. "Counterpoint." *Melody News* (November 1, 1934).
———. "BG: Part Two." *Down Beat* (February 22, 1956).
———. "BG: The Conclusion." *Down Beat* (March 9, 1956).
Herndon, Booton. *The Sweetest Music This Side of Heaven: The Story of Guy Lombardo.* New York: McGraw-Hill, 1964.
Lombardo, Guy, with Jack Altshul. *Auld Acquaintance.* Garden City, N.Y.: Doubleday & Co., Inc., 1975.
Maher, James T. Author's interview, October 16, 1987.
———. Author's interview, November, 1987.
———. *The Essential Gene Krupa.* Verve Records, 1964.
Metronome. "Saturday Dancing Party Will Run for Three Hours" (December 1934).
———. "Dancing Party" (January 1935).
Revell, Nellie. "New York Radio Parade." *Variety,* December 4, 1934.
Rollini, Arthur. *Thirty Years with the Big Bands.* Urbana and Chicago: University of Illinois Press, 1987.
Scholl, Warren. "Record Review." *Down Beat* (July 1935).
Simon, George T. *The Big Bands.* New York: Macmillan Company, 1967.
———. "Pick-Ups." *Metronome* (March 1935).
———. "Willard Alexander." *Metronome* (April 1935).
Uneeda. "Let's Dance," November–December, 1934.
Variety. "6-Hour Dance Parade May Be Extended," December 25, 1934.
———. "Ad Agencies' Showmanship," January 1, 1935.
Ward, Helen. Author's interview, April 20, 1987.
———. Author's interview, November 13, 1987.

CHAPTER EIGHT: Big Band, Small Band

Bailey, Mildred. "My Life." *Swing* (July 1940).
Chilton, John. *Giants of Jazz: Bunny Berigan.* Time-Life Records, 1982.
Connor, D. Russell. *The Record of a Legend.* Let's Dance Corporation, 1984.
Dance, Stanley. *Teddy Wilson and His All-Stars.* Columbia Records, 1973.
Down Beat. "Goodman to Make Trip West Soon." July 1935.
Erwin, Pee Wee, with Warren W. Vache, Sr. *This Horn for Hire.* Metuchen, N.J., and
    London: Scarecrow Press and Institute for Jazz Studies, Rutgers University, 1987.
Goodman, Benny, with Irving Kolodin. *The Kingdom of Swing.* New York: Stackpole Sons,
    1939.
———, with Richard Gehman. "That Old Gang of Mine." *Collier's,* (January 20, 1956).
Hammond, John, with Irving Townsend. *John Hammond on Record.* New York: Ridge
    Press/Summit Books, 1977.
———. "Blue Rhythm Band Or Else—!" *Melody Maker* (July 14, 1934).
———. "N.Y. as Backward as Chicago in Swing Music." *Down Beat* (June 1935).
———. "John Hammond's Lowdown." *Melody Maker* (July 20, 1935).
———. "Temperament on the Telephone for Benny Goodman's Benefit." *Melody Maker*
    (September 21, 1935).
———. "Landmark in White Jazz Circles." *Melody Maker* (September 28, 1935).
———. "BG: The Conclusion." *Down Beat* (February 22, 1956).
———. *Billie Holiday: The Golden Years.* Columbia Records, 1962.
Hentoff, Nat. "Dr. Jazz and His Son, the Professor." *New York Times Magazine,* April 14,
    1974.
Katz, Dick. *Teddy Wilson: Statements and Improvisations 1934–1942.* Smithsonian Collection,
    1977.
Melody Maker. August 24, 1935.
Metronome. "Going on Record." October 1935.
Rollini, Arthur. *Thirty Years with the Big Bands.* Urbana and Chicago: University of Illinois
    Press, 1987.
Rust, Brian. *Jazz Records: 1897–1942.* New Rochelle, N.Y.: Arlington House, 1978.
Scholl, Warren. "Record Reviews." *Down Beat* (September 1935).
———. "Record Reviews." *Down Beat* (October 1935).
———. "Release New Records on Mezz Mezzrow and All-Star White and Black Band."
    Down Beat (December 1935–January 1936).
Simon, George T. *Simon Says: The Sights and Sounds of the Big Bands.* New Rochelle, N.Y.:
    Arlington House, 1971.
———. *Giants of Jazz: Benny Goodman.* Time-Life Records, 1979.
Ward, Helen. Author's interview, April 20, 1987.

CHAPTER NINE: On the Road for MCA

Balliett, Whitney. "Bunny Berigan." *The New Yorker* n.d.
Connor, D. Russell. *The Record of a Legend.* Let's Dance Corporation, 1984.
Dance, Helen Oakley. "Goodman's Playing Defies Adequate Description." *Down Beat*
    (August 1935).
Down Beat. "Los Angeles—Hollywood—Pacific Coast" (October 1935).
Erwin, Pee Wee, with Warren W. Vache, Sr. *This Horn for Hire.* Metuchen, N.J., and
    London: Scarecrow Press and Institute of Jazz Studies, Rutgers University. 1987.

Goode, Mort. *Benny Goodman—The RCA Years*. RCA Records, 1986.

Goodman, Benny, with Irving Kolodin. *The Kingdom of Swing*. New York: Stackpole Sons. 1939.

———, with Richard Gehman. "That Old Gang of Mine." *Collier's* (January 20, 1956).

Hammond, John, with Irving Townsend. *John Hammond on Record*. New York: Ridge Press/Summit Books, 1977.

———. "John Hammond Investigates Chicago Style." *Melody Maker* (July 7, 1934).

———. "Counterpoint." *Melody News* (November 1, 1934).

———. " 'Dorsey Brothers Missed Golden Opportunity'—Says Hammond." *Down Beat* (July 1935).

———. "BG: The Conclusion." *Down Beat* (February 22, 1956).

Kappler, Frank K., and George T. Simon. *Giants of Jazz: Benny Goodman*. Time-Life Records, 1979.

Maher, James T. Author's interview, April 11, 1988.

Rollini, Arthur. *Thirty Years with the Big Bands*. Urbana and Chicago: University of Illinois Press, 1987.

Rust, Brian. *Jazz Records: 1897–1942*. New Rochelle, N.Y.: Arlington House, 1978.

Simon, George T. *The Big Bands*. New York: Macmillan Company, 1967.

Stacy, Jess. Author's interview, March 28, 1988.

Sudhalter, Richard M. "Benny Goodman: An Interview with the King of Swing." *American Heritage* (November 1981).

Tenny, Jack. "New York—Hollywood—Pacific Coast." *Down Beat* (September, 1935).

Tynan, John. "Jess Plain Stacy." *Down Beat* (July 11, 1957).

Vy. "Goodman Wakes Up West Coast with 'Swing' Style." *Down Beat* (September 1935).

Ward, Helen. Author's interview, April 20, 1987.

———. Author's interview, November 13, 1987.

Wilson, John S. "It Didn't Mean a Thing, Back Then, If It Had No Swing." *New York Times*, August 24, 1975.

CHAPTER TEN: Swing Is Here

Allen, Walter C. *Hendersonia: The Music of Fletcher Henderson and His Musicians*. Highland Park, N.J.: Walter C. Allen, 1973.

Bushell, Garvin, as Told to Mark Tucker. *Jazz from the Beginning*. Ann Arbor: University of Michigan Press, 1988.

Cesana, Otto. "Swing Is—Well, It's Here." *Metronome* (June 1936).

Connor, D. Russell. *The Record of a Legend*. Let's Dance Corporation, 1984.

Cons, Carl. "Society and Musicians Sit Spellbound by Brilliance of Goodman Band." *Down Beat* (December 1935–January 1936).

———. "What Is Swing?—Here Is The Answer!" *Down Beat* (April 1936).

Damai, Paul. " 'Swing? We'll Take Our Old Back Lawn Hammock Any Day.' " *Down Beat* (December 1935–January 1936).

Dance, Helen Oakley. Author's interview, August 3, 1987.

———. "Stuff & Nonsense." *Down Beat* (April 1936).

———. "Stuff and Nonsense." *Down Beat* (May 1936).

Dance, Stanley. "Jimmy Mundy." *The World of Earl Hines*. New York: Charles Scribner's Sons, 1977.

Davis, R. C. "Disagrees on King of Swing." *Metronome* (August 1936).

Down Beat. "Do You Know a Better Word for It Than 'Jazz'?" (August 1934).

———. "Goodman's Music Is a Classic in Modern Idiom" (November 1935).

———. "2nd Rhythm Concert Delights Local 'Cats' & '400' " (April 1936).

Driggs, Frank. *A Study in Frustration: The Fletcher Henderson Story*. Columbia Records, 1962.

Erwin, Pee Wee, with Warren W. Vache, Sr. *This Horn for Hire*. Metuchen, N.J., and London: Scarecrow Press and Institute of Jazz Studies, Rutgers University. 1987.

Feather, Leonard. *The Book of Jazz*. New York: Horizon Press, 1957.

Goode, Mort. *Benny Goodman—The RCA Years*. RCA Records, 1986.

Goodman, Benny, with Irving Kolodin. *The Kingdom of Swing*. New York: Stackpole Sons, 1939.

———. Letter to the Editor. *Life* (November 15, 1937).

Green, Abel. "Swing Stuff." *Variety*, November 5, 1935.

———. "Swing Stuff." *Variety*, December 4, 1935.

———. "Swing It!" *Variety*, January 1, 1936.

Hammond, John, with Irving Townsend. *John Hammond on Record*. New York: Ridge Press/Summit Books, 1977.

———. "Plenty of 'Swing' Talent Hidden in Chicago." *Down Beat* (May 1936).

Hentoff, Nat. "Dr. Jazz and His Son, the Professor." *New York Times Magazine*, April 14, 1974.

Kappler, Frank K., and George T. Simon. *Giants of Jazz: Benny Goodman*. Time-Life Records, 1979.

Ludwig, William F. "Why the Public Likes Swing." *Metronome* (October 1936).

Manone, Wingy, with Paul Vendervoot, II. *Trumpet on the Wing*. Garden City, N.Y.: Doubleday & Co., Inc., 1948.

Melody Maker. "Debunking the Frankenstein of Jazz . . . Swing!" (August 3, 1935).

Metronome. "Fats Waller Demonstrates Swing, Even Defines It" (February 1936).

———. "Swing Still Up in the Air" (March 1936).

Palmer, Robert. "Benny Goodman, Author, Swings for His New Book." *New York Times*, n.d.

Rollini, Arthur. *Thirty Years with the Big Bands*. Urbana and Chicago: University of Illinois Press, 1987.

Rose, David. Author's interview, May 23, 1988.

Rust, Brian. *Jazz Records: 1897–1942*. New Rochelle, N.Y.: Arlington House, 1978.

Shaw, Arnold. *The Street That Never Slept*. New York: Coward, McCann & Geoghegan, 1971.

Simon, George T. *The Big Bands*. New York: Macmillan Company, 1967.

———. "Pick-Ups." *Metronome* (December 1935).

———. "The Best Bands of the Year 1935." *Metronome* (January 1936).

Smith, Charles Edward. "The Street." *Swing Street*. Epic Records, 1962.

Stacy, Jess. Author's interview, March 18, 1988.

Tempo. "Jimmy Mundy" (n.d.).

Time. "Whoa-ho-ho-ho-ho!" January 20, 1936.

Variety. "October Music Survey," November 13, 1935.

———. "America Says 'Let's Dance to the Greatest Swing Band in the Country,'" December 25, 1935.

Voynow, Dick. "Nonsensical 'Spouting-Off' on Swing Amuses Old Swing Musician." *Down Beat* (March 1936).

Ward, Helen. Author's interview, April 20, 1987.

———. Author's interview, November 13, 1987.

Waring, Fred. "The Swing Mania Annoys Me." *Metronome* (September 1936).

[Wright, Gordon.] "Swing, Swing, Oh Beautiful Swing." *Metronome* (February 1936).

CHAPTER ELEVEN: Making It

Balliett, Whitney. "Back from Valhalla." *American Musicians*. New York: Oxford University Press, 1986.
Chilton, John. *Giants of Jazz: Bunny Berigan*. Time-Life Records, 1982.
Dance, Helen Oakley. Author's interview, August 3, 1987.
Erwin, Pee Wee, with Warren W. Vache, Sr. *This Horn for Hire*. Metuchen, N.J., and London: Scarecrow Press and Institute of Jazz Studies, Rutgers University, 1987.
Freeman, Bud. Interview with Helen Oakley Dance. Smithsonian Jazz Oral History Project, n.d.
Goode, Mort. *Benny Goodman—The RCA Years*. RCA Records, 1986.
Goodman, Benny, with Irving Kolodin. *The Kingdom of Swing*. New York: Stackpole Sons, 1939.
———, with Richard Gehman. "That Old Gang of Mine." *Collier's* (January 20, 1956).
———. Interview with Mr. and Mrs. Robert C. Franklin for the Oral History Research Project, Columbia University, January 1959.
Griffin, Chris. Author's interview, August 27, 1987.
Kappler, Frank K., and George T. Simon. *Giants of Jazz: Benny Goodman*. Time-Life Records, 1979.
Rollini, Arthur. *Thirty Years with the Big Bands*. Urbana and Chicago: University of Illinois Press, 1987.
———. Interview with Bob Rusch. *Cadence* (April 1988).
Simon, George T. *The Big Bands*. New York: Macmillan Company, 1967.
———. "Benny Goodman Revisited." *The Big Bands,* 4th Ed. New York: Schirmer Books, 1981.
Stacy, Jess. Author's interview, March 28, 1988.
Ward, Helen. Author's interview, April 20, 1987.
———. Author's interview, November 13, 1987.
West, Hollie I. "Benny Goodman: The Jazzman Remembers." *Washington Post,* September 15, 1974.
Wilson, Teddy. Interview with Milt Hinton. Smithsonian Jazz Oral History Project, September 2, 1979.

CHAPTER TWELVE: Return to the Palomar

Blackburn, Jane. "Hampton's Drummer Plays Vibraphone like Red Norvo." *Down Beat* (September 1936).
Connor, D. Russell. *The Record of a Legend*. Let's Dance Corporation, 1984.
Dance, Stanley. *The Complete Lionel Hampton: 1937–1941*. RCA Records, 1976.
Down Beat. "Goodman Sits In with New York Bands" (June 1936).
———. " 'Jitterbugs' Thrill at N.Y. Jam-Session" (June 1936).
———. "Goodman Signs for 'Big Broadcast' Movie" (July 1936).
———. "What a Band This Would Make! . . . Final Results of All-Time Swing Band Voting" (July 1936).
———. "Goodman Changes Men in His Band" (September 1936).
———. "Negro Press Runs Temperature" (October 1936).
Feather, Leonard. *The Book of Jazz*. New York: Horizon Press, 1957.
———. *The Jazz Years*. New York: Da Capo Press, 1987.
Goode, Mort. *Benny Goodman—The RCA Years*. RCA Records, 1986.

Goodman, Benny, with Irving Kolodin. *The Kingdom of Swing*. New York: Stackpole Sons, 1939.

———, with Richard Gehman. "That Old Gang of Mine." *Collier's* (January 20, 1956).

Griffin, Chris. Author's interview, August 27, 1987.

Hammond, John, with Irving Townsend. *John Hammond on Record*. New York: Ridge Press/Summit Books, 1977.

———. "Wilson Goes 'Boogie-Woogie' as Benny Relaxes—Trio Records Swing." *Down Beat* (October 1936).

———. "Predicted Race Riot Faced as Dallas Applauds Quartet!" *Down Beat* (October 1937).

Hampton, Lionel, with Bernard Seeman. "Me and Benny Goodman." *Saturday Evening Post* (January 20, 1956).

Kappler, Frank K., and George T. Simon. *Giants of Jazz: Benny Goodman*. Time-Life Records, 1979.

Meeker, David. *Jazz in the Movies*. New York: Da Capo Press, 1981.

New York Times. " 'Big Broadcast of 1937' Sets Paramount Mark," October 29, 1936.

Rollini, Arthur. *Thirty Years with the Big Bands*. Urbana and Chicago: University of Illinois Press, 1987.

———. Interview with Bob Rusch. *Cadence* (April 1988).

Shaw, Arnold. *The Street That Never Slept*. New York: Coward, McCann & Geoghegan, 1971.

Simon, George T. *The Big Bands*. New York: Macmillan Company, 1967.

Ward, Helen. Author's interview, April 20, 1987.

———. Author's interview, November 13, 1987.

West, Hollie I. "Benny Goodman: The Jazzman Remembers." *Washington Post*, September 15, 1974.

Wilson, Teddy. Interview with Milt Hinton. Smithsonian Jazz Oral History Project, September 2, 1979.

Winsten, Archer. " 'The Big Broadcast of 1937' Offers a Wealth of Talent Plus Story." *New York Post*, October 22, 1936.

CHAPTER THIRTEEN: Dancing in the Aisles

Ager, Cecilia. "Going Places." *Variety* (March 10, 1937).

Avakian, George. Author's interview, November 7, 1987.

———. "Benny Goodman, King of Swing, Enjoyed Long Career Before New Style in Modern Music Brought Him Fame." *Horace Mann Record*, November 25, 1936.

Baxter, Danny. " 'Amazing' Only Way to Describe James." *Down Beat* (April 1939).

Billboard. "Paramount, New York," March 13, 1937.

Boston Morning Globe. "New Films," May 21, 1937.

Connor, D. Russell. *The Record of a Legend*. Let's Dance Corporation, 1984.

Crease, Robert P. "Last of the Lindy Hoppers." *Village Voice* (August 25, 1987).

Down Beat. "Is Benny Goodman's Head Swollen?" (February 1937).

———. "Benny Goodman's Head" (May 1937).

Eisenberg, Emanuel. "Up Beat on Broadway." *New York World-Telegram*, April 3, 1937.

Erwin, Pee Wee, with Warren W. Vache, Sr. *This Horn for Hire*. Metuchen, N.J., and London: Scarecrow Press and Institute For Jazz Studies, Rutgers University. 1987.

Ferguson, Otis. "The Boy from the Back Row." *New Republic* (May 17, 1939).

Frazier, George. " 'Get The Lead Out of Your Fanny!' Critic Tells Talented Trumpeter." *Down Beat* (October 1936).

Gitler, Ira. *Swing to Bop*. New York and Oxford: Oxford University Press, 1985.

Goode, Mort. *Benny Goodman—The RCA Years*. RCA Records, 1986.

Goodman, Benny, with Irving Kolodin. *The Kingdom of Swing*. New York: Stackpole Sons, 1939.

————, with Richard Gehman. "That Old Gang of Mine." *Collier's* (January 20, 1956).

————. Interview for *First Person Singular*, 1962.

Goodman, Irving. Interview with Bill Spilka, April 5, 1987.

Griffin, Chris. Author's interview, August 21, 1987.

Hammond, John, with Irving Townsend. *John Hammond on Record*. New York: Ridge Press/Summit Books, 1977.

————. "Goodman 'Killer' Arrangements Detract from Band's Musicianship." *Down Beat* (February 1937).

————. "Bongo Player Thrills New York—Fletch Henderson's Band Ragged." *Down Beat* (March 1937).

————. "N.Y. Rhythm Concert." *Down Beat* (April 1937).

————. "Big Broadcast of 1938 Wants Benny Goodman's Quartette." *Down Beat* (May 1937).

James, Harry. "Jammin' with James." *Metronome*. (June 1938).

Kappler, Frank K., and George T. Simon. *Giants of Jazz: Benny Goodman*. Time-Life Records, 1979.

Lombardo, Guy, with Jack Altshul. *Auld Acquaintance*. Garden City, N.Y.: Doubleday & Co., 1975.

Maher, James T. Author's interview, September 9, 1988.

————. *The MGM Benny Goodman Treasure Chest*. MGM Records, 1959.

Maxwell, Jimmy. Author's interview, September 3, 1987.

Metronome. "In Person Policy of NY Paramount Shows Public Trend" (March 1936).

————. " 'Benny: Swell Head? Nix!' Say New York Boys" (April 1937).

Morgan, Alun. *Count Basie*. Tunbridge Wells and New York: Spellmount Ltd and Hippocrene Books, Inc., 1984.

N. E. W. "Outside the Groove." *Down Beat* (May 1937).

Rollini, Arthur. *Thirty Years with the Big Bands*. Urbana and Chicago: University of Illinois Press, 1987.

Rust, Brian. *Jazz Records: 1987–1942*. New Rochelle, N.Y.: Arlington House, 1978.

Simon, George T. *The Big Bands*. New York: Macmillian Company,

————. *Glenn Miller and His Orchestra*. New York: Thomas Y. Crowell Company, 1974.

————. "Harry James Revisited." *The Big Bands*, 4th Ed. New York: Schirmer Books, 1981.

Stacy, Frank. *Harry James*. New York: Arco Publishing Co., 1944.

Stacy, Jess. Author's interview, March 28, 1988.

Stearns, Marshall, and Jean Stearns. *Jazz Dance: The Story of America's Vernacular Dance*. Macmillan Company, 1968.

Steig, Henry Anton. "Alligator's Idol." *The New Yorker* (April 17, 1937).

Variety. "B'Way OK; Benny Goodman Swings 'Salem' to Wow 58G," March 10, 1937.

————. "Paramount, N.Y.," March 20, 1937.

————. "Swing into a New High in Entertainment and Box Office," March 10, 1937.

Ward, Helen. Author's Interview, November 13, 1987.

Zarchey, Zeke. Interview with Bill Spilka, February 23, 1987.

CHAPTER FOURTEEN: Carnegie Jump

Barnes, Howard. "Hollywood Hotel—Strand." *New York Herald Tribune*, January 13, 1938.

Condon, Eddie, with Thomas Sugrue. *We Called It Music*. New York: Henry Holt, 1947.

Connor, D. Russell. *The Record of a Legend*. Let's Dance Corporation, 1984.

Dance, Helen Oakley. "Call Out Riot Squad to Handle Mob at Goodman-Webb Battle." *Down Beat* (June 1937).

Down Beat. "Benny 'Hot-Fingers' Goodman—The Czar Of Bootleg Swing." December 1937.

Downes, Olin. "Goodman Is Heard in 'Swing' Concert." *New York Times,* January 17, 1938.

Eisenberg, Emanuel. "Up Beat on Broadway." *New York World-Telegram,* April 3, 1937.

Ewing, Annemarie. "Carnegie Hall Gets First Taste of Swing." *Down Beat* (February 1938).

Ferguson, Otis. *The Otis Ferguson Reader,* ed. Dorothy Chamberlain and Robert Wilson. Highland Park, Ill.: December Press, 1982.

Frazier, George. "Take Thirty." *Esquire* (June 1958).

Giddins, Gary. "King of the Savoy." *Village Voice* (August 30, 1988).

Gilbert, Douglas. "Goodman, Standing Where Toscanini Stands, Tells about Swing." *New York World-Telegram,* January 11, 1938.

Gilbert, Gama. "Swing It! And Even in a Temple of Music." *New York Times Magazine,* January 16, 1938.

Goode, Mort. *Benny Goodman—The RCA Years.* RCA Records, 1986.

Goodman, Benny, with Irving Kolodin. *The Kingdom of Swing.* New York: Stackpole Sons, 1939.

————, with Richard Gehman. "That Old Gang of Mine." *Collier's* (January 20, 1956).

————. Interview for *First Person Singular,* 1962.

Griffin, Chris. Author's interview, August 21, 1987.

Hammond, John, with Irving Townsend. *John Hammond on Record.* New York: Ridge Press/Summit Books, 1977.

————. "Big Broadcast of 1938 Wants Benny Goodman's Quartette." *Down Beat* (May 1937).

————. " 'A Damned Outrage to Throw Thousands out of Work!' " *Down Beat* (June 1937).

————. "Predicted Race Riot Fades as Dallas Applauds Quartet!" *Down Beat* (October 1937).

Hampton, Lionel. "Me and Benny Goodman." *Saturday Evening Post* (December 18, 1954).

Handbill. "S. Hurok Presents Benny Goodman and His Swing Orchestra." January 1938.

H. E. P. " 'Goodman Came, Saw, and Laid a Golden Egg!' " *Down Beat* (February 1938).

————. "The Deceased of Carnegie Hall Turn over in Their Graves as Jazz Lifts the Roof!" *Down Beat* (December 1938).

Hurok, S. Letter to Willard Alexander, January 10, 1938. In *Benny, King of Swing.* New York: William Morrow and Company, Inc. Stanley Baron, 1979.

Kappler, Frank K., and George T. Simon. *Giants of Jazz: Benny Goodman.* Time-Life Records, 1979.

King, William G. "Music and Musicians." *New York Sun,* January 15, 1938.

Kolodin, Irving. "Notes on the Program: Benny Goodman and His Orchestra," January 1938.

————. *The Famous 1938 Carnegie Hall Jazz Concert.* Columbia Records, 1950.

Life. "Life Goes to a Party." November 1, 1937.

Maher, James T. *The MGM Benny Goodman Treasure Chest.* MGM Records, 1959.

McDonough, John. "The Night Benny Brought Swing to Carnegie Hall." *Wall Street Journal,* January 7, 1988.

Melody Maker. "What They Say about Swing in the States." September 4, 1937.

Metronome. "Chick Webb Defeats Benny Goodman" (June 1937).

————. "Contest Comments—Roasts and Toasts" (July 1937).

————. "Hot Winter Ahead for New York" (August 1937).

————. "Benny Goodman Crashes Sedate Carnegie Hall" (January 1938).

————. "Benny's Barrage Baffles Critics" (February 1938).

————. "Goodman's Show Causes Riots" (February 1938).

Mok, Michel. "Mr. Goodman Swings the Alligators to Freedom." *New York Post,* February 3, 1938.

Morrison, Hobe. "Goodman's Vipers Slay the Cats, but Salon Critics Don't Savvy Jive." *Variety,* January 19, 1938.

New York Herald Tribune. "Swing in Carnegie Hall," January 18, 1938.

New York Times. "Hot Music at Carnegie," January 18, 1938.

Nugent, Frank S. "Hollywood Hotel." *New York Times,* January 13, 1938.

Rollini, Arthur. *Thirty Years with the Big Bands.* Urbana and Chicago: University of Illinois Press, 1987.

Simon, George T. *The Big Bands.* New York: Macmillan Company, 1967.

————. "Benny and Cats Make Carnegie Debut Real Howling Success." *Metronome* (February 1938).

————. "The Night When Carnegie Hall Swung." *New York Times,* January 10, 1988.

Stacy, Jess. Author's interview, March 28, 1988.

Sudhalter, Richard M. "Benny Goodman: An Interview with the King of Swing." *American Heritage* (November 1981).

Travis, Dempsey. *An Autobiography of Black Jazz.* Chicago: Urban Research Institute, 1983.

Tufts, Robert B. "Defending Goodman." *New York Times,* January 23, 1938.

Variety. "Inside Stuff—Vaude," March 24, 1937.

————. May 26, 1937.

————. "Variety Bills," December 1, 1937.

————. "Goodman, Lombardo, Fields Look No. 1, 2, 3 In N.Y. Par. Ballots," January 19, 1938.

————. "Variety Bills," January 19, 1938.

————. "Benny Goodman—West Boff B'way for $57,000," February 2, 1938.

————. "Paramount, N.Y.," February 2, 1938.

CHAPTER FIFTEEN: Farewell Blues

Balliett, Whitney. "Little Davy Tough." *The New Yorker* (November 18, 1985).

Baxter, Danny. " 'Amazing' Only Way to Describe James." *Down Beat* (April 1939).

Bernardi, Noni. Interview with Bill Spilka, November 9, 1987.

Breck, Park. "Did T. Dorsey Thumb Nose at B. Goodman?" *Down Beat* (April 1938).

Collins, Jack. "Copper Stands Guard for Krupa & Dorsey Gets 'Dr. of Swing.' " *Down Beat* (June 1938).

Connor, D. Russell. *The Record of a Legend.* Let's Dance Corporation, 1984.

Dexter, Dave, Jr. "Goodman to Europe in Good Spirits." *Down Beat* (July 1938).

————. "Handsome Harry: Hipster or Hollywood Ham?" *Hollywood Note* (March 1946).

Dorsey, Tommy. "From the Dorsey Dome." *Metronome* (May 1938).

Down Beat. "Goodman Changes Men in His Band" (September 1936).

————. "Krupa Signs New Contract with Goodman" (May 1937).

————. "G. Krupa Leaves Benny Goodman in Huff!" (April 1938).

————. "B.G.'s Draw Falls below T. Dorsey's" (July 1938).

————. "Should Leaders Have a Code of Ethics?" (September 1938).

————. "Why Artie Shaw Must Publicize His Clarinet" (October 1938).

————. "Will Benny Break Up His Band?" (February 1939).

————. " 'Broadway Bunk' Says B.G. about Split-Up of Band" (March 1939).

Emge, Charles. "Harry James." *Down Beat* (February 12, 1951).

Erwin, Pee Wee, with Warren W. Vache, Sr. *This Horn for Hire.* Metuchen, N.J., and London: Scarecrow Press and Institute for Jazz Studies, Rutgers University, 1987.

Feather, Leonard. *The Jazz Years.* New York: Da Capo Press, 1987.

Frazier, George. " 'Get The Lead out of Your Fanny!' Critic Tells Talented Trumpeter." *Down Beat* (October 1936).

———. "Stupid Critics Misjudge 3,000 Ickies' Action." *Down Beat* (June 1938).

Goode, Mort. *Benny Goodman—The RCA Years.* RCA Records, 1986.

Goodman, Benny, with Irving Kolodin. *The Kingdom of Swing.* New York: Stackpole Sons, 1939.

———, as Told to Ted Shane. "Now Take the Jitterbug." *Collier's* (February 25, 1939).

———. "My Ten Favorite Clarinetists." *Music and Rhythm* (October 1941).

Griffin, Chris. Author's interview, August 17, 1987.

Hammond, John, with Irving Townsend. *John Hammond on Record.* New York: Ridge Press/Summit Books, 1977.

———. "Hysterical Public Split Goodman & Krupa." *Down Beat* (April 1938).

———. "Hammond Throws Hat in Air for Shaw and Discovers More Blues Pianists." *Down Beat* (July 1938).

———. "Krupa Beat Weak & Lips Page Band Just Bad." *Down Beat* (September 1938).

James, Harry. "Jammin' with James." *Metronome* (June 1938).

———. Agreement with Benny Goodman, February 27, 1939.

———. Letter to Benny Goodman, January 16, 1942.

Jerome, Jerry. Author's interview, September 3, 1987.

Korall, Burt. *The Complete Artie Shaw.* RCA Records, 1976–1981.

Krupa, Gene. "Krupa Gets His Kicks." *Metronome* (February 1938).

———. "No Squawks on Criticism Before—Why Start Now? . . . Krupa." *Down Beat* (May 1938).

Locke, Ted. "White Man's Jazz No Good for Holiday?" *Down Beat* (August 1938).

Metronome. "Krupa Still In; Hunt Out" (May 1937).

———. "New York Votes Goodman Tops" (February 1938).

———. " 'I'd Sure Like My Own Band'—Krupa" (March 1938).

———. "Benny Goodman" (May 1938).

———. "Krupa's Band Kills Cats at Atlantic City Opening" (May 1938).

———. " 'We're Pals!' Benny and Gene—but?" (May 1938).

———. "Benny and Gene Kiss and Make Up" (June 1938).

———. "Phila. Cats Not So Sure about Krupa" (June 1938).

———. "Boston Debates Artie Shaw's Swing" (July 1938).

———. "Ickies' Antics Submerge Goodman-Basie Battle." July 1938.

———. "Krupa Shaping Outmoded Style" (July 1938).

———. "Benny's Boys at Sea" (August 1938).

———. "Goodman, Shaw Toe Together" (October 1938).

———. " 'I'm Kicking My Soul!'—Harry James" (May 1939).

———. "Wanted: Side-Men!" (September 1939).

———. "Don't Start a Band Now!" (October 1939).

———. "James, Norvo May Turn Pretty" (February 1940).

Monro, John. " 'Cripes! Shaw Doesn't Sound like Goodman!' " *Down Beat* (June 1938).

New York Times. "Swing Fiesta by Goodman," May 22, 1938.

———. "Swing Carnival Held to Benefit Charity," June 13, 1938.

———. Editorial, July 24, 1938.

Rollini, Arthur. *Thirty Years with the Big Bands.* Urbana and Chicago: University of Illinois Press, 1987.

Scanlan, Tom. "The Impeccable Mr. Wilson." *Down Beat* (January 22, 1959).

Simon, George T. *The Big Bands.* New York: Macmillan Company, 1967.
————. *Simon Says: The Sights and Sounds of the Swing Era 1935–1955.* New Rochelle, N.Y.: Arlington House, 1971.
————. "Harry James Revisited." *The Big Bands,* 4th ed. New York: Macmillan Company, 1981.
Stacy, Jess. Author's interview, March 28, 1988.
Variety. "Gene Krupa Mulls Idea of Own Band; Top-Priced Drummer." April 21, 1937.
Ward, Helen. Author's interview, April 29, 1987.
————. Author's interview, November 13, 1987.
Wilson, Teddy. Interview with Milt Hinton. Smithsonian Jazz Oral History Project, September 1979 and January 1980.
Yoder, Robert M. "High-Note Harry." *Saturday Evening Post* (July 24, 1943).

CHAPTER SIXTEEN: What Swing Really Does to People

Barron, Blue. "Swing Is Nothing but Orchestrated Sex . . ." *Music and Rhythm* (August 1941).
Barry, Edward. "This Mad Thing Called Swing!" *Chicago Sunday Tribune,* December 11, 1938.
Down Beat. "Dorsey Cut Off Air for Murdering 'Sacred' Tunes" (April 1938).
————. "Italians Ban Music by Jews!" (November 1938).
————. " 'Swing Is Not Insanity' Avers Lee Sowerby" (November 1938).
Downes, Olin. " 'Swinging' Bach." *New York Times,* October 30, 1938.
Gilbert, Gama. "Higher Soars the Swing Fever." *New York Times Magazine,* August 14, 1938.
Goodman, Benny, with Irving Kolodin. *The Kingdom of Swing.* New York: Stackpole Sons, 1939.
————. "What Swing Really Does to People." *Liberty* (May 14, 1938).
————. "Give Swing a Chance." *Look* (September 27, 1938).
————, as Told to Ted Shane. "Now Take the Jitterbug." *Collier's* (February 25, 1939).
————. "Audiences—Two Kinds." *New York Times,* December 8, 1940.
Hep Cat. "To Hell with the Jitter-Bugs." *Down Beat* (October 1938).
Jacobs, Dick. "They're Turning Swing into a Caricature." *Metronome* (October 1938).
Jerome, Jerry. Author's interview, September 3, 1987.
Life. "Speaking of Pictures . . . Swing Music Produces These" (February 21, 1938).
————. "Swing" (June 6, 1938).
Metronome. "How Long Will Swing Last?" (March 1938).
————. "They're Killing Our Swing!" (September 1938).
————. "They're Killing Swing" (November 1938).
Miller, Paul Eduard. *Down Beat's Yearbook of Swing.* Chicago: Down Beat Publication Company, 1939.
New York Times. "Reich Bars Radio Jazz to Safeguard 'Culture,' " October 13, 1935.
————. "Swing Music Barred for St. Patrick March; Only Irish and American Tunes Permitted," February 27, 1938.
————. "Swing Bands Put 23,400 in Frenzy," May 30, 1938.
————. "On Varied Fronts," June 19, 1938.
————. "Swing Music Held Degenerated Jazz," July 27, 1938.
————. "Swing away from Swing," August 14, 1938.
————. " 'Swinging' Bach's Music on Radio Protested; FCC Is Urged to Bar 'Jazzing' of Classics," October 24, 1938.
————. "Broadcasters Favor 'Swinging' of Bach," October 28, 1938.

————. "Radio's Policy on Swing," October 30, 1938.

————. "Swing Viewed as 'Musical Hitlerism'; Professor Sees Fans Ripe for Dictator," November 2, 1938.

————. "FCC Dodges 'Swing' Issue but Urges Care in Its Use," November 3, 1938.

————. "From the Mail Pouch," November 6, 1938.

————. "Let Freedom 'Swing,'" November 6, 1938.

————. "Wedding March in Swing Barred," November 18, 1938.

————. "Nazis Ban Swing Music as Not Fit for Germans," November 27, 1938.

————. "Group to Fight 'Jazzing' of the National Anthem," December 21, 1938.

————. "Music: Sweet Swing," February 19, 1939.

————. "Mail-Bag Excerpts," February 26, 1939.

————. " 'Jitterbug' Tunes Barred at Princeton Songfests," May 1, 1939.

————. "Burned Up by Hot Band; Hurls Instruments in Sea," May 17, 1939.

————. " 'What's Use of Goering?' Offered as a War Song," September 7, 1939.

————. "Sees 'Swing' on Wane," September 14, 1939.

Reisman, Leo. "Why I Won't Play Swing." *Liberty* (May 28, 1938).

Smith, Carleton. "On the Record." *Esquire* (October 1938).

Starr, S. Frederick. *Red and Hot: The Fate of Jazz in the Soviet Union 1917–1980.* New York: Oxford University Press, 1983.

Vogue. "It Don't Mean a Thing If It Ain't Got That Swing" (February 1, 1938).

Wittenmyer, Paul E. "Jitterbugs Wreck Chicago Stadium!" *Metronome* (October 1938).

CHAPTER SEVENTEEN: Contrasts

Connor, D. Russell. *The Record of a Legend.* Let's Dance Corporation, 1984.

Esquire. "Best Sellers." October, 1938.

Ferguson, Otis. *The Otis Ferguson Reader,* ed. Dorothy Chamberlain and Robert Wilson. Highland Park, Ill.: December Press, 1982.

Goodman, Benny, with Irving Kolodin. *The Kingdom of Swing.* New York: Stackpole Sons, 1939.

————. "Audiences—Two Kinds." *New York Times,* December 8, 1940.

————. "I Lead a Double Life." *House & Garden* (April 1951).

————. Interview for *First Person Singular,* 1962.

Hammond, John, with Irving Townsend. *John Hammond on Record.* New York: Ridge Press/Summit Books. 1977.

Jerome, Jerry. Author's interview, September 3, 1987.

Metronome. "Benny Slays Carnegie Cats" (February 1939).

New York Herald Tribune. "Iturbi Balks at Sharing Benny Goodman Podium," June 27, 1941.

New York Times. "On Varied Fronts," June 19, 1938.

————. "Concert and Opera," August 14, 1938.

————. "Two New Ventures," August 14, 1938.

————. "New Concerto by Bartók," October 9, 1938.

————. "Benny Goodman Turns to Classics," November 6, 1938.

————. "Goodman Assists in Szigeti Recital," January 20, 1939.

————. "Dinner Concert at Waldorf," January 16, 1939.

————. "Music: Sweet Swing," February 19, 1939.

————. "Mail-Bag Excerpts," February 26, 1939.

————. "Béla Bartók Plays Own Compositions," April 14, 1940.

————. "Goodman Soloist at Carnegie Hall," December 13, 1940.

Stevens, Halsey. *The Life and Music of Béla Bartók.* New York: Oxford University Press, 1964.

Straus, Noel. "Ovation to Bártok at Szigeti Recital." *New York Times,* April 22, 1940.

Szigeti, Joseph. *With Strings Attached: Reminiscences and Reflections.* New York: Alfred A. Knopf, 1967.

Taubman, Howard. "Records: Bártok's 'Contrasts.' " *New York Times,* November 10, 1940.

———. "Swing and Mozart, Too." *New York Times Magazine,* December 29, 1940.

CHAPTER EIGHTEEN: The Changes Made

Allen, Walter C. *Hendersonia: The Music of Fletcher Henderson and His Musicians.* Highland Park, N.J.: Walter C. Allen, 1973.

Avakian, George. *Benny Goodman Presents Eddie Sauter Arrangements.* CBS Records, 1975.

Balliett, Whitney. "A Sweet, Thin, Easygoing Person." *The New Yorker* (May 20, 1972).

Blesh, Rudi. *Combo: U.S.A.* Philadelphia, New York, London: Chilton Book Co., 1971.

Brooks, Michael. *Red Norvo and His All Stars.* Columbia Special Products, 1974.

Connor, D. Russell. *The Record of a Legend.* Let's Dance Corporation, 1984.

Dance, Stanley. *The World of Swing.* New York: Charles Scribner's Sons, 1974.

Dexter, Dave, Jr. "B.G.'s Book, Despite Errors by His Co-Author, Packs a Potent Punch." *Down Beat* (May 1939).

Di Michael, Don. *Giants of Jazz: Red Norvo.* Time-Life Records, 1980.

Down Beat. "Goodman Signs Sepia Girl Singer" (July 1939).

———. "Goodman Adds Noted Negro Pianist" (August 1939).

———. "Goodman Plans to Add More Negroes to Band" (September 1939).

———. "Benny Should Be Congratulated for His Courage—Jimmy Dorsey" (October 15, 1939).

———. "Should Negro Musicians Play in White Bands?" (October 15, 1939).

Ellison, Ralph. "The Charlie Christian Story." *Saturday Review* (May 17, 1958).

Feather, Leonard. *The Book of Jazz.* New York: Horizon Press, 1957.

———. *Inside Be-Bop.* New York: J. J. Robbins & Sons, 1949.

Gant, Charles. "Book Reviews." *Tempo* (July 1939).

Goode, Mort. *Benny Goodman—The RCA Years.* RCA Records, 1986.

Goodman, Benny, with Irving Kolodin. *The Kingdom of Swing.* New York: Stackpole Sons, 1939.

———. "I Wasn't Kidding Myself!—Benny Goodman." *Down Beat* (December 15, 1939).

———. Interview for *First Person Singular,* 1962.

Griffin, Chris. Author's interview, August 17, 1987.

Hammond, John, with Irving Townsend. *John Hammond on Record.* New York: Ridge Press. 1977.

———. "The Advent Of Charlie Christian." *Down Beat* (August 25, 1966).

James, Harry. "Here's Why Louise Tobin Is with BG." *Down Beat* (October 15, 1939).

Jerome, Jerry. Author's interview, September 28, 1987.

Maxwell, Jimmy. Author's interview, September 3, 1987.

Melody Maker. " 'The Kingdom of Swing' " (n.d.).

Metronome. "Bernstein and Cornelius Join Benny Goodman" (May 1939).

———. " 'My Greatest Band's Coming!'—Benny" (June 1939).

———. "Brother and Sister Gave Benny Bernstein" (July 1939).

———. "MCA and Goodman in Feud" (July 1939).

———. " 'Two Guys Can't Play First in One Band!' " (July 1939).

———. "Stacy Quits Benny; F. Henderson In; Changes Continue" (August 1939).

———. "Jess Stacy to Join Bob Crosby's Band; Sullivan Is Out" (September 1939).

———. "New Pop Records for Half a Buck" (September 1939).

———. " 'Goodman Cast-offs Couldn't Take Real Criticism!' " (October 1939).

———. "Musicians Are Human" (December 1939).

Rollini, Arthur. *Thirty Years with the Big Bands.* Urbana and Chicago: University of Illinois Press, 1987.

Russell, Ross. *Jazz Styles in Kansas City and the Southwest.* Berkeley and Los Angeles: University of California Press, 1971.

Sauter, Eddie. Interview with Bill Kirchner. National Endowment for the Arts Jazz Oral History Project, August 14, 1980.

Simon, Bill. "Charlie Christian." In *The Jazz Makers,* ed. Nat Shapiro and Nat Hentoff. New York: Rinehart & Co., 1957.

Simon, George T. *The Big Bands.* New York: Macmillan Company, 1967.

———. "Benny Goodman Revisited." *The Big Bands,* 4th ed. New York: Macmillan Company, 1981.

Stacy, Jess. Author's interview, March 28, 1988.

CHAPTER NINETEEN: The Hour of Parting

Atkinson, Brooks. "Swing Shakespeare's 'Dream' with Benny Goodman, Louis Armstrong and Maxine Sullivan." *New York Times,* November 30, 1939.

Brown, John Mason. "Erik Charell Presents 'Swingin' the Dream.' " *New York Post,* November 30, 1939.

Coleman, Robert. " 'Swingin' the Dream' Jitterbugs' Delight with Dull Spots." *New York Daily Mirror,* November 30, 1939.

Connor, D. Russell. *The Record of a Legend.* Let's Dance Corporation, 1984.

Dexter, Dave, Jr. "Shaw Grabs Goodman's Men." *Down Beat* (August 1, 1940).

Down Beat. "Goodman Band Takes First Vacation" (January 15, 1940).

———. "Pain Floors Benny; Band Goes West" (March 15, 1940).

———. "Benny Goodman Is 'Much Improved' " (April 1, 1940).

———. "Guarnieri Is New Goodman Piano Pumper" (June 1, 1940).

———. " 'My Band's Not Breaking'—Benny" (July 1, 1940).

———. "No Bookings for Ziggy; BG Rests" (July 15, 1940).

Family Health Guide and Medical Encyclopedia. Pleasantville, N.Y.: Reader's Digest Association, Inc., 1976.

Feather, Leonard. "BG Still Not Satisfied with His Band Boys." *Down Beat* (December 1, 1939).

Forrest, Helen, with Bill Libby. *I Had the Craziest Dream.* New York: Coward, McCann & Geoghegan, Inc., 1982.

Goodman, Benny. "I Wasn't Kidding Myself!—Benny Goodman." *Down Beat* (December 15, 1939).

Griffin, Chris. Author's interview, August 17, 1987.

Jerome, Jerry. Author's interview, September 28, 1987.

Korall, Burt. *The Complete Artie Shaw.* RCA Records, 1976–1981.

Maxwell, Jimmy. Author's interview, September 3, 1987.

Metronome. "I Still Don't Like Jitterbugs" (November 1939).

———. "Goodman Continues Tour Despite Intense Pain" (February 1940).

———. "B. G., Stokowski Plan Concert!" (April 1940).

———. "Sickness Stops Benny, but Only Temporarily" (April 1940).

———. "Catalina Island Casino to Feature Swing" (May 1940).

———. "Ziggy to Lead Goodman Band" (July 1940).

Miller, Sigmund Stephen, ed. *Symptoms: The Complete Home Medical Encyclopedia.* New York: Thomas Y. Crowell Co., 1976.

New York Times. "Swingin' That Dream," November 26, 1939.

———. " 'Swingin' Dream Closes," December 10, 1939.

————. "Benny Goodman at Mayo Clinic," July 13, 1940.

————. "Goodman Has Operation," July 14, 1940.

————. "Benny Goodman to Quit Hospital," August 3, 1940.

Rollini, Arthur. *Thirty Years with the Big Bands*. Urbana and Chicago: University of Illinois Press, 1987.

Savory, Bill. Author's interview, June 21, 1988.

Seldes, Marian. Letter to the author, April 9, 1989.

Shapiro, Nat, and Nat Hentoff. *Hear Me Talkin' to Ya*. New York: Rinehart and Company, Inc., 1955.

Shaw, Arnold. *The Street That Never Slept*. New York: Coward, McCann & Geoghegan, Inc., 1971.

Shaw, Artie. *The Trouble with Cinderella*. New York: Farrar, Straus and Young. 1952.

Simon, George T. *The Big Bands*. New York: Macmillan Company, 1967.

Stacy, Jess. Author's interview, March 28, 1988.

Swingin' the Dream. Playbill, November 1939.

Variety. "Swingin' the Dream," December 6, 1939.

————. "Swingin' the Dream," December 13, 1939.

Watts, Richard, Jr. " 'Swingin' the Dream.' " *New York Herald Tribune*, November 30, 1939.

Wright, Gordon. "Benny's Batch, Duke's Discs Top Records." *Metronome* (August 1940).

CHAPTER TWENTY: Benny Rides Again

Allen, Walter C. *Hendersonia: The Music of Fletcher Henderson and His Musicians*. Highland Park, N.J.: Walter C. Allen, 1973.

Balliett, Whitney. "Big Sid." *American Musicians*. New York: Oxford University Press, 1986.

————. "A Sweet, Thin, Easygoing Person." *The New Yorker* (May 20, 1972).

————. "Still There." *The New Yorker* (August 5, 1985).

————. "Discoveries." *The New Yorker* (August 18, 1986).

————. "What Ever Happened to Mel Powell?" *The New Yorker* (May 25, 1987).

Barrelhouse Dan. " 'New Goodman Surprises with Unique Type of Jazz.' " *Down Beat* (January 15, 1941).

Blesh, Rudi. "Flying Home." *Combo: U.S.A*. Philadelphia, New York, London: Chilton Book Co., 1971.

Bois, Sonny. "It's Benny Goodman's Bankroll—" *Music and Rhythm* (March 1941).

Connor, D. Russell. *The Record of a Legend*. Let's Dance Corporation. 1984.

Dance, Helen Oakley. "Inimitable Cootie Williams." *Down Beat* (May 4, 1967).

Dance, S. F. "British Fan Blasts BG's Cootie Deal." *Down Beat* (January 15, 1941).

Dance, Stanley. "Earl Hines." *The World of Earl Hines*. New York: Charles Scribner's Sons, 1977.

Dexter, Dave, Jr. "Goodman Changes Half His Band." *Down Beat* (July 1, 1941).

————. "BG Grabs Cootie for Hot Chair." *Down Beat* (November 1941).

Down Beat. "Pain Floors Benny; Band Goes West" (March 15, 1940).

————. "Benny Goodman Is 'Much Improved' " (April 1, 1940).

————. "Goodman's Mixed Band Plans Wait" (August 15, 1940).

————. "Benny in N.Y.; Set to Go" (September 1, 1940).

————. "Goodman Still Takes It Easy" (September 15, 1940).

————. "Wilson Back with Benny" (October 1, 1940).

————. "BG Begins Rehearsals" (October 15, 1940).

————. "Teddy Wilson May Rejoin Goodman" (February 1, 1941).

————. "BG Hires Guarnieri, Butterfield" (March 14, 1941).

————. "Rowdies Mar BG Program; on NBC Network in Fall" (May 1, 1941).

————. "Benny, Barnet, Clinton to Open Gigantic Dance Palace" (May 15, 1941).

————. "BG Ridicules Muggsy Charge of 'Sabotage' " (August 15, 1941).

————. "Helen Forrest on Her Own; Quits Goodman in Chicago" (August 15, 1941).

————. "Helen Forrest Out; Peggy Lee Joins BG" (September 1, 1941).

————. "Mess of Name Bands to Compete This Fall in New York Night Spots" (September 1, 1941).

————. "Cootie Only Colored Star Left as Catlett-BG Split" (October 15, 1941).

————. "Eye Trouble Fails to Halt Henderson" (October 15, 1941).

————. "Charlie Christian and Dick Wilson Seriously Ill" (November 15, 1941).

————. "Cootie Starts His Own Band; BG and Miller Change Their Lineups" (December 1, 1941).

————. "Goodman Now on Okeh Label" (December 1, 1941).

————. "BG Tour Set; Then Back to New Yorker" (December 15, 1941).

————. "Charlie Christian Dies in New York" (March 15, 1942).

Ellington, Duke. *Music Is My Mistress*. Garden City, N.Y.: Doubleday & Company, Inc., 1973.

Ellison, Ralph. "The Charlie Christian Story." *Saturday Review* (May 17, 1958).

Feather, Leonard. "Teddy Wilson Reveals He May Drop His Band." *Down Beat* (May 1, 1940).

————. " 'More Concerts This Fall,' Says Goodman," *Down Beat* (August 1, 1941).

Forrest, Helen, with Bill Libby. *I Had the Craziest Dream*. New York: Coward, McCann & Geoghegan, Inc., 1982.

Frazier, George. " 'Benny's New Band Is Too Much like Benny's Old Band." *Down Beat* (March 15, 1941).

Gitler, Ira. *Swing to Bop*. New York and Oxford: Oxford University Press, 1985.

Goodman, Benny, with Irving Kolodin. *The Kingdom of Swing*. New York: Stackpole Sons, 1939.

————. "Is Swing Dead?" *Music and Rhythm* (August 1941).

————. Interview for *First Person Singular*, 1962.

Green, Abel, and Joe Laurie, Jr. *Show Biz from Vaude to Video*. New York: Henry Holt & Co., 1951.

Hammond, John, with Irving Townsend. *John Hammond on Record*. New York: Ridge Press/Summit Books. 1977.

————. "The Advent of Charlie Christian." *Down Beat* (August 25, 1966).

Horvath, G. B. S. "Was Earl Hines Smart to Turn Down Benny Goodman?" *Music and Rhythm* (June 1941).

Kalman, Vic. "King of Swing Still Reigns." *Newark* (N.J.) *Sunday Star-Ledger* (September 15, 1985).

Larkin, R. L. "Is Benny Goodman's Comeback Doomed to Failure?" *Music and Rhythm* (December 1940).

Lee, Peggy. *Miss Peggy Lee: An Autobiography*. New York: Donald I. Fine, Inc., 1989.

Life. "New York Gets Biggest Jive Joint" (June 25, 1941).

Locke, Bob. "Coot Band on Upbeat." *Down Beat* (April 15, 1942).

Maxwell, Jimmy. Author's interview, September 3, 1987.

Metronome. "Sickness Stops Benny, but Only Temporarily" (April 1940).

————. "Teddy Wilson Plans Smaller Dance Band" (May 1940).

————. "Benny's Band Busts Up; Shaw Grabs" (August 1940).

————. "B. G. Swing King and Favorite" (August 1940).

————. " 'Nobody Knows What Benny Will Do!' " (September 1940).

————. "B. G. Plans Two String Quartets" (October 1940).

————. "Cootie and the King" (November 1940).

————. "Cootie Williams Joins Benny!" (November 1940).

———. "You're Telling Us" (December 1940).

———. "You're Telling Us" (January 1941).

———. "Goodman Takes Back Davey Tough; Shertzer Returns" (February 1941).

———. "Ex-Goodman Take Shaw Leave" (April 1941).

———. "Failing Eyes Brought Back Smack's Band" (April 1941).

———. "N.Y. Fight Arena to Swing" (May 1941).

———. "Cootie Williams" (June 1941).

———. "Dave Tough in & out, out & in, in & out of Goodman Band" (June 1941).

———. "Swing Rocks Mad. Sq. Garden" (June 1941).

———. "Artie Bernstein Back to Coast Studios Forsaking the Hot and Harrowed" (July 1941).

———. "B. G. Junks Rhythm Section!" (July 1941).

———. "Charlie Christian Rushed to Hospital" (July 1941).

———. "Garden, Floppo, Plans Tour" (August 1941).

———. "Goodman Makes More Changes" (August 1941).

———. "Duke, Benny, Artie Top 1941 Discs" (January 1942).

———. "Dancebandom Sure Misses Charlie Christian" (April 1942).

The New Yorker. "Wa-Wa-Wa" (June 1, 1963).

Powell, Mel. Author's interview, May 30, 1989.

Savory, Bill. Author's interview, November 13, 1987.

———. Author's interview, June 21, 1988.

Schuller, Gunther. The Swing Era. New York and Oxford: Oxford University Press, 1989.

Shapiro, Nat, and Nat Hentoff. Hear Me Talkin' to Ya. New York: Rinehart and Company, Inc., 1955.

Simmons, John. Interview with Patricia Willard. Smithsonian Jazz Oral History Project, January 1977.

Simon, Bill. "Charlie Christian." In The Jazz Makers, ed. Nat Shapiro and Nat Hentoff. New York: Rinehart and Company, Inc., 1957.

Simon, George T. The Big Bands. New York: Macmillan Company, 1967.

———. Giants of Jazz: Benny Goodman. Time-Life Records, 1979.

———. "Goodman Great." Metronome (December 1941).

Toll, Ted. "Simmons, with B. G. Another Negro, Bassist." Down Beat (August 1, 1941).

Tormé, Mel. It Wasn't All Velvet. New York: Viking Press, 1988.

Ulanov, Barry. "Goodman Band Thrills on N.Y. Stage." Metronome (May 1941).

Variety. "Terrace Room, N.Y. (Hotel New Yorker)," October 15, 1941.

———. "Bands at Hotel B.O.'s," October 22, 1941.

———. "Bands at Hotel B.O.'s," October 29, 1941.

———. "Benny Goodman Reserves Himself for Longhairs," November 5, 1941.

———. "Bands at Hotel B.O.'s," November 12, 1941.

———. "Bands at Hotel B.O.'s," November 19, 1941.

———. "Inside Stuff—Orchestras," November 19, 1941.

———. "Benny Goodman at New Yorker to Mar. 12," December 10, 1942.

———. "Glenn Miller's 'Choo Choo' Hits 1,000,000 Mark in Disc Output and May Become All-Time High," January 14, 1942.

Williams, Cootie. "Why I Quit Duke Ellington after 11 Years." Music and Rhythm (December 1940).

———. Interview With Helen Oakley Dance. Smithsonian Institution, May 1976.

CHAPTER TWENTY-ONE: Alice

Avakian, George. Author's interview, November 21, 1987.
Connor, D. Russell. *The Record of a Legend.* Let's Dance Corporation, 1984.
Down Beat. "Benny Weds" (April 15, 1942).
Goodman, Benny. Interview for *First Person Singular,* 1962.
Hammond, John, with Irving Townsend. *John Hammond on Record.* New York: Ridge Press/Summit Books. 1977.
———. "John Hammond Says." *Music and Rhythm* (May 1942).
———. "Why Has Benny Goodman Changed?" *Music and Rhythm* (June 1942).
Hughes, Spike. *Second Movement.* London: Museum Press, 1951.
Lee, Peggy. *Miss Peggy Lee: An Autobiography.* New York: Donald I. Fine, Inc., 1989.
Maher, James T. Author's interview, October 13, 1987.
Maxwell, Jimmy. Author's interview, September 3, 1987.
Metronome. "Goodman Wedding Imminent" (November 1941).
———. "John Hammond Leaves Post" (January 1942).
———. "There's a Hitch in It; It's Benny Goodman's" (April 1942).
New York Times. "Alice F. Hammond Marries a Briton." March 27, 1927.
Powell, Mel. Author's interview, May 30, 1989.
Savory, Bill. Author's interview, November 13, 1987.
———. Author's interview, June 21, 1988.
Townsend, Freddie. Author's interview, August 3, 1987.
Variety. "John Hammond Leaving Col" (December 3, 1941).
———. "Benny Goodman Weds" (March 25, 1942).
Ward, Helen. Author's interview, April 29, 1987.
———. Author's interview, November 13, 1987.
Who's Who 1942. "Duckworth, (George) Arthur (Victor)." London: Adam & Charles Black, 1942.
Young, Roland. "Will Gentleman Farmer BG Plow Under Corn?" *Down Beat* (March 1, 1942).

CHAPTER TWENTY-TWO: Wartime

Bank, Danny. Author's interview, October 20, 1987.
Barnet, Charlie, with Stanley Dance. *Those Swinging Years.* Baton Rouge and London: Louisiana State University Press, 1984.
Baron, Stanley. Introduction. *Benny, King of Swing.* New York: William Morrow & Co., Inc., 1979.
Berger, Morroe; Edward Berger; and James Patrick. *Benny Carter: A Life in American Music.* Metuchen, N.J.: Scarecrow Press, 1982.
Blesh, Rudi. *Combo: U.S.A.* Philadelphia: Chilton Book Company, 1971.
Carr, Ian; Digby Fairweather; and Brian Priestley. *Jazz: The Essential Companion.* New York: Prentice Hall Press, 1987.
Connell, Tom. "B. G.: The King of Swing Abdicates." *Metronome* (August 1946).
Connor, D. Russell. *The Record of a Legend.* Let's Dance Corporation. 1984.
Conrad, Earl. *Billy Rose: Manhattan Primitive.* New York: World Publishing Company, 1968.
Crowther, Bruce. *Gene Krupa: His Life & Times.* Tunbridge Wells: Spellmount Ltd., 1987.
Cummings, Rube. "Goodman Fans in Philadelphia Kill Policeman's Horse in Rush." *Down Beat* (May 1, 1942).

Dexter, Dave, Jr. "Bands' Big Bonanza in '42 on Movie Screens!" *Down Beat* (March 15, 1942).

Down Beat. " 'Hit the Road' Now a Big Headache!" (March 15, 1942).

————. "Virtually All Instruments Are Frozen" (June 15, 1942).

————. "Jim Jimmies the Jive" (July 1, 1942).

————. "Benny Sweeps Band Again" (August 1, 1942).

————. "Eddie Sauter on Shelf for Four Years" (August 1, 1942).

————. "BG Pays Pianist 2 Weeks Salary for 3 Numbers" (September 15, 1942).

————. "Gremlins Get Goodman, Also Some Mix Scratch" (November 15, 1942).

————. "Goodman Reverts to Original Setup" (January 1, 1943).

————. "Most Played Records" (January 15, 1943).

————. "BG's Opening Sets New Record" (March 15, 1943).

————. "Krupa Denies Plea of Guilt, Set for Trial" (May 15, 1943).

————. "Five 'Originals' in Goodman 'Line' " (June 15, 1943).

————. "Krupa Ork Folds. Gates Scatter" (July 1, 1943).

————. "Most Played Records" (July 1, 1943).

————. "Goodman Knocks Cats for Loop at Astor" (July 15, 1943).

————. "BG Crowned King Fifth Time" (January 1, 1944).

————. "And Don't Think It Ain't Been Charmin' " (July 1, 1944).

————. "BG's Band Plans Still Uncertain" (August 15, 1944).

————. "Benny Goodman to Play in Revusical" (October 1, 1944).

————. "BG Sets Band, Quintet for Para in March" (February 1, 1945).

————. "Diggin' the Discs" (June 1, 1945).

————. "Old Staff" (June 1, 1945).

————. "BG On Own as Contract Expires" (September 1, 1945).

————. "Diggin' the Discs" (October 1, 1945).

————. "Benny to Coast after Great Biz" (January 1, 1946).

————. "Woody & TD Win, Ten New All-Stars" (January 1, 1946).

————. "Benny Almost Has a Brand New Band" (January 28, 1946).

Emge, Charles. "BG Dissolves Band. MCA Pact Is Cause." *Down Beat* (April 1, 1944).

Feather, Leonard. *Inside Be-Bop.* New York: J. J. Robbins & Sons, Inc., 1949.

————. "Benny Goodman A−, 1." *Metronome* (April 1943).

————. "Benny Goodman." *Metronome* (August 1943).

————. "Benny Goodman." *Metronome* (April 1945).

————. "Benny Goodman." *Metronome* (December 1946).

Flinn, John C. "Bands No. 1 Theatre B.O." *Variety* (February 25, 1942).

Gaver, Jack. UPS release, December 2, 1944.

Gayer, Dixon. "Two Blows to Band Travel." *Down Beat* (October 15, 1942).

Gelatt, Roland. *The Fabulous Phonograph: 1877–1977.* New York: Macmillan Company, 1977.

Gitler, Ira. *Swing to Bop.* New York: Oxford University Press. 1985.

Goodman, Benny. Letter to Fletcher Henderson, May 7, 1945.

————. Letter to Paul Hindemith, December 10, 1946.

————. Letter to Aaron Copland, December 30, 1946.

————. Interview for *First Person Singular,* 1962.

Gottlieb, Bill. "Posin'." *Down Beat* (July 15, 1946).

Hammond, John. "BG's Quartet Rocks the Cradle Of Jazz." *Down Beat* (November 1, 1944).

————. Dave Dexter, and Elliott Grennard. "Music Faces Its Crisis." *Music and Rhythm* (August 1942).

Herman, Woody, with Stuart Troup. *The Woodchopper's Ball.* New York: E. P. Dutton, 1990.

Hodgkins, Barbara. "Benny Goodman." *Metronome* (August 1946).

Jewell, Derek. *Frank Sinatra.* Boston: Little, Brown and Company, 1985.

Kelley, Kitty. *His Way: The Unauthorized Biography of Frank Sinatra*. New York: Bantam Books, 1986.

Kernfeld, Barry, ed. *The New Grove Dictionary of Jazz*. London: Macmillan Press Limited, 1988.

Knight, Wayne. *Spotlighting Benny Goodman*. Giants of Jazz Records, 1980.

Lahr, John. *Notes on a Cowardly Lion*. New York: Alfred A. Knopf, 1969.

Lee, Amy. " 'Ray' Upsets Goodman Band." *Down Beat* (August 15, 1943).

Lee, Peggy. *Miss Peggy Lee: An Autobiography*. New York: Donald I. Fine, Inc., 1989.

Levin, Mike. "Recording Sliced One-Third." *Down Beat* (May 1, 1942).

————. "End of One-Nighters in Sight." *Down Beat* (May 15, 1942).

————. "Showdown Looms on Discs." *Down Beat* (July 1, 1942).

————. "All Recording Stops Today." *Down Beat* (August 1, 1942).

————. "Just Like Jack the Bear." *Down Beat* (August 1, 1942).

————. "What Goes with Goodman?" *Down Beat* (September 1, 1942).

————. "Tea Scandal Stirs Musicdom." *Down Beat* (January 15, 1943).

————. "Music Biz Just Ain't Nowhere!" *Down Beat* (November 18, 1946).

————. "Notes between Notes." *Down Beat* (December 2, 1946).

Maxwell, Jimmy. Author's interview, September 3, 1987.

————. Interview with Milt Hinton. Smithsonian Jazz Oral History Project, April 16, 1979.

McAuliffe, Arthur. "A Treatise on Moldy Figs." *Metronome* (August 1945).

Meeker, David. *Jazz in the Movies*. New York: Da Capo Press, 1981.

Metronome. "B. G. D.C. Concert Smash Success" (March 1942).

————. "Brother Enlists, Benny Goodman Put in 4-F" (June 1942).

————. "Benny's Changing His Band Again; but Even He Isn't Sure Now" (September 1942).

————. "Benny Casting for Veterans" (January 1943).

————. "Enormous Record Sales Reported" (May 1943).

————. "Krupa Admits One Charge; Savoy Closed" (May 1943).

————. "Krupa Jailed on Tea Charge" (June 1943).

————. "Benny Offers Gene Old Job" (July 1943).

————. "Cootie Nixes BG Booty" (September 1943).

————. "Gene in N.Y." (September 1943).

————. "Benny, Tommy Win Contests" (October 1943).

————. "Benny, Tommy, Gene, Lionel, Carney Swamp Contest" (January 1944).

————. "Gene to Tommy; BG Loses Stars" (January 1944).

————. "Krupa Valet Reneges" (March 1944).

————. "Benny Breaks Up Band" (April 1944).

————. "Records of the Year" (January 1945).

————. "Record Reviews" (May 1945).

————. "Record Reviews" (July 1945).

————. "Who's Who and Where" (August 1945).

————. "Record Reviews" (October, 1945).

————. "Herd, Flip, Diz, Harris, Slam, Tough New Winners" (January 1946).

————. "Who's Who and Where and When" (January 1946).

————. "Who's Who and Where and When" (July 1946).

New York Times. "Bernstein Leads Three Premieres," November 19, 1946.

————. "Views and Sidelights on the World of Music," December 1, 1946.

New York World-Telegram. "Gene Krupa Arrested on Marihuana Charge," January 29, 1943.

O'Day, Anita, with George Eells. *High Times, Hard Times*. New York: G. P. Putnam's Sons, 1981.

Pollack, Arthur. "Theater." *Brooklyn Eagle*, December 8, 1944.

Rosen, Paul. "Can Gene Krupa Come Back?" *Orchestra World* (September 1943).

Sauter, Eddie. Interview with Bill Kirchner. National Endowment for the Arts Jazz Oral
    History Project, August 14, 1980.

Shapiro, Harry. *Waiting for the Man.* New York: William Morrow & Co., Inc., 1988.

Sherman, Robert. "Life with Mother Was a Parade of Great Artists." *New York Times,*
    September 24, 1989.

Simon, George T. *The Big Bands.* New York: Macmillan Company, 1967.

————. *Woody Herman: The Thundering Herds.* Columbia Records, 1963.

————. "Benny Absolutely Stupendous on Stage." *Metronome* (July 1942).

————. "Benny Goodman." *Metronome* (February 1943).

————. "Benny, Barnet A, 1, Say Band Reviews." *Metronome* (November 1943).

————. "Simon Says . . ." *Metronome* (August 1943).

————. "Simon Says . . ." *Metronome* (May 1944).

————. "Simon Says . . ." *Metronome* (January 1946).

————. "BG Explains." *Metronome* (October 1946).

————. "Eddie Sauter." *Metronome* (November 1946).

Stacy, Frank. "BG, Duke & Bailey Lost, Moans Blesh." *Down Beat* (February 15, 1945).

————. "Swing." *Jazzways* (1946).

Stewart, Slam. Interview with Stanley Crouch. Smithsonian Institute Jazz Oral History
    Project, January 16, 1979.

Tirro, Frank. *Jazz: A History.* New York: W. W. Norton & Company, Inc., 1977.

Ulanov, Barry. "Benny Goodman." *Metronome* (December 1942).

————. "The One Lively Art." *Metronome* (January 1945).

————. "Oh, Benny, Oh." *Metronome* (May 1946).

Variety. "Paramount, N.Y.," January 6, 1943.

————. "Orchestra Grosses," January 13, 1943.

————. "Goodman, Sinatra Harmony Upset by Fan Mag's Popularity Awards," January
    20, 1943.

————. "Astor Roof," July 7, 1943.

————. "Krupa Got a 'Bum Rap,' S.F. Insiders Say; Appealing 1–6 Year Sentence," July
    7, 1943.

————. "Paramount, N.Y.," August 11, 1943.

————. "Krupa Joins Goodman for USO Camp Tour; Deferred by Army," September
    22, 1943.

————. "Terrace Room, N.Y.," October 20, 1943.

————. "MCA Refusal to Settle His Contract Key to Goodman Breaking Up Band,"
    March 15, 1944.

————. "BG's Plans to Re-Form Band Leaves Leaders Jittery; Portends Raids," February
    7, 1945.

————. "Goodman Balking at One-Night Dates," March 14, 1945.

————. "Goodman Denies Breaking Agreement with MCA to Play Series of One-Night-
    ers," March 21, 1945.

————. "Paramount, N.Y.," April 14, 1945.

————. "400 Club, N.Y.," May 9, 1945.

————. "N.Y. Fast; 'Utopia-Goodman Record," March 6, 1946.

————. "Paramount, N.Y.," March 6, 1946.

————. "Benny Goodman Deal with Commodore H., N.Y. Cold; Couldn't Agree,"
    September 26, 1946.

————. "Benny Goodman Orch," November 6, 1946.

————. "Bandsmen Befogged by B.O. Dip," November 13, 1946.

————. "B.G. Cuts Longhair Capers Again in N.Y.," November 20, 1946.

————. "Goodman Maps Classical Work," November 27, 1946.

————. "Band Folds Don't Scare Biz," December 11, 1946.
————. "Nat Moss Files AFM Charges vs. Benny Goodman for 'Laxity,' " December 18, 1946.
Williams, Tony. *Red Norvo's Fabulous Jam Session*. Spotlite Records, n.d.

CHAPTER TWENTY-THREE: Benny's Bop

Avakian, George. Author's interview, November 21, 1987.
Barnet, Charlie. Interview with Patricia Willard. Smithsonian Jazz Oral History Project, April 23, 1978.
Burns, Jim. "Wardell Gray." *Jazz Journal* (November 1968).
Capitol News. "Jess Stacy, Other Vets Rejoin Goodman for NBC Program" (January 1947).
————. "At Home with Benny Goodman" (March 1947).
————. "Benny Goodman in Capitol Debut" (March 1947).
————. "Goodman Pushes Capitol into Classics Field" (May 1947).
————. "Vine Street Gab" (May 1947).
————. "Swedish Stick Star Wins L.A. Acclaim" (February 1948).
————. "Young Clary Whiz Joins Goodman 6" (May 1948).
————. "Cap Capturing Top Bop (Mop!)" (February 1949).
————. "Tops in Bop and Progressive Jazz" (August 1949).
Connor, D. Russell. *The Record of a Legend*. Let's Dance Corporation, 1984.
Copland, Aaron, and Vivian Perlis. *Copland Since 1943*. New York: St. Martin's Press, 1989.
Down Beat. "BG Signs New Paper with Capitol Firm" (February 12, 1947).
————. "Diggin' the Discs" (March 26, 1947).
————. "BG Selects Jazz for Russia" (April 23, 1947).
————. "Diggin' the Discs" (April 23, 1947).
————. "Goodman Redeems Self at Concert" (May 21, 1947).
————. "Diggin' the Discs" (October 8, 1947).
————. "Diggin' the Discs" (October 22, 1947).
————. "Diggin' the Discs" (January 14, 1948).
————. "Carnegie Patrons Ignore Armstrong, Benny, Gene" (June 16, 1948).
————. "Bop-Styled Septet Stars All but Goodman" (July 14, 1948).
————. "BG Cries 'Nuff' as Costs Climb, Crowds Fall Off" (July 28, 1948).
————. "Henderson Calls Be-Bop Phenomenon of Cruelty" (September 8, 1948).
————. "Diggin' the Discs" (December 15, 1948).
————. "Well Worth Going 150 Miles to Hear Benny's New Band" (December 29, 1948).
————. "BG Takes Stage Shows in Hand; Pulls a Switch" (January 14, 1949).
————. "2,500 Hear BG On Coast" (March 25, 1949).
————. "Goodman to Do Philippine Dates" (November 4, 1949).
Downing, Terry. "Open Letter to BG." *Down Beat* (March 12, 1947).
Feather, Leonard. "A Bird's-Ear View of Music." *Metronome* (August 1948).
————. "The Changing of the Hasselgard." *Metronome* (September 1948).
————. "Blindfolding the King." *Metronome* (December 1948).
————. "Ah, Sweet Melody of Bop." *Metronome* (January 1949).
————. "Buddy De Frank One." *Metronome* (December 1949).
————. "Stan." *Metronome* (December 1950).
Finn, Mark. "Benny *Was* King." *Metronome* (December 1946).
Gardner, Mark. *Benny's Bop*. Hep Records, 1987.
Gelatt, Roland. *The Fabulous Phonograph: 1877–1977*. New York: Macmillan Company, 1977.
Gitler, Ira. *Swing to Bop*. New York: Oxford University Press, 1985.

Greco, Buddy. Author's interview, June 21, 1990.

Grut, Harald. "Meticulously Planned, but Rarely Did It Glow." *Melody Maker* (April 21, 1950).

Herman, Woody, with Stuart Troup. *The Woodchopper's Ball.* New York: E. P. Dutton, 1990.

Hoefer, George. "Benny & the Boppers." *Down Beat* (July 28, 1966).

Jaffe, William B. "B. G.'s Illness Held Key to Theatre Walk." *Variety* (January 19, 1949).

Jazz Record. "An Open Letter to Benny Goodman" (July 1947).

Jones, Max. *Talking Jazz.* New York: W. W. Norton & Company, 1988.

Korteweg, Simon. *Bebop Spoken Here.* Capitol Records, 1972.

Levin, Mike. "Long Disc Fight Looms." *Down Beat* (November 5, 1947).

Maher, James T. Author's interview, October 7, 1987.

Melody Maker. "Not Enough Goodman at the Palladium—but What There Is, Is Great" (July 23, 1949).

———. "Goodman: Continental Tour Is Off" (July 30, 1949).

———. "Return of the Thin Man" (July 31, 1954).

Metronome. "BG & the USSR" (February 1947).

———. "Record Reviews" (April 1947).

———. "Point and Counterpoint" (June 1947).

———. "Benny Goodman Complains" (August 1947).

———. "Record Reviews" (October 1947).

———. "Record Reviews" (November 1947).

———. "Benny Rides Again" (April 1948).

———. "Record Reviews" (January 1949).

———. "Records of the Year" (February 1949).

———. "Point and Counterpoint" (January 1950).

Millstein, Gilbert. "Apostle of Swing." *New York Times,* April 19, 1953.

Morgan, Alun. "Wardell Gray." *Jazz Monthly* (February 1956).

New York Sun. "Swing King Outswung by Dorsey," August 23, 1947.

New York Times. "Benny Goodman Wins Praise of Londoners," July 20, 1949.

———. "Goodman Tour Cancelled," July 28, 1949.

Noss, Luther. *Paul Hindemith in the United States.* Urbana and Chicago: University of Illinois Press, 1989.

O'Leary, Dorothy. "Jazz for Russia." *New York Times,* May 4, 1947.

Parmenter, Ross. "Sidelights on World of Music." *New York Times,* November 3, 1946.

Piazza, Tom. Interview with Benny Goodman. n.d.

Review of Recorded Music. "Tops in Pops" (November 1947).

Ronan, Eddie. "TD and BG Swap Blows on Set." *Down Beat* (September 20, 1947).

Simon, George T. "Benny Blows Bop." *Metronome* (August 1948).

———. "Bop Confuses Benny." *Metronome* (October 1949).

Variety. "Palumbo Disappointed in Goodman Biz, Asks Rebate on Philly Date," June 9, 1948.

———. "Goodman 'Cavalcade' Part of New Approach; Sets Production Scribe," December 15, 1948.

———. "Paramount, N.Y.," December 22, 1948.

———. "Storm, Xmas Shopping Slough B'way but 'Paleface'—Benny Goodman Brisk $75,000," December 22, 1948.

———. " 'Married'—Lancaster Happy $80,000," December 24, 1948.

———. "B'way Likes Sound of New Year's Biz." January 5, 1949.

———. "Benny Goodman Does Quick Fade at N.Y. Par," January 12, 1949.

———. "Cap Puts Major Accent on Bop; Pacts Big Roster," January 19, 1949.

———. "BG to Coast after Suffering 2nd Collapse; Las Vegas Date in Doubt," January 26, 1949.

————. "Bop Gets Band Biz's Brushoff," June 8, 1949.
————. "N.Y. Spotty; 'Fullback'—Goodman Mild," October 19, 1949.
————. "Roxy, N.Y.," October 19, 1949.
————. "Holdovers, Mayorality Campaign Nip B'way," October 26, 1949.
Ulanov, Barry. *"Variety* Lays an Egg." *Metronome* (July 1949).
Wilson, John S. "Why Barnet Had to Break Up." *Down Beat* (December 2, 1949).

Chapter Twenty-four: The Kell Interlude

Colbert, Henry. Letter to Dr. Smith, January 19, 1950.
Colbert, Mrs. Henry. Author's interview, June 18, 1987.
Copland, Aaron, and Vivian Perlis. *Copland Since 1943.* New York: St. Martin's Press, 1989.
Down Beat. "Record Reviews" (October 22, 1947).
————. "Benny's Clary 'Too Polite' " (January 14, 1948).
————. "Benny's Mozart Cuts Reggie Kell's Brahms" (May 7, 1952).
Downes, Edward. "Music: Festival Opens." *New York Times,* July 7, 1956.
Gelatt, Roland. *Music-Makers.* New York: Alfred A. Knopf, 1953.
————. "Clarinet by Kell." *Saturday Review of Literature* (May 27, 1950).
Haggin, B. H. "Music." *Nation* (December 28, 1940).
Kell, Reginald. " 'Dead Pan' or the Simple Art of Blowing a Clarinet." *Woodwind Magazine* (January 1949).
Larrabee, Eric. "Quiet Music." *Harper's Magazine* (February 1951).
Levin, Michael. "Goodman Returns to Carnegie!" *Down Beat* (May 20, 1953).
Maher, James T. Author's interview, October 7, 1987.
————. Author's interview, September 4, 1990.
Metronome. "Classical Records" (April 1947).
The New Yorker. "Pastoral" (July 7, 1956).
Noss, Luther. *Paul Hindemith in the United States.* Urbana and Chicago: University of Illinois Press, 1989.
Parmenter, Ross. "Clarinetist Seeks New Triumph Here." *New York Times,* December 17, 1948.
Peck, Seymour. "PM Visits: The King of Clarinetists. *PM,* December 6, 1944.
Powell, Mel. Author's interview, May 30, 1989.
Ross, Lillian. "Vibrato." *The New Yorker* (February 26, 1949).
————. "Quick Bash." *The New Yorker* (March 4, 1950).
Russianoff, Leon. Author's interview, August 17, 1987.
Simon, George T. "B. G. Explains." *Metronome* (October, 1946).
Straus, Noel. "Tajo, Kell Score in Local Debuts." *New York Times,* December 20, 1948.
Sylvester, Robert. "The New, Cool Benny." *New York Daily News,* July 15, 1954.
Taubman, Howard. "Goodman Is Soloist for Little Society." *New York Times,* December 16, 1947.
Time. " 'A Different Era' " (December 4, 1950).
————. "Personality" (January 5, 1953).
Woodwind Magazine. "Kell Announces Intention of Becoming U.S. Citizen" (December 1948).

Chapter Twenty-five: Carnegie Hall Revisited

Allen, Walter C. *Hendersonia: The Music of Fletcher Henderson and His Musicians.* Highland Park, N.J., Walter C. Allen, 1973.

Auld, Georgie. Interview with Bill Spilka, July 18, 1987.

Avakian, George. Author's interview, November 21, 1987.

———. *Benny Goodman 1937–38 Jazz Concert No. 2.* Columbia Records, 1952.

Bigard, Barney. *With Louis and the Duke: The Autobiography of a Jazz Clarinetist,* ed. Barry Martyn. New York: Oxford University Press, 1986.

Columbia Records Press Release. "Benny Goodman Signed to Exclusive Columbia Records Contract," July 19, 1950.

Connor, D. Russell. *The Record of a Legend.* Let's Dance Corporation, 1984.

Down Beat. "Goodman Back with Columbia" (August 29, 1950).

———. "Fletcher Ill" (January 26, 1951).

———. "Smack Very Ill; Benefit Planned" (March 9, 1951).

———. "Smack to Join Sister in Georgia" (March 23, 1951).

———. "Goodman Trio Reassembled for Air Show" (May 4, 1951).

———. "Benny Has a Ball on Big Band Date" (June 1, 1951).

———. "Record Reviews" (August 10, 1951).

———. "Band Business Begins to Boom" (May 21, 1952).

———. "Second Stroke Strikes Smack" (May 21, 1952).

———. "New Goodman LP Album Due" (November 19, 1952).

———. "Swing Era Lives Again in Great Goodman Album" (December 3, 1952).

———. "Goodman Lining Up Ork for Tour with Armstrong" (February 25, 1953).

———. "Fletcher Fund to Be Set Up by Goodman" (March 11, 1953).

———. "Goodman Lineup Nearly Complete" (August 8, 1953).

———. "Goodman Tour Ready to Go" (April 22, 1953).

———. "Concerts Go On without Benny" (May 20, 1953).

———. "Benny Still Very Ill as Concert Tour Winds Up" (July 1, 1953).

———. " 'Voice Of America' Interviews Benny" (February 8, 1956).

Feather, Leonard. "A Radio Programme from the Past." *Melody Maker and Rhythm* (April 28, 1951).

———. "BG-Louis Tour Is Cited as Bitterest Jazz Hassel Ever." *Down Beat* (June 3, 1953).

Gelatt, Roland. *The Fabulous Phonograph: 1877–1977.* New York: Macmillan Company, 1977.

Grauer, Bill. "Benny Swings Again." *Record Changer* (June 1951).

Hammond, John, with Irving Townsend. *John Hammond on Record.* New York: Ridge Press/Summit Books. 1977.

Harrison, Jay S. "Benny Goodman and Swing Era Are Back, at Carnegie Hall." *New York Herald Tribune,* April 18, 1953.

Jones, Max. *Talking Jazz.* New York: W. W. Norton & Company, 1988.

Jordan, Steve. Author's interview, May 1, 1987.

Levin, Michael. "Mix Reviews the Goodman Carnegie LP." *Down Beat* (January 12, 1951).

———. "Goodman Returns to Carnegie!" *Down Beat* (May 20, 1953).

Life. "Brief Comeback" (April 27, 1953).

Maher, James T. Author's interview, October 16, 1987.

———. Author's interview, October 5, 1990.

Metronome. "Dance Band Revival: Band" (July 1951).

———. "The Swing to Swing" (August 1951).

———. "Record Reviews" (September 1951).

———. "Record Reviews" (January 1952).

———. "Benny Sent Him!" (January 1953).

———. "Fletcher Henderson 1898–1952" (March 1953).

———. "Louis and the Other King" (March 1953).

———. "Big Rift" (July 1953).

Millstein, Gilbert. "Apostle of Swing." *New York Times,* April 19, 1953.

New York Herald Tribune. "Benny Goodman Collapses in Boston; in Oxygen Tent," April 20, 1953.
————. "Goodman Feeling Better," April 21, 1953.
————. "Goodman Won't Tour," April 29, 1953.
New York Times. "Fletcher Henderson Dies at 54; Important Cog in 'Swing Era,' Goodman Orch," December 31, 1952.
————. "Goodman Collapses, Put in Oxygen Tent," April 20, 1953.
Savory, Bill. Author's interview, June 21, 1988.
Schoenfeld, Herm. "Goodman-Armstrong 'Flashback' to '38 Jazz Idiom Dimmed by Time." *Variety* (April 22, 1953).
Simon, George T. "Bands, Bottles and Balls." *Metronome* (June 1952).
————. "Record Reviews: Jazz." *Metronome* (October 1952).
————. "BG Rides Again." *Metronome* (January 1953).
————. "Benny, Louis Take Off!" *Metronome* (June 1953).
Sylvester, Robert. "Exhaustion Fells Goodman, Perils Record Concert Tour." *New York Daily News,* April 21, 1953.
Taubman, Harold. "Benny Goodman and Satchmo Armstrong's All Stars Beat It Out." *New York Times,* April 18, 1953.
Time. " 'A Different Era' " (December 4, 1950).
————. "Personality" (January 5, 1953).
Ulanov, Barry. "BG: 1938." *Metronome* (February 1951).
————. "Benny Rides Again." *Metronome* (June 1951).
————. "Trends, Clear and Muddy." *Metronome* (May 1952).
Variety. "BG's Three-Year Col. Exclusive," July 19, 1950.
————. "B. G. Orch Pulls 10G in 2 Dates," April 15, 1953.
————. "Goodman-Satchmo P'kge Hit by Internal Beefs; B. G. May Not Come Back," April 29, 1953.
————. "BG's Bow-Out from Jazz P'kge Dents B.O. Slightly; Granz Switches Billing," May 6, 1953.
————. "BG-Satchmo Package Pulling Solid Grosses," May 13, 1953.
————. "BG (Krupa)-Satchmo Pull 9G in Chicago," May 20, 1953.
————. "BG (Krupa)-Satchmo Mop Up in Midwest," May 27, 1953.
Ward, Helen. Author's interview, November 19, 1987.
Wilson, John S. "Goodman and Company." *New York Times,* November 16, 1952.

CHAPTER TWENTY-SIX: The Benny Goodman Story

Allen, Steve. "That Old Goodman Gang in Movies." *New York Herald Tribune,* February 19, 1956.
Clayton, Buck, with Nancy Miller Elliott. *Buck Clayton's Jazz World.* New York: Oxford University Press, 1987.
Columbus, Ohio, *Citizen.* Untitled article. October 11, 1942.
Connor, D. Russell. *The Record of a Legend.* Let's Dance Corporation, 1984.
Crowther, Bosley. "The Benny Goodman Story." *New York Times,* February 22, 1956.
Down Beat. "U.-I. Gets Okay from Goodman for Biofilm" (May 5, 1954).
————. "Benny Goodman Sextet, Blue Note, Chicago" (May 19, 1954).
————. "Goodman 4 to Re-Form for Benefit" (June 2, 1954).
————. "Two Huge Memorials for Page Raise Almost 5 G's" (December 29, 1954).
————. "Basin Street's Where Folks All Meet for BG's Fine New Octet" (April 6, 1955).
————. "BG Name Magic" (May 4, 1955).
————. "Choice of Allen to Play BG Surprises Hollywood" (June 1, 1955).

———. "BG to Be Seen in Movie Biog" (September 21, 1955).

———. "BG Forms Record Firm, Waxes" (October 19, 1955).

———. "Ex-BG Sidemen Evince Mixed Emotions at Biofilm Selections" (October 19, 1955).

———. "Victor Readying BG Package" (November 2, 1955).

———. "Columbia Planning Large-Scale Goodman Record Package Project" (January 11, 1956).

———. "Victor Arranges 2 Strong Entries in BG Record Derby" (February 8, 1956).

———. "Goodman Sides Begin to Pour Out" (February 22, 1956).

Ebony. "Goodman Story" (February 1956).

Emge, Charles. " 'Won't Play Goodman as a Comedian,' Allen Asserts." *Down Beat* (September 7, 1955).

———. "Pic Does 'Credible Job' on Benny Goodman Story." *Down Beat* (February 8, 1956).

Farrell, Barry. *The Swing Era: Benny Goodman into the '70s: The King in Person.* Time-Life Records, 1972.

Hammond, John, with Irving Townsend. *John Hammond on Record.* New York: Ridge Press/Summit Books. 1977.

Hentoff, Nat. "Here We Go—and Benny's Band Did Not Dismay Them." *Down Beat* (March 21, 1956).

———. "Waxeries Cashing In on Resurgence of Goodman." *Down Beat.* April 18, 1956.

Holly, Hal. "Filmland Up Beat." *Down Beat* (August 10, 1955).

———. "Filmland Up Beat." *Down Beat.* (August 24, 1955).

———. "Filmland Up Beat." *Down Beat* (September 21, 1955).

———. "Filmland Up Beat." *Down Beat* (October 5, 1955).

———. "Filmland Up Beat." *Down Beat* (November 16, 1955).

Hyams, Joe. "Benny Goodman Consents to Film of His Life Story." *New York Herald Tribune,* April 1, 1954.

Life. "Benny Is Heard but Not Seen" (February 13, 1956).

Look. "Benny Goodman: The Life of a King" (February 21, 1956).

Maher, James T. Author's interview, November 2, 1987.

Metronome. "The Benny Goodman Story." March 1956.

The New Yorker. "Fresh Sound" (March 19, 1955).

———. "Ageless" (February 16, 1956).

New York Herald Tribune. "Goodman Story to Be Filmed," May 9, 1954.

Parsons, Louella. "Louella Parsons." *Pittsburgh Sun-Telegraph,* September 24, 1942.

Person to Person. CBS Television, November 5, 1954.

Simon, George T. "Benny's Back!" *Metronome* (September 1954).

———. "Benny Goodman: Basin Street." *Metronome* (May 1955).

———. "Steve Allen: Presenting Jazz on Television." *Metronome* (July 1955).

Stacy, Jess. Author's interview, March 28, 1988.

Time. "Benny Is Back" (February 20, 1956).

Variety. "Basin Street, N.Y.," July 21, 1954.

———. "Benny Goodman Story," December 21, 1955.

———. "All-Time Top Money Films," January 4, 1956.

———. " 'Goodman' Big (but Not Up to Miller)," March 7, 1956.

Wilson, John S. "Benny's Story." *New York Times,* February 12, 1956.

———. "Goodman's Early Career on LP." *New York Times,* February 26, 1956.

CHAPTER TWENTY-SEVEN: On the Road Again

Alden, Robert. "Hands of U.S. Tied in Asian 'Cold War.' " *New York Times,* June 11, 1956.
Beech, Keyes. "Goodman's Jazz Wows Thailand." *Chicago Daily News,* December 18, 1956.
Connor, D. Russell. *The Record of a Legend.* Let's Dance Corporation, 1984.
Dance, Stanley. *The World of Swing.* New York: Charles Scribner's Sons, 1974.
Down Beat. "Benny's Back with Band; Will Play the Waldorf" (February 8, 1956).
———. "Here's The Band Goodman Took into Waldorf-Astoria" (March 7, 1956).
———. "2000 Jam Floor—BG Is Pleased" (March 21, 1956).
———. "BG, Band to Take 6-Week Far East State Dept. Tour" (November 28, 1956).
———. "Benny Rides Again" (November 14, 1957).
———. "Hall of Fame" (December 26, 1957).
———. "The End" (February 6, 1958).
Farrell, Barry. *The Swing Era: Benny Goodman into the '70s. The King in Person.* Time-Life Records, 1972.
Gold, Don, and Dom Cerulli. "Newport Jazz 1958." *Down Beat* (August 7, 1958).
Goodman, Benny. "I'm Neutral about Musicians So Long As They're Good." *Music Journal* (June–July 1958).
Jordan, Steve. Author's interview, May 1, 1987.
Kalb, Bernard. "Kings of Swing and Thailand Jive." *New York Times,* December 7, 1956.
———. "Thai Ruler Opens Trade Exhibit." *New York Times,* December 8, 1956.
Maher, Jack. "BG Went Far in Far East." *Metronome* (April 1957).
McLellan, John. "Hub Reception Pleases Benny." *Boston Traveler,* October 21, 1958.
Metronome. "The Newport Jazz Festival" (September 1958).
Newsweek. "Benny Ma Lao" (December 17, 1956).
———. "Jazzman on His Beat" (November 16, 1959).
The New Yorker. "Ageless" (February 16, 1956).
———. "Let's Dance" (March 3, 1956).
New York Herald Tribune. "Goodman's Band to Play in Brussels," February 14, 1958.
New York Times. "Benny Goodman Sways Thailand," December 23, 1956.
———. "Goodman Decorated," December 30, 1956.
———. "Goodman Beats Drums for Asians; King of Swing Found Them 'Hep,' " January 25, 1957.
———. "The Brussels Fair," February 4, 1958.
———. "Benny Goodman to Play at Fair in Brussels," February 14, 1958.
———. "Goodman Going to Fair," May 3, 1958.
———. "Benny Goodman Scores New Brussels Triumph," June 1, 1958.
O'Day, Anita, with George Eells. *High Times, Hard Times.* New York: G. P. Putnam's Sons, 1981.
Suber, Charles. "The First Chorus." *Down Beat* (July 10, 1958).
Time. "Benny Is Back" (February 20, 1956).
———. "Facing the Music" (March 19, 1956).
———. "Cats in Asia" (January 21, 1957).
Tracy, Jack. "The First Chorus." *Down Beat* (June 13, 1956).
Variety. "Waldorf-Astoria, N.Y.," February 15, 1956.
Waggoner, Walter H. "Goodman's Music Makes Hit at Fair." *New York Times,* May 26, 1958.
Wilber, Bob, with Derek Webster. *Music Was Not Enough.* New York: Oxford University Press. 1988.
Wilson, John S. "Lecture on Dance Steals Jazz Fete." *New York Times,* July 6, 1958.

CHAPTER TWENTY-EIGHT: Mission to Moscow

Avakian, George. *Benny Goodman in Moscow*. RCA Victor Records, 1962.
————. Author's interview, November 7, 1987.
————. Author's Interview, November 21, 1987.
————. Author's interview, February 11, 1991.
Benjamin, Philip. "Goodman Gets in Practice Lick for His Swing through Soviet." *New York Times,* May 4, 1962.
Bracker, Milton. "Goodman Signs 12 for Russian Tour." *New York Times,* April 10, 1962.
Caruthers, Osgood. "A Top Soviet Orchestra Leader Tells Russians: 'We Need Jazz.' " *New York Times,* February 27, 1961.
Connor, D. Russell. *The Record of a Legend*. Let's Dance Corporation, 1984.
Coss, Bill. "Benny Goodman on the First Steppe." *Down Beat* (May 24, 1962).
Crow, Bill. "To Russia without Love: The Benny Goodman Tour of the USSR. Part I." *Gene Lees Jazzletter* (August 1986).
————. "To Russia without Love. Part II." *Gene Lees Jazzletter* (September 1986).
————. "To Russia without Love. Part III." *Gene Lees Jazzletter* (October 1986).
————. "To Russia without Love. Part IV." *Gene Lees Jazzletter* (November 1986).
Daily Worker. Untitled article. September 24, 1942.
Down Beat. "BG Selects Jazz for Russia" (April 23, 1947).
————. "The Editor Speaks" (July 10, 1958).
————. "Special Report from Europe" (September 4, 1958).
————. " '. . . A Good Orchestra" (January 8, 1959).
————. "The Reds and Dr. Stearns" (July 9, 1959).
————. "A Win in Moscow" (August 6, 1959).
————. "The Goodman Tour and the Teapot Tempest" (May 24, 1962).
————. "Benny Goodman" (July 5, 1962).
————. "Chords and Discords" (August 30, 1962).
————. "Goodman Men Sound Off about Soviet Tour" (August 30, 1962).
————. "Benny Goodman in Moscow" (December 6, 1962).
Duckworth, Sophia. "Letter from a Tourist." *Down Beat* (August 2, 1962).
Favoino, Gabriel. "Goodman Orchestra Warms Up for a Six-Week Tour of Russia." *New York Post,* April 27, 1962.
Feather, Leonard. *The Jazz Years: Earwitness to an Era*. New York: Da Capo Press, 1987.
————. "Moscow Diary." *Down Beat* (July 19, 1962).
————. "Feather's Nest." *Down Beat* (November 22, 1962).
Gelb, Arthur. "Goodman Scolds Soviet Scholars." *New York Times,* March 18, 1961.
Goodman, Benny. Interview for *First Person Singular,* 1962.
Kenworthy, E. W. "U.S. and Soviet to Expand Their Cultural Exchange," *New York Times.* March 9, 1962.
Klein, Howard. "Benny Goodman Appears in Bronx." *New York Times,* August 13, 1962.
Life. "Stompin' It Up at the Savoy-Marx" (July 6, 1962).
Maxwell, Jimmy. Interview with Milt Hinton. Smithsonian Jazz Oral History Project, April 16, 1979.
————. Author's interview, September 3, 1987.
Metronome. "BG & the USSR" (February 1947).
Morgenstern, Dan. "B. G." *Jaz* (October 1962).
New York Herald Tribune. "Benny Goodman Signed for Tour of Soviet Cities," April 18, 1962.
New York Post. "Our Benny Winning the Cold War," June 3, 1962.

————. "Shirley & Benny in Russia (Cont.)," July 21, 1962.
New York Times. "Goodman Thinks Russians Dig Jazz," January 25, 1959.
————. "Russian Musician Praises U.S. Tour," November 29, 1959.
————. "Soviet Changes Its Tune and Urges Jazz Clubs," April 7, 1961.
————. "Benny Goodman's Concert Pleases but Puzzles Khrushchev," May 31, 1962.
————. "Goodman Swings a Soviet Favorite," June 1, 1962.
————. "One-Man Session by Goodman Attracts a Crowd in Red Square," June 2, 1962.
————. "Soviet Blessing Goes to Goodman," June 3, 1962.
————. "Soviet Police Curb Goodman Jazz Band," June 5, 1962.
————. "Russian Youth Is Arrested in Goodman Band Incident," June 7, 1962.
————. "Tiflis Reds' Paper Applauds Goodman," June 9, 1962.
————. "Tiflis Crowd Hoots Down Song in Russian by Goodman Vocalist," June 10, 1962.
————. "Leningrad Hails Benny Goodman," June 21, 1962.
————. "Leningrad Hails Goodman, Janis," June 22, 1962.
————. "Goodman's Tour," June 24, 1962.
————. "Goodman's Choice of Music in Soviet Dissatisfies Band," July 1, 1962.
————. "Goodman Cheered in Moscow Return," July 4, 1962.
————. "Goodman's Band Ends Soviet Tour," July 9, 1962.
————. "Goodman Returns after Soviet Tour," July 19, 1962.
————. Untitled article, February 27, 1963.
————. "Izvestia Sees Cloak and Dagger in Goodman Band's Horn Cases," August 7, 1964.
New York World-Telegram and Sun. "Cool Sidemen Sound Sour Note as Benny Sticks to Old Standards," July 10, 1962.
Newsweek. "Benny Goodman in Russia . . . the Band Blew Hot and Cold" (July 2, 1962).
O'Leary, Dorothy. "Jazz for Russia." *New York Times,* May 4, 1947.
Parmenter, Ross. "Sidelights on World of Music." *New York Times,* November 3, 1946.
RCA Victor Records Press Release. "Benny Goodman in Moscow," September 1962.
Rich, Alan. "Benny Goodman to Tour in Soviet." *New York Times,* March 9, 1962.
Ruff, Willie. "Jazz Mission to Moscow." *Down Beat* (January 21, 1960).
Shabad, Theodore. "Russians Extend Goodman's Tour." *New York Times,* April 18, 1962.
————. "Russians Greet Benny Goodman." *New York Times,* May 29, 1962.
————. "Khrushchev Visits U.S. Embassy Fete." *New York Times,* July 5, 1962.
————. "Soviet Extends Campaign on Art," *New York Times.* December 8, 1962.
Simon, George T. "Mr. Jazz Man, Blow That Curtain Down." *New York Herald Tribune,* March 26, 1962.
Starr, Frederick S. *Red and Hot: The Fate of Jazz in the Soviet Union.* New York: Oxford University Press, 1983.
Talese, Gay. "Goodman's Band Assesses Its Trip." *New York Times,* July 10, 1962.
Topping, Seymour. "Goodman's Tour May Be Expanded." *New York Times,* April 12, 1962.
Wilson, John S. "Goodman Basks in Success of Soviet Jazz Tour." *New York Times,* July 20, 1962.

CHAPTER TWENTY-NINE: September Song

Avakian, George. Author's interview, April 24, 1991.
Balliett, Whitney. *New York Notes.* Boston: Houghton Mifflin Company, 1976.
————. *Night Creature.* New York: Oxford University Press. 1981.
Buckley, Tom. "Winging It with Old Goodman Gang." *New York Times,* June 29, 1973.

Campbell, Mary. "Benny's Clarinet Blowing Reaches All-Time High." *Plainfield* (N.J.) *Courier-News*, July 3, 1972.

Connor, D. Russell. *The Record of a Legend*. Let's Dance Corporation, 1984.

———. *Benny Goodman Live at Carnegie Hall 40th Anniversary Concert*. London Records, 1978.

Down Beat. "Goodman Tours Europe with Special Big Band" (March 5, 1970).

———. "Goodman Gets Degree" (July 10, 1973).

Farrell, Barry, and Joseph Kastner. *The Swing Era: Benny Goodman into The '70s. The King in Person*. Time-Life Records, 1972.

Feather, Leonard. "Jazz Beat." *New York Post*, May 16, 1965.

Forrest, Helen, with Bill Libby. *I Had the Craziest Dream*. New York: Coward, McCann & Geohegan, Inc., 1982.

Henshaw, Laurie. "King Benny Mellows with the Years." *Melody Maker* (February 7, 1970).

———. "Benny's Back—and Buying British." *Melody Maker* (September 18, 1971).

———. "No Compromise for Goodman." *Melody Maker* (December 22, 1973).

Horwitz, Dave. "When I'm 62." *Rolling Stone* (September 28, 1972).

Jampel, Dave. "Things Aren't Too Bad in Jazz Today, Goodman Sez: Raps Norman Granz." *Variety* (April 8, 1964).

Jazz Journal. "Benny Goodman" (March 1970).

Kelleher, Ed. "Goodman Carnegie Date Not like '38." *Billboard* (January 28, 1978).

Kwitny, Jonathan. "Others Come and Go, but Benny Goodman Plays On and On." *Wall Street Journal*, August 21, 1974.

Localio, Dr. Arthur. Author's interview, May 20, 1991.

McDonough, John. "Benny Rides Once More." *Down Beat* (October 29, 1970).

———. "Benny Goodman: *Benny Goodman Today.*" *Down Beat* (April 1971).

———. "Benny Goodman." *Coda* (September 1974).

———. "Television Tribute to John Hammond." *Coda* (October 1975).

———. "Benny Goodman." *Down Beat* (November 6, 1975).

———. "Benny Goodman." *Down Beat* (November 4, 1976).

———. "Benny Goodman: The King Swings On." *Down Beat* (November 17, 1977).

———. *Benny Goodman—Seven Come Eleven*. Columbia Records, 1982.

McGuffie, Bill. "The Greatness of Goodman." *Crescendo International* (August 1973).

McPartland, Marian. Author's interview, October 9, 1987.

———. "Benny Goodman: From the Inside." *Down Beat* (April 9, 1964).

Melody Maker. "Goodman's Back in Britain, and He Just Wants to Swing" (March 13, 1971).

Morgenstern, Dan. "Offbeat Goodman Reunion at Carnegie Hall." *Chicago Sun-Times*, January 19, 1978.

———. "Benny Rides Again." *Jazz Journal* (May 1978).

———. "Jazz in the '70s." *Down Beat*. (January 1980).

Morgenstern, Dan; Arnold Jay Smith; John McDonough; and Don Nelson. "Benny Goodman Returns to Carnegie Hall: Four Views." *Down Beat* (June 1, 1978).

New York Times. "City Honors Benny Goodman," September 14, 1966.

———. "Benny Goodman to Get Award," May 12, 1967.

———. "Goodman Band in Rumania," February 16, 1970.

———. "Prague Hall Is Jammed for Benny Goodman Concert," October 28, 1976.

Okon, May. "The King Still Swings." *New York Sunday News*, October 9, 1966.

Reidy, Frank. "Benny Goodman Is Very Happy with His British Band." *Crescendo International* (April 1971).

Tiegel, Eliot. "Hammond: Still Seeking Talent." *Billboard* (January 7, 1978).

Traill, Sinclair. "Benny Goodman: *Benny Goodman Today.*" *Jazz Journal* (February 20, 1970).

Variety. "Benny Goodman Orch," February 25, 1970.

———. "Goodman Scores in West Berlin Concert," March 11, 1970.

————. "Benny Goodman Show," January 25, 1978.

Webster, Daniel. "It Don't Mean a Thing, Says the Master of Swing." *Detroit Free Press*, July 20, 1974.

Welch, Chris. "A Night for Nostalgia." *Melody Maker* (February 21, 1970).

Welch, Dr. William J. Author's interview, May 16, 1991.

West, Hollie I. "Benny Goodman: The Jazzman Remembers." *Washington Post*, September 15, 1974.

Wilson, John S. "Benny Goodman: *Together Again!*" *Down Beat* (March 26, 1964).

————. "Jazz: Benny and His All-Stars Play Basic Goodman." *New York Times*, June 2, 1973.

————. "Goodman Goes On." *New York Times*, August 24, 1975.

————. "Goodman to Relive '38 Carnegie Jazz." *New York Times*, November 2, 1977.

————. "Goodman at Carnegie." *New York Times*, January 19, 1978.

CHAPTER THIRTY: Good-bye

Albertson, Chris. "Benny Goodman." *Stereo Review* (February, 1982).

Bank, Danny. Author's interview, October 20, 1987.

"Benny Goodman: Let's Dance, a Musical Tribute." Public Broadcasting System, 1985.

Connor, D. Russell. *The Record of a Legend*. Let's Dance Corporation, 1984.

————. *Benny Goodman: Listen to His Legacy*. Scarecrow Press, Inc. and Institute of Jazz Studies, Metuchen, N.J., and London: 1988.

Crutchfield, Will. "Music: Mostly Mozart Honors Goodman." *New York Times*, August 20, 1986.

Deffaa, Chip. "Goodman Ends 7-Year Break!" *Ridgewood* (N.J.) *News*, October 10, 1985.

Erwin, Pee Wee, with Warren W. Vaché, Sr. *This Horn for Hire*. Metuchen, N.J., and London: Scarecrow Press and Institute of Jazz Studies, Rutgers University, 1987.

Freitag, Michael. "Benny Goodman to Lead Band in Yale Benefit Concert." *New York Times*, December 8, 1985.

Gamarekian, Barbara. "5 in Arts Get Honors in Capital." *New York Times*, December 6, 1982.

Gussow, Mel. "Musical Hall of Fame Salutes 9 Songsmiths." *New York Times*, April 17, 1984.

Hamilton, Robert A. "Tapes by Benny Goodman to Finance His Archive." *New York Times*, November 10, 1986.

Holden, Stephen. "Admirers Gather in a Tribute to Goodman, King of Swing." *New York Times*, November 10, 1986.

Kalman, Vic. "King of Swing Still Reigns." *Newark* (N.J.) *Sunday Star-Ledger*, September 15, 1985.

Maher, James T. Author's interview, October 7, 1987.

————. Author's interview, November 2, 1987.

————. Author's interview, July 22, 1991.

————. Letter to the author, July 23, 1991.

McDonough, John. "Benny Goodman: *The King*." *Down Beat* (May 3, 1979).

————. "Benny Goodman," *Down Beat* (November 1979).

————. "Benny Rides Again." *Down Beat* (February 1986).

————. "Benny Goodman." *Down Beat* (August 1986).

————. "Benny Goodman, 1909–86." *Down Beat* (September 1986).

Molotsky, Irvin. "Kennedy Center Honors 5 in Arts." *New York Times*, August 16, 1982.

Morgenstern, Dan. "Warren Vaché: Classic Cornet." *Down Beat* (February 1983).

New York Times. "Benny Goodman's Wife, Alice H., Is Dead at 72," February 10, 1978.

————. "Swingin' for the King on a Night to Remember," August 9, 1980.

————. "333rd Rite at Harvard Honors Carlos of Spain," June 8, 1984.

————. "Funeral for Benny Goodman," June 16, 1986.

Nissim, Jeff. Author's interview, January 25, 1989.

Palmer, Robert. "Benny Goodman Swings with Octet." *New York Times,* June 26, 1979.

————. "Benny Goodman: 'I Just Love Music.' " *New York Times,* June 26, 1980.

Perlez, Jane. "Benny Goodman Hailed by Columbia Graduates." *New York Times,* May 15, 1986.

Phillips, Carol. Author's interview, July 30, 1991.

Rosenwasser, Marc. " 'King of Swing' Still Working Hard at His Music." Associated Press, May 30, 1979.

Samuel, Harold. Author's interview, August 22, 1991.

Schoenberg, Loren. Author's interview, July 8, 1991.

————. Author's interview, July 12, 1991.

Stacy, Jess. Author's interview, March 28, 1988.

Sudhalter, Richard M. "An Interview with the King of Swing." *American Heritage* (November 1981).

Tiegel, Eliot. "Benny Goodman." *Pulse* (July 1986).

U.S. News & World Report. "Benny Goodman: 'Popular Music Has Deteriorated' " (August 14, 1978).

Variety. "Jazz Giant Benny Goodman, 77, Dies in His Sleep at N.Y. Home," June 18, 1986.

Wilson, John S. "Swing: Goodman At 71." *New York Times,* June 9, 1980.

————. "Benny Goodman Joins John Hammond Tribute." *New York Times,* June 29, 1985.

————. "Benny Goodman, King of Swing, Is Dead." *New York Times,* June 14, 1986.

————. "Jazz: Big Band Revival at Carnegie." *New York Times,* January 18, 1988.

————. "Jazz: A Tribute to Benny Goodman." *New York Times.* November 6, 1988.

Zaslow, Jeffrey. " 'Ghost' Swing Bands Follow the Leader without the Leader." *Wall Street Journal,* May 27, 1986.

Index